D0203631

LIBERALISM DIVIDED

LIBERALISM DIVIDED

A Study in British Political Thought 1914–1939

MICHAEL FREEDEN

CLARENDON PRESS · OXFORD
1986

Oxford University Press, Walton Street, Oxford OX2 6DP
Oxford New York Toronto
Delhi Bombay Calcutta Madras Karachi
Kuala Lumpur Singapore Hong Kong Tokyo
Nairobi Dar es Salaam Cape Town
Melbourne Auckland
and associated companies in
Beirut Berlin Ibadan Nicosia

Oxford is a trade mark of Oxford University Press

Published in the United States
by Oxford University Press, New York

British Library Cataloguing in Publication Data
Freeden, Michael
Liberalism divided: a study in British political thought 1914–1939.
1. Liberalism—Great Britain—History
2. Great Britain—Politics and government—1910–1936
3. Great Britain—Politics and government—1936–1945
I. Title
320.5′1′0941 JC599.G7
ISBN 0-19-827432-7

Library of Congress Cataloging in Publication Data
Freeden, Michael.
Liberalism divided.
Bibliography: p.
Includes index.
1. Liberalism—Great Britain—History—20th century.
2. Political science—Great Britain—History—20th century. I. Title.
JA84.G7F66 1986 320.5′13′0941 85-15454
ISBN 0-19-827432-7

Set by Downdell Ltd.
Printed in Great Britain
at the University Press, Oxford
by David Stanford
Printer to the University

FOR IRENE

ACKNOWLEDGEMENTS

IN the preparation of this book I was fortunate to obtain expert and courteous assistance from staff at the Bodleian Library; the British Library; the British Library of Political and Economic Science; the House of Lords Record Office; the Marshall Library, Cambridge; the Library of King's College, Cambridge; the John Rylands University of Manchester Library; the Central Library, Manchester; the Scottish Record Office. I am grateful to the following for kind permission to quote from private papers: The Clerk of the Records, House of Lords; the Reform Club, London; Lord Layton; Mr R. Simon. Many individuals answered my queries or helped in other valuable ways; among them Mr N. Barker, Professor B. Delisle Burns, Mr J. D. Delisle Burns, and Mr D. Hubback. Mr F. B. Singleton, librarian at the *Guardian* offices in Manchester, placed the account books of the *Manchester Guardian* at my disposal, thus enabling me to identify dozens of unsigned leaders written by Hobhouse.

Colin Matthew, Ross McKibbin, and Sanjit Maitra generously devoted time and effort to reading parts of the typescript and I was guided on many issues by their perceptive comments. I would also like to thank the British Academy for awarding me a personal research grant.

My parents have, as always, taken a much-appreciated interest in my work, and I have benefited from their observations. My children Jonathan and Daniella have been tolerant of my odd working hours and their company has been a welcome diversion. As for my wife Irene, the dedication cannot do justice to the many ways in which this book is hers.

M. F.

Mansfield College, Oxford

CONTENTS

ABBREVIATIONS AND CONVENTIONS

CR	*Contemporary Review*	*NS*	*New Statesman*
DC	*Daily Chronicle*	*NT*	*Nineteenth Century and After*
DN	*Daily News*	*WG*	*Westminster Gazette*
FR	*Fortnightly Review*	*WW*	*Weekly Westminster*
FV	*Forward View*		
HJ	*Hibbert Journal*		
MG	*Manchester Guardian*	LSS	Liberal Summer School
NC	*News Chronicle*	NLF	National Liberal Federation

The following use of capital letters has been adopted: 'Liberal' pertains to the institutional and official aspects of the Liberal party; 'liberal' denotes the body of thought. The same applies to 'Conservative' and 'conservative'.

1

INTRODUCTION

WHAT happens when a sophisticated body of political ideas runs out of intellectual momentum after a long spell of ascendancy? What befalls an ideology when, after a sustained period of attachment to a successful and powerful political party, the latter suddenly collapses under a barely foreseen set of political and economic developments? These are two of the questions that prompted this study of the fortunes of British liberal thought in the years immediately following the triumphant accomplishments, theoretical and practical, of the new liberalism. The answers this book attempts to provide do not, however, dispose of such questions painlessly. The First World War was followed by two decades of ideological crisis for liberalism and, as is often the case, crisis is not only disruptive for those involved but—at least for the non-participant observer—illuminating. The shocks that jolted liberalism also disclosed its anatomy, as hairline cracks widened into rifts that would not heal, and its edifice was revealed to contain ill-fitting sub-structures: 'liberalisms' that could not be reduced to 'liberalism'. Hence while part of this story is one of ideological standstill, even of regression, another concerns itself with the continuing attempts of liberalism to recuperate from set-backs, to regenerate and to maintain vitality and relevance. Failure and success thus proceed side by side and the final account lies open to this day. The reasons for this complexity, and for the inadequacy of any approach that assumes the existence of a defined entity called liberalism within the time-limits of this study, may be found in the bifurcation and occasional fragmentation of liberalism itself. What makes the period under observation particularly interesting is that it brought into sharp relief the theoretical divisions that liberalism has always been liable to, but was usually able to paper over. This also lends an unusual and perhaps unexpected significance to an era in recent British history that has not appeared especially promising for students of Western political thought. At first glance the years between 1914 and 1939 seem to offer little in the way of the depth, scope and incisiveness that Continental political theory possessed, and in one sense that impression must persist as a final comment. But on another level of analysis the story of twentieth-century British liberalism, and through it our ability to comprehend current patterns of thought and organization, are enhanced by the realization that a Mill, a Green, or even a pre-war Hobhouse, seminal as they are, cannot in themselves constitute or epitomize the living and changing liberal tradition. In various and curious ways liberalism continued as an important political current, notwithstanding that both it and its institutional incarnation were being written off by friends and foes alike. Why this was so—why liberalism was deliberately made to suffer an eclipse that evidence does not wholly corroborate—and the methodological lessons that can be deduced from that phenomenon, are further questions this book will address.

Both popular and scholarly attitudes to political ideologies have suffered from three related misconceptions. The first is a tendency to gather under one label elements of ideological belief that differ on some important aspects, or that cover a wide range of positions that cannot always coexist. Thus 'socialism' may refer to mainstream opinion in the British labour movement as well as to Marxism or a commitment to nationalization. The second is to assume that ideologies are mutually exclusive and hence to insist that there are irreconcilable distinctions that permanently separate one ideology from another. In crude terms, the major Western ideologies are seen as *either* liberal *or* conservative *or* socialist. The third misconception is evident in the postulation of a one-to-one relationship between party and ideology, which would equate a liberal with a member of the Liberal party and liberalism with the pronouncements and programmes of that organization.

The methodological premisses concerning ideology, on which the analysis proffered in this book is based, diverge from the above, and are inseparable from the conclusions the book attempts to draw. While in one dimension this work is an examination of the development of the liberal tradition during a particular historical period, in another it is a case study in ideological morphology as a vital indicator of the nature, structure and pliability of political beliefs. In the main, ideologies are sets or conglomerates of ideas and concepts that have a dual function. They aim at directing the user to find his or her way within a socio-political system; that is, they provide a cultural and political map to guide the perplexed or persuade the obdurate. They then recommend political activities commensurate with the map provided, activities that can initiate action on the part of the committed or block the action of other groups that compete over the same social and cultural goods. Ideologies, however, are also distinguished by what may best be described as a modular structure. As it is impossible to appreciate the nature of modern British liberal thought without recognizing this structure, further elaboration is necessary. The following analogy may be helpful.

Imagine a furnished room. By means of its furniture every room has to supply solutions to a series of common problems: seating, lighting, storage, comfort, aesthetics and the like. Each problem in turn has a range of solutions attached to it. Seating, for example, may encompass chairs, sofas and stools. Each of these may have slightly different functions: it may be 'better' to sit on a chair rather than a sofa while typing. But the use of 'better' immediately suggests that the solution to one problem demands solutions to other problems as well. 'Better' may mean in one sense more comfortable, yet more comfortable could involve an unsatisfactory aesthetic solution. Ideologies, too, contend with basic and shared problems: human nature, justice and distribution, the relation between authority and liberty, the determination of the public interest, allegiance and social cohesion, to name some of the more central issues. Let us further assume that the furniture we have in mind is of the variety known as 'modular'. Modular furniture offers a basic range that is designed to be easy to adapt to specified needs, simple to link up with other units as a 'system', and capable of a large number of combinations. Equally, ideologies possess a number of fundamental units supplied to cope with each problem. Distribution, for instance, can be on the basis of need, or merit, or ascription. But what makes an ideology unique is the particular pattern of furniture it utilizes to make its room habitable. It is therefore misconceived to regard ideologies as mutually exclusive in their components, because there are simply more ideologies around than, say, fundamental approaches to the problem of distribution. It is inevitable that more than one ideology will share a concept or an idea. The stamp of uniqueness lies rather in the ordering of the furniture within the room, and in the decision as to which units are compatible with each other. Liberals may want to make liberty their centrepiece and to shove power behind the sofa. Conservatives will direct a spotlight on order and perhaps even temporarily pull a sheet over social responsibility and welfare, a sheet decorated with the motif of self-help. But all serious ideologies have to provide a unit that will cater for every one of the central issues of political thought.

No two normally lived-in rooms are identical and it is hence wrong to suggest one precise model of conservatism, liberalism or socialism. Liberal ideology will, as we shall see in these pages, allow for considerable variety in appearance and interpretation. Nevertheless, the contention here is that, despite the flexibility and differences that mark out empirical manifestations of liberalism, there are some basic characteristics that legitimate the label 'liberal'. When one enters a liberal room, one must be able to say: 'Well, even though this liberal uses curtains different from his next-door colleague's, I can still recognize this room as liberal. The central principles of liberalism are clearly visible, and there is no confusing this arrangement of furniture with any number of other rooms, Marxist, fascist and anarchist, that I have visited.' What makes a room a liberal room? This is a central issue which we shall examine. But it is worth noting at this point that inter-war developments in Britain highlighted as never before that liberals were engrossed in the furnishing of *two* liberal rooms, rooms that were considerably different from each other. Did they have enough in common to be called liberal? If not, which was the real liberal room? Could liberalism legitimately possess two different rooms? These are some of the key themes of this book.

To put all this somewhat differently: ideologies may be seen as a set of concentric circles with a core cluster of concepts and ideas, an adjacent band and a peripheral one.[1] For two instances of ideological thinking to belong to the same family, they must share an identifiable core. Among the core ideas that progressive liberals share—and this assertion is the result of empirical observation, of examining the recurring themes among a large number of liberals—one can locate liberty, rationality, a belief in gradual change, a commitment to legality and constitutionality, and a concern for the general good.[2] However, these ideas by themselves tell us nothing

[1] For a similar notion of a cluster concept see W. E. Connolly, *The Terms of Political Discourse* (Lexington, Mass., 1974), p. 14. Connolly follows W. B. Gallie, 'Essentially Contested Concepts', *Proceedings of the Aristotelian Society*, 59 (1955–6), pp. 167–98, who stresses the internal complexity of concepts, consisting of elements that, although shared by numerous thinkers, may both be accorded different interpretations and be placed in different rankings of importance.

[2] These, I have argued (in M. Freeden, *The New Liberalism: An Ideology of Social Reform* [Oxford, 1978], p. 22), are core components observable in all

about the nature of an ideology, just as an isolated piece of furniture conveys no sense of the room it stands in. The core exists within an idea-environment of adjacent and peripheral concepts, and this environment acts to colour and define the core. A table on its own is too generalized an object to be of use. But if it is surrounded by four chairs, or has a typewriter on it, or perhaps an anaesthetized patient, it takes on a distinct and separate character and function in each case. Similarly, the concept of liberty, by its mere appearance, tells us little; but if it is bordered on by the adjacent concepts of physical integrity and a notion of social atomism it will take on a completely different meaning than when bordered on, for example, by self-realization, mutuality and democracy. Further peripheral ideas on, for instance, sexual morality or immigrants will, in conjunction with the adjacent concepts, not only flesh out the core but may subtly change the entire nature of the ideology. This will, of course, vary further on a time dimension and it is even possible that a core component may disappear over a lengthy period. It is also essential to appreciate that the sharing of elements among ideologies or within sub-streams of one ideology does not signify compatibility or consensus. Identical tables may be part of the furniture of entirely different rooms. One's perception of that table and its function will vary according to its location in the room, the use to which it is put, and the context of the surrounding units of furniture. In other words, it is the morphology of the ideology—the ordering, the patterning, the interplay among concepts—that determines its unique nature.[3]

To sum up, then, a conception of ideology as composed of linked units does away with the misconceptions outlined above that have plagued ideological analysis in the past, and sets the scene for some of the central themes of this book. To postulate a flexible, though not infinite, combination of units under one rubric, can allow for

varieties of liberalism, though they are in no sense a sufficient indicator of the different ways liberals engage these concepts to work for them. But a commitment to some combination of these core ideas is a necessary precondition for designation as liberal.

[3] W. H. Greenleaf (*The British Political Tradition*, vol. ii. *The Ideological Heritage* [London, 1983], pp. 7–15) has drawn attention to ideological overlap, change and flexibility in an analysis with which I entirely concur. His objection to the notion of an ideological core does not contradict the approach offered here, which does not entail a static interpretation of an ideology. The core will bear different constructions depending on its changing idea-environment, as well as on the flexible internal relationships of the core components themselves.

the existence of more than one liberal variant.[4] To regard ideologies as consisting of a number of basic units, some shared, can account for the frequent overlap between different ideologies and do away with the type of boundary problems that mutually exclusive definitions of ideology create, and which are mainly problems of artificial oversimplification. Liberalism can then, for example, 'shade off' into socialism or, for that matter, socialism into conservatism. The 'confusion' caused by liberals who want to redistribute property forcibly, or socialists who fight for individual liberties, or conservatives who harness the power of the state to attain their ends, can be contained as long as it is realized that different adjacent and peripheral environments can surround any particular ideological core; even that what may be a core idea to one ideological pattern is adjacent or peripheral to another.[5] Finally, the insistence on a one-to-one relationship between party and ideology becomes an unnecessary strait-jacket which cannot account for the movement of ideologies across institutional boundaries. Such movement becomes imperative precisely because the original party framework no longer allows for a reasonably flexible adaptation and recombination of the idea-units that formed its ideology, and freezes a restrictive pattern so that, as in the liberal case, party organization is pitted against new ideological developments in a manner threatening to destroy the former and render the latter impotent.

Another problem concerning ideology relates to the school of analysis recently associated with the name of Quentin Skinner, not that it originates with him. Skinner has led a revivalist movement among historians of ideas that attempts to recreate a theorist's intentions within the historical and intellectual context of his times.[6] This approach is undeniably justified, but difficulties arise on two

[4] Max Weber's notion of elective affinity is helpful here, though applied not, as Weber suggests, to the relation between ideas and social organization, but to that between ideas and ideas. The notion of affinity inhabits an area somewhere between full choice and determinism, and would entail the possibility of a range of compatible ideas that an individual may choose within a framework of constraints, logical, moral, metaphysical or practical. Cf. Max Weber, *The Protestant Ethic and the Spirit of Capitalism* (New York, 1958), *passim*. See also A. Giddens, *Capitalism and Modern Social Theory* (Cambridge, 1971), p. 211.

[5] As Manning has noted, 'traditions of ideological writings do not have definable centres any more than they have fixed circumferences' (D. J. Manning, *Liberalism* [London, 1976], p. 62).

[6] Q. Skinner, 'Meaning and Understanding in the History of Ideas', *History and Theory*, 8 (1969), 3–53; 'Some Problems in the Analysis of Political Thought and Action', *Political Theory*, 2 (1974), 277–303.

counts. First, Skinner and his disciples are wary of using ideas themselves as units of analysis. They assume that traditions of ideas are artificial constructs that are frequently imposed by the scholar on his subject-matter. Undoubtedly, some scholars do erroneously reify an ideological tradition as if its meaning were a constant. But what if, as is usually the case, and certainly so in this study, the ideologues it examines *themselves* refer constantly to a tradition, which they feel influences them, and which they in turn seek to change? The idea of a tradition and the need to relate to it become in their own right a binding image upon the thinking of the protagonists in the liberal saga.

Secondly, the concern with intentions is indicative of a worthy line of argument, but one liable to distortion. It ignores one vital facet of ideological systems: they are not only produced but consumed. This is a crucial point if one recalls that the function of ideologies is to appeal to groups and to influence their behaviour. The study of intentions will necessarily be restrictive. It will aim at reconstructing what a theorist had in mind when he committed himself in a public utterance. But what if the theorist was only partially aware of the connotations of the terms of discourse that he employed and their cultural and political significance; what if his ideology is latent rather than manifest? This inevitably happens, as it happened to the liberals in this study, when they became confused over what liberalism meant because, unbeknown to most of them, liberal theory was being conditioned by reference to two different codes, two different idea-environments. Merely to reveal their intentions would leave us in the dark as to the actual ideologies they produced, because they themselves were unaware of the full significance of their creations. As one important context of any idea or set of ideas is that of other ideas available at the time, the theorist's use of language becomes meaningful only inasmuch as we can understand the debates and terms on which he was nourished. This, then, relates to the consumption of ideas by the theorist. At the same time the student of ideologies must focus on the consumption of the theorist's ideas by his contemporaries: what did individuals and groups within whose framework he discoursed, understand him to say? And is there a further latent significance in the arguments employed that eludes the participants altogether? Ideologies become the function of an interplay between the production and consumption of ideas, ideas that, for all we know, may have been misunderstood in a manner that makes a mockery of the intentions of their originators. The consuming of ideas by participants in a political system is the clue to *our* comprehension of their system, and the link to explaining their behaviour within its framework. This study of liberal ideology will try to explore its nature not in terms of the life histories and psychologies of its formulators (which is an interesting but separate approach) but in terms of the ways in which the liberal tradition was understood, misunderstood, debated and constructed by key individuals and groups, whether with intent or without.

Contemporary debates on liberals and libertarians,[7] on participationists and redistributionists,[8] on appropriators and developers of human attributes,[9] also gain in substance and lucidity when the above interpretation of ideological structure is projected on to the historical case study of liberalism that will follow. From this perspective inter-war liberalism becomes a signally important breeding-ground for the theoretical distinctions and terms without which current liberal debate would be impoverished, if not incomprehensible. By having recourse to this recent period in history, new light can be shed on the nuances of modern liberal theory itself. A *rapprochement*, if not a marriage, can be effected between history and theory, and between ideology and philosophy, as the concerns of each are reflected, embellished and refined by the others. This book is designed to address different reading publics—political theorists, historians, students of ideologies. Some portions, such as those that relate to notions of the state, to political obligation, to the meanings attached to equality and to the complexities of the concept of liberty, confront problems that political theorists are particularly acquainted with. Others, such as the sections on the Liberal Summer Schools, have a story to tell and look at the development of modes of thought and behaviour. Behind this lies the conviction that both techniques, that of conceptual analysis and that of sequential analysis, are mutually enhancing.

The quarter-century that began in 1914 experienced major changes that any intellectual historian would want to record. The destructive

[7] See e.g. R. Nozick, *Anarchy, State, and Utopia* (Oxford, 1974); M. J. Sandel, *Liberalism and the Limits of Justice* (Cambridge, 1982).

[8] See A. Gutmann, *Liberal Equality* (Cambridge, 1980).

[9] See C. B. Macpherson, *Democratic Theory: Essays in Retrieval* (Oxford, 1973), ch. 2.

power of mass bureaucracies, foremost among which was the state, overshadowed the hopes for human and social improvement that those organizations had formerly held out for optimistic reformers. The certainties of a civilization that had ruled the world were eroded by the evils it produced, not only through bouts of mutual physical annihilation, but through its inability to anticipate and thus smooth out the course of social change. This is true even of Britain, relatively unscathed by the upheavals that were Europe's fate throughout the nineteenth century, but paying for this immunity in an inability to generate political flexibility and leadership or to adapt institutionally and ideologically to novel technologies and emerging social forces. The Victorians could indulge in massive exercises of self-reassurance because the shining stars in their firmament enjoyed relative fixity: for the rulers, a beneficent class system; for the moralists and preachers, the earnestness and convictions derived from clear codes of behaviour; for the businessmen, models of political economy that endorsed their self-seeking ends. Added to those was a cultural and intellectual confidence that drew sustenance from all-embracing scientific and ethical systems based on the notion of evolution. Evolution both reaffirmed man's primacy in and over nature and accorded a rhythm of gradualness and predictability to the universe in which he resided. In such circumstances, liberalism became a dominant, even if not exclusive, ideology that could preach the virtues of openness and tolerance, precisely because it thrived in a sanguine world whose settledness was not endangered by such virtues.

Nineteenth-century liberalism was a creed nourished by the certain belief in orderly progress. Its successor, the new liberalism, continued in the same vein. Realizing that the price of Victorian smugness had been a heavy one in terms of human welfare, it affirmed its faith in the power of an intelligent, rational, and sociable humanity to overcome the defects of social organization. Post-1914 liberalism entered a different mood. The immutable laws of social intercourse had been defiled by the war; the economic prosperity that had shored liberalism up diminished rapidly. Liberalism, removed from its position of power and influence, had to fight against a system it had dominated for so long: this was no less than a humiliation. Tactical retreats disguised potential routs: individual and political liberty was once again at risk and had to be defended; the state—that creation of intelligent humanity—was turning upon its maker; the increasing intrusion of power, struggle, and class into social relations found liberalism unequipped to cope; and the certainties of the liberal *Weltanschauung* were displaced by an attitude to social thought and action euphemistically called experimentation. The latter masked a sometimes floundering search for new systems to act as signposts for a confused multitude, epitomized by the failure of psychology to serve in a surrogate role to evolution as the new science of human behaviour, and by the inadequacy of the new formulas to replicate in the industrial field the successes liberalism had achieved with political democracy. Added to this were grave epistemological problems that affected liberal thought and deserve scrutiny. What, after all, do liberals do when the goodness of human nature is called into question by a horrific war, or by the manipulative, self-interested and socially injurious acts of capitalists? Up to what point can society be changed to accommodate and supply the outlets for reasonable and altruistic behaviour in line with liberal beliefs, when observable human behaviour frequently does not accord with those beliefs and, moreover, economics and philosophy no longer provide compelling and simple explanations of human action? How can the universalism embodied in liberal theory survive the uncompromising hostility among sectional groups that appear closer to the 'herd instinct' than to the overarching rational notion of community or even to the calculating rationalism of the utilitarian 'greatest happiness of the greatest number'?

These issues forced liberals to seek new solutions in their political theorizing. But all too often the quality of that theorizing was itself a victim of the incertitudes it was called upon to dispel. A belief in liberalism was adhered to mechanically, almost dogmatically. The difficulties that beset the Liberal party reverberated on to the ideology, as most supporters could not detach the one from the other.[10] This deterioration in the status of politics and the calibre of politicians was but a further example of the pernicious linkage between party and ideology in Britain. The decline of the serious press, especially the periodicals that had been the mainstay of liberal-

[10] As J. A. Hobson correctly surmised, most liberals mistakenly anticipated the extinction of their political tradition because 'they identify the future carrying power of liberalism as a philosophy with the survival of the Liberal party as an effective instrument of government' ('Liberalism in British Politics', *New Republic*, 3.3. 1926).

ism, and the growing popularization and deintellectualization of the daily newspapers, robbed liberals of a traditional mode of disseminating ideas and programmes. Not least, central supportive disciplines, especially philosophy, moved away from socio-political concerns and could no longer be utilized to invigorate liberal theory, to supply it with ethical and moral arguments, and to accord it the respectability of academic standing, in the manner that, for example, T. H. Green's Idealism had done in the past. Indeed, the professionalization of both philosophy and economics removed them from political accessibility and thus alienated political thought from two centres of intellectual creativity that had been vital to the health of liberalism. Furthermore, those liberal theorists that remained were, with the few exceptions that had reached their creative apex before the war, low-key and remote from the higher reaches of intellectual life, nor did they seem capable of reacting to the new fashions in thought that were rocking the Continent. The result was a political and ideological deracination of liberalism that merely sustained the social flight from Liberalism of both the middle and the working classes. At the end of it all, many liberals themselves no longer knew what, if anything, had survived of their liberal beliefs.

Yet this is no simple tale of ideological regression. As will be made clear in the following chapters, liberalism was not dormant between the wars, nor was its path one of unmitigated failure. In the long run, it succeeded in one important mission—to keep alive the hopes and aims of British progressives; to pass them on, in slightly different form, to different bodies, perhaps for a future time. One of the main purposes of this study has been to explore the achievements, however modest, as well as the deficiencies, of liberalism between 1914 and 1939. The pre-1914 generation has in recent years yielded many of its intellectual secrets to modern scholars. It is perhaps time for historians of ideas and political theorists to turn to the inter-war period with the same questions in mind. Inter-war liberalism especially still suffers from having been perceived mainly through the eyes of Labour historians, a fate that befell its predecessor, the new liberalism, for many years. The unearthing of post-war liberalism is an exercise that, not surprisingly, may challenge existing knowledge and opinions in a number of areas. Many of the perspectives this book offers on liberalism are, as already indicated, a concomitant of subscribing to the version of ideological structure that I have proposed above. It may, however, be useful to mention some of the central propositions this study wishes to argue.

As a result of the First World War, the new liberalism which for a relatively short while had intellectually dominated liberal ideology underwent a partial rethinking of its positions; indeed, for many progressive liberals the war did not signal the persuasive strength of collectivism but, conversely and unexpectedly, the dangers of state intervention. Though many new liberals moderated some of their immediate hostility to the state, that shift indicated the importance of individual liberty to liberal thought—a rather obvious point that had nevertheless been neglected through the pre-war emphasis on social welfare. Indirectly, this assisted in the re-emergence of another variety of liberalism, as the new liberalism was perceived to return to older tenets and its emerging doubts weakened its hold upon the liberal intelligentsia. The consequence was a development implicit in the nature of liberal theory, but one that surfaced clearly from the early 1920s onwards. When the new (or left) liberals recovered some of their poise, liberalism experienced a bifurcation into two main streams, left and centrist, each of which could claim to represent cardinal components of the liberal tradition and, further, could with some justification call itself progressive. The use of the label 'progressive' is a convenient one to distinguish supporters of the liberal propensity to improve and reform individuals and their social arrangements from the libertarian propensity merely to unshackle the individual and assume that this will be conducive to the social good.[11] No doubt, there were progressives at the time who would not have called themselves liberal, but the designation of the term throughout this study relates to individuals who all shared a liberal core of ideas.

Both liberal traditions had existed earlier; what was new was the lack of certainty as to which wing of liberalism was liberalism. By studying the two variants side by side it is possible to examine their nature with greater precision; it is also possible to endorse the case of both wings for inheriting the liberal mantle—that is, to accept the theoretical and practical bifurcation of liberalism as immanent in

[11] K. Minogue, *The Liberal Mind* (London, 1963), pp. 61–8, 201, also identifies two strands in liberalism, which he calls the libertarian and the salvationist. I would argue that *within* progressive, non-libertarian liberalism there were important divisions, whereas libertarianism was alienating itself from liberalism (cf. Chapter 7).

its ideology, and as becoming manifest in its reaction to modern industrialism. Centrist-liberalism used adjacent concepts such as individuality, private property and security to surround its liberal core; left-liberalism made social justice, welfare and community pull in another direction. There is a further need here for analytical 'fine tuning', as each of these two liberalisms employed the adjacent concepts of the other, but in a more peripheral position. For example, centrist-liberals *were* concerned about standards of welfare; left-liberals *did* accept the rationale behind some degree of private property. But in the first case, welfare was frequently made to bow to efficiency and productivity; in the second, private property was severely restricted by social needs and communal priorities. To confuse matters more, both streams often used identical concepts, such as liberty and equality, but then proceeded to stretch them to cover a range of diverging interpretations, or placed them in idea-environments that gave them different meanings. Centrist-liberalism was an older, capitalist, commercial and more individualist tradition that re-emerged strongly as a reaction to economic and institutional weaknesses in the 1920s, seeking liberal hope in past images of man and society, though often attached to new institutional and technical solutions. Left-liberals were the new liberals of a decade earlier, sadder though not much wiser, who upheld the radical and egalitarian traditions of liberalism, though without the momentum that the new liberalism had sustained for a brief moment in British history. Centrist-liberals became more narrowly political and in their wake the cultural horizons of liberalism receded. In their hands liberalism became a dour instrument of politics, not a vision of society. Left-liberals tried to retain the fire of liberalism but even they had to resign themselves to the fact that, at a time when British political thought had little excitement to offer, their ideology was no longer at the hub of intellectual, scientific, and moral advancement. Although left-liberalism may have been intellectually more sophisticated, it is not intended to suggest that either branch espoused superior values or established a standard by which to measure the other. Both left-liberalism and centrist-liberalism attempted valid ideological responses to perceived needs and both experienced successes and failures. The existence of these two traditions became salient and evident to their more perceptive adherents only a few years after the end of the war; this is why the terms do not come into their own in Chapters 2 and 3. At the same time it is right to note that both varieties of liberalism attest to the demise of a sharp dichotomy between individualism and collectivism. It is also true that in practice communities of progressive liberals were often intermeshed; that the groups and coteries of liberal thinkers each contained left-liberals and centrist-liberals; and that some individuals themselves moved between the two liberalisms. The distinction, though vital, is more analytical than historical; whether or not liberals were aware of it at the time (and some like Hobhouse were) has no bearing upon its existence, and cannot detract from its usefulness in comprehending liberalism.

The ideological framework of analysis employed here is not merely helpful in dissecting liberalism 'internally'; it also supports a further cardinal assertion, namely, that the liberal tradition was partially 'externalized' and carried on by individuals who formally adhered to 'socialism'. The moment one discards the confinement of an ideology to a political party, it is possible to extend one's perspective to the existence of that ideology outside those boundaries. Liberalism certainly pervaded other institutions and was absorbed by neighbouring ideologies. The position advanced here, by way of illustration, is that some major British socialist thinkers—Laski, Tawney and, to a lesser extent, Cole—were at times within the left-liberal tradition in all senses save that of self-awareness. Moreover, the Labour party—both in terms of personnel and of ideas—became host to clearly left-liberal beliefs which, though they could not claim to be exclusive, overlapped heavily with some of the socialist components of Labour ideology and vied with others for a say in its fortunes. A plea is consequently entered here for a reassessment of the nature of the British liberal and socialist traditions and their complex relationship. No doubt the same could have been done for the relation between some variants of conservatism and centrist-liberalism, but the association of liberalism with socialism comes more naturally to a book that is primarily concerned with the progressive tradition. Limitations of space, too, have excluded this avenue of exploration, as they have a consideration of land and education issues. These latter questions were, furthermore, not located at the heart of the industrial preoccupations of inter-war liberal thought. As for international relations, liberal attitudes deserve a study on their own, and have only been alluded to in order to illustrate their closeness or 'linkage' to thinking on domestic issues.

A detailed tour through inter-war liberalism must observe further phenomena to which little consideration has been given to date. The role of liberals in forging an approach to industrial relations cannot be overlooked. The achievements and relevance of that approach may be queried, but it does at least demonstrate that there were some creative areas in liberal theory and that ideological innovation was still possible. The success story of the liberalism of the 1920s, in theory and practice, is the Liberal Summer School, which itself encapsulated divergent attitudes on social reform versus economic reorganization, on redistribution as social ethics and planning as social engineering. The dominance of Keynes must be contended with, though it is proposed that his political thinking was neither original nor radical; that his economic concerns were set in a framework of centrist-liberal making, and that to treat him as a liberal in isolation from those influences is to abandon a vital dimension of analysis. The interesting, though unsatisfying, connection between psychology and left-liberalism also deserves attention as an example of an ideology searching for new scientific truths on which to rebuild confidence in its fundamental beliefs. The 1930s are also a focus of interest for the part played by liberalism in buttressing democracy as well as in consolidating what has been termed 'middle opinion', though here again the nature of ideological structure must deter the scholar from referring to a false conception of consensus. Overlapping ideological positions, sharing adjacent and peripheral concepts but with different cores may create the semblance of consensus or of ideological convergence; time and a closer look usually prove these illusory.

A few words are due on the structure of the book, which reflects its methodological concerns. The strategy employed for each chapter has been the one judged most suitable for the subject it encompasses. Chapters 2 and 3 examine the impact of the war and the post-war period on liberal thought, while drawing especial attention to its repercussions on liberal theory. Chapter 4 deals with the development of an important institution that fashioned liberal theory, crystallized many of the major liberal groupings, and sustained some of the more significant liberal thinkers examined in this study. Chapter 5 is devoted mainly to the theoretical assumptions explicit and implicit in centrist-liberalism, especially those pertaining to human nature and social reorganization, though the necessary comparisons with left-liberal thought are drawn. Chapter

6 shifts attention to the attitudes of both centrist-liberals and left-liberals to the developments on the 'left' of liberalism—the tortuous attraction-repulsion relationship with socialism and the Labour party and, to a lesser extent, trade unionism. Chapter 7 is the inverse of Chapter 5: it scrutinizes left-liberal ideology and sets its core ideas within their contexts. Because of the higher theoretical complexity of left-liberalism, the chapter also contains a more analytical treatment of three central concepts: equality, property, and liberty. It also casts a comparative glance at centrist-liberalism to indicate similarities and divergences. Abetted by this theoretical discussion, the theme of Chapter 6 is further amplified in Chapter 8, when a mirror-image tactic is adopted, namely the chapter analyses, for their liberal content, some representative socialist theorists, hitherto believed to be located just beyond the vague and imaginary boundary that divides socialism from liberalism. Finally, Chapter 9 looks at liberalism in the 1930s, though many of its characteristics in this period have already been discussed under previous headings. Nevertheless, the 1930s posed particular problems for liberalism that demand attention in a historical-institutional context which can illustrate some of the theoretical conclusions drawn earlier. The conclusion by way of Beveridge is a slight leap in time, but in view of the importance both of his Report and of his putative role in liberalism, it is useful to conclude the chapter with some comments on the relation between the Report and inter-war liberalism.

It will be realized by now that this study deliberately abstains from employing any particular research strategy. Its consistency inheres in an allegiance to a theory of ideological structure that requires a multi-faceted approach, and in a desire to uncover the complex nature of inter-war liberalism. The history of ideas tolerates no clear-cut narrative boundaries, while the recourse to issues of political theory—ultimately the main concern of this study— necessitates perspectives that cut across temporal ones and attempt to synthesize empirical evidence in order to discover general trends. A similar flexibility in the use of source material is required. For much of the period, a few liberal dailies and weeklies became the focus of intellectual ferment and these afford the most thorough insight into the liberal mentality; Hobhouse's leaders and occasional articles, continuing their pre-war function, deserve special mention. In contradistinction to Edwardian liberalism, both

Parliamentary debates and official Liberal publications lose much of their pertinence as indicators of the frontiers of liberalism. Some private papers have proved unexpectedly useful in probing liberal minds, and quite a few letters evince a surprising willingness to ruminate on theoretical issues.

Post-war liberalism has no classics, no single book by a Mill, Green or Hobhouse that epitomizes the current state of liberal thought. In neither quality nor range can even Hobhouse's *The Metaphysical Theory of the State* aspire to that status, nor any single book by J. A. Hobson.[12] Instead, there exists a large number of thoughtful, exploratory works side by side with more humdrum productions. Some of the writers that figure frequently on these pages, such as Hobson, Ramsay Muir, and C. Delisle Burns, were very prolific; others, such as E. D. Simon, published little of direct relevance to liberalism, but left many unpublished thoughts for posterity. Examination of these thinkers is supplemented through reference to books and articles by a host of other liberal luminaries so as to tap what is, after all, not the product of any individual but of a number of interlocking groups. It is interesting to note in this connection the many protagonists of this study who referred to each other in prefaces and footnotes. Who influenced whom becomes a barren question when one is confronted with a plethora of mutual acknowledgements and book reviews by figures such as Hobson, Hobhouse, Tawney, Laski, Wallas and C. D. Burns, sustained over a period of many years. Inter-war liberalism is undoubtedly the creation of a group mind, though one that was increasingly exhibiting alarming schizophrenic symptoms. The label 'liberal' no longer entailed a choice between left or centre; it had become both left *and* centre. And inasmuch as this fragmented but extended liberalism still represented a major element of the indigenous political mind, British ideology and political culture were overwhelmingly preoccupied with the issues of individualism and self-determination together with those of democratic equalization as the foci of a well-constituted social life. Whether these issues were distinct or complementary was the question that, then as now, hung in the balance.

[12] Much of Hobhouse's and Hobson's opus had been written by 1914 and is outside the scope of this study.

2

THE WAR ON LIBERALISM

THE study of twentieth-century politics and history is inextricably bound up with issues of war and peace, but this classificatory perspective has often been applied at the cost of accuracy. The world wars have on the whole been the subjects of separate studies and their dates have helped neatly to demarcate eras in European history. The First World War especially has been seen as the great divide between a century of harmony and peace and the unleashing of the irrationalism that blemished the world after 1914. Within the British context the war has further been portrayed as 'a triumph of state planning' to many people of progressive sympathies and as an impetus to the advance of collectivism.[1] A close examination of the impact of the war on the domestic ideological scene, however, reveals continuities as well as changes; indeed, the analysis of British liberalism can only be harmed by treating the war as a separate unit of study or as a *deus ex machina* or 'rampant omnibus'.[2] In terms of political thought it eliminated some tendencies but exacerbated others: the ideological development of liberalism was powerfully influenced by the war, yet the war created little that was totally new in political thinking. The aftermath of the war—reconstruction and the debates of the 1920s—also had its roots in the pre-war period as well as in the war itself. No new phoenixes arose out of its ashes, but when the dusts of war had settled some of the older phoenixes looked rather more menacing, while others were scarred with the burst fragments of ideological dogmas and political illusions.

The advent of the war saw a curious development among liberal thinkers. The confident and combatant mood of the pre-1914 new liberals had stretched the limits of liberal theory to a point where mutual responsibility, social welfare and common ends had staked claims equal to, and occasionally prior to, the liberty of the in-

[1] A. Marwick, *The Explosion of British Society 1914–1970* (London, 1971), pp. 13–14; W. H. Greenleaf, *The British Political Tradition*, vol. i. *The Rise of Collectivism* (London, 1983), pp. 74, 76.

[2] T. Wilson, *The Downfall of the Liberal Party 1914–1935* (London, 1968), p. 20.

dividual. In the climate of opinion surrounding the National Insurance Act progressives did not feel the need to account for the paradoxical semblance of quasi-Rousseauist utterances which held that compulsion simply meant a larger freedom.[3] The war channelled this assertive and energetic liberalism in an entirely unexpected direction. Unexpected, that is, to those who not unnaturally assumed that the case for individual liberty had been presented in its ultimate form by J. S. Mill, and that the attainment of individual and civil liberties was a chapter of history now virtually closed. Moreover, the liberal creed suddenly appeared to its subscribers as a beleaguered rather than dominant doctrine. While it still benefited from the high intellectual and moral standards of its espousers and from an unimpaired sense of justice, liberals were dismayed and perplexed by the abrupt and completely unanticipated downswing in their fortunes, political and ideological. Their reaction set the tone for inter-war liberalism and was to determine the way in which the rich legacy of the new liberalism would be spent.

By the beginning of 1915 the first gnawing doubts were being voiced. Leonard Hobhouse—liberal theorist, sociologist and journalist—converted the leader columns of the *Manchester Guardian* into a stronghold of liberal rhetoric. Hobhouse, as well as other prominent liberals, did not engage in mere anti-war invective. Their opus was within the pre-war liberal tradition of a detailed commentary on current affairs, to which liberal principles were meticulously applied, side by side with more general theoretical frameworks to which detailed events could be related. In Hobhouse's case this framework was constructed in his more contemplative essays as well as in works such as *The Metaphysical Theory of the State*. He and his co-liberals reverted during the war to a restatement of liberal essentials in plain and pristine form, not least because the war vulgarized, as war often does, the finer distinctions of political argument; but also, and more pertinently, because the internal repercussions of the war challenged the hard-won achievements of nineteenth-century British liberalism as a whole. Hobhouse especially—ever sceptical, ever gloomy as the depressions of his later years increased their deadening hold on him—reflected the bewilderment that accompanied the clash of opposing social philosophies. The power of the state, competitive versus co-operative versions of

[3] Freeden, *The New Liberalism*, pp. 231–3.

human nature, social revolution and the rise of new classes, the possible failure of humanitarianism and doubts about the inevitability of progress—all combined in a seething witches' brew of beliefs.[4]

1. CONSCRIPTION AND THE LIBERAL CONSCIENCE

As the hopes of an early end to the war receded, liberal concerns, practical and theoretical, began to crystallize round a number of issues. First and foremost came that of compulsion, as the debate over conscription began to gather momentum during 1915. The liberal aversion to compulsion provides in effect the key to wartime liberal attitudes and illuminates the old/new directions liberalism was beginning to follow. The debates on the Ministry of Munitions Bill in mid-1915 exposed a wide front of liberal feeling against compulsion, the issue at stake being the liberties of workers (and the rights of trade unions) in munitions-related industries. Liberals reaffirmed their faith in the power of the 'voluntary traditions of this country [which] have accomplished things of which we have every reason to be proud'.[5] At the same time a plethora of intriguing and contradictory developments in liberal thought was taking place. A willingness to condone limited compulsion began to emerge among those liberals who, while undoubtedly progressive, were not among those pre-war liberal collectivists who had come to terms with restrictions on individual liberty for the sake of the common good. Conversely, those reared in the new liberal interventionist tradition suddenly turned away from the imminence of coercing individuals to fight for their country.

The more moderate liberal press argued that, unpleasant as any affront to the voluntary principle was, other considerations prevailed. J. A. Spender's *Westminster Gazette* asserted that 'we place no limits on the claims of the State to the service of its individual citizens in a struggle in which its honour, and it may be its existence, is at stake'.[6] And the *Daily Chronicle* made a rare entry into political theory when contending that those problems were 'all part of a wider problem which is set by every great war for every

[4] See L. T. Hobhouse, *Questions of War and Peace* (London, 1916); also the following reviews: J. A. H[obson], 'Philosophy in War-Time', *MG*, 28.6.1916; 'Professor Hobhouse's Dialogue', *Saturday Westminster Gazette*, 8.7.1916.

[5] 'Munitions and Compulsion', *DN*, 8.6.1915.

[6] 'Methods of Controversy', *WG*, 2.6.1915.

democracy'. Curtailment of liberty was necessary for national survival, but in order to preserve liberty, popular submission should as far as possible 'be that of enlightened free-will, not that of mechanical compulsion'.[7]

The gist of this moderate liberal position was that there was nothing 'necessarily anti-Liberal or anti-democratic in compulsory service in time of war',[8] provided that the objects of compulsion could be persuaded of its rationality and fairness. Most of the liberal press, however, was still bound up by ties of personal loyalty to the Liberal government. Serving the flag had always been considered by liberals to be a fundamental citizen duty. But a schism in liberal opinion was in the making. The *Daily News*—not an overt organ of the new liberalism but often to be found on its fringes—began to adopt a more sceptical stance. It condemned the so-called 'equality of sacrifice' of general conscription, both because of the differential value of individuals and because of the inefficient removal of workers from spheres of productive labour. It averred that this 'Prussianization' of the labour force, the system of forced military service, had in German hands been one of the prime causes of the war.[9] By early 1916, when a limited conscription Bill was being debated by Parliament, it declared that the Bill introduced 'a principle which is alien to our spirit and which once introduced will remain as a permanent menace to our conceptions of liberty'.[10] On the very same day, the *Daily Chronicle* continued its path of reconciliation with governmental action, and proclaimed: 'Let us say at once that if compulsory service is to be introduced it could hardly be introduced in a more unobjectionable form'.[11] The third of the London trio also cast its lot in favour of conscription, recalling that although the voluntary system had served the nation splendidly, it was now exhausted by the course the war had taken. Liberty was transformed from an absolute end into a variable: 'The only way to regain our liberty after the war is to be willing to sacrifice some of our liberty so that success in the war may be sure and decisive'.[12]

[7] 'Labour and Munitions', *DC*, 17.6.1915.

[8] 'Labour and Military Service', *WG*, 8.9.1915. See also 'Service in Life and Property', *WG*, 26.6.1915.

[9] 'Conscription in the Lords', *DN*, 15.7.1915.

[10] 'The Crisis', *DN*, 6.1.1916.

[11] 'The Limited Compulsion Bill', *DC*, 6.1.1916.

[12] 'Liberty and War', *WG*, 13.1.1916. See also the discussion on liberty in Chapter 7, Section 5.

The new liberals, in the meantime, were embarking on a remarkable and unexpected route of their own. Already in the early days of the war Hobhouse was condemning plans for the temporary nationalization of industries to sustain the war effort, 'a definite nationalisation of a vast branch of industry, superseding private management, disregarding private ownership', as 'a departure of immense significance . . . the most sweeping interference with private rights that the war has yet produced'.[13] This developed into widespread concern and resentment pertaining to the Defence of the Realm Act—its censorship, powers of secret arrest and trial, and restrictions in the industrial sphere—and focused into an onslaught by left-liberal intellectuals on the government. What, they asked, was the purpose of the war if it destroyed what it intended to preserve? 'We go to war professedly to fight for freedom, and are rapidly introducing industrial and military slavery here.' Already at this stage the future portents were visible: 'There will be no Liberal Party as we have known it. It is abdicating its birthright; it will have lost its soul'.[14] The Liberal government was no longer the liberal government. Hobhouse, who from his early Oxford days had decried the cultural and philosophical influence of Germany, now discovered the spectre of things German in the erosion of British freedom. This was more than simple identification with nationalist public opinion; rather, it must be seen as a severe indictment of the rationale behind the domestic activities of the Asquith Administration: 'Conscription means discipline and order. It provides a way of dealing with strikers. . . . It will help to keep the working classes "in their place". It will, in fact, re-create in England the German model'.[15] Indeed, continued Hobhouse, even in terms of the argument for efficiency (one of the obsessions of the Edwardian age spurred on by competition with Germany), the best were already serving under the voluntary system. A few days later Hobhouse returned with the theoretical backdrop. Compulsion, especially when applied to conscientious objectors—who were rapidly becoming the test case for the protection of fundamental individual liberties[16]—raised an issue that was 'the final crux of

[13] [L. T. Hobhouse], 'Socialism in War', *MG*, 10.3.1915.

[14] J. R. Tomlinson, 'Liberalism and the War', letter to the Editor, *Nation*, 23.10.1915.

[15] [L. T. Hobhouse], 'The Cry for Conscription', *MG*, 1.6.1915.

[16] See e.g. C. P. Trevelyan, *Hansard*, 5th Ser. LXXVIII 275 (18.1.1916).

political theory and practice'. Interestingly enough, the case against compulsory military service was not argued along the traditional liberal lines of sanctity of life or absolute natural rights. Hobhouse's argument reflected the concerns of his mentor T. H. Green, for compulsion struck at the 'authority of conscience and the moral autonomy of the individual' that formed 'the kernel of the *modern* principle of liberty'.[17] As Green had repeatedly observed, morality could not be enforced and law was but an insistence on external conformity.[18]

It was significant that Hobhouse nailed his epistemological colours to the mast at that point in time. The new liberalism had gone some way towards merging individual identity within a common entity (though Hobhouse had never accepted the extremes of this approach). By postulating both methodological individualism and voluntarism as corner-stones of his theoretical position, Hobhouse moved emphatically away from that collectivism and towards resurrecting essentials of the liberal creed that had been underplayed by new liberals, and did so more convincingly than many of his more moderate liberal contemporaries. Indeed, he practically overtook them in his zeal for stressing individual rights against the community. In an imaginary dialogue Hobhouse wrote in 1916, the narrator describes the movement of the liberal pendulum, first away from the old liberalism with its one-sided concept of liberty, then—through the new liberalism—swinging too far in the opposite direction, but possibly regaining its balance. His hopes are tempered by Hobhouse's *alter ego*, Pentire, pessimistically worrying about the nation's lack of will or capacity to achieve that moderate resting point.[19]

It is illuminating to find another liberal acquainted with Green's teachings—Herbert Samuel—adopting a rather different theoretical standpoint over the very same issues of compulsion. In what may be seen as an official Liberal reply to the liberal critics of the government, Samuel conceded that conscription entailed the

[17] [L. T. Hobhouse], 'Compulsion', *MG*, 12.6.1915. My italics. Hobhouse's relative, Stephen Hobhouse, was an active conscientious objector who was imprisoned during the war (S. Hobhouse, *Forty Years and an Epilogue* [London, 1951]). Cf. also J. Rae, *Conscience and Politics* (Oxford, 1970).

[18] See T. H. Green, *Lectures on the Principles of Political Obligation* (London, 1941), pp. 34–41; L. T. Hobhouse, *The Metaphysical Theory of the State* (London, 1918), p. 122. Cf. 'The State God', *Nation*, 7.12.1918.

[19] Hobhouse, *Questions of War and Peace*, p. 112.

greatest sacrifice of liberty, but added that 'It is one of the virtues of British liberty that it knows when to limit itself. If it did not, it could not have survived'.[20] In the industrial sphere, urged Samuel, compulsion in the form of the prohibition of restrictive trade practices was vital to the well-being of the nation.[21]

The reasons that liberals such as Hobhouse were not prepared to recognize what their fellow-liberals, and even more so liberals in the 1920s and 1930s, could accept without difficulty—namely, that conscription may be argued in terms of national interest and common good—are complex. On the most basic level, they were out of sympathy with the war aims. Many would have endorsed the strong case put by J. A. Hobson—the liberal social theorist and economist—to the effect that the

> assaults on civil liberty are not the mere products of emergency, but belong to the considered defences of Conservatism . . . the object and the effort of the long campaign against civil liberty are to habituate the people to acquiesce in the deprivation of their historic rights, and so to undermine the moral supports of democracy.[22]

Certainly C. P. Scott used the full force of the *Manchester Guardian* to rail against the conscription measures of early 1916.[23] There was further a greater sympathy for the hardships of the working classes and for their interests. While moderate liberals did not hesitate to recommend a modicum of compulsion of the working classes as part of an élitist assertion of what was good for the nation, left-liberals employed the traditional liberal paraphernalia of individual rights to protect the hard-won and now imperilled social and political gains of the less privileged. Beyond that, however, there was a clear reaction away from the *terra incognita*, in terms of socio-political theory, that the new liberalism had been exploring. The residual liberal belief that voluntarism was the

[20] H. Samuel, *The War and Liberty* (London, 1917), p. 46.

[21] Ibid., pp. 61–3.

[22] J. A. Hobson, 'The War and British Liberties. IV. Liberty as a True War Economy', *Nation*, 29.7.1916. Hobson together with many other new liberals was active in anti-war groups such as the British Neutrality Committee and the Union of Democratic Control. See M. Swartz, *The Union of Democratic Control in British Politics During the First World War* (Oxford, 1971), ch. 2 and *passim*; C. A. Cline, *Recruits to Labour: The British Labour Party 1914–1931* (Syracuse, 1963), pp. 8–23; P. Clarke, *Liberals and Social Democrats* (Cambridge, 1978), pp. 166–71.

[23] [C. P. Scott], 'The Coming Bill', *MG*, 3.1.1916; 'The Compulsion Bill in Parliament', *MG*, 12.1.1916.

mainspring of social progress was restated with conviction. This had not been such an issue among liberals before the war because of the tentative and restricted scope of state regulation and compulsion. Most social reform legislation had been directed at specific underprivileged or exposed sections of society and even if the principle of compulsion for all had been recognized, it did not have widespread practical effect. DORA and the Munitions Acts changed all this because of their general application and because, one is tempted to say, the conscientious objector was too close to the liberal intelligentsia for comfort. The fate of Bertrand Russell threatened the very livelihood of the liberal social critic. No wonder that Hobhouse and others rallied to his support. 'Above all things we stand for freedom', asserted the long leader of the *Manchester Guardian* after Russell's dismissal from Trinity College, Cambridge, 'and the world judges us, and at bottom we are forced to judge ourselves, by the kind of freedom that we maintain in test cases.'[24] Freedom and the voluntarist organization of society underpinned the moral support of governmental action[25] as well as ensuring that the nature of the war was truly determined by the people, because voluntarism alone made the people effective masters.[26] In sum, the curtailment of liberties during the war posed a universal threat to individual consciences and life styles in a way that the restricted social reform compulsion before the war did not. Liberal-democracy was perceived as under serious attack for the first time since it had emerged as a leading strand of British ideology and politics.

Left-liberals were especially pained by the reverses their own creed was suffering. The *Nation* had made the astounding discovery of an infant sibling to free trade—free service—and considered both to be endangered by the war.[27] In an article entitled 'The "Letting Down" of Liberalism' it listed Home Rule and the Right of Asylum as further casualties of governmental policy. 'Whether the instrument to these changes be force or assent,' it commented, 'it was inevitable that with them much of the sap of the old Liberalism

[24] 'Moral Impediments', *MG*, 15.7.1916. See also 'Liberty and the Government', *DN*, 2.9.1916. Many liberals also followed the activities of pacifists and quasi-pacifists closely. On those activities during the war, see M. Ceadel, *Pacifism in Britain 1914–1945: The Defining of a Faith* (Oxford, 1980), ch. 4.

[25] J. A. Hobson, 'The War and British Liberties', *Nation*, 29.7.1916.

[26] [L. T. Hobhouse], 'Pressure and Compulsion', *MG*, 25.9.1915.

[27] 'The Country and its Rulers', *Nation*, 22.1.1916. See also [L. T. Hobhouse], 'The English Way', *MG*, 20.5.1916.

should go too.'[28] The Russian revolution of March 1917 was the occasion for a surprising outpouring of praise that only makes sense in the domestic British context. As Hobhouse put it, 'the spirit of the new democracy in Russia is what the spirit of democracy should be. . . . To feel this deep and genuine sympathy with Russian freedom we must recover the sense of freedom among ourselves.'[29] The extolling of Russia as an example for Britain was a bitter reaction to 'this disappearance of Liberalism from the effective government of England'.[30] By 1918 the gloom was all-pervading: 'The Liberal organization has almost ceased to exist. The Liberal attitude, the Liberal habit of mind, has gone out of fashion.'[31]

This was far more than mere frustration with the leadership feud within the party, or with Lloyd George's increasing conservative links. It was a deep feeling that the fundamental ideals of traditional liberalism had been damaged beyond repair:

> Thirty or forty years ago, [liberalism] was the main expression of a policy morally timorous indeed, but humane and progressive. Peace, Liberty, Economy, Free Industry were the watchwords of this older Liberalism. It attached a restricted meaning to them all. But in their full significance, Peace, Liberty, Economy, and Free Industry remain the master-keys of the society of the future.[32]

In a decided shift towards stressing continuity rather than change, the unity of liberalism rather than its evolution, the *Nation* observed that 'nearly all the later political movements have been more or less conscious expansions' of the old liberal principles. The radical, pioneering ethic of the new liberalism was exchanged for a return to the basic building blocks, the removal of which now seemed to threaten the entire edifice.

2. THE STATE: AN IDEA IN DECLINE

The rediscovery of liberty was however but one, and perhaps not the most crucial, development of liberalism after 1914. Of central

[28] 'The "Letting Down" of Liberalism', *Nation*, 5.8.1916.

[29] [L. T. Hobhouse], 'The Dawn', *MG*, 14.4.1917. Cf. Samuel, *The War and Liberty*, p. 12.

[30] 'The Defeat of Liberalism', *Nation*, 6.5.1916.

[31] 'The State of British Parties', *Nation*, 6.7.1918.

[32] 'A Message from Laodicea', *Nation*, 14.9.1918. Cf. Clarke, *Liberals and Social Democrats*, p. 182.

importance was the searching treatment accorded to the concept of the state. Despite the pre-1914 adoption of some mildly socialist policies that involved state intervention in order to guarantee minima of social welfare, the scope and scale of state activity during the war were clearly unprecedented. When coupled with the fact that such activity was on the whole offensive from the liberal viewpoint, it is not surprising that the optimistic and sometimes naïve attitude of the new liberalism to the state evaporated rapidly. Gone was the notion of the state as neutral and benevolent broker among interests, or as the political manifestation of the common good and the social will, the agent of a rational society.

A number of paths converged upon the reassessment of the state as idea and as institution. The first was a direct corollary of the question of compulsion, for it was the state that now appeared as the instrument of coercion. As Hobson noted: 'In war, not only does the State become absolute in its relations towards the individual, but militarism becomes absolute within the State.'[33] Hobhouse, reviewing Hobson's book, quoted the latter with approval: 'Hard personal experience will have taught . . . what an instrument of destruction and oppression a state may be' and endorsed Hobson's conclusion that the state would have to be 'conquered' by means of democracy.[34] The 'heavy inroads upon . . . ordinary liberties of speech, meeting and Press, of travel, trade, occupation and investment'[35] had written a new chapter in the curious history of the word 'socialism'. Associated in the 1890s with the idea of mutuality and social responsibility, narrowed down to Labour schemes of nationalization in the Edwardian era, socialism now became a state socialism unconnected with its original ideological roots. In the words of Havelock Ellis:

> We were in presence, not of a collapse of Socialism, but of a readjustment of our whole politico-social ideal . . . Socialism is not only a great and remote abstract ideal in which it is possible to believe that the salvation of humanity may be found. It is also a very concrete, systematic, and detailed process, the weaving of a vast web of endless regulations, the construction of a huge bureaucracy to supervise these regulations, together with the glorification of the idea of a supreme State representing a power which no

[33] J. A. Hobson, *Democracy After the War* (London, 1917), pp. 13–14.

[34] [L. T. Hobhouse], 'The Recovery of Liberty', *MG*, 29.12.1917, quoting from Hobson, *Democracy After the War*, pp. 160–1.

[35] Hobson, *Democracy After the War*, p. 14.

autocratic despot could ever hope to wield. Now, it so happens that the same moment which saw the eclipse of Socialism as an abstract ideal, also saw the incorporation of a sort of Socialism as a concrete fact, involving a bureaucratic system of the most minute regulation and the most unlimited scope in the name of an all-powerful State.[36]

The novelty was not so much in this conception of socialism as in the exclusion of any other.

As the war drew to an end, the evaluation was quite conclusive: 'The war experience has dealt, for the time at any rate, a deadly blow at State Socialism . . . all this enhanced distrust and contempt for the State is a very grave matter for the future of the country. For nobody can seriously argue that at the end of the war . . . the State will or can return to pre-war conditions and the competitive *laissez-faire* which prevailed over the wide fields of industry and commerce.'[37] This latter point had been accepted by progressive thinkers, and their case was adroitly put by the publicist and lecturer C. Delisle Burns. He dissociated the current attack on the state from the nineteenth-century antagonism to state regulation of socially-harmful phenomena:

The moral issue is not a mere repetition of the old problem of the rights of the individual against the state. We have lived down the controversy between the Individualists and the Idealists[38] of the nineteenth century. We take it for granted that 'The State' whatever that means, cannot be simply the 'hindrance of hindrances': the ideal of government is not, as the extreme Individualists said, the abolition of government. There are no 'rights' of the individual against the state. But neither are there any 'rights' of the state against the individuals . . .[39]

The ascendency of so-called state socialism seemed, nevertheless, a mixed blessing. Hobhouse in particular gave vent to feelings of confusion. The new power of the state created theoretical ambiguity: 'For good as for evil it is the reverse of the *laissez-faire* principle of

[36] H. Ellis, 'The Future of Socialism', *Nation*, 13.10.1917.

[37] 'Capital, Labor, and the Government', *Nation*, 16.3.1918. The *Westminster Gazette* wrote a few years later: 'The one direction in which war experience was decisive was in enlightening us all as to what State management meant in actual practice. A set-back for years was given to the large ideas of nationalising the means of production and distribution which had served the Socialist section of Labour for so long.' ('Towards an Industrial Policy', 10.8.1922).

[38] And, one may add, socialists and new liberals.

[39] C. D. Burns, 'When Peace Breaks Out', *International Journal of Ethics*, 26 (1915–16), 85.

the old Liberalism.'[40] This new awareness of evil was described by Hobhouse thus:

> . . . the bitter experience of the war has everywhere made many critical of the wisdom of Governments. We believe that experience of State control has given renewed life to the idea of liberty, while the common sufferings of war-time have endowed us with a new sense for equality. Thus it is true that the leading ideas of the older Liberalism have entered on a fresh life.[41]

Nowhere was this more evident than in the astonishing rehabilitation that Hobhouse and other liberals offered the theories of Herbert Spencer. The very same Hobhouse who before the war had utterly rejected Spencer's individualistic and atomistic political thought could write on the occasion of Spencer's centenary:

> . . . after a lapse of years, the strange turn of events is giving Spencer his revenge. For the 'State' to which his opponents unceasingly appealed is rapidly becoming almost as unpopular with them as it was from the first with him, and it is well within the bounds of possibility that the reaction from war politics will ultimately produce a new liberty movement, a revised twentieth-century Cobdenism which may look back to Spencer as one of its progenitors.[42]

Havelock Ellis, too, had recognized this potential in the once-despised Spencer. While admitting that Spencer's individualism was extreme and that he had failed to see the importance of socializing material needs with no loss to freedom, Ellis saw him as 'an Englishman with a special message to Englishmen to-day. . . . We overlooked his central vision of the dangers that attend the hypertrophied State with its inevitably militaristic tendencies, and his warnings were unheeded. Now we have reached the abyss that Spencer foresaw.' The somewhat premature conclusion was that 'the Great War has set the final seal on the fame of Herbert Spencer, and henceforth he takes his rightful place in the great

[40] Hobhouse, *Questions of War and Peace*, p. 58.

[41] [L. T. Hobhouse], 'The Future of Liberalism', *MG*, 5.9.1919.

[42] [L. T. Hobhouse], 'Herbert Spencer', *MG*, 1.5.1920. See also [L. T. Hobhouse], 'Cobden's Letters' (review of J. A. Hobson, *Richard Cobden: The International Man* [London, 1919]), *MG*, 3.4.1919). This significant change in Hobhouse's political thinking is missed out by S. Collini in his observations on the post-war Hobhouse. (*Liberalism and Sociology: L. T. Hobhouse and Political Argument in England 1880–1914* [Cambridge, 1979].)

English tradition'.[43] This temporary revival of Spencer's reputation is indicative of the fundamental changes that liberalism had undergone within half a decade. It would have been unthinkable for new liberals before 1914 to refer to Spencer's political, as distinct from evolutionary, ideas, except to use them as a foil to their own antithetical arguments.

The reaction to the role of the state was of course bolstered from another, not unexpected, quarter. Anti-German feeling, prevalent even among war sceptics and opponents, identified the Prussian idea of the state as the corrosive ingredient in the denial of British liberties. State socialism was not only iniquitous, it was German. Hobson warned against the establishment of Prussianism in England. But what was this Prussianism? 'Political thinkers tell us that it is a theory of the absoluteness of the State, psychologists that it is a tyrannous and a submissive state of mind.' Ultimately, it was 'the arbitrary power of a military-bureaucratic State claiming to override all rights of civil life and private personality'.[44] Ellis endorsed this viewpoint, while admitting that the association of socialism with its German protagonists may have unjustly 'accentuate[d] the temporary depreciation of the Socialist ideal'. Nevertheless, the German apostles of socialism based themselves on a 'quite un-English faith in the iron rule of System and the ruthless domination of the Idea'.[45] The growing identification of socialism with rigid ideological dogmatism certainly abetted the process of disentangling liberalism from socialism. This process now became a cardinal concern of post-war liberals, in contradistinction to their new liberal predecessors. But in the shorter run the immediate problem was 'the danger lest our present temporary imitations of the German system should be maintained in the name of State necessity after the war'.[46] At the root of this debate was the

[43] H. Ellis, 'The Triumph of Herbert Spencer' (review of H. Elliot, *Herbert Spencer* [1917]), *Nation*, 3.3.1917. For a similar assessment see J. M. Hone's review of the same book in *DN*, 7.8.1917: '. . . the Spencer who was a social and political thinker seems to us more than any other to typify an era for the return of whom—who would have believed it possible ten or fifteen years ago?—we have already begun to sigh in secret . . . had Europe but followed Spencer in his views of individual freedom and the limitation of State action, there would have been no war.'

[44] J. A. Hobson, 'The War and British Liberties. I. The Suppression of Free Speech', *Nation*, 15.4.1916. Cf. Hobhouse, *Questions of War and Peace*, p. 56.

[45] H. Ellis, 'The Future of Socialism', *Nation*, 13.10.1917.

[46] '"Eternal Vigilance"', *Nation*, 5.8.1916.

ultimate inability of British theorists to come to terms with the concept of the state, a concept that many found alien and difficult to assimilate.[47] Even progressive liberals, who only a few years earlier had enthusiastically embraced the reformist and ethical potential of the state, were concerned with the unanticipated consequences of acknowledging its centrality in social life, and now faced an acute dilemma: 'You cannot have liberty by halves. You cannot be at one and the same time belauding the State and seeking in it the consolation of all human ills, and yet depreciating patriotism as a sentiment that leads to warfare and destruction.'[48]

3. AN ALLY ABANDONED: THE ASSAULT ON IDEALISM

The culmination of the deep unease with the state—on a higher theoretical level of argument, but lurking behind many concrete discussions—was the all-out attack that British liberal thinkers, with only a few exceptions, launched against Idealism. This was no mere intellectualized reaction to the climate of war, though Hobhouse prefaced his book on the subject with the following ruminations: 'In the bombing of London I had just witnessed the visible and tangible outcome of a false and wicked doctrine, the foundations of which lay, as I believe, in the book [by Hegel] before me.'[49] Rather, Hobhouse's anti-Hegelianism was of long standing and had been voiced as a response to what he believed was the pernicious infiltration of German Idealism via Oxford to British universities.[50] He reiterated those views from time to time in his journalistic writings, as when accusing the 'so-called idealists' in England, who were following German thinkers with their mystic conception of the state, of being 'ready to take up any stick with which they could beat Liberalism and political Rationalism'.[51] He also traced their influence on British politics, via Balliol, to the Liberal imperialists and ultimately, from 1911, to the Liberal

[47] For a good example of traditional liberal anti-statism see E. S. P. Haynes, 'Liberty and the State', *English Review*, 28 (1919), 59–66.

[48] Hobhouse, *Questions of War and Peace*, p. 86.

[49] Hobhouse, *The Metaphysical Theory of the State*, p. 6.

[50] Cf. L. T. Hobhouse, 'The Intellectual Reaction', *Speaker*, 8.2.1902; L. T. Hobhouse, *Democracy and Reaction* (London, 1904), p. 77.

[51] [L. T. Hobhouse], 'Compulsion', *MG*, 12.6.1915. See also Hobhouse's direct attack on German philosophy in L. T. Hobhouse, *The World in Conflict* (London, 1915), pp. 100–4.

government. The latter ushered in one of the prime institutional achievements of the new liberal ideology—national insurance—which Hobhouse had whole-heartedly endorsed[52] but about which Hobhouse's *alter ego*, Pentire, was now curiously made to observe: 'It was not without reason that a Labour member in the conscription debate argued that if the State may compel a man to insure, it may compel him to serve. Both forms of compulsion are integral parts of the German idea.'[53]

This is not the place to discuss the fascinating question of the misrepresentation of Hegelianism in British political and philosophical thought. But the unfairness of Hobhouse's position was exacerbated by the fact that he had always condoned T. H. Green's liberal version of Idealism. Even though Green owed more to Aristotle than to Hegel, Hobhouse could not but have been aware that British Idealists covered a wide range of socio-political positions, which included interpretations of the role of the state along liberal and progressive lines.[54] Indeed, the *Nation* may have been closer to the truth when it described the occupation of the English neo-Hegelians as a 'cloistered academic discipline'. Critiques of actual states, programmes of reform—these were not their predominant interest.[55] It may have been conservatism, but it was conservatism by default, hardly the breeding-ground of a reputedly ferocious and reactionary Hegelianism.

Hobhouse succeeded, however, in carrying most of his colleagues' opinions with him. Hobson elaborated on Hobhouse's anxieties: 'Our Neo-Hegelians in Oxford and elsewhere had not been remiss in adopting and applying to the purposes of our nation and Empire the characteristic features of the German State theory, and during the war their teaching, narrowly confined in its early appeal, has been spread broadcast in our universities, our churches and our patriotic Press.'[56] Henry Jones, the Idealist, was condemned as mouthing 'the pure milk of Prussianism' in a speech from which Hobson quoted: '. . . the State had a right to compel, provided that it stood for its own welfare. It owned us, we belonged to it. We

[52] See Freeden, *The New Liberalism*, pp. 233–5.

[53] Hobhouse, *Questions of War and Peace*, pp. 60–1.

[54] Moreover, E. Caird, who had been a close associate of Green and was Master of Balliol while Hobhouse taught at Oxford, was concurrently a liberal and a devout Hegelian.

[55] 'The English Utilitarians', *Nation*, 11.12.1915.

[56] Hobson, *Democracy After the War*, pp. 117–18.

derived the very substance of our soul from the organized community in which we lived and which we called the State.'[57] Others were just as dismissive of Idealism. Burns, drawing closer to the new liberal coterie in his intellectual and journalistic pursuits, wrote: '. . . of all the nonsense that ever pretended to be a description of fact, the Hegelian state is the worst.'[58] Ellis saw the failure of Marxism in England as due to its Hegelian form.[59]

Hobhouse's *The Metaphysical Theory of the State* was the most considered, critical, and influential examination of Hegelianism to emerge out of the war. It closely mirrored the concerns and passions to which four years of militarism and state control had subjected British political thinking, and succinctly expressed the mood of progressive liberalism and the limits to which its adherents were prepared to go in their theoretical assumptions. Whether or not Hobhouse was right in his assessment of Idealism is a separate question. Far more important is his role as an evaluator, consumer, and disseminator of Idealist notions, for the formation and impact of a political ideology can be understood through such activities.[60] The Hegel that Hobhouse saw was a sinister influence, providing 'by far the most serious opposition to the democratic and humanitarian conceptions' of the French, Dutch and English traditions.[61] Hegelian Idealism postulated the notion of the state as a totality, an end to itself, to which the lives of men and women were mere means.[62] In analysing Hobhouse's perception of Hegelianism one can identify a number of crucial components, and his responses to those components illuminated his liberal beliefs. Hobhouse's reservations about compulsion through law were elaborated by means of a discussion of freedom. As he maintained when setting out his general position, the Hegelian conception of the state 'was designed to turn the edge of the principle of freedom by identifying freedom with law; of equality by substituting the conception of discipline; of personality itself, by merging the individual in the state; of humanity, by erecting the state as the supreme and final form of human association'.[63] Hobhouse's consideration of freedom went a long

[57] Ibid., p. 118. Cf. J. A. Hobson, 'The War and British Liberties. III. The Claims of the State Upon the Individual', *Nation*, 10.6.1916.

[58] Burns, 'When Peace Breaks Out', 90.

[59] H. Ellis, 'The Future of Socialism', *Nation*, 13.10.1917.

[60] See below pp. 303–4 for the influence of Hobhouse's critique on Laski.

[61] Hobhouse, *The Metaphysical Theory of the State*, p. 23.

[62] Ibid., p. 19.

[63] Ibid., pp. 23–4.

way towards reinforcing the barrenness of the much-vaunted distinction between negative and positive liberty as a possible elucidator of the development of modern liberalism. Certainly, liberalism had begun emphasizing the importance of 'positive' state activity in order to underpin individual liberty and in order to protect the individual not only from the ravages of his fellows, but from impersonal forces that impinged upon his humanity. But granting the individual powers that enhanced his freedom and enabled him to exercise meaningful control over his life did not, argued Hobhouse, supplant the 'negative' concept of liberty, as absence of constraints on the actions of individuals. In contrast, Hegel had posited true freedom as something positive, as self-determination by a rational will. Its objective expression was law, and consequently the state, as the sustainer of law, upheld the fabric of rationality, morality and freedom.[64] The sequence and quality of Hobhouse's summary need not concern us here. What is vital is Hobhouse's conclusion when rejecting Hegel: 'Grant, for the sake of argument, that self-determination is something more than absence of constraint. But it is *not less* than absence of constraint.'[65] The significance of this statement was twofold: it insisted on the compatibility of the so-called 'negative' and 'positive' aspects of liberty, and it posited absence of constraint as the uncompromising minimum of the liberal position.[66] The naïve optimism of the pre-war new liberalism had been eroded. No longer would it be possible for liberals to indulge in fond hopes of an activist state treading the narrow tightrope between persuasion and compulsion in order to ensure the primacy of social welfare among human ends.

The second element of Idealism that Hobhouse repudiated was its notion of individual and social structure. Much of Hobhouse's displeasure was directed against the British Idealist Bosanquet (indeed, the title of his book was an uncomplimentary mirror-image of Bosanquet's well-known defence of Idealism entitled *The Philosophical Theory of the State*), though in singling out the conservative Bosanquet as representative of the entire British school Hobhouse was guilty of a severe distortion. Bosanquet, no less than Hegel, had by his denial of isolated individuality dismissed the view that

64 Ibid., pp. 32–3.
65 Ibid., p. 35. My italics.
66 See also the discussion in Chapter 7, Section 5.

state interference constituted the intrusion of others upon the self. The reason for this, observed Hobhouse, was simple: 'To [Bosanquet] there are no others.'[67] By regarding the individual as part of a system called the universal,

> the Hegelian logic abolishes on the one side the independence of the individual living human being, and on the other side the universal ties of identity of character which relate the individual to the human species as a whole [i.e. via membership of specific groups], and substitutes for it as the reality the organized body of human beings, which in its highest manifestation is the state.[68]

Here again Hobhouse countered with a liberal fundamental: 'We are contending for individuality, for the irreducible distinction between self and others.' The principle of freedom sprang from the nature of the self as a coherent whole for—a further liberal tenet—'the self is a whole capable of a harmonious development'.[69]

From here Hobhouse moved to a third fundamental thesis. Continuing his previous argument, he now assailed 'the sum and substance of Idealist Social Philosophy'—the assumption of a common self identified with the real will. Idealists asserted that 'the state . . . [was] the true self in which the mere individual is absorbed'. Hobhouse's liberal training refused to accept the disappearance of the division between the individual and the state, both because the self was a finite and distinct area of experience and because the state could not, on his understanding, be elevated to the level of a super-personal entity.[70] Furthermore, the identification of the state with the entire social fabric suggested a confusion between state and society that the essential non-reductionism of liberalism could not entertain. As Hobson had pointed out, one reason for this was that 'the State is only a single aspect or instrument of society. . . . This arrogant assumption of a suzerainty of the State over all other social relations, as if a man were only incidentally a father, a workman, a friend, a student, a human being, and always first and foremost a subject of the State, is the very kernel of the Prussian idea.'[71] Another reason was implicit in Hobhouse's Millite

[67] Hobhouse, *The Metaphysical Theory of the State*, pp. 57, 50.

[68] Ibid., p. 68.

[69] Ibid., pp. 62, 36.

[70] Ibid., pp. 41, 43, 54, 30.

[71] J. A. Hobson, 'The War and British Liberties. III. The Claims of the State Upon the Individual', *Nation*, 10.6.1916.

understanding of political freedom as not consisting 'in like-mindedness, but in the toleration of differences; or, positively, in the acceptance of differences as contributing to richer life than uniformity'.[72] This traditional concept of human nature was occasionally tinged with more of Hobhouse's pessimism than his rational predecessors would have countenanced. His central belief entailed that 'the institutions of society are not the outcome of a unitary will but of the clash of wills, in which the selfishness and generally the bad in human nature is constantly operative, intermingled with but not always overcome by the better elements'.[73]

In summing up the components of Hobhouse's liberal creed the following characteristics emerge: a concept of freedom that has to include absence of coercion (though it also contains another Millite ingredient—active citizenship—as well as Hobhouse's idea of harmony among individuals);[74] the identification of the individual as the main unit of social analysis; the assumption of human rationality—expressed as a capacity for harmonious self-development—though tempered in this specific case by a quasi-conservative disbelief in unmitigated human goodness; the further assertion that human rationality entailed a divergence rather than a convergence of human nature; the expression of that pluralist notion of human nature—and its social manifestations—in a state limited to prescribed social roles and to one facet of social structure. Many of these themes were contained in the prominence Hobhouse and liberals of that ilk accorded to the question of political obligation, so central to Green's explorations in political philosophy. It is an interesting aspect of Hobhouse's treatment of Idealism that, parallel to his mediate reading of Hegel via Bosanquet, he consistently tended to regard Green as standing apart from the Idealists he criticized, thus conveniently overlooking Green's essentially Idealist positions. Hobhouse was attracted to Green's deviations from Idealism, deviations that were part and parcel of the liberal outlook. One of these was Green's refusal to abandon the construct of a common, actually shared good emanating from individuals. The retention of the liberal distinction between individual and state enabled Green to discuss politics in terms of the ethical principles of obligation. This, indeed, distinguished the Hegelian from the traditional liberal approach to

[72] Hobhouse, *The Metaphysical Theory of the State*, p. 60.
[73] Ibid., p. 83.
[74] Ibid., pp. 61, 143.

the relation between the individual and the state. If for Hegelians the individual realized himself within, and only within, the framework of the state, and if the state was none other than the ethical (*sittlich*) consciousness of its members willing themselves in rational and free behaviour, then questions of political obligation were rendered superfluous.[75] For once we define the state as a moral community,[76] political obligation, which is the moral sense of commitment to that community, follows automatically. Question obligation and you question the existence of the Hegelian state.[77] Even though Hobhouse did not entertain such a charitable view of the Hegelian state, his conclusions clearly reinforced the dualism between man and the state that underlies questions of political obligation. Such questions have been at the heart of the liberal tradition simply due to the historically nourished suspicion that the state, as a concentration of force, can develop interests that many of its citizens do not share, and use its depositories of power to impose those interests. If the pre-war new liberals eschewed the problem of political obligation, it was because they saw no problem. The state had doffed its mantle of potential oppressor and donned that of benefactor, of realizer of rational collective interests. Though there is a certain Idealist ingredient in this point of view, its origins reached beyond Idealist sources of inspiration and were rooted in biological and evolutionary argument.[78] The war, not surprisingly, produced once again a debate on the subject of political obligation. This reflected the two-pronged impact of the war—a reassessment of the practicalities of politics (why should one obey a state that adopts these particular methods and aims?), and a theoretical evaluation of the rationale of politics (what type of state deserves obedience?). It also meant that the new liberalism had obscured rather than solved problems which by their very nature liberalism was fated to grapple with interminably. Liberal ideology was yet again in transition: the day-by-day concerns stimulating the construction of general frameworks of analysis that, in turn, reacted upon future political awareness and behaviour.

[75] Cf. H. J. Laski, *The Grammar of Politics* (London, 1925), p. 30.

[76] See text to note 84 below.

[77] Cf. L. Siedentop, 'Political Theory and Ideology: The Case of the State' in D. Miller and L. Siedentop (eds.), *The Nature of Political Theory* (Oxford, 1983), p. 70 for similar observations on political obligation.

[78] Freeden, *The New Liberalism*, ch. 3.

It is understandable, therefore, to find Hobhouse writing: 'To confuse the state with society and political with moral obligation is the central fallacy of the metaphysical theory of the state.'[79] What he meant by this was that political commitment was devoid of anything but the appeal to force if it could not be argued on moral grounds, thus reinstating the conventional liberal argument that limited the activities of the state to pursuing moral ends agreed upon or accepted by individuals. A further consequence of Hobhouse's argument was a denial that the highest duty of the individual was to be a member of the state. Hobson elaborated on this idea in an important article entitled 'The Claims of the State Upon the Individual'. The war had raised the question 'Does the individual owe an absolute and unlimited obedience to the State at such a time?' In rejecting any absolutist justification of the state, Hobson dismissed the narrow interpretation of political obligation: 'Religious and philosophic thinkers have always striven against the false limitation of the view which regards a man as a mere repository of social activities and duties.' There were people 'who at all times have insisted that in their religion, their science, their morals and their politics, they owed their first allegiance to a higher authority than the State, an authority to which they sometimes gave the name of Conscience, God, Humanity, or the Truth'.[80] In other words, an ethical view of man in society applied binding criteria of behaviour which could challenge the priority that any social institution or cultural framework demanded, and could deny—as more and more theorists were in fact doing[81]—that individual allegiance was primarily owed to the state. C. D. Burns also addressed himself to this problem. At an early stage of the war he had realized that the fundamental questions of political obligation had been thrown wide open. In the searching and sometimes naïve style that was so typical of the moral earnestness of progressive thinkers, the essential question seemed to him to be: 'What precisely is the state?' Between those acts condoned by state absolutists and those the state could effectively command, 'there is a vast region as yet almost unexplored by the moral philosopher'.[82] The establishment of limits to one's

[79] Hobhouse, *The Metaphysical Theory of the State*, p. 77.

[80] J. A. Hobson, 'The War and British Liberties. III. The Claims of the State Upon the Individual', *Nation*, 10.6.1916.

[81] See Chapter 3 on guild socialism and syndicalism.

[82] Burns, 'When Peace Breaks Out', 84.

obedience to the state was necessary so as to prevent 'those who deify the state' from excusing every governmental command. The moral right involved in state activity was obscured by the theory of state absolutism, precisely because the state was 'not any longer an all-inclusive institution'.[83]

The anti-Hegelian presentation of Idealism was indisputably dominant among liberals, but the balance has to be redressed through recalling the progressive wing of British Idealism itself. One of its main representatives was J. H. Muirhead, a self-defined liberal. In face of the mounting criticism of German philosophy at the outset of the war, he felt compelled to defend the German Kantian and Hegelian traditions from their detractors. According to those traditions, argued Muirhead, '*Might* the State must possess, but it is only the might of the *State*, when it is employed in the service of law and freedom.'[84] Those German philosophers responsible for creating the climate of ideas in which war was possible constituted 'a violent break with the ideas for which Kant and the whole early idealist movement stood'.[85] Muirhead insisted that Hegel had repudiated the doctrine that the state was founded on force. Rather, it rested on the will of the governed. Typical of British Idealists, Muirhead discovered in Hegel's standpoint an affinity with Aristotle's assertion that 'the abiding purpose of the state was the good life, not life alone'.[86] Hetherington, Muirhead's colleague, gently rebuked Hobhouse for boiling down Hegel's theory to the doctrine that the end of the state is power. '. . . a genuine idealist theory of the State is a justification neither for State absolutism nor for autocracy', for all civilized states occupied 'a special position in the organised world of moral institutions'.[87] As they both clarified in a joint book, the state was no end in itself, but 'its highest function consists precisely in the extension of [citizens'] interests to what lies beyond itself'. Nor did these two Idealists differ from progressive liberals in their attitude to the war.

[83] Ibid., 85–6.

[84] J. H. Muirhead, *German Philosophy and the War* (Oxford, 1915), p. 6. Italics in original. See text to note 76 above.

[85] Ibid., p. 3.

[86] Ibid., p. 24. Muirhead expanded his treatment of the subject in his book *German Philosophy in Relation to the War* (London, 1915). In the 1930s he returned to this theme, commenting with some exasperation on Hegel's reputation: 'To-day he is the double-dyed villain of the Dictatorial State both in Western Europe and in Russia' (*Reflections by a Journeyman in Philosophy* [London, 1942], p. 174).

[87] Review by H. J. W. Hetherington in *HJ*, 17 (1918), 328–31.

The lesson it had taught them was the importance of common citizenship and a democratically controlled community to counter sectional interests.[88] In the main, though, the liberal press followed Hobhouse's line. The *Nation* endorsed his 'able and vigorous onslaught on Hegel's philosophy of politics' and continued: 'Hegel's doctrine of the State is so strange and extravagant that it is amazing how many apparently sober thinkers in this country have adopted it.'[89] And Hobson, adding another essay to the mutual exploration of their works that he and Hobhouse undertook for each other, deemed *The Metaphysical Theory of the State* a better book for not pretending to be impartial on Hegelianism.[90]

4. THE DIMINISHED STATE: INSTRUMENT OF A REAL COMMUNITY

It remains now to examine the repercussions of these developments in political thinking upon the notion of the state. That this word was not common currency within the British confines of political thought is best illustrated by the sudden and (in comparison with the Continent) belated discovery of the 'state' in essays and in popularized political discussion during the first quarter of this century. As Hobson remarked: 'The traditions and the needs of Britain have never favoured close theorizing upon the nature of the state or upon any political foundations, nor have the social and economic interests of the ruling classes hitherto supported the practical development of a strong, highly centralized state.'[91] The various strands of socialism and new liberalism at the turn of the century, no less than Idealism itself, had changed all this. But further developments were now at hand. As A. D. Lindsay had written just before the war:

> The old theories of individualism and socialism went wrong because they thought of politics as concerned entirely with the relations between State and individual. Any theories which ignore the fact that man's social nature

[88] H. J. W. Hetherington and J. H. Muirhead, *Social Purpose: A Contribution to a Philosophy of Civic Society* (London, 1918), pp. 95, 20–1, 24.

[89] 'The State God', *Nation*, 7.12.1918. But see the favourable review of *Social Purpose* in the *Saturday Westminster Gazette* ('The Citizen and the State', 8.3.1919), which welcomed its 'timely protest' against the profound distrust of the state.

[90] J. A. H[obson], 'The Theory of the State', *MG*, 23.11.1918.

[91] Hobson, *Democracy After the War*, p. 116.

expresses itself in many forms ignore the chief problem of politics. This multiplicity of forms of social organization other than the State is especially characteristic of the modern State . . . [92]

Lindsay was a pluralist writing at the height of the influence of allied theories such as syndicalism and guild socialism, theories that intruded conspicuously upon British political thought in the early part of the period that this study encompasses. The liberal reaction to those ideas will be examined in the next chapter, but at this stage it is worth noting their reflection in the demoting of the state and in the increasing emphasis on the range of groups comprising a society. Some thinkers believed that the war, with its bankruptcy of the nation state, called for 'a new conception of sovereignty' not concentrated in one institution.[93] Unworried as yet by the excesses of state intervention during the war, however, Lindsay claimed that although the state undertook more functions, its development was accompanied by a growth in the individuality and independence of its members. This Durkheimian attitude[94] was made explicit by Burns, writing in the early months of the war and happy on this level of argument to use Durkheim to refute Spencer: 'Spencer did not see that the activity of the individual could increase and *at the same time* the activity of society.'[95] Hence even at the peak of revulsion from state socialism and absolutism, progressive theorists were still pointing out the inevitability of the state as the central agency for promoting social ends. By one of those strange quirks of ideological transformation, middle-of-the-road liberals were suddenly drawing collectivist lessons from the war, just when their left-liberal counterparts were trying as hard as they could to unlearn them. A. G. Gardiner of the *Daily News*, apparently oblivious to the achievements of the new liberals before 1914, credited the war with illuminating the folly of the anarchic hostility between capital and labour. It was because 'we have seen that in the time of emergency the community is supreme' that it was possible to substitute 'the

[92] A. D. Lindsay, 'The State in Recent Political Theory', *Political Quarterly*, 1 (February 1914), 132.

[93] B. Villiers, *Britain After the Peace: Revolution or Reconstruction* (London, 1918), pp. 260–1.

[94] Durkheim's influence was making some inroads into British political debate. See e.g. J. W. Scott in *HJ*, 17 (1918), 332.

[95] C. D. Burns, *Political Ideals* (3rd edn., Oxford, 1919), pp. 241, 249. Italics in original. See E. Durkheim, *The Division of Labour in Society* (New York, 1964), especially Durkheim's critique of Spencer, pp. 200–29.

law of co-operation for the law of competition'.[96] Contrary to new liberal thinking, the *Daily News* saw the war as an indirect instrument of community-building.[97] Even in the early phases of the war, when the paper was still promoting voluntarism, it called for 'intelligent direction', for the organization of labour towards the war's domestic ends.[98] An odd time-warp was in force: while moderately progressive liberals were working their way towards the semblance of a communal and quasi-organic perspective on society, new liberals—one step ahead—held the attractions of the state and of organicism in clearly diminished regard.

There was, however, no question of new liberal opinion returning full circle to an older liberalism. It was Hobson who was alerted, in the midst of his own relentless attack on the abuses of the state, to the practical dangers of proceeding too far:

> In fact, it is self-evident that any sudden lapse from the State Socialism of war-time, with its enormous governmental control of engineering, agriculture, mining, transport and other vital industries, and its correspondingly enlarged expenditure, into the pre-war conditions, would spell disorder and disaster. The State must continue to retain a large proportion of this control and this spending power, if unemployment, industrial depression, a fall of wages and something like social revolution are to be averted.[99]

It would have been nearly impossible for new liberals to have discarded their fundamental beliefs, even in the face of a catastrophe such as the war. Having demolished the 'metaphysical' state, Hobhouse was eager to set the record straight. The state remained for him the organized power of the community, operating through universal laws. Though fallible, its business was to act according to its best judgement. Harking back to turn-of-the-century assurance, Hobhouse could still see the state as 'trustee for the final good of society' though that trusteeship could only be discharged, as new liberals had always emphasized, by recognizing the freedom of its members.[100] This was but another version of

[96] A. G. G[ardiner], 'A New Way of Life', *DN*, 30.6.1917.

[97] 'National Welfare', *DN*, 8.10.1917.

[98] 'Munitions and Compulsion', *DN*, 8.6.1915.

[99] Hobson, *Democracy After the War*, pp. 164–5. In economic terms, Hobson noted that the war had revealed the prevalence of underconsumption and hoped that both the state and the workers would maintain their higher levels of spending after the war. (J. A. Hobson, 'The Economics of High Productivity', *English Review*, 25 [1917], 225–37).

[100] Hobhouse, *The Metaphysical Theory of the State*, pp. 89, 93.

Hobson's liberal organic analogy, restated by him thus: 'In opposition to the Prussian State, which is absolutely centralized in its power and control, the British State is organic in the sense that it is a free corporation of cells and organs which, while contributing to the life of the organism, preserve also their private liberties and ends.'[101]

Above all, for both Hobson and Hobhouse the state was an organization for the attainment of human good. Commenting on the evolving idea of the state, Hobson wrote:

> . . . the British conception regards the State itself as the means or instrument to subserve and to promote the personal ends of its citizens. Although modern Socialism and the doctrine of the general or collective will have modified or confused this simpler individualism, it still remains the case that in the British idea of the State the individual is an end as well as a means.[102]

But even this mild concession to the good of the community as a separate entity would have been too much for Hobhouse,[103] for whom the value of the state lay entirely in service to the harmonious development of its component members. The pitfall of the alternative approach was the postulation of the state as a separate and fictitious whole.[104] In similar vein, Burns reiterated the idea of the state as an independent institution for the attainment of a common political good, thus preserving the pre-war liberal faith in its neutrality. But that good was—as Green had also maintained—always that of individuals. 'Speaking English, not philosophy,' Burns went on to say, 'the state is one of many institutions, admirable, slightly ineffective even for the partial purpose for which it exists, but not sovereign over others and certainly not the sole bulwark of the civilised life.' And he concluded: 'We do not say that government has fewer claims; it may have more, but they are utterly different from what they were even in the nineteenth century. . . . All the difficulty in discovering what the limits are to the first commands of the state are due to attempts to make the modern

[101] J. A. Hobson, 'The War and British Liberties. III. The Claims of the State Upon the Individual', *Nation*, 10.6.1916. See also Freeden, *The New Liberalism*, ch. 3.

[102] Hobson, ibid.

[103] See Chapter 7, Section 2 on the organicism of Hobhouse and Hobson.

[104] Hobhouse, *The Metaphysical Theory of the State*, p. 97.

state into the πόλις or the Renaissance "sovereign".'[105] The last word on this matter belongs to Havelock Ellis, epitomizing the relaxed and prosaic attitude of many of his compatriots to political questions. It was, he observed, a mistake to assume that the Englishman rejected the state: 'The Englishman regards the State as he regards his trousers, as useful indeed, even indispensable, scarcely to be worshipped.'[106]

Notwithstanding the developments surveyed in this chapter, the war was not perceived as the great divide between an era of reason and the unleashing of a destructive irrationalism. In a moment of confidence, Hobhouse asserted: 'The ideal of unreason and immoralism is nonsense, and we may fairly hope, without relying on an optimistic faith which is itself irrational, that the chastening of adversity will itself shake this nonsense out of the world.'[107] Hobson, too, dismissed the attack on reason as based on a misunderstanding. Reason was part of the original human outfit endowed with biological utility to effect gains and avoid injuries, and vindicated the enduring purposes of mankind.[108] In darker moods, Hobhouse abandoned his unwavering belief in progress, but here too an important caveat was registered: the inevitable march of progress as an evolutionary *law* was denied; the *possibility* of progress was reaffirmed.[109] Both Hobhouse and Hobson saw the salvation of the world in the supremacy of reason, but for Hobhouse this was no longer a scientifically based prediction concerning human development, but an act of 'faith in reason' born out of contemplation of the horrific alternatives.[110] This faith was to sustain liberals through years of growing turbulence.

[105] Burns, 'When Peace Breaks Out', 86, 91.

[106] H. Ellis, 'The Triumph of Herbert Spencer', *Nation*, 3.3.1917.

[107] Hobhouse, *The World In Conflict*, pp. 73–4.

[108] J. A. Hobson, *Problems of a New World* (London, 1921) pp. 265–6. See Chapter 7 for a further discussion of the liberal reassessment of reason.

[109] Cf. also H. Samuel, *Belief and Action* (London, 1937), p. 240.

[110] Hobhouse, *Questions of War and Peace*, pp. 123–4, 142, 179; L. T. Hobhouse, *Social Development* (London, 1924), p. 207; Hobson, *Problems of a New World*, p. 272.

3

THE WORKER AS CITIZEN

1. HOPES OF A NEW WORLD

The post-war years found Britain distraught and uncertain.[1] Political confusion and a crisis of confidence in the national leadership, a social unrest that hinted at a grave underlying malaise, economic instability within two years of the end of the war, and the questioning of moral and ideological principles confronted a liberalism that hardly knew what it was or where it should go. Its organizational vehicle, the Liberal party, had been ravaged by the personal feud between Asquith and Lloyd George, and, for many of its supporters, had irreparably blemished its reputation as the party of peace—the first pillar of the ideological trinity that had traditionally included retrenchment and reform as well. Now two further threats materialized: the Coalition, which initially had held out the promise of comprehensive social reform,[2] threatened to divest Liberalism of its identity and to subsume it under a lack-lustre Conservatism, and the much-strengthened Labour party, invigorated by the infusion of enfranchised blood, seemed capable of eclipsing the Liberal party—certainly in terms of enthusiasm and purposiveness, if not yet in votes. If Hobson had written about a crisis of liberalism in 1909, that crisis was now compounded and augmented as the liberals, winded by a series of body blows, gasped for breath. This lack of oxygen lasted for half a dozen years, during which some liberals' faces turned blue with the inertia of conservatism, while others reddened in the struggle for new life as they found themselves uncomfortable members of a Labour party they never

[1] C. F. G. Masterman, Liberal politician manqué, writer and journalist, lent his eloquence to the occasion: '. . . the forces of malignancy, some blind or capricious power which turns the sight of men into darkness, and the reason of men into lunacy, are to-day dancing [a] "Devil's Dance" over the ruins of a world' (*England After War* [London, n.d. (1923)], p. 11).

[2] See the interesting reappraisal of the Coalition by K. O. Morgan, *Consensus and Disunity: The Lloyd George Coalition Government 1918–1922* (Oxford, 1979), ch. 4 and *passim*. Few progressive liberals at the time, however, felt inclined to praise the Coalition for its social reform measures of 1919 and 1920.

quite came to trust. As for the rest, later chapters will investigate whether a resuscitated liberalism emerged without noticeable brain damage to its thinkers and spokesmen.

The war itself, which had goaded liberals into discussing issues of state socialism and individual liberty, did not find them quiescent on other matters of prime importance. Reconstruction was a question that loomed large from 1916 onwards, and liberal minds were actively engaged in mapping out the problems that a new world would have to tackle.[3] In order to appreciate some of the vital concerns of post-war liberals, an analysis of their understanding of reconstruction is essential. On the official level, reconstruction had commenced as the strengthening of economic institutions[4] and the restoration of the damage caused to them during the war.[5] Although reconstruction goals began changing by the end of 1916, they had been widely conceived of from the start by liberal thinkers. The coming reorganization of society, it was hoped, would be based on a new order.[6] The opportunity was a challenge, though to call it an exciting one would have belied the mood of the age. 'The organic fabric of Britain's social arrangements of pre-war times [lay] in ruins', observed the *Nation*. A transformation had taken place within a few months that could not have been anticipated within a generation. The possibility now existed of a final break with 'the unrestricted, often wasteful, competition of private enterprise'. Instead, 'there may arise a determination to develop, from conditions which even before the war were proving unsuitable to twentieth-century demands, an organized society, more rational and more just.'[7] Many progressives hoped for a 'great moral revolution' side by side with an economic one.[8]

Reconstruction, then, entailed from the outset a grand design, a social blueprint that offered various rewards in its implementation. But governmental thinking, as is often the case, constituted only the rearguard among the possible options entertained by liberals. Although there now existed a unique opportunity to consolidate and

[3] Viz. Hobson, *Problems of a New World*.

[4] P. B. Johnson, *Land Fit For Heroes* (Chicago, 1968), p. 12.

[5] See e.g. E. Halévy, 'The Policy of Social Peace in England: The Whitley Councils (1919)' in *The Era of Tyrannies* (London, 1967), p. 82.

[6] 'The Country and its Rulers', *Nation*, 22.1.1916. See also Morgan, *Consensus and Disunity*, p. 23.

[7] 'Reconstruction', *Nation*, 12.8.1916.

[8] Villiers, *Britain After the Peace: Revolution or Reconstruction*, pp. 25, 34.

expand the pre-war advances made in the field of social reform, the ambivalence of liberals was unmistakable, fuelled also by the reaction to state socialism. Herbert Samuel absurdly anticipated entering an era which could prove to be a new renaissance, one of political, social, and economic changes that would fashion ordered progress. But, as he admitted, the machinery of the state was old and would have to be modernized. Moreover, devolution away from the state would be imperative in order to relieve the pressures on its capacities. Ultimately, he maintained, 'we come back, as the chief agency in the work of reconstruction, to the free action of the individual'.[9] Other liberals were not so sure. Natural monopolies, it was generally assumed by new liberals, were 'likely to develop along Socialistic lines, with complete State ownership, or State regulation and control'.[10] It was conceivable that the state would also move towards establishing a general minimum wage and towards further regulation of employment. But official Liberals and new liberals were, as they had often been in the past, out of step with each other with respect to the significance of social reform.[11]

To the extent that reconstruction encompassed the pre-1914 reformist ends, it also embodied the bifurcation between their moral and material aspects. More houses, more wages, less poverty, were social goods but could not, for advanced thinkers, be detached from wider considerations. As the *Daily News* wrote: 'The problems of material reconstruction . . . are likely to be earlier and more effectively faced than the problems of moral and physical reconstruction. It is much easier to legislate for the welfare of a particular industry than for the welfare of the whole population that forms the first responsibility of the State as a political entity.'[12] Other liberals explicitly questioned the assumption 'that the one test of successful reconstruction [was] to be the test of output'. It was not, they countered, to be found in industrial production but 'in quality of life . . . in the opportunities of leisure, happiness, and freedom that are thrown open to the mass of the nation'.[13] Hobhouse insisted

[9] Samuel, *The War and Liberty*, pp. 99, 100–2, 113–16, 122.

[10] 'Reconstruction', *Nation*, 12.8.1916.

[11] As Morgan has observed, in the immediate post-war years this was especially true of the Independent Liberals, who were 'notably silent on the root themes of social deprivation, economic recession, and unemployment'. (*Consensus and Disunity*, p. 203.)

[12] 'National Welfare', *DN*, 8.10.1917.

[13] 'The World of Labor', *Nation*, 25.8.1917.

that 'there is something deeper than material poverty . . . It is the [workers'] new demand for freedom, already sounded in the days before the war . . . a freedom which . . . looks to self-direction as its ideal.'[14]

This final note was the decisive one in the progressive liberal conception of reconstruction. It demoted the restorative aspect of social reform—the material aid to disadvantaged individuals and groups—as secondary to the ethical aim of a regenerated society. Consequently, two characteristics of liberal social thought emerge directly from the war: the amount of time and energy devoted to concrete proposals diminished, and attention was diverted to the role and importance of the industrial sphere as a prime arena for the maintenance of social well-being. Why was it that while the Coalition was immersed in questions of housing, health and unemployment, these issues frequently played a secondary role in liberal thinking? Partly this is so because the breakthroughs of principle had been attained before the war, and liberal intellectuals no longer felt the need to argue the details of, say, the case for a minimum wage. Partly it reflected the linking of the broad concept of social reform (as social regeneration) to the broad concept of reconstruction (as redesigning social arrangements and relationships). Only with the advent of the Liberal Summer School movement was there a return to the discussion of concrete issues, although even there, by comparison with pre-war liberalism, such activities were reduced by the growing influence of Keynes, in a move away from traditional redistributive measures towards economic management.[15] But increasingly this change in emphasis expressed the crystallization of two central and interconnected themes of inter-war liberalism: the place of the worker in a modern industrial society and the rediscovery of the importance of power in the body politic.

Within the above framework, progressive liberals construed the question of reconstruction as encompassing humanitarian and socially oriented activity. Delisle Burns, able to draw upon his practical experience at the Ministry of Reconstruction, saw this as an extension of the notion of productivity, to include all the material and mental force that went to create the resources of civilized life. The exasperation with social reform as tinkering was evident: '. . .

[14] [L. T. Hobhouse], 'Reconstruction', *MG*, 28.7.1917.

[15] Cf. D. Winch, *Economics and Policy: A Historical Survey* (London, 1972), p. 22. See also Chapters 4 and 5.

we must face the undeniable fact that it is not the banking system or the property system or the old education only that is at fault but the fundamental and all-powerful system of the relations of man to man.'[16] In the last resort the question was moral, though the claims of ethics were expedited by a reminder that 'revolution is in the air', a feeling reinforced among many liberals both by the events in Russia and by the immediate post-war situation in Britain. It was precisely the attempt to buy off revolution that Hobson spotted in the motives of the Coalition to promote their much narrower policies of reconstruction. Writing in 1921, he was equally dismissive of the series of concrete measures that signalled for him the failure of official reconstruction. If its aim was the preservation of the existing order, then 'education, housing, land settlement, public health, infant welfare, Whitley Councils, eight-hour days, statutory wage boards, represent an advance of social reform and capitalist concessions not ill adapted to this object'.[17] Later he criticized the strategy of social reconstruction as too narrowly economic.[18]

2. THE NEW STATUS OF LABOUR

The increased interest of liberals in the industrial worker was not directly related to the political emancipation of Labour. The beginnings of the debate preceded the 1918 Representation of the People Act by a considerable margin, whereas the early years of the Labour party had seen liberals far more concerned with working-class poverty, the vicissitudes of disadvantaged groups such as old age pensioners and the inability of labour to find work. The war had again underscored some home truths and created others. It was difficult to ignore the vital importance of workers in the munitions industry, to take one salient example. The prohibition of strikes was not only a testimonial to the power and primacy of the state but an implicit recognition that the strategic position of some workers afforded them a potential veto over public policy. The realization, reluctantly conceded, that certain groups among the working class could dictate the pace of events, with its suggestion

[16] C. D. Burns, 'Productivity and Reconstruction', *International Journal of Ethics*, 28 (1917–18), 402, 404.

[17] Hobson, *Problems of a New World*, p. 178. See also J. A. Hobson, 'Expression of Religion in Daily Life', *The Humanist*, 1.1.1922, where he referred to 'the lamentable failure of the process called social reconstruction'.

[18] J. A. Hobson, 'The Reformulation of Politics', *CR*, 129 (1925), 431.

of an alternative hierarchy of power to that enshrined in constitutional usage, and with its anti-Parliamentary threat of direct action, impelled liberals and others to do some fast thinking. This new awareness fostered important developments in liberal theory and encouraged a decisive shift towards debates on social structure, towards reinterpretations of democracy, and towards an appreciation of both work (as distinct from capital or production in the abstract) and power as central political facts and social concepts.

It took some time to disentangle questions of conscription and industrial compulsion from those of industry proper. At the beginning of 1916 the *Nation* was still writing in terms of organized workers' opposition to the Conscription Act, observing ominously that the threat of enlistment conferred upon employers the power to keep labour in bounds.[19] But the new issues were crystallizing quickly. 'It used to be thought that the working man wanted two things—good wages and security', wrote J. L. Hammond, the historian and liberal journalist. 'It is now evident that he wants something more—a sense of freedom and responsibility in his work.' Working-class discontent, he noted, was spreading

> partly because education is stimulating the self-consciousness of the working classes, partly because industrial as well as political developments seem to be increasing their dependence on the direction of authority in the State and in the mill. The working classes are, in fact, trying to demand the introduction of the atmosphere of democracy into their working lives.[20]

Hammond's liberal faith in the power of education may have been a trifle sanguine, but the stirrings among the workers could not be ignored. The *Daily News* declared magnanimously: 'Never has the nation—a nation of workers and employers and consumers—been more ready to recognize the justice of the reasonable claims of Labour.'[21] The striving for status was now considered to be central to workers' aspirations. 'It is more than a question of a quarrel for material things', was the opinion of the *Nation*. 'Our own inclination is to look for a definite improvement of status as a way out of the mere wage-receiving lot.'[22] For many liberals the issue of status pointed the way to dampening down the immediate rumblings of dis-

[19] 'Thoughts on the Present Discontents', *Nation*, 29.1.1916.

[20] J. L. H[ammond], 'Legislation and Liberty', review of E. S. P. Haynes, *The Decline of Liberty in England* (London, 1916), *MG*, 28.8.1916.

[21] 'The Claims of Labour', *DN*, 22.1.1917.

[22] 'Reconstruction', *Nation*, 12.8.1916.

affection now emanating from wage earners, and to their integration into a more equal, or at least more harmonious, community. Hobhouse succinctly summarized this position: '. . . the old labour questions were bread and butter questions, but . . . the new ones are rather those of responsibility, independence, and, in a word, industrial self-government.'[23]

The *Nation*, still under the capable and energetic editorship of H. W. Massingham, quickly emerged in the forefront of this movement within liberalism, thus maintaining its tradition of invaluable service to the cause of modernizing liberal ideology. It began to realize that the solution to industrial discontent lay in a decisive and new arrangement. The days of the worker solely as purveyor of a commodity—labour—appeared to be numbered. But the change in status was not motivated purely for ethical reasons.[24] Rather, as the *Nation* wrote with an astuteness not common among liberals:

> If the war has made the position of the workman at the moment more dependent and precarious, it has emphasized in another sense his power and his importance, and it has made him conscious, as never before, of the necessity of using his power. The State, its institutions, its industries, these are not to be active forces pressing on his life, ruling his habits; they are to be a world that feels and reflects his power.[25]

These sentiments represent a change in liberal theory so important that it merits separate treatment later.[26] Suffice it to say at present that notions of social justice and humanitarianism were bolstered by the recognition of a dramatically altering balance of social forces. As Hobhouse warned:

> The new labour movement . . . wants to control its own destiny. It is working for a share in management—a far more difficult claim [than improved material circumstances]. Nor is it satisfied with such an indirect control as would fall to the citizens of a Socialist State . . . the worker . . . begins to suspect that there will be less liberty for him, not more, as a mere cog in the wheels of the State machine.[27]

23 [L. T. Hobhouse], 'Industrial Self-Government', *MG*, 29.6.1917.

24 The ethical case for the integration of workers into industrial life and the necessity of regulating industry with reference to 'supra-economic ends' was advanced by the progressive Idealists Hetherington and Muirhead, *Social Purpose*, pp. 184, 191, 205. See also H. Jones, *The Principles of Citizenship* (London, 1919), pp. 170, 175.

25 'A Constitution for Industry', *Nation*, 30.6.1917.

26 See Chapter 7, Section 6.

27 [L. T. Hobhouse], 'The Attitude of Labour', *MG*, 27.6.1917.

The argument from ethics had never survived on its own in the harsh world of politics. But whereas pre-war discussions had been accompanied by an appeal to efficiency and its attractions for business, the post-war assignment of new status to the worker appealed to the instinct of communal survival and stability. This argument, based on an inevitablist view of the world, would find it increasingly hard to coexist with the insistence on the spontaneity of morality inherited from the liberal world of T. H. Green.

But moral perspectives persevered for quite a while. As the *Nation* wrote in 1919: 'The bond between a people and its Government is a moral relationship.' It was the breaking up of that relationship by the government 'and not the wickedness of the workman . . . [that was] the root of the disorder in England'. Liberals were, however, eager to forge a new social morality and were encouraged to see, in their pursuance of that aim, that 'for the first time [the country] is becoming alive to its full capacity for citizenship'. In institutional terms, which will presently be explored, this meant '*the demand for the revision of the social contract*'.[28] The words status and contract were of course reminiscent of Maine's distinction, and some liberals consciously referred to it. Elliot Dodds, an up-and-coming young Liberal, argued that the movement established by Maine from status to contract now had to be reversed. In its earlier stages Labour had concentrated on the terms of its 'contract' with its employers. Now it was seeking the status of a partner in the industrial commonwealth.[29] Dodds was using the terms in a way that differed greatly from that of Maine. Modern status was not ascribed or predetermined, nor was it to be understood in a hierarchical sense. It was derived from liberal ideas of community and inherent worth, thus uniting two important facets of citizenship—equal worth of the individual unit and active participation in communal life, facets that the new liberalism had been stressing since the 1890s.

C. D. Burns brought a more critical mind to bear on this topic and added an important consideration. The relation between employer and worker was not contractual at all in any real sense. Like many progressives, he regarded industry as a public service within the economic community. But, Burns argued, no personal relation-

[28] 'A Treaty with Labor', *Nation*, 26.7.1919. Emphasis in original.

[29] E. Dodds, *Is Liberalism Dead?* (London, 1920), p. 126, and *Liberalism in Action* (London, 1922), p. 214.

ship was involved and justice, not benevolence, determined the positions of the parties, '. . . therefore the new dominant word describing the relation of men is neither status nor contract but function'. The industrial relationship was one of 'functions complementary to each other, within the whole complex of relations in the organization of the community'.[30] The idea that all those engaged in the industrial process were performing an essential social and human function was one influenced by current sociological and psychological theories. Burns's acquaintance with Durkheim's work has an evident outlet here, for function denoted in part the mutual contribution of members of a society to its stability and efficient operation. Furthermore, it alluded to an assessment of human worth in the ethical light of social service and communal interdependence, an analysis proffered in particular by R. H. Tawney.[31]

Implicit here also were those psychological theories that Burns's friend, Hobson, was reflecting in his post-war work. Hobson had been profoundly influenced by the Ruskinian perspective that equated wealth with life or, in Hobson's terminology, vitality and consumption. The thrust of his pre-war writings had been directed against a narrow conception of economics as the production of quantifiable wealth. As an alternative he promoted the demolishing of the systemic barriers existing between economics and other social sciences—mainly politics but also sociology—and between economics and social philosophy. Burns had read Hobson's *Work and Wealth*, published in 1914, and had assimilated Hobson's extended view of economics.[32] His understanding of productivity[33] was hence entirely at one with that of Hobson: work was creativity, an expression of human potential. But for that to be the case in practice, the existing work context would have to be transformed radically. In Hobson's words, 'the real object is to rescue humanity from the thraldom of mechanical industry'.[34] Even if industrial work could not, on the whole, be made pleasurable, it could become 'tolerable and of willing acceptance'.[35] Here Hobson employed his recent explorations into psychology[36] in order to combine economics

[30] C. D. Burns, *Government and Industry* (London, 1921), pp. 306–7.
[31] See Chapter 8, Section 2.
[32] Burns, *Government and Industry*, p. 304.
[33] See above p. 48.
[34] Hobson, *Problems of a New World*, p. 197.
[35] Ibid., p. 196.
[36] See Chapter 7, Section 2.

with that rising branch of knowledge as well. He now saw liberation from industrial domination not merely in terms of social and political control, but as grafted on to a psychology that had discovered the links between biological instincts and their sublimation in social behaviour. Of course, Hobson conceded, one could argue superficially that 'the reduction of certain primary activities to routine subconscious processes liberates more energy for conscious and creative work in higher spheres'.[37] This accorded with the turn-of-the-century distinction he had made between the uniform and the artistic, as a guide to a possible delimitation of social from individual activity. But Hobson's unitary perspective, once harnessed to a denial of the dualism between man and nature,[38] now applied to psychology as well. Instead of a widening gulf between the physical and spiritual processes, human nature was the outcome of the constant interaction of both.[39] Work should express the totality of the human personality. It was in this sense that Hobson applied the idea of liberation to industry.[40] But in line with Hobson's total, organic approach, work was to undergo two transformations. It was to reflect 'the freedom of pleasurable production' as a sphere of self-chosen activity in which physical, emotional and rational aspects of human personality were to be invested. But it was not the be-all and end-all of personality which, precisely due to its release from the oppression of mechanical thraldom, could increasingly engage in the non-industrial side of human life.[41] That would secure what Hobson called 'the conception of organic unity in social self-government', a new social order to be realized simultaneously in terms of industry and politics.

Moves towards a fundamental restructuring of the labour side of industry must hence be seen not only as a response to political exigencies but also as fashioned within a series of continuing intellectual debates about the nature of the social sciences, the significance of community and citizenship, and the ethical determinants of

[37] J. A. Hobson, 'The Ethical Movement and the Natural Man', *HJ*, 20 (1922), 673.

[38] See the controversy surrounding T. H. Huxley's 1893 *Evolution and Ethics* lecture (Freeden, *The New Liberalism*, ch. 3).

[39] Hobson, 'The Ethical Movement and the Natural Man', 677.

[40] J. A. Hobson, 'The New Industrial Revolution', *CR*, 118 (1920), 639.

[41] Hobson, 'The New Industrial Revolution', p. 639; Hobson, *Problems of a New World*, pp. 196–7, 139. Cf. J. Allett, *New Liberalism: The Political Economy of J. A. Hobson* (Toronto, 1981), pp. 58–9.

social life. These had all been central concerns of the major new liberal theorists. Liberals were still in the grips of nineteenth-century theories of progress with their optimistic, oft-teleological unfolding of the course of human history. But progressive liberal theory had always excelled in the concrete and detailed application of principles to political action. It stands to reason therefore to find liberals of all shades and affiliations engaged prolificly in constructing and evaluating practical proposals about the role of industry in post-war Britain, with the result that within a few years the reform of the industrial system was considered to be at the centre of liberal policy.[42] For Ramsay Muir—the liberal publicist and organizer—the industrial system was unfair and ripe for reform for three reasons: it permitted 'excessive inequality in the distribution of the products of industry'; it dissociated 'the enjoyment of income from the performance of social service'; and it did not 'give a fair chance to every man of making the best of his own individuality, and thereby impoverish[ed] the whole community'.[43] Muir thus encapsulated many liberal concerns—the defects of capitalism as a system of sharing wealth, the quest for a just method of apportioning social rewards, and the establishment of optimal conditions for the development of the individual. Unlike some of his more radical liberal colleagues, though, Muir did not, in 1920, organize his analysis round the seemingly crucial question of industrial democracy and workers' participation. Whether this was an oversight or an important theoretical distinction is a matter to be deferred for the time being. That there were clear divisions among liberals on the industrial issue is not in doubt. It may be best to commence an examination of those divisions by looking at a concrete proposal: the Whitley Councils.

3. WHITLEYISM: SOCIAL HARMONY OR EMPLOYERS' PEACE?

In 1916 a subcommittee was established within the framework of the Committee on Reconstruction. It was chaired by the senior Liberal MP J. Whitley and instructed to make proposals on the relations between employers and employed. Its report in June 1917 suggested creating joint standing industrial councils for each

42 'Lessons from Cambridge', *DN*, 10.8.1923.

43 R. Muir, *Liberalism and Industry* (London, 1920), p. 70.

industry on a national basis. It further proposed subordinate district councils and works' committees. The Whitley Councils, as they were known, were to consist of equal numbers of representatives of the employers' associations and of trade unions and were assigned permanent functions. These included negotiations on wages and the conditions of employment, the improvement of industrial techniques, technical education and research, discussions on security of earnings and employment, the prevention of differences between the two sides of industry, and proposals for industrial legislation.[44] A number of these councils were set up and they received governmental support and encouragement. For official Liberals the Whitley Councils seemed to offer an exciting potential. As Samuel saw it, 'the workman would become a citizen of the workshop as well as of the State. A free constitution would be established in industry as well as in national government.'[45] Moderate progressives followed suit, portraying the proposed industrial councils as incarnations of the new co-operative spirit generated by the war, the expression of a communal change in values.[46] The *Daily News* waxed enthusiastic: 'There has been no document of more weight and more promise issued since the war began.' Unfortunately it then undermined its own appraisal of the new 'democratic arrangement' by an inappropriate reference to 'masters and men'.[47] Even from left-liberalism initial responses were cautiously welcoming. Hobhouse was attracted by the insistence of the subcommittee that participation and discussion should be substituted for the cash basis of the present relations between workers and employers. Believing as he did in the principle of social harmony, he appreciated the role of the national industrial councils as promoters of co-operation. Their failure was of course a possibility to be reckoned with. But 'we can also conceive them succeeding and becoming a power in the land such that the definition of their relations with the State . . . may become the central question of politics.'[48] Hobson thought the proposals marked 'an almost revolutionary advance in the status of labour'.[49] For the

[44] See Halévy, 'The Policy of Social Peace in England', and Samuel, *The War and Liberty*, pp. 80–2.

[45] Samuel, *The War and Liberty*, p. 83.

[46] 'Industry in War and Peace', *WG*, 29.6.1917.

[47] 'The New Industrial World', *DN*, 29.6.1917.

[48] [L. T. Hobhouse], 'Industrial Self-Government', *MG*, 29.6.1917.

[49] J. A. Hobson, 'Representative Government in British Industry', *New Republic*, 1.9.1917.

Nation they represented a principle of vital importance: 'an industry is not the property of an employer, but a form of national service undertaken by a body of persons, all of whom have a recognized and conscious share in its control.'[50] Here, then, was an effective application of the ideas new liberals were now propounding: communal ownership of, and control over, processes that were socially useful and dependent upon social co-operation; the organic interconnection between major areas of human conduct; and the mutuality of give-and-take between individual and society. Indeed, the latter was now reinforced by the war experience, for the conscription of industry as well as of an army had emphasized the essential indispensability for social survival of these two social institutions. If it was true that during the war the state claimed to possess 'an equal right of disposal over the lot of the soldier and that of the civilian worker',[51] surely the corollary was that the obligations of both automatically earned them pride of place in the web of citizenship.

The issue of Whitley Councils was quickly subsumed within the larger debate on industrial partnership. Dodds summed up the different approaches: 'The phrase "industrial partnership" has been interpreted in three ways—as a share in profits; as a voice in the control of working conditions; and as a participation in the duties of management.' Whitleyism went quite some way towards achieving the second of these goals, but left the other two untouched.[52] An examination of the various paths pursued by liberals towards the 'democratization' of industry illustrates the ideological divides to which liberalism was increasingly prey. It would have been a brave man indeed who, by the end of the war, would have set himself up against the amelioration of working conditions. Liberals who presented this as their main plank for industrial reform were virtually indistinguishable from conservatives on this count. One step further, but a modest one at that, was the demand to accord workers the right to decide under what conditions they were prepared to labour. B. S. Rowntree, the liberal reformer and pioneer of social surveys, was one who clearly found it difficult to make the leap from his well-justified interest in social reform to questions of industrial reconstruction. In 1919 his top priority was still a minimum wage for workers, followed by the reduction of working

[50] 'A Constitution for Industry', *Nation*, 30.6.1917.
[51] 'What Has Become of Liberalism?', *Nation*, 3.8.1918.
[52] Dodds, *Is Liberalism Dead?*, pp. 127–8.

hours and insurance against unemployment. He then recommended giving workers 'more control over the industry in which they are engaged' but added: 'I do not believe that at present they have any wish to control it either financially or commercially.'[53] Indeed, participation by workers in management would, if it were permanent, result in their losing touch with their rank and file or, if it were rotational, deny them the expert knowledge to be useful—arguments that the business element within the Liberal party was prone to formulate. What is one to make of this? As with the meaning of reconstruction, the new liberal avant-garde that had achieved so much prior to 1914 was failing to keep up with events. It was slow to grasp that, in the words of the *Nation*, 'the new fact in the practical direction of Labor since the war is that it is no longer wholly absorbed with the problem of poverty. The stress is laid on the question of control.'[54] Rowntree was still obsessed with the success of the old formulas. The new ones were untried and potentially harmful to the task of increasing production. Even among the liberal faithful, the slippage towards conservatism had begun.

Élie Halévy, that most perceptive French observer of the British scene, identified this fatal flaw of Whitleyism in a series of characteristically brilliant pieces of instant history published between 1919 and 1922. On the one hand it was a vehicle for 'philanthropic employers to break up the solidarity of the union and to create a special community of interest between themselves and the workers in their factories, as opposed to the solidarity that united, or could unite, their workers to unionized workers in other firms'.[55] Divide and rule, though, was a failure of the Whitley spirit but not necessarily, from the viewpoint of the establishment, a negative consequence of this industrial policy. Yet paradoxically enough, the shortcomings of Whitleyism as a bare minimum programme of industrial reconstruction could have constituted its advantage from the workers' perspective. For, as Halévy remarked, 'leaving the doctrinaires aside, what interests the workers deeply is not industrial management but wages, or, in more general terms, the conditions of labour'.[56] Halévy's conclusion went straight to the heart

[53] B. S. Rowntree, 'Labour Unrest and the Need for a National Ideal', *CR*, 116 (1919), 502–3.

[54] 'The Future of Industry', *Nation*, 11.10.1919.

[55] Halévy, 'The Problem of Worker Control (1921)' in *The Era of Tyrannies*, p. 130.

[56] Ibid., p. 137.

of the problems confronting post-war liberal practice and theory:

> the Whitley Council sought to innovate and to create a kind of mixed institution, half worker, half employer, from which the idea of the class struggle would be absent . . . Must we willingly blind ourselves, shutting our eyes to an annoying reality, and . . . deny this very real conflict of interests and passions? . . . utopia is the Whitley Council and the dream of a fusion of classes.[57]

At worst, Whitleyism was a conservative scheme to ensure social peace and continuous production. 'In exchange for a guarantee of high wages, the workmen's leaders are expected to take their hand off the regulator.'[58] But even if, as Hobson preferred to see it, industrial peace and high productivity were mutually dependent,[59] the Whitley Councils still reflected the fundamental weakness of the liberalism of their supporters—the conviction that institutional devices could bring about a social harmony that would eradicate conflict from human relationships, and could constitute machines that 'will be directly responsible to every movement of thought, and should be not only a solvent of difficulties, but a means of preventing difficulties arising'.[60] Gilbert Murray—the Oxford classicist—saw it simply as a question of applying that liberal invention, representative government, to the sphere of industrial relations.[61] These themes, as will be shown repeatedly, represented an innocence about social structure and political power that prevented liberals from modernizing and adapting their ideology in the way that the pre-war new liberals, under entirely different circumstances, had succeeded in doing. Liberals who knew this and tried to change the course of liberal ideology ran up against a further fact of life. Most members of the working class seemed less interested in far-reaching plans for reform, either from socialists or from liberals, than in doing precisely what progressive ideologists thought they no longer wanted to do, that is, they wished to concentrate on bread and butter questions.

Some of Halévy's British contemporaries were arriving at conclusions similar to his. Even on the less substantial issue of control

57 Halévy, 'The Policy of Social Peace in England', 121–2.

58 'The State of British Parties', *Nation*, 6.7.1918.

59 Hobson, 'Representative Government in British Industry'.

60 A. G. G[ardiner], 'A New Way of Life', *DN*, 30.6.1917.

61 G. Murray, 'Liberal Policy and the War: III. The New Order at Home', *DN*, 25.8.1917.

over conditions of work, progressive liberals were insistent on showing it in a different light from those who promoted Whitleyism as the main thrust of industrial reform. Charles Trevelyan, who was to join the Labour party a year later, linked the notion of such control with the nationalization of key industries and services.[62] Liberalism of the left was adamant that control over industrial conditions should not be symbolic, but should constitute a 'real partnership'.[63] A more interesting distinction among liberals was, however, developing with respect to the radical approaches to industrial reconstruction—participation in management and sharing in profits. Moderate progressives such as Dodds and C. F. G. Masterman interpreted these terms in a more genteel fashion than their radical counterparts. For Dodds, participation in management was the intermediary stage and profit-sharing the ultimate one.[64] This gradation is not without significance. Joint management on an equal footing allowed Dodds to describe it as "self-government" in inverted commas; it was no more than 'an adequate share in the functions of management' but would hardly constitute a revolution. On the other hand, he was vague about a system of profit-sharing which, while conceded, was not spelt out.[65] For most liberals this was a question of maintaining the incentives necessary to the functioning of capitalism. If industrialists were to be shorn of too much profit, of the fruits of capitalism, the system would no longer be viable. Conversely, and validating the Halévy thesis, the *Daily Chronicle* could uphold the case for labour sharing in the benefits of increased production in terms close to the hearts of the employers: 'Only if the worker gets a joint interest with the employer . . . can we hope to see the necessary maximization of British output . . .'[66]

4. ONE PARTY IN SEARCH OF A POLICY

By the beginning of the new decade the journalistic activities of Liberals such as Dodds and Masterman had penetrated the policy-

[62] C. Trevelyan, 'Can Radicalism and Socialism Unite?', letter to the Editor, *Nation*, 2.2.1918.

[63] 'State Mines', *Nation*, 28.6.1919.

[64] But see Dodds, *Is Liberalism Dead?*, p. 109, where he recognized the claim for a share in the control of industry.

[65] Ibid., p. 122.

[66] 'Dr. Addison on Reconstruction', *DC*, 24.9.1917. For Brougham Villiers, too, profit-sharing was 'essentially conservative, being intended to reconcile employer and employed, by giving the worker a subordinate interest in the profits of the business' (*Britain After the Peace*, p. 108).

making forums of the Liberal party. Masterman was appointed by the executive of the National Liberal Federation to head its Industrial Policy Committee,[67] which reported early in 1921. It recommended among others a growing popular variant on the Whitley Council theme—the establishment by Parliament of a National Industrial Council consisting of representatives of the employers, the workers and the community. Its function would be 'to promote increased production and the full and proportionate reward of labour where the returns to capital are on the increase'.[68] The limits to which the recommendations were prepared to go and the debate they occasioned in the pages of the liberal press are instructive. For a political party preoccupied with the developing crisis in the British economy, the stress on production is understandable. But the proviso that was attached to the participation of labour in the just fruits of its efforts was unclear. Was labour to bear the brunt of economic dislocation until profits were up? The foreword of the NLF executive dramatically illustrates the gulf between official Liberalism and its advanced thinkers, a gulf that did much to hasten the demise of the party. The executive dusted the old slogans and reapplied them to 1921: 'individual freedom in industry . . . the removal of disabilities and the restraint of tyrannical powers'—these were the ends of Liberal industrial policy couched in terms perfectly consistent with nineteenth-century *laissez-faire*.[69] State regulation and restraint, and a vague equality of opportunity that referred to optimal *individual* initiative and choice, were the suggestions that bore virtually no resemblance to the debate of the past five years.

The leader of the *Manchester Guardian* was courteous but unenthusiastic. Too many important questions were left open. What, it asked, was the full and proportionate reward of labour?[70] The *Nation* was more scathing:

> Our Liberal reformers proceed more carefully (one might almost say more gingerly) when approaching the great issues of industrial control and

[67] Another member was J. M. Robertson, a liberal theorist of force and vigour, but now isolated by his rationalist individualism from the new concerns of liberalism. See *MG*, 22.1.1921.

[68] Ibid. The failure of the national industrial conference (see R. Lowe, 'The Failure of Consensus in Britain: The National Industrial Conference, 1919–1921', *Historical Journal*, 21 (1978), 649–75) did not dissuade progressives from thinking along those lines.

[69] *MG*, 22.1.1921.

[70] 'Liberal Industrial Policy', *MG*, 22.1.1921.

property, where Liberalism has hitherto stood for a minimum of political interference. The precision of their attitude upon the acquisition of land, for instance, is in almost humorous contrast with the vague brevity of their declaration upon the heated subject of nationalization of industries . . . if it be any part of the purpose of Liberal reformers to retain the confidence of social Radicals in the new constructive claims of Liberalism, and to stop their desertion to the Labor Party, this delicacy is quite misplaced.[71]

Both newspapers failed to pick up the point concerning the disproportionate treatment of labour and it was left to Hobson to raise the question at the first meeting of the Liberal Summer School later that year. He 'most severely criticised' Muir's scheme for the sharing out of profits on lines developed from the NLF report. Once the minimum wage had been paid and adequate reserves had been secured for the capitalists, 'freely competitive businesses would not have anything to divide'. Hence, 'it differed little from the profit-sharing schemes of the past that had failed mostly from workers' opposition'. As a result of the discussion, which also included the converse opinion that profit-sharing was unworkable in principle, Muir withdrew his proposals.[72]

Immediately after the publication of the NLF industrial policy report, Muir also crossed swords with Masterman. If Hobson's caveats did not attract the attention of progressive liberals, the issue of compulsion—on which liberals were by now well-versed—did. The *Manchester Guardian* had misunderstood the report as endorsing the conferral of compulsory powers on the separate industrial committees under the National Industrial Council. Echoing the new liberalism of a decade earlier, it welcomed compulsory fixing of hours and wages as an important addition to Whitley Council practice: 'To a Liberal the grant of such extensive powers will always seem open to objection, but it seems likely on the whole that it would extend rather than curtail the enjoyment of real liberty.'[73] Muir, however, interpreted the report differently. 'It isn't clear whether they are to have compulsory powers or not', he protested.

[71] 'A Liberal Challenge to Liberalism', *Nation*, 29.1.1921.

[72] *MG*, 1.10.1921.

[73] 'Liberal Industrial Policy', *MG*, 22.1.1921. The *Westminster Gazette* had already in 1919 called for 'a supreme Whitley Council' with large authority and responsibility, the power to arbitrate and act in labour disputes and to formulate a general labour and industrial policy—in other words, a body that would also accommodate the functions of what later became the proposal for an economic general staff ('For Industrial Peace', *WG*, 4.2.1919).

A purely advisory body might not take its duties seriously. On the other hand, the ultimate authority of Parliament had to be preserved. That could be achieved by charging the industrial councils with the duty of drafting schemes, but making them compulsory only after Parliamentary endorsement.[74] Masterman was provoked to reply. Certainly, he agreed, 'advisory councils are futile and worthless'. Neither did he dismiss the delegation of powers to the councils by Parliament, provided that their decisions, 'if they appear to be unfair, must be challengeable in Parliament'. The emphasis was, however, on getting away from state imposed and regulated machinery: '. . . the whole object of the system is to magnify the advantage of agreement and minimise the exercise of force.'[75] Muir, endowed with a verbosity of Fabian proportions, was quick to issue a rejoinder. The National Industrial Council, as proposed, would be a vast and unmanageable body, overriding the more important functions of the particular councils under it. Instead, it should stand in relation to them as the TUC stood in relation to individual trade unions. The question of compulsion still irked Muir, for whatever Masterman's intentions were, they were not, he complained, reflected in the resolutions of the NLF executive.[76]

On the eve of the Nottingham NLF special conference that was to consider these proposals, Muir contrived to streamline his scheme, now presented in the press as a conflict between the NLF and the Manchester Liberal Federation.[77] Although, Muir argued, it was true that in some ways the state meddled too much with industry, in another sense it did not meddle enough. Its role with respect to industry was to establish representative and effective institutions outside the realm of Parliamentary action, 'a real and powerful system of industrial self-government, subject always to the supreme control of the State, but not to the incessant intervention of its agents'.[78] This policy was supported by the *Daily News* in the face of the official recommendations of the NLF executive that

74 'The New Liberal Programme: Some Manchester Comments and Criticisms', *MG*, 24.1.1921.

75 'The New Liberal Industrial Policy: Mr. Masterman's Reply to the Manchester Critics', *MG*, 26.1.1921.

76 R. Muir, 'The New Liberal Industrial Policy: Mr. Masterman's Explanation: A Rejoinder', *MG*, 28.1.1921.

77 'Business and Government', *DN*, 24.2.1921.

78 R. Muir, 'Liberals and Industry', *DN*, 23.2.1921.

would establish a cabinet minister at the head of a national council of industry.[79]

What does this tell us about the state of liberal thought? It demonstrates both its continuous preoccupation with the salient socio-industrial questions of the day and the tortuousness of its responses: torn between conflicting pulls of class and party, ransacking the liberal repertoire for an adequate formula, but finding only confusing directives as the cohesive system of the new liberalism was cracked wide open by theoretical doubts and practical complexities that seemed insurmountable. Compulsion and liberty, state control and self-government, community and group—the fissure in liberal ideology was in the making, and the uncertainty all-pervading. Only on the liberal left did the heirs to the new liberal tradition continue to pontificate with some degree of certitude and self-assurance; but not without significant theoretical modifications-cum-compromises.

The radical liberal viewpoint on reconstruction was represented by Hobson. It was not profit-sharing that was seen to be the challenge to the existing system, but 'the management of the industry . . . in the hands of a body representing those whose activities contribute to the value of the product'. True, Hobson agreed that 'labour of brain and hand, capital and the market, are all dynamic factors in an industry, and . . . must all have a voice in management'.[80] In practice this may not have seemed too different from Dodds's position, for in typical liberal fashion it recognized the co-operative plurality of society. But the aim of these proposals was not simply the co-option of workers to industrial efficiency[81] or 'the appeasement of unrest and the encouragement of effort in a whole race of men',[82] nor even the attainment of self-respect or abstract justice. 'Political democracy [was] impossible without industrial democracy'[83] because the economic and social structure and functioning of the nation would otherwise be severely

[79] Masterman later wrote: 'In a desperate attempt to prevent the appearance of division, I swallowed the whole of [Muir's] programme *en bloc*, as the lean kine swallowed the fat kine in Scripture, and yet got no fatter' ('The Liberal Convention', *Nation*, 7.2.1925).

[80] Hobson, *Problems of a New World*, pp. 241–2.

[81] B. S. Rowntree, 'Prospects and Tasks of Social Reconstruction', *CR*, 115 (1919), 6.

[82] C. F. G. Masterman, *The New Liberalism* (London, 1920), p. 117.

[83] Hobson, *Problems of a New World*, p. 241.

distorted. This was ultimately a question of ethics, of ideology and of scientific observation. Even if the workers' demands were only half-conscious, even if (as Halévy knew) those demands 'did not originate in socialistic or other revolutionary propaganda, or indeed in any sort of intellectualism' but in 'the concrete grievance of the stoppage and reversal of the wheels of working-class progress',[84] the social recognition of their 'status' had to proceed from 'first, the insistence that the workers have a vested interest in the industry that employs them; secondly, that in virtue of that vested interest, *or property*, they also have a right of representation in the actual government of the business and industry'.[85]

By shifting the grounds of argument on to the question of rightful ownership, Hobson was challenging basic capitalist assumptions. A claim to property was founded on identifying the producers of values. If the location of those creative forces and the repossessioning of what was lawfully theirs constituted 'the most radical challenge to the established Industrial Order',[86] that order would have to be educated to change. It is important to appreciate that this was no socialist argument. Not *all* value was created by the workers of hand or brain. It was central to the liberal persuasion to insist that the role of industrialists, of businessmen, of entrepreneurs could not be eliminated, for a variety of economic, ethical and psychological reasons.[87] No group, however, had an *exclusive* claim. Hobson therefore dismissed the Whitley Council solution as 'based on a belief that labour will be satisfied with an "equal voice" in all matters "directly" affecting conditions of labour, and will leave the employer's other functions intact, including his right to make whatever profits he can under the new circumstances of restricted control'.[88] But the type of profit-sharing Hobson had in mind outstripped conceptually even the ultimate goal that Dodds and others were groping towards. Hobson's notion differed 'from that commonly in vogue, inasmuch as it aims at the participation of labour in the surplus profits on monopoly, not merely the sharing of a gain attributable to the greater care or efficiency of labour'.[89] This was an extension of Hobson's well-known theory of surplus value

84 J. A. Hobson, *Incentives in the New Industrial Order* (London, 1922), p. 14.
85 Ibid., p. 20. My italics.
86 Ibid.
87 See Chapter 5, Section 1.
88 Hobson, *Incentives in the New Industrial Order*, pp. 106–7.
89 Ibid., pp. 107–8.

which attempted to distinguish the elements of wealth that went to maintain the factors in production from those that were socially created and therefore had to be redirected to social use. The novelty in his post-war approach to the surplus—in accord with the new trends in liberal theory—was a reluctance to claim all for the community through the state and the readiness to entertain the possibility of smaller groups such as the workers acting *qua* group as an integral part of the social whole and thus entitled to a share of the social produce.

5. GROUPS AND CITIZENS

So far we have been concerned in this chapter with the 'middle range' theoretical responses of liberals to the growing impingement of industrial problems on post-war society. But there was another backdrop to liberal thought, parallel to the above, that operated on the general level of social theories and ideologies. Here notions of the state, concepts of human nature, reassessments of political power were grappled with, attesting to the continuing existence of specifically liberal modes of political discourse. Even in a period when political argument and speculation lacked the force and the status accorded them by their past reputable vehicles of expression —a respected press, a leisured class—liberal thinkers were hard at work, innovating, synthesizing, often unsuccessfully but, in the long run, not without impact. It is necessary to extract their ideas from mundane and routine reaction to events and to demonstrate the interconnectedness between these running commentaries on the life of a nation and the more refined and analytical theorizing within the traditions of political thought. Though liberals may have expressed themselves badly, what they said is crucial to an understanding both of twentieth-century British politics and of the evolving nature of liberalism itself.

The great post-war vogue in British political thought revolved round guild socialism and, to a lesser extent, syndicalism. Though the antecedents of this movement of ideas are evident before 1914, it was only after the war that it became, for a short while, a force to contend with. G. D. H. Cole, S. G. Hobson and, to a lesser extent, Harold Laski and the Webbs were captivated by a theory that, in a variety of permutations, offered a radical solution to the role of industry in society. The widespread need of progressives to address themselves to the challenge of guild socialism reflected its popularity and its intimate connection to political exigencies. In line with our interest in liberal thought, we shall not be examining guild socialism as such but rather observing its 'consumption' by liberals and the extent to which they were willing to assimilate or reject it. Inasmuch as progressive liberalism was a central constituent of British social-policy thinking, the rise and fall of guild socialism can be studied through the liberal reaction to that doctrine.

From the very outset, liberal analysts were ambivalent towards guild socialism. Inevitably, in the aftermath of the war, it was seen as an obvious outlet for the worker who had lost enthusiasm for state socialism and as a reflection of his growing power.[90] Eventually, it was recognized by liberals that the guild socialist dissatisfaction with 'the unnatural divorce between the worker and his work' was a valuable insight.[91] But the real fascination of liberal theorists with guild socialism can be accounted for by the heavy overlap they believed existed between it and liberalism. Some of its attractions were described by Dodds:

> In their attack on the 'commodity' theory of labour, in their demand for the democratization of industry, in their belief in man as a free and self-governing being, the Guild Socialists have struck the right note. It is true that where Collectivism leaves one coldly hostile, Guild Socialism strikes a responsive chord. In its spiritual ideals, at all events, it is in keeping with the best Liberal tradition.[92]

The guild socialist emphasis on liberty as self-determination appeared to some liberals to be the logical extension of their own creed. Having recognized the significant shift in labour aims away from the social reformist problem of poverty towards the question of control, it was easy to note that 'the spontaneous growth of the shop-stewards' movement ran parallel with the cult of Guild Socialism among the intellectuals' in the direction of freedom and self-government. The *Nation* asserted boldly: 'what we suggest is an evolutionary process, and if it led in the end, as the workers gain in education and ambition and status, to something like Guild

[90] Cf. B. Villiers, *England and the New Era* (London, 1920), pp. 64–7; Hobhouse, 'Industrial Self-Government', *MG*, 29.6.1917; 'A Constitution for Industry', *Nation*, 30.6.1917.

[91] 'The Liberal Position', *DN*, 9.8.1922.

[92] Dodds, *Is Liberalism Dead?*, p. 119.

Socialism, we should not shrink from that development.'[93] But there were further similarities between liberalism and guild socialism. The increasing liberal wariness of the state found its extreme reinforcement in guild socialist, not to mention syndicalist, hostility. The *Nation*, disseminating during the early 1920s the most sympathetic among liberal opinions towards the guild socialist movement, saw its influence in 'the recognition of the fatal burdens of cast-iron systems, and the need for adjusting industry to human nature'.[94] The bias towards empiricism, the malleability of human nature, and the desire to experiment appealed to the liberal mind. Moreover, the decentralist and devolutionary motive power within liberalism could welcome the guild socialist idea as a 'useful crystallization of local forces'.[95] Bertrand Russell, always something of an ideological maverick, reinforced this affinity from outside the liberal camp. Guild socialist solutions were, to his mind, available for 'all those who still care for the ideals which inspired liberalism, namely the problem of combining liberty and personal initiative with organization'. The devolution of power and of economic decision-making to voluntary bodies would confine the state—as in the traditional liberal formula—to maintaining peace among rival interests.[96]

[93] 'The Future of Industry', *Nation*, 11.10.1919. At the very least, argued a reviewer of the *Nation*, 'Freedom and happiness are things of the spirit, and no machinery on earth can make them. The Guilds cannot make them, but they could make the Guilds'. ('Freedom Made Easy', review of S. G. Hobson, *Guild Principles in War and Peace* [London, 1917], 4.8.1917.)

[94] 'A Policy for Labor', *Nation*, 22.4.1922.

[95] 'The Real War After War', review of J. A. Hobson, *Democracy After the War*, *Nation*, 2.2.1918.

[96] B. Russell, *Principles of Social Reconstruction* (London, 1916), pp. 71–5. See also his *Roads to Freedom: Socialism, Anarchism, and Syndicalism*, 3rd edn. (London, 1920), pp. 141–5. It is difficult to categorize Russell, who shared many of the central liberal assumptions about human reason, the dangers of the centralized state and the importance of the individual, but in other senses remained committed to forms of social organization and economic distribution unacceptable to most liberals, and was only marginally associated with the thinkers examined in this study. In 'Socialism and Liberal Ideals', (*English Review*, 30 [1920], 449–55; 499–508) he announced his movement away from liberalism to socialism because those liberal ideals to which he subscribed could not be achieved without transforming the economic structure of society. He is, however, a further example of the flexibility of the boundaries of liberalism (see Chapter 8), and his books were warmly, though not uncritically, welcomed by liberal progressives. See review of *Principles of Social Reconstruction* by C. D. Burns, *International Journal of Ethics*, 27 (1916–17), 384–7; 'Roads to Freedom', *WG*, 21.12.1918; and review of the same by M. Ginsberg, *HJ*, 17 (1919), 760–2.

Nevertheless, the ultimate liberal verdict on guild socialism was decidedly unfavourable. On the question of freedom, the possibilities of oppression were as great as those of expression. Dodds believed that the tyranny of the majority would operate within each guild,[97] exacerbated of course by the lack of constitutional guarantees available on the national political level. Muir gave guild socialism short shrift. Not only was it hard to see how liberty could be increased within the guild, but 'it is obvious that it would not increase the liberty of the consumers'. Perhaps it would even reintroduce that great liberal bugbear, the monopolist trust, but unlike its capitalist counterpart, unchecked by the state.[98] The liberal fear of sectionalism was here at work, coupled with distrust for a class that had not yet enjoyed the benefits of a liberal, rational education. Hence Muir's summation: '[Guild socialism] is inspired partly by a well-meaning loose-thinking idealism; but it is also partly inspired by mere impatience, by venom and by hate; and hate cannot be the parent of justice.'[99] Even the *New Statesman* found fault with guild socialism on the issue of liberty. Reviewing Cole's *Labour in the Commonwealth*, it was struck by his individualistic, if not 'anarchist' tendencies. Cole was 'really insisting on every act and volition of the individual springing from his own contemporary impulse, immediately expressing his own personality, and being separately justified by its advantage in promoting his own well-being'. Cole's conceptual weakness was that of guild socialism, for 'he cannot bear to call any man, or the community, or even the whole of humanity "master" '. But it was precisely the notion of conscious and deliberate service, and service to the community, that was 'perfect freedom'.[100]

Hobhouse, commenting on an earlier book by Cole, had already warned in 1917 that for guild socialists 'the idea of freedom culminates in a system of self-governing monopolies . . . Those that control the essentials of life will clearly be in a position to dominate the entire community.'[101] In other words, concentrated and unequal power was merely being transferred from the state to the guild. Depriving the state of sovereignty could not augment the liberty

97 Dodds, *Is Liberalism Dead?*, p. 121.
98 Muir, *Liberalism and Industry*, p. 64.
99 Ibid., p.65.
100 'The Quest of Freedom', *NS*, 11.1.1919.
101 [L. T. Hobhouse], 'The New Socialism', review of G. D. H. Cole, *Self-Government in Industry* (1917), *MG*, 1.2.1917.

of the individual. Some compulsion was necessary in any society and the state was entrusted with that inevitable function in the name of the entire community. Three years later he elaborated on that theme, describing Cole's attempt to make social co-operation the expression of personal freedom as 'putting the part above the whole . . . it is here that he will be at issue not only with the old Collectivist but with the old-fashioned Liberal'. Hobhouse's liberalism was thus reflecting the strange synthesis between the new liberal predilection for communal control and the old liberal pursuit of the general welfare by means of governmental co-ordination. As he explained with an air of reluctance: 'After a prolonged course of Fabian economics and Hegelian metaphysics one departs wishing that one could never hear the word "State" again. But I think we ought to control the sense of nausea due to repletion for the sake of the many who use the term "State" in all innocence for the supreme legal authority.'[102]

Hobhouse was adamant that no liberal could tolerate a division of sovereignty, but this must also be interpreted in the light of his later extension of the industrial issue: 'Industrial regulation . . . sprang up first to meet the human needs of the worker . . . but at the present time the demand has gone farther than this and is urging the need of the community in general for co-operation and good will in the industrial system.'[103] Other liberals supported the sovereignty argument for a mixture of reasons. From one vantage point, the general interest of all citizens could only be promoted by a body that represented them all. From another, the theme of efficiency was drawn upon to insist that no society could function with a divided decision-making process. Both points were reiterated by Dodds: 'It would be impossible to separate political and industrial issues into water-tight compartments . . . In the event of a conflict, who would decide—"producers" or "users"?'[104] Or as Ernest Barker maintained, 'any doctrine of separation of powers, such as Guild-Socialism advocates, is bound to collapse before the simple fact of the vital interdependence of all the activities of the "great

[102] [L. T. Hobhouse], 'The New Democracy', review of G. D. H. Cole, *Social Theory* (1920), *MG*, 19.4.1920.

[103] L. T. Hobhouse, 'The Problem', in J. A. Hobson and M. Ginsberg, *L. T. Hobhouse* (London, 1931), p. 274.

[104] Dodds, *Is Liberalism Dead?*, pp. 119–20.

society" of to-day . . . If there is to be a State, it must have the final responsibility for the life of its citizens.'[105]

Aversion to the separation of society into discrete watertight systems was a recurrent theme of Hobson's writings, and it was entirely in character to find him a source of sustained and methodical critique of guild socialism for a period of over twenty years. As early as 1912 Hobson attacked syndicalism for advocating states within a state, but at that time he was deterred by its revolutionary anarchic and Marxist leanings. After the war Hobson's reaction to guild socialism was specifically related to his core beliefs concerning organicism and human nature. Even more emphatically than Hobhouse, as shown in the previous chapter, Hobson insisted on the retention of a democratically constituted state, for he foresaw that 'the economic and the political systems of the nation are destined to be more intimately interwoven than ever'.[106] As he later elucidated, syndicalism, guild socialism, and Bolshevism rested their cases on three assumptions: economic issues would play an increasing part in politics; economic justice and security for the workers could only be obtained by a proletarian government; and such government would only be possible through functional, rather than regional, representation.[107] But while other liberals rested content with dismissing guild socialism for ignoring the importance of the consumer and, indeed, the sovereignty of the consumer-cum-citizen—a perspective for which they were primarily indebted to Hobson himself—Hobson had moved one step ahead. To assert the primacy of the consumer under present conditions misrepresented social facts. 'It is only in a formal sense that consumption of wealth can be represented as the end or aim of economic processes. The productive processes of industry absorb nearly all the time, energy, thought, and continuous interest of the great majority of men and women . . . Moreover, man, as worker, is closely associated with his fellow man, as consumer is a detached unit.' If guild socialism were to be repudiated, this could not simply be accomplished by turning a blind eye to the rise of the 'politics of the workshop' which characterized the post-war era.[108] The solution lay rather in

[105] E. Barker, *Political Thought in England 1848–1914* (London, 1963; 1st edn. 1915), p. 203.

[106] Hobson, *Democracy After the War*, p. 181.

[107] Hobson, 'The New Industrial Revolution', 638. See also *Problems of a New World*, pp. 188–9.

[108] Hobson, 'The New Industrial Revolution', 638; 'The Form of the New State', *Nation*, 23.3.1918.

promoting a notion of human nature liberated from industrialism, as discussed above.[109] Economic values would play a reduced role in personal and social life. One could aspire to minimizing, though not eliminating entirely, the disagreeable aspects of production, and also—through scientific and administrative innovations—to developing other activities and interests: 'Friendship, family life, knowledge, recreation, travel, citizenship, the cultivation of unexplored riches of personality, all await this economic deliverance.' Only when this aspect of human life asserted its supremacy as part of the true trend of social evolution, could 'the bond of neighbourhood . . . prevail over that of the workshop, as the groundwork of social co-operation in politics'.[110] Hobson's organicism was thus transferred to the post-war world as an insistence on the multifariousness of mutually dependent aspects of human nature, as an increasingly rearguard attempt, in the face of the disintegration of the social sciences, to preserve their systemic unity, and as a strongly held political stance pertaining to the communal nature of human interaction and citizenship.

For the same reasons Hobson reacted unfavourably to the proposal drawn up by the Webbs in *A Constitution for the Socialist Commonwealth of Great Britain*. They had suggested reorganizing British political institutions on a two-fold basis: a political and a social parliament, both to be territorially elected on a universal franchise. The political parliament would be responsible for defence and foreign affairs, would administer justice, and would safeguard personal liberties. The social parliament would supervise economic and social activities and utilize national resources for communal ends. It would concern itself with property, taxation, the administration of public services, and control over national economic resources and cultural affairs. The relationship between the two parliaments would entail separation of functions and the courts would be entrusted with the settling of jurisdictional conflicts.[111] Though this proposal differed fundamentally from guild socialism in retaining nationally responsible and representative legislatures, Hobson considered it deficient in two contradictory

[109] See pp. 53–4 above.

[110] Hobson, 'The New Industrial Revolution', 645. 'Bond' becomes 'unity' in *Problems of a New World*, p. 200.

[111] S. and B. Webb, *A Constitution for the Socialist Commonwealth of Great Britain* (London, 1920), pp. 111–31.

senses. On the one hand it was too remote from some of the more acceptable ideas of guild socialists in that it made no allowance whatsoever for functional representation, and mistakenly assumed that local constituencies could cope with the tasks of economic organization. On the other hand it dispensed with the need for a supreme representative body, for the final settlement of economic, social and cultural issues 'must rest with the political government and its expert advisers'.[112] Hobson's outlook was sufficiently influenced by the transformations of the 1920s to include a recognition of economic and industrial functions as integral components of the political sphere, but he remained a liberal in his adherence to a hierarchy of spheres in which politics, when inspired by the general good, was the ultimate arbiter and limiter of the other realms of human activity. Even then, the need for a political centre derived not so much from the traditional liberal desire to establish a focus of political obligation, as from the need to co-ordinate an organically linked society.

Delisle Burns was not far off the mark when he wrote in 1925: 'Mr. J. A. Hobson's *Work and Welfare*[113] has affected the outlook [of this book] so intimately in the criticism of industrial practice that it is hardly possible to say what sentence is not dependent upon his work.'[114] That was not the only work by Hobson to have shaped Burns's mind, for when discussing the problems of guild socialism he showed the same changing pattern of treatment one finds in Hobson's writings. Burns believed that guild socialists had the trade unions in mind when talking about producers' organizations. This contrasted them with 'the community', and it also meant they did not form a complete economic unit. In arguing that the industrial community included consumers as well as producers, Burns distanced himself from the 'economic conception of the activity of consumers as simply absorbing services'. In Hobsonian terms he referred to consumption as a 'fine art . . . the creation of a type of life; its social function is not mere absorption for further production, but creative imagination'.[115] However, while Hobson was prone to emphasize parliamentarianism and electoral systems

[112] J. A. Hobson, *Democracy and a Changing Civilisation* (London, 1934), pp. 95–6.

[113] The actual title was *Work and Wealth* (London, 1914).

[114] C. D. Burns, *Industry and Civilisation* (London, 1925), p. 7.

[115] Burns, *Government and Industry*, pp. 295–6.

incorporating federalism and proportional representation side by side with empirical social evolution as the mainstays of organicism, Burns reflected his civil service background when conceiving of administration 'as the first basis for the organization of the industrial community'. The emergence of a community, on a historical perspective, paralleled the growth of an administrative system. In 1925 Burns was again following Hobson's concessions to the present importance of economic organizations. Because both current problems and current intellectual interests were economic, it was perhaps 'morally right to concentrate attention upon economic life', even up to the point that Hobson, the greater organicist, was reluctant to grant, namely, 'situations in which the economic [community] should predominate [over the political]'.[116] And Burns went on to elucidate: 'It does *not* mean that in *any* crisis the state should take precedence of any other association or kind of community.'[117] However, Burns reasserted the statism of left-liberalism by claiming moral priority for the modern state on two grounds: as the junction point for various types of social co-operation, and as part of a single world system.

Other liberals saw in guild socialism dangers of a different kind. For Dodds, the conflict and antagonism among guilds, with the possibility of holding society to ransom, that was grafted on to a system that lacked incentives to produce and that encouraged standardization, would 'be fatal both to enterprise and efficiency'.[118] This had also worried Hobhouse, for guilds repelled 'the suggestion of an underlying unity of aim and insist on a radical and insuperable antagonism'. Not only was this the divisive language of the class war liberals had always sought to avoid, but the directing and managerial skills of guildsmen had yet to evolve. A new managerial class would again reinstitute divergencies of interest between themselves and the workpeople. The re-emergence of these dubious characteristics was, Hobhouse felt, in the nature of industry.[119] As the *Nation* formulated it: 'With size will come centralization: with centralization death.'[120] Masterman also questioned whether guild socialism could maintain, for example, the Lancashire cotton industry in the face of fierce individualistic competition from abroad

[116] Burns, *Industry and Civilisation*, p. 241.
[117] Ibid., p. 242.
[118] Dodds, *Is Liberalism Dead?*, pp. 121–2.
[119] [L. T. Hobhouse], 'The New Revolution', *MG*, 6.10.1917.
[120] 'Freedom Made Easy', *Nation*, 4.8.1917.

and whether workers' management could emulate that 'miracle of organisation and enterprise'.[121] Similarly Graham Wallas, abandoning much of his earlier socialism, now maintained that the economic motive of gain should not be accorded a subordinate place in the organization of industry. Reviewing Tawney's *The Acquisitive Society*, Wallas singled out inefficiency as the scourge of British industry. Social equality and social service were ends he felt he could agree on with Tawney, but he was sceptical about the ability of self-government to increase public spiritedness. To the contrary, 'attempts to contrive means by which the economic motive of earning shall help instead of hindering social good are not necessarily wasted'. One must 'be careful to secure that civil servants and professors and miners shall know that if they work they will be sufficiently paid, and if they do not work they will be dismissed'.[122] Words to bring great cheer to any industrialist, liberal or otherwise, but also a development of the quid pro quo implications of Tawney's notion of social service. All this had been explored at greater length in Wallas's *Our Social Heritage*, where Wallas took G. D. H. Cole to task for suggesting (in *Social Theory*) that vocational organization allowed the differences between people to develop, whereas the state imposed the common and the uniform in the form of consumption. Rather, argued Wallas, trade unions and, presumably, guilds, were characterized by identity, reluctance to change, and conservatism. They were also far from conducive to social and economic development, because they diverted potential capital—necessary to make future labour more productive—into higher wages.[123] This was notably not an underconsumptionist argument of the type Hobson was prone to suggest, though it did hint at the fact that taxation was an alternative to private initiative in the creation of investment capital. Nor was this a conservative argument, for Wallas saw the community through its agent, the state, as the innovative mechanism which by controlling mobility between professions, guaranteed a general progressive interest that guilds were unable to cater for.[124] Even Laski, at that time in his guild socialist (or pluralist) stage, had to concede that Wallas's discussion was 'a distinguished one', though at the same time

[121] Masterman, *The New Liberalism*, p. 126.
[122] G. Wallas, 'Acquisitive Society', *Nation*, 11.6.1921.
[123] G. Wallas, *Our Social Heritage* (London, 1921), pp. 113–16.
[124] Ibid., pp. 152–4.

Wallas's alternative proposals lacked concreteness. This was particularly regrettable, lamented Laski, because the immediate post-war situation demanded 'that task of affirmation which I should argue is now the first business of political philosophy'.[125]

The failure of the General Strike in 1926 symbolized the final demise of guild socialism and syndicalism in Britain. If the strike was the ultimate weapon of those movements against democratic representative government, against the citizen as consumer, then their potential power petered out against a background of economic weakness and ideological rejection by the workers. The latter occurrence had been anticipated by liberals early on: 'we think it incorrect to assume that the extreme doctrines of Socialism or Syndicalism, embodying nothing less than the destruction of "the capitalist system," with the conscious "class-war" as its weapon, are the animating motives of any large section of the discontented workers or even of their leaders.'[126] When the strike came, however, liberals were divided, the more advanced urging moderation. Unfortunately, as was wont to be the case, the divide was superimposed on the Asquith Lloyd-George feud and caused much acrimony. Thus while the *Westminster Gazette* understood the issue to be the defence of Parliamentary government, the *Daily News* felt that Liberalism had done great damage to itself by its attitude to the strike and had now to demonstrate that it wanted neither reaction nor revolution.[127] Maurice Bonham-Carter, representing the Asquith faction, wrote to Hubert Henderson, then editor of the *Nation*, to complain of the conciliatory note of the left-liberal press and to demand an affirmative to the following queries:

Is it an essential part of the Liberal tradition to maintain the sovereignty of Parliament . . .? Is it possible seriously to believe that the success of the General Strike would not have struck an irremediable blow at this Sovereignty, and is it unreasonable and unworthy of a Liberal to hold that compromise with the authors of the General Strike offered risks of undermining this sovereignty . . .?[128]

[125] H. J. L[aski], 'Mr. Wallas as Social Thinker', review of G. Wallas, *Our Social Heritage*, *Nation*, 9.4.1921.

[126] 'What Does Labor Want?', *Nation*, 1.2.1919.

[127] 'Party Leaders and Strike Issues', *WG*, 22.5.1926; 'Liberalism and the Strike', *DN*, 19.5.1926.

[128] Henderson Papers, Box 21, Bonham-Carter to Henderson, 2.6.1926. Lloyd George had in fact attacked the strike for the challenge it posed to democratic

Henderson was moved to reply, proffering a wider political perspective: 'It is important to assert sound constitutional principles as effectively as one can, but when the note is pitched too high, a soupçon of the ridiculous begins to creep in. The Government is not and cannot be, in practice, entirely free from the pressure of extra-Parliamentary events.'[129] Such exchanges aside, the General Strike occasioned few discussions of principle among liberals. The specific issues concerning workers' democracy had in part been repelled, in part assimilated within existing institutional and ideological frameworks. Other, more pressing themes within liberalism had come to dominate the stage, and these centred to a large extent round the Liberal Summer School movement, to which we now turn. But the problems of industrial democracy had left an important heritage. In its dual reaction to the benefits of self-government and its dangers, in its sympathy for workers and its abhorrence of sectionalism, in its pursuit of social justice and its concern for efficiency, a dialectical split was forming within progressive liberalism that was to characterize the course of its development in the inter-war years.

government as well as advocating a reorganization on the lines of the Sankey Report (*Hansard*, 5th Ser. CXCV 83–91 [3.5.1926]).

[129] Henderson Papers, Box 21, Henderson to Bonham-Carter, 4.6.1926.

4

THE LIBERAL SUMMER SCHOOL: THE FIRST DECADE

IN more senses than one, the Liberal Summer School movement was the linchpin of liberal and progressive thought during the 1920s. It witnessed the only serious attempts to revive liberalism as an intellectual force; it supplied the Liberal party with a radical ideology that gradually assumed salience and centrality in its programmes; and it served as a source of inspiration, often discreet, sometimes acknowledged, for a wide spectrum of political activists outside the Liberal party, even if its practical influences had to await the advent of another world war. The Liberal Summer School (LSS) movement is of crucial importance for an understanding of British liberal thought between the wars: in its successes, its failures, its tensions, it mirrored the dilemmas and difficulties of a struggling ideology. A sustained period of crisis will frequently highlight issues and magnify cracks, and so it was with liberalism, whose nature and structure as a belief system was revealed for all to see.

It is interesting that the LSS has not engaged the attention of many scholars of liberalism,[1] a phenomenon that itself is characteristic of the considerable problems that faced liberal thought. The British propensity to identify party with ideology not only abetted the rapid decline of liberalism as the party was rent from within and squeezed from without, but has bequeathed a perspective that overemphasizes the demise of the Liberal party while tending to overlook the partially successful disengagement of liberalism from its institutional fetters.[2] That disengagement was not without cost to

[1] Notable exceptions are J. Campbell, 'The Renewal of Liberalism: Liberalism Without Liberals', in G. Peele and C. Cook (eds.), *The Politics of Reappraisal 1918–1939* (London, 1975), pp. 88–113, and M. W. Hart, 'The Decline of the Liberal Party in Parliament and in the Constituencies 1914–1931' (Oxford University D.Phil. Thesis, 1982), ch. 6.

[2] M. Bentley, *The Liberal Mind 1914–1929* (Cambridge, 1977), p. 160 and *passim*, provides a useful corrective to this viewpoint.

liberal theory, for it is undeniably true that its finest manifestations in the past had benefited immensely from a thriving and confident organizational framework. But to take the converse argument to its logical conclusion is to deny oneself insights both into the tenacious persistence of ideological patterns and into the development of an important mainstream of British socio-political thought.

1. THE FORMATIVE YEARS

The post-war Liberal crisis of leadership has been amply reconstructed in political analyses of the period. What is less often noted is that the internal dissatisfaction of liberals with their leaders was not merely a question of the lack of a guiding hand, or the absence of unity and poor Parliamentary and electoral performances. E. D. Simon, a wealthy Mancunian industrialist, who had been directed in his first political steps by the Webbs and was now poised to embark upon an influential career as a Liberal mayor, MP, and national figure, acutely located some intellectual roots of the malaise. He considered the Liberal leadership incapable of assimilating the new demand for an industrial policy. Of R. B. Haldane, Simon had originally entertained high hopes—'the only present or ex-liberal leader' to show a 'real interest in industrial policy', he recorded.[3] Shortly afterwards, a seventeen-hour session with Haldane disabused him of any lingering hopes: 'He was most disappointing on Liberalism . . . Even after 10 hours of competent attack, he did not budge an inch; our time was almost wasted.'[4] Haldane's obsession with education as a cure-all hardly touched upon the main concerns of social reformers. Keenly aware of the intellectual challenge from Labour, Simon was even more scathing in his opinion of Herbert Gladstone, then running the Asquithian Liberal organization, apparently 'as a happy family, all on Christian name terms . . . Knows literally nothing about the N[ational] L[iberal] F[ederation]; no touch with MPs; never heard of "Labour and the New Social Order" . . . The absolute limit of amiable helplessness. What a party! No leaders. No organisation. No policy! Only a Summer School!'[5]

[3] Simon Papers, Diary, p. 4. Quotations are from selections from Simon's personal diary transcribed by Joan Simon in 1976.

[4] Ibid., p. 5.

[5] Ibid., p. 8.

But the Summer School proved the seed of a new beginning. Its origins lay in the emergence of the Manchester Liberal Federation as host to a group of radical liberals, a new 'Manchester School' that grew from ginger group to determinator of national Liberal politics and faintly echoed its illustrious predecessor in its resonance, though not in its ideas. Predictably, the *Manchester Guardian* and its editor, C. P. Scott, were well placed to maintain the newspaper's prominence as mouthpiece of the liberal intelligentsia, combining its national role with a close ear to the resurgence of Manchester liberalism. Simon was the moving spirit behind this liberal revival and in 1919, together with Colonel Thomas F. Tweed—at the time the Manchester Liberal Federation's agent and later the north-west Liberal organizer—prevailed upon Ramsay Muir, then professor of Modern History at Manchester University, to attend the meetings that a number of Liberal Manchester businessmen had been having since 1918 to discuss the problems of industry. Their main purpose was the formulation of a 'clear and definite' liberal policy to replace the 'vague generalities' of the Liberal leadership.[6] As Muir explained a few years later:

No enthusiasm could be aroused by mere negations of the attitudes of other parties, by mere opposition to protection and to Socialism, or by the assertion that an undefined 'middle course' between 'reaction' and 'revolution' was the line of safety . . . accordingly there arose a demand that there should be a clear definition of what the party stood *for*, and not merely of what it stood *against*, in the new post-war world.[7]

After listening in on a number of debates on a subject he knew little about, Muir was converted (and in future was to acknowledge that Simon had drawn him into politics).[8] But the original intention of the group to proceed by resolution proved impossible and Muir was requested to produce a book, *Liberalism and Industry*,[9] which he then read out to the Manchester Liberal Federation—an unusual infusion of theory into a political forum, rarely to be found in Britain outside small socialist coteries.[10] Hobhouse publicized the

[6] E. D. Simon, 'The Liberal Summer School', *CR*, 130 (1926), 298–9. See also S. Hodgson, 'The Story of the Liberal Summer Schools', *DN*, 24.7.1926.

[7] R. Muir, 'The Liberal Summer School and the Problems of Industry', *CR*, 132 (1927), 283.

[8] See below, p. 350.

[9] Its main themes will be discussed later in this chapter and in Chapter 5.

[10] E. D. Simon, 'Liberalism and Industry', in S. Hodgson (ed.), *Ramsay Muir* (London, 1943), p. 181. See also Hodgson, 'The Story of the Liberal Summer Schools', *DN*, 24.7.1926.

book in a long leader, describing it as extolling 'the guidance by the collective thought of the community of existing institutions and tendencies in the ways of freedom and justice'. The book itself offered no theoretical breakthroughs, and certainly Hobhouse did not think it to be more than a 'considered statement of the Liberal attitude to the economic well-being of society'.[11] But it filled an important gap by providing liberals with the middle range of theorizing that could be translated into political programmes and policies.

By early 1921 the Manchester Liberal Federation had not only adopted Muir's book as 'a basis for the solution of the many social and industrial problems with which the nation is confronted', but had successfully pressed its case for the adoption of a stance on industrial questions upon the NLF, as discussed in the previous chapter. Simon jotted down in his diary with justifiable pride: 'I have been in close touch with Manchester Liberalism for the last few years—am responsible both for the production of Muir's book and (almost entirely) for the fact that the NLF is meeting today to adopt an industrial policy.'[12] Even if the NLF proved somewhat more resistant to radicalism than Simon would have liked, the new Manchesterism was acclaimed by advanced liberals beyond the confines of Manchester. The London *Nation* hailed Muir's book as 'a bold and comprehensive attempt to formulate a new Liberal policy on its industrial side', adding that 'If the general body of free Liberals were ready to advance with Professor Muir and his new Manchester school, it might be that a quick and glorious resurrection were awaiting the otherwise doomed Liberal Party.'[13] But the *Nation* sounded a cautionary note which, in the light of future developments, signalled a parting of the ways within liberalism, both political and theoretical. How many liberals, it asked, could be trusted to accept that policy? How strong was the older Manchesterism, with its refusal to enlarge the functions of the state? And how far along the necessary road of co-operation with the Labour party were liberals prepared to go and, for that matter,

[11] [L. T. Hobhouse], 'Economic Liberalism', *MG*, 30.12.1920.

[12] Simon Papers, Diary, p. 6. Hodgson regarded the Manchester group's triumph at the Nottingham NLF conference as the end of the militant phase of the movement, besides which 'nothing in effect happened. The resolutions disappeared with other heterogeneous matter into the limbo of general Liberal policy' (S. Hodgson, 'The Story of the Liberal Summer Schools', *DN*, 24.7.1926).

[13] 'The New Manchesterism', *Nation*, 1.1.1921.

were Labour members—suspicious of a recalcitrant liberalism—ready to combine with liberals to create a common progressive movement?

There followed rapid progress on another front. In the summer of 1921 Simon organized a meeting on his farm in Herefordshire with Muir, Philip Guedalla, the liberal journalist, E. T. Scott, son of C. P. and future editor of the *Manchester Guardian*, and Colonel Tweed. The result was a preliminary summer school that met at Grasmere in September 1921. Significantly, its purpose as originally conceived was not party political; it was to be 'a stimulation of co-operative, exploratory thinking by people whose training and experience enabled them to make useful contributions . . . the essential thing was discussion and criticism'.[14] Authoritative pronouncements by party leaders or resolutions for conferences were ruled out by Muir; Simon later recollected that 'he wanted an annual meeting on the lines of the British Association for the Advancement of Science, to discuss all kinds of problems on scientific lines from the Liberal angle'.[15] Muir had realized that ideological innovators were rarely to be found within the upper ranks of a party machine and that a wider net had to be cast in order to reformulate the core and range of liberal thinking: 'many of the best minds engaged in the study of the economic and political sciences were in fact Liberals, though not active politicians; and they planned to provide for them at once a nucleus and a platform.'[16] Moreover, the entire approach of the LSS was issue-oriented, not, as the traditional party perspective would dictate, person-oriented. Programmes for the sessions 'began by drawing up a list of the subjects upon which not orthodox platitudes but new light seemed to be needed. They then discussed who would be most likely to be able to shed some fresh light, from a Liberal point of view, upon these subjects . . . whether his name was known to the public or not.'[17] It was a daring move within the British political context to recognize the centrality of ideology and its systematization and to accord it a durable institutional presence.

The Grasmere meeting, originally limited to fifty participants, nearly doubled that figure.[18] The composition of the audience in-

[14] Muir, 'The Liberal Summer School and the Problems of Industry', 285.
[15] Simon in Hodgson (ed.), *Ramsay Muir*, p. 182.
[16] Muir, 'The Liberal Summer School and the Problems of Industry', 285.
[17] R. Muir, 'The Summer School Movement', *WW*, 9.8.1924.
[18] *MG*, 2.9.1921. But see Simon in Hodgson (ed.), *Ramsay Muir*, who mentioned

dicated the future appeal of the LSS to younger liberals—a 'League of Youth', as Stuart Hodgson, the liberal editor, called it.[19] No invitations were sent to party officials or MPs—a practice later abandoned as the LSS moved from periphery to centre. The strong Mancunian element was balanced by invitations to prominent liberals and progressives that included J. A. Hobson, R. H. Tawney, Eleanor Rathbone, the economists Walter Layton and D. H. Macgregor, W. H. Beveridge, and A. D. McNair, secretary to the Sankey Commission. Layton later recalled: 'The backbone of the agenda was naturally Ramsay Muir's book. But even at Grasmere and in increasing volume in ensuing years the thinking of the Liberal Summer School was fed by a series of tributary streams, one or two of which ultimately became great rivers of thought.'[20] Thus a dual pattern was set: not only did much British social policy thinking originate in the LSS, but it became the stage for unravelling different strands of post-war liberal theory.

Small differences of opinion, indicating diverging groups within the liberal mainstream, had already surfaced at Grasmere. Attention has been drawn to the clash between Muir and Hobson over profit-sharing.[21] Another strongly critical discussion took place over the presentation by Eleanor Rathbone of the case for family endowment and a basic wage rate for married couples, with special allowances for children.[22] The *Nation*'s doubts were not entirely laid to rest. Business experience and interests operated to curtail industrial democracy in favour of expert management, and the 'frequently recurring note' of suspicion of bureaucracy 'turned the general sense of the meeting against full nationalization of mines and railways'. The anti-statist shadow of the war stretched out to Grasmere: 'the present unpopularity of the State and its officials operated, both in this and in the urgent matter of unemployment,

the figure of sixty and Muir in 'The Summer School Movement', *WW*, 2.8.1924, who assessed participation at seventy. Hodgson later recollected that there had been 150 ('The Story of the Liberal Summer Schools', *DN*, 24.7.1926). So much for the reliability of witnesses!

19 Hodgson, 'The Story of the Liberal Summer Schools', *DN*, 24.7. 1926: 'The abler sort of young man turned after Grasmere as naturally to the Summer School movement as in an earlier generation he turned to Fabianism.'

20 W. Layton, 'The L. S. S.' in *80th Birthday Book for Ernest Darwin Simon* (Stockport, private printing, 1959), p. 32.

21 See above, p. 62.

22 *MG*, 30.9.1921.

to disparage unduly the part which here, as in every modern nation, the State must play as a controlling factor in industrial life.' Instead of, for example, regulating that avowed enemy of the new liberalism, the trust, by means of the state, it was thought sufficient to rely upon informed public opinion (another liberal fetish that would naturally exclude the uneducated from an active political role). Ultimately, the *Nation* detected in Grasmere 'the almost complete failure to recognize that society was a directly operative force in the determination of economic values' and the corollary that the surplus to be divided should accrue to the state rather than to the owners of the factors of production.[23] Since this patently Hobsonian thesis was precisely the substance of Hobson's argument with Muir, it comes as a surprise to read in Simon's diary that 'after a week's discussion J. A. Hobson said it was much the best thing of the kind he had been at; that all discussions had been carried on in a truly liberal spirit'.[24] Perhaps Hobson had low expectations from such forums—to Rowntree a liberal friend (Simon again?) wrote that Hobson had found Grasmere 'far better than any similar Fabian meeting he had ever been to'.[25] Deeds, however, speak louder than words and Hobson did not continue his association with the LSS.

Following Grasmere the LSS settled down into a regular pattern, meeting alternately in Oxford and Cambridge. Muir and Layton were appointed joint directors of the School and a committee was formed to co-ordinate its work and prepare future summer sessions. Apart from the initiators, the committee included E. H. Gilpin, later co-opting Maurice Bonham-Carter, Major Crawfurd, H. D. Henderson, W. McG. Eagar, Hodgson, and Keynes. Simon was unrepentant about its functioning 'in a thoroughly undemocratic way'; Muir considered it to be 'a large and representative council' despite the lack of elections. The committee held numerous small and private conferences which were not given publicity. It was also instructed, after Grasmere, 'to consult Mr. Asquith in order to make sure that the movement did not in any way run counter to his ideas'.[26] Hence, despite its non-party pro-

[23] 'A Lake School of Liberals', *Nation*, 8.10.1921.

[24] Simon Papers, Diary, p. 7 (2.10.1921).

[25] Quoted in A. Briggs, *Social Thought and Social Action: A Study of the Work of Seebohm Rowntree 1871–1954* (London, 1961), p. 199.

[26] R. Muir, 'The Summer School Movement', *WW*, 2.8.1924; Simon, 'The Liberal Summer School' (1926), 299.

file, the LSS movement attempted from its very inception to secure the co-operation and ears of the party élite, and after 1921 Manchester liberalism obtained a national liberal podium.[27] Layton still looked back on the LSS as 'a pressure group designed to force the pace on the official party machine'.[28] But it was always more than that. Writing in 1922 after the second LSS, the *Manchester Guardian* commented: 'The Oxford school that ended yesterday was widely representative of Liberalism, and was in no sense the creation of a clique or the beginning of a schism.'[29] The 1922 session papers, published in book form, bear testimony to that claim. For one thing, Asquith and Grey were invited to open and close the School respectively. For another, the speakers included Robert Cecil, perhaps best described as a radical conservative, again indicating the gradual release of liberal ideology from party structure ('One or two of the speakers were, indeed, not even professed Liberals. They were invited to speak because it was known that on their subjects they would express the true mind of modern Liberalism').[30] Other speakers included J. M. Robertson, J. A. Spender, Hobhouse, and Muir. A strong complement of economists consisted of Keynes, Josiah Stamp, Layton, and Henderson. Two of the lectures are of particular interest: Layton's 'The State and Industry' reflected the general mood of the School on the possibility of radical reform, and was heartily endorsed by the liberal press.[31] Many listeners found it 'a stiff dose of gloom'.[32] McNair's 'The Problem of the Mines' was important in a different sense—it marked the beginning of LSS ventures into policy proposals that eventually became central planks of the nationally acclaimed Liberal programmes and Reports. Layton voiced the increasingly heard liberal position that state management in industry could neither be ruled out nor encouraged—it was a question of expediency—though he endorsed limited workers' representation and profit-sharing, a National Industrial Council and further restrictions on the right of inheritance. On the vexed question of compulsion, a consensus of sorts was emerging, with Hobhouse and Henderson joining Layton in

[27] *MG*, 2.9.1921.
[28] Layton in *80th Birthday Book for Ernest Darwin Simon*, pp. 32–3.
[29] 'Liberals at Oxford', *MG*, 10.8.1922.
[30] *Essays in Liberalism* (London, 1922), p. vi.
[31] See e.g. 'Towards an Industrial Policy', *WG*, 10.8.1922; 'The Liberal Position', *DN*, 9.8.1922.
[32] *MG*, 9.8.1922.

opposing universal compulsory state systems, while agreeing that compulsion would have to be attached to minimum wages. Henderson stressed that, with respect to unemployment relief, 'not a legal but a moral obligation lies upon each industry to do its best to work out a satisfactory . . . scheme'.[33] The general thrust of the discussion, against a backdrop of growing economic despondency, was that the present system could be mended but not ended. In Layton's words: 'My object . . . is to show how a system which embodies a large amount of private enterprise can be made tolerable and acceptable to modern ideas of equity.'[34]

McNair developed the ideas that had been unsuccessfully floated by the 1919 Sankey (Coal Industry) Commission. Though that commission had not spoken with one voice, all the commissioners had agreed on the need to transfer the control and possession of mineral rights to the state.[35] The rejection of the recommendations by the Coalition government and the association of the Labour party point of view with outright nationalization cleared the way for pursuing what Layton termed a solution 'on characteristically Liberal lines'.[36] For McNair, indeed, the solution was 'emphatically not the Nationalisation of the industry'.[37] The mines would remain private; the coal itself and the royalties on it would be nationalized. The state would then be 'placed in a strategic position for the control and development of this great national asset',[38] and would also determine leases to the mining companies. McNair and Layton could adopt these suggestions as 'inspired by the Liberal point of view'[39] because they combined two perspectives that were emerging as central to liberal thought in the 1920s. The state was the ultimate repository of responsibility for industrial affairs but it was simply not competent to undertake managerial as well as supervisory functions. 'That is where', McNair underlined, 'we part company with our Socialist opponents.'[40] As for joint control, measures on both the local and national levels were necessary, especially if some degree of profit-sharing with miners were to materialize. The war

[33] *Essays in Liberalism*, p. 189.
[34] Ibid., p. 149.
[35] See below, pp. 188–9.
[36] *Essays in Liberalism*, p. 154.
[37] A. McNair, 'Liberalism and the Coal Mining Industry', *WW*, 1.12.1923.
[38] *Essays in Liberalism*, p. 201.
[39] Ibid, p. 210.
[40] *WW*, 1.12.1923.

may not have popularized state socialism but, in McNair's view, it certainly constituted a point of no return for the key coal-mining industry. Mining labour would never again be content with its subordinate position.[41] Pre-war new liberalism had alternated between outright communal responsibility via the state and arrangements, such as national insurance, that shared responsibility among other bodies as well. For liberals such as McNair, the war had one main social and industrial lesson to impart—co-operation with the state, rather than exclusive state activity, was the only viable method. McNair's pluralistic notion of friendly partnership among the various units constituting a society was indeed a liberal one, but at the cost of abandoning hope for the impartial, benevolent, and efficient state the new liberals had sponsored. It is interesting therefore to note that the 1922 LSS also heard early mention of an idea that was increasingly to be suggested as an alternative institutional solution to balancing the public and the private domains. This was the public corporation on the Port of London Authority model, mooted by Muir and McNair as the proper method of undertaking an industrial or commercial concern on behalf of the community, by substituting Parliamentary for ministerial control.[42]

The second secretary of the LSS recalled that 'the Liberal Summer School at Oxford in 1922 was a landmark in the lives of forward-looking Liberals', especially those of the younger generation. The reason for this was that 'the Grasmere meeting had been one for the intellectually expert; to Oxford all were free to come.'[43] Violet Bonham-Carter was tingling from the experience: '. . . the whole school was kindled by a curious corporate vitality which I have never felt so strongly anywhere, and which went through one like a current as one dropped into one's socket in the crowded row.' Youth and the constant bombardment of lecturers by questions were her predominant impressions.[44] In 1922 600 members were present. Attendance rose constantly, peaking at about 900 in the mid-1920s. Considerable effort was made to attract young people: the *Weekly Westminster*, for example, offered scholarships and prizes, based on essays to be submitted to the newspaper, to cover

[41] Ibid.

[42] *Essays in Liberalism*, pp. 143, 209.

[43] S. Brown in Hodgson (ed.), *Ramsay Muir*, p. 204.

[44] V. Bonham-Carter, 'The Faith of the Future: Some Impressions of the Oxford School', *DN*, 11.8.1922.

the costs of residence and transport for the 1924 and 1925 Schools.[45]

2. THE *NATION* TRANSFORMED

Between the 1922 and 1923 sessions an important event in liberal journalism took place which deserves separate consideration. For some time Simon had been casting around for a forum which could amplify and spread the views of the LSS movement. Through his close association with the Webbs, Simon had become a director and subsidizer of the *New Statesman*.[46] By late 1922 both the *New Statesman* and the *Nation* were faltering financially. Simon put £2,000 into the *Nation*, 'to get a constructive Liberal paper, to push Summer School idea' but at the same time he 'tried hard to combine *Nation* and *Statesman* with [Clifford] Sharp as editor'.[47] Webb objected because of Sharp's 'gradual "Liberalization"' but resigned himself, in view of the financial crisis, to the *New Statesman* becoming liberal ('though of the Manchester variety') and to his quitting the project.[48] Two other directors, however, objected and one of them found further money with which to enable the *New Statesman* to survive; it is curious to reflect on this when, eight years later, a reinvigorated *New Statesman* swallowed the *Nation* and put an end to efforts to disseminate broadly its peculiar brand of liberal thinking. But a more important drama in the fortunes of liberalism was about to unfold. The Rowntree family, who had been supporting the *Nation* by means of the Rowntree Trust, had become increasingly concerned during 1921 and 1922 about the heavy losses incurred by the weekly. In the middle of financial negotiations in December 1922, its illustrious editor, H. W. Massingham—for some time in indifferent health—submitted his resignation.[49] The Rowntrees accepted with alacrity having, unknown to Massingham, opened another front a month earlier. In November Arnold Rowntree had heard that the Summer School liberals were casting around for a weekly and had com-

[45] See *WW*, 17.5.1924; 8.8.1925. This tradition was then continued at a more modest level by the *Forward View*.

[46] M. Stocks, *Ernest Simon of Manchester* (Manchester, 1963), p. 29.

[47] Simon Papers, Diary, p. 7.

[48] Simon Papers, M11/16/33, Webb to Simon (3.1.1923).

[49] See A. F. Havighurst, *Radical Journalist: H. W. Massingham* (Cambridge, 1974), pp. 293–302.

menced talks with 'two or three of them'.[50] By March 1923 Keynes (who had become the driving force in this transaction), Simon, and others had purchased the *Nation*. Keynes became chairman of the new board; the Rowntrees kept a share.[51] The eminent group of *Nation* journalists loyal to Massingham greatly resented the way he had been treated. Letters of protest poured in from Hobson, Hammond and Nevinson,[52] as well as from C. P. Scott.[53] The old guard withdrew their services, with the exception of Leonard Woolf, despite attempts by the new editor, Henderson, to retain their co-operation.

The significance of this change extends far beyond the boundaries of journalistic history. Massingham had resigned mainly because of the impossible situation in which a reunion of the Liberal party under Lloyd George would place him. He had made up his mind to go over to the Labour party in such an eventuality.[54] Although, as will be argued in Chapter 6, this would not have excluded him from the embrace of liberalism, a split was beginning to develop among liberal intellectuals over the nature of liberalism itself. Simon and Keynes acquired the option on the *Nation* because of 'their belief in the possibility of finding a progressive policy in National affairs not based upon a collectivist dogma'.[55] And elsewhere Simon wrote: 'Those who have acquired the paper did so for the purpose of expressing a definite constructive policy of Liberalism, on the lines which the Summer School Committee is trying to work out. These are totally different from Massingham's views.'[56] Thus the new liberalism so closely associated with the *Nation* appeared in the bleak light of 1923 to be sadly antiquated. In ideological terms it was too staunchly collectivist; in practical

50 A. Rowntree to J. A. Hobson, 16.4.1923 (copies in Simon [M11/16/33] and Hammond [vol. 34] Papers).

51 Cf. R. F. Harrod, *Keynes* (Harmondsworth, 1972), pp. 394–5.

52 Simon Papers, M11/16/33, Hammond to Simon, 29.3.1923; Rowntree to Hobson, 16.4.1923. Hammond requested C. P. Scott's help in convincing Keynes to give the *Nation* up; Scott was unable to oblige and reluctant to approach Keynes (*Guardian* Archives, A/H19/25, Scott to Hammond, 18.2.1923).

53 Hammond Papers, vol. 34, 24.1.1923, 11.3.1923. But see the fascinating contrary assessment of Massingham by Leonard Woolf in his *Autobiography*, part iv, *Downhill All the Way* (Oxford, 1980), pp. 254–7.

54 Massingham to A. Rowntree, 10.12.1922, quoted in Havighurst, *Radical Journalist*, p. 296.

55 Simon Papers, *Nation* file M/11/16/33, undated.

56 Ibid., 3.4.1923.

terms, too critical and too negative[57] to serve as the platform of an aggressive, politically minded liberalism. Not all held that view. C. P. Scott commented: 'To pass from that [Massingham's feeling for the liberal spirit] to the arid intellectualism of Keynes will be a change indeed.'[58] Clearly, the bifurcation within liberal thought had risen to the surface and been formally acknowledged in crisp institutional demarcations.

Within this basic bifurcation between liberal left and liberal centre there were, of course, a large number of currents. In the LSS movement alone, Keynes, Muir and Simon were all to move in different directions. In fact, no sooner had the *Nation putsch* against left-liberalism been set in motion, a second split emerged between Muir on the one hand and the economists Keynes, Henderson and Layton on the other. Once the idea to use Sharp as joint editor for both the *Nation* and the *New Statesman* had been discarded, the choice of editor fell on Muir, who envisaged the *Nation* as catering both for the younger intellectuals and the non-expert but politically interested progressive, the 'chosen people' and the 'philistines'.[59] Keynes objected to the proposed appointment, plainly regarding himself in the first category and Muir in the second. According to Muir, Keynes had offered him too low a salary, and had insisted that the editor write little or nothing himself and that some sub-editors be responsible to Keynes directly.[60] Muir was deeply offended by the figure mooted for his salary, a mere £750. This was 'less than any corresponding editor receives; less than the present assistant receives'. He reacted to the sum 'as if I had received a smack in the face; and from that moment resolved that on no consideration whatever would I accept less than £1,000'.[61] But the other issues were at least as serious. For a compulsive writer such as Muir, 'the sole attraction of the position is the opportunity of saying some things I want to say, and of persistently expounding not so much a

[57] Harrod, *Keynes*, p. 394. The *Daily Chronicle* had unsympathetically described the *Nation* as 'militant' during the war, on the occasion of its being banned by the Government for views it expressed on the conduct of the war. Other liberal newspapers, though not necessarily in agreement with the *Nation*, had leapt to its defence ('The "Nation" and the Government', *WG*, 18.4.1917: 'The Case of the "Nation"', *DN*, 9.4.1917; 'The Censorship and the "Nation"', *MG*, 4.4.1917).

[58] Hammond Papers, vol. 34, Scott to Hammond, 11.3.1923;

[59] Keynes Papers, NS 1_1, Muir to Keynes, 2.2.1923.

[60] Simon Papers, M11/16/33, Muir to Simon, 17.3.1923.

[61] Keynes Papers, NS 1_1, Muir to Keynes, 9.2.1923.

body of doctrine as an attitude of mind'.[62] Keynes's views on the functions of an editor were so different from those of Muir that the latter 'was reluctantly driven to the conclusion that their real motive was a complete distrust of myself'.[63] Certainly a clash of personalities existed, provoking the sensitive Muir to write to Keynes:

> But let us be frank, without offence. Isn't your view on this question coloured by your view of me? You know, of course, nothing about me, and have probably never read a line I've written. But you naturally think of me as an inexperienced middle-aged provincial ex-professor, imposed upon the paper because of my half-accidental association with the Summer School group. You are honestly (and naturally) dubious about my capacity to do the work. And you weren't impressed by the results of our two talks: I watched you with interest at work upon the formation of a judgment.[64]

This was only a thin veneer of disguise on the problems besetting post-war liberalism. Muir's sense of inferiority[65] reflected the relative paucity of liberal analysis and thinking, especially when confronted with the new brilliance emanating from Cambridge. Keynes saw the *Nation* as an instrument for the scientific reinvigoration of liberalism. Muir, in his eyes, was not up to that task—one over which the Cambridge school of economics was ordained to preside—and was moreover a traditionalist with rigid beliefs that would fall foul of the experimenting spirit Keynes wished to introduce. As Keynes's first biographer wrote, no doubt mirroring his subject's opinion: 'One had the feeling that locked within [Muir's] breast was a sacred text in which the answers to all the problems could be found. He was always ready with an answer, and that a sincere one; and this was a valuable gift in a politician.'[66] This insight focuses aptly on the malaise of a declining ideology falling back on routine enunciation of long discovered truths. Though not entirely accurate, it is a useful comment on the post-war condition of liberalism: the new liberals were losing their central hold on advanced liberalism; the new generation of liberal thinkers had regressed in terms of intellectual ability and sophistication as well as having shifted more towards the centre; and the brighter intellects

[62] Ibid., Muir to Keynes, 2.2.1923.
[63] Simon Papers, M11/16/33, Muir to Simon, 17.3.1923.
[64] Keynes Papers, NS 1_1, Muir to Keynes, 9.2.1923.
[65] Ibid., Muir to Keynes, 20.2.1923.
[66] Harrod, *Keynes*, p. 395.

within the liberal camp—mostly economists—regarded the new theorists with suspicion and preferred to be professionals first and liberals second. For Keynes, Muir was a failed intellectual reduced to the level of a politician. C. P. Scott's acerbic evaluation of the two is revealing: 'Ramsay Muir would certainly not fill [Massingham's] shoes. He is a militant imperialist and if in addition the object of the new management is to emphasize the differences between Liberalism and Labour, instead of interpreting their essential unity of spirit and aim, it will injure instead of aiding any possible Liberal revival.' As for Keynes, he was a 'brilliant and original thinker and writer, in his own subjects, but he is also about the most obstinate and self-centered man I ever encountered'.[67] Liberalism appeared to be torn between those who identified themselves with a broad, progressive, communitarian approach and those who were retreating into the more narrow confines of liberal interpretation; but, reading Scott between the lines, it was further split—as indeed was the Summer School—between unexciting theorists and capable 'technicians' of liberalism, the latter, Keynes included, displaying little originality as political thinkers.[68]

Layton, who had initially defended some of Muir's claims,[69] was quick to locate this second discord. Writing to Keynes, he argued: '. . . the *only* essential so far as I am concerned is that the political complexion of the Nation must be in harmony with that of the summer school group. It is because of our political opinions that the option was offered to us, and that the capital has been put up. A difference on fundamental political views would be fatal to collaboration between you, Muir and me.'[70] As Layton realized, Muir was worried that the *Nation* would reflect Keynes's personal views or those of the Cambridge school of economics.[71] Neither option would cater for liberalism as a central interest, which is why Layton at first hoped that Muir would serve as the necessary bridge. Nevertheless, it is probably due to the pressure of economists such as Layton that the bridge was not burnt. Simon, who had returned from abroad to find himself in the middle of this row, was initially inclined to withdraw from the entire scheme and wired Layton to

67 Hammond Papers, vol. 34, Scott to Hammond, 24.1.1923.

68 See Chapter 5.

69 Keynes Papers, NS 1_1, Layton to Keynes, undated (early Feb. 1923), and 17.2.1923.

70 Ibid., Layton to Keynes, undated (Feb. 1923).

71 Ibid., Layton to Keynes, 17.2.1923. Cf. Muir to Keynes, 9.2.1923.

that effect. Layton replied by return of post: 'there is every reason to suppose that the paper will reflect the political views of the summer school. This is for me the *sine qua non* and with you in the scheme we can ensure it.'[72] Simon recanted and noted in his diary: 'Muir, who is not only sensitive but touchy, and likes to be treated as a great man, got huffy, failed to stand up for himself, and resigned. And now hates Keynes like the devil. I am sorry I was away, as Muir is a real loss to the *Nation*, and I *might* have prevented it.'[73]

Muir got his own paper nevertheless. He was appointed editor of the *Saturday Westminster Gazette*, which then appeared as an independent weekly (the *Weekly Westminster*) from November 1923 till January 1926. Its rambling style was in stark contradiction to the reflective essays of the old *Nation* or the terse, slightly insipid efficiency of the new. But for a while the offshoots of the new Manchester liberalism were well equipped with platforms from which to preach. The Keynesian *Nation* underwent a marked ideological shift within the liberal spectrum. Although Harrod insisted that 'Keynes made it a rule never to interfere with the editorial policy',[74] this directly contradicts Keynes's remark to Layton on Muir's conditions for editorship: '. . . it would be impossible for me to be in a show of this kind as a sleeping or semi-sleeping partner.'[75] Nor was this to be the case, as a comparison of Massingham's last issue with Henderson's first bears out. Massingham highlighted the social question as a central theme of the *Nation*. It had not always been possible to treat it within 'the strict lines of Liberal doctrine' but, Massingham assured his readers, 'we have endeavoured to apply to it the spirit of Liberalism, which is, we think, a larger and a more fruitful thing'.[76] Henderson signalled an end to endorsing the oft-expressed hope of co-operation with the Labour party, while calling for a Liberal party 'which has its centre well to the Left'. But the concerns of this liberalism were being transformed. Pre-war liberal policy—'the development of social

[72] Simon Papers, M11/16/33, Layton to Simon, 21.3.1923.

[73] Ibid., Diary, pp. 7–8. In the light of this episode, it is difficult to agree with Bentley, *The Liberal Mind*, p. 177, who describes Muir's liberalism as 'an intellectual brand dedicated to overcoming personal squabbles in order to reach deeper truths'.

[74] Harrod, *Keynes*, p. 396.

[75] Keynes Papers, NS 1_1, Keynes to Layton, 7.2.1923.

[76] 'Vale', *Nation*, 28.4.1923.

services involving public expenditure, and the raising of the money by stiffer taxes upon wealth'—had been shattered by the new facts of economic life, especially the War Debt. The social question was to give way to the question of economic structure.[77] Whether this was the voice of Henderson or Keynes or, most likely, a fundamental consensus of opinion between the two, this stark switch from one week to the next speaks volumes for the changing nature of British liberalism in the 1920s. The old *Nation* had been Ruskinian and Hobsonian in tenor, preferring quality of life to volume of output.[78] The new *Nation* was to write without hesitation: 'it is clear that the technique of Capitalist production requires a degree of specialization and a strictness of discipline which are bound to be distasteful, and which involve some sacrifice of the quality of human life.'[79] And Henderson's prediction of future political issues sounded suspiciously Keynesian: 'Proportional Representation, Divorce Reform, Prohibition, Eugenics, freedom of opinion and of propaganda on sex and birth-control problems.'[80] In the oscillating liberal balance between humanism and efficiency, the latter seemed to be again in the ascendant. But back to the Summer School movement.

3. THE HALCYON YEARS

1923 was another important session in terms of producing a liberal 'groundwork of thought and knowledge'.[81] Gilbert Murray gave the inaugural address and others included Muir, McNair, Simon (in his first talk to the LSS), Henry Clay and H. A. L. Fisher. But the novelty lay in the first clear call to liberals from the group of Cambridge economists, Layton, D. H. Robertson and Keynes, their home ground inspiring them to a shared confidence. Robertson's message was simple:

Our remedial thought and effort must be directed not merely to providing stimulants for the depression, but sedatives for the boom. The whole matter is summed up in one word, a word which has become increasingly

[77] 'Editorial Foreword', *Nation*, 5.5.1923; 'Liberalism and Labour', *Nation*, 12.5.1923.

[78] See above, p. 47.

[79] 'Hints for Socialists', *Nation*, 21.7.1923.

[80] 'Editorial Foreword', *Nation*, 5.5.1923. Cf. Keynes, 'Am I a Liberal?' discussed in Chapter 5.

[81] A. G. G[ardiner], 'The Spirit of Liberalism', *Nation*, 21.7.1923.

fashionable in recent years, and which it seems to me that the Liberal Party in particular should adopt once for all as the first plank in its social policy—the word 'stabilization'.

Moreover, another item on the Liberal programme, industrial self-government, could also be beneficial to that end. Though enlightened self-interest was essential, stabilization could only be underpinned by a national policy 'endorsed and enforced by Government', to include long-distance planning and financing of public works.[82] Keynes added his voice to the need to stabilize domestic prices, as a general expectation of falling prices could inhibit the productive process altogether and create unemployment. 'For this reason, a modern industrial community organized on lines of individualistic capitalism simply cannot stand a declared policy of Deflation.' A resolute policy on the part of the Treasury and the Bank of England could remedy that lack of confidence. The reform of the standard of value was a question that liberalism was well adapted to attack.[83]

Keynes's direct and indirect impact on liberal, rather than economic, theory is a theme we shall return to. The emphasis of this study—bearing in mind the consumptionist approach to ideology—is on the perception and assimilation of Keynesian ideas into liberal thought. Predictably the *Nation* under its new management drew attention to the introduction of what it saw as a vital theme: 'A marked feature of the School was the new emphasis which was laid on the idea of securing a stable standard of value by means of monetary policy. At Oxford last year this question was not alluded to . . .' (a double barb, perhaps?). And it went on to reflect: 'Monetary policy has not so far received any notice in party programmes or the speeches of party leaders. This is not surprising; for the question is a technical one, upon which responsible politicians naturally hesitate to move.'[84] But the *Manchester Guardian*, whose editor, Scott, held Keynes in high professional esteem, also gave full coverage to his talk, and its leader commented on limiting unemployment through currency control: 'The novelty is less in the belief that it could be done, which has long been maintained by economists, than in the assertion that it should be done, which, as far as we know, has never been said by any responsible politician

[82] D. H. Robertson, 'The Trade Cycle', *Nation*, 11.8.1923.
[83] J. M. Keynes, 'Currency Policy and Unemployment', *Nation*, 11.8.1923.
[84] 'The Evolution of Liberal Policy', *Nation*, 11.8.1923.

and would probably be vehemently denied by . . . many life-long Liberals.'[85] Is it strange, then, that when Asquith looked in at the LSS, on the day of Keynes's lecture, and sat between platform and audience, it was 'a position, as he seemed to find it, of embarrassing isolation'?[86] Certainly the *Manchester Guardian* was concerned that, despite some danger of a dispersal of energy, the valuable work of the LSS was not having the necessary effect upon the official policy of Liberalism, adding, in a self-consoling tone, 'perhaps it is too soon to grow impatient'.[87] It was, no doubt, too soon for Keynes to have any noticeable impact.[88] For the time being, the Cambridge economists were suggesting—to those liberals prepared to listen—new techniques for attacking some of the moral and social defects that liberals had identified, notably unemployment; they were proposing state intervention in order to facilitate that end, while recognizing the multi-faceted structure of the industrial and commercial worlds; they were indicating that stability was a desired goal, in language that suggested that liberals were occupying the sensible middle ground between the economic crassness and protectionism of a Conservative policy and the dangerous wholesale measures that Labour might be tempted to adopt; and their practical proposals were consonant with the new mood of experimentation which the LSS was grooming. With these impressions in mind, progressive liberals could regard the Cambridge economists' analyses as further variants on the theme of a modern enquiring liberalism, making a bid to be the future policy-formulator of Britain.

The 1923 LSS was a success. Some of the talks given under its auspices became the basis for the New Way Series, published by the *Daily News*. Two further issues that were to be taken up in the future were given an early airing by the School: inheritance rights, dealt with by Clay,[89] and a housing policy—an attempt by Simon to develop the traditional liberal cause of social reform through relieving the burden of taxation on houses and securing a minimum wage for willing workers.[90] McNair revived the plan for a national in-

[85] *MG*, 9.8.1923; 'The Liberal Summer School', *MG*, 10.8.1923.

[86] *MG*, 9.8.1923.

[87] 'The Liberal Summer School', *MG*, 10.8.1923.

[88] Neither the *Daily News* nor the *Westminster Gazette* commented on Keynes's talk.

[89] See below, pp. 253–4.

[90] For Simon's policy, see below, pp. 255–6. See also 'Lessons from Cambridge', *DN*, 10.8.1923.

dustrial assembly. Education, agriculture, and land were given their due. By 1924 the LSS had entered on its second phase. The official leadership of the Liberal party now readily acknowledged its existence and, with the reunification of the party and the re-emergence of Lloyd George, even its role as 'think-tank'. It was generally perceived to be a 'bold appeal to the intellect of democracy', to occupy the important ground between 'practical politics and theoretical political thought' and, although unofficial, to be representative enough to supply the party platform with information and ideas.[91] It set up a research department with the help of the party organization,[92] and began to play an active role in the preparation of the Liberal reports of the 1920s, the first of which was *Coal and Power*. Although the report, published in July 1924, appeared over Lloyd George's signature, liberals hastened to point out its intellectual pedigree, stretching from the Sankey Commission via McNair's LSS activities and pamphlet.[93] Muir and Simon may have been less than accurate when they traced *Coal and Power* (and its later endorsement by the Samuel Commission in 1926) to Summer School discussions;[94] nevertheless, the LSS had something to do with the dissemination of the proposals and with the creation of a favourable climate of opinion. It is also only fair to point out that the miners were adamant that nationalization of the mines was the only solution, while both Labour and Conservative governments simply ignored this.[95] The report also made recommendations concerning the generation of electricity, similar to those on the mines, though the *Nation* believed that it might well be made the business of the state, as electricity was an area for large-scale operation.[96]

[91] 'The Liberal Summer School', *DN*, 29.7.1924; 'Elbow Room for Ideas', *WG*, 10.8.1923.

[92] R. Muir, 'The Summer School Movement', *WW*, 2.8.1924.

[93] 'New Mines for Old', *Nation*, 19.7.1924. See A. McNair, *The Problem of the Coal Mines* (London, 1924).

[94] Muir, 'The Liberal Summer School and the Problems of Industry', 282; Simon, 'The Liberal Summer School' (1926), 301.

[95] See J. Campbell, *Lloyd George: The Goat in the Wilderness 1922–1931* (London, 1977), pp. 96–7. Liberals were of course equally unhappy with any solution that would give miners control of the mines ('Coal and Power', *DC*, 12.7.1924). See also Chapter 6.

[96] 'New Mines for Old', *Nation*, 19.7.1924. Cf. also 'A Liberal Land Policy', *MG*, 16.10.1924. For the relevant sections of the report, see *Coal and Power* (London, 1924), part i, chs iii, iv; part ii, chs ii–iv.

Another interesting by-product of the LSS, or rather of its committee, was Beveridge's *Insurance for All and Everything*, published in 1924.[97] Beveridge's relationship with the LSS was a curious one and, like his liberalism, blew alternately hot and cold. Though present at Grasmere and at a 1922 Cambridge meeting of the committee, Beveridge stood outside the progressive liberal mainstream of the 1920s. In 1923 he requested his name to be deleted from LSS committee literature,[98] but he apparently had long discussions on his insurance proposals with committee members before his pamphlet appeared under the New Way imprint. Beveridge was instrumental in persuading liberals, and eventually the Conservative government, that the community should accept responsibility for widows with young children by extending state pensions or allowances to them. He also successfully argued the case for reducing to sixty-five the age at which old age pensions could be paid.[99] Both additions to the pensions scheme were firmly grounded in the view that insurance should, with a few exceptions, be contributory. As Beveridge explained:

> The problem is not that of guaranteeing an income at all times to everybody irrespective of his work and services. That way lies communism. The problem is the narrower one of giving security against all the main risks of economic life to those who depend on continuous earning . . . This is the line of Social Insurance, maintaining individual freedom and responsibilities and the family as the unit of the State.[100]

For many liberals, the contributory principle did not rule out the exclusive assumption of communal responsibility in other spheres, though Beveridge himself never adopted the new liberal argument that society was ethically committed to care for all its members.[101] As with the 1911 Insurance Act, however, liberals were attracted by the tripartite sharing of responsibility among the employer (industry), the worker (the individual) and the state (the community).[102] They also appreciated the assumption of communal respon-

[97] New Way Series, no 7.

[98] J. Harris, *William Beveridge* (Oxford, 1977), pp. 312–13.

[99] R. Muir, 'Security of Livelihood', *WW*, 9.2.1924; 'Pensions for Widows', *WW*, 1.3.1924. See also Simon, 'The Liberal Summer School' (1926), 301.

[100] W. H. Beveridge, *Insurance for All and Everything* (London, n.d. [1924]). pp. 31, 16–18, 25–8.

[101] See Freeden, *The New Liberalism*, pp. 184–5.

[102] R. Muir, 'Security of Livelihood', *WW*, 9.2.1924.

sibility *in order* to give workers a sense of 'self-reliant security'.[103]

Beveridge made no special attempt to promote his views via the liberal movement. In 1924 he wrote for Muir's *Weekly Westminster*;[104] a year later he pleaded too heavy a workload when declining an invitation by C. P. Scott to write a similar article on family endowment for the *Manchester Guardian*.[105] Family endowment was another issue which hovered tenuously behind the scenes. The ideological roots of the family endowment movement can be traced back both to the endowment of motherhood proposals of Fabians and eugenists and to the field surveys of living standards on the Rowntree model. After the war Eleanor Rathbone spearheaded and organized the Family Endowment Society, which also assimilated the feminist cause in a progressive framework. Most of its members were left-liberals or moderates, and the Society was skilful in adapting its policies to the language of the political groups it tried to persuade.[106] The Society intended to challenge the notion of a uniform living wage for an 'average' family and, while reluctant to opt for a particular alternative, it stressed that any system would have to take into account the number of children as well as the financial condition of the parents. Rathbone's book, *The Disinherited Family*,[107] made an immediate impact. Beveridge later wrote of his 'total conversion' on reading it,[108] and he responded with an enthusiastic review which suggested that a new principle of redistribution was involved. To the vertical distribution between the classes was added a horizontal one within each class by reference to family needs.[109] This fitted in well with the pre-war progressive emphasis on redistribution as the main cure for economic and social maladies. It also moved in the direction of greater equality between the sexes by raising the mother to the status of recipient of (preferably) state allowances. Beveridge's work on family allowances was to intersect with the LSS in the future but the link was not entirely of his making. Rathbone, as we

[103] 'Insurance Against All Risks', *WG*, 4.4.1924.

[104] Sir W. Beveridge, 'The Endowment of the Family', *WW*, 10.5.1924.

[105] *Guardian* Archives, A/B43/1a [no date], 2 [19.2.1925], 3 [29.3.1925; 2.4.1925].

[106] See J. Macnicol, *The Movement for Family Allowances 1918–1945* (London, 1980), pp. 19, 24, 27.

[107] E. Rathbone, *The Disinherited Family* (London, 1924). See especially chs 1,4,7.

[108] Ibid., epilogue, p. 270.

[109] Beveridge, 'The Endowment of the Family'.

have seen, had been invited to Grasmere; other liberals, such as Gilbert Murray, contributing a foreword, found her book 'completely convincing'.[110] D. H. Robertson, while critical in insisting on a contributory system of allowances and proposing lower payments, told the 1924 LSS that since the publication of *The Disinherited Family* any treatment of that question could only be a commentary on it. Rathbone herself was in the audience and defended the details of her case.[111] Muir and Simon served on the Council of the Family Endowment Society, and Simon—whose work later reflected its ideas—had further channels of communication with the Society, as its two other major figures, Mary Stocks[112] (who wrote Simon's biography) and Eva Hubback (with whom he collaborated on a book) were close friends.

Beveridge himself did not attend the 1924 LSS, but other participants were keen to rope him in as an inspiration to the School. Masterman, giving his first LSS talk—'a first-class fighting speech'—thought that Beveridge's insurance scheme was more likely to be adopted by liberals than an alternative scheme based on friendly societies.[113] As one of the architects of the pre-war Health Insurance Act, Masterman's opinions still carried weight, but this also indicates the growing involvement with, and impingement, of the larger Liberal world, upon the cosy coteries of the Summer School. The 1924 LSS had seen a number of old faces: McNair, Layton, Henderson, Keynes, Murray, but Donald Maclean spoke on Poor Law reform and the School was opened by John Simon and closed by Lloyd George. Muir was concerned 'lest [the LSS] become too much of an institution, lest it come to be regarded as "correct" and "orthodox"'. This was already true with regard to some of the local summer schools that had been formed to emulate the larger group and had 'mostly been organised by official

[110] Rathbone, *The Disinherited Family*, Foreword, p. v.

[111] 'At the Oxford Summer School', *WW*, 9.8.1924. The *Westminster Gazette* commented oddly: 'It is perhaps a disadvantage that this scheme should have been introduced to the public by a bachelor professor and a bachelor woman social investigator.' It was also concerned that it would be 'a revolution indeed to bring about a change by which the family burden was made the basis of wages, instead of, as now, what is regarded as the general economic value of the work done' ('Wages and the Family', 6.8.1924).

[112] See M. Stocks, *My Commonplace Book* (London, 1970), pp. 120–1.

[113] *MG*, 5.8.1924. Lucy Masterman observed that her husband was 'enjoying his new friends of the Summer School'. (L. Masterman, *C. F. G. Masterman* [London, 1939], p. 344.)

bodies'. But the influx of MPs into the Summer School movement was dangerous; instead of stimulating fresh thought 'an M.P. is almost debarred from original thinking by the very conditions of his treadmill life' (Muir had just lost the seat he held for only one year—Rochdale). If enquiry were to be replaced by propaganda, Muir warned, the movement would be stillborn.[114]

Politicians and ideologists were working concurrently in tandem and at cross purposes. Both wanted a revival of liberalism, but for politicians this was primarily a vote-catching exercise. Certainly the 1924 Liberal programme, signed by Asquith and Lloyd George, reflected some of the values of the LSS. It replaced the outdated and ambivalent 'peace, retrenchment, and reform' with 'Peace, Social Reform, and National Development' as the Liberal slogan, and gave prominence not only to housing, town planning, land reform and improved social insurance but to the co-operation of all elements in industry and to the *Coal and Power* recommendations.[115] But this still only skimmed the surface of the complex LSS debates. The ideologists were sceptical. Simon doubted 'whether a somber [sic] constructive Summer School policy can ever be made to appeal to more—or even be understood by—the mass of voters. I don't think any democracy has ever been interested in such a policy of reason and hard thinking.'[116] Muir agreed that LSS methods were unsuitable for 'the capture of masses of electors' but concluded more optimistically that the battle was over the future leaders of the younger generation.[117]

1925 and 1926 continued to be good, if not particularly exciting, years for the LSS. The 1925 session saw the beginning of a tradition that the School maintained in future years: the invitation of foreign, mainly Continental, lecturers to talk on their national problems and on international affairs. It also witnessed a few disappointments, notably Seebohm Rowntree's inability to get to grips with the means for attaining a new industrial policy[118]—not unexpected given his cautious approach.[119] Simon gave a paper on inheritance rights that was remembered in the years to come[120] as a

114 R. Muir, 'The Summer School Movement', *WW*, 9.8.1924.
115 *DN*, 13.10.1924.
116 Simon Papers, Diary, p. 9 (27.2.1925).
117 R. Muir, 'The Summer School Movement', *WW*, 9.8.1924.
118 Outis, 'The Cambridge Summer School', *WW*, 8.8.1925.
119 See below, p. 247.
120 See 'The Liberal Summer School', *Nation*, 17.7.1926.

recurring theme among progressive liberals. J. Stamp—the economist and statistician—gave a talk on the equalization of individual incomes, and argued against the redivision of the present economic cake, and in favour of the whole community setting itself to baking a bigger one.[121] In retrospect the most important talk to emerge from the 1925 session was due to the speaker rather than to its contents: Keynes's 'Am I a Liberal?'[122] The Council (former Committee) of the LSS also decided to circulate six questionnaires in order to explore the subjects of drink, trade union policy, inheritance, rural and urban land questions, fair wages and family allowances, and population.[123] In the meantime Masterman and Muir were appointed to the committee that produced, in late 1925, *The Land and the Nation* (the Green Book), while Simon wrote a section in its sequel, *Towns and the Land* (the Brown Book).[124] The latter report was particularly welcomed by the liberal press as 'immensely valuable' and offering 'for the first time in our political history . . . an orderly and beneficent development of our urban life' on issues such as town-planning, slums and taxation of site-values, though it was also recognized that 'most of these proposals have long been parts of Liberal and Radical policy'.[125] Both reports, however, were still indicative of the digressionary if not pernicious hold that the once all-embracing land question had on liberal minds. But the most important event in the life of the LSS took place in early 1926. Lloyd George gave it £10,000 and the services of a secretariat to finance an industrial inquiry,[126] which occupied the energies of the School for

[121] *The Times*, 3.8.1925.

[122] This will be discussed in the next chapter.

[123] See the questionnaires and the summaries of the answers submitted in the *Guardian* Archives, file 145/3: Liberal Party (mainly cuttings) 1924–1929. The questionnaires differ slightly from those projected in 'The Questioning Spirit', *DN*, 25.7.1925 and in R. Muir, 'Inquiry in Politics', *WW*, 8.8.1925.

[124] Eagar Papers, ms. 13. The Land Report embodied radical measures, recommending tenure for cultivators, a living wage and housing for labourers, a county authority to assist farming activities and—crucially—state ownership of the land itself, though not nationalization of farming. (See Campbell, *Lloyd George: The Goat in the Wilderness*, pp. 120–2.) The renewed land campaign helped reconcile progressive liberals with Lloyd George (Wilson, *The Downfall of the Liberal Party 1914–1935*, pp. 308–11).

[125] [C. P. Scott], 'Urban Land Reform', *MG*, 24.11.1925; 'Towns and the Land', *DN*, 24.11.1925; 'The Urban Land Report', *WG*, 24.11.1925. See also R. Muir, 'The Liberal Land Policy', *CR*, 129 (1926), 424–32; 554–63 and Hobson's favourable evaluation ('Lloyd George's Land Campaign', *Nation* (NY), 11.11.1925).

[126] Simon in Hodgson (ed.), *Ramsay Muir*, p. 183.

eighteen months, and cemented its ties with official Liberalism. The 1926 session was therefore the last before the LSS embarked on its third stage of quasi-official policy formulator for the Liberal party. Significantly, it was in 1926 that Muir joined the executive of the NLF and commenced upon a career that took him to some of its top organizational posts.[127] Among the speakers in 1926[128] were to be found Carr-Saunders, the population expert, Guedalla, J. A. Spender, Henderson, and Graham Wallas, who, in 1922, had written to Murray about his political position: 'I think I am nearest to the Manchester Guardian and E. D. Simon.'[129]

An interesting figure in the 1926 session was Philip Kerr, former secretary to Lloyd George. From the mid-1920s he had been urging Lloyd George to take up the industrial question, and soon progressive liberals were receiving support from that quarter.[130] With the shock of the General Strike still well in mind, Kerr saw the existence of two nations as the main challenge to Britain, and especially 'to the title of the possessing class to rule the economic life of the country'. He identified the post-war concern with the granting of responsibility to labour as the root question, but charged the employers with the prime duty of producing full employment and a rising standard of living. This end could be attained by co-operation, in a constitutional framework outside Parliament, between employers and trade unions.[131] The novelty here was hardly in the substance—which fell short of the progressive liberal position that accorded the state a more central role in safeguarding industrial democracy—but with Kerr winning Lloyd George's ear, a turning point in the consciousness of the Liberal party could be foreseen. Kerr still harboured the naïve liberal optimism about a harmonious blending of class interests with the help of the right machinery. He was also far closer to the employers' viewpoint with regard to the satisfaction of human ends through baking bigger cakes, producing higher wages, falling prices, and a high standard of life—precisely the material interpretation of social reform that

127 Lord Meston in Hodgson (ed.), *Ramsay Muir*, pp. 195–7.

128 See Simon, 'The Liberal Summer School' (1926), 300.

129 Murray Papers, Box 53, Wallas to Murray, 14.4.1922. And Muir commented on Wallas's talk on trade-unionism: '. . . it was clear that he found in the temper of Liberalism the best mode of approach to these problems' (R. Muir, 'Summer Politics', *WG*, 31.7.1926).

130 See Campbell, *Lloyd George: The Goat in the Wilderness*, p. 192.

131 *MG*, 27.7.1926.

the ethically oriented new liberals had dismissed before the war as insufficient. But his ideas were definitely within the orbit of LSS thinking and appeared to augur well for the reviving fortunes of British liberalism as a whole. As the *Nation* anticipated: 'Is it too much to hope that from the union of the gifts of Mr. Lloyd George and the Summer School there may emerge the new radical impulse which we need?'[132]

The 1927 LSS met under the comforting shadow of the expected industrial report. It was opened by Samuel, whose speech underscored the fact that—Lloyd George's gifts notwithstanding—the Liberal leadership existed in a world only tangentially related to the LSS. Most of it was devoted to an attack on the Labour party.[133] Tacked on to the end was what might have been generously called, by 1927, a minimalist progressive programme: the distribution of the product of industry; workers' share in controlling the conditions of their employment (but no mention of industrial democracy as such); the development of national resources with special reference to unemployment and the diffusion of the ownership of property—'all these in their bearing on the establishment of peace in industry'.[134] The *Manchester Guardian* dismissed Samuel irritably: 'The need at the moment is to get ahead with the definition of the Liberal policy, and that is the primary object with which these Liberal Summer Schools are held.'[135] Others did get along with the job. E. H. Gilpin, a member of the industrial inquiry, proposed a worker's charter which would include statutory consultation in large industrial and commercial establishments, and Keynes, another member, discussed semi-socialized enterprise, not as a preliminary to extending it, but in order to increase its administrative efficiency.[136] Simon, also a member of the inquiry, added his voice to the plea for peace in industry, based on the principle of a living wage as high as the trade could bear. Increased production, with its concomitant of increased wages, was possible in an atmos-

132 'The Liberal Summer School', *Nation*, 17.7.1926. Muir portrayed Kerr, in a good indication of the temper of his politics, as one who in the past was probably a conservative, but who now recognized that the best hope for progress lay in the liberal approach ('Summer Politics', *WG*, 31.7.1926).

133 See below, p. 191.

134 H. Samuel, 'Liberals and the Labour Movement', *CR*, 132 (1927), 419.

135 'Liberalism and Labour', *MG*, 29.7.1927.

136 'Events of the Week', *Nation*, 6.8.1927; 'The Nationalisation Fetish', *WG*, 1.8.1927.

phere of co-operation.[137] The session was also attended by Lloyd George, who attempted to fuse the interests of the party with those of the LSS by suggesting that elections could only be won on a clear programme. In the mid-1920s many liberals had expressed concern over the limiting constraints of a programme or over its irrelevance, thus reversing the role programmes had come to play in the Liberal party since Newcastle in 1891. The *Nation* asserted that cut-and-dried programmes would not secure the confidence of the country, and that the initiative in national policy properly rested with the government of the day.[138] Lloyd George however felt that recapturing office had no attractions unless it was 'in order to carry out a definite programme of work which the party has devoted its years of leisure to thinking out and planning . . .'[139] The *Daily News* hailed his speech as brilliant and identified the dislike of programmes with distrust of democracy. Political parties had a duty to define their aims 'with the utmost possible precision'.[140] Within a year liberals had published the most important political programme to be produced between the wars.

4. BRITAIN'S INDUSTRIAL FUTURE

Britain's Industrial Future, the report of the Liberal Industrial Inquiry, appeared in February 1928. It was to a large extent, though not exclusively, the product of active members of the LSS movement. Layton, Henderson and Keynes represented the Cambridge economists; Muir and Simon and, more peripherally, Gilpin, spoke for the originators of the School; Lloyd George and Kerr were the sympathetic wing of the party; Masterman (who had died in November 1927) and H. Nathan were progressive party activists mainly outside the LSS; Rowntree still reaped the fruits of his earlier reputation; Samuel and John Simon (the latter, significantly, refusing to sign the report[141]) put in appearances for the top echelons of the party leadership. Five special subcommittees were formed: on the functions of the state in relation to industry

[137] *MG*, 3.8.1927.

[138] 'The Liberal Revival', *Nation*, 31.1.1925. Cf. R. Muir, 'The Liberal Summer School and the Problems of Industry', 284 and *Politics and Progress* (London, 1923), p. 178.

[139] *MG*, 2.8.1927.

[140] 'Honesty and Policy', *DN*, 2.8.1927.

[141] Stocks, *Ernest Simon of Manchester*, p. 85.

(chaired by Muir), on industrial and financial organization (Keynes), on labour and the trade unions (E. D. Simon), on unemployment (Lloyd George), and on worker renumeration and status (Gilpin). Among other subcommittee members were Guedalla, Hobhouse, Hodgson, Eva Hubback, McNair, Robertson, Stamp and L. F. Urwick (a proponent of rationalization[142]). The Yellow Book, as it was popularly known, reflected a large and reasonably coherent segment of progressive liberalism and as such deserves analysis. On the whole it was a consolidating rather than an innovating document,[143] but from the perspective of liberal theory it was an attempt to give institutional answers to two of the most pressing post-war issues: the role of the state and the integration of the worker into the political system. Despite having 'no intention of writing a treatise on political philosophy'[144] its authors provided an excellent example of one of the guises in which modern political thinking is to be found. Concrete discussions of policy proposals, interspersed with statistical data, may not seem the natural domain of political theories. But both consciously and unconsciously, the report illustrates how political principles direct people to seek certain sets of solutions to social problems and why, in a more general sense, the study of political thought cannot be restricted to an examination of philosophical texts alone, but can benefit from an acknowledgement of the ubiquity of *theoria* in *praxis*.

The Introduction spelled out the framework of analysis. The extension of democracy into the economic sphere was a question both of justice and of efficiency. Discontent led to friction and conflict. Fair treatment of individuals throughout society held out the possibility of greatly improved conditions of life, though to that was attached a Ruskinian/Hobsonian rider: 'We believe with a passionate faith that the end of all political and economic action is not the perfecting or the perpetuation of this or that piece of mechanism or organisation, but that individual men and women may have life, and that they may have it more abundantly.'[145] Nevertheless, democracy in industry could in no way parallel political democracy. Contrary to the aspirations of the post-war left-liberals, the tension between the industrial status of the worker

[142] See Chapter 5, Section 2.

[143] See H. Phillips, 'A Short Answer to Certain Criticisms', *FV*, Mar. 1928, Supplement.

[144] *Britain's Industrial Future* (London, 1928), p. xix.

[145] Ibid., p. xxiv.

and his political status 'as a free and equal citizen and a maker and unmaker of governments' was irreconcilable: 'To a certain extent this inconsistency is inherent in the necessities of industrial organisation.'[146] A stringent static and hierarchical model was proffered, beyond the pale of even the most élitist concept of democracy:

> It would, we think, be wrong and dishonest to hold out hopes to the ordinary man that he will ever be in a position to choose at each moment of the day whether he will do this thing or that, or even to take a direct part in the election or dismissal of those from whom he receives his immediate instructions.[147]

The second issue concerned the legitimate sphere of community action via the state. Clearly, by the late 1920s the pendulum that had swung between new liberal enthusiasm and post-war *tristesse* had come to rest at a point of reluctant acceptance. The authors of the Yellow Book were emphatic in disclaiming 'love for State intervention in itself. On the contrary, we attach the greatest importance to the initiative of individuals and to their opportunity to back their opinion against that of the majority and to prove themselves right.'[148] But the facts spoke for themselves, above all the fact that had always been at the root of the *empirical* liberal argument for the state: over the past century it had made inroads into functions that closely affected industry and commerce, which could not be repealed without backtracking on the course of history at an incalculable cost. Moreover, the authors were eager to eschew the turn-of-the-century debate between individualism and socialism, recognizing how the latter notion, once a popular progressive term, had become a monopoly of a political party and thus useless for liberal ends. But state activity was not tantamount to socialism: 'If no one had ever generalised about Socialism, or used the word, or made it the rallying cry for a party, these measures might have been universally welcomed. It would be folly to reject what is right because some would have it lead to what is wrong.'[149] Of course, the Yellow Book was deliberately not political theorizing of a high calibre. The new liberal and moderate socialist arguments of the previous generation—to the effect that individualism and socialism were compatible and complementary ideas—were unavailable to its

[146] Ibid., pp. xxii–xxiii.
[147] Ibid.
[148] Ibid., p. xix.
[149] Ibid., p. xx.

authors, nor would they have warmed to them. A significant theoretical distinction obtained between these two approaches. New liberals had interpreted the assumption of communal responsibility for defined areas of human activity as itself conducive to the development and perfection of the individual, just as true individuality would manifest itself in socially oriented behaviour. For the next liberal generation, as represented by the Yellow Book, individualism and state activity existed side by side but in separate spheres. At best, the liberal vision of beneficial harmony and coexistence could be conjured up:

> The task is one of guiding existing tendencies into a right direction and getting the best of all worlds, harmonising individual liberty with the general good, and personal initiative with a common plan—of constructing a society where action is individual and knowledge and opportunity are general, and each is able to make his contribution to the efficiency and diversity of the whole . . .[150]

This was assuredly progressive language but the tell-tale signs were there: an acceptance of human nature as it was, an identification of the individual as the central social unit, a stress on the co-operation of unique individuals, a relegation of the community to the role of regulator and co-ordinator—elements that diverged from the insistence on the essentially social nature of the individual and the distinct needs of the community.[151] The report was at pains to assert the attractions of individualism on 'the purely practical side', though of course important theoretical considerations were here at stake. Individualism in the form of decentralization of decisions was a concrete expression of diffused power and the direct connection between action and responsibility. It was also a vindication of undogmatic experimentalism as a means of arriving at solutions to problems and hence offered the possibility of choice and competition among different methods. Finally, it was tailored to the necessity of eliciting performances by means of rewards, that being perceived as a given fact of human nature.[152] Any state or centralized action would have to devise ways to minimize losses on those counts.[153] The Yellow Book liberals evidently wished to promote

150 Ibid., p. 63.
151 See Freeden, *The New Liberalism*, ch. II, and below, Chapter 7.
152 For further discussion, see Chapters 5 and 7.
153 *Britain's Industrial Future*, pp. 64–5.

individualism: 'We appreciate the real advantages of the decentralised society of the pure Individualist's dreams; and wherever force of circumstances compels a departure from pure individualism, we have endeavoured so to frame our proposals as to retain as many as possible of its advantages.'[154] On the surface it might appear that the theoretical bias was individualist, with practical departures from that rule dictated by the exigency of the hour. As we shall see in the next chapter, things were not quite as simple.

The proposals that were forged within the above theoretical guidelines were very varied. The Public Concern, national and local, was held up as an example that combined governmental control with experimental diversity.[155] It was controlled individualism initiated and underpinned by the agents of the community. The Public Corporation would be a further category applied to semi-monopolistic companies, publicity and openness to inspection being the approved methods of control.[156] The Joint Stock Company seemed especially attractive as it embodied the principle of the separation of responsibility from ownership. Though not the ideal solution it was a pointer to the future, for 'private enterprise has been trying during the past fifty years to solve for itself the essential problem, which the Socialists in their day were trying to solve, namely, how to establish an efficient system of production in which management and responsibility are in different hands from those which provide the capital, run the risk, and reap the profit'.[157] Curiously, then, the joint stock company was proposed not as an alternative to socialism, but as a realization of one of its original ends, without in any way conceding that diffused ownership was different from communal ownership.

A significant digression from the liberal tradition was the blessing bestowed by the report on trusts and monopolies. For the previous generation of liberals, monopolies had been unacceptable concentrations of economic power that served particular groups at the expense of the community, distorted whatever benefits competition could contribute to the development of individuals, and challenged the new egalitarian ethos that liberals had been carefully

[154] Ibid., p. 66.
[155] Ibid., p. 75.
[156] Ibid., p. 95. The BBC and the Electricity Board were already such examples.
[157] Ibid., p. 100.

nourishing.[158] The report, fearing the wastefulness of competition, came up with a new message for the times:

> In modern conditions a tendency towards some degree of monopoly in an increasing number of industries is, in our opinion, inevitable and even, quite often, desirable in the interests of efficiency. It is, therefore, no longer useful to treat trusts, cartels, combinations, holding companies, and trade associations as inexpedient abnormalities in the economic system to be prevented, checked, and harried.[159]

This condoning of a shift in the balance of social power was merely enhanced by the nature of the safeguards the Yellow Book sought to apply to the wielding of monopolistic power. The notion of publicity as the mainstay of public accountability may have reflected the strong connections of the authors of the report with the liberal press, but it was hardly sufficient to exert effective control in the interests of the public at large.

Another suggestion in the report was the establishment of a Board of National Investment to finance new capital expenditure, by directing investment into neglected but profitable fields of domestic enterprise. This manifestly Keynesian body was created to bridge the gap, ignored by Hobson's underconsumptionism,[160] between savings and their channelling towards nationally desirable outlets that would be economically advantageous.[161] Also making a reappearance was the mooting of an economic general staff, an idea originally floated by Beveridge in the *Nation*,[162] but itself the product of the fermenting of guild socialism within post-war liberal minds. The need for such a general staff reflected, in the understanding of the authors, a two-fold development: politico-governmental decisions inevitably affected industry—a position reinforced by the interconnected perspectives of liberal organicism; and an acknowledgement of the highly technical and expert knowledge that governments required. This 'need of systematic thought' was one that a democracy could not always create from within.[163] The general staff was far removed, however, from any notion of an authoritative

[158] See Freeden, *The New Liberalism*, pp. 44–7.

[159] *Britain's Industrial Future*, pp. 93–4; and see the discussion of rationalization in Chapter 5, Section 2.

[160] See next chapter.

[161] *Britain's Industrial Future*, pp. 111–14.

[162] Sir W. H. Beveridge, 'An Economic General Staff', *Nation*, 29.12.1923, 5.1.1924.

[163] See Chapter 9.

organ directly responsible for economic affairs, and hence its name was hardly apposite. There was certainly no breach in the vigorously reasserted liberal doctrine that sovereignty was indivisible, a doctrine now bolstered by the newer recognition that spheres of social activity could not be artificially separated.[164]

In the sphere of industrial relations, the Simonite argument voiced at the 1927 LSS[165] was reiterated. The causal chain leading from the just treatment of workers to increased efficiency, industrial peace, and higher wages was a carrot and stick combination that coincided with that managerial point of view which sees happiness and satisfaction as mere signposts on the road to productivity. The solutions tended decidedly towards the minimalist pole: a 'fair deal' for labour did not include participation in decision-making but was contingent upon increased productivity and reified as a share in the fruits of economic efficiency. Workers' grievances such as a low income, no security of livelihood, inferior status, little consultation on work practices, and a belief in an unjustifiable division of society into the class that supplies labour and the class that owns capital, were 'legitimate' and 'liberal discontents' but did not include the further possibility that workers might themselves want to participate as co-equal owners or managers.[166] Neither did the Yellow Book do anything to mitigate the sense of unease with which liberals of the 1920s regarded the trade unions. The old sin of sectionalism, which liberals had laid at their door from their very inception, was compounded by the blatant identification of the unions with the Labour party, a link that liberals had only recently and grudgingly accepted, but which they were now heavily overstating. Yet whatever their private thoughts may have been, liberals did not contemplate a public out-and-out attack on organizations that so keenly offended their sense of right. Some conciliatory remarks were made: 'On the whole, the trade-union organisation materially contributes to the smooth working of industry.' They were 'essential organs for the common regulation of industry and trade, and vital forces in the life of the nation'.[167] But especially un-

[164] *Britain's Industrial Future*, pp. 116–18.

[165] See above, p. 104.

[166] *Britain's Industrial Future*, pp. 147–50. See the remark by Layton quoted on p. 173 below.

[167] Ibid., pp. 156, 159. See R. Muir, 'Trade Union Reform', *CR*, 131 (1927), and *Trade Unionism and the Trade Union Bill* (London, 1927), which was published for the Liberal Industrial Inquiry.

satisfactory was the state of the law, subject to a tug-of-war between courts and unions for a generation, with the liberals standing unhappily on the sidelines and then doing too little too late to pacify union anger. The unions, still not—or, rather, again not[168] —regarded as legal entities, had 'in some way' to be 'worked into the recognised framework of our social system, and [crucial liberal phrase!] given responsibilities corresponding with their power'.[169] Singled out for particular criticism was that central component of trade-union behaviour—collective bargaining. The idea of dividing the product of industry consequent upon a hostile power struggle could not compensate for the advantage the worker gained by acting as member of a group. Liberals, aided by the persuasive arguments of T. H. Green, had long rejected the competitive individualism that in the past had regulated the drawing up of contracts between worker and employer. They now felt threatened by a group-individualism that was equally damaging to the social fabric. The report believed that in some industries unions were 'driven by a desire to weaken or undermine "the existing system"' but added: 'The greatest need of British industry to-day is not (as some foolishly suppose) to weaken the power of the Trade Unions, but to foster in the minds of Trade-Unionists the already dawning recognition that efficiency in production is of the first importance to them.'[170] The conclusion, however, is of special interest: 'The nation, represented by the State, forms a third party whose interests cannot be disregarded . . . The State cannot look on indifferently while civil war rages between organised bodies of its citizens, for its primary function is to substitute the rule of reason and law for that of force.'[171]

Why was it that, whereas in the realm of economic activities the state was assigned a residual role, in the field of industrial relations it once again was called upon to occupy centre stage? This discrepancy was a plainly liberal one, though it was enhanced by differences of approach between Keynes and Muir. For the former, as for most liberal economists, social harmony was attainable primarily through the encouragement of responsible individual enterprise, with the state adopting a supporting role when the fundamental mechanism proved insufficient. The economic sphere was seen as

[168] Cf. A. Birke, *Pluralismus und Gewerkschaftsautonomie in England: Entstehungsgeschichte einer politischen Theorie* (Stuttgart, 1978).
[169] *Britain's Industrial Future*, p. 159.
[170] Ibid., pp. 151, 156.
[171] Ibid., pp. 165, 166.

virtually isolated from power factors and hence, when the state made an appearance, it exchanged its primary political role for a secondary economic one, smooth, undisturbed and free of conflict. The activities of trade unions, on the other hand, were deftly removed from the category of beneficial economic human behaviour into a category which for liberals was dysfunctional, if not deplorable—that of irrational, disharmonious and irresponsible power-wielding. The restraint of such behaviour, if necessary by force, was for such liberals the natural arena of state activity, for industrial strife threatened stability as well as harmony.[172] Muir, however, had assimilated, even if imperfectly, elements of the new liberal heritage and identified the state with rationality ('It exists to maintain peace, justice and liberty for all its citizens'[173]) rather than with force. Hence even in the area of its primary activity—the management of conflict—the state had to act through regulation and law, both of which appealed to reason in preference to their alternative sanction, force.

In an obvious reversal of the new liberal position, the Yellow Book referred to the enlargement of the industrial functions of the state with apprehension, pointing out that 'there has also been a steady movement of opinion towards the view that the voluntary organisation of industries for self-regulation offered the true line of advance'.[174] It took up a strong stand against compulsory arbitration of disputes as practically unworkable, and as retarding the growth of industrial self-government by discussion and agreement. Whether this was in praise of human reasonableness or a condemnation of externally imposed general rules is difficult to say. On the question of wages a clear concept of human ends as related to the economic process was emerging. The notion of man as producer was replaced by that of consumer: 'Industry is not an end in itself; it exists in order to provide livelihood for the whole community . . . high real wages are an end in themselves, because high wages mean general well-being.'[175] Profit-sharing was recommended mainly to facilitate co-operation through a sense of partnership. The 1921 NLF resolutions were referred to as guiding outlines for the construction of machinery to align workers' and employers' interests.[176]

172 See the attitude of liberals to the General Strike, in Chapter 3.
173 *Britain's Industrial Future*, p. 166.
174 Ibid., p. 171.
175 Ibid., pp. 180, 181.
176 Ibid., pp. 199, 206.

Here the vexed question of compulsion was side-stepped. A council of industry (more limited in scope than a national industrial council) would advise a minister of industry whether to sanction compulsory orders requested by wage boards and joint industrial councils, primarily on the issue of wages, hours and working conditions. But due to the mixed composition of those various bodies, majority agreement of both workers' and employers' representatives would necessarily have to precede compulsion, thus restricting its effectiveness.[177]

A further key liberal theme sounded in the Yellow Book was that of the diffusion of ownership, intended in the main to reduce the tensions between a small owning class and a large working class.[178] This would simultaneously contribute to two of the other ends the report was promoting. By way of forging a more durable link between the worker's interest and that of his employer, shareholding by workers within their industry would be encouraged. The Hobsonian argument had lost out, though. While identifying the problem of surplus profit, the Yellow Book merely considered the alternatives of assigning it to distribution within the company or to reinvestment.[179] The second end to be attained would be the Keynesian 'wider diffusion of the banking habit' as long as it entailed 'the encouragement of popular investment'. All these would constitute 'a real advance towards that goal of Liberalism in which everybody will be a capitalist, and everybody a worker, as everybody is a citizen'.[180]

The pressing political question was unemployment, and here it was deemed correct to call upon the services of the state. State intervention in this field was made palatable by the supposition that much unemployment was the result of the dislocation of trade that followed the war; hence the state would not need to adopt permanent measures. True, a vast programme of national development (by the standard of the times) was hatched—of which more later—and this certainly was in the tradition that placed the responsibility for grave defects of social organization squarely on the shoulders of the community.[181] At the same time Keynesian discoveries suggested that unemployment could be tackled through indirect communal con-

[177] Ibid., pp. 222–4.
[178] Ibid., p. 242.
[179] Ibid., pp. 248–9.
[180] Ibid., pp. 260, 261.
[181] Ibid., book iv.

trol, based on co-operation between the Treasury and the Bank of England. Rejecting the idea of nationalizing the latter, the report regarded the Bank of England as 'an admirable specimen of the "semi-socialised" institutions which represent, on our view, the true line of development'.[182]

The publication of the Yellow Book was followed by an extensive debate in the press, liberal and otherwise, though its popularization had to await the 1929 election campaign. Initially, there was wide disagreement over the nature of the measures it proposed. Some of the less discerning spokesmen of conservatism saw it as unbridled socialism—witness the *Daily Dispatch* which wrote: 'Not even the members of the Committee of Inquiry can feel surprised should the followers of Karl Marx and the standard-bearers of the Red Flag complain somewhat belligerently that practically every plank in their platform has been taken to bolster up the tottering Liberal grandstand.'[183] Certainly the *New Statesman*, though hardly the mouthpiece of communism, published a congratulatory and rather envious article by G. D. H. Cole, calling the Yellow Book 'a formidable and an exceedingly interesting document' and going on to reflect: 'It would be a public service of the first importance if the Labour economists would get together and . . . endeavour to think out their ideas of Britain's economic future on the same scale as the Liberal intellectuals have now attempted.'[184] On the other hand, the *New Leader* predicted for the report 'a large sale at the Individualist Bookshop' and some conservative newspapers played down its importance by calling its proposals vague or sedative.[185] Even among the authors of the Yellow Book ambivalent feelings existed. Immediately prior to its publication Henderson, believing that public interest was shifting away from economic and industrial questions, doubted the attractiveness of the report and felt the need for new inquiries into other spheres of internal reconstruction.[186] While the report was still in the making Kerr had feared that it

[182] Ibid., p. 414.

[183] Quoted in 'The Reception of the Industrial Report', *Nation*, 11.2.1928. The MP Austin Hopkinson accused the report of abandoning liberty and the rationale of liberalism. ('Liberalism's Epitaph', *English Review*, 46 (1928), 515–22).

[184] [G. D. H. Cole], 'Liberalism and the Industrial Future', *NS*, 11.2.1928. And Kingsley Martin wrote a few years later that the Yellow Book 'contained the germs of a genuine Socialist programme' ('Opposition Policy', *NS*, 19.9.1931).

[185] Quoted in 'The Reception of the Industrial Report', *Nation*, 11.2.1928.

[186] Layton Papers, LSS files, Henderson to E. D. Simon, 29.1.1928.

would fall flat, as liberal reluctance to invoke remedial governmental action—a reluctance that Kerr endorsed—left little scope for impact on the public mind. Kerr pressed for an alternative policy aimed at persuading Labour and the trade unions to accept a more efficient and productive capitalism. Until more work could be devoted to the industrial rather than the governmental side of the report, Kerr thought it better to postpone it.[187] Eagar replied that he was worried about Kerr's conclusion that the state could do so little, and warned that the effect of the report would be:

(a) To convince Labour men generally that Liberalism is Conservatism without the courage of its convictions. (b) To prove to Conservatives that Liberalism is Socialism without the moral appeal of Socialism or its intellectual tidyness. (c) To settle for a considerable number of Liberals that their philosophy is mainly of antiquarian interest and that they must make up their minds finally whether their intellectual home is in Conservative [sic] or the Socialist Parties.[188]

And Keynes too wrote to Kerr: '. . . personally I think there is a great deal more to be done than you do by direct State action'.[189]

The liberal response after publication, while predictably enthusiastic, illuminated the different shades of opinion within liberalism. For the more progressive liberals, the report vindicated the liberal precepts that had been advocated over the past fifty years. 'The last thing which seems to have occurred to anybody is that the Report might be a development of Liberal principles', wrote the *Manchester Guardian*.[190] On the other hand, the *Daily Chronicle* proudly declared that 'no inquiry of comparable calibre has ever before been carried out by private enterprise in this country', though it welcomed the report's plans for national development.[191] Hubert Phillips, the economic adviser to the Industrial Inquiry and director of the Liberal Research Department, described the aims of the report in Millite terms as 'the evolution of order out of chaos', order being the pre-

[187] Lothian Papers, GD40/17/229, Kerr to Layton (copy to Eagar), 25.8.1927; Eagar Papers, ms. 14, Kerr to Lloyd George, 2.9.1927; Kerr to Keynes, ibid., 2.9.1927.

[188] Eagar to Kerr, Eagar Papers, ms. 14, 27.8.1927. Copy in Lothian Papers, GD40/17/229.

[189] Keynes to Kerr, Lothian Papers, GD40/17/229, 31.8.1927.

[190] 'A Mixed Reception', *MG*, 6.2.1928. This reaction must be contrasted with the *Manchester Guardian*'s attitude to the Beveridge Report. See below, p. 371.

[191] 'A Masterly Report: Liberalism in Industry', *DC*, 3.2.1928.

requisite for progress.[192] Hobson talked of 'a new era of Liberalism', which he described in glowing terms.[193] The *Daily News* saw the report as supplying a practical answer to 'the question for the plain man . . . ought he to be content to be the slave and puppet of forces which are in themselves nothing but the combined activities of himself and his fellows? Or ought he to seek at least to direct them?'[194] This conception of a rationally emerging order that insisted, as Muir elaborated, that 'an intelligent community ought to be able in some degree to guide and plan its own development',[195] was perhaps the last faint echo of the assimilation by the new liberals of the evolutionary process, which had confirmed the triumph of mind over matter in the course of the movement of history.

Phillips endorsed the liberal position that, although intervention must always be justified, it could make for freedom, opportunity and progress. Even the Yellow Book had voiced the new liberal sentiment that 'often more law may mean more liberty'.[196] Phillips went on to claim that 'our freedom to choose is a freedom that operates only within a framework of necessities that the social will has imposed. *And that framework of necessities the social will also can alter.*'[197] This succinct expression of the new liberal outlook reasserted the social-liberalism that the post-Green generation had developed as a sustained attack on 'inalienable rights' and 'freedom of contract'. But Phillips also inherited, along with most of his colleagues, an incurable faith in the possibility of consensus. The very idea of a council of industry, whose proposals would 'have the approval not only of both "sides" to the bargain but also of "neutral" members participating in the business of negotiation',[198] postulated the ultimate unanimity of a Rousseauist 'general will' acting as the rational interest of the community. But because it lacked the compulsory element that the worldly wise Rousseau had to introduce, this naïve version of rational decision-making was bound to break down in the face of recalcitrant individuals or groups. For Phillips, 'the keynote of the Liberal proposals is a

192 H. Phillips, 'Liberalism and Industrial Relations', *FR*, 130 (1928), part I, 603.

193 J. A. Hobson, 'The Liberal Revival in England', *Nation* (NY), 20.6.1928.

194 'The Plain Man and the Report', *DN*, 3.2.1928.

195 R. Muir, 'Liberalism and Industry', *CR*, 133 (1928), 561.

196 *Britain's Industrial Future*, p. xix.

197 Phillips, 'Liberalism and Industrial Relations', part II, 730; part III, 71 (italics in original).

198 Ibid., part II, 734.

distribution of responsibilities, in the sphere of industrial relations, which in itself provides at every stage the strongest incentive to co-operation on the part of every interest affected'.[199] Here was the crux of the liberal *Weltanschauung*: social harmony and individual happiness could be achieved by bringing all components of a community into the system and, through offering a set of rules by which everyone could play, the game (whatever it was) would be played willingly, even enjoyably.

There were liberals, however, whose interest in the report lay in rather different areas. From Samuel's comments the report may as well have been the product of a high-level group of managers, whose principles embodied industrial efficiency, low production costs and capable management.[200] Muir, adopting a middle position, was at least keen to strike a more philosophical note than Samuel who, despite his amateur philosopher's status, kept his political speeches free from theory and contemplation. The Yellow Book demonstrated for Muir that, for the progressive liberal as well as for his nineteenth-century predecessor, the driving force of all progress was to be found in the energy and initiative of individuals, but that the community had to supply the machinery to make this possible.[201] This stress on machinery reflected the liberal preoccupation with rules as prime guarantors of justice. The role of the state, too, had caused concern among some signatories to the report. Kerr's anti-statism was balanced by Keynes's pragmatic support for state action. As Keynes told Kerr: 'My real difficulty lies in the impracticability, or uselessness, of inscribing pious ideas on a political banner of a kind which could not possibly be embodied in legislation.'[202] Paradoxically, though the intentions of most Inquiry members were less radical than those of the new liberals twenty years earlier, the result of the Yellow Book was to incorporate state interventionism decisively within liberal ideology as no document had ever done before.[203]

[199] Ibid., 732.

[200] H. Samuel, 'The Liberal Industrial Report', *CR*, 133 (1928), 278.

[201] Muir, 'Liberalism and Industry', 560–1.

[202] Lothian Papers, GD40/17/229, Keynes to Kerr, 31.8.1927; Kerr to Keynes, 2.9.1927.

[203] See also the assessment of its wide influence in Greenleaf, *The British Political Tradition, vol. ii. The Ideological Heritage*, pp. 175–7.

5. REVIVAL AND CONTROVERSY

The Yellow Book was only an industrial policy, despite occasional divergences into other areas, not a comprehensive statement of liberal, or even LSS, policy and ideology about a well-constituted society. But it injected a real revivalist spirit into the flagging fortunes of liberalism and could not have come at a more opportune moment. From the liberal perspective, the run-up to the 1929 elections revolved almost entirely round the Industrial Inquiry, which was adopted at a special convention of the NLF in March 1928. Only E. D. Simon, among the more daring of the LSS liberals, queried the sketchiness of the Yellow Book on many issues, especially its eschewal of exploring financial governmental action 'to equalise economic opportunity and to abolish the evils of poverty'. Here the report had shown itself to be superficial and half-hearted.[204] The 1928 LSS, however, displayed a united front on the report, its showpiece being a debate between Keynes and Tom Johnston of the Labour party over some of the Yellow Book proposals. That debate, according to the *Nation*, did not reveal sharp and clear-cut controversy, though there was an altercation over the idea of the public concern, to which Johnston objected. Another curious event at the LSS was the fact that proportional representation was only carried by a narrow majority.[205]

The 1929 election campaign saw the translation of some of the Yellow Book proposals into the more popular versions of two pamphlets: *We Can Conquer Unemployment*, under Lloyd George's name, and *Can Lloyd George Do It*?, by Keynes and Henderson.[206] The first spelled out a concrete programme of national development to include a trunk road system, the provision of low rental housing, telephone and electrical schemes. It found it necessary to reject the wage fund theory, namely, 'that the State is providing unemployment with funds which would otherwise be used by private individuals at least as effectively, and that, therefore, at the best, the aggregate of employment can be no greater'. That view was 'hoary with antiquity' and had to be replaced by the notion that the state could enter new areas and create work where it would not conflict with or displace private enterprise. This was combined

[204] E. D. Simon, 'The Liberal Summer School', *CR*, 136 (1929), 277.
[205] 'The Liberal Summer School', *Nation*, 11.8.1928.
[206] Both London, 1929.

with the Keynesian insistence on the utilization of savings for investment, though the role of the state in encouraging that was only hinted at.[207] This must have relieved the *Daily Chronicle*, for whom liberals had demonstrated conclusively how unemployment schemes could be 'financed on sound business lines, without involving the addition of a penny to the burdens of the taxpayer'.[208] G. D. H. Cole, however, read into the Lloyd George pamphlet much that was sound and praised him for carrying liberalism 'a long way from its old faith in the sovereign virtue of letting private enterprise alone'.[209]

Keynes's and Henderson's pamphlet expanded on the advantages of paying more people wages instead of unemployment pay, in terms of increased effective purchasing power and the cumulative stimulus to trade.[210] As for state intervention, their typical position was:

> it is not a question of choosing between private and public enterprise in these matters [concerning capital development]. The choice has already been made. In many directions—though not in all—it is a question of the State putting its hand to the job or of its not being done at all . . . the object is not to develop State enterprise as such. The object is to develop and equip the country through the instrumentality of such forms of organisation as already exist and lie ready to our hands.[211]

This technical statement masked the ideological willingness to use the state in order to manipulate individual behaviour towards attaining collective ends.

The failure of the Liberal party in the 1929 elections—in which, despite polling more than five and a quarter million votes, it obtained only fifty-nine seats, marked another turning-point in the fortunes of liberalism. It seemed as if progressive liberalism had invested its entire energies in the Yellow Book and its aftermath, and with the growing realization that its policies would not be implemented, it gently petered out, all passion spent. Certainly this would have been a just verdict on the LSS movement which survived for another

207 *We Can Conquer Unemployment*, pp. 53–5.

208 'Use the Workers: Liberal War on Waste', *DC*, 28.3.1929.

209 [G. D. H. Cole], 'Can We Conquer Unemployment?', *NS*, 23.3.1929; 'The Two Problems of Unemployment', *NS*, 30.3.1929. In general, the pamphlet 'created a sensation' (R. Skideslky, *Politicians and the Slump: The Labour Government of 1929–1931* (Harmondsworth, 1970), p. 72.

210 Keynes and Henderson, *Can Lloyd George Do It?*, p. 25.

211 Ibid., pp. 32–3.

year or two on the laurels of its industrial policy, but faded in the 1930s both from the public eye and as a force within liberalism. With a Labour government again in power, Simon was left to ponder the indirect influence of liberalism, via the Yellow Book, on the Labour party.[212] This self-appointed role of mover behind the scenes was one that liberals were now reluctant to accept. The Yellow Book became the liberal bible and during the 1930s it served as a point of reference to which progressives delighted in relating. The LSS, however, became increasingly the party think-tank rather than an independent and innovative ideological entrepreneur. Thus the dominant issue at the 1929 School was that of electoral reform, as a tired Liberal party tried to maximize its possibilities within what it now hoped would remain a three-party system. This time proportional representation obtained an overwhelming majority. As Muir pensively observed: 'once you have reached the conclusion that a three-party system is a good thing in itself, and will yield better results than a two-party system, the objections to Proportional Representation shrink to insignificance.'[213] This exercise in self-reassurance indicates more than anything the mood of liberalism at the half-way point between the wars.

There was one final episode that caused a few sparks to fly in the 1930 LSS. Simon momentarily entered into the role of *enfant terrible*, in an attempt to reconstitute the function of the LSS as the experimental sounding-board for new or, in this case, heretical ideas. He questioned whether enough was being done to protect the export trade—especially the motor industry—and to prevent the consequent unemployment that its poor performance caused, and suggested that they should consider a revenue tax of 10 per cent on all imports apart from raw materials.[214] This official assault on free trade, amplified by full press coverage,[215] created a storm. Layton responded immediately, concerned not so much about the low tax proposed as about the breaching of a principle. He acknowledged an inevitable decline in the British proportion of world trade, but reiterated the classic free trade position that a balance in the exchange of goods and services had to be maintained. Muir joined battle, not unpredictably donning the mantle of official Liberalism

[212] *MG*, 2.8.1929.
[213] R. Muir, 'The Younger Liberals and the Labour Party', *Nation*, 17.8.1929.
[214] *MG*, 4.8.1930.
[215] Cf. Stocks, *Ernest Simon of Manchester*, p. 94.

and discarding the original spirit of enquiry of the LSS. He excoriated Simon for raising the free trade question—it had 'embarrassed his work as chairman of a party that was already fighting under great handicaps'. Substantively, both Muir and Layton saw Simon's position as leading to a rise in the cost of living and a decrease in real wages, precisely the charge that had always been levelled against Conservative protectionism.[216]

Simon and Muir continued to argue through the pages of the *Political Quarterly*. For Simon, this was a challenge to existing liberal dogma, but also an expression of concern from a social reformer alarmed at unemployment and the declining standard of living. The urgent need for revenue dictated a search for new sources of national income, and direct taxation would, in his opinion, become dangerous if too high. The voice of a progressive liberal could be heard in the preaching of governmental intervention 'with the free play of economic forces by conscious and deliberate control'. Free trade was too much associated with that free play.[217] Muir circumvented these more general issues by repeating the arguments that protection would lower the standard of living and would increase employment only in trades working for the home market at the expense of export markets.[218]

Simon's 'unintentional indiscretion', as it was called, caused 'alarm and indignation' among many LSS members. Dingle Foot, reporting on the session, hinted at the main liberal fear—that creeping protection would destroy the distinctions between the Liberal party and its enemies on the right.[219] Outside the LSS Hammond expressed concern and regret to Murray.[220] But the challenging of free trade was of wider significance. The *Nation*, unexpectedly, rallied to Simon's defence, noting that his heresy was

[216] *MG*, 5.8.1930. See S. Hodgson, 'The Tenth Liberal Summer School', *CR*, 138 (1930), 296–8; and *Liberal Magazine*, 38 (1930), pp. 347, 402–5, in which Simon's 'outbreak' was regretted. See also Layton Papers, Free Trade Controversy File, which contains voluminous notes and correspondence with Simon as well as various drafts of Layton's rebuttals of the case for tariffs. For Layton's activities during the 1920s see D. Hubback, *No Ordinary Press Baron: A Life of Walter Layton* (London, 1985), pp. 70–8.

[217] E. D. Simon, 'Some Questions about Free Trade', *Political Quarterly*, 1 (1930), 479–95.

[218] R. Muir, 'Mr. Simon's Questions about Free Trade', *Political Quarterly*, 2 (1931), 23–9.

[219] D. Foot, 'The Liberal Summer School', *Nation*, 9.8.1930.

[220] Murray Papers, Box 23a, Hammond to Murray, undated.

'essentially agnostic'. It was, of course, politically unwise and perhaps there was no obvious alternative in sight, but, added the *Nation*, 'we agree with Mr. Simon that the case for Free Trade needs restatement in the light of modern conditions, and we are willing to re-examine that case with the utmost candour'.[221] Other liberals had felt qualms about free trade prior to the LSS furore. Ted Scott, then editor of the *Manchester Guardian*, had written earlier in the year to his father-in-law, Hobson, asking for theoretical reassurances about the validity of the doctrine and speaking in the tones of a believer whose faith was inexorably being eroded: 'Even for my own part I find very great difficulty in accepting the theoretical Free Trade case with the confidence I felt in 1906.'[222] Hobson was unable to provide the solace, in the form of a couple of articles, that Scott had hoped for. Instead he wrote Scott a letter, ambiguous in its content and indicative of the dilemmas of divided loyalties that liberals were experiencing: 'I wish I could produce a satisfactory reply. . . . But I don't think I can.' For the underconsumptionist Hobson, the weak link in the free trade chain was the assumption that cheap imports would increase home demand by releasing more money for consumption. But this increased consumption could be applied to imported goods and thus do nothing to reduce unemployment. The free trade argument questionably presumed 'that all powers of production are employed and argues that Tariff will direct them from a more productive to a less productive use'. But was the converse true? In the overriding bleak reality of the post-war British economy, 'neither free trade theory or practice will cure unemployment'.[223] Keynes, too, was losing interest in the traditional case for free trade.[224] A revenue tariff would provide scope for increased investment and employment, an argument he began to promote in 1930 and 1931.[225] Among the Industrial Inquiry members,

[221] 'Mr. Simon's "Indiscretion"', *Nation*, 9.8.1930. Henderson himself adopted a more traditional line on this issue. See Layton Papers, Free Trade Controversy File, Henderson to Simon (extract), 7.8.1930.

[222] *Guardian* Papers, A/H69/16, Scott to Hobson, 9.2.1930.

[223] Ibid., Hobson to Scott, A/H69/17, 10.2.1930. See also Layton Papers, Hobson to E. D. Simon, 21.10.1930 in which Hobson supported Simon, noting that he had put that argument to free traders twenty years earlier but could not get them to grapple with it.

[224] He wrote to support Simon (Stocks, *Ernest Simon of Manchester*, p. 94). See also J. M. Keynes, letter to the Editor, *Manchester Guardian*, 17.8.1930.

[225] See Winch, *Economics and Policy*, pp. 149–50, 160–1. For Keynes no less than for Simon and Hobson the support for a revenue tariff was a response 'to the pressure of immediate policy circumstances' (p. 161).

Phillips expressed agreement with Simon's inquisitive mood.[226] Even for supporters of free trade, the confusions of the times required fresh evidence and hard thinking.

Simon emerged unscathed from all this. His ability to raise the issue in the first place must have reflected 'his personal ascendancy in the School'.[227] He himself was aware of this, as a number of entries in his diaries show: 'Founded the Liberal Summer School, with Muir, and have been mainly responsible all thru first for collecting the committee, then for keeping them together and alive . . . Biggest achievement the Yellow Book—I think it is fair to say it would never have been written but for me.'[228] His clash with Muir was evidence of a parting of the ways between the two, but also demonstrated the growing ambivalence of Simon towards the Liberal party.[229] In fact, by the 1931 LSS, the free trade incident had almost been forgotten, and Dingle Foot, no friend of Simon's on that issue, reported that 'this year [Simon] had no doubts at all and made it abundantly clear that he did not look to the customs-house for salvation'.[230] Hobson, too, had recovered his equilibrium. The nationalistic implications of protection proved too much for him to stomach. He sympathized with those liberal economists who now were 'reluctant concessionaires' out of concern over reduced revenue and wages, and admitted the advantages of tariffs in periods of depression. But the desirable control by the state over key domestic spheres of human activity was the obverse of existing attempts of the state to act in the international system.[231] For there it appeared as separatist and selfish, harmful to other peoples as well as to its own. The solution lay in 'skilled conscious guidance' for international economic forces. Paradoxically, free trade could only really function in a controlled situation, for 'economic liberalism' would degenerate into a nationalistic free-for-all.[232]

[226] H. Phillips, letter to the Editor, *Nation*, 16.8.1930.

[227] Hodgson, 'The Tenth Liberal Summer School', p. 298, although Simon did not succeed in convincing his colleagues that the LSS should conduct an inquiry on free trade (Layton Papers, Simon to Layton, 8.9.1930).

[228] Simon Papers, Diary, p. 11.

[229] See pp. 349–51 below.

[230] D. Foot, 'The Liberal Summer School', *CR*, 140 (1931), 325.

[231] Similarly, Keynes argued (in 'National Self-Sufficiency. I', *NS*, 8.7.1933) that national self-sufficiency and economic isolation could work in the cause of peace, and that geographical remoteness between ownership and operation had evil consequences. See also below, p. 365.

[232] J. A. Hobson, 'A World Economy', *NS*, 18.4.1931. Cf. also G. D. H. Cole, 'Free Trade: Negative and Positive', in the same issue.

As for the LSS, by 1930 it was being side-tracked into relatively minor issues. 'The condition of England question figured less than ever before in the programme, presumably because men do not stop to furnish the dug-outs when the enemy is making a massed attack all along the line', wrote Foot.[233] The LSS, now trapped in the web of party politics, was beginning to display signs of the paralysis of the organization it had set out to reform. Like the party, it was reacting to emergencies, and not doing it well. Hodgson was moved to

a melancholy reflection. What will happen to the Summer School if the Liberal Party passes out of its present chaos only to disappear altogether? Its able leaders . . . have been the greatest driving force in public life in recent years . . . It is hard to think that all this bubbling energy, this zeal for social betterment and reform, this real knowledge and sparkling wit is nothing but a Midsummer Night's interlude in the rather frowsy drama of modern politics.[234]

Was the first, and only active, decade of the LSS movement a success or a failure? It is difficult to pass an unequivocal verdict. It served as a hatching-ground for the attempts of liberalism to strike a modernist pose, but it had the misfortune to do so at a time when organized Liberalism was on the decline and when its brand of progressivism no longer had access to the corridors of power. It produced the most important policy statements of inter-war Britain, but the accumulative effect of its programmes and plans did not come into its own before 1945, by which time much of liberal progressivism had been integrated into a broad Labourite social-democratic front, or had succumbed to the allure of a more confident liberal-conservatism. It was an intellectualist movement, but not intellectual enough to be innovative in the sphere of political thought. Though it contributed to the many-coloured mainstream of left-of-centre reformist ideology, it fell short of supplying liberalism with a desperately needed integrating framework with which to fire the imagination of a nation.[235] Most crucially, it failed to retain the allegiance of those left-liberals who by the time of Grasmere were beginning to move beyond the fold. Whether such a move was theoretically possible will concern us in forthcoming chapters. But

233 Foot, 'The Liberal Summer School', *Nation*, 9.8.1930.

234 Hodgson, 'The Tenth Liberal Summer School', 301–2.

235 True, as Simon observed of the LSS, 'we have . . . done something to bring the economist and the politician into closer touch, to interpret the economist to the politician'. ('The Liberal Summer School' [1929], 276.)

the ability and the insight to prevent the ideological splintering of progressive liberalism was beyond the capacities of the LSS activists. There is much in the notion that events—such as the new era of economic and political foreboding after the war—destroyed the urge to productive and inventive political thinking. There is also much to attract in the suggestion that ideologies age or, like institutions, routinize, to use Weberian terminology. The fact is that even a proselytizing and explorative phenomenon such as the LSS could not prevent the alienation of key individuals and groups among advanced liberals. Many committed new liberals began to withdraw from politics in the 1920s, disillusioned with liberalism but unwilling to make the breach formal by supporting the Labour party. Others, as we shall see, joined the Labour party while remaining, on their own understanding, loyal to liberalism. The LSS had nothing to offer any of these. Party allegiance triumphed over ideology when, in the wake of the *Nation* takeover and the rise of the Cambridge economists in the LSS, a clear and eventually dominant section opted against co-operation with Labour. Even with Labour in power, backed by the Liberal party and with a programme that had a great deal in common with the liberal one, the LSS voted in 1929 not to work for 'a reunion of the progressive forces'—i.e. an alliance with Labour minus its left wing.[236] Nor could the LSS, despite a few modest starts, supply radical liberalism with the comprehensive social vision it had in the past obtained from its intellectuals. The salience of the industrial issue and of unemployment is indisputable and liberals were correct to engage these problems, but they did so while paying far too little attention to questions of social justice, to the indispensable normative mainstays of political theory, and to the integration of a conception of human nature that they could accept into a workable structure of social institutions. Or rather, if they did, they did not do so deliberately and consciously, for in the time-honoured tradition of British political thinking, 'here, as elsewhere, theory followed rather than preceded practice'.[237] It will be the aim of the next chapter to try and analyse the legacy of political thought that liberals of moderately progressive views, both inside and outside the LSS movement, bequeathed to their generation.

[236] R. Muir, 'The Younger Liberals and the Labour Party', *Nation*, 17.8.1929.
[237] 'The New Manchesterism', *Nation*, 1.1.1921.

5

HUMAN NATURE, ECONOMIC LAWS, AND THE RECONSTITUTION OF CAPITALISM

HARDLY a decade had passed since the outbreak of the Great War before the legacy of late-Victorian liberalism began to adopt a new form. From the vantage point of 1914, one is tempted to regard the new liberalism as the logical development of a tradition of political discourse that reunited ethics and politics, linked the notion of community firmly to liberalism by way of a socially oriented and interdependent concept of human nature, and welcomed the state as the central agency of a solidaric society, through which collective mind would triumph over matter and the continued evolution and progress of humanity would be assured. Ten years later the long-term perspective on liberalism would have had, of necessity, to be altered dramatically.[1]

Propelled by the experience of the war itself and by the savage reality of an accelerating economic decline, British liberalism underwent a theoretical fragmentation that paralleled the shattering of its political confidence. Those liberal elements that still maintained allegiance to notions of reform, progress and individual betterment, evinced a fundamental bifurcation between a liberalism of the left and a liberalism of the centre. Each of these two streams had its sub-currents, not all of which seemed to be flowing in the same direction. Both streams, however, could with some justification claim that they contained important components of the liberal heritage. To follow this crucial divergence of the liberal

[1] The confusion surrounding the liberal tradition is well illustrated by the intriguing responses to a questionnaire circulated among young liberals (average age 28.2) by the centrist-liberal *Forward View* in 1928. Answering the question whether nineteenth- and twentieth-century liberalism were based on the same principles, 55 per cent (base not given) assented and 38 per cent demurred. The *Forward View* interpreted dissent as a negative verdict on the present quality of liberalism, but failed to establish what those principles were. (*FV*, December 1928, Apr. 1929.)

tradition, a degree of 'fine tuning' in ideological analysis is both necessary and revealing. It is here in particular that the ideological morphology of liberalism must be appreciated. The liberal core was shared by both streams but they differed in the adjacent concepts that defined and coloured the core ideas. As has been noted in Chapter 1, liberty, rationality, and a concern for the general good were retained by liberals of all persuasions, but these central concepts were bordered on by different sets of idea-environments: individuality, property, and security were made to work in one direction while social justice, welfare, and democracy put another interpretation on the core. The need for 'fine tuning' is compounded by the characteristic stretching of concepts such as justice, individuality, equality of opportunity and even property to cover a wide range of meanings which can only be located within the specific context of use.

This chapter will explore the moderate brand of progressive liberalism that enhanced its salience during the 1920s, to a large extent due to the efforts of the LSS, but also to a considerable degree by default, as the pre-war new liberalism inched its way towards the labour movement and the cohesive nucleus of its proponents bowed to the inevitable biological cycle. Progressive centrist-liberalism overlapped on a number of issues with the aging new liberalism but differed in emphasis on some key questions. First, although it accepted a certain role for the state, perhaps no smaller than that suggested by the new liberals in the early years of the century, it refused to subscribe any further to a faith in the state as the disinterested agent of the community, reverting instead to a more individualistic conception of human nature and social relations. Secondly—and this is the subject of Chapter 6—it insisted on magnifying the ideological differences between liberalism and a socialist/trade-unionist Labour party. Thirdly, centrist-liberalism was less reflective, philosophically oriented, or synthetic in the broad cultural sense of integrating various branches of human knowledge. Consequently, there was a notable aura of impoverishment about the quality of its political thinking. Even its crowning achievement, the LSS, lacked the intellectual *gravitas*, perceptiveness, and originality that had given the new liberalism its range and vitality. This is precisely why Muir epitomized the liberalism of the 1920s. He combined tireless work for the Liberal party with intense propagandist activities through speeches, books, and journalism. His writings, however, occupied the unsatisfactory middle ground between political thought and party proselytizing and, as Barker pointed out,[2] he never distinguished himself in either of his two careers, as he himself came to realize.[3] Virginia Woolf described him as 'on all hands a dull dog'[4] but he was undeniably a faithful one to liberalism; indeed, in more senses than one he was a pale shadow of his great socialist counterpart, Sidney Webb. Liberalism in the 1920s was, like Muir, earnest, worthy, hopeful, and uninspiring.

1. THE RETURN OF ECONOMIC MAN

Reflecting at the end of the war on the defeat of liberal ideas 'in the grand cataclysm', the *Nation* posed the question: 'Is it that the Liberal concept of liberty is too poor, that it cannot feed the positive desire for a fuller rational life, that men look beyond its conception of a fixed capitalist class, a fixed labour class, and a slightly varied but still unsocial division of the product?'[5] A persistent feeling of inadequacy indicated that the new liberalism had not provided a secure resting place for progressive liberals or, if it had, the interluding years had once again brought confusion in their wake. As a letter to the editor suggested: 'Professor L. T. Hobhouse before the war laid down the principles of Economic Liberalism in his illuminating little volume "Liberalism," . . . but these principles have not been appreciated, much less proclaimed and defended by the political leaders of the Party'—and, one may add, by most liberal thinkers too. 'What Liberalism wants', the letter continued, 'is . . . a chart, mapping the dangerous channel between the Scylla of uncontrolled individualism on the one hand and the Charybdis of an ennervating State-aid upon the other.'[6] Inheriting a pervading feeling that liberalism was past its prime, the emerging theorists attempted to avoid the disaster they believed would befall their creed from either a resurrection of a mid-Victorian liberal ideology —still enunciated by Liberals such as Beauchamp, who identified liberal principles as 'Peace, Free Trade, Economy, Education'[7]—or

2 *Dictionary of National Biography, 1941–1950.*

3 Simon Papers, M11/16/32, Muir to Simon, 15.2.1934. (See Chapter 9.)

4 *The Diary of Virginia Woolf*, vol. ii. *1920–1924*, ed. A. O. Bell (Harmondsworth, 1981), p. 232.

5 'A Chance for Liberalism', *Nation*, 25.1.1919.

6 S. P. Turnbull, '"A Chance for Liberalism"', *Nation*, 8.2.1919.

7 Lord Beauchamp, 'The Liberal Party', *CR*, 130 (1926), 1.

from what many thought were the collectivist excesses of the new liberalism. Muir, Dodds, Masterman, and Murray propounded their version of a new liberalism (witness the titles of Masterman's 1920 book and Muir's 1923 pamphlet), which was in many ways older than its pre-war predecessor both in its effort to salvage elements of liberal ideology that other advanced liberals had condemned, and in its deflation of areas of social thought that the original new liberals had helped to pioneer. Unsurprisingly, that remnant of the new liberalism, the *Nation*, when reviewing one of Dodds's books, saw it as illustrative of the failure of liberalism to confront fully the problem of social reform. Despite this the *Nation* situated Dodds on the 'Left Wing of Free Liberalism'.[8]

As with any political theory, the reassertion of a moderate progressive liberalism hinged upon a particular concept of human nature. Interestingly, the new Manchesterism revived aspects of the old, harking back to an entrepreneurial, initiative taking, energetic and efficient notion of man or, perhaps, 'business man'. Thus D. H. Robertson, in recommending his economic policies, observed: 'Note that it is strictly in accord with the most old-fashioned Liberal principles—with the doctrine of the Invisible Hand which causes those who seek their own advantage to promote indirectly the advantage of society.'[9] Dodds, while conceding that the old Manchester School ignored the true nature of economic liberty, stressed that 'the self-reliance and independence for which it pleaded must remain the object of a wise government'.[10] And the *Daily News*, in classic liberal mould, identified self-reliance as 'the real life-blood of a healthy industrial system'.[11] The return to enlightened self-interest based on managerial and economic utility-maximizing models was, more surprisingly, endorsed by liberals previously associated with the breakaway from the social dogmas of political economy. As we have seen, Graham Wallas, once a leading Fabian, crossed swords with R. H. Tawney, because of 'the

[8] 'A Champion of New Liberalism', *Nation*, 10.6.1922. By the 1930s the assessment of Dodds was less kind. For 'middle-way' planners he had become an 'old-fashioned' liberal (A. E. Douglas-Smith, 'A Political Survey', *New Outlook*, Aug. 1936).

[9] D. H. Robertson, 'The Trade Cycle', *Nation*, 11.8.1923.

[10] Dodds, *Is Liberalism Dead?*, p. 32. Dodds became editor of the centrist-liberal *Forward View*, organ of the Yorkshire Council of Young Liberals, which he used to air similar opinions (see, e.g. 'Our Job', Feb. 1927; 'A Declaration of Liberal Faith', Feb. 1932).

[11] 'Industry and Politics', *DN*, 17.7.1919.

subordinate place which [Tawney] assigns to the economic motive of gain'.[12] Not that the new liberals, or even moderate socialists, had made away with that motive, but they would not have felt the need to accord it salience and centrality. Even Hobhouse was moved to write, in another of his many reassessing essays:

I think we can understand better than we did in our youth something of the feeling about Governments which animated our grandfathers and great-grandfathers in the struggle for political, social and economic liberty. We can understand why they thought of Government as the champion muddler, why they made a thing so prosaic as public economy a cardinal point, why they clamoured so persistently for individual initiative and relaxation of control as sometimes to drown the plea of those who were suffering from unrestricted liberty in the wrong place. I do not think we shall ever go back to *laissez-faire* precisely as it was understood by Cobden and Bright. But I do think that economic and political liberty will play a revived and larger part in our political programmes, and that the real problem of the thinker to-day is to find for the term a new and fuller definition suited to the changed structure of our time.[13]

It was Muir, however, who provided the most detailed exposition of post-war centrist-liberalism. For Muir, too, human nature was structured round the central principle that 'private initiative is the source of all human progress'.[14] On the face of it, this was an eminently liberal claim, entirely consonant with Mill's famous remark at the end of *On Liberty* that the worth of a state is the worth of the individuals composing it. But a caveat must be registered immediately. To echo a Millite tenet may be a tribute to the timelessness of liberal essentials, but it ignores the immense distance that liberalism had travelled in the intervening period towards an acknowledgement of the social interdependence of individuals. There is a prima-facie case for probing such a statement carefully in the light of new knowledge and different circumstances. Muir's assertion has to be seen in the context of the conditioning ideas that transformed this general liberal principle into a particular expression of centrist-liberalism. Within a largely shared vocabulary, the clues to ideological diversity are provided by differences of stress and priority as well as by the presence or absence of specific terms.

[12] G. Wallas, 'Acquisitive Society', *Nation*, 11.6.1921. See Chapter 3, p. 75 above.

[13] [L. T. Hobhouse], 'Reaction', *MG*, 29.5.1920.

[14] R. Muir, 'The Meaning of Liberalism', *CR*, 130 (1926), 549.

Muir often expressed himself in language that did not easily distinguish his brand of liberalism from the new liberal one. The preservation and enlargement of liberty were a condition of the highest human welfare; liberty could be realized only in organized societies with the co-operation of all; nationalism, efficiency and material comforts were secondary to liberty; individuality and the cultivation of the highest human types were the ultimate ends of society, and were extolled over doctrinaire individualism. The Greenian end of encouraging people to make the most and the best of themselves was reiterated, while the predominance of the communal interest—defined in the above terms—was established.[15] At the same time Muir's political writings were determined by the choice of subject for the volume produced by the originators of the LSS—*Liberalism and Industry*—and through him and his colleagues the link between the two provided a dominant framework within which to work out problems of liberal theory.

Muir's resurrection of economic-cum-business man was not, of course, a return to the myth of *laissez-faire* that had bedevilled liberalism in its desire to cut loose from the old Manchesterism. Muir specifically repudiated that doctrine while pointing proudly to the social reform achievements of liberalism over the past century.[16] But there is no mistaking his emphasis on freedom as the core and, in the ultimate analysis, sole component of the liberal creed. The preservation and increase of 'the real liberty of all citizens' was especially tied to the granting of 'reasonable freedom of thought and action to those exceptional, adventurous, original men who are always the pioneers of human progress'.[17] A later passage reveals the degree of restructuring the liberal ideological core was again undergoing. Writing on the importance of research, Muir stated: 'There is scarcely any function of importance to the welfare of the community which so clearly illustrates how directly that welfare depends upon freedom for individual enterprise.'[18] One of the features of the new liberalism had been the establishment of liberty and welfare as twin, mutually defining, central notions of liberalism. Subtly but unequivocally, welfare was demoted once again to the status of a secondary, dependent goal, while the alternative

[15] Muir, *Liberalism and Industry*, pp. 19–27.
[16] R. Muir, *Politics and Progress* (London, 1923), p. 104.
[17] Muir, *Liberalism and Industry*, p. 21.
[18] Ibid., p. 168.

route proposed by new liberals—the identification of communal welfare as a facet of individual liberty—was barely hinted at, and often abandoned to the socialists. This standpoint was spelled out by Masterman—whose book Muir had just read and commended:

> Liberty is an end in itself . . . It is not a stage leading towards some ultimate goal. It is itself an ultimate goal . . . Liberty may be a means to happiness, to comfort, to material prosperity, to success. It is good even if it leads to none of these things. Liberty is greater than Prosperity. It is better to be free in rags than to be a pampered slave.[19]

The confusion is obvious: if liberty were an end unto itself, what was one supposed to gain from it? If nothing, this countered the repeated liberal claim that 'the progressive emancipation of all human individualities from the restraints which forbid the development of their full potentialities' in order to release 'individual character, energy and inventiveness' was what liberalism stood for.[20] If, however, as seems to be the case, Masterman also recognized liberty as a means to other human ends, it would be more useful to talk about a cluster of ends, of which liberty was an indispensable member. But the simplistic notion that liberty was good even if it led to nothing else was reminiscent of dogmas that liberalism had already discarded.[21]

Muir accepted that 'liberty is not a merely negative thing, a mere absence of restraints; it is a positive thing, the existence of a real opportunity to make the most and the best of our powers'.[22] This unacknowledged paraphrase from Green's *Liberal Legislation and Freedom of Contract* would appear on the face of it to confirm the movement of liberalism towards a more activist communitarian ideal based on the notion of man as a social animal. But when Muir wrote those words, a reference to Green was more likely to be used as a symbol of accreditation to a noble and elevating liberal tradition than as a radically innovative position within the progressive mainstream. Indeed, when Muir did invoke Green, it was to give Green's philosophy the very traditionalist gloss (in the liberal context) that it merited. It was, he quoted Green, 'the business of the State to maintain the conditions without which a free exercise of

[19] Masterman, *The New Liberalism*, p. 27.
[20] Muir, *Politics and Progress*, p. 7.
[21] See the discussion in Chapter 7, Section 5.
[22] R. Muir, *The New Liberalism* (London n.d.[1923]), p. 7.

the human faculties is impossible'.[23] For both Green and Muir, this denied the community any direct involvement in the choice or furtherance of such faculties. Muir saw the issues of liberty and individuality as inextricably interrelated with the economic concerns of the time. This central theme in his writings marked a further divergence of centrist-liberalism from new liberalism. The latter had adopted the Ruskinian-Hobsonian expansion of economics to include all vital functions of life, to embrace qualitative consumption and social health. It was therefore inevitable that politics and economics should heavily overlap. Muir and his co-liberals upheld that link between politics and economics, concentrating on 'those questions of civic and economic organization with which politics are primarily concerned'.[24] But this now turned into an exercise in intellectual curtailment, because the sphere of economics itself was in the process of contracting. Industrial production, trade and national prosperity had become the delimiting boundaries. Conversely, some liberals reduced politics to the arena of state activity and concluded, as did John Murray: 'Politics and business ought to be kept separate with the utmost scrupulousness . . . Integrity in public life and high standards in industry depend on the rigorous separation of the two realms.'[25]

The salience of national economic hardship and the detachment of economics as a discipline and field of reform from a humanist social philosophy did much to deny colour and sheen, as well as scope and range, to post-war progressive liberalism. Initiation, organization, direction—a combination of those abilities was deemed more important than ever.[26] On the one hand, Muir resuscitated the Victorian value of thrift, not only as the best way of providing capital, but 'as one of the most valuable and useful ways of expressing individuality, of stimulating individual energy, and of diffusing interest in and knowledge of the industrial activity of the country'.[27] On the other hand he echoed Hobsonian underconsumptionism in suggesting the creation of public works to increase workers' spending power and hence to enlarge demand for products in other industries.[28] If there was a way of reconciling these two

[23] Muir, *Politics and Progress*, p. 15.
[24] Ibid., p. 69.
[25] J. Murray, 'Can Liberalism Revive?', *CR*, 127 (1925), 720.
[26] Muir, *Liberalism and Industry*, p. 53.
[27] Ibid., p. 59; *Politics and Progress*, p. 40.
[28] Muir, *Politics and Progress*, pp. 135–6.

policies, Muir did not propose it, being unaware of the tensions between them. Indeed, the question of thrift seemed to have shed its marked individualistic connotations, to the extent that Muir was able to make an assertion impossible for pre-war progressives: 'the principle that the help given by the State should not displace, but should stimulate and help, individual effort and thrift' was 'the first principle of Liberal social reform'.[29] The choice of words was more significant than the idea, for political discourse and theorizing, as much as political propaganda, are conducted by means of codes with symbolic and expressive value. The new liberals had not ditched thrift, but the term evoked shades of the Charity Organization Society and its anti-communitarian philosophy. The LSS was, however, the creation of a group of businessmen, and Muir's ideas, which on his own admission were moulded by them, reflected their somewhat different view of life.

One should not overstate the case for the reintroduction of economic individualism. The pendulum had swung back, but not all the way. When one of the industrialists behind the LSS, R. H. Brand, claimed that 'everything in this uncertain world depends on personal management, personal capacity, personal initiative and enterprise', and that 'nothing can prevent the unfit going to the wall—if they insist on remaining unfit',[30] he was gently castigated for being 'a little over-insistent on the rights of Capital'.[31] Nevertheless, for many liberals the acid test of individual development, indeed character, had reverted to the arena of material productivity. Not only was a consideration of the economic structure of the liberal state vital in securing a larger liberty,[32] but citizenship too was made out to be primarily an economic issue. Thus Muir wrote of the 'sense of citizenship *in the industries* to which [working people's] lives and strength are given'[33] and linked citizenship to the creation of the nation's wealth.[34] The notion of citizenship as membership of the community was devalued in line with the decline of the centrality of the community as a social grouping. The interest of the community was described as the maximum production of wealth and the maintenance of the conditions necessary to that end;[35] the community

29 R. Muir, 'Security of Livelihood', *WW*, 9.2.1924.

30 R. H. Brand, 'Socialism and Social Reform', *Nation*, 11.8.1923.

31 'Liberal Fundamentals', *Nation*, 15.12.1923.

32 Muir, *Politics and Progress*, p. 38.

33 Ibid., p. 17 (italics added).

34 Ibid., p. 58.

35 Muir, *Liberalism and Industry*, pp. 57, 42. See also Watchman, 'The Oppor-

was in fact relegated to the status of one of five co-equal factors in industry, the other four being individual ability, labour, capital, and the consumer. Rather than constituting the overarching entity than an earlier liberal organicism had postulated, none of those five factors, not 'even the community as a whole', could claim 'that industry exists exclusively for its benefit'.[36] If social health was now defined in terms of private enterprise, it was quite logical to reduce social utility—an idea the new liberals had boldly attached to a general social will—to the *economic* health of the community.[37]

For Dodds, too, the change in emphasis made it imperative for liberalism to 'interpret its political theory in the term of industrial freedom',[38] for 'in the eyes of Liberals, industry itself is a kind of commonwealth'.[39] In a revealing remark he explained that 'man is not only, as Aristotle taught, "a political animal", but "an industrial animal" as well'.[40] This implied that industry was a co-equal but separate sphere of human activity, and that the reach of politics did not by definition embrace that sphere together with all the others, as the Aristotelian–Idealist–new liberal perspective had held. And if for Aristotle justice was a principle firmly embedded in the economic structure of the community, it is curious to read the following observation by Muir:

> . . . it is necessary to distinguish between the attainment of justice in human relationships, the only sphere to which the democratic procedure through discussion and agreement is possible or healthful, and the more creative functions of industry which depend so much upon individual genius and personal leadership that they can never be satisfactorily decided by discussion and voting.[41]

Was one to assume from the above that industry did not concern human relationships but was entirely monadist in its creativity? Was justice excluded from the workings of industry? Was the democratic process so inadequate that even its cardinal liberal virtues of discussion and agreement were less creative accomplish-

tunity of Liberalism. III. A Liberal Programme for the Consumer and the Salaried Worker', *Nation*, 16.4. 1927.

36 Muir, *Liberalism and Industry*, p. 58.
37 Muir, *Politics and Progress*, p. 149; *Liberalism and Industry*, p. 186.
38 Dodds, *Is Liberalism Dead?*, p. 104.
39 Dodds, *Liberalism in Action*, p. 210.
40 Dodds, *Is Liberalism Dead?*, p. 124.
41 R. Muir, 'The Liberal Ideal', *Nation*, 11.8.1923.

ments of the human mind than the skills of material invention and of management? Undoubtedly, there had been a restructuring of liberal priorities together with a devaluation of justice, as Muir later clarified when listing the functions of the state in industry: '*first* to create the most favourable conditions for the free operation of enterprise; and *secondly* to regulate the activities of this enterprise so as to ensure that justice is done'.[42] The new liberals had attempted to impress upon the public that efficiency—a theme harnessed to the political ends of the Boer War—was subservient to justice. Yet increasingly liberals such as E. D. Simon were insisting that economic efficiency was as equally important as social justice.[43] When the *Daily News* insisted that a liberal was 'a man who rates liberty higher than order, and justice than organisation',[44] the reference was not necessarily to *social* justice. Rather, it contained an appeal to the centrist-liberal view of human nature, voiced by Samuel: 'No ingenuity of organization can give to the official the qualities of initiative and energy that distinguish the born leader of industry.'[45] This, and not only economic exigency, is surely one explanation for the decline of the attractiveness of industrial democracy, especially workers' participation, by the mid-1920s.

2. EFFICIENCY AND RATIONALIZATION: THE LIBERAL CASE

The relegitimization of the concept of efficiency fitted in well with the current mood. Whereas previously progressives were inclined to refer to efficiency mainly in the context of the physical well-being of the dispossessed, both the war and the economic difficulties of the 1920s spurred on the demand for productive efficiency.[46] If the 'root problem' was 'the reconciliation of technical efficiency with personal freedom',[47] it was not always accompanied by a reconciliation with citizenship and the material necessities of life. In 1918

42 R. Muir, 'How Liberalism Would Reform the Mining Industry', *WW*, 19.7.1924.

43 *MG*, 7.8.1929.

44 Interestingly, among other liberal essentials it mentioned a favourable disposition to change as well as a rejection of materialism, but nothing about a commitment to social welfare ('Loyalties', *DN*, 27.9.1924).

45 Samuel Papers, E/7A, Samuel, draft chapter on 'Socialist and other Theories' (*c.* 1927), p. 17.

46 See e.g. 'Theory and Practice: Labour, or Liberal?', *DC*, 15.9.1924.

47 'Hints for Socialists', *Nation*, 21.7.1923.

the *Nation* still paid tribute to the fact that the country was committed to

> the provision of economic security for all, irrespective of individual efficiency or merit. To the older individualism, sustained by the conviction of the necessity of the struggle for life on a basis of merely personal fitness, such a policy spells national suicide. But the common-sense alike of peoples and of statesmen has rightly condemned this *laissez-faire* policy.[48]

But other liberals were having second thoughts. Muir commended industrial councils not for their consultative potential but for the great increase in efficiency they would occasion.[49] Efficiency was not only identified as the prime national interest but participation and a sense of justice had to take second place in the liberal liturgy. Elsewhere there was a noticeable tightening of the reins on the loose, reciprocal nexus of human exchange relationships that the new liberals had tried to outline. They too had been concerned with a quasi-contractual approach to the rights of citizenship conditional upon the fulfilment of social duties. But that reciprocity had both a strong uncalculating element beyond economic considerations and was prepared to offer a less formal and explicit 'service-rendering' definition of duties for which full citizenship would ensue.[50] Muir spelled out the nature of the 'social contract' in crisper concrete language: 'the material basis of Liberty shall be guaranteed to all who make their fair contribution, by work and by thrift, to the common weal.'[51] He later elaborated on this in no uncertain terms, attacking the 'socialist scheme' in which 'the citizen will be sure of his income, without variation, whether he is sick or well, whether he is idle or working, whether he is young and strong or old and past work'. This was a fallacious promise because it undermined the 'motives of effort and thrift to such an extent that the community would soon cease to produce sufficient wealth to maintain all its members'.[52]

These statements exemplify emphatically the direction in which British social policy thinking was moving. An ideological tug-of-war had existed for a generation between radicals intent upon extending and operationally equalizing the notion of citizenship

[48] 'A State Bonus for All', *Nation*, 25.5.1918.

[49] R. Muir, 'The Organisation of Industry. III', *WW*, 5.9.1925.

[50] See Freeden, *The New Liberalism*, pp. 222–4.

[51] Muir, *Liberalism and Industry*, p. 202.

[52] R. Muir, 'Security of Livelihood', *WW*, 9.2.1924.

and channelling national development towards a mutually responsible, socially aware community, and those who considered effort and achievement alone to be passports to full membership in the community. Muir's analysis was an indication that views had crystallized among progressives. The material base of the underperformers, let alone their full citizenship, would be put at risk: a modern echo of the nineteenth-century policy of less eligibility. Further, and more critically, the central targets of social reform—illness, unemployment, and old age—which had already been accepted as disadvantages beyond the scope of individual responsibility, were once again made the excuse for differential treatment. The community was no longer directed to make full compensation for what had in the past been regarded either as social defects or as inescapable crises of the human condition. In retrospect it was the centrist-liberal view that became established policy, though this is not to ignore the safety net, in the form of minimal standards of communal succour, that all progressives now accepted without question. Perhaps it was more hope than evidence that prompted the *Daily News*, commenting on the Mond–Turner Report, to preach the new gospel of a revolution in industrial attitudes: 'The old, dull, ferocious heresy that efficiency is incompatible with humanity goes here altogether by the board . . . on a wide view, efficiency and humanity go hand in hand.'[53]

One interesting offshoot of the renewed focus on efficiency was the debate on rationalization in the late 1920s. The tendency to advocate rationalization in industry was by no means one associated with liberalism, being mainly a scheme for securing greater efficiency in production and reducing manufacturing costs. But it incorporated elements that were particularly attractive to progressive liberals and illuminated some of the complex interrelationships among liberal ideas on industry. One of those ideas, grown nebulous with time, was competition. In the past, advanced liberalism had tried to steer a course between the Scylla of unrestrained competition and the Charybdis of monopolies, both conceived as incarnations of a dangerous particularism. As enthusiasm for the

[53] 'The New Age in Industry', *DN*, 14.3.1929. The Mond–Turner Report was the result of a series of talks in the late 1920s that attempted to promote understanding between employers and trade unions, reflecting the rising ideas on industrial co-operation. (See P. Renshaw, 'The Depression Years 1918–1931' in B. Pimlott and C. Cook (eds.), *Trade Unions in British Politics* [London, 1982], pp. 111–12.)

state soured, the alternative notion of collectivism as the controllable and disinterested will of the community lost its attraction. The *Nation* noted that 'the issue is no longer between competitive enterprise and monopoly, but between privately owned and publicly owned monopoly',[54] and both aspects had liberals worried. Competition had never been ruled out by liberals, as long as it produced excellence rather than destruction. As the *Nation* asserted elsewhere, if liberty was the first and governing idea in private conduct, it was so also in business, and economic liberty hinged upon effective competition. Still, what was clear to all was the emergence of organized labour and capital in a single trade, with the result that 'combination will largely displace competition as the principle of trade activity'. Methods of public control would have to be devised to ensure a balance between the protection of the public and the initiative of these combinations.[55] The modern *mot d'ordre*, claimed the *Nation*'s reviewer, was organization.[56]

Eventually, rationalization became the counter-cry to nationalization among forward-looking businessmen. One of its foremost proponents, L. Urwick, who had also been involved in the Liberal Industrial Inquiry, described rationalization as the general process of reorganization and unification in terms of a whole industry, based on 'the belief that a more rational control of the economic life of the world was possible and desirable'.[57] Although competition was not condemned on principle, it was certainly not self-regulating. Indeed, a significant modification of the business ethic was announced: '. . . there is a purpose in industry and commerce beyond and above the profit of particular business enterprises. Our economic machinery exists not to enrich individuals—that is incidental—but to serve the community.' That end would be achieved by 'eliminating the wastes while at the same time retaining all the advantages inherent in the existing economic system'.[58] For the devotees of the term, rationalization also denoted the application of scientific inventions and the 'mechanism of thought evolved by the physical sciences', including that knowledge gleaned from physiology and psychology known as scientific management.[59] The

[54] 'Liberalism and Nationalization', *Nation*, 25.9.1920.
[55] 'The Post-War Business State', *Nation*, 26.10.1918.
[56] 'The Case for Nationalization', *Nation*, 27.11.1920.
[57] L. Urwick, *The Meaning of Rationalisation* (London, 1929), p. 19.
[58] Ibid., pp. 26, 25.
[59] Ibid., pp. 17–19.

attractions for centrist-liberals were manifold. For one, rationalization suggested continuity with the post-war aims of reconstruction. For another, its etymological kinship with rationality inspired a hope that this latter prime constituent of liberal ideology was finally materializing in the world of trade and industry. The *Nation* observed of those who advocated it: 'Whether their schemes are desirable or not, there is no question of a verbal trick. The idea which rationalization is *intended* to convey is precisely that of the rational organization of industry.' Ultimately, it was compatible with the evolutionary process that advanced liberals had hailed as their version of social Darwinism: 'Surely to enlarge the sphere of conscious direction is of the very essence of progress. It is thus that mankind gradually masters his environment.'[60]

Not all liberals welcomed rationalization. Although the Yellow Book had been seen by some to propose the application of rationalization, of control and co-ordination, to industry, the 1930 LSS session hosted a critical debate on the subject. The view that rationalization would secure greater efficiency and economy and would correlate productive capacity and demand was attacked as ignoring the human factor, disregarding the equal obligations of industry to capital and labour, removing the spur to free competition, and exposing the community to exploitation by virtual monopolies.[61] Liberals were also ideologically split over the merits of size and concentration: was individual welfare to be promoted by dispersing agglomerations of socio-economic power that upset the social balance, or by a harmonious co-ordination of differing interests within large groups? Hobson succinctly identified the tension between the two: 'The desire to maintain private enterprise and initiative in business, while trade after trade suspends internal competition and takes on the character of a cartel, leads to difficulties which there is no serious attempt to overcome.'[62] Hobson, of course, thought he could reconcile those two 'inconsistent and, indeed, contradictory principles' by means of his organic approach which, much as it had influenced liberals of the left, failed to carry weight among those of the centre.[63] Rationalization appealed to

60 'What is Rationalization?', *Nation*, 10.12.1927.

61 W. L. Hichens, 'The Rationalisation of Industry', *FV*, September 1930; A. Watson, 'The Human Factor in Rationalisation', Ibid.; *MG*, 6.8.1930.

62 J. A. Hobson, 'Liberalism and Labour', *MG*, 7.2.1929.

63 See e.g. E. Barker, 'Democracy and Social Justice', *CR*, 137 (1930), in which he discussed Hobson's *Wealth and Life* (1929).

Hobson not only on grounds of waste reduction and efficiency but because it was an 'extension of [a] reasonable policy from the business unit to the trade, conceived as an organic whole'. Furthermore, this new phase of capitalism could be seen as desirable in itself, for it encouraged the perception of the organic interdependence of trades within the economic system.[64] For Hobson this was a step towards communal control. The state itself would have to become an instrument of rationalization, because regulative and representative machinery was needed to secure 'the greatest good of the whole community'—a social utility not to be measured simply as the aggregate of parts. While still falling short of nationalization, Hobson's perception of industry as an integrated organic whole, and his further insistence on a bond between industrial and other social interests, led to a demand for a conscious, community interest-oriented policy not only of maximum production but aimed at 'a distribution which shall satisfy the claims of common justice'.[65] When Hobson therefore summed up that 'Rationalisation thus comes to mean pumping into the conduct of the economic system as an organic whole a sufficient quantity of reason to eliminate the waste of friction and conflict from which it has hitherto been suffering',[66] he was in accord with much of what centrist-liberals claimed, with one crucial exception. What for Hobson was a logical extension of combination into co-ordinated control of all major aspects of communal life, was for the more individualistic liberals of the centre a path on which, for reasons we shall see below, they would not tread.

3. THE RETREAT FROM SOCIAL REFORM

Parallel to the restrictions placed by centrist-liberals on the mingling of social and economic interests, a transformation was occurring with respect to notions of welfare and social reform. The new liberals had broken the conceptual barrier surrounding social reform by interpreting it not solely as an improvement of the material standards of life, but first and foremost as an ethical

[64] J. A. Hobson, 'Liberalism and Labour', *MG*, 5–6.2.1929.

[65] J. A. Hobson, 'The State as an Organ of Rationalisation', *Political Quarterly*, 2 (1931), 32, 34.

[66] Ibid., 45.

reformulation of social relationships. Centrist-liberals referred to ethics tangentially, if at all, and were loath to talk about the need for a fundamental social regeneration. On issues of industrial organization, asserted Muir, 'the Liberal holds that no moral question is involved, and that the question should not be discussed under the terms of abstract doctrinaire theories, but as a problem of practical efficiency and advisability'.[67] The early enthusiasm for social reform had receded as the gravity of the constraints on national expenditure unfolded, and most liberals agreed that 'further large measures of social reform (of the public expenditure type) must be ruled out for the time being'.[68] The major breakthroughs of principle had after all taken place before the war, most further measures proposed being incremental additions to the existing basis, rather than new departures (with the possible exceptions of housing and family allowances).[69] No wonder that a Liberal MP, reporting in the *Nation* on debates on education, unemployment insurance and housing, could only ruminate on how the cause of social reform was declining in the public esteem:

You would think that there would be crowded audiences, fierce interest, suggestions and recommendations pressed with eagerness or anger. Instead you have had a Chamber most of the day scantily filled, in which specialists with incredible earnestness have pressed forward amendments, technical, and altogether incomprehensible to the general, while that general has gazed at them with a wild surmise, and after a time has marched off to tea on the Terrace.[70]

A significant change, however, had occurred within the notion of social reform itself. Witness Muir's transmutation of liberty and welfare—the interlinked guidelines for reformers promoted by the new liberals—into liberty and security. Though naming security as a main concern of conservatism,[71] Muir was not deterred from identifying it as the primal need the liberal state would have to satisfy.[72] To speak of security of life and livelihood was of course consonant with the ideals of the liberal tradition. To refer to liberty

[67] Muir, *Liberalism and Industry*, p. 120.

[68] Editor's reply, *Nation*, 19.11.1927.

[69] On the practical level, progressive liberals were still active on many social reform fronts (for example Masterman and E. D. Simon on insurance and housing respectively) both in and out of Parliament (see e.g. the 1924 session).

[70] MP, '"Social Reform"', *Nation*, 26.7.1924.

[71] Muir, *Politics and Progress*, p. 6.

[72] Muir, *The New Liberalism*, pp. 8–14.

within the law, to a subsistence wage, and to unemployment maintenance was a progressive stance that needed reaffirmation when public policies appeared to threaten them all. But by the 1920s this position was *traditionally* progressive. In elevating security as the quintessential human end, Muir evinced a tendency, typical of his colleagues, to settle for life rather than the good life, and to evade discussions of spiritual, intellectual, and moral values as justifications for life. As he noted, 'almost the whole of the social policy of modern Liberalism' could be reduced to the production of sufficient wealth and its distribution, so as to secure general well-being without weakening incentives to effort. While conceding that this devalued the 'higher and more spiritual ends of social life', he hastened to remind his readers that 'after all, the Social Problem is primarily a material problem'.[73] New liberals would not have dissented; they would, however, have treated this as one facet of wider issues. Holding the view that the vital forces of humanity were simply there to be emancipated, Muir could not have subscribed to the left-liberal belief in an active social philosophy, whose aim it was to design and restructure society according to newly available theories of human nature.[74]

While Muir was undoubtedly concerned with the question of maldistribution, his main preoccupation with social reform was in the mitigation of the various risks that modern workers were running: industrial accidents, sickness, unemployment, unprovided old age, and unprovided widowhood.[75] What was palpably lacking in his writings, and in the utterances of many members of the LSS group, was empathy with the endemic poverty and unequal life chances of a large section of the population. Other liberals on the spectrum from centre to left were more cognizant of what had been, at least since Rowntree's first survey of York, an abiding liberal concern. Massingham's Cassandra-like admonishments through the pages of the *Nation* expressed the opinions of the more radical liberals:

It is needless for *The Nation* to argue, as it has often argued, that with any . . . dissociation from the principle of life and growth in the modern State the function of Liberalism, as its masters conceived it, comes to an end. Let us say at once on the question of Socialism that while we believe it to be

[73] R. Muir, 'Liberalism and the Social Problem', *WW*, 31.1.1925.
[74] See Chapter 7.
[75] R. Muir, 'Security of Livelihood', *WW*, 9.2.1924.

impossible to abolish private property, and that the Liberal Party cannot even try, it is possible to abolish poverty, and the Liberal Party ought to try.[76]

As an external observer, the *New Statesman* criticized a liberalism which regarded itself as a liberating force for not having undertaken the liberation of the people from poverty, preferring middle-class freedom to freedom for all.[77] Nevertheless, Masterman—though moving slowly towards the centre—was able to summon the eloquence Muir lacked in the service of a deeply felt social ideal: 'The Liberal war against poverty . . . is not in the least incompatible with the principle of freedom. For poverty is itself slavery, and those lying in bondage in its prison-house are in effect as much deprived of freedom as of comfort.' Yet Masterman too found it necessary to underpin his plea to eradicate poverty with arguments from the LSS lexicon concerning waste and social unrest.[78] Perhaps this is why Simon, some years later, needed to single out the absence in the Yellow Book of proposals for the equalization of economic opportunity and the abolition of poverty,[79] and another progressive young liberal deplored the lack of 'heart' in LSS discussions, which displayed little evidence of tackling those issues.[80] In contrast to the technical cheese-paring of so many planners for reform, Simon was one of the few who always insisted on the wider view. A self-made expert on housing, he pointed out 'most emphatically the impossibility of solving the housing problem by merely building houses. The whole wage system must, at the same time, be thoroughly overhauled. In truth, the reformer is continually forced to recognise that all the aspects of the social problem are interrelated and mutually dependent'[81]—thus voicing an argument that the organicism of the new liberals had always promoted.

4. CAPITALISM: THE PRODIGAL RETURNS TO THE FOLD

If turn-of-the-century liberalism had reacted strongly against nineteenth-century notions of capitalist production and wealth-amassing

[76] 'A Word to the Liberal Party', *Nation*, 2.12.1922.

[77] 'The Two Liberalisms', *NS*, 31.1.1920.

[78] Masterman, *The New Liberalism*, pp. 30, 45, 46. See also Masterman, '"Labour Unrest"', *DN*, 11.2.1919.

[79] Simon, 'The Liberal Summer School' (1929), 277.

[80] A. Herbert, 'The Liberal Summer School', *CR*, 142 (1932), 327.

[81] E. D. Simon, *Houses for All* (The New Way Series, no. 7, London n.d. [1923]), p. 26.

as glorious ends of human activity, post-war liberals—encouraged no doubt by the large business element among them—appeared not only reconciled to the continuation of the capitalist system, but up to a point supported the values it stood for. They retained and reasserted some aspects of the redistributionary component of liberal policy,[82] especially with regard to inheritance, graduated taxation, and the diffusion of ownership. As long as wealth was given, it was important to switch emphasis to welfare and its integral dependence on redistribution. But in an era when the production of wealth was on the wane, liberals felt no need to maintain a tactful silence on the subject. Experts such as Stamp had convinced most of them that the number of rich people was so small relative to the population that even if all their wealth were to be redistributed equally, it would not suffice to keep the nation in comfort.[83] Accordingly, Dodds could confidently state that 'what Liberals desire is first of all to secure a maximum production of wealth, and next to see the product more equally distributed',[84] though the *Nation* in reviewing his book censured him for giving a 'false precedence to productivity', thus eschewing the complementary nature of productivity and distribution as the basis of social reform.[85] Masterman was more cautious when demanding two changes in the war against poverty: 'a greater effort at Production, a fairer method of Distribution . . . Liberalism believes that it has the secret of both'.[86] But the *Daily Chronicle* virtually threw progressivism to the winds when announcing: 'Labour dogma says that poverty is founded on bad distribution. Research and evidence suggest that it is founded rather on the total insufficiency of existing wealth . . . we must not war against riches so much as against waste. We must enable the community to produce more per head, if its members are to enjoy more.'[87] Centrist-liberals in particular abandoned any false pretences when confronted with the awful alternative of

[82] See e.g. H. Johnson, 'The True Line of Liberal Advance', *FV*, December 1929.

[83] This view was widespread. See 'If All Incomes Were Equal', *DC*, 3.2.1921; R. Muir, 'The Socialist Case Examined', *WW*, 24.1.1925, Supplement, p. 4; J. A. Hobson, 'Liberalism and Labour', *MG*, 9.2.1929; Samuel Papers, E/7A, Samuel, draft chapter on 'The Labour Movement' (*c.*1927), p. 9.

[84] Dodds, *Is Liberalism Dead?*, p. 196.

[85] 'A Champion of New Liberalism', *Nation*, 10.6.1922.

[86] Masterman, *The New Liberalism*, p. 46. By the 1930s, however, as will be seen in note 165 below and in Chapter 8, socialists were also emphasizing the need for more production as essential to welfare.

[87] 'Further Thoughts on the Manchester Speech', *DC*, 1.5.1923.

socialism. Perhaps capitalism was not entirely blameless, conceded its liberal supporters, but the greatness of its achievements was indisputable.[88] J. A. Spender delighted in the first Labour budget reflecting Snowden's 'old Liberal' economics, claiming that it proved that capitalism was capable of doing all that was important in socialism much more efficiently.[89] Left-inclined liberals, on the other hand, offered an early version of Keynes's and the Yellow Book's blurring of the distinctions between individualist capitalism and socialism, and denied the need for an absolute choice between them. Satisfaction was expressed with the existing combination of the two principles, 'an extraordinarily efficient machine for achieving the common ends of society'.[90]

It was again left to Muir to offer the strongest defence of capitalism that progressive liberals were prepared to make. Muir, too, relegated redistribution to a secondary position and located the root of the evil in the insufficient creation of wealth.[91] The distinction he wished to draw was between the capitalism of the past—attached to a 'master class' that directed the processes of industry—and modern capitalism, which had been completely transformed by the growth of limited liability. The latter 'immeasurably widened the range of interest and participation in industrial operations'[92] and created a social structure of far greater utility in channelling human nature to achieve optimum results. This new brand of capitalism offered the thrifty, those paragons of character and capability, full access to the economic hub of society, thus extending the circle of participation, rewarding the most beneficial social traits, supplying the wherewithal for industry, and guaranteeing the type of social justice that centrist-liberals applauded. The traditional individual capitalist entrepreneur, whose concentrated and socially irresponsible power was anathema to liberals of all shades, had made way for a two-tier division into directors and investors. Hence, in Muir's words, 'it is *not* capital which controls industry, it is expert direction—acting, no doubt, in the interests of capital, but acting

88 'Socialism: True and False Issues', *DC*, 21.3.1923.

89 J. A. Spender, 'A Word for "Capitalism"', *WG*, 1.5.1924. Bentley's comment that liberals gloried in capitalism (*The Liberal Mind*, p. 154), overstates the case for most centrist-liberals.

90 'Socialism and Common Sense', *DN*, 20.3.1923.

91 R. Muir, 'Liberalism and the Social Problem', *WW*, 31.1.1925.

92 R. Muir, 'The Reward of Capital', *Nation*, 10.9.1921.

with very great freedom'. Both the captain of industry and the *rentier* were indiscriminately merged into the term 'capitalist'.[93]

These were by no means the only merits of modern capitalism. In effect, it contained an industrial version of the élitist model of democracy close to the centrist-liberals' hearts. The expert control of the directors was nominally subservient to the control of the shareholders, but 'everybody knows that this element of control by the shareholders is in the last degree unreal, except on rare occasions when the company is on the rocks'. Not that present capitalism was perfect. While conceding the conventional argument that 'the claim to profits is rightly proportionate to the amount of the risks run', Muir complained that the state was currently allowing shareholders to enjoy the reward of services they did not perform.[94] A solution to this inequity would be a mild form of profit-sharing, once interest to the shareholder had been discharged; any surplus profits being allocated to create a reserve for the company and then to the state, and perhaps to the workers.[95]

Progressive liberalism thus maintained the idea of a partnership between the different factors in production or, more accurately, the groups and interests that bore upon the vital centres of human action. The *Nation* had seen this 'as the most ambitious, because the most difficult, part of economic reconstruction'—the representation of capital, labour, management, consumers and the state in the government of industry.[96] If one excludes consumers from a direct stake in profits, what meets the eye is Muir's ordering of the financial claims of the other groups: first, the two types of capitalist, then the state, finally the workers. This is an apt indication of the social perspective of the centrist-liberals. At the apex of their pyramid were creative individuals. Further down, the organized community supplied the conditions for the effective functioning of these individuals, at the same time clamping down on some of their excesses. In the usual quasi-contractarian language of modern liberalism, the state deserved a quid pro quo for its co-operation and for conferring legal privileges on the entrepreneur. The persistent reference to the worker as last in the pecking order was precisely the

[93] Ibid.

[94] R. Muir, 'The Reward of Capital', *Nation*, 17.9.1921.

[95] Cf. Chapters 3 and 4.

[96] 'The New Manchesterism', *Nation*, 1.1.1921. Cf. Muir, *Liberalism and Industry*, pp. 53–8.

flaw, if not betrayal, of which liberals of the left accused their ideological colleagues.

Muir simplistically assumed that the pejorative connotations of capitalism would be forgiven and forgotten under its new dual structure. The economists of the *Nation* preferred instead to distinguish sharply between the ideological and non-ideological aspects of capitalism, as it now existed. Thus, 'Capitalism is a *technical* order of industry, under which goods are produced in large masses by elaborate and costly machinery: it is also a *juridical* order, under which the ownership of these instruments and the responsibility for their use are left in the main in private hands.' Inasmuch as capitalism was elevated to the status of a science, and science in the service of progress was unquestioningly accepted by liberal economists as part of their rationalistic ethos, its consequences were inevitable. Despite the human costs of capitalism, it was the sole technique for procuring increasing comfort for increasing numbers.[97] This exuded a strong traditional utilitarian aroma, one in which the greatest happiness of the greatest number could be arrived at through a committed adherence to scientific method. It also constituted a return to the idea of a political economy outside human control and volition, bolstered by the fact that, as Kerr maintained, the rationale of capitalism was 'inherent in a material world in which man's primary concern is to satisfy in ever ampler degree his physical needs'. That given concept of human nature was beyond the sphere of politics, though it could possibly be changed by education or religion.[98] At the same time, the man-made aspect of capitalism—the system of property rights—was open to improvement and modification. Although not responsible for the instability of industry, the existing arrangements of property ownership and administration were recognized as a potentially aggravating factor.[99] As Murray put it, 'Socialist legislation is bound gradually to increase . . . The enormous advantages of capital and of capitalism will be utilized for more public ends.'[100]

[97] 'Hints for Socialists', *Nation*, 21.7.1923.

[98] P. Kerr, 'The State and Industry', *FV*, Sept. 1927. See also section on Keynes later in this chapter.

[99] Though in fact they were themselves subservient to improved scientific perspectives (see section on Keynes later in this chapter). Economic science, even more than biology in the past, was seen to supply ideology with the backing of certainty.

[100] G. Murray, 'Resurgamus', *Nation*, 15.3.1924.

Hobson, as a liberal of the left, was in the meantime fighting his own battle of conscience with capitalism. In his fierce indictment of the forces that brought the world to war in 1914, he identified a culpable alliance between capitalism and militarism. 'This bad system', capitalism, utilized war to further the economic domination necessary to the maintenance of profitability, though protection and economic imperialism were equally valid means to that end.[101] Apart from the unsavoury motives and methods of capitalism, it stood accused of flouting the communal interest so precious to liberals, and in particular to Hobson's organicism, and replacing it with the exclusive interest of a small group of private owners, which appropriated communal wealth. Unfortunately, however, even state socialism could become a new kind of capitalism with cartels under state direction, pursuing a monopolist policy in conjunction with protection. This latter trend absorbed Hobson's interests after the war, for now that the brutality of men's instincts was no longer blatantly exposed through aggressive conflict, 'the logic of capitalism and of imperialism is everywhere impaired in the clearness of its working by concessions made to humanitarianism and sentimentalism'.[102] By the end of the decade, inspired perhaps by the reformed utterances of the Yellow Book, which he applauded, Hobson traced a movement from capitalism to socialism by harnessing, as we have seen, the forces of efficiency and rationalization to the service of the community, under the strict supervision of the democratically controlled state. Both capitalism and socialism had, to his mind, major shortcomings, but the relation between the two was not mutually exclusive.[103] Especially intriguing was Hobson's retention of a system of incentives. His discovery of psychology after the war rekindled his interest in what he regarded as scientific aspects of human nature not accorded sufficient prominence by most socialist ethical theories. Progressive liberals wanted to repress capitalism and profiteering, but—unlike moderate socialists such as Tawney—they fully accepted the inevitability, even desirability, of capital and profits. As Muir argued,

> The profit-making motive may be a sordid one, as Labour idealists assure us. But it works; while the motive of public service (by which, we are told,

[101] Hobson, *Democracy After the War*, pp. 29, ch. 2, and *passim*.

[102] Hobson, *Problems of a New World*, p. 127.

[103] J. A. Hobson, 'Liberalism and Labour', *MG*, 5–9.2.1929. See also J. A. Hobson, *From Capitalism to Socialism* (London, 1932), and Chapters 7 and 9.

it ought to be replaced) is not always incompatible, even among men in whom it is quite genuine, with a certain slipshodness in the handling of funds for which they are not personally liable.[104]

Hobson attempted to steer a middle course between profit and service. It was, he believed, 'a sound public economy to encourage a high output of energy, enterprise, initiative and risk-taking, in . . . non-essential industries by offering high prizes for conspicuous success'. As he had always maintained, it only made sense to socialize vital routine industries, for the creativity of gifted individuals could be best put to use in private enterprise. In order to elicit it, material incentives were necessary. This centrist-liberal position was, however, immediately qualified: 'When it can be shown that fuller recognition, or the essential interest of a successful career, will dispense with the profiteering motive, why then these industries are ripe for social services.' And although 'these abstract terms, state, public, community, must carry very little of pleasant emotion to recommend them to a miner or a railway porter', an interim position could be attained, not 'by substituting a directly social interest and gain for an individual interest and gain, but by giving new expression and validity to the latter', through introducing the personal link between worker and industry that industrial representation and democracy would forge.[105]

5. THE CAPITAL LEVY

An episode of practical policy that illustrates some of the divides discussed above was the proposal made at the end of the war to introduce a capital levy to defray the massive national debt incurred by the hostilities. Initially, the capital levy acquired widespread support among progressive liberals as well as party leaders, who regarded it as 'a perfectly legitimate method of emergency taxation' and 'the best mode of escape from our present distresses'.[106] The *Daily News* declared unequivocally: '. . . the ultimate choice is between some such drastic expedient as the capital levy and the abandonment of social reform. Can there be any question what the progressive choice must be?'[107] The justification for the levy was

[104] Muir, *Politics and Progress*, pp. 171–2.

[105] Hobson, *Incentives in the New Industrial Order*, pp. 92, 113, 116.

[106] See e.g. Dodds, *Is Liberalism Dead?*, p. 101; J. M. Hogge, 'Free Liberalism', *CR*, 116 (1919), 631; Muir, *Liberalism and Industry*, pp. 177, 182.

[107] 'A Progressive Program', *DN*, 21.6.1920.

seen to lie in the considerable war profits made by traders and industrialists. It was thus a communitarian idea, since national activities and needs had been the cause of unjustified individual wealth. At the same time, many technical difficulties remained: valuation of capital, a just and graduated distribution of the levy, and a possible dislocation to industry. Initially, these seemed surmountable. Masterman, one of the strongest advocates of the tax, attempted to allay Muir's fears that it could become a permanent annual levy—which would have endangered the motivation and incentives that liberals were sworn to uphold. Masterman reasoned that the capital levy was not in the nature of a redistributionary tax, like other liberal measures, but went one step further—it was an investment in the nation's future (even, arguably, a form of planning), 'a means of transferring obligation . . . from the young to the old'. However, the levy was not a good thing in itself, but 'the only alternative to bankruptcy or revolution.'[108] Predictably, Hobson adopted a much less ambiguous line. The acquisition of wartime wealth was a surplus that 'is not needed for the maintenance of the owner's adequate standard of consumption'. It was therefore 'reasonable and equitable' that the nation should take a share for urgent national needs when, after all, those capital gains resulted from the special protection afforded by the state during the war.[109] A general levy on capital was admissible as a one-off measure, based on the principle of the ability to pay. Interestingly, Hobson resorted to his usual communal stance in asserting that 'the urgent need of the State is held to override the private rights which each competent citizen has in the vital resources of his personality',[110] an argument he had abandoned when attacking conscription during the war. It was not an urgent need by Hobson's lights to be compulsorily harnessed to the war-chariot of a capitalist-militarist clique, even in the midst of a world conflagration. When weighing the pros and cons of a war-profiteering as against a general levy, Hobson came to the conclusion that although the first may have been the more popular, the second would be the only one capable of denting

[108] *MG*, 26.1.1921. See also C. F. G. Masterman, 'The Radical Programme', *DN*, 21.10.1919. The *Daily Chronicle*, though ('Hybrid Programme for the NLF', 22.1.1921), condemned the appearance of a capital levy item on the NLF programme at the controversial Nottingham special conference (see Chapter 3).

[109] Hobson, *Incentives in the New Industrial Order*, p. 186.

[110] Ibid., p. 193.

the national debt while simultaneously bypassing that wealth whose taxation could impair incentives.[111]

By 1922 a shift had occurred among many liberals, especially the liberal economists. Keynes, who had originally supported the capital levy,[112] now declared it impractical, since the post-war boom was over, though it should still be kept as a reserve policy. Price inflation would make it easier to repay the national debt without a levy, but a levy would be preferable to the damage caused by a depreciation of currency.[113] Muir picked this theme up. A capital levy in 1922 would defy the purpose for which it had been devised—'to defend the livelihood of poor men'—because it would hit industry so hard that trade depression and unemployment would increase.[114] Stamp emerged as one of the most uncompromising opponents of the levy. He saw it as competing for the same monies as death duties and thus costly in its future effect on revenue. The deflationary tendency of the levy would exacerbate the business slump. Beyond that, Stamp anticipated a 'storm of resentment and . . . [a] vertigo of panic', for even if the tax were economically desirable, 'in this matter psychology is at least as powerful as arithmetic, and it is what men *do* think about values and taxes and not what they ought to think, that determines their economic action.'[115]

Thus the capital tax debate amply illustrates the divides within liberal opinion. It was now generally acceptable to posit a national interest that could not be resolved into its component units. It was also agreed by virtually all that excess profits were a legitimate source of national revenue and that many redistributionary policies were both economically sensible and socially just. But it was the received wisdom of all liberals that incentives, too, were part and parcel of a scientific (economic and psychological) as well as a moral approach to social organization. Even Hobson's radical tendencies had to accommodate the empirical evidence offered by those developing sciences of society.[116] Once again, ideology was

[111] Ibid., pp. 190–229. See also J. A. Hobson, *Taxation in the New State* (London, 1919), pp. 225–9 and the approving comments in 'Taxation in the New State', *Saturday Westminster Gazette*, 19.7.1919.

[112] J. M. Keynes, *The Economic Consequences of the Peace* (London, 1919), p. 263.

[113] *MG*, 26.10.1922.

[114] Muir, *Politics and Progress*, p. 125.

[115] Sir J. Stamp, 'Why the Levy Won't Do', *WW*, 1.12.1923.

[116] See Hobson's reservations about the capital levy in a talk he gave to the Rainbow Circle (Rainbow Circle Minutes, British Library of Political and Economic Science, 14.11.1923).

buttressed by science. But rather than simulating the acclamatory alliance the new liberalism had forged between biology and liberal collectivism, the present alliance was one of level-headed resignation, as if economics could not help but introduce a dismal note into social thought. Nevertheless, differences in nuance abounded. Massingham, for example, was positioned at the end of the spectrum that regarded the levy above all as a question of the just spreading of social burdens, and its opponents as those who wanted property to be left alone.[117] Libertarians such as Francis Hirst, former editor of the *Economist*, regarded the capital levy as on a par with socialism and protection.[118] The economists subsumed questions of justice under those of economic utility, while other centrist-liberals flirted with issues of right and obligation but allowed themselves to be swayed by considerations of entrepreneurial motivation and the 'extra-moral' industrial crisis that Britain was experiencing. Here was a clear example of the fragmentation of liberal thought between the poles of left and centre.

6. 'WAS KEYNES A LIBERAL?'

In 1925 Keynes published his well-known essay 'Am I a Liberal?'[119] Apart from his involvement in the peace treaties and the post-war settlement, Keynes's direct writings on politics were few—mainly short articles published throughout the 1920s. In order to reconstruct his political thinking one has to turn to those essays, as well as attempt to glean political attitudes from some of his specific economic proposals. The interest in Keynes as a liberal is obvious; he was one of the organizing spirits of the LSS and a keen Liberal publicist; indeed, as he once stated: 'My own aim is economic reform by the methods of political liberalism.'[120] Beyond that, of course, larger questions loom: what did one of the most influential minds between the wars contribute to the modes of thinking about society? Was Keynes as great a liberal as he was an economist? What was his impact on the liberal tradition? All these questions, which have concerned scholars for the past half-century, are distinguished chiefly

[117] H. W. Massingham, 'The Case for a Labour Government', *FR*, 121 (1924), 124; 'A Word to the Liberal Party', *Nation*, 2.12.1922.

[118] F. W. Hirst, letter to the Editor, *MG*, 11.12.1923.

[119] J. M. Keynes, 'Am I a Liberal?', *Nation*, 8, 15.8.1925.

[120] J. M. Keynes, letter to the Editor, *NS*, 11.8.1934.

for the variety of responses they elicit. Any attempt to elucidate them further must assess Keynes as a liberal within the context of the production and dissemination of liberal ideas that were taking place at the time he was developing his own theories. Within the spectrum of centrist-liberalism, Keynes—and to a lesser extent some of his fellow economists—occupied a curious position. On the one hand he lacked the commitment to and interest in the central tenets of liberalism, and could thus be distinguished even from the less penetrating of the progressive liberal theorists. There was little attempt to develop new theoretical positions that could integrate with the liberal creed, yet modernize it. If efficiency appeared to precede justice in the analyses of the economists, it was not because this reflected a thought-out philosophical view or ideological stand, but because questions of ideology often seemed irrelevant to the quest for scientific truth.[121] Hence the contributions of inter-war economists to liberal theory were marginal or indirect. On the other hand, Keynes and his colleagues were far more innovative, more radical and more likely to attach themselves to ideological positions (though often not consciously) that were compatible with either left-liberalism or centrist-liberalism. This is not to suggest that Keynes's liberalism defies analysis. Rather, it was dispersed over a wider range of the ideological spectrum than was the case with most liberals at the time. The consequence was that one young contemporary of Keynes, A. L. Rowse, could write that Keynes's 'economic views are Socialist in their implication',[122] while a more recent commentary has remarked on his 'conservative, even archaic view of society'.[123] And latterly it has been claimed that Keynes's political outlook was in essentials that of the new liberalism.[124]

I would like to argue that none of these opinions is accurate, although all contain elements that are discernible in Keynes's

[121] For the importance Keynes attached to true beliefs see R. Skidelsky, *John Maynard Keynes: Hopes Betrayed 1883–1920* (London, 1983), pp. 133–47. For Keynes, truth had a moral component, though one not always explicitly acknowledged.

[122] A. L. Rowse, 'Socialism and Mr. Keynes', *NT*, 112 (1932), 329. The *New Statesman*, however, denied Keynes's socialism because he seemed to distinguish conceptually between economic reform and liberty ('Liberty and "Marxism"', 18.8.1934).

[123] E. S. Johnson and H. G. Johnson, *The Shadow of Keynes* (Oxford, 1978), p. 29.

[124] P. Clarke, 'The Politics of Keynesian Economics, 1924–1931', in M. Bentley and J. Stevenson (eds.), *High and Low Politics in Modern Britain* (Oxford, 1983), pp. 175–7.

writings. Nor would it be proper to suggest that Keynes displayed a discrepancy between an advanced economics and a more moderate politics, 'a failure to draw out the necessary political conclusions from the right economic premises'.[125] In fact, there is a marked correspondence between his direct political utterances and the indirect political assumptions behind his economic thinking. 'Am I a Liberal?' reflects many of the perennial themes of Keynes's opus: a strong élitist intellectualism; a rationalist faith in the possibility of depoliticizing economic issues, allowing science to reduce controversy and inconclusiveness; a preoccupation with social stability and a consequent concern with reform in order to facilitate that end. Unlike left-liberals,[126] Keynes adopted the liberal viewpoint that regretted the Labour appeal to class, while at the same time announcing that the class war would find him 'on the side of the educated *bourgeoisie*'.[127] This was certainly not a statement that a radical or a new liberal would have made, and it shows Keynes's disregard for the emotional symbolism of political labels as well as the social preferences that hardly qualified a member of the Bloomsbury set for an active role in bridging the social abyss. Keynes undoubtedly was the moving spirit behind the changing emphasis in the social policy of the *Nation*,[128] when he prematurely declared that

> Civil and Religious Liberty, the Franchise, the Irish Question, Dominion Self-Government, the Power of the House of Lords, steeply graduated Taxation of Incomes and of Fortunes, the lavish use of the Public Revenues for 'Social Reform,' that is to say, Social Insurance for Sickness, Unemployment, and Old Age, Education, Housing and Public Health—all these causes for which the Liberal Party fought are successfully achieved or are obsolete or are the common ground of all parties alike.[129]

Questions of liberty, as we have seen, deeply concerned liberals as a result of their war experience and were again to be a major focus of liberal debate in the 1930s. The problem of taxing inheritances was still being examined by Keynes's colleagues in the LSS. As for social reform, it was optimistic to confuse initial breakthroughs with actual and final attainments, nor were the wider implications

125 Rowse, 'Socialism and Mr. Keynes', 331.
126 See Chapter 6.
127 J. M. Keynes, 'Am I a Liberal?', *Nation*, 8.8.1925.
128 See above, pp. 93–4.
129 J. M. Keynes, 'Am I a Liberal?', *Nation*, 8.8.1925.

of the term—as a cohesive policy of redesigning social relationships—shared by most progressives in the 1920s. The conclusion seems to be not that social reform was a spent force for an advanced liberalism, but that Keynes was uninterested in what he believed was a *passé* area of concerted social activity. Even with respect to the traditional liberal doctrine of free trade, its attractions for Keynes were not ideological and philosophical, but technical and intellectual.

Nevertheless, Keynes was no conservative. He attacked the old individualism of conservative capitalism which was based on enervating hereditarian principles, afraid of innovation, and attached to *laissez-faire*. This theme was taken up in his 'The End of Laissez-Faire', which has erroneously been hailed as signifying a major ideological departure from traditional tenets. Curiously indifferent to or uninformed about the development of liberalism since the 1890s, Keynes was as late in drawing a veil over the myth of *laissez-faire* as were some members of the Labour party when they, for the very different reason of perpetuating a deliberately misleading propaganda point, berated the Liberal party. Hence Keynes was heralding no new truths when he restated the propositions that there was no natural harmony of interests among individuals, that the public interest was in principle distinguishable from enlightened self-interest, and that no social contract could affirm natural property rights.[130] What made Keynes's analysis interesting was that he then proceeded, a couple of pages later, to rehabilitate in part those very propositions he had so peremptorily dismissed. Keynes posited a 'natural line of evolution' which, distinct from the existing unsatisfactory state of social organization, manifested itself in 'the tendency of big enterprise to socialise itself'. As a consequence, the dissociation between capital owners and managers signified the emergence of a new motive for industrial and economic activity side by side with the more conventional one of making profits, namely, furthering 'the general stability and reputation of the institution'.[131] Two central points are discernible here. First, the motive of commitment to an institution recalled the service incentive that many socialists thought more worthy of human nature than selfish materialism. In promoting the idea of a semi-autonomous corporation (Keynes's term for a public concern),

[130] J. M. Keynes, *Essays in Persuasion* (London, 1931), p. 312.
[131] Ibid., pp. 315, 314.

Keynes converged upon a perspective with strong socialist undertones. Not only was his notion of a corporation responsible to Parliament[132] consonant with the liberal assimilation of aspects of guild socialism, but the idea of economic units acting as agents of the social interest had a respectable Hegelian pedigree which fed into the socialist tradition. This connects with the second point. Keynes's applauding of state socialism for engaging 'men's altruistic impulses in the service of society',[133] grafted on to his designation of this process as evolutionary, suggests that in the course of events a new identification of enlightened self-interest (now socially oriented) with the public interest would emerge, and that a new natural, rational harmony between individual and society—mediated by the group—was possible.

In sum, it was possible to detach what Keynes thought was essential to *laissez-faire* from that doctrine and to form with it part of the idea-environment of other incarnations of liberalism. As he explained in 'My Early Beliefs', though he had escaped from Benthamism, he belonged to a group comprising 'the unrepentant heirs and last upholders' of another eighteenth-century 'heresy'—meliorism. It was 'because self-interest was *rational* that the egoistic and altruistic systems were supposed to work out in practice to the same conclusions'.[134] And while Keynes recognized the defects of this attitude, and modified it by engineering what Halévy called an artificial harmony of interests, contrived by a social intelligence, he admitted that he could not shake off his fundamental faith in the overriding rationality of human feeling and behaviour at large. It is, of course, wrong to conclude that such a perspective is more democratic or non-élitist. Quite the reverse can happen, as in the case of Keynes, for when one's expectations of the rationality of others are confounded, the superiority of one's own rationality takes on élitist dimensions. Conversely, for the liberal-democrat, the acceptance of a flawed rationality in human beings often encourages acquiescence in their choices and paths of self-development.

The above discussion also points to a central, if partially implicit, philosophical-cum-scientific assumption that Keynes held in conjunction with new liberals such as Hobhouse and Hobson. The

[132] Cf. J. M. Keynes, 'Am I a Liberal?', *Nation*, 15.8.1925.

[133] Keynes, *Essays in Persuasion*, p. 316.

[134] J. M. Keynes, *The Collected Writings of John Maynard Keynes* (London, 1971–83), vol. x, p. 447.

evolutionary theories adopted by the latter postulated the development of the human mind as a crucial factor in directing the patterns of human behaviour towards an altruistic social awareness. Organization and reason—as aspects of sociability—were being expressed in collective co-ordination, in purposive control.[135] Although direct reference by liberals to biological and evolutionary theories was on the wane after the war (with the notable exception of Hobson), the impact of those theories had been culturally absorbed by most progressives. Keynes was a product of that world, with its firm belief in the inevitability of rationality, buttressed by scientific evidence that appeared to bestow certainty on the interpretations of social philosophers and ideologists. He simply applied those insights to the field he knew best—economics—when proposing measures to facilitate 'the transition from economic anarchy to a regime, which deliberately aims at controlling and directing economic forces in the interests of social justice and social stability',[136] measures which 'would involve Society in exercising directive intelligence through some appropriate organ of action'.[137] This was the language the new liberals had been using for a generation. It was, as Keynes himself put it, 'the true destiny of New Liberalism' to seek solutions to social problems on such lines.[138]

Yet, clearly, Keynes was no new liberal. His appeal to directive intelligence came less out of the egalitarian and communitarian ethos of the new liberalism than from a selective and rather hierarchical endowment of humanity with mental ability. This can explain, among other factors, why Keynes was so interested in 'a considered national policy' on population which would take account not only of its size but of the eugenic question of its 'innate quality'.[139] Beyond that, Keynes had little patience for the holistic, ethical, and to his mind too abstract philosophizing of the left-liberals. Unlike them, he was torn between a desire to depoliticize issues and a hope that a new system of values would come to dominate social transactions. Scientific methodology taught that knowledge progressed

[135] Cf. Freeden, *The New Liberalism*, ch. 3.

[136] J. M. Keynes, 'Am I a Liberal?', *Nation*, 15.8.1925.

[137] Keynes, *Essays in Persuasion*, p. 318.

[138] J. M. Keynes, 'Am I a Liberal?', *Nation*, 15.8.1925.

[139] Keynes, *Essays in Persuasion*, p. 319. Some new liberals were in sympathy with eugenics, but for a variety of reasons, not necessarily élitist. (See M. Freeden, 'Eugenics and Progressive Thought: A Study in Ideological Affinity', *Historical Journal*, 22 [1979], 421–43.)

by inductive experiment, and it made sense for Keynes to settle for what centrist-liberals were inclined to prefer—handling questions on their merits in detail rather than attempting to formulate universal guidelines for action. At the same time he recognized that 'the fiercest contests and the most deeply felt divisions of opinion are likely to be waged in the coming years not round technical questions, where the arguments on either side are mainly economic, but round those which, for want of better words, may be called psychological or, perhaps, moral'.[140] There is, in fact, a better word: ideological. For, as Keynes observed elsewhere, the creative, original intellects who are obsessed with making money rather than reconstituting society 'have . . . no creed whatever. That is why . . . they fall back on the grand substitute motive, the perfect *Ersatz* . . . Money.'[141]

Whether or not economic arguments can be merely technical, Keynes clearly pined for 'a new set of convictions',[142] even if in actual fact they were less radical than those of some of his liberal predecessors.[143] In 'Am I a Liberal?' he listed current questions under the following headings: peace, government, sex, drug, and economic. On peace he advocated pacifism, arbitration, and disarmament. Government called for augmented responsibility concurrent with decentralization and the establishment of the 'intermediate' corporation between individual and state. His divergence from left-liberals was exemplified by the eccentric choice of wording for the third and fourth items, and also by some of their contents.[144] In one sense Keynes was at the forefront of social thinking, for to identify birth-control, marriage laws and the treatment of sexual offences as prime areas of reform was to join an enlightened but unpopular minority. The economic position of women, too, was a subject of interest only to the few liberals, such as Simon, who followed the affairs of organizations like the National Union of

[140] Keynes, *Essays In Persuasion*, p. 319.

[141] Ibid., p. 356. Keynes still found the money motive useful for channelling more dangerous proclivities (J. M. Keynes, *The General Theory of Employment, Interest and Money* [London, 1973], p. 374).

[142] Keynes, *Essays in Persuasion*, p. 322.

[143] And aimed at shoring up the principles of capitalism (cf. W. Parsons, 'Keynes and the Politics of Ideas', *History of Political Thought*, 4 [1983], 367–92).

[144] The divergence was not in the methods attached to furthering these ends. Indeed, less radical liberals were plainly disconcerted by Keynes's suggestion that it was the duty of the state to concern itself with the size of the population (see 'Sex in Politics', *DN*, 3.8.1925).

Societies for Equal Citizenship. Only on family allowances could a reasonable backing be mustered among liberals. But it is instructive to see that Keynes presented those issues as suggesting 'new liberty, emancipation from the most intolerable of tyrannies'.[145] Rather than describe such measures as essential to working-class welfare, or the nourishment of a true feeling of community, or the promotion of human equality, Keynes chose to argue the case from the standpoint of liberty alone, thus stressing the individualist idea-environment of his proposals.[146] Under the heading of drugs Keynes meant drink, an issue which most progressive liberals no longer considered of pressing urgency, and one now divested of an aura of radicalism. He also repudiated his undergraduate views, with their assumption of the organic unity of states of mind.[147] Though new liberal organicism was of a far more concrete nature—one that related to social structure—it was clearly alien to Keynes's thinking.

A few words on the internal balance of Keynes's views are called for. He himself described the 'political problem of mankind' as combining three things: economic efficiency, social justice, and individual liberty.[148] This disingenuous reference to efficiency is revealing, for in according it prime of place and in reducing it to 'technical knowledge' Keynes was turning a blind eye to its notorious emotional and ideological undertones. Was Keynes simply too headstrong to bow to the conventional use of language? Was he oblivious to the way in which political concepts were endowed with partisan content? Or was his resurrection of the term an indication of a reshuffling of components within the structure of liberalism? There is some truth in all these claims. Efficiency for Keynes was not a value to be chosen at the expense of other values, following a deliberate weighing of alternative social ends. Keynes employed efficiency simply because he was trained in the economic tradition that applied scientific principles to human lives as the only rational way to go about organizing a society.[149] However, even on less technical

[145] J. M. Keynes, 'Am I a Liberal?', *Nation*, 15.8.1925.

[146] See R. A. Soloway, *Birth Control and the Population Question in England, 1877–1930* (Chapel Hill, 1982), for a discussion of some of these different idea-environments.

[147] Keynes, *Collected Writings*, vol. x, pp. 436–7.

[148] J. M. Keynes, 'Liberalism and Labour', *Nation*, 20.2.1926.

[149] As Skidelsky (*John Maynard Keynes*, p. 154) has observed, Keynes linked rationality to expediency.

grounds liberals who were economists had for some time contrasted one central economic end—the attainment of welfare—with the notion of waste. And waste, if anything, was inefficient. They could do this without subscribing to the full complement of beliefs encompassed in the 'national efficiency' ethos, which had often veered towards notions of political and imperial aggrandizement and extreme individualistic competitiveness.[150] In a more modest sense, efficiency referred to issues of dignified physical survival and greater productivity for the enhancement of national (and potentially redistributable) wealth. Not surprisingly, when questions of economic organization were at the heart of political controversy in the 1920s, efficiency was a word spoken on almost all lips.

But Keynes's particular de-ideologizing of efficiency held dangers for liberal theory, for in the neutral form he gave it he allowed efficiency to play a greater role than most progressive liberals would have tolerated. Had Keynes's ideas been interpreted within the traditional range of meanings that efficiency denoted, liberalism might have undergone a fundamental change not dissimilar to the Fabian message that H. G. Wells conveyed to the LSS in 1932. On that occasion Wells had called, in an extraordinary outburst, for a disciplined, reinvigorated and militant liberalism, 'for a Liberal Fascisti, for enlightened Nazis . . . a greater Communist Party, a Western response to Russia'.[151] It is a measure of Keynes's relative unimportance as a liberal theorist that his formulations never aroused the sort of criticism from his liberal colleagues to which Wells was subjected.[152] Certainly Keynes's following remark reads as a departure from the ethical predilections of progressive liberalism: '. . . Liberals tend to . . . suspect that in the present blind striving after justice [Labour] may destroy what is at least as important and is the condition of social progress, namely efficiency.'[153] And he went on to argue: 'It is useless to suppose that we can pursue ideal justice regardless of ways and means in the economic world. No one can look at the evolution of society and not admit to himself that some measure of social injustice has often been the necessary condition of social progress. If society had

150 See G. Searle, *The Quest for National Efficiency* (Oxford, 1971).

151 H. G. Wells, *After Democracy* (London, 1932), p. 24.

152 As Rowse remarked: 'When [Keynes] writes on politics he displays little of the characteristic excellences of his technical work' ('Socialism and Mr. Keynes', 336). Wells on the other hand caused a furore with his talk (see below, pp. 331–2; 337).

153 *MG*, 6.1.1927.

always been strictly just, I am not at all sure that we might not still be monkeys in a forest.'[154] He concluded that liberals had to guide the aspirations of the masses for social justice along channels not inconsistent with social efficiency. It is only when one realizes that Keynes's criteria of social analysis were largely economic ('an economically just and efficient society') that his overriding of justice assumes less alarming proportions. Elsewhere he was more explicit, claiming that though capitalism could be made more efficient in attaining economic ends, it was still 'in many ways extremely objectionable'. The problem consequently was 'to work out a social organisation which shall be as efficient as possible without offending our notions of a satisfactory way of life'.[155]

The question then hinges upon Keynes's understanding of social justice. Only disjointed evidence exists. In the main, Keynes was content to assume that its nature was adequately clear. Further elaboration from him was neither necessary nor, in truth, possible. Social justice emanated from 'an unselfish and enthusiastic spirit, which loves the ordinary man'[156]—no more than the fundamental altruistic impulse he referred to on other occasions. Justice also related to limiting the forces of supply and demand 'by reference to what is "fair" and "reasonable" having regard to all the circumstances'.[157] When it came to a more specific discussion of the ethical and organizational expressions of justice, the typical Keynesian disjuncture emerged. On the one hand, he argued that 'many of the greatest economic evils of our time are the fruits of risk, uncertainty and ignorance',[158] thus implying that the absence of intelligence, reason and knowledge—as well as unpredictability—were the barriers to the elimination of social ills. Nowhere was this linked to the concept of society or community that had become so central to the modern liberal treatment of justice. On the other hand, Keynes was explicit in spelling out the third element in his trinity of economic efficiency, social justice, and individual liberty. The latter could only thrive under conditions of 'tolerance, breadth, appreciation of the excellencies of variety, and independence, which prefers, above everything, to give unhindered opportunity to the

[154] J. M. Keynes, 'Liberalism in Industry' in H. L. Nathan and H. Heathcote Williams (eds.), *Liberal Points of View* (London, 1927), p. 206.

[155] Keynes, 'The End of Laissez-Faire' in *Essays in Persuasion*, p. 321.

[156] J. M. Keynes, 'Liberalism and Labour', *Nation*, 20.2.1926.

[157] J. M. Keynes, 'Am I a Liberal?', *Nation*, 15.8.1925.

[158] Keynes, *Essays in Persuasion*, p. 317.

exceptional and to the aspiring'.[159] Obviously, this was a gloss on Keynes's notion of social justice, in which empathy for the ordinary person had to give way to concrete measures for the advancement of the unordinary. Justice did not entail equality of opportunity for all—a principle most progressive liberals supported —but merely freedom of action or development for individuals of superior value or motivation. Finally, Keynes excluded social justice from the main concerns of liberalism, calling it instead 'the best possession of the great party of the Proletariat',[160] whereas efficiency, economic individualism, and liberty required the qualities of the Liberal party. Keynes was not, however, a committed party loyalist and was quite prepared to see a restructuring of party alignments. On the occasion of the publication of Oswald Mosley's 1930 manifesto, with its recommendations for national economic planning, he welcomed the spirit which informed it as an embodiment of a 'peculiar British Socialism, bred out of liberal humanitarianism, big-business psychology, and the tradition of the public service'. The party of Keynes's choice would not necessarily be the Liberal party, now typified in his opinion by Samuel and Snowden. It could equally be that of Lloyd George, Ramsay MacDonald, Bevin, and Mosley[161]—all of whose ideas corresponded to the new spirit of collectivist planning for which Keynes craved. His indiscriminate categorization may have been confused; not so his list of priorities in which social reform was completely overshadowed by economic and social stability tempered with a traditional individualism.[162]

The clear link that exists between Keynes's economics and his direct ideological utterances also contributes to an understanding of his political views. When Keynes promoted efficiency, planning and unequal opportunity as pillars of his social vision, he further demoted the linchpin of the new liberal ideology—redistribution—which for Hobson had integrated ethical and economic arguments, and which, as we have seen, centrist-liberals had played down. By the end of the 1920s, as Winch has observed, 'arguments derived from Hobson merely tended to strengthen the case for old-fashioned redistributive measures'.[163] Whether they were old-

[159] J. M. Keynes, 'Liberalism and Labour', *Nation*, 20.2.1926. [160] Ibid.
[161] J. M. Keynes, 'Sir Oswald Mosley's Manifesto', *Nation*, 13.12.1930.
[162] Keynes, *General Theory*, p. 380.
[163] Winch, *Economics and Policy*, p. 130.

fashioned or not depends upon one's point of view. Henderson, in an article later endorsed by Keynes, definitely thought an important change was under way:

Hitherto the State, for the most part, has stood outside the economic system. It has not concerned itself with questions as to what goods should be produced, or how they should be produced or marketed. It has waited until the work of industry has been done and its proceeds divided up and paid out in money-incomes to individuals, and then it has intervened, by taxation and social expenditure, to modify the resulting distribution of purchasing power, and to prescribe to some extent its use.[164]

The issues involved here were further instances of the growing divisions within liberal thought. The first point was more apparent than real, for the state had been intervening in the economic system for quite a while. In dispute was the timing of the intervention and the sophistication of the economic methods used. The more fundamental issue—fundamental, that is, for political thought rather than for economics—was the eclipse of redistribution by other concerns. Some of these were articulated by the *Nation* in late 1929, when advising the new Labour government on its forthcoming Budget. It maintained that graduated taxation would be counterproductive beyond a certain point, that its yield would decline as evasion practices increased, and that both money and citizens would end up abroad. It concluded that in a world in which external developments, financial and other, restricted the power of the national state, 'the a priori justice or injustice of redistributing wealth by taxing the rich for the benefit of the poor is beside the point'. Britain could not practice an 'insular socialism' that did not conform to international practice. Consequently, there was 'no escape from the conclusion that we should eschew for the time being measures which are primarily redistributive in character, and concentrate our energies for the next few years on the attempt to restore and improve our national productivity'.[165]

[164] [H. D. Henderson], 'The Future of Liberalism and Labour. IV. The Riddle of Socialism', *Nation*, 9.1.1926.

[165] 'The Limits of Insular Socialism', *Nation*, 30.11.1929. Even G. D. H. Cole accepted the logic of the critics of 'insular socialism', though he believed that efficient production could run concurrently with redistribution ('The Limits of Socialism', *NS*, 17.5.1930). See also H. Wright (editor of the *Nation* in 1929), 'How it Looks to a Liberal', *NS*, 17.10.1931, who, while expressing loyalty to ideals of social reform, was prepared to ditch increased unemployment insurance and free trade—as were many progressives in the wake of the 1931 crisis—in order to persuade the international community of Britain's financial stability.

Because redistribution was both an ethical and an economic device, its relegation by Keynes and his colleages into relative insignificance had some important repercussions. As a replacement for the economic function of redistribution—that of countering underconsumption—Keynesian economics were innovative and virtually unchallengeable from a progressive point of view. But a revolutionary change in technique did nothing for the ethical ends to which redistribution was harnessed. At most it can be maintained that Keynes was using new economic theories to further the accepted new liberal aims of enabling everyone to benefit from the fruits of social life, through eliminating or minimizing unemployment—and hence doing away with one of the aspects of non-participation in the social system. Employment could then be construed as a sub-set of the liberal goal of participation. But on a more severe analysis Keynes abandoned, by jettisoning redistribution as a major tool of socio-economic policy, a key component of new liberal ideology and resurrected an older liberal tradition.[166]

Throughout the 1920s Keynes aimed economic messages with political import at his fellow liberals. In the 1923 LSS he described the reform of the standard of value as the most urgent economic question before the country.[167] Behind this lay of course the stabilization of the domestic price level and hence of employment. For Keynes there was a strong connection between economic and social stability. Progressive liberals could embrace his ideas wholeheartedly even if the economic analysis was often above their heads, because he seemed to point to a new scientific way of furthering two articles of liberal faith: the reintegration of the economically dispossessed into the community, and the substitution of state for voluntary decision-making in crucial areas of public policy and interest. The second, though not the first, article of faith was keenly pursued by Keynes himself, as usual preferring to present it as a technical rather than an ideological matter. The area that was 'technically social' involved 'decisions which are made by no one if

[166] Keynes himself acknowledged the 'moderately conservative' implications of his theory (*General Theory*, p. 377), though the following may be overstating the case: '[Keynes's] received view of the world was of a society in which each man had his appointed place, and it was an injustice for him not to be allowed to feed his family and retain his self-respect in fulfilling the task ordained for him.' (Johnson and Johnson, *The Shadow of Keynes*, p. 25).

[167] J. M. Keynes, 'Currency Problems and Unemployment', *Nation*, 11.8.1923.

the State does not make them'.[168] Keynes did not consider what had become the crux of the social-liberal argument: decisions that *were* taken by private individuals and associations, but which were inimical to the social interest, even if 'efficient'. Among the four areas he designated for state activity, two—publicity and the dissemination of information, and planned population control—were measures widely entertained by progressives. The novelty lay in the other two: currency and credit control, and co-ordinated planning of savings and investment.[169] Certainly Keynes's proposals for currency control impressed his liberal audience. The *Manchester Guardian* hailed Keynes's exhortation to implement his ideas as practical policy, which had never been openly enunciated on the political level, and which would inevitably arouse furious opposition among many bankers and loyal Liberals.[170] Here Keynes's contribution to inter-war liberalism is most salient. His high-powered crusade for the adoption of his economic theories had a marked impact on shifting liberal techniques, and thus indirectly some liberal ends, away from the concerns of the new liberalism. Because his relative lack of interest in redistribution, taxation and social reform measures as instruments of economic policy weakened the public appeal of those items, they figured less prominently within the ethical nucleus of the centrist-liberals to whom Keynes was attached through the LSS. In contrast, Keynes's economic credo buttressed other progressive liberal beliefs—especially the notion of the permanence of state interventionism, the balance of functions between the individual and the community, and the retention of a moral approach to politics (though the latter was not always consciously and lucidly held by Keynes himself). Keynes therefore provided a parallel method to that advocated by the new liberals for mastering the problem of rational social self-control—not via redistribution or a reallocation of political power in the industrial system, but via a deft and not directly visible state manipulation of the credit and investment systems. In no sense did he change or renew liberal ideology as such. In liberal terms Keynes was primarily a continuer and secondarily a rejectionist; he was himself no creator. Nevertheless, his role was the important one of forcing some liberals to choose

[168] Keynes, *Essays in Persuasion*, p. 317.
[169] Ibid., pp. 318–19.
[170] 'The Liberal Summer School', *MG*, 10.8.1923.

among the different ideological options that the existing range of liberal beliefs offered.

In political terms, control of the credit system was a disavowal of the individualistic nature of capitalism and a recognition that 'conscious and deliberate control of economic forces for the public good'[171] was the only alternative to chaos. The retention of individualistic private enterprise was incompatible with material well-being, argued Keynes, unless interest rates fell beneath the uniform level—harmful to British prosperity—now imposed by an economic internationalism. And such a fall would only come about through the activity of the state, an activity which would detach the British system from international forces.[172] In other words, private enterprise would only be possible within a system manipulated by the state. Keynes thus reiterated the view, now common among progressives, that economic systems were not self-balancing ones. His paper, the *Nation*, wrote: 'We regard a stable standard of value as a perfectly feasible objective, fraught with immense possibilities of social advancement. There is a sense in which it may be called a Socialist proposal; for it involves the substitution of conscious control with a deliberate aim for a laissez-faire reliance upon gold.'[173] Yet Keynes himself carefully dissociated himself from the socialist implications of such a view. When his ideas were embodied in the Liberal programme, he denied its 'Socialistic character . . . Whether we like it or not, *it is a fact* that the rate of capital development in the transport system, the public utilities and the housing of this country largely depends on the policy of the Treasury and the Government of the day.' The state would, however, determine the volume, not the direction, of actual employment.[174]

Central to his economic argument was a distinction between savings and investment which that earlier underconsumptionist, Hobson, had failed to make. Hobson had assumed that governmental control of redistribution would increase the general propensity to consume, thus augmenting production and avoiding the

[171] *MG*, 6.1.1927. Such control was in effect an alternative to nationalization, too.

[172] J. M. Keynes, 'National Self-Sufficiency. II', *NS*, 15.7.1933.

[173] 'Labour in Office', *Nation*, 26.1.1924. The relevance of 'socialistic' political control to Keynesianism is stressed in R. McKibbin, 'The Economic Policy of the Second Labour Government 1929–1931', *Past and Present*, 68 (1975), 122.

[174] J. M. Keynes and H. D. Henderson, *Can Lloyd George Do It?* (London, 1929), pp. 32–3 (original italics); Keynes, *General Theory*, p. 379.

periodic crises of capitalism. But Hobson made an automatic connection between saving and investing, which Keynes challenged.[175] Because saving could exceed investment, Keynes preferred to introduce state activity not at the point of redistribution—which in his opinion would not guarantee the movement of funds to optimal economic/social uses—but at the point of converting savings into investment. It was through an expansion of credit, and through enticing individuals to place their savings at the disposal of the state (an activity the state could control, among others, by manipulating the terms of borrowing),[176] that the intelligent will of the community would express itself. This may have been healthy economics but it did not consider, as the new liberals had done, the question of how to provide the public in general (as distinct from entrepreneurs) with enough money to attain a reasonable standard of living and to leave something for saving and/or investment. In fact, Keynes's pronouncements on the ethical importance of a reasonable standard of living are confusing. While exhorting the government to regard the regulation of the wages and the gradual betterment of the economic welfare of the workers as 'a first charge on the wealth of the community', this was to be achieved 'by the control of the volume of credit and the general direction of the flow of investment by the big public',[177] as well as through the planning of labour mobility. And this was coupled with the following admonishment: 'It is not only wages and hours of labour which are going to determine the health and prosperity of the labouring classes.'[178] Indeed, given Keynes's aversion to expensive social reforms,[179] which *were* aimed at the health and prosperity of the workers, it is hard to see how the measures he proposed would resolve the problem of the disadvantaged (which extended beyond the question of unemployment), as distinct from the problem of how to attain a healthy and

[175] See the correspondence between Hobson and Keynes in Feb. 1936 (Keynes, *Collected Writings*, vol. xxix, pp. 208–11) and the useful discussion in Clarke, *Liberals and Social Democrats*, pp. 227–34. See also the interesting suggestion in Allett, *New Liberalism: The Political Economy of J. A. Hobson*, p. 129, that the distinction between the two related to different views of capitalist behaviour, active (Hobson) and passive (Keynes).

[176] Winch, *Economics and Policy*, p. 168.

[177] *MG*, 6.1.1927. Curiously, this point was deleted in the revised version of the talk printed in Nathan and Williams (eds.), *Liberal Points of View*, p. 215.

[178] *MG*, 6.1.1927.

[179] *MG*, 26.10.1922. This would not necessarily be true for the final years covered by this study.

stable economy. In the early 1920s especially, when Keynes cited free trade as the principal alternative policy against poverty,[180] he seemed unaware of the core of social malaise and, like other centrist-liberals, prone to pin his hopes for social welfare on economic and industrial welfare, with relative disinterest in the equalization of the conditions of life.

In the 1930s, however, Keynes's terminology underwent some modifications. It is intriguing to find him arguing in favour of state expenditure on the arts[181] and attacking 'a perverted theory of the State' which denies its right to spend on non-economic purposes. True, the object of expenditure was not one of vital and immediate necessity for the masses, not at least before more basic needs had been attended, and it is slightly ominous to see Keynes's article opening with a reference to bread and circuses. Although he appeared to be using advanced progressive language concerning the 'common man' being 'one with, and part of, a community', it was naïve if not patronizingly conservative of him to assume that the feeling of belonging to a community could be attained through 'ephemeral ceremonies, shows and entertainments' more successfully than by any other means.[182] What is revealing, though, is Keynes's unstinching approval of state activity and his allusion to 'our conception of the duty and purpose, the honour and glory of the State'. Nevertheless, this was no product of an adulatory ideology of the state, but simply a common-sense, unemotional utilitarian attitude towards it. Like other progressive liberals, Keynes had consciously discarded Benthamism but not some of the utilitarian considerations that Bentham had bequeathed to future generations. If Keynes thought he was concocting a new political philosophy, he was both flattering himself and misjudging the extent to which he had been 'amongst the first of our generation, perhaps alone among our generation, to escape from the Benthamite tradition'.[183] He matched new liberal optimism about the benevolence, or at least neutrality, of the state, but he opposed a 'highly centralized system of State Socialism', and even when pressing for rationalization and combination in the business world, stressed the need for 'the maximum degree of decentralization which is compatible with large units and regulated

[180] Ibid.

[181] This reflected Keynes's strong personal connections with the arts.

[182] Keynes, 'Art and the State' in *Collected Writings*, vol. xxviii, pp. 341–9.

[183] *Collected Writings*, vol. x, p. 445 (referring to the pre-1914 generation).

competition'.[184] Even his *General Theory*, whatever its long-term influence may have been, did not change the nature of inter-war liberal debate, nor did it more than restate Keynes's political ideology.[185]

Keynes's curious mix of statism and individualism remained all along one of the hallmarks of his thought, emphasizing once again that while his ideological predilections were certainly centrist-liberal, if not slightly to the right of that,[186] he had not been caught up in the progressive liberal backlash against the state which was set in motion by the war. In a conversation with the editor of the *New Statesman*, Kingsley Martin, in 1939, Keynes indicted the out-of-date character of private capitalism while stating categorically: 'In contemporary conditions we need, if we are to enjoy prosperity and profits, so much more central planning than we have at present that the reform of the economic system needs as much urgent attention if we have war as if we avoid it.' Yet private capitalism was not to be ditched entirely, and Keynes was equally insistent on the importance to the individual and value to society of private property: 'From the days when I served on the Liberal Industrial Enquiry, I have felt that there was too little organized sympathy for attempts to make the private property system *work better*.' For Keynes, as for the natural rights theorists, there was 'a profound connection between personal and political liberty and the rights of private property and private enterprise'.[187] In this uncomplicated view he differed significantly from the liberals of the left.[188]

Keynesianism, though liberal-interventionist, was nevertheless a departure from new liberal doctrine, because it lacked an ethos of *participation*, conscious and rational, in the making of public social policy. Redistribution was an ethical end in which all could participate; it was easily recognizable and, no less important,

[184] Keynes, 'Liberalism and Industry' in Nathan and Williams (eds.), pp. 211–12. As Alec Cairncross has written: 'The dominant forces at work making for increased state intervention were not let loose by Keynes nor would they have enjoyed his unqualified approval.' 'Keynes and the Planned Economy' in A. P. Thirlwall (ed.), *Keynes and Laissez-Faire* (London, 1978), p. 55.

[185] See especially *General Theory*, ch. 24.

[186] See the interesting comments by B. Corry, 'Keynes in the History of Economic Thought: Some Reflections', in Thirlwall (ed.), *Keynes and Laissez-Faire*, pp. 3–34.

[187] 'Democracy and Efficiency', *NS*, 28.1.1939.

[188] See Chapter 7. M. Cranston (in 'Keynes: His Political Ideas and their Influence' in Thirlwall, *Keynes and Laissez-Faire*, pp. 111–12) argues that Keynes displayed strong affinities with the Lockean liberal tradition.

understandable to the general public. Keynes's economic policies were a return to minority decision-making: manipulative, incomprehensible to the layman because too technical, and therefore not directly under democratic control. They signalled a reversion to an impersonal, even dehumanized, economics, not manifestly the outcome of rational human action. True, this was no rediscovery of 'natural' laws, because economic behaviour was subtly directed by a select band of individuals. But the human beings affected by those experts were unconscious or, at best, nebulously aware of such influence. Hence, the liberal ideal of rational, immediate, democratic self-control suffered a set-back. Unlike Hobson's conception, it again removed economics from politics—not in the sense that the two were uncoupled, for the obverse was true—but in the no less valuable sense that a direct connection was not popularly *seen* to exist, or understood.[189] The price of Keynesianism was that economics had been, if not depoliticized, de-democratized. *General* control of economics via politics was brought to an end; a new élitism was born, remote in spirit from the inclusivist ethics that had animated the new liberalism.[190]

While Keynes was indisputably the dominant economic figure between the wars, other economists—mostly of his circle—reinforced many of his political opinions. D. H. Robertson, as we have seen, saw stabilization as central to liberal social policy.[191] Henderson hailed the direct entrance of the state into the economic sphere, though on administrative rather than on social-philosophical principle: 'the case is just as strong for insisting that the state should exercise a general supervision and direction of the economic system, as for insisting that every large concern should have a managing director.'[192] Layton preached the liberal virtues of variety and harmony and, like Keynes, denied the sanctity of private property as such while acknowledging its usefulness to the public interest.[193] And, like other liberal economists, Layton lacked a social vision to give a greater sense of purpose to his professional studies. In one

[189] See for example the comment of a participant in the 1929 LSS: 'The average voter has neither the knowledge nor the training to pass judgment on the merits of rival economic plans.' (M. Deas, 'Is There a Liberal Ideal?', *FV*, December 1929.)

[190] Cf. Keynes, *General Theory*, p. xxi.

[191] See above, pp. 94–5.

[192] [H. D. Henderson], 'The Future of Liberalism and Labour. IV. The Riddle of Socialism', *Nation*, 9.1.1926.

[193] *Essays in Liberalism* (London, 1922), pp. 147, 149.

debate, he announced surprisingly that state-initiated publicity to inform the worker what the product of industry was, and how it was divided, was 'easily the most important single thing that the State can do to create industrial peace'.[194] No wonder that left-liberals were inclined to complain that 'liberals were sitting so devotedly at the feet of social plumbers like economists that they were forgetting something of the utility of social architects'.[195]

7. THE IDEOLOGY OF EXPERIMENTATION

The disintegration of a unified progressive liberal tradition, compounded by the failure of the new liberalism to maintain its former pre-eminence, was sustained by an interesting methodological development. As present uncertainties obscured the possibility of forming confident intellectual judgements, the holistic new liberal approach fell into disrepute. True, many liberals still insisted—and rightly so—that 'the various lines of Liberal policy are something a little more intelligent than a mere fortuitous collection of inconsequent items—surely there is in them something of a connected political philosophy'.[196] But the tendency to make political points through universal statements about man and society, propped up by an organic, comprehensive outlook on the community, belonged to a bygone age. Instead, the return to more tentative and piecemeal proposals was dressed up in the methodological finery of experimentation, as the liberal 'faith in the relation between knowledge and control'[197] searched for new bases. Understandably, experimentation was close to the liberal inductive spirit and to the openness and choice espoused by most liberals. As Samuel saw it, this tradition judged ideas, laws and actions by their consequences, combining intuition and reason.[198] Adherence to experimentation legitimated the centrist-liberal eschewal of general theories, and furthered the perennial search of liberal ideology for scientific status.[199] Liberals frequently defined the task of government as discovering 'by experiment the new and ever-changing balance of

[194] Nathan and Williams (eds.), *Liberal Points of View*, p. 117.
[195] *MG*, 28.7.1926. (P. Guedalla at the LSS.)
[196] See F. Milton, 'Is There a Liberal Ideal?', *FV*, February 1930.
[197] J. A. Hobson, 'Liberalism in British Politics', *New Republic*, 3.3.1926.
[198] Samuel, *Belief and Action*, pp. 116–17.
[199] Indeed, science and experience were often mentioned in the same breath. Cf. 'The New Programme. Further Thoughts on the Manchester Speech', *DC*, 1.5.1923.

economies in [the] co-operation between public and private business enterprise'.[200] This was justified in typically liberal terms of harnessing the capacity and adventurousness of individuals to the public benefit. Freedom of initiative and development would be pursued by encouraging experimentation, which in itself exercised those faculties most conducive to individual and social welfare alike. Experimentation was also conducive to another liberal essential: 'an infinite variety of method . . . , in order that, as conditions change, each form of activity may find the mode of organisation best fitted for it'.[201] The pluralist nature of social conditions and development was such 'that no single formula could possibly cover all . . . needs'.[202]

A. G. Gardiner took this position to its extreme in contrasting the 'practical and experimental genius of the race' (for which the liberal tradition was a fitting vehicle) with abstract and doctrinaire socialism.[203] For the *Daily News*, the necessary synthesis of socialism and individualism was a slow, experimental, and fluctuating progress towards social ideals, remote from immutable principle.[204] The concept of experimentation was evidently fodder to one of the central myths of British politics—the a-theoretical and *ad hoc* nature of political thinking. Keynes elaborated upon a variant of this attitude in *My Early Beliefs*, when recalling the discussions he had had with his friends under the guidance of G. E. Moore:

> We entirely repudiated a personal liability on us to obey general rules. We claimed the right to judge every individual case on its merits . . . for the outer world it was our most obvious and dangerous characteristic. We repudiated entirely customary morals, conventions and traditional wisdom. We were, that is to say, in the strict sense of the term, immoralists.[205]

Keynes felt it was too late for him to change that attitude, which clearly had a bearing upon his social philosophy. But he also made the important observation that it entailed an a priori view of what human nature was like. This accurately exposed the error that lay behind the apparently pragmatic and non-principled nature of ex-

[200] 'The Post-War Business State', *Nation*, 26.10.1918.

[201] Muir, *Liberalism and Industry*, p. 119. See also E. Dodds, 'Liberalism, Labour and the Future', *FV*, February 1930.

[202] Muir, *Liberalism and Industry*, p. 71.

[203] A. G. G[ardiner], 'The Spirit of Liberalism', *Nation*, 21.7.1923.

[204] 'Socialism and Common Sense', *DN*, 20.3.1923.

[205] Keynes, *Collected Writings*, vol. x, pp. 446–7.

perimentation. At the very least, it embodied unconsciously held beliefs which in practice restricted experimenting to narrow limits determined, for instance, by some of the closely argued positions on state activity and individual initiative that have been examined in this chapter. At most, the extolling of experimentation itself aspired to become a dogma with which to rule out of court the dogmas of opposing ideologies. Besides, the scientific assumptions behind experimentation did not exclude the belief in the existence of a truth.

The liberal quest for truth had already been established by Mill as a prime liberal end. Keynes's attempt to scientize social knowledge did not remove him from that path. The nature of his theorizing, he asserted, was aimed at 'the elaboration of a new standard system [to replace nineteenth-century economics] which will justify economists in taking their seats besides other scientists'.[206] Significantly, in denying the truth of the old system Keynes did not dismiss the search for truth *per se* as the basis for scientific thinking. It was, however, essential to converge upon the truth by continuously testing existing knowledge. For Keynes, to ignore that was to dogmatize.[207] But to adopt experimentation was not to negate the possibility of guiding principles and theories. Hence, the concept of dogma was contrasted with theoretical or ideational truth as well as with science. Induction and scientific experiments were compatible with adherence to abstract principles. Unawareness of this point has been the most distinctive lacuna of British ideological thinking. Hobson, however, had consistently promoted it, spelling out what Keynes was not quite prepared to admit, namely, that even the distinction between technical and ideological, towards which Keynes was working his way, was often spurious. The theme to which Hobson periodically returned was the 'struggle between the disinterested urge of the social scientist and other motive forces which tend to influence and mould his processes of inquiry, reasoning and formulation'.[208] The subservience of science to moral ends, paramount in liberal economic argument, cast a shadow on the possibility of a fully disinterested science.[209] Rather, 'a pre-existing deposit of social interests, themselves infused with certain ideas of social

[206] Keynes, *Collected Writings*, vol. xxviii, p. 32.
[207] Ibid., p. 33.
[208] J. A. Hobson, *Free-Thought in the Social Sciences* (London, 1926), p. 6.
[209] Ibid., pp. 12–13.

betterment'—better described as 'social art'—preceded social science, but was in turn nourished by it.[210] When C. P. Scott wrote of an experimental and fact-finding liberalism that it 'has no panacea, but it has a method and a purpose', he was adumbrating one of its most important attributes.[211] Liberalism lacked a panacea as a dogmatic and total vision, but this was quite compatible with its remaining a purposeful ideology. That purpose was instructed by ideas of reform and improvement that allowed for freedom of interpretation and flexibility of implementation, as well as being evident in the gradualist and tentative nature of the liberal method itself.

210 Ibid., p. 19.
211 [C. P. Scott], 'A Great Enterprise', *MG*, 15.7.1926.

6

LIBERALISM, SOCIALISM, AND LABOUR

THE previous two chapters have looked at the development of liberal ideology from within, against the socio-economic backdrops that stimulated it. Throughout the 1920s, however, the tortuous relationship with the Labour party constituted the major *political* environment of liberalism. Operating simultaneously on two levels —the ideological and the organizational—liberalism at times seemed engaged in a life-and-death struggle with the other main progressive force in the land. This chapter will examine the way in which liberals interpreted that dual relationship and the effect it had on their self-image. On the seminal questions of a progressive alliance, the attitude to socialism and the role of the trade unions, liberals were subjected to opposing forces and pressures. Inasmuch as Liberalism as a political movement began to be replaced by Labour as the left-of-centre party, some important questions need to be explored. Was the boundary between the Liberal and Labour parties essential and inevitable? What was their degree of compatibility in terms of ideological structure? Did the heritage of liberalism survive the partial demise of the party and, if so, in which form? How central to the bifurcation of liberal thought were its perceptions of its ideological rivals on the left?

From the end of the nineteenth century, the relations between liberalism and socialism/Labourism were more complex than historians and political theorists, let alone official Labour historiographers, have—until very recently—allowed for. Two central problems are immediately prominent. First, the identification of party with ideology has contributed to an over-simplified version of events by which the progressive function of liberalism was taken over by the Labour party. This version postulates the smooth succession of a vigorous and popular Labour movement to an antiquated liberalism which—easy to see for all but liberals themselves —was merging into conservatism in much the same way as Liberal Unionism had done in the 1880s.[1] It is in the nature of the

[1] The parallel error is to collapse Labour party ideology into socialism, an error of which the greater number of liberals in this study—as will be shown—were guilty.

successful creed to interpret events in the most favourable light. As Hobson astutely commented on Labour ideology,

> the aggressive 'myth' has, in its very appeal for strong immediate action, a potency greater than that contained in the defensive 'myth' . . . the fact that socialism is the aggressor, alike in the intellectual and the practical fields of conflict, will lead us to expect in it larger elements of fallacy and fiction.[2]

The second problem becomes that of unravelling the respective influences of the Liberal and Labour movements. Is it true that liberals served the cause of civil and political liberty, leaving Labour to pick up the thread of progressivism for the onward trail to social liberty? Is it accurate to portray Labourite socialism as promoting the economic equality which liberals refused to contemplate? Or is it preferable to entertain an alternative set of propositions, which enable the terms 'liberal', 'labour' and 'socialist' to encompass a loose coalition of meanings and positions, with both overlap and divergence? Does this perspective apply to the policies and programmes that various progressive groups espoused? And is one to evaluate the heritage of a political movement by reference to its leadership, its élites, its routinized and conservative forms, or should one also consider its ideological entrepreneurs and innovators, even when they no longer display allegiance to their parent party?

1. SOCIALISM: EXPLORING SIMILARITIES

In the late nineteenth century, Sir William Harcourt's 'we are all socialists now' had been a byword for liberals. For those just discovering their social conscience, it was an adequate and conveniently imprecise symbol of their desire to attract the goodwill of the masses. For those genuinely concerned about a more egalitarian society, it signified a departure within liberalism that was nevertheless condoned by fundamental liberal principles. For few liberals did the word 'socialism' cause embarrassment. With the rise of the Labour party, firmer lines were drawn. Liberals found no ready answer to the quick and effective co-option of socialism by the Labour party. On the whole they went along with the narrowing down of socialism to a party political concept, successfully

[2] Hobson, *Free-Thought in the Social Sciences*, p. 159.

achieved by the Labour party. Indeed, having shrugged off the term as confusing the lines between the parties, some liberals outdid self-styled socialists in reducing socialism to a range of meanings entirely beyond the orbit of liberalism. Outside the coteries of left-liberals, the issue lay dormant for a while, then regained prominence with the emergence of the Labour party as a central political force in the early 1920s. This was aided by the concurrent switch in organizational loyalties, as many liberals joined the Labour party and were under pressure to state their ideological proclivities unequivocally. Centrist-liberals argued, on the occasion of the formation of the first Labour administration, that 'Socialism is so vague a word, meaning so many different things to different people, and to most declared Socialists little more, it may be suspected, than a worthy if somewhat hazy aspiration, that it is almost silly to pass resolutions about it, as though it were a definite, clear-cut issue.'[3] Its mixture of vagueness and visionary dogma was held to act 'as a drag on useful and practical reforms'.[4] In fact, socialism was only vague when all its meanings were brought together. For its various proponents and opponents, who singled out particular ranges of the concept, it appeared to be clear enough; clearer, at any rate, than in the pre-war period. 'A generation ago', explained the *Nation*:

> those were the days of the development of municipal enterprise, . . . They were the days when the extravagances of a *laissez-faire* philosophy had made natural an undiscriminating reaction, in which it was easy to confuse together under the common label of Socialism the utterly different projects of the State management of industry, and the taxation of wealth to promote measures of social reform like Old Age Pensions.[5]

For left-liberals and moderate socialists alike, the major philosophical issue was whether a 'possible organic connection between Liberalism and Socialism really exist[ed]'.[6] As could be expected, Hobhouse had become greatly concerned with this question when reassessing his general ideological position. In common with many of his colleagues, he had become increasingly detached from the Liberal party. Unlike many of them, however, he did not join the Labour party, even if 'his sympathies continued to lean heavily in

[3] 'Labour in Office' *Nation*, 26.1.1924.

[4] 'What is Socialism?', *WG*, 5.8.1924.

[5] 'The Husks of Socialism', *Nation*, 11.4.1925.

[6] H. Langshaw, *Socialism: and the Historical Function of Liberalism* (London, 1925), p. 8.

that direction'.[7] But he refrained from attaching himself to the restrictive, antagonistic variant of socialism that he detected in the Labour party.

On a higher analytical level, Hobhouse maintained the need for three principles of rational reconstruction. The first was the effectiveness of the social system. A society was workable if it constituted a community, 'if men living under it so far serve one another, providing for personal and common needs, that the community is actually maintained'. This was philosophic conservatism.[8] Philosophic liberalism was the second principle, closely linked to Hobhouse's guiding tenet of harmony. A society of liberated personalities would contribute mutually towards the rational harmony, as well as towards the fulfilment of each personality, that was the ethical end of life.[9] The third principle involved philosophic socialism, which was grounded on the notion of human similarity. It was intended not only to compensate for the unequal distribution of goods, but to resist any 'zero-sum' idea of essentials, for 'A good must be shared. In anything that by its nature can only be the privilege of a few, still more in any gain which by its nature is another's loss, there is a radical disharmony.'[10] Socialism provided the fairness, equalization and common good elements, based on shared human needs and, combined with the elements of community and development, constituted a reformist ideology acceptable to the radical progressive. Here was an example of a pluralistic social philosophy which could cut across organizational allegiances.

Unlike some of his fellow liberals, Hobhouse was not embarrassed by the term socialism. Perhaps, having retreated from active involvement in party politics, he felt more free to allude to it. Some of his practical proposals concerning wealth ownership and the management of industry stood 'at the border line between State Socialism proper and the semi-Socialism or Social Liberalism to which most modern communities seem to be committed'.[11] Hobhouse identified the socialist position with respect to industry as holding that 'the true basis of industry is social service and [that] conditions of labour ought to be not matter of privilege won by hard bargaining but matter of general right secured for strong and

[7] Hobson and Ginsberg, *L. T. Hobhouse*, pp. 66–7. But see below, pp. 219–20.
[8] L. T. Hobhouse, *The Rational Good* (London, 1921), pp. 131–2.
[9] Ibid., p. 108.
[10] Ibid., p. 134.
[11] L. T. Hobhouse, *The Elements of Social Justice* (London, 1922), p. 172.

weak alike by the common sense of the community'. His characteristic conclusion was that 'on this view we get the interesting result that the permanent function of Liberalism is to teach Labour the true principles of Socialism'[12]—a perspective entirely consonant with his more scholarly analyses. One must remember, though, that Hobhouse conceived of socialism in a specific sense, fundamentally ethical and humanitarian. In the early stages of the war he had castigated German social-democracy not only for being revolutionary but for being 'Socialistic and not Liberal in the true sense, for the claim of personality, and its correlative the rule of right, has never focused itself in a political party with the Germans'.[13]

Hobhouse's theoretical integration of the liberal stress on personality and the socialist demand for equal consideration for its development,[14] held together by a communal framework, pointed to a tenable philosophical/ideological stance that few other liberals were prepared to think through. Significantly, this approach was far more in line with that of some socialist thinkers to be discussed in Chapter 8. It is hardly surprising that the unsigned review of Hobhouse's *The Elements of Social Justice* that appeared in the *Nation*, which said of the book: 'It is liberal; but it has learned much from the teachings of Socialism', was in fact written by Laski.[15] Even Hobson eschewed such a general consideration of the interconnections between liberalism and socialism, preferring instead to explore concrete compatibilities. And remaining, as he did, on the level of existing rather than 'true' socialism, Hobson was more prone to criticise its defects than extol its virtues. It is instructive that his membership of the Labour party in no way inhibited Hobson's critical perspective on socialism, which adopted numerous forms. Like Hobhouse, Hobson valued a total, community-related and organic attitude to social bonds and structure. But whereas Hobhouse thought this descriptive of true socialism, Hobson saw socialists, especially working-class ones, wavering between a 'narrow class allegiance' and 'the wider claims of the community as an organic whole',[16] and was loath to use the term as an ideal.

[12] L. T. Hobhouse, *MG*, 21.11.1924.

[13] L. T. Hobhouse, 'The Past and the Future. IX. The Spirit of the West', *MG*, 29.5.1915.

[14] See Hobhouse, *The Elements of Social Justice*, pp. 101–2 and his ch. 7 on equality (p. 117).

[15] [H. J. Laski], 'The Individual and the Common Good', *Nation*, 13.5.1922. See *Holmes–Laski Letters*, 31.12.1921.

[16] Hobson, *Free-Thought in the Social Sciences*, p. 249.

The shortfalls of socialism equated it with a group interest so that, in one sense, there was nothing to choose between it and unattractive 'isms' such as capitalism and imperialism. With respect to core arguments, Hobson was wary of a socialism that disparaged non-economic factors in politics and industry, and offended his organic perception of the interconnections among the various spheres of human thought and activity. He berated socialism for exhibiting 'intellectual defects' such as 'a too simple and superficial psychology and a too rigid and intransigeant presentation of the world of affairs'.[17] Subtlety and totality of perspective would have protected socialism from 'too often miss[ing] its intellectual mark by labelling equally as plunder all payments taken by classes whom it calls capitalists, and in claiming for labour, narrowly confined to the work of wage-earners, "the whole product" of industry'.[18] Thus socialism failed to follow Hobson in his extension of the discipline of economics to all that was vital in human life and consumption; it adopted reductionist positions with regard to human nature; and its economic analysis, too, ignored the complexities of the creation of value and the distribution of remuneration. Moreover, socialists created uniform people and ignored deviations from those standards. '. . . such a socialist society would have to ignore certain important qualitative facts which should rightly play an important part in determining any aggregate of economic welfare.'[19]

Some socialist objectives, Hobson insisted, were unattainable in principle, bearing in mind the familiar argument that preferences for and attitudes to work were unequally distributed.

> Equality of sacrifice, in other words, involving impossible subjective estimates, could not be even approximately secured. Nor could a socialist society, apportioning the product according to some objective standard of need, allow for the wide differences in capacity of enjoyment or utilisation in persons possessing different tastes or trainings.[20]

Hence, if socialism, in its quest for what was common in human needs and nature, thought to solve the arising problems by criteria of measurability, it was making unsustainable assumptions about people. These crypto-Benthamite assumptions were in need of constant refutation. It was not that Hobson ruled out the possibility of

[17] Hobson, *Democracy After the War*, pp. 7, 139.
[18] Ibid., p. 32.
[19] Hobson, *Free-Thought in the Social Sciences*, p. 135.
[20] Ibid., p. 136.

general laws, or a scientific interpretation of human affairs. However, 'A science of ethics cannot pretend to be advancing towards quantitative exactitude.'[21] It should be envisaged as closely based on qualitative and organic considerations, with reference to 'vital', life-sustaining functions.

To concentrate on Hobson's objections to socialism is to paint a one-sided picture, for he was of course well disposed to many of its core ideas. But, unlike Hobhouse, he remained involved in the day-to-day assessment of political ideas and action throughout the 1920s and the socialism he encountered seemed flawed. In his later writings his favourable commendations of socialism are outweighed by doubts. As he saw it, 'the socialistic and other revolutionary movements have wallowed in a moral sentimentalism of their own, in which elements of genuine feeling for the general good are intertwined with greed, envy, pugnacity, and self-assertion, the whole complex being rationalized by loose and hasty reasoning brought to bear on ill-collected and ill-assorted facts'.[22] Nevertheless, even the *New Statesman* had acknowledged socialism to be a multiple doctrine, a source of ideas from which one could select and reject.[23] Hobson proceeded to do just that. He rejected Shaw's undemocratic and élitist socialism, with its 'championship of discipline against liberty'. Most British socialists, Hobson asserted, 'have presented Socialism not as crushing individual liberty, but as enlarging it, by removing the barriers which poverty, ignorance, social and other disabilities place upon personal freedom'.[24] As he had noted approvingly when comparing new trends in socialism with the older state socialist variety:

> . . . The new Socialism . . . severs ownership from operation, and entrusts the latter function to a body mainly constituted of different grades of workers in the industry. This situation would materially affect their feelings towards their work, would introduce a new element of free will into its performance.[25]

Conversely, the state socialist 'claim to "rationalise" the creative activities, to organise freedom itself, and plan inspiration, is of most dubious validity', and the paralysis it would induce was 'a

21 Ibid., p. 223.
22 Ibid., pp. 246–7.
23 'The Position of British Socialism', *NS*, 20.5.1922.
24 J. A. Hobson, 'Must We Scrap Democracy?' *Nation*, 3.12.1927.
25 Hobson, 'The New Industrial Revolution', 642.

final argument for a limited as against a complete socialism', namely, 'the necessity for leaving an unchartered liberty to the play of the creative faculties of the individual in life, whether those faculties fall under the categories of science, art or play'.[26]

What, then, did Hobson's practicable and limited socialism look like? In an important series of articles he published in 1929, Hobson pointed out that the supposedly 'impassable gulf between a Liberalism which takes personal freedom for its aim, and freedom of enterprise in all activities for its method, and a Socialism which subordinates individual will and effort to the direction of some State machine'[27] was chimerical. Hobson was coming over to the view that a convergence was not only possible, but actually taking place, between a modified capitalism and the rationalizing, co-operative tendencies that progressive thinkers wished to encourage.[28] In this movement he identified a theme that had been of concern to liberals for some time. The abandonment of *laissez-faire* in the late nineteenth century had been spurred on by the liberal fear of monopolies, which distorted the market relationship that the *laissez-faire* system itself was supposed to maintain, apart from raising major ethical questions about unequal distribution of wealth and power. The renewed spectre of rationalized cartels prompted further measures of representation and regulation in order to neutralize their potential dangers. As J. M. Hogge, the spokesman of Free Liberalism, had written after the war: 'The problem of the future will not be between theories of Socialism and Individualism, but will concern itself with the question as to whether the individual is to be the helpless victim of capitalist trusts over which he has no control or whether he will become a member of a commonwealth whose Government controls capitalist monopolies.'[29] This was reiterated by Hobson in only slightly different language, when he predicted that a rapid advance towards practicable socialism would follow the realization that the conflict between capital and labour was likely to become secondary to a conflict between weaker and stronger trades.[30]

But practicable socialism entailed much more. The seeds of its new industrial order were already contained in 'Its enlargement of

[26] Hobson, *From Capitalism to Socialism*, pp. 36–7.
[27] J. A. Hobson, 'Liberalism and Labour', *MG*, 5.2.1929.
[28] See Chapter 5.
[29] Hogge, 'Free Liberalism', 634.
[30] J. A. Hobson, 'Liberalism and Labour', *MG*, 6.2.1929.

public services, its policy of higher wages, improved conditions, and participation in self-government by workers, its limitation of profits, its direction of savings into channels of public utility, its development policy, its advocacy of a national economic Government'. These, however, were the policies contained in the Liberal Yellow Book and the subsequent Liberal programme, which Hobson readily admitted was '"Socialistic" both in its general tendency and many of its specific proposals'. Not that Hobson endorsed the Yellow Book in its entirety. He had reservations about its failure to realize 'the social or organic nature of industry', a failure that related to the lack of provision for the social utilization of surplus profits, and about the separatist view of each trade which penalized the workers in the weaker ones.[31] Conversely, he added, 'The "Socialism" of Labour is . . . no more advanced than that of the New Liberals.'[32] Here Hobson recycled his old argument that harnessed a holistic perspective to an economic analysis of the orgins of value and the interdependence of industrial activities. It is of little consequence that he now preferred to call it liberal socialism, whereas Hobhouse's variant on the theme was social liberalism. Both theorists were clearly pointing not to a middle ground, but to a reasoned and consistent progressive position that, ideologically speaking, had become both a theoretical and a practical norm. It was dedicated to a peaceful and experimental transformation of capitalism into a moderate socialism. From this perspective, other progressive or revolutionary theories were deviations which were neither carefully thought out, nor suitable for the British political culture. When Hobson wrote in 1936 about 'A British Socialism',[33] he implied that his was a pivotal position, not a half-way house, and that other progressive rivals could only be regarded as minor ideological variants, distinctly off course as far as the British political spectrum was concerned.

From the liberal vantage point, one of those minor variants was the type of state socialism discussed in Chapter 2. Especial exception was now taken to two of its aspects—centralization and bureaucratization—though the sinister connotations of a regimented Prussian-style state tyranny had faded into oblivion. Hobson underlined the general opposition to those principles of organization:

[31] Ibid., 7.2.1929.
[32] Ibid., 8.2.1929.
[33] J. A. Hobson, 'A British Socialism', *NS*, 25.1.1936; 1.2.1936.

'[Labour's] aversion from a bureaucratic machine, working with rigid uniformity from a single centre, is as intense as that of Liberalism.'[34] This anti-bureaucratic sentiment had a long liberal pedigree.[35] Some liberals took this argument a stage further, linking centralization with 'the ultimate stultification of Parliamentary government', the ominous implication being that the arrival of socialism would destroy the system of representative democracy.[36] More serious was Hobson's conclusion that a balance would have to be struck between syndicalism and bureaucracy in any practicable version of socialism.[37] This was an attractive theoretical synthesis between two principles that had something useful to contribute to social organization, but which could prove dangerous if taken in large doses. In fact, those principles acted as an antidote to each other.

Liberals, however, levelled more criticism against two distinguishing characteristics of the socialism(s) they opposed: class conflict and nationalization. The less thoughtful liberals, or those prone to electioneering slogans, were reluctant to make the intellectual effort to differentiate between Marxist and non-Marxist versions of socialism, though in mitigation it must be noted that the Western interpretation of Marxism at the time exhibited great superficiality. As a Lloyd George Liberal explained:

> The enemy of Liberalism is Socialism. Between these two there can honestly be no truce, for their differences are fundamental . . . We have heard a great territorial magnate exclaim that we are all Socialists now; and the ordinary man of sound instincts thinks that Socialism means merely a little extra sympathy with the lower classes, a keener sense of social justice, a determination that all shall have a fair chance. But that is not Socialism in the continental sense . . . it is the gospel of Karl Marx slightly revised to meet the demands of a new generation. This creed has two main tenets. One is the materialistic conception of history; in other words, the view which regards man as merely the product of his environment, and history as only the record of his efforts to satisfy his bodily needs. The other tenet

[34] J. A. Hobson, 'Liberalism and Labour', *MG*, 8.2.1929.

[35] See Chapters 2 and 3. By 1924 Masterman had slid further into simplistic invective, asserting that 'Socialism is the construction of the insect State' and that it was identical to communism except in the choice of political rather than revolutionary means ('The Three Creeds', *DN*, 15.11.1924).

[36] R. H. Brand, 'Socialism and Social Reform', *Nation*, 11.8.1923. On the question of devolution, see Chapter 9 on democracy.

[37] J. A. Hobson, 'How Much Socialism?', *Nation*, 22.6.1929.

is that of the Class Struggle—an eternal war between the rich and the poor, between those who have and those who have not.[38]

This passage is highly representative of the other polar liberal attitude to socialism, and succinctly spells out those ideological constructions put on socialism that divided it so sharply from liberalism. This liberal perspective–admittedly an extreme one hardly distinguishable from conservative attitudes to socialism–saw redistribution predominantly as a question of supplying physical requirements and of catering to an acquisitive and amoral notion of human nature. It regarded socialism as a particularist ideology, serving the interests of the dispossessed alone. The passage followed the common misinterpretation of conflict as permanent, rather than the ephemeral outcome of changing social conditions, and therefore suggested that the socialist model of human relations was essentially one of adversity and instability. Evidently, if this was socialism, it was incompatible with the assumptions that liberals generally accepted about human rationality, individual character and potential, the possibility of social harmony, and the universality of their creed. What liberals could neither fathom nor tolerate was the introduction of the concept of 'class' into politics, a concept they considered to be contrary to the public interest and to the spirit of rational politics.[39] As Gilbert Murray saw it, 'The Labour Party . . . seems to me to be essentially a class party . . . We [Liberals] act rather less in the direct interest of the oppressed class, rather more in the interest of the whole community.' The fundamental theory of socialism, which Murray believed was state interference, presented to him no difficulty, being so unpopular. What really concerned him was the tendency to appeal constantly to class feeling and to stimulate anti-social passions.[40] In the words of the *Nation*, there was an element in the Labour party for which socialism was simply a slogan in the class war, '"rebels" against the existing social order, who are moved, not by a positive belief in the virtues of public

[38] W. W. Davies, 'The New Liberalism', *Lloyd George Liberal Magazine* (1921), 8–9. For a similar though slightly milder version see E. Dodds, 'Liberalism, Labour and the Future', *FV*, Feb. 1930.

[39] See Chapter 7, Section 6. Bentley (*The Liberal Mind*, pp. 156–7) has rightly drawn attention to the *naïveté* of the liberal rhetoric of classlessness. See also his 'The Liberal Response to Socialism 1918–1929' in K. D. Brown (ed.), *Essays in Anti-Labour History* (London, 1974), pp. 42–73.

[40] G. Murray, 'What Liberalism Stands For', *CR*, 129 (1925), 683, 694.

management, but by a desire to "overthrow" something which they call "capitalism"'.[41]

2. NATIONALIZATION

The debate over nationalization was complex enough to develop a momentum of its own. The number of liberals active and vocal against nationalization *per se* was small. One such group formed a 'Liberal Anti-Nationalization Committee' in 1920, at a time when feeling against the state was still running high. The *Nation* dismissed them peremptorily, as hardly qualifying for serious discussion of the industrial problem.[42] From some new liberal quarters the case for nationalization could still be heard forcefully, but no one was prepared to plead for total nationalization of the means of production, distribution, and exchange. Percy Alden, the social reformer, offered a new liberal programme at the end of the war which linked liberal progressivism with the socialization of industry. This was the 'acid test' of liberalism, as applied to railways, mines, canals, and the means of transport. Quoting from one of the figures in the new liberal pantheon, Arnold Toynbee, Alden attempted to settle the question, how much nationalization? It would be determined in relation to the following two cases:

> The *first* was when the individual finds it impossible to supply for himself something that is a vital need, then the State must supply it for him. The *second*, which may be regarded as its corollary, was that where the individual is in possession of something which in the interest of the community as a whole should belong to the State there the State should step in and claim ownership.[43]

With the post-war bifurcation of progressive liberalism, this was, however, at odds with most liberal opinion in its unmistakable preference for associating the interest of the community with nationalization, rather than with other organizational solutions.

The publication of the report of the Coal Commission in 1919 was a focal point of the nationalization debate immediately after the war. R. H. Tawney, a member of the Commission, enthused about the Sankey recommendations, and saw them as 'a new part-

[41] 'The Husks of Socialism', *Nation*, 11.4.1925.

[42] 'Liberalism and Nationalization', *Nation*, 25.9.1920.

[43] P. Alden, 'A New Liberal Programme: Liberalism and Labour', *CR*, 115 (1919), 396–7, 400.

nership between the consumers, the mine workers, and the State' which would transform the coal industry into a public service, and pointedly excluded employers, capitalists or owners from this summing up.[44] The *Nation*, too, felt sympathetic towards the form of nationalization Sankey had proposed, 'midway between State ownership and administration as conceived by the early Socialists, and the full control by the workers which is the aim of Guild Socialism'.[45] But few liberals were prepared to consider the question from this perspective alone, nor did many display interest in ethical considerations. Serious doubts were entertained about a potentially costly experiment, especially in view of the perceived intransigence of the workers, that could result in a conflict with the state.[46] The behaviour of the striking miners, contended the *Daily Chronicle*, had set public opinion decidedly against the nationalization policy it had supported early in 1919.[47] The *Daily News* attempted to steer a vague course between complete and no nationalization, but offered no guidelines except for a slow and measured policy.[48] Masterman advocated the nationalization of railways and coal mainly because of the financial imperative of cheap transport and energy, though both he and Samuel approached the question as the time-honoured liberal one of restricting the abusive power of monopolies.[49] Limited nationalization was, as Masterman pointed out, a long-standing plank in the Radical programme.[50] When *Coal and Power*, with its Sankey Report-type recommendations, was published in 1924, liberals saw it as a vindication of the formula that sought to balance the public interest and individual rights; they also reaffirmed their belief in the impartial role the state could play in catering to all interests.[51]

[44] R. H. Tawney, 'What the Coal Report Means', *DN*, 25.6.1919.

[45] 'State Mines', *Nation*, 28.6.1919. See also L. T. Hobhouse, 'Psychology in the Coal Pit', *MG*, 6.6.1919.

[46] 'The Nationalisation Question', *WG*, 11.10.1919.

[47] 'Miners' Conference: Federation's Plan to Push Nationalisation', *DC*, 3.9.1919. Cf. also 'Railway Policy: Trade Union Support for Sir E. Geddes', *DC*, 22.1.1921.

[48] 'Parliament's Task', *DN*, 22.10.1919; 'A Progressive Program', *DN*, 21.6.1920.

[49] C. F. G. Masterman, 'Cheap Coal', *DN*, 17.7.1919; H. Samuel, 'The Liberal Outlook. III. What is Wrong with Industry?', *DN*, 1.11.1919; Masterman, *The New Liberalism*, p. 108.

[50] C. F. G. Masterman, 'Mr. Masterman on Mr. Thomas', *Nation*, 11.12.1920.

[51] C. F. G. Masterman, 'Coal and Power: A Great National Program', *DN*, 12.7.1924; 'The Two Tests', *DN*, 12.7.1924.

The question of nationalization was soon taken up by larger issues. Hobson, with his newly tempered attitude to state intervention, and deliberately eschewing, contrary to his past practice, the 'barren controversy about the inherent value of the institution of private property, or the "proper" limits of the State',[52] restricted his recommendations to the socialization of essential monopolistic industries. The recognition of the case for workers' participation now seemed to offer an alternative approach to nationalization altogether. Public control could replace ownership in the left-liberal vocabulary as long as industrial representative government could effectively provide protection to employees.[53] On the other hand, the consumer and his interests—as Hobson had always maintained—had to remain paramount,[54] and nationalization could be the means to ensuring this appeal to the sovereignty of the whole citizen over any of his parts. Liberals felt that consumers ought to be protected against combinations of both capital and labour.[55] Nevertheless, centrist-liberal opinion was adamant that the protection of the consumer did not necessitate any special measures. As McNair put it to the 1923 LSS, 'I do not think this question is vital, as the consumer is well represented in the ultimate body—Parliament.'[56] Nationalization—an extreme case of consumer representation—would therefore be ruled out as a general policy.

The liberal treatment of nationalization assumes special importance in view of the well-established tendency to divide British opinion on the subject into two strong pro-nationalization and anti-nationalization sectors. In effect, the bulk of liberal attitudes to nationalization contained most of the practical and ideological options one could encounter, while avoiding the extremes of total nationalization or strict adherence to a private economy that were found respectively within labour or conservative ranks. As Hobhouse reminded his readers,

> nationalisation is a term covering more than one meaning . . . ownership is one form of nationalisation. Centralised management from Whitehall is another form of nationalisation. Management by all the workers of all grades in an industry subject to State supervision is a third, and there are other variations which might be distinguished.

[52] Hobson, *Incentives in the New Industrial Order*, p. 36.
[53] Ibid., p. 23.
[54] See Chapter 3, and 'The New Industrial Order', *Nation*, 15.4.1922.
[55] 'Constructive Liberalism', *Nation*, 18.11.1922.
[56] 'A National Industrial Assembly', *Nation*, 11.8.1923.

For Hobhouse, the difference between the Labour and Liberal parties on nationalization was one either of emphasis or of ulterior aims. In the latter guise liberals regarded nationalization as outside the realm of politics. Their concept of social change was married to a developmentalism that disregarded terminal points in history, and to an idea of progress that operated on a time-scale firmly linked to the present. They refused to countenance the possibility, much mooted in the Labour party, of two distinct time-scales, short term and long term. The question that remained was that of emphasis. For most liberals nationalization occupied a more marginal position within their ideological structure than it did within socialist creeds. It was at best an element adjacent to their core beliefs, integrated into their methodological preference for experimental incrementalism. Hobhouse expressed this attitude using the usual liberal stock phrases. Nationalization deserved 'further trial. It has to be judged on its merits in each case as a working method of industry.'[57] For Hobhouse personally, as was to be expected, any scheme of nationalization that could further the moulding of a community of interest was to be welcomed.

The minimalist liberal experimental acceptance of nationalization was represented by Samuel. Writing in 1927, and limiting any consideration of the idea to 'a practical means of securing concrete results', he expressed readiness to condone the socialization of some industries, while insisting it was unsafe to assume that the success of the principle so far would extend to its general application. He also drew attention to an argument that deserved careful consideration. Nationalized industries were not self-contained, but functioned within a larger world of competitive enterprise. Was this environment not imperative for their adequate functioning? On the whole, nationalization would bring in its wake a slackening of energy and a lessening of initiative,[58] and would be detrimental to human nature, as centrist-liberals perceived it. By 1934, exuding a taste of sour grapes as the Liberal party fought for survival, Samuel was categorical in his denunciation of nationalization. The experimental extension of the sphere of useful state action was one thing, but the commitment of the Labour party to the nationalization of industry had blocked the formation of a single, effective, united progressive force.[59]

[57] [L. T. Hobhouse], 'Liberalism and Labour', *MG*, 24.1.1920.

[58] Samuel, 'Liberals and the Labour Movement', 414–16.

[59] H. Samuel, 'Liberty, Liberalism and Labour', *CR*, 146 (1934), 265–6.

The stiffening of attitudes among centrist-liberals was unmistakable. Kerr, who had defined himself in 1922 as in tune with a left-central position,[60] was arguing by 1935 against the nationalization of banks, mines, cotton, iron and steel, railways and transport, and the land.[61] The role of the state, as Kerr clarified elsewhere, was limited to running monopolies, laying down conditions to which private enterprise had to conform, and taxing the rich for the benefit of the common good.[62] Kerr's stand on nationalization was in marked contrast to the more relaxed attitude of another centrist-liberal, Seebohm Rowntree, who in 1919 foresaw 'enormous economies' from the nationalization of railways, and was prepared to consider investigation into the advisability of nationalization for canals, mines, insurance, banking, afforestation, electric power and—shades of nonconformism—the drink trade.[63] Rowntree stood by most items on this list in later years[64] and, unlike Kerr, did not see them as a prelude to a takeover of society by the state. However, a centrist-liberal group such as the LSS—with which both Kerr and Rowntree were later associated—had tended to adopt a stance half-way between these two. Even when considering the relatively popular cases of the mines and the railways, the sense of the Grasmere meeting was against their full nationalization.[65]

The liberal economists also came to look upon nationalization with growing disfavour. Henderson ruled out the nationalization of the great mass of industries, mainly because it did nothing to further the cause to which he and Keynes in particular were committed, namely, 'the gradual substitution of the deliberate purpose of the community' for the haphazard operation of the economic system. The economic law of supply and demand could not be overruled by a social reformism to which nationalization was thought to belong, nor was nationalization a good instrument of social reform, understood as redistribution of purchasing power.[66] Stamp welcomed this distinction between nationalization and better distribution,

[60] Lothian Papers, GD/40/17/1030–1, Kerr to Lloyd George (17.1.1922).

[61] Ibid, GD/40/17/312 (20.12.1935).

[62] Lord Lothian, *Liberalism in the Modern World* (London, 1933), pp. 9–10. See also P. Kerr, 'The Fundamental Obstacle to Socialism' in H. L. Nathan and H. Heathcote Williams (eds.), *Liberalism and Some Problems of To-Day* (London, 1929), pp. 105–33.

[63] Rowntree, 'Prospects and Tasks of Social Reconstruction', 3.

[64] See Briggs, *Social Thought and Social Action*, p. 320.

[65] 'A Lake School of Liberals', *Nation*, 8.10.1921.

[66] *MG*, 5.8.1924.

observing that 'there has hitherto been a quite unnecessary confusion and connection between the two policies'.[67] Liberal economists, joining many other progressives, preferred to use the public concern to bypass the question of nationalization entirely. The *Westminster Gazette* approvingly commented on a speech by Keynes at the LSS that the evolution of a type of management which retained 'the best incentives and methods of private ownership combined with a growing amount of public control' rendered the nationalization panacea obsolete.[68] Ultimately, nationalization was portrayed as a gross irrelevancy, which was exploited occasionally as a magic incantation to fly in the face of science. In the *Nation* Henderson continued to attack it as a device designed to increase the political strength of the workers, especially their wage-raising potential, by relying on 'the bottomless purse of the Exchequer'. Liberals, asserted Henderson, ought to be suspicious of an idea that sprang from a dislike of the criterion of profit and loss[69]—thus again demonstrating that in their attempt to 'rescientize' economics, Cambridge liberal economists were removing it from social control—that is, dehumanizing it by the standards of Hobsonian economics.

3. SOCIALISM: UNDERSCORING DIFFERENCES

Not the least cause for the liberal unease with socialism was the curious anti-intellectualism that pervaded the political thinking of so many reformers and commentators. Take Samuel, commenting on Labourite socialism with respect to nationalization: 'It shows the danger of government by philosophers.'[70] It was an odd statement to come from one who dabbled in philosophy himself. The *Nation*, musing on the Fabian Society, felt that its middle-class socialism evoked among working-class socialists a feeling of contempt and suspicion for intellectual support given by the educated and well-to-do. Fabian socialism was not really theory but 'intellectualism, in the sense of erudition, dialectics, and mental superiority'.

[67] Sir J. Stamp, 'Inheritance and Inequality', *Nation*, 20.11.1926.

[68] 'The Nationalisation Fetish', *WG*, 1.8.1927. See also Chapter 4 above and pp. 315–16, 324–5 and 356ff. below.

[69] 'The Future of Liberalism and Labour. IV. The Riddle of Socialism', *Nation*, 9.1.1926.

[70] H. Samuel, 'The Political Outlook', *CR*, 138 (1930), 412.

The result was 'a certain preference for complexity, indirectness, and paradox' which obliged Fabians to adopt a highly critical tone against liberalism as well as 'proletarian' socialism.[71] Muir, on the other hand, located the bane of socialism not in its sophistry but in its adherence to general ideas. Although the average Englishman distrusted them, he was paradoxically dominated by two such false simplifications: socialism and *laissez-faire*.[72]

Granted that the new liberalism was in large part a reaction to the separation of state and economy, the recoiling of centrist-liberals from a socialism that attempted to fuse the two was an abdication of much of the spirit of reforming liberalism. As if to illustrate his aversion to inclusive perspectives, the increasingly polemical Muir submitted the socialist case to a detailed, if myopic, examination in a special nine page supplement to the *Weekly Westminster*. Muir's consumption of socialist ideology reveals intimately the workings of the centrist-liberal mind and, more particularly, those of a mind close to the production and dissemination of the moderately progressive liberal creed. Opposing his arguments to Fred Henderson's *The Case for Socialism*, Muir denied that the equal distribution of the national income would eradicate poverty. Such total redistribution would be insufficient to keep the entire population in comfort, and would erode the foundations of wealth production without which the general welfare would be unattainable.[73] The structure of this presentation was highly traditional in its complete ignorance of Hobsonian–Keynesian underconsumptionist theory and in its assumption that wealth production was the *sine qua non* of welfare, rather than one of its manifestations. True, in the purely technical sense, any distribution had to posit the prior existence of wealth, but the questionable point was the location of wealth production within the small entrepreneurial groups close to centrist-liberal affections, and on whom their concept of human nature was modelled. Although distribution was a core principle of socialism —the operative definition of equality—it was merely adjacent to the liberal core which, on Muir's account, included the reification of personal talent in the form of production. Personality, expressed through production, created the preconditions for general welfare.

[71] *Nation*, 26.8.1916.

[72] Muir, 'The Meaning of Liberalism', 549.

[73] 'The Socialist Case Examined', *WW*, Supplement, 24.1.1925. This had been Stamp's assertion (see above, p. 146).

Muir also objected to the socialist distinction between owners and labourers, while conceding that the general ownership of property was still a long way off. Ownership was already widely diffused, however; it was the directing class that was small in numbers. Thus the justification of class conflict was not borne out by the social structure nor was the liberal model of ownership consonant with the Marxist anticipation of increasing polarization.[74] Most significantly, Muir eschewed the ethical case for socialism, concentrating his rebuttal rather on the vagueness of its economic and organizational aspects. This was indicative of the image of socialism as narrowly materialist and falling short of a workable set of prescriptions for running a society. Principally, Muir took socialism to task for offering no provision for the adequate operation of industry. In a world in which capitalism would still exist, any socialist economy would be unable to offer the attractions of its capitalist rivals. State enterprise would also be bereft of the mechanisms of economic failure which weeded out the unsuccessful. As Muir saw it, the cost to bear was theirs alone, rather than the state accruing 'a rapidly increasing dead weight of permanent debt'.[75] The new liberal notion of a social safety net was inapplicable to industrial life. The gamble that market forces offered the entrepreneur—'the chance of making big gains at the risk of heavy loss'[76]—reduced the degree of rational control that progressive ideologies had been insisting on as the hallmark of a civilized society. Muir would not even countenance the limited communal self-control that liberal economists espoused. This shift towards conservatism[77] was epitomized by his querying whether '*men being what they are*, we shall get the same drive towards the increased production of wealth if the motive of profit is wiped out?'[78] The motive of service was not an option that students of human nature could muster evidence for under existing conditions. Nor was the environmentalism of socialists a realistic substitute for the inborn faculties of great men of business.

Evidently, the centrist-liberals bore no love for the state. This was not merely on grounds of inefficiency, bureaucracy, unoriginality,

74 See Chapter 7, Section 4.

75 'The Socialist Case Examined', *WW*, Supplement, 24.1.1925.

76 Ibid.

77 See below, p. 350.

78 'The Socialist Case Examined', op. cit. My italics. See also R. Muir, 'A Catchword Analysed', *Weekly Westminister Gazette*, 19.5.1923.

and the like, but also because the liberal conception of the state appeared directly opposed to the socialist one. For all shades of progressive liberals, left and centre—the lessons of the war notwithstanding—the state was capable of attaining benevolent neutrality. Socialism would undermine that status, as in the crucial case of labour disputes:

> To-day, when a dispute takes place, it is fought out between employers and employees: the State stands aloof, offers conciliation, and tries to secure that the national interests are damaged as little as possible. Under Socialism, the State would be the employer, and there would be no appeal. The State would be the enemy against whom the workers were fighting. Would that be a healthy state of things?[79]

Obviously not, when the central agency of the rational communal will allied itself with a section of the community against the rest.

Even Muir could not entirely deny socialism membership in the progressive club. Socialists had 'genuine if vague aspirations' with respect to social ills.[80] Indeed, 'if Socialism means no more than the use of the power of the State for the welfare of its members, then all politicians, and certainly all Liberals, have always been Socialists.' The 'essence of Socialism'—its core—was, however, contrasted with liberal ideology because of its disavowal of 'private initiative as the motive power of progress' and because of its 'disbelief in the moral or social justice of private ownership of property'.[81] This dual assertion will be tested later: accepting the first core component, was private initiative incompatible with what socialists were saying? And, conversely, was the second component—private ownership—a rightful contender for 'core status' within liberalism? What was clear was the emergence of a divide between centrist-liberals anxious to see the term 'socialism' delimited and removed from the arena of serious political possibilities, and left-liberals eager to extend their liberalism into those areas where a common language with socialists was being forged. For the first type there was a tactical retreat from the aggressive optimism of the late nineteenth-century, for as Dingle Foot now argued, dismissing Harcourt's famous assertion which had been a motto for all social

[79] 'The Socialist Case Examined', op. cit.

[80] Ibid.

[81] Muir, 'The Meaning of Liberalism', 548; 'The Liberal Idea', *Nation*, 11.8.1923. For similar views, see 'Socialism', *Liberal Magazine*, 31 (May 1923), 267–73.

reformers, 'we are none of us Socialists now . . . the diversity of programmes . . . is the least part of the gulf. There are differences of outlook, temperament, and construction which are at least equally important and certainly far more abiding.'[82] For the second type, there was enough theoretical overlap to carve out a common position and to maintain that 'the Socialism which simply puts the common good over private rights is indistinguishable from Liberalism'.[83]

4. THE QUANDARY OF TRADE-UNIONISM

Given the rise of working-class organizations and the consolidation of the working-class vote after the war, one can understand why so many liberals, in making up their minds about the Labour party, could not dissociate their views on trade-unionism from a general assessment of their neighbours on the left. Interesting parallels are evident in attitudes towards socialism and towards the trade unions, though the two were seen as different components of the Labour party. For Masterman, Labour could be divided into three sections: the first was social reformist; the second preached bureaucratic socialism, syndicalism or Bolshevik egalitarianism; the third was trade-unionist which exploited the desire of working people for representation. 'And there is a war in these members, one with another. The third is at present obviously triumphant . . .'[84]

Keynes echoed that distinction and identified the three elements in the Labour party as the trade-unionists—'once the oppressed, now the tyrants', the communists—'the advocates of the methods of violence and sudden change', and the socialists—'who believe that the economic foundations of modern society are evil, yet might be good'.[85] Comparing these two listings, one is struck by Masterman's own distinction between a party of a class and a party of ideas[86]—the two ill-fitting components of the Labour party since its inception. But this fundamental cleavage was complicated by the existence, side-by-side and within the realm of ideas, of a responsible and an irresponsible radicalism, which cut across trade-union behaviour. From the liberal perspective, these contradictions were

82 Foot, 'The Liberal Summer School', 328.
83 '"Socialism in Our Time"', *MG*, 6.4.1926.
84 C. F. G. Masterman, 'The Case for a Liberal Party', *Nation*, 22.5.1920.
85 J. M. Keynes, 'Liberalism and Labour', *Nation*, 20.2.1926.
86 'Mr. Masterman and the Future of the Party', *MG*, 5.1.1924.

dangerous because irrational. Quite apart from those ideological precepts that liberals had little sympathy with, the political mixture that the Labour party offered seemed destabilizing and socially disharmonious. On the other hand, liberal attitudes towards these components of the Labour party were inconsistent, in particular—as the quotation from Keynes shows—towards the working-class vote liberals had once wooed out of sympathy with the lot of the dispossessed. They now awoke to a political situation in which organized labour posed a political threat to liberalism and compensated for its economic frustrations by a more than adequate flexing of political muscle. Hence, in conjunction with their retreat from the state and from socialism, liberals became wary, if not actively hostile, towards the trade-union movement. C. D. Burns located the problematic contact area between liberals and the trade unions precisely:

> . . . the trade union movement in England shows the characteristic ideals of democratic England, in their strength and in their weakness. For English trade unionism as a political force has all the strength of confidence . . . But trade unionism, like English democracy in general, is deficient first in its incurable separatism and secondly in its lack of appreciation for intelligence and intellectual qualities.[87]

This anti-intellectualism was not merely a distrust of theorizing about politics, but a masked class tension in which working-class contempt for middle-class education and culture vied with middle-class exasperation at working-class reluctance and inability to take a broad view of social issues. As the centrist-liberal empathy with the 'condition of the people' question declined, trade unions symbolized all the dangers of pursuing a radical progressive policy towards the dispossessed, without any of the social advantages that such a policy was held to have had in the past.

During the First World War, the unions had come in for a battering. Their right to strike had been curtailed and trade-union rules and customs, established in order to regulate working conditions, had been swept away. Hobhouse expressed concern that the pledge to restore those rules on the conclusion of peace would be difficult in the light of the changing structure of industry.[88] Samuel feared

[87] C. D. Burns, 'Ideals of Democracy in England', *International Journal of Ethics*, 27 (1916–17), 442.

[88] [L. T. Hobhouse], 'Industrial Self-Government', *MG*, 29.6.1917.

that producers were now endangered and that the mere protection of the worker by industrial laws was insufficient to prevent a return to *laissez-faire*.[89] At that point none foresaw the failure of industrial self-government even in the moderate form of the Whitley Councils. Very soon the liberal tune began to change. Walter Runciman delivered a veiled warning when he wrote: 'Trade Unions have a great future before them, and they have their own policy to advocate, on which I would say nothing, except that the attitude of the old Manchester School towards labour and labour legislation has now no place in Liberal policy. The unions, on the other hand, will surely not fail to recognise their national obligations.'[90] But what were those obligations? Above all, not to pursue a policy of sectionalism, which for liberals attacked the heart of their own creed—the promotion of the public good.

If anything united progressive liberals of all colours against the trade-union movement, it was the perception that the latter was a pressure group attempting to dominate national politics for sectional ends. Their critique can be divided into a political case and a social/ethical case. On the first count, liberals feared that trade unions were introducing an alien dimension into the modern political scene, a blinkered approach to the national interest. The *Nation* feared that the Labour party would be composed almost exclusively of trade-union secretaries, and that such narrowness of outlook and experience would hinder its Parliamentary and governmental effectiveness.[91] The solution seemed to lie in welcoming more non-union candidates into the Labour party—a marked divergence from the late nineteenth-century insistence by radical liberals on the opening of Liberal party doors to trade-union activists. The almost automatic link prevailing between trade unions and the Labour party gave much cause for concern among progressive liberals.[92] Labour had monopolized the market for class feeling and in the liberal view that monopoly, as any other, was just a further instance of the pernicious effects of concentrated power. Masterman

89 Samuel, *The War and Liberty*, pp. 71–2.

90 W. Runciman, 'The Radical Outlook', *CR*, 113 (1918), 5.

91 'The Future of the Labor Party', *Nation*, 15.11.1919. For a similar view, see 'Labourism and Liberalism', *WG*, 9.1.1920.

92 Among non-liberals, Sharp of the *New Statesman*—always friendly to liberalism—agreed that no party should be based on the defence of class interests, though he also argued that liberals should accept trade-unionism in order to prevent the advent of class politics ('Liberals and Trade Unionism', *DN*, 7.11.1925).

saw it as 'a repetition of the tyranny of the old feudal and landlord system. Members of Trade Unions, in meetings where Trades Unions are present in bulk, are sometimes . . . afraid to lift up their hands in support of the Liberal candidates.'[93] Vital democratic processes were themselves under threat, and the advised use of the term tyranny resurrected liberal fears about populist majority rule which Mill had anchored to the British liberal tradition. For middle-class progressive liberals, argued Henderson, 'the traditions and psychology of trade-unionism are foreign'.[94] While it may be a moot point which tradition was 'foreign' and which 'indigenous', there is little question as to which was at the time the more articulate and influential in Westminster, which has always enjoyed relative security from mass opinion. But liberals were not convinced that this would continue to be the case and feared the intrusion of populist illiberal values into national politics. Gilbert Murray thought this to be the outcome of bad political training, through strikes and picketing, with the result that the trade unions could 'possibly become an anti-social influence'. This was the danger of 'progressive blackmail, or the holding of the nation to ransom'—an interesting inversion of Joseph Chamberlain's attack on the rich, forty years earlier, and one that reflected the growing preoccupation of liberals with monopolies of labour rather than of capital.[95]

Concurrent with the above doubts about the political nature of trade-unionism, left liberals expressed great unease at the social and ethical role the unions were playing or, rather, failing to play. The perspicacious Brougham Villiers remarked: 'The new state of things is disturbing to the agitator of the 'nineties, now middle-aged and respectable, who has become used to the conception of peaceful evolution towards an orderly collectivist State.'[96] Once again, Hobhouse presented the most interesting example of the change in views that new liberals were prone to undergo. On ethical grounds Hobhouse felt that union sectionalism fell short of participation in the rational, harmonious and common-good seeking community that liberals should aim for.[97] This once keen fighter

[93] Masterman, *The New Liberalism*, p. 193.

[94] 'The Future of Liberalism and Labour. II. The Limitations of the Labour Party', *Nation*, 26.12.1925.

[95] Murray, 'What Liberalism Stands For', 689–90.

[96] B. Villiers, *England and the New Era* (London, 1920), p. 61.

[97] L. T. H[obhouse], 'The True Socialism', letter to the Editor, *MG*, 21.11.1924.

for the rights of the Labour movement[98] recalled his great rapport with trade-unionism, 'even, he would venture to say, his passionate and enthusiastic sympathy *as long as they stood for the bottom dog*'.[99] Once, indeed, they were a 'natural expression of fellowship among the workers' and 'the necessary instrument for the maintenance of their standard of life . . . Thus to the Liberal of the later [Victorian] generation, trade unionism appealed as a means of class emancipation from economic bondage.' Now, however, the unions were not only 'powerful but dominating'. This remarkable analysis epitomizes some of the problems liberals were having with social power structures. There existed a logical trap, whereby successful support for the underdogs necessitated their organization as a political force. But the emergence of such a force—to compensate for the economic weakness of the group—created a social imbalance virtually as iniquitous as the one the reformer sought to remove. Even in the heyday of the new liberalism, its proponents had wavered between propping up the weak and furthering the good of the whole. In the past, it was believed the two were complementary ends, once a spirit of ethical humanitarianism could be made to prevail. Now it appeared that the facts of social structure and of human motivation differed from what liberal theory had expounded. Society was more a collection of groups than an organic community, and the common interest was elusive and easy to lose sight of. This may have been regrettable, but it could not be ignored. In practice, reformers had to promote the interests of groups they thought were worthy of special treatment, which fundamentally contradicted the liberal ethos that was supposed to transcend group interests. The consequence that confronted Hobhouse, but which he was loath to accept theoretically, was that social reform—applied to redistribution of goods and power—would have to rest content with a balancing of inequalities[100] which would never quite succeed because of the relative weakness of the communal perspective when competing with a sectional one. Hobhouse recognized that trade

See e.g. the response to the National Liberal Enquiry, Questionnaire No. 2, *Liberalism and Trade Unionism*, which challenged the assumption that trade-union members had common interests opposed to those of the rest of the community (*Guardian* Archives, C. P. Scott Papers, 145/3/5).

[98] L. T. Hobhouse, *The Labour Movement* (London, 1893), ch. 2.

[99] L. T. H[obhouse], 'A Liberal's View of Trade Unionism', *MG*, 14.11.1925. My italics.

[100] See G. Sartori, *Democratic Theory* (New York, 1965), pp. 344–5.

unions could not but 'retain their sectional character', but the ethical bonds uniting such a group internally, and externally with the rest of society, were deficient. Hence a political party could not function adequately on a trade-union basis. It should 'consist of men bound together not by identity of material interests, but by community of political views, and it should surely consist not of bodies of men organised for partial interests, but of individuals exercising as citizens their free judgment over the general range of public affairs'.[101]

We shall return to this theme in the next chapters, but it is instructive to note the affinity of views on this issue between Hobhouse and his left-liberal colleague, Hobson. The abhorrence of particularism was even more central to the theoretical edifice in Hobson's mind, with its comprehensive organicism. Trade unions did not figure prominently in any of Hobson's proposals for industrial regulation and social peace, though in the late stages of the war he had assumed that future bargaining on conditions of employment would take place between them and the state.[102] The divide between socialism and trade-unionism was especially regrettable to Hobson because, with all his reservations about the former, it at least offered a general theory of society. But 'most trade unionists are primarily workers and only secondarily citizens'. In thus ignoring the communitarian perspective on social life that socialist organicism provided, 'they remain for the most part local trade individualists'.[103] This particularist trend effectively transposed the despised nineteenth-century system of free market bargaining on to the behaviour of those very groups that had suffered from it most. As Hobhouse elaborated, when commenting upon the abandonment of all but minimum needs to market forces:

> The more powerful Trade Unions are not ill disposed to this view, for it means that they will get what they can, and they think that they can get a good deal. But from the social point of view it is a counsel of despair . . . it leaves each quarrel to be determined by the strength of the parties at the moment, without reference to the permanent needs of industry.[104]

No wonder that the new liberals of yore regarded the political role that trade unions adopted as a betrayal of the sanguine liberal

[101] L. T. H[obhouse], 'A Liberal's View of Trade Unionism', *MG*, 14.11.1925.

[102] Hobson, *Democracy After the War*, p. 177.

[103] J. A. Hobson, 'Liberalism and Labour', *MG*, 8.2.1929.

[104] L. T. Hobhouse, 'The Problem' in Hobson and Ginsberg, *L. T. Hobhouse*, p. 275.

ideals of a solidaric society co-operating for the common good and, in Hobhouse's case, as a challenge to a wholly positive view of human nature.[105]

It was left to a progressive like Delisle Burns to concede that 'a working-class party introduced a new factor in politics', based on a feeling of companionship, an association of workers 'conscious of one another as workers'.[106] This was not the phenomenon of class consciousness, maintained Burns, but the expression of a group mind which based bonds on occupational and local solidarity. Harnessing popular psychological insights to his cause, Burns concluded that any moral reforming of society would have to take certain empirically observable facts into consideration. Among those were two 'general characteristics of the mental outlook of trade-unionism'—a tendency to opposition and a sense of growth, with its accompanying self-assurance. This was often combined with a conservatism that reflected the sharing of common customs and practices.[107] In short, here was an attempt to elevate, in so far as it pertained to trade-unionists, a different concept of human nature, mediated by the influence of the small or medium-sized group. Introverted group behaviour was a 'fact of life' that any ethical solutions to the issues of social organization would have to bear in mind. Once again, new fashions in science were called upon to buttress reason and to underpin ethics. The subordination of the group to the whole through assimilation or self-negation was not a useful basis from which to construct an ethical society.

Burns's views on this subject were nearer to the position of centrist-liberals. Rejecting the left-liberal notion of a communitarian social entity, they regarded society as the product of the interplay of diverse groups which, ideally, would mediate between individual wants and a common good. As Murray observed: 'The fact is that in our highly complex modern societies the welfare of the whole absolutely depends on the good will—and, at times, the self-sacrifice—of a great many groups.'[108] Harmony was attainable through the voluntary activities of groups and not, as Hobson would have preferred, through a rational awareness on the part of

105 Hobhouse, *The Elements of Social Justice*, p. 71.

106 C. D. Burns, *The Philosophy of Labour* (London, 1925), pp. 37–8.

107 Burns, *Industry and Civilisation*, pp. 95–6, 253–4, 255–60. See also below, pp. 239–41.

108 Murray, 'What Liberalism Stands For', 689.

the individual that he constituted a contributory unit, indispensable to the social whole. Understandably, Hobson could not condone the indiscriminate use of the strike weapon, nor were left-liberals favourably inclined to the General Strike of 1926. As Hobson explained:

> Was it possible to acquiesce in a situation where the private quarrel between employers and workers in an essential industry could bring ruin to other industries, threaten social order and imperil public finance, without any right of intervention on the part of any of these vital interests? Never has there been a more striking testimony to the need of some conscious regulation of the industrial system in virtue of its social or organic unity.[109]

The right to private war had to disappear from industry and, as Hobson went on to insist:

> The absolute right to lock-out or strike must go. It is unjust, in that it is an appeal to force in a matter of disputed right: it is inhuman, because of the misery it causes to the workers: it is wasteful of the resources of capital and labour: it is wicked, because it stirs up hate: it is anti-social in that it denies and disrupts the solidarity of the community.[110]

Major Hobsonian themes were here intertwined: the substitution of reason for force (an extension of the argument he had already applied to international relations); the economic case for the optimal utilization of vital resources; and, of course, the damage caused to the social entity. And what of individual liberty? Once again, the pendulum seems to have swung. Before the war, new liberals had approved of compulsion to further unmistakably communal interests. Then, as we have seen, came the reaction to state impingement on individual freedom. Now the disruption caused by trade unions justified legitimate state intervention because the strike reproduced a market situation of the monopolistic use of force that threatened the very status of the state, and re-established the conditions that had given rise to new liberal theorizing against the unsocial behaviour of the 'haves'. Hobson justified compulsory arbitration as a replacement for the right to stop work, because that latter liberty involved risks or injuries to third parties. In other words, the limit of the right to self-defence was the point where its exercise inflicted harm on someone other than the attacker. This was a 'definitely moral test'.[111]

[109] J. A. Hobson, *The Conditions of Industrial Peace* (London, 1927), pp. 29–30.
[110] Ibid., p. 30.
[111] Ibid., p. 120.

As he had often done in the past, Hobson plumped for a strong affirmation of the primacy of social as against individual rights whenever the two clashed. Though present conditions would not allow it, 'In principle a strong case can be made for total prohibition of organised strikes or lock-outs as breaches of public order and injuries to otherwise defenceless third parties. A completely socialist community could not permit any group of workers to refuse to do their share towards the social upkeep.'[112] These clear Rousseauist undertones demonstrate how thin the dividing line between freedom and control could be, and how often new liberals were tempted to cross it, relying not so much on a conservative concern for public order as on a communitarian identification of exclusive areas of social need and interest. Masterman supported railway nationalization for the very reason that strikes against the state ought to be an impossibility. Only if the state assumed responsibility for the welfare of railway workers could it defend its refusal to accede to their demands. And such a refusal was justifiable because declarations of war on the community were contrary to its interests.[113]

Conversely, Phillips showed more sensitivity to the issues at stake. There were cases where 'the respective claims of "individual liberty" and of "social well-being" evaluate themselves differently in relation to one another'. Arguing from premises opposed to Hobson's, Phillips contended that 'The Liberal view has always been that the "right to strike," *i.e.*, the right of the worker to refuse employment under conditions of which he disapproves, *is* a right.' And contrary to Hobson, the right to individual liberty was presumed to override the well-being of the community on the grounds that, as a rule, the damage done was insufficient to tamper with that right. On the question of essential public services, however, the relation between the social interest and individual liberty could be redesigned so as to deny the right to strike.[114]

This discussion may be referred to the general assumptions on the structure of liberalism that have guided this study. On the question of strikes, Hobson seems to have adumbrated a clear-cut relationship between the two political concepts of liberty and social welfare. Had he always maintained that clearly defined relationships

[112] Ibid., p. 21.

[113] Masterman, *The New Liberalism*, p. 110. This was another instance of the liberal underestimation of conflict (see Chapter 7, Section 6).

[114] Phillips, 'Liberalism and Industrial Relations', 736–8.

existed among political concepts, his liberalism may indeed have been suspect. But, although he did tend to proffer a general commitment to a system of social thought, his particular organicist system allowed for sufficient flexibility on a number of other issues to retain a firm foothold in the liberal camp. In fact, liberalism did not eschew systems: Hobhouse, too, was a system builder who incorporated findings from various fields of knowledge in order to formulate a series of reinforcing and interconnected statements about man and society. On the whole, however, liberalism was also characterized by a subscription to tenets and to concepts whose boundaries were deemed to be unmarked in principle. In other words, although there may have existed a general liberal vision of society, its interlocking components were not usually riveted to each other. The social interest did not always override individual liberty, nor individual liberty the social interest. A hallmark of liberalism was its exhibition of methodological flexibility. That flexibility was by no means the *ad hoc* laxity of an untheoretical mind, but the inbuilt consequence of subscribing to the view that political concepts could not be clearly demarcated and that, further, the dimensions which these concepts occupied intersected.

To take an illustration, social well-being and liberty could in theory be mutually exclusive components. Solutions to practical problems could simply be presented as a choice between the one or the other. Liberals rejected that position, insisting that the components of those two concepts, as of any other, were partially shared. Social well-being included some version of liberty; liberty was rendered meaningless without an underlying guarantee of social well-being. But there was no fixed formula that applied to their common ground. If liberty expanded to fill the entire concept of social well-being, no theoretical tension between the two would exist; to be free would be identical to enjoying a state of social well-being. The practical policy this entailed would involve one of two possibilities, depending on one's point of reference. One could argue that social well-being was reduced to individual liberty alone, and the result would be the minimalist state. Or one could argue, conversely, that individual liberty was reduced to social well-being, and the practical consequence could then be a Rousseauist position of 'forcing men to be free'. The flexibility of liberalism was the logical concomitant of an experimental and open commitment to thinking about politics, and the resulting vagueness of conceptual borders allowed for any reasoned combination of conceptual overlap to be proposed. Whether this was woolliness or realism is beside the point. In raising flexibility to a methodological principle, liberalism ruled out any system that offered static points of contact between concepts.[115] In general, an argument based on core liberal concepts such as liberty, rationality, perfectibility and the common good is liberal so long as: 1. No fixed relation between the concepts is postulated; 2. No one concept is reduced to another. These two conditions are, of course, necessary but not sufficient. They tell us something about the structure of liberalism but not about the content of the concepts that liberals believe in, or the range of interpretations within which a concept may be considered to be compatible with liberalism.

It would be incorrect to create the impression that progressive liberals were implacably antagonistic to the aims of trade unions as well as suspicious of their methods. Phillips suggested over-optimistically that liberals regarded unionism as a civilizing, not disruptive, element in the social structure, 'since unionism primarily implies organisation, and where there is organisation there is at least the possibility of order'. For Phillips, unions had a role to play in the evolutionary process that fashioned order out of chaos. Many liberals, apparently, were better disposed towards the unions after the collapse of the General Strike. If that strike signalled, as Phillips put it, the death of political trade-unionism, there now existed an opportunity to reconsider the place of *industrial* trade-unionism in society. Especially deplorable was the 'vindictive attack upon the status and privileges of trade unions which finds expression in the Trade Disputes and Trade Unions Act of 1927'. It was time to assess the constructive possibilities of trade unions in a well-balanced society, based on the principles of the Liberal Yellow Book.[116] Muir had initially regretted the fact that the relations between trade unions and employers' associations were not regulated by law,[117] but when the Conservative government introduced the 1927 Act he thought it a folly and quickly changed his mind: 'the thing to do is to let well alone, to cultivate cordial relations, to explore every possibility of frank and mutually respecting

[115] Cf. Chapter 1, notes 2, 3.

[116] Phillips, 'Liberalism and Industrial Relations', 607–9. See also *MG*, 3.8.1927.

[117] R. Muir, 'The Problem of Industry', *WG*, 3.7.1926.

co-operation', though this was very much the language of conciliating a former enemy. Indeed, the time had come to discard the view which 'thinks of the Trade Union primarily as an organisation of defence and attack, a quasi-military organisation where the primary duty is to wrest from more or less hostile employers more favourable conditions for their members'.[118]

The root problem that trade unions had presented to liberals was the inability of the latter to assimilate those organizations and their methods into an ideology that allotted no room for endemic conflict. In a world of harmony and conciliation, trade unions were a grave embarrassment, an obstacle to the clearly chartered road to progress, a throw-back to primordial passions and to social practices that should have long been abandoned. Contrast this with Muir's vision of a well-tempered trade union, performing its functions for the general social good. These functions included operating as benefit societies and adjusting wages and conditions of labour. Furthermore, trade unions had been

> called in by the State as indispensable and invaluable partners in the administration of schemes of social insurance which are the greatest contribution of our generation to the improvement of social conditions . . . they have established for the working men of England a real partnership in the regulation of the industries in which they are engaged . . .[119]

This liberal vision accorded centrality to the concept of partnership. Even if not quite attaining the 'social organism' perspective of some new liberals, it suggested the existence of a T. H. Green-like common area of rational goods, which the participants in the social system could gravitate towards, given the will to co-operate. Partnership, however, retained the stress on the private and voluntaristic nature of those wills and renounced the central co-ordination of a social will that Hobson sought.[120] As the *Nation* warned in 1918, referring to the right claimed by the state to dispose over the lot of the workers, the latter were improperly portrayed as having 'no individual will; nor even the organized, collective working-class will . . . Here is a claim that cuts both against trade unionism and against the Liberal concept of an individual will, not indeed in independence

[118] Muir, 'Trade Union Reform', 409, 412. See also R. Muir, 'Liberals and the Trade Unions Bill', *FV*, June 1927.

[119] Muir, 'Trade Union Reform', 413.

[120] See Chapter 7, and Hobson, *The Conditions of Industrial Peace*, p. 116.

of the community, but of real validity within it.'[121] This notion of group autonomy modelled on the relationships among separate individuals could, if taken just a bit too far, result in Hobson's trade individualism. For Muir, specifically, the partnership function of the unions was attached to the centrist-liberal ends of the production and dissemination of wealth. The new liberal notions of community and citizenship were conspicuously absent.

5. A QUESTION OF BOUNDARIES

As with the other issues discussed in this chapter, the question of Liberal-Labour relations acts as a sensitive barometer to the emerging nuances within liberalism, a question in which the themes explored above are inextricably interwoven. It has to be reiterated that a perspective that attempts to regard the liberal and 'labour' traditions as mutually exclusive is condemned to irrelevance. In the 1920s, the notion of a Labour party, even if not always its concrete manifestation, overlapped with liberalism on a number of counts. Those who identified the Labour party with socialism, could argue that socialism also had an important theoretical kinship with liberalism. For those who saw the Labour party as the working-class party, competition over the allegiance of that class was still a possibility that liberals could contemplate. And for those hostile to either the socialist or the class/trade-unionist base of the Labour party, a limited co-operation on a partially shared platform was within the realm of practical politics. Although differences still existed, there was no clear boundary. Liberal ideology could reach out beyond the confines of the Liberal party; indeed, not *all* its credal varieties related to the party. This last development, if any, was a landmark in Liberal party history, for it meant that the party no longer functioned as the necessary and sufficient vehicle of liberalism. As Keynes wistfully observed: 'Possibly the Liberal Party cannot serve the State in any better way than by supplying Conservative Governments with Cabinets, and Labour Governments with ideas.'[122] With its monopoly shattered, the political *raison d'être* of the Liberal party was undermined, especially for the left-liberals who now transferred to the Labour party, taking their ideological

121 'What Has Become of Liberalism?', *Nation*, 3.8.1918.

122 J. M. Keynes, 'Liberalism and Labour', *Nation*, 20.2.1926.

baggage with them. One of those was Charles Trevelyan, who spelled out his reasons for doing so: 'The Labour Party is now such an enormously better instrument for fighting economic wrongs and profiteering and monopoly than Liberalism ever was or could be, that it has become waste of time for earnest social reformers to bend the Liberal Party to their ends.' And, to dispel all doubts about an ideological shift, he added: 'I have not been required to shed anything of my Liberalism, except the party name, in joining the Labour Party.' For Trevelyan, democracy, free trade, personal freedom, respect for national liberties, were elements of liberalism integrated into the Labour creed: 'The Labour Party is, indeed, the safest custodian of these cherished Liberal principles.' As for questions of social and economic justice, it was not so much that liberalism was unaware of them, as that it stammered when fearless leadership was needed.[123] With one proviso one can accept Trevelyan's account. It was centrist-liberalism that stammered; left-liberalism, through the political realignments of Trevelyan and his colleagues, executed on the whole a remarkable coup of permeation, one that the Webbs—had their eyes been open—would have regarded with ill-concealed envy.

At the end of the war great confusion reigned among liberals with respect to their attitudes towards the Labour party. At one end of the spectrum moderate liberals such as J.M. Robertson cautioned that 'however much some Labour leaders might personally antagonise the Liberal Party, their party as a whole was consciously a wing—they might say, the vanguard—of the progressive parties in general. Liberalism, so-called, had its "wings" within itself . . .' Robertson was perturbed by the possibility of the Labour party accepting non-working-class elements while still retaining its name. The parting of the ways depended on whether the 'new Labourism' would 'accept politics as the unending series of adjustment of wills . . . that has been thus far carried on by Liberalism'.[124] Labour,

[123] C. P. Trevelyan, introduction to H. Langshaw, *Liberalism and the Historic Basis of Socialism*, pp. vii–viii. Christopher Addison, the only leading Coalition Liberal to join the Labour party, wrote: 'Liberalism is a living thing but there is no hope for the Liberal "party" as it is until insincerity is cleared out.' (Quoted in Kenneth and Jane Morgan, *Portrait of a Progressive: The Political Career of Christopher, Viscount Addison* (Oxford, 1980), p. 162. As the authors observe, Addison was aware that the division within the Liberal party was also 'between rival ideologies and visions of the Liberal ethic' (p. 83).

[124] J. M. Robertson, 'The Idea of a Labour Party', *CR*, 113 (1918), 616, 619.

then, had a claim to a share in political life as a glorified pressure group operating under the aegis of the Liberal party, or in close consultation with it. One step removed from this view, but representing a much larger range of liberal opinion, was the acceptance, however reluctant, of the Labour party as an independent political grouping towards which a variety of liberal feelers could be directed. Even here, political hyperbole must be separated from cooler assessment. Masterman, not immune to the former, expressed in 1920 confidence that liberalism could 'look for an enormous access in strength from that large and uncertain chaos which at present supports the Labour Party'. Although those supporters appeared to combine socialism, class politics and a liberal enthusiasm and energy, they were 'animated by similar ideas, working for the same ends, as the historic Liberal Party'.[125] In practice, Masterman saw two paths of co-operation between the two parties. First, they were united by a common antagonism to the Tories, in Masterman's case exacerbated by his distaste for Lloyd George coalition politics. He identified the issue as 'how Labour and Liberalism combined can obtain a majority over the Coalitionists at an election? The question of what they are to do when they get it is unimportant, so long as they both determine that it should never be got.'[126] Tactical voting may have been the first priority, but the second and major reason for co-operation lay in the acknowledgement of the similarity of the practical programmes of Labour and the new liberals. Like Robertson, Masterman felt a sense of possessive outrage at having been overtaken by the Labour party on items which liberals had initiated, for the Labour party was itself 'a great storehouse of Liberalism'.[127]

Unlike Robertson, however, Masterman did not simply wish away the existing political structure, but believed it feasible to engineer a coalition of convenience and partial ideological overlap on practical measures. Ultimately, he hoped that the common denominator of the removal of injustices would engender support for 'the Social Reform State as against the Socialist State; the State,

[125] Masterman, *The New Liberalism*, p. 25.

[126] C. F. G. Masterman, 'Labor and Liberalism', letter to the Editor, *Nation*, 6.11.1920.

[127] Masterman, *The New Liberalism*, p. 194. Another liberal wrote that 'Labour is in process of appropriating the Liberal tradition' but accepted the inevitability of the Labour party and the need for Liberals to come to terms with it (G. G. Armstrong, 'Liberalism and Labour', *DN*, 17.12.1921).

that is to say, in which all liberty is maintained as is compatible with the abolition of poverty, against the State in which, in the desire to abolish poverty, liberty itself is destroyed'.[128]

The Liberal press, especially the *Manchester Guardian* and the *Nation*, played an important part in directing and channelling the debate over Liberal–Labour relations. C. P. Scott repeatedly urged the two parties that between them held 'the future of democratic progress' to work together, hoping for 'something like a consolidated party of progress'.[129] Under Massingham's editorship, the *Nation* became increasingly supportive of Labour party aims, while remaining a liberal paper. Although moving to the end of the liberal spectrum furthest away from Robertson, it continued to allocate space to a plethora of progressive liberal opinions. In the immediate post-war period, it regarded Labour as an arriving political army which lacked 'the reserve of intellectual resources which the older parties retain, even in the hour of their enfeeblement'. Left-liberals patently hoped they could play the part of mob tamers, and that the Liberal party would become one 'with which Labor could work, and form the Government of the future'.[130] Concurrently, the *Nation* insisted on the advantages of Liberalism—its open-mindedness, its freedom from dogma and from commitment to specific institutions, its practical experience. Again, the case for a coalition seemed overwhelming: '. . . two confessedly imperfect parties, each moving in the same direction, might do worse than help and complement each other. It is unlikely that either Labor or Liberalism, by itself, can govern the country; it is very probable that together they can do it better than the present Ministry.'[131] But it was not to be more than an anti-Lloyd George coalition. The *Nation* asserted in 1921 that fusion between the Labour and Liberal parties was impossible and undesirable. More ominously, with the increased confidence of the Labour party in its policies, 'Anything like detailed agreement on the whole principles and practice of internal social policy seems also impossible.'[132] The

[128] Masterman, *The New Liberalism*, p. 198. See also C. F. G. Masterman, '"Little Tags of Socialism"', *DN*, 24.3.1921. E. David has rightly drawn attention to Masterman's conservative political rhetoric ('The New Liberalism of C. F. G. Masterman, 1873–1927' in Brown, *Essays in Anti-Labour History*, p. 37).

[129] [C. P. Scott], 'Labour and Liberalism', *MG*, 13.2.1920; 'Mr. Asquith and the Liberal Party', *MG*, 11.3.1920.

[130] 'The Future of British Parties', *Nation*, 6.12.1919.

[131] 'Liberalism and Labor', *Nation*, 27.9.1919.

[132] 'Wanted, An Electoral Arrangement', *Nation*, 26.2.1921.

clue to common action, understandably for liberals, was to be in support of proportional representation and an agreement not to fight three-cornered contests. The feeling that progressive forces were reduced to be long-term minorities pitted without hope against a dominant coalition was widespread towards the end of Lloyd George's seemingly entrenched coalition. But liberals with ears close to the Labour ground realized that an attempt to form a united opposition was far from merely being a question of meeting half-way. Many left-liberals would have readily conceded that an ossified Liberal party constituted a major obstacle and that it would not only be against Labour's interests, but against those of truly progressive liberals, to compromise with the Liberal party.

Thinkers openly affiliated with the Labour party certainly expressed this view. Laski suggested that although 'a member of the Labour Party like myself would have no difficulty in finding an active basis of immediate alliance', liberalism was regrettably not always evident in the policy of the Liberal party.[133] And Massingham, more radical than the weekly he edited, called in 1924 upon the Liberal party to support a Labour government. With respect to the central task of organizing and humanizing the capitalist state, he stated bluntly: 'It is enough to say that . . . the Liberal qualification does not suffice.' Not inaccurately, he identified the reverse movement within liberalism when accusing the party of being 'content to look on while social reform was sent to the scrap-heap, as if the reversion to unrestricted capitalism were either a good thing in itself, or were consonant with the social Liberalism of the 'nineties'.[134] As Massingham realized, the tide of liberalism had shifted. The Edwardian new liberals were no longer making the running within institutional Liberalism: the battle-cry of social reform did not inspire its progressives; and many of its radicals were deserting for the Labour camp. Liberalism had 'lost its main source of recruitment, no less than its character as a living and renewable force, a refuge from Tory Philistinism, and a centre of enthusiasm and moral energy'.[135] It was a similar sense of passion spent that moved even a loyal liberal such as Gilbert Murray to ruminate:

133 H. J. Laski, 'A Radical Revival', *Nation*, 21.5.1921.
134 Massingham, 'The Case for a Labour Government', 119, 121.
135 Ibid., 121.

> Liberalism has lost not only its Vicars of Bray—who will duly return when fortunes change—but, what is sadder, almost all of those whom I would respectfully describe as its Hatters and March Hares, its wild enthusiasts and born rebels . . . This whole type of thought, or rather of emotion, has gone from Liberalism and found refuge in Labour, and to this extent Liberalism has been left a sort of moderate or central party.[136]

Unlike Massingham, Murray did not regard this as a strong enough inducement for embracing the tenets of the Labour party, with its anti-property and anti-capitalist stance and its unequivocal backing for trade unions. But while reiterating the appeal of liberalism to reason, Murray was caught in the paradoxical position of recommending Labour for its 'emotional attractiveness', for its rebelliousness, and uncompromising support for the poor against the rich. If liberalism was indeed, as Murray's reflections indicated, wearing its heart on the left but its reason where its head was—on the centre—a bifurcation of liberalism was inevitable.

Under Massingham the *Nation* became increasingly militant in its support for Labour. By the time it was purchased by Keynes, it had ceased to be the effective voice of progressive liberalism on this subject. Instead, it specialized in the narrower slice of opinion that clustered round those left-liberals who had despaired of liberalism as an independent political force. Massingham's parting shot adjured the Liberal party to cede to the Labour party a large share of the promise of the future.[137] And the letters to the Editor reflected a Labour viewpoint that grew more critical of, and often openly hostile to, liberalism.[138] After 1923, with the change of ownership, centrist-liberalism asserted its hold on this as on so many other objects. Sharing with Hobhouse an increasingly pessimistic disposition, Murray anticipated the possibility, consequent to the demise of organized Liberalism, that the nation would be rent between a Conservative party of the rich and a Labour party of the poor. Something curious and significant was happening to Murray. The fear of what Labour stood for, or could stand for, was driving him into the opposite direction. This in itself was no new thing, as conservatism had always cannibalized a dissatisfied liberal element. What was different this time was the motivation. It was no longer the 'bitter cry of the middle classes' anxious at their impending dis-

[136] G. Murray, 'The Future of the Liberal Party', *Nation*, 29.11.1924.
[137] 'Vale', *Nation*, 28.4.1923.
[138] See e.g. *Nation*, 25.11.1922.

possession by a radical liberalism. The threat now came from outside liberalism and, furthermore, was not motivated by immediate material considerations but by ideological revulsion. Socialism and class war together would destroy liberal ideas and a liberal spirit. Hence by default, the attractions of conservatism suddenly became salient. For as Murray saw it, 'Both Liberalism and Conservatism, as opposed to Revolution, start by a fundamental reverence for Civilization and an acceptance of the existing social system as the result of long ages of human effort and progress.' True, this was not a predilection common to most centrist-liberals in the 1920s, but Murray's preferences seemed delicately poised between the more humane side of conservatism and treading the downward path of a democracy out of control. At that point in time, however, the die had not been cast. Conservatives may 'wish to stand for civilization and good government, but will inevitably confound these good things by the old lust for big profits, class ascendancy, and coercion'.[139] Yet even if liberalism could still prevail, it would at the most keep up a struggle, not resolve it favourably. From Murray's academic citadel, nourished by a Greek cultural élitism, the choice between 'education and circuses' had to be permanently available. If this tension within human nature were to be removed, reaction and revolution would vulgarize man and vindicate the Marxist prognosis.

In the early days of the 1924 Labour government, progressive liberals were inclined to stretch out a hand of friendship towards it. Hodgson of the *Daily News* condemned the quarrel between the two parties as 'about nothing at all'; while a leader reminded liberals that 'the Labour program is much wider than any mere class legislation'. Proportional representation, just about to fail in Parliament, was seen as the essential institutional device to prevent conflict between Liberalism and Labour.[140] C. P. Scott, however, now adopted a more critical line, challenging the Labour party to decide whether it wanted to work with or against the Liberals. He warned it against any hopes it might entertain of superseding the Liberal party 'and alone to control the progressive movement of political thought and policy in this country'. Its future lay in 'taking up

[139] G. Murray, 'Resurgamus', *Nation*, 15.3.1924.

[140] S. Hodgson, 'Liberals and Labour', *DN*, 26.4.1924; 'P. R.', *DN*, 2.5.1924. See also 'Liberal–Labour Relations', *WG*, 1.5.1924 and [C. P. Scott], 'The P. R. Bill', *MG*, 2.5.1924.

the work of Liberalism and carrying it further'.[141] As the year went by, liberal attitudes to the Labour party, among centrist-liberals in particular, began to harden.[142] Under the provocative caption, 'Should Liberals Vote Tory?', the *Nation* warned: 'With Labour in its present mood, there is no basis for co-operation between Liberalism and Labour.' In the past, liberal tolerance for Labour had been justified. Now that time had passed. 'Labour has declared war on Liberalism; it means to show no quarter; it can expect, and should receive, no quarter in return.' After a year of Labour government it was evident to liberals that a progressive alliance was not to be, that however large Labour might loom in their plans, there was no reciprocal interest on the part of Labour in the Liberal party or in liberalism itself. In a complete reversal of its policy under Massingham, the *Nation* unequivocally welcomed the defeat of Labour in the 1924 election: 'We do not wish to see the Conservatives obtain an independent majority; but, short of that, it seems to us desirable that they should gain as many seats as possible at the expense of Labour.'[143] The pre-war new liberal perspective would have rejected this unholy alliance out of hand; instead, the ideological waverings of Murray were assuming concrete form as potential electoral pacts between Liberals and Conservatives. This drifting apart of left-liberalism and centrist-liberalism became more marked as the years went by, but one major divide emerged in sharp relief: centrist-liberals were fighting for the survival of a beleaguered institutional tradition, and this organizational conservatism alone was enough to hamper their innovative and progressive drives. Left-liberals were fighting for the victory of a radical ideology, under whatever institutional guise, and in so doing were sometimes tempted to propel the liberal creed into twilight zones. Many of them were either already in the Labour party or, in notable contrast to their new liberal predecessors before 1914, situated on the fringes of liberalism, if not outside it. Centrist-liberals were being slowly reduced to an ideological, though not yet a numerical, rump—their residual ideological structure consisting of a core now deprived of those adjacent concepts that could sway it in a radical direction. The reasons for this, as we have seen throughout, were multifold, relating to the differential consumption of new political ideas and

[141] [C. P. Scott], 'A Crucial Decision', *MG*, 23.4.1924.
[142] See Wilson, *The Downfall of the Liberal Party 1914–1935*, pp. 285–302.
[143] 'Should Liberals Vote Tory?', *Nation*, 25.10.1924.

to the differential impact of political and economic events. This chapter has further suggested that these processes were exacerbated by the physical/institutional divides that induced so many liberals to go into voluntary exile from their party, and that reinforced the perception of ideological incompatibility as seen by both liberals and non-liberals within the progressive camp.

The anger and frustration roused by the first Labour administration gave way to more restrained counsel. Once again, centrist-liberals resumed talk of Liberal-Labour co-operation, though on a lower and cooler level than before. Now that the problems of Liberal leadership had been solved, in a spirit of renewed confidence, liberals felt they could again play a vital role in devising a constructive alternative policy together with Labour: '. . . while there can be no formal alliance between the two parties in the near future, it is eminently desirable that they should work together, as cordially as may be.' Borrowing a term from the French political experience, progressives believed that 'something like a Left *bloc* in Parliament may well prove indispensable'.[144] This proposal was reiterated by Masterman a year later: 'I can testify that during all the four years of the Coalition, both in the Press and in conversation with my friends of the Labour Party, in every talk or article, we found ourselves in agreement that Liberal and Labour should unite in a kind of 'Bloc des Gauches' against the dominant Tory majority.' Unfortunately, claimed Masterman, the Labour party had refused such approaches and it was possibly too late to reverse the processes of time in this generation.[145] C. P. Scott, too, returned to plead for Liberal-Labour co-operation, warning Lloyd George that an alliance with the Conservatives would be 'fatal to the whole spirit and future of Liberalism'.[146]

Meanwhile, on the official Liberal level, Samuel was blowing hot and cold in line with his assessment of the tactical situation. In 1927, dismissing the extremism and the socialism of the Labour party, he suggested that 'the right policy for Liberalism to adopt in relation to the Labour movement is to continue the policy that it would have adopted if a separate Labour Party had never come into

[144] 'The Liberal Revival', *Nation*, 31.1.1925. Sharp of the *New Statesman* had already used the idea. (Cf. p. 326 below).

[145] C. F. G. Masterman, 'The Future of Liberalism and Labour', letter to the Editor, *Nation*, 16.1.1926. See pp. 341–3 below for the revival of this idea.

[146] [C. P. Scott], 'A Call to Duty', *MG*, 21.1.1926.

existence'.[147] This ostrich-like pose enabled Samuel to revert to the assumption that the 'essential purposes of the Labour Movement are included within the aims of Liberalism'[148]—a statement that, even if true, would hardly have applied to Samuel's liberalism, rapidly moving away from the left pole of the spectrum. With the 1929 elections in sight, Samuel became even more adamant, declaring that the Liberals would on no account put Labour in office. Even the now centrist *Nation* drew the line at that utterance, asserting that 'our true role lies on the Left rather than on the Right' and expressing the hope 'that Liberal leaders will always keep in view the ultimate goal of a united progressive party'.[149] In 1930, however, Samuel was prepared again to concede that many beliefs and purposes were common to the two parties, and entertained the idea of co-ordinated action on certain measures, a proposal repeated again in 1934.[150] But socialist theory and the concrete policy of nationalization constituted for Samuel unbridgeable gulfs.

The idea of a united progressive party was one dearer to Hobhouse than to most other liberals. As the war drew to a close, his hopes were high that Labour sectionalism would disappear and enable a *rapprochement* with the new liberalism:

> . . . the Labour party is nationalising itself, and in so doing will inevitably draw closer to the really democratic section of the Liberal party. In time we shall have the unified democratic party—the fusion of men of progress with humanitarian faith—for lack of which our politics since the decay of the old party system have moved in a circle.[151]

Hobhouse came nearer than most progressives to realizing that the correlation between the ideology he espoused and Liberal party structure had been nullified, but his immediate post-war energetic application to reconstruction and reform was sanguine. Naturally, during the final phase of the war his perspective had shrunk: 'It cannot be beyond possibility that the two [Liberal and Labour] par-

[147] Samuel, 'Liberals and the Labour Movement', 418–19.

[148] Ibid., 411.

[149] 'Liberalism and Labour', *Nation*, 2.2.1929. After the economic crisis of 1931 J. L. Hammond wrote to E. T. Scott, expressing hope that the break-up in politics would enable the formation of a new progressive party that would include 'good stuff among Liberals' like E. D. Simon (*Guardian* Archives, A/H19/88, 19.11.1931).

[150] H. Samuel, 'The Political Outlook', 412; 'Liberty, Liberalism and Labour', 266.

[151] [L. T. Hobhouse], 'An Effective Labour Party', *MG*, 22.10.1917.

ties should come to a working agreement on concrete war aims, which would also put them in line with President Wilson', and which was to be distinguished from the military victory the government desired.[152] Beyond that, ideological and practical collusion was possible on the basis of the national minimum policy—which had already united moderate socialism and the new liberalism before 1914. For Hobhouse, the Liberal party stood at the parting of the ways, poised to change from 'the party of political democracy' into 'in the true and deep sense of the term, the party of social democracy'.[153] A year later he was still hopeful that the progressive battle to be fought by liberalism—the utilization of an organized but not repressive society to further freedom and equality of conditions—was 'precisely the battle that Labour is fighting . . . the two parties which tradition keeps apart are constantly brought together by a common aim'.[154]

By 1922 Hobhouse's tone was mellowing. The ideal of a united progressive party was no longer on the cards: 'Between Liberals and Labour differences will remain, but the Liberal who is true to his own principles will be tolerant enough to wish strength and sanity rather than distraction and weakness to a party which represents a living element in the opinion of the day and is a necessary makeweight in the balance of political power.'[155] The realities of the political situation and the acceptance of the democratic process, rather than positive arguments in favour of Labour institutions or ideology, were cited in support of the Labour party's existence. Hobhouse did not make the institutional transition into the Labour party that his close friend, Hobson, undertook. This difference in temperament and attitude is an intriguing one. Like Hobhouse, Hobson acutely felt what he termed the 'break-up of creeds and parties'. But he was more of a pragmatist when it came to seeking a platform for his beliefs and more eager than Hobhouse to disseminate them, once post-war aspirations had receded. He resigned from the Liberal party during the war as a protest against the abandonment of free trade, a protest that must have seemed to him quite pointless fifteen years later. He then stood unsuccessfully as an Independent in the 1918 elections. But while becoming a

[152] [L. T. Hobhouse], 'Liberal Policy', *MG*, 5.9.1918.
[153] [L. T. Hobhouse], 'Towards the Clean Peace', *MG*, 28.9.1918.
[154] [L. T. Hobhouse], 'The Future of Liberalism', *MG*, 5.9.1919.
[155] [L. T. Hobhouse], 'Socialists and Reconstruction', *MG*, 20.6.1922.

member of the Labour party in the mid-1920s, the marriage, even more so than in Trevelyan's case, was one of convenience:

> Though since then [1918] my sympathies have been with the Labour Party, I have never felt quite at home in a body governed by trade union members and their finance, and intellectually led by full-blooded Socialists. For neither section of this Labour Party avowedly accepts that middle course which seems to me essential to a progressive and constructive economic government in this country.

By the 1930s, given a coalition with a Liberal party that would adopt a programme similar to that of *The Next Five Years* group, he assumed that many Labour electors would vote Liberal.[156]

Hobhouse, possibly because he was more of a philosophical purist, was harder on Labour (though disenchanted with Liberalism too). A leader most probably written by him went out of its way to welcome J. M. Robertson's pamphlet on 'Liberalism and Labour', which argued for the permanent value of a Liberal party. Robertson had been distancing himself from Hobhouse's ethical, communitarian, new liberal ideas, but his anti-Labour stance now seemed valid. In 1918 liberals went over to Labour because they had hoped to find in it a stouter liberalism. But, noted the leader, 'Three years of experience have sadly disillusioned them. It is not the principles of the Labour party but its Parliamentary nullity which has made them feel the necessity for a revived Liberal party.'[157] Hobhouse's fundamental faith in the possibilities of co-operation was not diminished, however. If the two parties 'would consent to put the public welfare above party pride' and concentrated instead on practicable policies, there could arise 'magnificent opportunities for urgently needed political, economic, and social improvement'. Such a programme would include works of social utility, especially housing, the encouragement of trade by easing international relations, educational measures to stem the economic and social deterioration of the young, a general industrial benefit scheme, and improvement of workers' conditions.[158]

By 1924 Hobhouse was voicing explicitly his fast-crystallizing opinion that a realignment of politics was the only alternative to the eventual demise of non-sectarian social-liberalism. As he empha-

[156] J. A. Hobson, *Confessions of an Economic Heretic* (London, 1938), pp. 126, 125. For *The Next Five Years* plan, see Chapter 9, Section 5.

[157] 'Liberalism and Labour', *MG*, 6.1.1922.

[158] L. T. Hobhouse, letter to the Editor, *MG*, 11.12.1923.

sized: 'The true divisions of political thought often wander far from the lines dividing parties'—the clearest realization among thinkers of the time that ideology and party were out of step.[159] His criticism of the Labour party was unabated. It was mostly to blame for the lack of harmony in political life, because of its 'honest conviction' that the Liberal party was standing in the way of Labour dominance of non-Conservative opinion. But a two-party system, of which Labour would be one, was not a true reflection of British political thinking:

> The real divisions would in the first place put the extremists at each end by themselves, where they would not disturb other people, and, this done, would group the bulk of the Labour and the bulk of the Liberal party together as men who, discarding cast-iron formulae, are resolute to find the way to . . . [the] realisation of freedom through co-operation . . .[160]

In similar vein Hobhouse wrote to C. P. Scott, airing parallel private doubts about the Liberal party to those he had publicly expressed about Labour. His 'difficulties about the Liberal Party' arose on the one hand from the Trevelyanite belief that 'moderate Labour—Labour in office—has on the whole represented essential Liberalism—not without mistakes, but *better* than the organised party since C.[ampbell]-B[annerman]'s death'. The other side of the coin was that the residual Liberal party, 'however you divide it up, never seems any better agreed within on essentials'. One part leant to the Tories, another to Labour, and a third had 'nothing distinctive' but was a kind of 'Free Trade Unionist group'. The conclusion was a reinforcement of the view in Hobhouse's earlier leader: a confirmation of the obsolescence of the distinction between the Labour non-nationalizer and the Liberal proponent of social progress. For Hobhouse, the British ideological spectrum exhibited a fourfold division into communist and theoretical socialist, 'ordinary Labour' and 'good Liberal', 'bad Liberal' and 'ordinary Tory', and diehard. In any institutional realignment Hobhouse, together with the entire group of left-liberals, would have supported a new or renewed party based on the second ideological category. At present, though, a grave problem existed for organized Liberals. They constituted a rump of 'bad' liberals, against whose preponderance

[159] See also A. P. Marshall (an officer of the National League of Young Liberals), 'Liberalism, Labour and the Future', *FV*, Oct. 1929: '. . . it is makebelieve to pretend that party names represent definite divisions of thought.'

[160] [L. T. Hobhouse], 'What is Socialism?', *MG*, 10.6.1924.

all attempts to retain a spirit of progressivism had little indigenous backing. Moreover, such attempts were hardly encouraged by the unhelpful reaction of the Labour party,

> and the Liberals then drew away and inevitably gravitated towards the other side. They failed to present a third view because outside the enthusiasts there is really no third view. Liberals may be full of fight, but, as against the main body of Labour, what have they to fight for? Internationalism, Free Trade, Ireland, India, any particular kind of social reform? No, on all these there is agreement. There is really nothing, till you come up against doctrinaire Socialism, which is really outside 'moderate' Labour.[161]

Hobhouse grasped with particular succinctness what the real crisis of liberalism entailed. It was not a question of readaptation to difficult times, nor one of formulating a more aggressive programme or even a more effective party machine. The ground had been swept under liberals' feet because they had failed to solve the problem that had threatened liberalism ever since the cracks had appeared in the 1860s. That problem was to maintain the vital triple alignment between party, ideology and voting base which was the key to political success. Not that left-liberals were able to conduct liberalism towards a more secure future. Their plea for a better fit between party and ideology still left unanswered the question concerning the source of mass electoral support—the Achilles heel of liberalism.[162] But the rifts among liberals had become virtually irresolvable, contributing also to a heightening of ideological tension between left-liberalism and centrist-liberalism. The next chapter will explore the consolidation of left-liberal theory as part of this disintegrative process.

[161] *Guardian* Archives, C. P. Scott Papers, 132/318, Hobhouse to C. P. Scott, 7.11.1924.

[162] Cf. H. C. G. Matthew, R. I. McKibbin and J. A. Kay, 'The Franchise Factor in the Rise of the Labour Party', *English Historical Review*, 91 (1976), 723–52.

7

THE ELEMENTS OF LIBERAL HUMANISM

1. THE SURVIVAL OF ETHICAL LIBERALISM

THE one characteristic that clearly separated the tone of left-liberalism from its centrist counterpart was the salient linking of its arguments to a communitarian ethic. Most centrist-liberals were abandoning references to the ethical ends of the community or to the moral role of the state—other than to hint vaguely at the importance of social justice or to identify, in Murray's words, moral reform with a Puritan recoiling from drink, vice and gambling.[1] Even Barker, one of the few centrist-liberals to accord the state a moral role, saw it as the facilitator not of a *social* morality but of a network of individual moral obligations, in which personally responsible individuals exercised claims on each other.[2] Left-liberals, however, preserved the cardinal insistence of the new liberalism on the interpenetration of politics and social ethics. Neither the First World War, nor the post-war pessimism that engulfed many liberals, ended that tendency in British political thought. Rationalist beliefs plainly survived the war; indeed, the rationalism of a Hobson or a Hobhouse was *ipso facto* conterminous with a community-based morality. Hobhouse's post-war social-philosophical works sustain this assertion. As he wrote in 1922: 'Politics must be subordinate to Ethics, and we must endeavour to see Ethics not in fragments but as a whole.'[3] This double theme, despite some significant variations among left-liberals, sums up the organic holism that still pervaded the left-liberal assessment of social structure and function, one in which politics was restored both to the Greek ideal on which most university trained liberals had been nourished, and to dominant nineteenth-century Idealist or utilitarian perspectives that refused to detach politics from ethics. If some interpreters of Benthamism regarded it as a scientization of politics, Hobhouse was right in recognizing its important moral message and in realizing that its

[1] Murray, 'What Liberalism Stands For', 684.
[2] E. Barker, *The Citizen's Choice* (Cambridge, 1937), pp. 128–9.
[3] Hobhouse, *The Elements of Social Justice*, pp. 13–14.

heritage had outlasted its original guise. Benthamism had contributed to modern social thought 'a simple and comprehensive theory of the good as the touchstone of all personal and social relations alike', and although its simplicity and comprehensiveness were also its prime defects, it strengthened an appreciation of the equality of human feelings, supplying the social reformer with a basis for an altruism that transcended Bentham's own impact on social thought.[4] Concurrently, Hobson attempted to give a sound foundation to his ethical comprehension of welfare by substituting conscious satisfaction for 'vague conceptions of self-realisation', thus moving away from an Idealist notion of human good to 'a New Utilitarianism in which physical, intellectual, and moral satisfactions will rank in their due places'.[5]

Essential to the Hobhousian/Hobsonian analysis of social life was their insistence on an integrating sphere of public morality, created and recognized by thinking individuals, upheld by social and rational components of human nature. For Hobhouse the conceptual device to which this notion was anchored was the idea of harmony; for Hobson it was his organicism. Both concepts led them to reassert the supremacy of communal values without having to compromise on the liberal exaltation of individuality. Starting from the individual, Hobhouse identified elements of harmony within each person 'between feeling and action and experience'.[6] While avoiding rational reductionism, Hobhouse allowed reason to penetrate the system of feeling and justify it. The harmonious development of the personality depended on the expression, rather than repression, of fundamental human needs and impulses.[7] When it came to social relationships, Hobhouse saw those same principles at work writ large. Departing both from Benthamism and from a notion of superimposed Idealist reason, Hobhouse conceived of the common good as 'neither the sum of individual "goods" as independently determined, nor another kind of good opposed to them. It is the harmony of which each individual good is a constituent.'[8] Based on the notion of a rational and self-expressing personality, social interaction was unproblematic, as 'the individual

[4] Ibid., pp. 14, 18–19. Delisle Burns, in contrast, was still a captive to the view that Benthamism was a vindication of egoism (*Industry and Civilisation*, p. 31).

[5] J. A. Hobson, *Wealth and Life* (London, 1929), p. 16.

[6] Hobhouse, *The Elements of Social Justice*, p. 23.

[7] Ibid., pp. 24–5.

[8] Ibid., p. 30.

has no moral rights which conflict with the common good, as therein every rational aim is included and harmonized'.[9] Consequently, Hobhouse could not accept the centrist-liberal exaltation of competition as a positive human characteristic, because of the friction it caused and because of its eschewal of the common perspective.[10] This hopeful vision was, as will be argued later, a fundamental weakness of liberal theory.

Hobson approached the question of ethics from a somewhat different angle, though his conclusions were not far adrift from those of Hobhouse. Both endorsed collectivism as the ethical expression of human relationships, but Hobson did not see the issue as one of the internal harmony of personality simply externalized to account for the ethical community. In one of his major post-war works, *Wealth and Life*, he addressed his appeal to ethics as 'the doctrine of the social determination of values',[11] embodying the need to promote life-sustaining qualities and activities within the framework of a community. Hobson remained loyal to his early organicist views, which considered the community 'as an organic structure with a life "of its own" both on the producing and consuming side'.[12] But beginning with a social understanding of man, Hobson traced a path back to liberal individualism. The 'supreme problem of humanity, at once ethical, intellectual, aesthetic' was

> how to integrate the capacities of man, as a social animal, so as to enable him to make the most of a life that consists in the progressively complex control of an environment which, by the very expression of this control, is calling forth and educating new cooperations of inborn capacities.[13]

Human purposiveness enabled Hobhouse and Hobson to entertain an evolutionarily sustained pattern of progress. Evolution itself was not ethical, but allowed for the emergence of human morality, which in turn left an irradicable imprint on the evolutionary process.[14] For Hobson as economist it was of special interest that the term 'value' was shared by economics and ethics. This supported one of his favourite themes—the extension of economics beyond a

[9] Ibid., p. 40.
[10] Hobhouse, 'The Problem' in Hobson and Ginsberg, *L. T. Hobhouse*, p. 268.
[11] Hobson, *Wealth and Life*, p. xv.
[12] Ibid., p. xxii.
[13] Ibid., p. xxiv.
[14] Hobson, *Wealth and Life*, p. xxiv; Hobhouse, *The Elements of Social Justice*, pp. 14–15.

quantitative science to a systematic study of human welfare subordinated to the claims of ethics. The fragmentation of the ethical sphere was, Hobson maintained, a comparatively recent development. A tension between private vices and public virtues had of course underlain the emergence of Western individualism, but even the old teachings had their attractions for him. Those teachings had at least approached the question of a natural harmony of interests as a moral doctrine, one which through an invisible hand rendered egoistic behaviour socially beneficial, and which saw in the realization of natural tendencies an intrinsically moral event in the natural law tradition.[15] If left-liberals were now conscious of an increasing estrangement between private and public interests, Hobson located a parallel occurrence in the field of economics: '. . . within the last few generations economic processes, the business life, have become an essentially autonomous system of human activity, with more and more complex relations, operated by rules worked out by business men for business purposes, and embodying a commercial ethics which differs sensibly from the private ethics of the family or other forms of the community.'[16] The invisible hand doctrine was abandoned in favour of 'a scientific conception of the play of economic forces, in which spiritual direction was displaced by laws almost as immutable as those discoverable by physics, chemistry, or geology'.[17] The depreciation in those theories of human will, purposiveness and control neutralized both the moral component and the individual or personality-oriented component, which together were at the heart of progressive liberalism. The reversion of post-war liberal economists to mechanistic explanations of laws of cause and effect that obviated human volition placed them at the opposite pole to the left-liberal position, if not on the fringes of liberalism. Ultimately, Hobson hoped that the growing sense of the unity of life and conduct would 'exercise a dissolvent influence upon economics as a separate science and art' and that it would come to be directed by, and in the interest of, social philosophy. This complemented his belief that social progress would diminish the part played by economic activities in human life.[18]

[15] Hobson, *Wealth and Life*, pp. 115–16.

[16] Ibid., p. 94. In contradistinction, such dualism lay at the heart of Samuel's extolling of egoism side by side with altruism as mainsprings of welfare and the common good (*Belief and Action*, pp. 129–41).

[17] Hobson, *Wealth and Life*, p. 123.

[18] Ibid., pp. 137, 446–7.

Hobson thanked his friend Delisle Burns for the latter's comments on *Wealth and Life*. But Burns himself had written in his *Industry and Civilisation* that Hobson's earlier book, *Work and Wealth*, had closely affected his critical thinking;[19] indeed, Hobson's influence must have been strengthened by the frequent contacts between the two in the inter-war years. Like Hobson, Burns treated industrial and economic problems within an ethical framework. Like Hobson, also, Burns saw economic science as 'an abstraction which, in order to be brought more closely into relation with real life, needs to be supplemented by the moral science or ethics dealing with actual law and custom'.[20] Burns related his moral perspective on economics and industry to the 'good character and good conduct' of the persons concerned—workers, employers (both entrepreneurs and owners). But it was 'not to be thought of as if moralising meant only making their intentions virtuous, for here it is taken to mean an extending of intellectual and emotional powers in harmony'[21]—a point plainly reminiscent of Hobhouse's analysis. Furthermore, morality in industry was not only related to the individual, but expressed 'at least a dim feeling of community in economic relationships'. In turn, 'the fundamental relationship . . . of the economic community to community life as a whole is one of subordination'.[22] Politics was assigned a role in suffusing human life with morality:

> The existence of the state and the development of its activities are more important morally than the maintenance of the organisation of exchange, and this not simply because liberty is morally more excellent than marketable goods, but because the political has in fact become the central meeting place for the systematisation of all communal life.[23]

The increasing complexity of social life, as Hobhouse had earlier recognized,[24] necessitated the state, but it was a state of a peculiar kind, devoted not only to the direct maintenance of order and of liberty, but to the attainment of wealth and social development. Behind these lay the twin moral ends Burns had identified: self-development and social service.[25] Though, unlike Hobhouse, he

[19] Burns, *Industry and Civilisation*, p. 7.
[20] Ibid., pp. 19, 232.
[21] Ibid., pp. 228, 226.
[22] Ibid., pp. 236, 242.
[23] Ibid., p. 244.
[24] See Freeden, *The New Liberalism*, p. 70.
[25] Burns, *Industry and Civilisation*, pp. 243–5, 250.

acknowledged that morality could be served by pursuing either end separately, he preferred a social system that would engineer their pursuit in tandem, paying attention to the interests of the individual as well as those of the community.[26] In particular, Burns concentrated on the moralization of professional standards (with reference to Durkheim), of consumer demand as defined by the moral utility of goods and services (again echoing Hobson) and—of which more later—the moralization of property.[27]

2. THE QUEST FOR NEW SCIENTIFIC SUPPORT: THE TENTATIVE CASE OF PSYCHOLOGY

One of the more interesting sidelights on the development of social thought in the 1920s relates to the impact of the psychological theories that were widely popularized after the war. Pre-1914 new liberalism had been profoundly influenced by biological and evolutionary ideas, and those remained in the cultural background of post-war thinking, but with little direct articulation. It is not suggested that psychology leapt in to fill the breach, for in its embryonic forms, lacking central unity and acceptance, it could not serve as powerfully a moulder of human thought as evolution had in the past. Nevertheless, the inevitable tendency of any ideology to seek scientific validation, combined with the concrete interests of many left-liberals and their intellectual circles,[28] found liberal thinkers attempting to incorporate recent psychological findings and trends into their socio-political discourses.[29] Hobhouse had himself been active in conducting psychological experiments in animal behaviour before the war and had published in the field of comparative psychology. Graham Wallas's incursions into the non-rational aspects of political behaviour, however dilettante they may have been,[30] brought him more acclaim than his contributions to progressive thought. Above all, William McDougall's elaboration of a social psychology, linking the study of mind to that of behaviour in

[26] Ibid., pp. 41–2, 250–1.

[27] Ibid., pp. 167, 175, 183, 192, 195.

[28] See e.g. the frequent reviews of psychological books in the liberal *Saturday Westminster Gazette* after 1920.

[29] The dependence of modern thought in turn on physics, biology, and psychology was also observed by Idealists. See Hetherington and Muirhead, *Social Purpose*, p. 34.

[30] See T. H. Qualter, *Graham Wallas and the Great Society* (London, 1980).

a social context,[31] was an important departure that reached the peak of its influence among liberal thinkers in the early 1920s. The consumptionist approach to ideology does not require to examine those psychological theories in detail, but rather to ascertain their utilization by left-liberals. The reliance of British political thought on psychological insights had a long pedigree stretching back to associationist psychology. The revival of this connection between the disciplines was eased by the mixture of philosophy, social philosophy, and empirical scientific observation that characterized psychology in the early part of the century. New theories of community interaction, a re-evaluation of the concept of rationality, and work-oriented studies of efficiency all vied with each other for scholarly attention.

A. The Group Mind

McDougall's *The Group Mind*, published in 1920 and dedicated to Hobhouse, was a central focus of liberal discussion. The delineation of a field which he termed collective psychology was bound to interest proponents of ideologies with a communal bias. McDougall's ideas were inadvertently or consciously redolent of some of the core concerns of progressive thought. He took issue with Spencer's extreme individualism, allying himself with an opposed organicism that claimed that 'since . . . the social aggregate has a collective mental life, which is not merely the sum of the mental lives of its units, it may be contended that a society not only enjoys a collective mental life but also has a collective mind or, as some prefer to say, a collective soul'.[32] He cited with approval Barker's exposition of the theory of a group mind existing entirely in the minds of the members of a group, united by the common substance of an idea.[33] On the face of it one would have expected McDougall's enunciation of extreme organicist views to have been enthusiastically acclaimed by Hobson. After all, when McDougall

[31] Cf. R. Thomson, *The Pelican History of Psychology* (Harmondsworth, 1968), p. 178; L. S. Hearnshaw, *A Short History of British Psychology 1840–1940* (London, 1964), pp. 188–92.

[32] W. McDougall, *The Group Mind* (Cambridge, 1920), p. 7.

[33] Ibid., pp. 18–19 (citing Barker's *Political Thought in England 1848 to 1914* [London, 1915]). McDougall failed to realize that Barker was far from being a 'sympathetic student of German idealism' (*The Group Mind*, p. 17) and was merely explaining Bosanquet's views. Barker's liberalism was a philosophy that cautioned against both state and group, preferring the individual unit in conjunction with like units. Cf. *The Citizen's Choice*, ch. v and *passim*.

wrote that 'a society, when it enjoys a long life and becomes highly organised, acquires a structure and qualities which are largely independent of the qualities of the individuals who enter into its composition and take part for a brief time in its life',[34] he appeared to coincide with Hobson's postulation of a community as a distinct entity. Initially, Hobson's reaction was favourable to this 'new and hazardous intellectual adventure'. McDougall's book was an 'exceedingly stimulating volume'. Hobson had no quarrel with the concept of the group mind as such, but was concerned about McDougall's eschewal of the biological foundations of nations and expressed reservations about the nationalistic exaltation of the nation over internationalism or humanity as the highest achievement of the social mind.[35] He then became increasingly hostile to McDougall's theories, perhaps sustained by the harsher reactions of some of his colleagues. By 1926 he was criticizing the *Realpolitik* implications of McDougall's theories, for self-assertive instincts seemed to equip the group with a licence to subject those members who had an instinct to obey.[36] Hobson was especially unhappy with the liberties McDougall had taken with the organic analogy when defining the nation as a 'self-contained and complete organism'. The suggestion that loyalty to a nation overruled ties to other groups was an attitude reminiscent of 'the great war', and reinforced Hobson's long-standing antipathy to power politics. When combined with the use of the gregarious instinct to inflame combative passions, this was 'an instructive illustration of the most insiduous abuses of 'social psychology''.[37]

McDougall, suffering from past criticism and anticipating future attacks, had in fact gone out of his way to distance himself from that other source of anti-state feeling, German Idealism, staunchly supporting Hobhouse's strictures in *The Metaphysical Theory of the State*, and discoursing at length on his attitude to German philosophy and science. This apology began with the statement that 'in my youth I was misled into supposing that the Germans were the possessors of a peculiar wisdom; and I have spent a large part of my life in discovering, in one field of science after another, that I was mistaken'. It ended with a progressive liberal avowal of belief:

[34] Ibid., p. 9.
[35] J. A. H[obson], 'The Group-Mind', *MG*, 24.8.1920.
[36] Hobson, *Free-Thought in the Social Sciences*, pp. 207–9.
[37] Ibid., pp. 255–6.

'I wish to state that politically my sympathies are with individualism and internationalism.' McDougall begged to shrug off 'the cloven foot of individualism'—as anti-collectivism—or 'leanings towards the aristocratic principle'. Aligning himself with F. H. Bradley, he identified with a normative ideal 'which would aim at a synthesis of the principles of individualism and communism, of aristocracy and democracy, of self-realization and of service to the community'.[38] Put this way, there seemed to be common ground between his credo and various Idealist and liberal positions. It is therefore all the more significant that his professed communities of intellectual allegiance rejected his advances.

One of the attacks that McDougall had to endure was from the Idealists Hetherington and Muirhead. True, they complimented psychology on the new advances it had occasioned, in demonstrating that society was a union of minds. But Idealists were sceptical about the validity of experimental sciences. The 'science of the actual' could establish facts and illuminate origins, but shed no light on the 'status and value' of conscious experience in the life of the mind.[39] McDougall, despite his attempt to incorporate T. H. Green's views into his own, confused the actual character of a man with his 'true' self, something Green had strenuously resisted.[40] McDougall's social psychology also exaggerated a narrow understanding of self, which over-emphasized the parts at the expense of the whole. However,

> the parts cannot afford to dispense with organisation . . . if there is one lesson which social psychology teaches more than another, it is that society is all of one piece. If you look for the principle of progress in the ebullitions of instinct or the vagaries of 'intuition' instead of in the sense of what is logically implied in the 'social idea', there is nothing to stand between you and the old individualism from which the whole modern movement of thought is an effort to escape.[41]

The Idealist critique was concerned with individualist implications in McDougall's theories. Hobson, however, had taken issue with him on different subjects, opposing the nationalist connotations of group-mind theory and (despite Hobson's interest in eugenics)

[38] McDougall, *The Group Mind*, pp. ix–xi.
[39] Hetherington and Muirhead, *Social Purpose*, pp. 43–4.
[40] Ibid., pp. 71–2.
[41] Ibid., pp. 45–6.

McDougall's support for the theory that associated inferior intelligence with the lower classes.[42] On the question of the group mind itself, however, Hobson's and McDougall's ideas coalesced. In fact, McDougall supplied Hobson with an escape-hatch from a problem that had clearly become an embarrassment. Shortly before the war Hobson, vacillating between physical and non-physical interpretations of the social organism, opted for a physical explanation and suggested 'the existence of a social body corresponding with and related to the social mind'.[43] He repeatedly debated the question with Hobhouse, complaining of the latter's limited conception of the organic whole as not more than the sum of its parts in co-operative activity.[44] Hobhouse reiterated his position in every one of his major publications. In *Social Development* he accepted that the common will of a group (a 'mental network') would differ from the wills of its members acting in isolation, but insisted that those were several co-operating selves, not a group mind.[45] This book attracted Hobson's most outspoken critique, attacking Hobhouse for disparaging the physical aspects of herd and family life, for declining to extend the unity of personality to the relations of personalities in a society, and for his refusal 'to apply the noun organism, but only the adjective organic, to Society'. To Hobson's mind, this was a rejection of 'the softer psychological doctrine' with its leaning towards a federal self or an *esprit de corps*. Hobson implicitly accused Hobhouse of over-rationalism and an arid or perhaps academic intellectualism: 'Sympathy is a warmer word than harmony, and furnishes the emotional current lacking in the more formal and static metaphor.'[46]

Hobson found no support for his views and by 1929 felt the need to recant: 'It would . . . be foolish to suggest that any human society or association displays any such order or organic structure on its

[42] Hobson, *Free-Thought in the Social Sciences*, pp. 214–15.

[43] J. A. Hobson, review of L. T. Hobhouse's *Social Evolution and Political Theory*, *MG*, 22.2.1912. See Freeden, *The New Liberalism*, pp. 105–9.

[44] e.g. J. A. H[obson], 'The Theory of the State', *MG*, 23.11.1918.

[45] Hobhouse, *Social Development*, pp. 178–87. For an amplification of Hobhouse's position, see M. Ginsberg, *The Psychology of Society* (London, 1921), especially chs 4 and 5.

[46] J. A. Hobson, 'Society and the Individual', *WW*, 15.3.1924. Hobhouse in fact discussed sympathy at length, recognizing its older psychological pedigree [as for Hume and Bentham] and identifying it as a social impulse on the road to harmony and reason (*Social Development*, pp. 152–7). Cf. G. F. Gaus, *The Modern Liberal Theory of Man* (London, 1983), pp. 58–9, 92–3.

physical side.' He now also denied that 'there is any such solidarity of social purpose as appears to be exhibited in the instinctive and self-sacrificing coöperation of the hive or ant-hill'.[47] The notion of the group mind as popularized by McDougall introduced a new and shared dimension to the discussion that Hobson and Hobhouse had conducted with each other for so long. For both, the idea of a common element in social thinking essentially underpinned their theories of community and humanistic ethics. The construct of the group mind revived the possibility of using a scientifically based conception of community as a formidable weapon against the vociferous forces of doctrinaire individualism. Hobson now felt it safer to refer to the mental and cultural consequences of organicism and cautiously sought to advance the frontiers of knowledge in an agreed direction:

> It will, I think, be admitted by all these thinkers [including Hobhouse and R. M. McIver] that organised coöperation, the voluntary participation of individuals in some common activity, can produce a valuable effect, spiritual or even material, different both in quantity and in character from that which the unorganised activities of the individual participants could compass.[48]

Bowing to pressure, Hobson was prepared to accept that 'consentient feeling' existed only in individuals. He conceded that it might be convenient to have a separate term to distinguish the federal unity of a group from the unity of the individual mind, and provisionally adopted the term 'co-organic'.[49]

It would be unwise, however, to conclude that these modifications reflected any departure from Hobson's essentially organistic outlook. He simply now attached it to the new psychology instead of the old biology. The well-read Hobson was ever assimilating new information and synthesizing it impressively with his own system of thought. Central to that system was the assertion that 'there is a general spirit, will,[50] and achievement that have value, and that this spirit is embodied in physical forms and activities which contribute to the "value"'.[51] This allowed for the institutions and conduct commensurate with liberal communitarianism—the market-place

[47] Hobson, *Wealth and Life*, p. 25.
[48] Ibid., p. 27. See also Hobhouse, *The Elements of Social Justice*, p. 188.
[49] Hobhouse, *Wealth and Life*, p. 28.
[50] See also ibid., p. 387.
[51] Hobson, *Wealth and Life*, p. 30.

side by side with social property.[52] Hobson was keenly conscious of the potential impact of psychology—a subject which 'left free, is busily undermining the rotten foundations of a civilisation which has proved itself at many points incapable of adaptation to the vital needs of humanity'.[53] The social reformer in him embraced the challenge that psychology seemed to pose to 'vested intellectual and spiritual interests'.[54]

B. The Roots of Reason

In addition to the notion of the group mind, psychology offered a range of attractions to liberals. First, it had an important 'unmasking' function to perform, in 'claiming to unearth and reveal the real supports of accepted and authoritative doctrine in all branches of social conduct'.[55] For a heretic like Hobson this was irresistible, especially bearing in mind that his onslaught on economic imperialism had concentrated on its 'conspiratorial' nature and its insiduous manipulation of power. More importantly, psychology provided insights into human nature and rationality that were crucial to maintain the appeal of progressive liberalism during a period of relative reaction. To appreciate this one must relinquish the commonplace association of early twentieth-century psychology with a simplistic irrationalism. As Hobhouse commented disapprovingly,

> in the world of mind, which might seem to be her own domain, reason in these days seems sadly out of fashion. Psychology, which begins to reduce the play of mental activity to a science, has not fostered the conception of conduct as a reasoned art. On the contrary, its tendency is to emphasize the primacy of feeling, the sway of instinct, the prevalence of the irrational in the mass movements of mankind.[56]

Left-liberals such as Hobhouse, Hobson and Burns—and indeed Wallas before them—set out to prove the contrary and to bend the new psychology to the needs of progressive rationalism. On the Continent the rise of social Darwinism (as struggle), flavoured with an emphasis on heredity and the Bergsonian and Freudian 'recovery of the unconscious', had challenged the role of conscious

[52] Ibid., pp. 29, 163.
[53] Hobson, *Free-Thought in the Social Sciences*, p. 278.
[54] Ibid., p. 277.
[55] Ibid., p. 52.
[56] Hobhouse, *The Rational Good*, pp. 19–20.

choice, so that the positivism that 'had started as an ultra-intellectualist doctrine became in effect a philosophy of radical anti-intellectualism'.[57] The British story was a different one. The new liberals had claimed to identify a rational and sociable rhythm in Darwinist evolution, and had offered out hopes for a deliberate control over the environment and, via eugenics, over heredity as well. Similarly, left-liberals were eager to integrate psychology into the rationalism for which they had always felt allegiance. Wallas's *The Great Society*, though expressly indebted to McDougall's *Social Psychology*, differed from the latter's approach precisely on McDougall's refusal to raise reason to the status of instinctive impulses. Wallas described his own book as 'an argument against certain forms of twentieth-century anti-intellectualism'[58] and insisted on dividing all impulses into instinctive and intellectual, in order to account for the development of dispositions such as thought and language.[59]

Hobhouse, too, was alarmed by the anti-intellectualism contained in what he believed was a misinterpretation of psychological findings. At the very least the relation between 'the unconscious and the conscious, the emotional and the rational, impulse and idea' was problematic, because man 'formulates his impulses into ends, and explains them by reasons which are mutually intelligible'. He was prepared to accept that idea and impulse were 'equally essential to the developed purpose'.[60] Indeed, psychology was performing a vital function in the retention of reason as an explanatory device for human conduct. Previously reason had attracted misunderstanding and prejudice because it was 'often taken as a thing apart', divorced on the side of knowledge from experience and on the side of conduct from feeling.[61] The reintegration of reason and feeling was, through Mill's example, as true to the liberal tradition as an exclusive appeal to reason, if not truer. Psychology now supplied the empirical data which could detail the place of rational thought in everyday life. Adapting these findings to his developmental

[57] H. S. Hughes, *Consciousness and Society 1890–1930* (London, 1974), pp. 38–9; ch. 4.

[58] G. Wallas, *The Great Society* (London, 1914), p. v. On the early impact of Hobson on Wallas see M. J. Wiener, *Between Two Worlds: The Political Thought of Graham Wallas* (Oxford, 1971), p. 132.

[59] Wallas, *The Great Society*, pp. 39–45.

[60] Hobhouse, *The Rational Good*, pp. 22–3, 24.

[61] Ibid., p. 29.

teleology, and acknowledging McDougall's influence,[62] Hobhouse saw a development of root interests (a wider concept than interest and one which determined the 'general trend of thought, feeling, and behaviour') from natural impulse to rational will, the latter through intelligence and mind purposefully directing and shaping oft-contradictory impulses towards a harmonious whole. Notable among these was the social impulse itself. The organizing function of reason was to ensure that no 'ineradicable impulse' should be left frustrated, 'for if so the whole is not satisfied'. Passing or detached impulses, however, had to be subordinated to the permanent requirements of the whole, thus allowing for social control.[63]

Hobson, who had read and criticized a draft of Hobhouse's *The Rational Good*, was not entirely convinced. Reviewing the book, he queried the total dependence of the will on the mass of impulse-feeling. If the will, according to Hobhouse, was an organizational power of decision between volitions, desires, or impulses (desire being impulse directed towards an anticipated end, and volition being the direction of *effort* towards an end through the control of impulses and desires), did not the will have a quasi-independent source?[64] Hobhouse, however, emphasized the developmental and evolutionary implications of natural psychic drives, and the interplay of impulse and desire within a social and harmonizing context that could account for the emergence of consciousness, intelligence and ultimately reason, which was itself *ipso facto* social.[65]

Though Hobson may have questioned the uncomplicated flow of Hobhouse's evolutionary vision, he had no readier solutions to offer. Like Hobhouse, he saw psychology as bringing social conduct to the 'bar of reason',[66] and welcomed the emergence of a more sophisticated understanding:

[62] McDougall's approach was known as 'hormic psychology'. It stressed purposive striving that emanated from instincts and expressed itself in drives (Hearnshaw, *A Short History of British Psychology*, pp. 189–91). Cf. also Hobson and Ginsberg, *L. T. Hobhouse*, pp. 149–177, 238.

[63] Hobhouse, *Social Development*, pp. 143, 169, 173–4; *The Rational Good*, pp. 30–1. See Gaus, *The Modern Liberal Theory of Man*, pp. 122, 137, 144–8, for an edifying discussion of Hobhouse's psychological theories.

[64] J. A. H[obson], 'Professor Hobhouse's New Book', *MG*, 16.2.1921; Hobhouse, *The Rational Good*, pp. 44–8.

[65] Hobhouse, *The Rational Good*, pp. 42, 45, 48, 91, 127.

[66] Hobson, *Free-Thought in the Social Sciences*, p. 52. Cf. Hobhouse, *The Rational Good*, p. 47.

The shallow psychology of the age of rationalism played into the hands of the enemy by an excessive appraisal of the directive power of reason. If the new psychology has seemed to plunge to the opposite extreme, by disparaging reason as the mere tool of the full-blooded instincts, there are already signs of the recovery of a juster balance . . . the necessity of effecting some harmony or co-operation among the instincts will endow [curiosity] with a constantly increasing importance as a co-ordinating and controlling power.[67]

Hobson also shared Hobhouse's attraction to the dynamic, instinct-propelled, energy-expending notion of human nature that contemporary psychology was promoting, though he remained sceptical over one of the main unsolved problems of the time—whether there existed an instinct of gregariousness. But his old loyalties to the biological roots of human behaviour and his extension of economics into the sphere of life-sustaining activities both found an echo in psychology. Hobson had always strenuously opposed the dualism of matter and spirit, and had consequently rejected those psychological theories that centred on sublimation. Sublimation was, he believed, a dangerous term that held out the possibility that animal life could be transcended.

The notion that we are shedding animalism, letting ape and tiger die, in the evolution of civilisation is erroneous. We are only evolving and elaborating the potentialities of animal life. If we resent the materialistic degradation of such a view, we had best proceed, not by constructing some new turn of fallacious dualism, but by lifting the whole process of evolution into some neutral zone where neither the grossness of materialism nor the vagueness of idealism is chargeable.

This, however, could also have serious disadvantages for social reform and 'may oblige us to concede the impossibility of the total extinction of physical conflict between individuals and groups. It may lead us to dismiss for ever the notion of expelling profiteering completely from the whole economic system.'[68]

If conflict and property were instinctual, the irrelevance of socialist utopianism for Hobson becomes evident. While the persistence of conflict could pose a problem for liberals, however, it eased the assimilation of the 'naturalness' of property into left-liberal thought. Primarily, however, the retention of the role of instinct

[67] Hobson, *Free-Thought in the Social Sciences*, pp. 274–5.
[68] Hobson, 'The Ethical Movement and the Natural Man', 677, 675–6.

guaranteed for Hobson a diversity of human creativity that could sustain his total approach to human nature. In a series of articles for the *Nation*, Hobson elaborated on his recent discovery that 'safety, order, calculability' had repressive repercussions for liberty and the value of human life.[69] The case against conservatism became, in Hobson's systemizing hands, cultural and psychological as much as political. The amount of standardization and 'law and order' a society needed had to be weighed against the burdens of monotony and routine, and 'risk, chance, and skill in the game of life'. Defying the vestiges of Victorian morality, Hobson commented: 'How much wiser the Catholic Church with its allowance for revelry than the repressive regularities of Puritanism!' A margin of disorder was essential especially 'at a time when science conspires with ethics to impress the dominance of physical and moral order'. Psychology alone among the sciences delimited the realm of reason and its systems. When Hobson criticized the 'pride and a sort of aesthetic craving' that 'impel thinkers to piece together their bits of intellectual order onto a completeness and an objectivity they do not possess', he should in all fairness have included himself. Even if psychology 'performs no greater service than in . . . turning the light of comedy upon the pretence of Reason to be Master—or even Freeman—in the human household', Hobson deliberately restricted disorder to areas of individual expression which would benefit rather than endanger central communal control. They were, after all, '*margins* of free living and free thinking'. Disorder was carefully built into a system under the rational guidance of a socially aware community.[70]

The lessons of psychology involved a curious reversal of Hobson's arguments for the socialization of the economic surplus. Stressing humans as sources of energy was linked to a 'broad survey of an evolutionary process which presents a continually increasing surplus of organic energy over and above the requirements for specific survival'.[71] Hence racial survival was the first charge on human energy, and the surplus was devoted to individualization rather than, as with the economic surplus, being appropriated by society. Clearly, Hobson did not deny that in important spheres of

[69] See also ibid., 672–3.

[70] J. A. Hobson, 'Notes on Law and Order', *Nation*, 24.10.1925, 14.11.1925. My italics.

[71] Hobson, *Wealth and Life*, p. 15.

life the sources of value and creativity were individual, as distinct from economic activity which was already the product of a *social* system involving exchange, supply and the like. Thus Hobson's use of psychology, despite his sympathy with the group mind, offered a combination of collectivism and individualism that reinforced his left-liberal views. In the final analysis, nevertheless, the following conclusion was crucial: 'For though modern psychology everywhere displays the craft with which the passions "rationalise" their cravings, it is none the less true that the whole development of the orderly institutions and practises of civilised societies attests the normal supremacy of reason.'[72]

C. *The Energy of Creativity*

The impact of psychology on left-liberalism can be further illustrated through the work of Delisle Burns. Burns still regarded the ethical assumptions underlying economics as based on an egoistic individualism, in which 'production and consumption as well as supply and demand, which are in origin psychological terms, are still used in economics in some senses which imply an entirely obsolete psychology. That psychology belongs to the utilitarian period in English philosophy.'[73] No doubt this was correct of many centrist-liberal economists, but Burns was a little less than generous towards the recent more social tenor of utilitarianism. His analysis of psychological approaches to industry and politics, however, was in many aspects more detailed and original than that of his colleagues. Burns saw the new psychology as offering an alternative to both utilitarianism and Idealism; indeed, it had undermined them both. It was now clear, he declared, that the Benthamite distinction between egoism and altruism was not fundamental, because the unit of analysis known as the self was not 'presented to thought as separate from "others"'. Furthermore, it was not pleasure as such that people were after; rather, 'the fundamental psychic fact is the expression of personality or even of racial and group tendency'.[74] As for Idealism, despite an affinity on the notion of a group mind, the new psychology exposed groups as grounded on 'primitive appetites' such as a repressed 'sex complex'. Consciousness or thought were not motive forces in explaining

[72] Ibid., pp. 15–17.
[73] Burns, *Industry and Civilisation*, p. 43.
[74] Ibid., pp. 31, 53.

or directing their behaviour. Like Hobson and Hobhouse, Burns adopted the concept of psychic energy as the basis of human thought and action. It was of particular use when applied to industry, since two of the 'instincts and conations' included in the systems of psychic energy were production and consumption.[75] The interesting conclusion demonstrated the deft use of new scientific findings to buttress old truths: 'The ideal . . . of industry, is no longer conceived in terms of individual liberty or rational social organisation in the old senses of those phrases. It is rather to be conceived by reference to the discharge of psychic energy of diverse kinds, . . .'[76] Not that individual liberty or rationality were ruled out; they were simply subsumed under other phenomena. Burns agreed with left-liberals and Idealists that individuality and society were inseparable. He also followed Hobhouse's argument that 'out of the instinctive expression arises intelligent plan'. But psychological insights refined the liberal conception of human nature. Importantly, the wants-oriented approach—linked to associationist psychology—that characterized both utilitarians and modern economists was found lacking.[77] Human nature was 'primarily *expressive*', rather than receptive to external stimuli, and hence concerned with 'initiation or creation'.[78]

This formulation combined Hobsonian insights with typical liberal interpretations of man. Man as doer and actor was never a preserve of Marxist theory alone. But whereas nineteenth-century liberalism singled out activities that had measurable results in the spheres of business and industry, and whereas Mill had talked of exercising the moral and mental faculties by means of political activity and participation, the Ruskinian-Hobsonian restatement of life as qualitative consumption was now put to new use. Instead of regarding consumption as the passive end of the economic process, receptive of economic productive activity, consumption itself was endowed by Burns with creative capacity. Both production and consumption displayed energies that were 'expressive of character, personality, or life'.[79] Drawing directly on Ruskin, Burns distinguished between types of demand on the basis of their psycho-

[75] Ibid., pp. 35, 37.
[76] Ibid., p. 39.
[77] Ibid., pp. 47–8.
[78] Ibid., p. 51. Original italics.
[79] Ibid., p. 54. But cf. Hobson, *Free-Thought in the Social Sciences*, p. 132, who makes a similar point.

logical and moral utility, as whatever 'expands, increases, or intensifies psychic or mental energy'. Among others, the activity of the consumer would express itself in 'originat[ing] ideas as to possible goods and services and mak[ing] new and more subtle demands'. Consumer activity would not only transmute consumption into valuable conduct, it would initiate production. Thus the totality and interconnectedness of human life was doubly emphasized. Giving a new and clever twist to Hobson's analysis, Burns observed that 'the age is suffering from an "under-consumption" which appears not simply as bodily starvation, but as imaginative weakness'.[80] Under the influence of social psychology, furthermore, consumption was seen as the reflection of a group mind, for 'demand or public taste is hardly ever individual, because the social group or the social "set" in which a person lives determines his choice of a house, of dress, and of food'.[81] Burns dismissed as a 'persistent superstition' the notion that consumption was 'individual' even where production was 'social': 'Even those economists and social philosophers with a bias towards what is called "socialism" seem to imagine that the use of goods and services is individualistic or atomic and personal, in a sense in which the supply of goods and services is not; but this is mistaken.'[82] It was the group mind, not the individual Briton, that demanded bacon and eggs for breakfast. But individual self-expression in diversity was an important part of social life as well, and had to reflect the pluralistic structure of society, which in turn contributed towards the unique configuration of each personality.[83]

D. The Incentive Motive

Psychology also had a part to play in the sphere of incentives. Although the adoption by liberals of psychological tenets could reinforce the left-liberal conception of the total personality, a more narrow alternative use was available. On a minimalist interpretation even centrist-liberals could welcome a theory that concentrated on creativity and activity, simply by associating these with industrial productivity and entrepreneurship. It is noteworthy that left-liberals, too, were not averse to considering that subject; though in

[80] Burns, *Industry and Civilisation*, pp. 210, 220.
[81] Ibid., p. 50.
[82] Ibid., p. 196.
[83] Ibid., pp. 200, 215.

line with their treatment of incentives this was a concession on their part to a weakness in human nature rather than an enthusiastic discovery of its core. The 1920s had seen a proliferation of technical research linking psychology and industrial efficiency, such as time-and-motion studies. The experience of the First World War and the urgent need for post-war industrial and commercial recovery acted as further stimuli.[84]

Hobson, who was familiar with this literature, used it to cast doubts on 'socialist experiments, which are based upon assumptions about common needs and common human nature'.[85] Instead, he was impressed by the wide differences in subjective enjoyment of work. In criticizing communism, Hobson saw the crucial test as its ability 'to evoke and maintain all the necessary economic incentives. This is a problem of practical psychology.'[86] The experimental mood of liberalism[87] found an outlet in the rising science, for 'the problem of economic organisation for the common good is one of experimentation chiefly in the field of industrial psychology'.[88] The link between incentives and the motive forces of human nature was summed up by Hobson as follows: '. . . where a physical capacity to work is impeded by a want of will to work derived directly from the nature of the work, or the conditions under which it was done, the extra payment required to liberate the labour-power must be brought under the economy of payment according to needs.'[89] The need identified was the overcoming of a psychological reluctance and was significantly divorced from any 'natural', 'instinctive', or 'impulsive' repugnance for work, which would have signalled a defect of character. Burns, on the other hand, while recognizing the role of incentives, tried to play down their importance as 'subordinate', on the grounds that work or effort were themselves expressive and pleasurable. Economists, he asserted, confused 'the emotional attitude towards a conceived purpose with the emotional accompaniments of achieved purpose'.[90] This must be superimposed on Burns's previous argument,

[84] See Thomson, *The Pelican History of Psychology*, pp. 345–9, 355; Hearnshaw, *A Short History of British Psychology*, pp. 275–82.

[85] Hobson, *Free-Thought in the Social Sciences*, p. 135.

[86] Hobson, *Wealth and Life*, p. 224.

[87] See Chapter 5, Section 7.

[88] Hobson, *Wealth and Life*, p. 242.

[89] Ibid., p. 435.

[90] Burns, *Industry and Civilisation*, pp. 52, 55.

which noted the worker's 'recognition of the social necessity of the work he does'.[91] Hobson commented, obliquely referring to opinions such as those of Tawney,[92] that 'neither Mr. Burns, nor any other exponent of the workers' point of view, would maintain that this "sense of the social value of work" would go far as an actual incentive to its due performance'.[93] Previously Hobson had warned against the adoption of a 'soft' psychology which assumed that workers, although no longer willing to toil for the profit of the employer, would work for the community. This was no other than a 'preposterous pretence'.[94] Burns himself returned to liberal quid pro quo premisses when he wrote: 'It is reasonable to assume that no one should receive service unless he renders service.'[95]

E. Organicism: Aftermath of an Analogy

From liberal attitudes to psychology it is clear that no liberal entertained organicist images that conclusively separated the social entity from the sum of its parts. However prevalent the discussion between Hobson and Hobhouse, it was not at the heart of liberal organicism. Despite lack of agreement on the physical implications of the term, the notion of organism was used by liberals to convey a common ethical and political message, epitomized in the following passage by Hobhouse:

> A machine is in one sense an organisation of parts contrived to effect some combined purpose. A living organism is another sort of organisation of many parts to one result, the well-being of the whole. The difference between the two is that in the machine the inanimate parts are quite indifferent to the work they do . . . In the organism, on the other hand, each cell has a certain life of its own and contributes by its vital activities to the life of the organism, which in turn sustains its being. Now, society can be neither a mere machine nor a purely physical organism, for it is made up of conscious, sentient, reflecting beings. But it makes a vast difference whether these sentient beings have an order imposed on them which shapes them to some end of which they know little and perhaps for which they care less, or whether they freely, and as the expression of their own sense of what is best for man, build up organs of common will to achieve great ends in co-operation . . . In this sense, and without the metaphor which has too often

[91] Burns, *The Philosophy of Labour*, p. 36.
[92] See Chapter 8, Section 2.
[93] Hobson, *Wealth and Life*, p. 226.
[94] Hobson, *Free-Thought in the Social Sciences*, pp. 157–9.
[95] Burns, *Industry and Civilisation*, p. 121.

been abused, it is the ideal of society not merely to be organised but to become organic.[96]

A moral community was a collection of consciously co-operating individuals. Their highest faculties would be developed through and only through the incorporation of this awareness into their wills and activities. Liberal organicist theories distanced themselves categorically from authoritarian interpretations that imposed a central will on the parts. They portrayed the state as 'a fellowship of *persons*: that is of moral beings for moral ends: it is an ethical entity. And as the organic manifestation of the personality of a people it may properly be called an organism or a person.' Far from glorifying the state, the emphasis was on service to the individual, on 'ethical beings bound together in the unity of an ethical organism'.[97] Burns's reading of organicism, like Hobhouse's, held both that 'when we come to consider the contact between minds, the individual remains a hard and irreducible substance' and that 'the common good is a different kind of good from the goods of separate individuals'.[98] The reality of individuals did not negate their inherent interdependence in the spheres of mind and morality; nor did the ability of the parts to serve the good of the whole clash with the promotion of their own ends.[99] Hobson himself, whatever the nature of his dispute with Hobhouse, had reaffirmed this liberal understanding of organicism during the war.[100] Of course, he also used the term 'organic' in the further senses of interconnected, total, vital and social. It was in the first and last of these senses that he hailed the Yellow Book as a programme of social legislation with a common spirit and purpose—a policy of interdependent parts.[101] Similarly, Hobson approved of that aspect of rationalization that conceived of industries as organic wholes.[102]

As for the notion of the general will, liberals appeared ambivalent. Inasmuch as it signified a Rousseauist bending of a mistaken

[96] L. T. Hobhouse, 'The Organised State', *MG*, 12.8.1916.

[97] W. S. Lilly, 'The Reward of Labour', *NT*, 81 (1917), 102, 107.

[98] C. D. Burns, *The Contact Between Minds* (London, 1923), pp. 122, 115–16; *Government and Industry*, p. 8.

[99] In contrast Samuel, who preferred the term 'organization' to 'organism', asserted: 'There is no force in politics other than the action of individual men, acting upon their individual judgements.' (Samuel Papers, E/7A, draft of chapter on 'Political Illusions', p. 16.)

[100] See above, p. 43.

[101] J. A. Hobson, 'Minority Government', *Nation*, 11.5.1929.

[102] J. A. Hobson, 'Liberalism and Labour', *MG*, 5.2.1929.

individual will to a correct social one, an apparently authoritarian collectivism, they were alarmed. Hobson contrasted the idea of the general will with the notion of self-government through elections, implying that the former looked down upon democratic procedure as a transient majority opinion.[103] But he also used the concept in the loose meaning of 'social', when berating Laski for failing to link the social good with a directly operative social or 'general' will,[104] or when demanding of state officials and politicians that they enable the free, strong and intelligent functioning of the general will.[105] Even Hobhouse commended the Idealists Muirhead and Mackenzie for developing a concept of the general will in the manner of T. H. Green rather than Hegel: 'the conception of the general will and of the freedom of the individual as completed in social life rather than thwarted by it was susceptible of a more liberal and democratic application . . . that liberal Collectivism which has been a political power since the eighties.'[106] It was the notion of the real will, rather than the general will *per se*, that outraged left-liberals.

The employment of psychological insights by liberal theorists, Hobhouse excepted, was never more than dilettante dabbling. In comparison with the turmoil in social thought unleashed by psychology on the Continent, the reaction among British social thinkers was trivial. Furthermore, whereas biology and evolution had set liberal theory on new paths of intellectual exploration at the end of the previous century, liberals now simply gleaned selective items from popularized psychological studies that confirmed some of their social and political ideas. Psychology had no trail-blazing role to perform. What it could do was lend its tentative weight to four components of liberal thought: communitarianism with its special blend of the social and the individual and its emphasis on socially important human characteristics; a dynamic and developmental conception of human nature and character; the defence and upholding of rationality as the highest mode of thought, action and organization; and issues of social justice and reward pertaining to work and remuneration. Liberalism continued in its efforts to move

[103] J. A. Hobson, 'On True Self-Determination', *Nation*, 11.12.1920.

[104] Hobson, 'The Reformulation of Politics', 432.

[105] Hobson, *Wealth and Life*, p. 387. Clarke observes (*Liberals and Social Democrats*, p. 194) that Hobson no longer referred to the general will in his *Democracy After the War*, but fails to note that he returned to it in later works.

[106] [L. T. Hobhouse], 'Social Idealism', *MG*, 12.12.1918.

with the times, but its lack of confidence was hardly mitigated by its alliance with young sciences bereft of intellectual authority.

3. LIBERAL EQUALITY

In order to establish the conceptual particulars of left-liberal ideology, to draw some comparisons with centrist-liberalism, and to illustrate the range of positions occupied by liberals, this and the following two sections will respectively analyse three main components of its ethical system: equality, property, and liberty. With regard to the first concept, the questions that arise are: what type of equality does a communitarian theory lend itself to, and is there a specific interpretation of equality held by liberals? One of the problems with the concept of equality is that it so often is discussed under the heading of equality of opportunity. That notion, however, covers a spectrum of meanings from the minimalist to the maximalist. It can simply reflect the absence of formal restrictions on the occupation of social roles, as with the assertion that any citizen over thirty-five may become the President of the USA; or it can denote a radical social reorganization in which all available resources are put at the disposal of any member of society. As Hobson observed, equality of opportunity was one of the phrases which have been 'a terrible impediment to disinterested science, not only by reason of its slipperiness, but because of the interested and often impassioned burdens it carries'.[107] Although many liberals employed the term, centrist- and left-liberals were situated at different points on the spectrum. For Hobhouse, the revival of the discussion on equality was another outcome of 'the common sufferings' of the First World War.[108] The transfer of power to the working class also fomented the feeling that 'this power should be used to extend the principle of equality from the political into the social sphere'.[109] Centrist-liberals, however, treated equality in the main as a service-concept in relation to liberty. As the *Nation* remarked approvingly on the winds of change in the NLF, its new programme was essential to 'the policy of equality of opportunity which gives reality to personal liberty'.[110]

[107] Hobson, *Free-Thought in the Social Sciences*, p. 21.
[108] [L. T. Hobhouse], 'The Future of Liberalism', *MG*, 5.9.1919.
[109] H. B. Usher, 'Liberalism and its Future', *CR*, 123 (1923), 165.
[110] 'A Liberal Challenge to Liberalism', *Nation*, 29.1.1921.

Rowntree presented the centrist-liberal position as follows:

Now, what would practical 'equality of opportunity' involve? Manifestly, not that everyone should have the same opportunities, but that everyone should have the opportunities suited to his or her development. Here, most emphatically, the rule which should be observed is: 'The best tools to the man who can use them best'.

While accepting that 'each personality should be regarded as something of ultimate value', Rowntree dismissed the equal worth of personality as such. Equalization was not an aid to the fostering of community, nor was it a recognition of the common needs of humanity, with its concomitant belief in the sharing of natural and social bounties. It was plainly harnessed to a conception of human nature which treated the overriding claims of individual personality in isolation from the notion of common humanity, and in association with a stratified model of social structure. Rowntree foresaw 'a new *régime*' with 'a new kind of class distinction, founded upon the value of an individual's life to the community, and on the measure of his faithful service in whatever capacity he labours'.[111] Although this was put in terms of a contribution to the common good, it emphasized a measurable and therefore differential value to individual work and achievement, at odds with that ethical approach which accepted differential contributions as indicative of equal efforts and intentions and hence of equal worth.

Not that left-liberals wanted to do away with individual uniqueness. Hobson was dismayed with the American transition, as he saw it, 'from the libertarian to the equalitarian factor in democracy' because it was an equality that was compatible with the herd mind, rather than with personal liberty. The pressures to conform displaced individual reason and judgement. In contradistinction, the liberal viewpoint was a denial of equality as sameness. As Hobson argued, 'if every man is equal, in the sense that he is substantially the same as every other man, his aptitudes and needs the same, then his views and sentiments must be the same.'[112] Only that equality which served the development of human personality was socially and individually

[111] Rowntree, 'Labour Unrest and the Need for a National Ideal', 497–8. See Briggs, *Social Thought and Social Action*, pp. 157, 219, 339, who clearly shows the combination of religiously inspired humanitarianism and stress on business efficiency that characterized Rowntree.

[112] J. A. Hobson, 'I. The Good American. The American Attitude Towards Liberty', *Nation*, 7.2.1920.

valuable. Hobhouse, commenting on Hobson's article, observed that the American concept of equality of *opportunity* was in effect Green's *liberty*—a right to make the best of oneself—whereas the American idea of equality as such was uniformity, and differed from the embryonic British notion which was a creation of the war.[113]

The type of equality left-liberals held up as desirable eschewed sameness. It was directed towards the twin goals of the expression of personality and the pursuit of the common good. Hobson identified three components in the concept of social equality. The first was the equal political opportunity for individuals to form and express public opinion. The second extended that right to groups and recognized their equal need to express their interests and valuations. The third aimed at transcending the barriers of class and enabling unique personal attributes to contribute to public policy. The organization of society with a view to social equality recognized 'in each individual a unique personality, a member of a class or group, and a member of the wider community, of which the classes or other groups are sections'.[114] But though Hobson acknowledged 'the fact that in body and mind we are, say 95 per cent., alike'[115] he realized that a difficult balance had to be struck. True, equality of opportunity was 'a sound working principle' because 'there is so much likeness in the make-up and environment of most individuals that their differences may safely be ignored for certain purposes'. But it was far more than an assertion of equal liberty for all to go their own ways. Here Hobson broke with the liberal individualist tradition and its contractarian interpretation of equal rights owed to the individual and innate to his or her individuality. A communitarian approach taught that rights had social origins and were ultimately conferred to enhance social needs. It was socially useful to treat all alike when capacities and needs could not be estimated, but when they could, 'opportunities should be distributed according to capacity to use or enjoy them'.[116] This did not entail, as in Rowntree's analysis, a hierarchical society, because crucially the criterion for distribution was not use alone, but enjoyment. The

[113] [L. T. Hobhouse], 'Liberty in the Mass', *MG*, 21.2.1920.

[114] J. A. Hobson, *Towards Social Equality* (L. T. Hobhouse Memorial Trust Lecture no. 1, Oxford, 1931), p. 5.

[115] Ibid., p. 25.

[116] Hobson, *Wealth and Life*, p. 42.

ability both to produce and to consume was taken into account. Reverting to Aristotelian language, Hobson saw social equality consisting 'in treating persons alike so far as they are alike, as well as in treating them differently so far as they differ'.[117]

In almost all cases, the development of personality remained central to the liberal exposition of equality. But because the understanding of personality, its attributes, and the forces that sustained it, differed greatly—because in effect the notions of human needs were at variance with each other—the operational definition of equality of opportunity had vastly diverse manifestations. Hobson cautioned that serious steps were required to secure a genuine equality of economic opportunity, which would 'involve an attack upon the present system of exclusive rights of property almost as revolutionary as the wholesale schemes of socialism and communism'.[118] Nevertheless, he and other liberals would not tolerate a total attempt at standardization. The distinction between the claims of personality and community had to allow for a high degree of individuation. A levelling process would stifle personality in a 'live organic society'.[119] It was important not to be deceived by 'false assumptions of equality in human nature'.[120] The keynote to Hobson's analysis, whether of equality or of property, was that 'community in the sense of citizenship, nationality, humanity, is in the last resort resolvable into enriched personality'. Yet this was no simple assertion that personality had a social aspect, for membership of a community introduced a different dimension. The correct formulation was to talk about an individual personality and a social personality (a community) that were closely linked.[121]

Hobhouse also viewed equality from the perspective of the common good, though within a less directly communitarian framework than that of Hobson. Consequently, he did not share the latter's reluctance to connect the discussion of equality to that of individual rights. Those rights were based on a conception of common nature, and here Hobhouse took out double indemnity by resting his case on empirical and non-empirical evidence alike. The ability of all beings to feel entitled them to consideration, for on the principle of

[117] Hobson, *Towards Social Equality*, p. 26.

[118] J. A. Hobson, *Property and Improperty* (London, 1937), p. 56.

[119] Hobson, *Towards Social Equality*, pp. 25, 29, 32.

[120] Hobson, *Democracy After the War*, p. 186.

[121] J. A. Hobson, *Rationalism and Humanism* (Conway Memorial Lecture, London, 1933), pp. 23–4.

harmony happiness as comfort was part of the good. Human beings, however, shared also a soul, or reason, a 'generic' common nature which 'had no reason to fear the test of our ordinary experience of life'. On this foundation Hobhouse proposed to begin with the differences among individuals and, again in Aristotelian fashion, to regard equality 'as essentially an adjustment in which differences of persons (in whatever respect) is made a basis of corresponding differences of treatment'. In this analysis of distributive justice Hobhouse quarrelled with the economists' view—and by implication with the opinions of many centrist-liberals—for having grounded their quantitative determination of proportionate equality 'on the hard facts of the human market rather than on ethical principles'.[122] Hobhouse's reading of Aristotle included qualitative as well as quantitative considerations, mitigated the notion of desert by that of need, and further proposed to include effort as well as attainment as a measure of desert.

At the heart of Hobhouse's analysis were the claims of the individual personality. Unlike Hobson, he stressed reciprocal obligations that arose from the choice of individuals to enter into relationships with one another, and that derived only from direct expressions of personality, such as will or effort. When determining the practical aspects of equality, however, he insisted on identifying 'the point of difference between Socialism proper and the Social Liberalism which seeks the harmony of the communal and the individual'.[123] Like Tawney, as we shall see in the next chapter, he emphasized the importance of maintaining necessary economic functions when providing for equal needs. The provision of needs without equivalent service would have to be severely controlled (here again the Victorian heritage revived by the economic stringencies of the 1920s is obvious) 'as to lay no crippling burden on production and offer no encouragement to idleness'.[124] It was equally important, however, that wealth could only be acquired by social service and that there would be no functionless or socially injurious wealth. Exceptions to the rule of reciprocal provision for services applied to children, the aged, the disabled and the permanently defective. Idlers would have to receive an allowance to meet their needs 'at the judgment of the community', for this was not an un-

[122] Hobhouse, *The Elements of Social Justice*, pp. 95, 97, 99.
[123] Ibid, pp. 101–2, 146.
[124] Ibid., p. 133.

qualified right, nor a licence to behaviour that burdened the community. A further important exception was the unemployed, for 'the whole of our argument substantiates the alternative right to labour or maintenance'.[125] Unemployment was the fault of bad industrial organization and was not to be seen as a default on the reciprocity of social provision and individual contribution. As for the employed, increased effort and ability deserved greater remuneration. Remaining firmly within the liberal orbit, Hobhouse contended that 'it is in the larger interest of the common good itself that private interests should maintain themselves, and that in particular capable men should be able to make their own way, provided always that . . . their advancement is secured . . . by sound social service.'[126] This latter proviso was reaffirmed in a reassertion of the new liberal ethic: 'the elementary human needs are a matter of common concern, . . . mutual aid is a better ideal than individual self-sufficiency, and public service a better motive than personal profit.'[127]

The difference between left-liberals and centrist-liberals was profound, despite similar terminology and overlapping ideas. Centrist-liberals did not regard equality as adjacent to community and as necessary to the development of personality. Neither did they extend the notion of equality to embrace the distribution of socially useful goods and services. Muir saw variety rather than equality as adjacent to liberty, and insisted that in the liberal state there would be no attempt 'to establish an artificial equality among men who are naturally unequal and different. The only forms of equality which it will pursue will be equality before the law, and equality of opportunities for all citizens to make the most of their varying powers'.[128] This minimalist position was far less than left-liberals were prepared to countenance; what was palpably lacking was the *rationale* of the maximization of citizens' powers—the common good, the benefit of the community, as well as, and including, their own. Masterman, for instance, warned against those who would 'establish an equality which would allow no prize for unusual talent or energy, trusting that patriotism and general desire for fellowship and welfare will cause every man to work his hardest, animated by the sense of duty

[125] Ibid., pp. 138–9.
[126] Ibid., p. 144.
[127] Hobhouse, 'The Problem', p. 279.
[128] Muir, *Politics and Progress*, p. 32.

to the whole community'.[129] Left-liberals also allowed for such prizes, but believed that it was ethically essential to cultivate a sense of duty as fundamental to the social relationship. Masterman proceeded to change tack and to argue that liberalism could not guarantee 'the continued prosperity of an equalitarian state in a world of fierce competition'.[130] This converged upon the views of those economists whom Hobhouse had berated. One of them, T. E. Gregory, a liberal, insisted that the share of each individual in what was produced had to be 'proportionate, and strictly proportionate, to the market value of his services'. Any equalization would be restricted to recycling incomes and would not allow direct state intervention in the market; indeed, the wealth of the rich was essential to further social and economic experiment. The crux of the different approaches was reflected in the following: 'I am not in favour of giving great masses of people something for nothing . . . it is broadly desirable that anybody who receives a sum of money from the state should have contributed to the sum which he receives.'[131] Thus the notion of social relationships was reduced to a commercial one, and the idea of catering to human needs was rendered subservient to the rule of market forces.

Among Summer School liberals, the most persistent advocate of a more committed and passionate regard for equality was Simon. The signs of a future estrangement from the placid and genteel progressivism of his LSS colleagues are more easily discerned on this theme than on any other. As early as 1920 Simon wrote in his diary: 'I believe economic equality (at least of opportunity) is probably the acid test as to whether the Liberal party still represents a Liberal spirit.'[132] By 1925 he was identifying that equality of opportunity as one of the hallmarks of a radical liberalism and formulating a doctrine that many of his co-liberals must have regarded with perturbation: 'it is necessary not only to make the poor richer, but to make the rich—especially the very rich—poorer. [The Radical Liberal] is prepared to support any steps, however drastic, that are needed to fight inequality and vested interests wherever they are hostile to the public good . . .'[133] On the whole Simon stood by this

[129] Masterman, *The New Liberalism*, p. 153.

[130] Ibid.

[131] T. E. Gregory, 'The Production and Distribution of Work', in Nathan and Williams, *Liberal Points of View*, pp. 50–3, 56, 69–75.

[132] Simon Papers, Diary, p. 18.

[133] E. D. Simon, *The Inheritance of Riches* (London, 1925), p. 13.

interpretation of radicalism. He repeatedly told the LSS that they were not doing enough to further equality of opportunity, a subject which—he felt—even the Yellow Book had failed to deal with adequately.[134] He provided the term with a content that placed him on the liberal left: 'My political aim is to give the best chance to every child, and to remove the excessive inequalities of today. That is practically the aim of Labour.'[135] Simon distinguished himself sharply from the 'social reform' liberal who believed in social insurance, some public services and a national minimum but who was closer to the left wing of the conservatives in his refusal to interfere with the existing rights of property.[136] In effect, his proposals differed in degree rather than in kind from those of more moderate progressives in two important areas—the inheritance of wealth and housing. Only in the sphere of family allowances did he depart significantly from mainstream progressivism.

The proposals Simon supported with respect to inheritance policy had been aired by liberal economists such as Clay, Stamp, and Henderson. They favoured ownership based on earnings and saw restrictions on inheritance as essential prerequisites for the former. Stamp and Henderson had backed the erosion of accumulated fortunes by means of the 'Rignano scheme' which differed from death duties by taxing not what a bequeather saved himself but only what was passed on by him from previous generations. The ideal of a nation of small capitalists, close to the heart of centrist-liberals, was only possible if the large fortunes which had been amassed could be redistributed. This redistribution was less a question of catering for human or communal needs than of creating the conditions of personal freedom and development, once again demonstrating the importance of assessing an ideology not only on its proposals, but on the idea-context in which those proposals are presented. Nearly all progressive liberals supported taxation of inherited wealth, but the adjacent purposes which it could serve differed. For Henderson, its prime attraction was the possibility it held out for a more speedy repayment of the national debt. The Rignano

134 Simon, 'The Liberal Summer School' (1926), 303; 'The Liberal Summer School' (1929), 277. See above, p. 119.

135 Simon Papers, Diary, 27.2.1925. Stuart Hodgson also supplied an extensive interpretation of equality of opportunity in work and leisure, while stressing its value for the individual (J. Stuart Hodgson, 'The Liberal State', in Nathan and Williams (eds.), *Liberalism and Some Problems of To-Day*, pp. 17–42).

136 Simon, *The Inheritance of Riches*, p. 13.

scheme had to his mind important value undertones—a 'very powerful, profound social effect'—in that each generation would have the incentive to earn fresh money. 'It would become very much more the general tradition that everybody would be expected to earn a considerable income in order to make good for their children the losses on their own inherited fortunes.'[137] Hence industry, family responsibility, and productivity were the 'healthy' ideological by-products of this centrist-liberal set of proposals. Clay, too, integrated his discussion of inheritance with a centrist-liberal assumption concerning the natural inequality of people, but was more anxious to emphasize that inequality of income was a result of 'the inequalities of opportunity which the existing economic inequality involves'. He supported a limitation of the right of bequest because it offered the best way to 'promote the diffusion rather than the extinction of property', which was in turn 'the most *conservative* way of securing this greater equality that suggests itself'.[138] Significantly, the main beneficiaries of such equalization were to be 'the non-commercial, small propertied middle class', not the dispossessed.[139]

Not all centrist-liberals approved of the Rignano scheme. The *Westminster Gazette* saw it as no better than confiscation and, while in favour of death duties in principle, believed such a scheme would destroy all incentive to work and deflect money away from productive purposes.[140] Muir, describing the inequality in the distribution of capital as 'the most unwholesome feature in our economic system', nevertheless objected to the Rignano scheme for the practical reason that it would be virtually impossible to distinguish between different kinds of inherited wealth. He suggested instead graduated legacy duties which, rather than persuading a man to keep his money in his family, would act to make him distribute it widely. Muir's main objection to the Rignano scheme, as could be expected, was that 'it takes the money ultimately for the State: it does

[137] H. D. Henderson, 'Liberalism and the Problem of Inheritance', in Nathan and Williams, *Liberal Points of View*, p. 201. See also J. Stamp in *Nation*, 20.11.1926. Hobhouse, too, spoke of the scheme favourably ('The Problem', pp. 284–5).

[138] H. Clay, 'Property and Inheritance', *Nation*, 11.8.1923.

[139] H. Clay, 'Liberalism, Laissez-Faire and Present Industrial Conditions', *HJ*, 24 (1926), 738.

[140] 'The Right of Inheritance', *WG*, 8.8.1923. However, the then editor, J. A. Spender, commended a similar scheme as proposed by Henderson in the 1926 LSS ('The Family Versus the State', *WG*, 31.7.1926).

not bring about its distribution'.[141] This sparked off an immediate response from Simon that illustrates the growing divide between centrist-liberalism and left-liberalism: 'The general impression left by your leader is that you prefer to distribute what is left by inheritance among a larger number of people, rather than to take more of it for communal purposes by death duties.' For Muir taxation of inheritance had become a means of shoring up an individualistically based capitalism, whereas Simon saw death duties as a remedy for social injustice which would help increase workers' earnings. Unlike his LSS colleagues, he was prepared to reduce inheritance to the lowest possible point that did not interfere with incentives to production or saving.[142]

Simon's more radical approach to equalization was coupled with a co-ordinated—in fact, organic, in one sense of the word—series of social policies, one of the mainstays of which was housing. Despite Lloyd George's homes for heroes programme, liberals felt bereft of a housing policy[143] and Simon attempted to remedy this deficiency through the 1923 LSS. While acknowledging the contribution of the Addison scheme to lower middle and upper working-class housing, Simon declared that the aim of liberals was to give 'every working-class family the chance of occupying such a house'.[144] Two paths led to that objective. The first derived from the view that 'as Liberals we hold that it is the duty of the State to provide the conditions under which private enterprise can function and to exercise the control necessary to ensure that the best type of house shall be built'. Furthermore, 'we are perfectly willing that houses should be built municipally rather than that they should not be built at all, but our preference is always in favour of private enterprise and initiative, properly regulated by the State.'[145] This was the balance that the LSS preferred: the state as encourager and supervisor but not as direct actor. In practice Simon recommended the exemption of new houses from personal rates—those that covered services required by individuals—and the financing of such services on liberal principles, i.e. the ability to pay. He also reiterated the long-standing liberal

141 [R. Muir], 'How to Break Up Swollen Fortunes', *WW*, 26.12.1925.

142 E. D. Simon, letter to the Editor, *WW*, 2.1.1926.

143 Cf. A MacCallum Scott, 'Attacking Socialism', *Lloyd George Liberal Magazine* (1922), 459.

144 E. D. Simon, 'The Housing Problem', *Nation*, 11.8.1923. See also E. D. Simon, *How to Abolish the Slums* (London, 1929), p. 1.

145 Simon, *Houses for All*, p. 18.

proposal of a rate on site values. Conversely, Hobson now expressed his doubts about universal house ownership, because 'such localisation might gravely interfere with the desired mobility of modern industry'. Instead, 'public ownership should afford the necessary security with better hygienic conditions and with freedom of movement in accordance with economic changes.'[146] It is interesting that Simon later confided to his diary: 'got Muir to help me with "Houses for All". Now think he spoilt it, and should not dream of asking similar help!'[147] The stated preference for private enterprise must have rankled.

The second path, which linked Simon with left-liberalism, was the insistence on a regular living wage for workers: 'We can never solve the housing problem until we have solved the wages problem.'[148] Simon's concerted attack on the slums also came into play here, for their replacement could only be effected by enabling workers to pay the rent of good houses. All this was part of the new liberal legacy: the interconnected assault on social evils seen as a reinforcing chain, and therefore necessitating a general view of social structure and purpose. Here also was the rationale for introducing the more radical proposals concerning family allowances, hatched by Beveridge and keenly adopted by Simon; as a 'family wage' it would be one method of regularizing and increasing the incomes of the poorly paid.

Simon was first and foremost a municipal activist and often called for a revival of 'municipal liberalism' which on its own terms would give substance to the quest for equality. Hence the notion that slums should be provided with the same services as suburbs was a form of geographical area redistribution as well as an insistence on equal chances for every child.[149] On the future of children a housing policy coalesced with family allowances. As the *Nation*, commenting on Simon's *How to Abolish the Slums*, observed, his proposals—which involved paying a special rent allowance to tenants in accordance with their means and number of children—represented 'at once the most satisfactory solution available of the problem of housing finance and the most satisfactory way of applying Miss Rathbone's principle of "Family Endowment"'. With a clearly

[146] Hobson, *Property and Improperty*, p. 197.
[147] Simon Papers, Diary, 'My First 50 Years', *c.*1930.
[148] E. D. Simon, 'The Housing Problem', *Nation*, 11.8.1923.
[149] E. D. Simon, 'Liberalism and Municipal Policy', *Nation*, 14.1.1928.

organic perspective, the *Nation* applauded a full housing programme for saving unemployment pay, stimulating trade, and preserving human character, and added: 'It is no longer appropriate to treat housing and unemployment in water-tight compartments.'[150] Subsidized housing through children's rent allowances was a policy that centred once again, as the new liberalism had tried to do, on the needs of disadvantaged individuals who could not care for themselves. This interpretation of equality, superficially concerned with the life chances of individuals in the same way as centrist-liberalism, differed in its adjacent concepts and in the justification for that idea-environment. Centrist-liberals wanted individual development on lines of efficiency and productivity, aiming at an ultimate differentiation that would erode equality. Left-liberals, in Simon's words, harboured a view of human nature that believed that 'human beings respond well in almost every case to good conditions and generous treatment'.[151] They were more concerned with the universal improvement of the human lot, of social conditions, and with an extension of the assault on poverty, than with the establishment of the prerequisites for excellence. Both approaches professed to embody principles of social justice and both could lay claim to a liberal pedigree. Through analysing the structure and patterns of argumentation that characterize liberal ideology, both approaches have been shown as reconcilable with aspects of the liberal tradition.

The above discussion is not intended to suggest that questions of inheritance, housing or family allowances exhaust the practical ramifications of equality, but that inter-war liberals concentrated on those issues as the most promising areas of further equalization. At the same time left-liberals were prepared to integrate general ethical considerations of equality into their theories with greater resolve than the new liberals of a former generation. For left-liberals, the emphasis on equality signalled no departure from liberalism; furthermore, as we shall see in Chapter 8, their ideas constituted a community of thought shared with well-known British socialists who also believed that equality was compatible with patently liberal beliefs.

150 'The Slum, The Taxpayer, and the Unemployed', *Nation*, 2.3.1929.
151 E. D. Simon, *Liberalism in Local Government* (London, 1924), p. 21.

4. PROPERTY: AN INSTITUTION RECLAIMED

The question of property in liberal thought had, by the twentieth century, undergone considerable modifications since its designation as a natural right, but it had certainly not succumbed to the challenge of some nineteenth-century socialist doctrines. Two extreme positions were ruled out from the start: the unlimited right to appropriation and the abolition of all private property. Within these poles important differences existed among liberals, differences corresponding on the whole to the centrist and left outlooks. Hobhouse adumbrated the two progressive approaches to a socially beneficial organization of property:

> The first is by the method of individualist production—the peasant-proprietor, the one-man business. This method is the economic expression of that view of liberty which regards it as an emancipation of individual life from the social nexus . . . The alternative method is the economic expression of liberty as a social function and as dependent on social control. On this method property as economic power must be vested in the last resort in a self-governing community, while the individual will require property—as distinct from the prescribed use and permitted enjoyment of material things—for the free conduct of his personal life.[152]

Centrist-liberals made much of certain modifications to the property system which, they believed, would improve social organization, cater to their concept of human nature, and serve the ends of social justice. They asserted that the system of property ownership had changed markedly through the introduction of the joint-stock company.[153] Share-owning served, parallel to the wider distribution of land and the breakdown of large concentrations of wealth, as the means of diffusing private property and rendering it available for all. When Muir listed security of property as part of the first condition of liberty, together with security of life and livelihood, he went on to explain that modern liberalism qualified the right to private property in three ways: the community was to maintain direct power over it by taxation; the distinction between earned and inherited wealth, inasmuch as it did not discourage saving, would have to be observed; and respect for legitimate wealth (that wealth which reflected an individual's contribution to the co-operative process of its creation) would be upheld.[154] The wide ownership of

[152] Hobhouse, *The Elements of Social Justice*, pp. 157–8.
[153] See above, pp. 147–9.
[154] Muir, *The New Liberalism*, pp. 12–13.

property expressed the desire of centrist-liberals to optimize the conditions under which individual talents would flourish; private property had, in Murray's words, moral and vital value.[155] The freedom it offered—material independence from others—was a source of self-respect.[156] The adoption of this concept of property illustrates more than anything else the growing fissure within progressive liberalism, commensurate with the rise of strong anti-communitarian feelings among the centrists; while for left-liberals the concept of property moved further away from their ideological core and donned, as shall presently be shown, social dimensions. Hobhouse was at pains to remind his readers that property was not necessarily private; rather, it denoted a form of regulated control that could be either private or collective.[157] Centrist-liberals, however, shied away from the latter option and became increasingly insistent on the need for private property as the guarantor of individual initiative and responsibility. But that responsibility was not of the variant that made the plight of the unfortunate the concern of the rest; it was the kind that encouraged respectability in terms of financial and moral prudence.

Some liberals took the further small step of reintroducing the concept of property as its own reward, as an indicator of self-emancipation rather than a means to it. This, however, was borderline liberalism, on the verge of alienating itself from the progressive variety and allying itself with a middle-class economic conservatism. Take for example the views of Hirst, who declared unequivocally that 'Liberalism is Libertarianism' and that 'Enlightened selfishness is the best substitute in public policy for the private morality of the Sermon on the Mount.' For Hirst, private property was a protection against the state and the community: 'Strip men of their private property, and they are helpless to resist the tyranny of a bureaucratic State.' Hirst's mid-Victorian interpretation of the right of private property associated it with 'the right to compete freely in business, to buy in the cheapest market, to sell in the dearest . . .', and further with the right to unlimited earnings.[158]

155 G. Murray, 'The Future of the Liberal Party', *Nation*, 29.11.1924.

156 By the 1950s this had become mainstream Conservatism. Cf. Anthony Eden, quoted in V. Bogdanor and R. Skidelsky, *The Age of Affluence* (London, 1970), p. 61.

157 Hobhouse, *The Elements of Social Justice*, pp. 152–3.

158 F. W. Hirst, 'Liberalism and Liberty', *CR*, 145 (1934), 283; 'Is British Liberalism Alive or Dead?', *CR*, 149 (1936), 426–7.

Centrist-liberals, though no radicals, remained—in contradistinction to the above—firm reformers. Liberals in general may, in view of socialist attacks on property, have expressed themselves more strongly about the importance of private property than before, but they were far from satisfied with the rights and distribution of property as they now stood. They no longer justified property rights within a family immune to state intervention, because their society had failed to establish a 'relationship between the ownership of property and social obligations'.[159] Centrist-liberals like Muir were also perturbed by the divorce of ownership from responsibility that widespread shareholding introduced. The old fears concerning the powers of monopolies were simply transferred to the new directors of joint-stock companies: 'It is not wealth as such that now threatens British liberty. It is the power of those who wield an almost irresponsible control over the accumulated wealth of millions. The new ruling class may be described as the Director-class.'[160] Thus the wider distribution of property would not on its own buttress liberty unless counter-measures were taken. Muir realized that it was the state that, through its legislation, had created the problem and that should now be called upon to solve it. Some of the solutions he envisaged entailed stricter controls on large companies, but 'the greatest contribution which can be made by the joint-stock system to the diffusion of ownership is the readiness with which it can be adapted to schemes of profit-sharing.'[161] The resurrection of the idea of worker-participation, not in the running of a concern, but in its profits and prosperity, underlined the interest-oriented, 'stake in the country' approach to human nature of centrist-liberalism. Nevertheless, Muir aspired to get rid of the 'worst defect' of capitalism—its assumption that every industrial concern is the property of those who have invested capital in it. It is ironical that the quotation from Bacon, much favoured by centrist-liberals as a reflection of their philosophy—'Money is like muck, not good except it be spread'—was probably picked up by them from Tawney's *The Acquisitive Society*.[162] But Tawney had used it as a comment on fifteenth to seventeenth-

[159] National Liberal Enquiry, Questionnaire No. 3, *The Inheritance of Wealth* (*Guardian* Archives, C. P. Scott Papers, 145/3/6).

[160] R. Muir, 'Property and Liberty', *CR*, 154 (1938), 556.

[161] R. Muir, 'The Diffusion of Ownership', *CR*, 155 (1939), 157. Cf. also P. Kerr, 'The State and Industry', *FV*, September 1927.

[162] R. H. Tawney, *The Acquisitive Society* (London, 1921), p. 62.

century thought, and elsewhere expressed a preference not for breaking large incomes into fragments but for securing that the purpose of most wealth would be the common advantage.

By the end of the 1930s the slogan 'ownership for all' had become a central plank of official Liberalism. A report carrying that name was published, and prompted a party resolution condemning both socialist state ownership and the 'capitalist collectivism' of the present (Conservative) government. In the light of the growing concern for civil and political liberties, private property was seen as an essential defence against both the right and the left. The *Manchester Guardian* saw the report as breaking new ground—a claim only correct with respect to party policy—and attempted to portray it within the context of a general onslaught by liberals on inequality.[163] But the report mainly restricted itself to dealing with inheritance on the lines of Muir's legacy tax. If evidence is required for the gulf between a progressive ideology and its party political incarnation, the following remark by the *Manchester Guardian* supplies it: 'The Liberal Summer School did some good work on the problem fifteen years ago, and the party may be congratulated on now taking it up officially with definite proposals.'[164] Any sarcasm was unintentional, but this is certainly a pointer to the reasons for the failing image of the Liberal party.

Left-liberals unanimously supported the institution of private property, but hedged it with considerable restrictions, connected it to different functions, and allowed for the parallel institution of public property. Hobhouse, who before the war had argued the case for the social origins of individual property rights, criticized Bertrand Russell for denying the morality of the possessive impulse altogether. 'To Mr. Russell the impulse to hold what one has is barely distinguishable morally from the impulse to take what another has.' But, contended Hobhouse, human creativity was sustained by the impulse to possess.[165] He further went along with centrist-liberals in regarding private property as a bulwark of freedom, and was no less insistent on identifying it also as a potential source of dangerous power. The amount of property necessary to the free conduct of one's personal life was modest, however, and—for the

[163] *MG*, 28.3.1938. See also 'Ownership for All', *Liberal Magazine*, 46 (1938), 158–61.

[164] 'Property', *MG*, 30.3.1938.

[165] L. T. H[obhouse], 'An Apostle of Peace', *MG*, 16.12.1916.

sake of that very liberty property was to abet—its final control in the economic and industrial spheres 'must be in communal hands, since, if exercised by individuals, it gives them the disposal of the lives of others'.[166] Unlike centrist-liberals, Hobhouse would not entrust private organizations with that role. Indeed, the rationale behind the wider diffusion of property was meaningless for advanced industrialism. In a modern society, 'economic freedom lies, not through the partition of property, but through the control of power'.[167]

This leads to a further issue that both united and divided liberals. Most of them had come round to accepting that the community, rather than the individual, was the arbiter of property rights. As Phillips had observed, the right to property, especially the assumption that 'what's mine's my own', had to give way to the realization that the social will defined the framework of such rights.[168] Similarly, Burns saw the ownership of property as a liberty 'extended by grace of society'.[169] But if the community was the source of property rights, or validated them, it could still decide that any one among a plethora of distributive mechanisms was socially advantageous. For centrist-liberals the pattern was one of many small individual property holders, a large number of private concerns regulated by the state, and the state itself as owner of a few essential services. For left-liberals the pattern differed.

Already at the turn of the century Hobson had observed that 'every defence of the principle of individual property is likewise a plea for social property' and had argued that common property was necessary for the self-realization of the community.[170] Hobhouse had echoed that contention in 1913[171] and was to reiterate it in 1922: 'If property is the economic basis of freedom and self-dependence, the possession of *some* property is desirable for individuals, and for any corporate body that has to direct its own affairs.'[172] This was a skilful extension of the individualist-

[166] Hobhouse, *The Elements of Social Justice*, p. 159.

[167] Hobhouse, 'The Problem', p. 283.

[168] Phillips, 'Liberalism and Industrial Relations', 70–1.

[169] Burns, *Industry and Civilisation*, p. 183.

[170] J. A. Hobson, 'The Ethics of Industrialism', in S. Coit (ed.), *Ethical Democracy: Essays in Social Dynamics* (London, 1900), p. 104. See Freeden, *The New Liberalism*, p. 46.

[171] L. T. Hobhouse, 'The Historical Evolution of Property, in Fact and in Idea', in C. Gore (ed.), *Property: Its Duties and Rights* (London, 1913), p. 31.

[172] Hobhouse, *The Elements of Social Justice*, p. 155.

liberal case to groups and ultimately to states as well; skilful in that it avoided an explicit reference to the social origins of property, preferring to take the line that communities needed independence and means in order to run their own affairs. Social property was thus defensible because the community was invested with the duty of performing certain functions 'which require their due return'.[173] But there was also a residual sense in which the community was the owner of property that was not clearly created by the productivity of individuals *or* of society. In such cases, 'the basis of exclusive ownership fails, and all have an equal right to participate, i.e. the only rational claim is that of the community.'[174] This argument applied especially to unearned wealth in natural resources or in inherited income. Under conditions of war, however, the egalitarian assumptions underlying the claims of the community to wealth could be taken to an extreme, as the *Nation* had insisted: 'the nearest approach to the equality of sacrifice is obtained by placing at the disposal of the State the whole available property and income of the non-fighting citizens.'[175] Though this was to be 'an exceptional act of State' and was labelled communism by the *Nation* two years later,[176] it was but an extension of the logic that saw the community as the arbiter of property rights and the determiner of optimal social functions. A softer version of this role, commensurate with peacetime needs and using a different scale of socially approved values and activities, was one the community would always be called upon to play.

Towards the end of the war Hobson developed a distinction between property and improperty, one he was to abide by for the rest of his life. The concept of 'improperty' had a dual purpose in that it singled out the gross abuses of the present economic system for attack while implying that property within certain constraints was acceptable, even desirable. Property itself was not an evil, but it could be a vehicle for socially damaging behaviour, 'the chief channel through which the lust of power sought and found satisfaction'. Capitalism was 'the use of property as a tool of commerce, industry or finance, for the acquisition of profit'.[177] But, as Hobson continued to contend,

[173] Ibid., p. 161. [174] Ibid., p. 163.
[175] 'Your Money or Your Life!', *Nation*, 22.1.1916.
[176] 'A State Bonus for All', *Nation*, 25.5.1918.
[177] Hobson, *Democracy After the War*, p. 26.

property, like power, is not essentially bad. On the contrary, some property, some portion of useful matter reserved for the use of a particular person, is necessary for any sort of life . . . Everyone, in order to be a free person, ought to have access to some share of the natural and developed resources of the world, and to the general stock of knowledge which will help him to realize his purposes with such materials. This right to property flows from the conception of a free personality in a world of equal opportunity . . . property is good which is the instrument or the embodiment of the wholesome creative impulses of human beings.[178]

The dividing line between liberals was not on the condoning or condemning of private property, nor on the notion of property as a means for expressing personality. As always, it returned to human traits it was individually and socially beneficial to develop. But the left-liberalism of a Hobson further indicated an equality of access that surpassed the minimalist centrist-liberal stipulation of property ownership. It expressly mentioned a share in natural and developed resources, as well as in information and hence education, thus identifying what it considered to be beneficial types of property. Improperty, on the other hand, was doubly injurious in that it laid its claims as a result of the use of (economic) force and appropriated a 'surplus' which was socially created and therefore illegitimately held by individuals or groups.[179] Twenty years later Hobson elaborated on that theme. Whereas in primitive societies the distinction between property and improperty was a simple one—the first being created by an individual's labour, the second by seizure or usurpation of another's property—the owners of improperty in modern societies were advantaged by the lack of any such clear differentiation. Although improperty could be found in interest, profit, and rent, they were not always manifestations of improperty. Consequently, 'the fact that improperty is everywhere mixed with property enables the possessing classes to accept the view that whatever the "laws" (which they have made) recognise as legal ownership is property, and that the charges brought against improperty are the inventions of envy and malice.'[180] Improperty, suggested Hobson, related to any land, labour or capital that were owned without being applied to the production of wealth, understood in its wider sense. Conversely, property should designate only

178 Ibid., pp. 28–9.
179 Ibid., pp. 30–1.
180 Hobson, *Property and Improperty*, p. 211.

what was necessary to induce optimal utilization of these factors. As to the payment of rents, 'whether they fall under the term "improperty" depends upon the question whether we count human motives as they are or as they ought to be in a fully developed commonwealth in which every man thinks and feels he ought to put his best abilities at the service of the community'.[181]

While Hobson rejected the accepted view that 'whatever income a man can obtain in accordance with the legal rules of the business or professional game is his rightful property',[182] he also dissociated himself from socialist conceptions of property. Socialist theory drew a distinction between property for personal use and social property in the means of production. But even personal property such as shelter, contended Hobson, could return unearned income. Moreover, workers everywhere owned personal capital. Socialists confused the issue by refusing to distinguish between 'the legitimate and the illegitimate payment for the use of capital' (an example of the first being the purchase of production tools), and between 'capital as a productive factor and the question of its ownership'. A blanket condemnation of property was no solution to the liberal who would differentiate between economic processes 'which are rightly socialised because they supply the common needs of consumers and those left to private enterprise because they supply individual needs'.[183] Hobson would not entertain the progressive capitalist argument (liberal or otherwise) that maintained that private enterprise, properly constituted, could cater to common needs as well. Only the community could provide the necessary organic viewpoint.

Hobson was a communitarian in that he believed in 'the social determination of the value of any particular goods by the interplay of the entire body of producers and consumers'. This invalidated 'the notion that any property in its form or its value can be the product of any individual worker, entrepreneur, manufacturer or trader'.[184] Rather, in order to realize the common life, the community required control over the property it had helped to make.[185] But Hobson also insisted that, shorn of industrial control as an

[181] Ibid., pp. 95, 99–100.
[182] Ibid., p. 68.
[183] Ibid., pp. 72–4, 104.
[184] Ibid., p. 164.
[185] Hobson, *Wealth and Life*, p. 163.

instrument of profit, 'property is a permanently valuable institution',[186] and rightly administered, 'private property is a social force making for genuine community of life and interests'. Consequently, because 'property is indispensable as a support of personality *and* community', the balance or harmony between the two was of paramount importance.[187] Left-liberals had come to believe that one way of attaining such balance was by redressing 'the overemphasis on the rights of property and underemphasis on economic equality, and the excessive antipathy to State intervention'[188] that characterized Liberal party activity in the 1920s and 1930s.

5. LIBERTY: THE CORE OF LIBERALISM?

A. The Environments of Liberty

To observe that a belief in liberty is a core element in liberal thought is a truism. To hold that liberals were ideologically united through a belief in liberty is an error. Like other political concepts, liberty covers a wide range of positions. Indeed, a subscription to some variant of liberty features in almost all British political thinking, conservative and socialist as well as liberal. In examining the concept of liberty in the progressive liberal context vital differences emerge, which indicate not only the divergences within liberalism but a fundamental divide that conservatives and socialists, drawing on the insights derived by liberals from their treatment of liberty, proceeded to utilize in their own skirmishes.

By way of an opening gambit, two quotations can be set side by side. Both are from the pens of progressive liberals, both of them theorists and publicists. Barker provides the first, significantly culled from that archetypal conservative, Burke:

> . . . true liberty must be 'manly and moral' in the sense of being based on the moral quality of the individual man, as a being vested with the divine gift of personality, in virtue of which he is an end in himself and a free agent in realising his own end. This is the essential nature of liberty; and the thing or being which must essentially be free is neither the State nor any other form of group, but man himself—the individual man.[189]

[186] Hobson, *Problems of a New World*, p. 199.
[187] Hobson, *Wealth and Life*, p. 164. My italics.
[188] 'The Liberal Convention', *MG*, 18.6.1936.
[189] E. Barker, 'Group Idols and their Loyalties', *Listener*, 18.7.1934.

Delisle Burns provides the second: 'if liberty is essentially an individualistic and negative factor in life, the sooner we abolish liberty the better.'[190] How could two exponents of liberal thought have produced statements that ostensibly appear to differ so powerfully? No easy dichotomies emerge in attempting to answer this question. Progressive liberals of all shades shared some aspects of an understanding of liberty, but each subscribed to different parts of the package, adopting concepts of liberty that were saliently at variance with each other or, as has been argued all along, located in different idea-environments. One thing, though, was manifest, as Wallas noted: Mill's '"one very simple principle" subject to unexplained exceptions'[191] would no longer do as an adequate approach to a liberty now conceived of as complex and intricate, and reflective of new conditions and knowledge that demanded redefinitions.

The centrist position on liberty was itself by no means unambiguous. It was distinct from the libertarian position, epitomized by Ernest Benn, who complained of the effect of law-making: 'Day by day, in the well-meaning effort to ease somebody's little trouble, we take away a little bit of discretion or liberty from the rest of the 40 millions of us.'[192] Benn had previously attracted criticism for a letter he had published in *The Times*. In its promotion of the conditions for optimum individual advantage, he had maintained, liberalism should restrict itself to peace, economy and free trade.[193] For the *Daily Chronicle*, this was political nihilism, not liberalism. For the *New Statesman*, in an article sympathetic to liberalism, this was a shibboleth of fifty-years vintage that had *ipso facto* become conservatism.[194] Most liberals, however enthusiastically or reluctantly, had rejected that idea-environment for liberty and had accepted that 'liberty was not merely the employment of the minimum of restraint, the removal of disabilities, the permission of that which had hitherto been forbidden. They had got beyond that. They were thinking of a kind of freedom which could not be realised without the aid of the State.'[195] For John Macdonell, the writer and legal

[190] C. D. Burns, 'The Conception of Liberty', *Journal of Philosophical Studies*, 3 (1928), 195.

[191] Wallas, *Our Social Heritage*, p. 168.

[192] E. Benn, 'Liberty Submerged by Law', *Listener*, 10.4.1935.

[193] E. Benn, letter to the Editor, *The Times*, 26.8.1926.

[194] 'A "Liberal." What Does it Mean?', *DC*, 27.8.1926; '"True Liberalism"', *NS*, 4.9.1926. See also H. Storey, 'Types of Liberalism', *Liberal Magazine*, 34 (Oct. 1926), 560–5, for a critical reaction.

[195] J. Macdonell, 'The Modern Conceptions of Liberty', *CR*, 106 (1914), 194.

expert, this was not a new kind of freedom. Rather, what was involved was an extension of the measures that were thought essential, or at least legitimate, to the increasing of liberty. But he took offence at 'the persistent employment of old language to designate new conception[s] and to the describing of coercive measures as if they were merely liberating measures'. As with Spencer over a generation earlier, what seemed to irk such liberals were 'laws which seek to carry out certain important national objects . . . the encouragement of temperance, the increase and maintenance of health, the spread of knowledge, the improvement of the race, the equalisation of wealth'.[196] For Macdonell, liberty was in a 'zero-sum' relationship with those other social ends. To pursue them was to diminish the available sum of liberty. And liberty itself was

> the 'maximising of life' and . . . the multiplication of private associations and of persons living their own lives in their own way, each a centre of spontaneous activity . . . With liberty so understood Mill's teaching and his pleas for the free expansion of the individual are not obsolete.[197]

Liberty, then, thrived in an idea-environment which saw the individual as the be-all and end-all of life, with voluntarism maintaining an area sacrosanct from immediate social direction and organization.

Centrist-liberals such as Muir had, of course, assimilated Green's famous comment on liberty, as 'not a merely negative thing, a mere absence of restraints; it is a positive thing, the existence of a real opportunity to make the most and the best of our powers'.[198] But in the 1920s, as has been argued above, this was far from a radical statement; indeed, Green himself had not attached a particularly innovative interpretation to the realization of liberty. The centrist-liberal position unequivocally accepted the need for formal social intervention to enlarge and refine liberty.[199] Crucially, however,

[196] Ibid., 198, 197. Spencer had warned that the popular good could only be attained by decreasing restraints, i.e. by furthering liberty as he understood it, rather than through direct measures (H. Spencer, *The Man Versus the State*, [Harmondsworth, 1969], p. 70).

[197] Macdonell, 'The Modern Conceptions of Liberty', 201–2.

[198] Muir, *The New Liberalism*, p. 7.

[199] See the responses to the questionnaires of the National Liberal Enquiry, which indicated widespread support (hedged by practical limitations) for compulsory arbitration of industrial disputes, compulsory provision for widows and children, and compulsory purchasing power for local authorities. (*Guardian* Archives, C. P. Scott Papers, 145/3/5, 6, 8).

the image Muir adopted was one of an individual seizing opportunities to develop. As with Mill, no content was affixed to such development, nor was there any suggestion concerning the mechanisms which assured it. The concept of human nature that was adjacent to that of liberty was one of an active, achieving, initiating self. Consequently, the duties of society towards maintaining liberty would be discharged when it managed 'to create the conditions in which human faculty can freely flourish'. Predictably, Muir grouped some of those conditions under the heading of security. Stability and self-sufficiency (once account had been taken of minimal social dependence) enabled his model individual to 'freely enjoy what his capacity and efforts deserve', namely, to benefit from the goods that were available for those who could utilize their opportunities well. A further condition of liberty was, Muir insisted, self-mastery, but this simply served to confirm the original assumptions. When he wrote that man 'should have the means of obtaining this mastery. For this he cannot but be dependent upon the society to which he belongs',[200] he was depicting society as a reserve force, subservient to individual needs. Man, as it were, formed a liaison with society only to disengage himself and to assert self-control and independence. The assistance society rendered in areas such as health and education were apt illustrations of this principle. The function of the first was to ensure the physical fitness of the individual as potential entrepreneur; of the second, to socialize, in a manner of speaking, against society, in order to protect against uniformity and communal pressures and thus to ensure mental fitness. Finally, self-government enhanced individuals' senses of themselves as voluntary agents and gave them 'a real share of control over the conditions of their lives'.[201] All these conditions serviced what Muir loosely called liberty. But he more exactingly described 'the end towards which all these other conditions look' as

> an open career for talent, unchecked either by prescriptive and hereditary privileges on the one hand, or on the other, by a rigid and mechanical organisation which in aiming at equality will destroy liberty; in order that, whencesoever they may come, the men and women who have the gifts that make for leadership may be free to win and wield the power they deserve.[202]

[200] Muir, *The New Liberalism*, pp. 8, 16, 17.
[201] Ibid., p. 22. [202] Ibid., p. 28.

Clearly, this idea-environment of liberty included a conception of human nature that not all liberals could accept, as well as a further set of linked concepts. When Dodds declared in the 1930s that 'liberty, property, security' formed an indissoluble trinity,[203] that cluster went to the heart of the differences in liberal ideological structure. It marked a divide between those who saw a conservative notion of security and an individualism that maximized unique and unequal abilities, rewarding and further nourishing them by means of private property, as adjacent to liberty, and those who surrounded liberty with concepts of equality and communal responsibility.[204] Left-liberals, who proffered the latter interpretation, accorded the notion of liberty a more analytical treatment, not necessarily because they were better theoreticians, but because centrist-liberals relied on battles already fought and, as far as they were concerned, won, by master analysts such as Mill and Green.

Left-liberals also displayed a variety of approaches to liberty, in the course of which a number of themes emerged. We have already noted that the impact of the First World War was to reinvigorate liberal interest in liberty, often at the expense of other precepts of the new liberalism. Hobhouse was one of those most intensely engaged in a reassertion of its importance. An examination of his utterances on liberty shows that it is impossible to demarcate totally the differences between the left-liberals and the centrist-liberals. They had at the very least travelled together into the twentieth century, though from that point in time they cast around for different anchors for their few shared positions. The plight of conscientious objectors reinforced Hobhouse's deeply felt conviction that 'the authority of conscience and the moral autonomy of the individual form the kernel of the modern principle of liberty'.[205] Hobson, too, returned during the war to a determined defence of liberty as a personal right, for 'British liberty does not consist merely in the negative condition of not being subject to a foreign power, but in the positive enjoyment of those personal rights which are now passing'. In that context he had reiterated the unusually liberal and anti-holistic interpretation he had previously put on the organic

[203] E. Dodds, letter to the Editor, *MG*, 15.5.1936. See also F. Milton, 'Is There a Liberal Ideal?', *FV*, February 1930: 'Property is the main key-word to liberty . . .'

[204] Some liberals were aware of these different idea-environments and warned against the 'subtle twisting into perverted interpretation' of concepts such as liberty and equality (K. Griffith, '"Go Forward!"', *FV*, Apr. 1927).

[205] [L. T. Hobhouse], 'Compulsion', *MG*, 12.6.1915.

analogy, and which stressed the preservation of the private liberties and ends of individuals.[206] But a change in emphasis in comparison to his pre-war stance cannot be overlooked. Then he had supported individual rights and liberty as conducive to the health of the whole. The climate and concerns of the war now induced him to stress private liberties and ends as *distinct* from the ingredients of social life, for there was 'a net economy of political strength and progress in encouraging the free play of personal views and sentiments, even when they impede the smooth activity of some particular State function'.[207] Hobson's reidentification of the individual personality as an analytical unit may never have been expressed so succinctly again. For his colleague, Hobhouse, however, it was always an important element in the cluster of concepts which included liberty. Even a loyal disciple of Green, Hobhouse thought of 'the freedom of the individual as completed in social life'. He would not reduce the individual to a completely egocentric being, engaged in want-maximization through competition with other individuals, but neither would he subsume the individual within an autonomous social or common will. Hobhouse thus occupied the middle ground which regarded human rationality as imbued with a sense of 'common interest and fellowship'.[208] Hence individual liberty existed in social life, but not entirely in and inseparably from social life, as many Idealists would claim; and it existed in the personal spheres of conscience and action, but not entirely so, as Bentham and some of his fellow-individualists seemed to be saying.

B. Many Liberties?

The works of Hobhouse and other liberals of his time are replete with references to negative and positive liberty, but their use of the concepts differed sharply from recent practice. Berlin's exposition has promoted the two concepts as 'either-or' types.[209] Many left-liberals saw the one as complementing the other, however. Hobhouse recognized both that freedom 'seems a negative condition' and that this was an unsatisfactory statement to make, as freedom could also 'involve power or, at lowest, opportunity'. In other

206 J. A. Hobson, 'The War and British Liberties. III. The Claims of the State Upon the Individual', *Nation*, 10.6.1916. See above p. 43.

207 Ibid.

208 Hobhouse, 'Social Idealism', *MG*, 12.12.1918.

209 I. Berlin, 'Two Concepts of Liberty', in *Four Essays on Liberty* (Oxford, 1969), pp. 118–72.

words, external constraint was a necessary but not sufficient condition for liberty. Hobhouse's psychological studies led him to regard liberty as 'living in accordance with the impulses of which [man] is sensible within himself'; it meant self-determination which entailed wilful control over emotions, impulses and interests; and this, as will presently be shown, denoted making certain kinds of choices.[210] It is revealing to compare this approach with Wallas's examination of liberty. Wallas adopted Mill's more restrictive conception of liberty, which related to '*human* hindrances to our impulses',[211] whereas Hobhouse also included in those constraints external barriers, physical disturbances such as disease and self-imposed obstructions.[212] Even more than Hobhouse, Wallas had related his discussion explicitly to psychology, as when he wrote: 'The psychological facts . . . on which the usefulness of the principle of liberty depends consist of the results which follow from the obstruction of human impulses.'[213] Unfortunately, his psychology was singularly uninfluenced by the professional work conducted at the time, being simply confined to the stipulation of certain instincts, the suppression or blocking of which led to the emergence of another instinct—a feeling of unfreedom. Burns, however amateurishly, at least invoked the rising reputations of Freud and Jung when he noted that 'restraint is bad because there is in each man or group of men an inner force which grows upward to a natural height if obstructions are absent. This inner force is the fundamental fact which explains liberty. Liberty is the natural growth of this force.'[214] True, Wallas made an observation that was an important one for liberal thought. He analysed freedom in terms of the subjective pain its absence invoked in the individual, thus linking it to personal experience and judgement. For Wallas 'the immediate reaction-feeling of unfreedom is . . . a definite psychological state produced by facts in our biological inheritance'.[215] But what distinguished Wallas's analysis both from Hobhouse's evolution-

[210] Hobhouse, *The Elements of Social Justice*, pp. 47, 50.

[211] Wallas, *Our Social Heritage*, p. 157.

[212] This is of course still a source of contemporary disagreement. Cf. F. Oppenheim, *Political Concepts: A Reconstruction* (Oxford, 1981), p. 84 versus G. C. MacCallum, 'Negative and Positive Freedom' in P. Laslett, W. G. Runciman and Q. Skinner (eds.), *Philosophy, Politics and Society*, 4th Ser. (Oxford, 1972), pp. 174–93.

[213] Wallas, *Our Social Heritage*, p. 156.

[214] Burns, 'The Conception of Liberty', 191.

[215] Wallas, *Our Social Heritage*, p. 161.

ism and Burns's 'psychologism' was the lack of a developmental theory of human nature, which Burns described as 'the enjoyable expansion of personality or activity which is characteristic of every normal individual or group of men'.[216] Hence for Wallas progress would not automatically ensue from the liberation of men from constraints.

Wallas further endorsed Matthew Arnold's insistence on the need for organizing human life 'with a deliberate and constructive intellectual effort'. Had British liberals learnt from Arnold, 'they might have realized that Liberty only led to "great energies guided by vigorous reason" in a people who, instead of waiting for energy and reason to appear of themselves, were willing to make the organized effort of will necessary to achieve them'.[217] In contradistinction, Burns argued that 'the complaint of Matthew Arnold that liberty was only a means [to the rational exercise of energies] falls to the ground, for life is clearly not a means but an end'.[218] Burns's conclusion rested on the assumption that liberty as the life-force within the individual would naturally develop into Wallas's organized and conscious will. Hobhouse's evolutionism also allowed for the natural development of rationality, though also for assisting this process, if necessary. Wallas, however, did not believe that liberty was compatible with all the factors necessary for a progressive and civilized society. He therefore criticized Mill on two grounds. First, men left to their own devices would not inevitably contribute to human and social progress. Beyond that, 'a complete absence of the feeling of unfreedom' was neither 'possible or desirable for mankind'. Indeed, 'the impulse to follow the lead may be as natural for us as the impulse to give the lead, and that scope for the impulse to follow may also produce "great energies," "strong wishes," and "native pleasures".'[219] Writing to Samuel a few years later, Wallas elaborated:

> More and more the efficiency and elasticity of government depend upon subtle processes of appointment which can only be called 'free choice' by straining of language, and these subtle processes result in a kind of trust on the part of the politicians and the feeling of responsibility on the part of the

[216] Burns, 'The Conception of Liberty', 191.
[217] Wallas, *Our Social Heritage*, pp. 171, 174–5.
[218] Burns, 'The Conception of Liberty', 191.
[219] Wallas, *Our Social Heritage*, pp. 161, 166.

more or less independent experts, which are the very texture of modern well-organized society.[220]

From the Idealist side, Muirhead objected to Wallas's references to liberty because he had failed 'to arrive at a reconciliation between the negative and the positive ideas of freedom that so confusingly run in and out of the discussion'.[221] Left-liberals insisted they were two sides of the same coin. Hobhouse drew an analogy between man and the physical world:

> There seems nothing to prevent us from describing a mechanical system as working 'freely' in so far as its operations are the total result of internal factors, and as 'constrained' in so far as its operations depend on external factors. We thus arrive even in the physical world at a positive conception of freedom which precisely matches the negative. Freedom is determination by internal factors and the absence of constraint from without.[222]

Both Muirhead's notion of reconciliation and Hobhouse's idea of harmony were intended to demonstrate the total compatibility of the self and the social world.

What left-liberals certainly did not do was to reduce the question of liberty to the structure of language. If they did dismiss the separateness of negative and positive liberty, they never suggested that a discussion of the concept could be collapsed into this single, ultimately secondary issue.[223] They perceived clearly that what dictated the various interpretations of liberty was not a correct or incorrect technical definition, but the different ends to which liberty was linked. One way of approaching this was to maintain that the single concept of liberty should be broken down into a multiplicity of 'liberties'. Samuel expressed this when he wrote: '. . . the matter will not be rightly understood unless we realise at the outset that the term Liberty does not mean, as is usually assumed, a single thing, but covers a number of things, different from one another, and sometimes at variance with one another.'[224] Samuel went on to list national, political, intellectual, personal and economic liberty and suggested the possibility of conflict among them; hence the increase

220 Samuel Papers, E/17, Wallas to Samuel, 16.3.1927.

221 J. H. Muirhead, review of Wallas, *Our Social Heritage*, in *HJ*, 20 (1921), 179–81.

222 Hobhouse, *The Elements of Social Justice*, p. 49. Cf. also 'A Chance for Liberalism', *Nation*, 25.1.1919.

223 As does MacCallum, 'Negative and Positive Freedom'.

224 H. Samuel, 'Liberty', *CR*, 131 (1927), 567.

of one could only be achieved through the restriction of the other. Hobhouse too had posited that 'It is not . . . a question of liberty in general against constraint in general but of one liberty against another or one constraint against another.' He then commented significantly that any preferred position on the question of liberty could only be maintained in the light of the other values attached to it:

> Which of the two is to be preferred depends, of course, on the conditions of the common welfare. Now the relevant conditions may be such as have no especial bearing upon liberty in general, e.g. they may be conditions of health, security, economic efficiency, etc. But it may be also that 'Liberty' itself has something to say, i.e. of two alternative 'liberties' one is of a higher kind or has a larger application.[225]

This illustrates the difficulties such a discussion was liable to enter. On the one hand, Hobhouse and Samuel set liberty in a series of contexts or environments, a constellation of ends without which the exercise of liberty, the making of choices, the expression of impulses, the autonomous self-determining personality, were vacuous.[226] Yet Hobhouse also seemed to fall into the trap of arguing that those ends had no special bearing on liberty in general, thus implying first, that liberty could be understood independently of the ends that surrounded it and, secondly, that there was something that could be designated 'liberty in general'. As we shall presently suggest, the 'liberty in general' that Hobhouse had in mind was in fact of a specific type.

But what of Hobhouse's view that liberty was composed of higher and lower 'liberties'? Hobson expanded on this proposition and set it to work for a utility-maximizing theory, when he suggested that the surrender of certain individual liberties could be seen as an act of free will, 'based on a rational estimate that the aggregate gain will be greater than the loss, or that lower liberties are exchanged for higher liberties upon a scale of welfare values'.[227] As he had earlier argued, 'each repression of personal liberty involved in social order, . . . each provision of security against the primary risks of life, is the opening up of larger and loftier areas of freedom, adventure, and personal achievement', as long as a sphere

[225] Hobhouse, *The Elements of Social Justice*, pp. 77–8.

[226] Samuel's context was really the application of liberty to different areas, not the outlining of different *kinds* of liberty.

[227] J. A. Hobson, 'Democracy, Liberty and Force', *HJ*, 34 (1935), 38–9.

of more instinctive, disorderly behaviour would be retained.[228] If the loss of some liberties was balanced by the acquisition of others, a net gain could only be attained in one of two ways: either the quantity of liberty held after this exchange would be larger—and neither Hobhouse nor Hobson suggested this possibility—or the values attached to the liberties lost were inferior to those attached to the liberties gained. This in fact was specifically stated by Hobson: 'Narrower liberties may be suppressed in favour of broader liberties, lower liberties in favour of higher, *i.e.* of such liberties as are essential to the achievement of finer personal and social values.'[229]

C. The Value of Liberty

Burns contributed a forceful and provocative essay to the debate on the values associated with liberty. He maintained that the purely negative approach to liberty as the removal of restraints was closely associated with a conception which regarded 'the individual or the group, whose liberty is under discussion, . . . [as] essentially a segregate atom in a social void'.[230] The presuppositions Burns identified were of a dual nature, for they revolved round a conception of social structure and a theory of human nature which, while mutually reinforcing, were analytically distinct. In a structural sense, negative liberty was a denial of human relationships:

> Now in explaining liberty, any man or group was assumed to be *over against* some other men or group; and liberty consisted in a sort of removal to a distance or elimination of one of the terms in the relation. Thus liberty came to be a conception of social dissolution; and this is pure individualism or, in the case of groups of men, crude nationalism.

As a portrayal of human nature, liberty was adjacent to a particular individualism: '. . . the individualistic assumptions led to identifying liberty with what was called independence—a tell-tale word.'[231] This assumption defied empirical observation; it was founded on a 'fantastic psychology' and on a belief in the ability and responsibility of the isolated self.

Naturally, Burns opposed that old view to the 'facts' and 'experience' of today. To criticize him for doing what he would not be

228 Hobson, 'The Ethical Movement and the Natural Man', 673.
229 Hobson, 'Democracy, Liberty and Force', 40.
230 Burns, 'The Conception of Liberty', 186.
231 Ibid., 188–9.

done by is beside the point, if one accepts the ideological nature of all social statements. The validity of his case rested simply on applying the most recent scientific and social theories to his analysis. This itself was the outcome of the liberal belief in progress; it was basically enamoured of the proposition that the new must displace the old. In ideological terms, Burns still felt the old to be dominant; those assumptions lay 'at the base of most current economic and political theory'.[232] The new theories were consequently those that extolled sociability and community, but as the social applications of both biology and psychology prove, science can always be put to the service of the ideologist in furtherance of either new or old ideas. Burns's premiss, that man is fundamentally social, proceeded to the logical derivative that liberty, as the natural growth and expression of one's inner force, meant spreading one's personality 'over the frontiers of another personality . . . Thus freedom is increased by personal contacts. For not only is the outward flow of persuasiveness an aspect of freedom, but the return from the other personality thus in contact increases the growth-power of the first.'[233]

Hobhouse, always qualifying communitarian notions, never took his perception of liberty to the extreme of reducing it to a social concept, but he was certainly nearer in outlook to Burns than to the centrist-liberals. Like Burns, he dismissed any association of liberty with individualistic atomism. It was not only that he rejected Mill's self-regarding acts, on the grounds that 'the good of each is, on the principle of the common good, matter of concern to all'.[234] He could also not accept a concept of self-determination that abstracted from time and space, from an individual's past and from his environment. Hence human will and responsibility were a function of a continuity that, even if not definitely binding, had to be taken into account as part of oneself. This nod in the direction of history was obviously aimed against utilitarianism, with its a-historical self-restriction to the here and now. What ultimately characterized Hobhouse's approach was his idea of harmony, and his subsequent assertion that 'there is freedom just as far as there is harmony'.[235] The essence of this harmony was two-fold: it related

[232] Ibid., 186.
[233] Ibid., 192.
[234] Hobhouse, *The Elements of Social Justice*, p. 61.
[235] Ibid., pp. 51, 52–3.

to the elements within the individual, and to 'a community as a collective whole and all its members as individuals in close interaction'. Co-operative unity and social harmony *were* liberty. The reason for this lay in the left-liberal assumptions—anchored to the psychic energy theories of current psychology—that the individual had to work out his or her potential (possible only under conditions of harmony among individuals) and that, furthermore, that potential developed as a social personality.[236] When the concept of liberty was broken down into its components, maintained Hobhouse, it would be found that liberties were defined by rights. Indeed, 'the bare idea of right is essential to liberty, for it is the distinctive value of a right . . . that it is a basis upon which its possessor constructs his own course of action having therein a measure of initiative and free choice.' Concurrently, Hobhouse signalled in the direction of communitarianism when he wrote: 'The formula that liberty is limited by rights requires . . . the addendum that rights must include, in addition to the rights of individual members, the right of the community as a whole.'[237]

There nevertheless remained an important difference among left-liberals, which ranged Hobhouse and Hobson against Burns on the question of liberty as the expression of human personality. For the former, the exercising of choice was crucial. They regarded the individual as free when he *could* develop certain desirable characteristics and *willed* their attainment, whereas for Burns the individual was free when he *did* develop such characteristics. In either case, one could not be free without expressing those characteristics. Yet Hobhouse and Hobson preserved their belief in the subjective feeling of freedom and in the demonstrable existence of freedom as voluntary, unconstrained choice, mediated through the individual will. Communal intervention had to be constraint by conviction, and respectful of self-development, rather than mere coercion.[238] Burns underplayed the view of liberty as the absence of restraint, preferring instead to emphasize that 'all good government assists and does not interfere'.[239]

In comparison, the centrist-liberal Samuel acknowledged the existence of instances when 'more law means more liberty', but

[236] Ibid., pp. 59, 68, 85, 90. [237] Ibid., pp. 84, 62, 63.

[238] Ibid, pp. 68, 70. See also Gaus, *The Modern Liberal Theory of Man*, pp. 175, 181.

[239] Burns, 'The Conception of Liberty', 194, 191.

gave no blanket approval for a wholesale increase in legislation. Not every restriction meant greater freedom, since 'a law may be coercive and stop at that'.[240] Left-liberals would have concurred, as did Burns, observing that 'clearly there may be bad laws, which do in fact restrict liberty'.[241] Equally, Hobhouse's contention that some 'liberties' make for liberty and others do not[242] was common ground among liberals. It is therefore not easy to delimit categorically centrist-liberalism from left-liberalism at that stage of the debate. The clues that enable one to establish different attitudes to liberty appear later on. Burns assured his readers that 'there is nothing in the nature of law or government which should make us desire to diminish them in the interests of liberty. Law is the sphere of existing liberties, and new laws, if they are good laws, extend that sphere.'[243] Samuel, by contrast, remained suspended between a nineteenth-century libertarian position and the avant-garde of modern liberalism. He was perfectly willing to accept that liberty was not the ultimate human value: 'A clear deduction from individual freedom may sometimes bring other advantages, and result in a net gain to human welfare.'[244] But this very utterance was in another sense traditionalist, for it saw liberty as potentially assailable by other desirable human values, rather than compatible with them. For Samuel human variety underpinned a world of pluralist but competing values. In later years, however, Samuel adopted a different view, returning to the Idealism that had influenced him in early life and quoting Muirhead in order to deny that liberty was a fixed quantity which would diminish under corporate control.[245]

Such differences of emphasis were illustrated by a letter to the *Nation*, in which T. H. Green was co-opted for the position that 'man fulfils himself and gains true significance through his association with the community and through nothing else. From his relation to society he derives all his liberty and all his rights, and

240 Samuel, 'Liberty', 570.

241 Burns, 'The Conception of Liberty', 194.

242 Hobhouse, *The Elements of Social Justice*, p. 79.

243 Burns, 'The Conception of Liberty', 194. It is a measure of the degree to which Hegel was alien to the British that such an Idealist opinion could have been held unacknowledged by a declared anti-Hegelian like Burns.

244 Samuel, 'Liberty', 570.

245 Samuel, *Belief and Action*, p. 155 (quoting J. H. Muirhead, *The Service of the State* [London, 1908], p. 37).

individual liberty is a meaningless fiction apart from this relation.' The now-centrist *Nation*, accused of neglecting to apply those principles to the solution of the social problem, stuck by its guns. While accepting that Mill was outdated, the editor, Henderson, insisted that an area of conduct could be identified 'with which society should interfere as little as possible, this being the area in which individual actions affected minimally the interests of others'.[246] Typically, experience and psychology were mobilized to endorse this position, though one ought to recall that prior to the war and the emergence of new fashions, Hobson had likewise linked psychology to Mill's vindication of eccentricity.[247]

D. The Structure of the Concept

Any attempt to shed light on the above complexities must relate to the understanding of liberty current at the time. Progressive liberals regarded it as a two-faceted concept which encompassed the feeling and state of freedom gained from non-constraint (liberty A) and the working out of one's potential (liberty B).[248] The meaning of potential was a value judgement defined by desirable human characteristics and endorsed by psychology. These two facets varied independently, though they affected each other, and liberals differed as to the stress they put on either. Left-liberals vacillated between preferring liberty B and advocating both facets equally. Centrist-liberals, conversely, laid greater emphasis on liberty A (which they interpreted as the absence of constraints by other people's actions) and were prone to call attention to a potentially competitive relationship with liberty B. They recognized liberty B as socially valuable, as a human end, but preferred not to call it liberty at all. For centrist-liberals, the pursuit of liberty B could either reduce or promote liberty A. The reverse was, however, untrue, as liberty A was always conducive, in their opinion, to liberty B.

Left-liberals disagreed with centrist-liberals not only because they believed in a greater volume of cases when the loss of liberty A could enhance liberty B, but above all because they would never accept that the pursuit of the social good could restrict liberty *in toto*.

246 'J. S. Mill v. T. H. Green', letter to the Editor, *Nation*, 17.10.1925.

247 See Freeden, *The New Liberalism*, p. 112.

248 Feeling and being free are not identical (see W. L. Weinstein, 'The Concept of Liberty in Nineteenth Century English Political Thought', *Political Studies*, 13 (1965), 156–9), but the distinction hardly concerned liberals. Weinstein prefers not to call facet B by the name of liberty. Most centrist-liberals would have agreed.

The social good, essential to humanity and society, was in effect equated with liberty B. Its pursuit could only restrict liberty A, which was permissible as long as liberty A was not eliminated and its restriction was rationally justified. Left-liberals preferred to surround liberty B with the values they believed to be fundamentally good or useful; centrist-liberals surrounded liberty A with such values. Because for left-liberals liberty entailed the optimization of the human potential for development, any value and any activity that contributed to such development *ipso facto* promoted liberty. This is why Hobhouse could affirm that 'liberty so understood is itself the most far-reaching principle of the common welfare'.[249]

In terms of ideological structure, liberty B was comprehensible only within the context of other values. To seek health, knowledge or security was desirable because they were all aspects of self-development, i.e. they contributed to liberty B, to working out the human potential. Liberty B itself served as the idea-environment of human nature. What then about liberty as a distinct or separate value? In one sense the concept of liberty was stretched to include its idea-environment ('liberty *is* knowledge, welfare', etc.) and hence was divested of a separate existence. But in another sense left-liberals wished to construct the right environment for the emergence of a new appreciation of liberty A, the feeling of no constraint, by educating the public to interpret constraint or unfreedom as the withholding of conditions for the development of human potential.[250] After all, what counts in liberty A is the subjective feeling of not being interfered with, a feeling that can be attached to different external conditions and internal states of mind. Left-liberals believed that they could, to a large extent, shift the feeling of non-interference to areas of human experience that were new to it. A rational perception of the conditions necessary for human development and the knowledge of, and participation in the establishment of, such conditions, would evoke a new sense of relief from constraints. Though the old liberty A as simple physical unencumbrance admittedly still had residual value, a revised liberty A would emerge side by side with it.

In the final analysis a centrist such as Samuel supported only that liberty which encouraged self-reliance and personal initiative. But

[249] Hobhouse, *The Elements of Social Justice*, p. 79.

[250] Connolly is thus harsh in his condemnation of liberals for having ignored these kinds of constraints (*The Terms of Political Discourse*, pp. 158, 169).

even centrist-liberals had advanced beyond a Spencerian position in recognizing that such a cluster of values was insufficient for maintaining the decencies of modern civilization. They therefore allowed for its supersession by laws 'which do good in a measure'[251] as long as such occasions were few and the sacrifices of liberty A small. The vision of society held by left-liberals was more complete, if naïve: their *Weltanschauung* did not seriously permit irrational disharmonies (though Hobhouse's growing pessimism conceded the possibility that 'so far as a man is free to do right he is also free to do wrong').[252] Consequently they could not conceive of liberty as threatened by the pursuit of other humanly and socially beneficial ends. Those ends were mediated by a social understanding of human nature; thus for Burns liberty associated with self-reliance and independence was no ideal at all, but an 'absurdity'.[253] For the libertarian, in contrast, the reason that liberty as non-restraint was valuable lay precisely in that it enabled the expression of independence and self-reliance. The assumption here was that human nature unfolded solely through the exercising of an individual's will. As for social structure, an extreme atomism saw society as necessitated by defects in human nature, or by a scarcity that justified small acts of intervention. Human nature flourished as an autonomous unit, and this autonomy, in circular fashion, encouraged the growth of sterling human characteristics. For left-liberals, liberty A could never suffice to optimize human nature because that nature was social. Liberty B became essential not only because it extended over a number of valuable ends, but because the individual will might not suffice to achieve it. Individuals might *need* intervention in order to be fully human. Those theorists partially abandoned liberty A because they asserted that individuals were mutually dependent, and therefore collective action (which often involved intervention) was inevitable for liberating their potential. This partial abandonment of liberty A forced theorists who still valued the feeling of freedom to try and find it in the now dominant liberty B, by affirming that collective action was itself a natural rational outgrowth that did not entail *uninvited* interference; hence even liberty A would not be violated.

[251] Samuel, 'Liberty', 571.
[252] Hobhouse, *The Elements of Social Justice*, p. 71.
[253] Burns, 'The Conception of Liberty', 193.

Finally, was liberty an end or a means? To pose the question thus is unfortunate, for if liberty is identified as part of a reciprocally defining cluster of values the 'chicken and egg' perspective becomes redundant, as does the dependent or independent variable issue. Superficially, liberty could appear to be an end, indeed *the* end of a proper social order. When this idea was entertained by centrist-liberals, arguing that the human essence was revealed by definition through non-intervention, the logical conclusion was a defence of liberty that would override the pursuit of any other social end. This argument was implied by Keynes when asserting that liberty had to be defended 'on principle'.[254] But of course, liberty A could also be expressed as a *condition* for initiative, independence, 'character', and so on. Indeed, if the feeling of not being interfered with was a valued sensation, it was only valued because of the idea-environment which defined that value. The approach suggested here would not allow for a concept of liberty 'as such'. This was well put by Hobson: 'I cannot accept [the] view that freedom has a value independent of the use to which it is put, nor can I share [the] related assertion that "ultimately we either believe intuitively that freedom is good or we do not".' Samuel seemed to be moving in that direction too when he wrote: 'Welfare is the aim, individual action is the means, and liberty the condition. Liberty by itself is not enough. Men say that they are ready to die for the sake of liberty; but it is really for the sake of what liberty makes possible.'[255] Thus liberty had no value on its own, but only when set in a cluster of adjacent ideas such as welfare or, in the left-liberal case, social personality:

> In order to be real, liberty must be associated with opportunity. Follow out this line of thought and you will come to the conclusion that liberty cannot be valued for its own sake, but only as a means or condition of a desirable life. Whether such a life is to be evisaged in terms of happiness, welfare or personality, and whether such ends are computed wholly in terms of individual achievement, or have a directly social significance attached to them—these important questions will have intimate bearings upon what may be termed 'the economy of freedom'.[256]

Hobson's unfortunate choice of the words 'means' and 'condition', must not suggest a separatist notion of liberty that exists prior to

[254] J. M. Keynes, letter to the Editor, *NS*, 11.8.1934.
[255] Samuel, *Belief and Action*, pp. 243–4.
[256] Hobson, 'Democracy, Liberty and Force', 38.

the ends it services. Hobson himself regarded the concept of liberty as 'barren' when detached from 'the achievement of higher personality and larger welfare'. The 'positive meaning' of liberty was increased knowledge of one's environment, a release from custom and superstition, and the enlarging use of mind for explorative purposes. Liberty was not a means to those ends; it was tantamount to their attainment. Liberty was vacuous unless linked to a specific set of desirable values, a cluster of ends that infused liberty with a special meaning. The denial of the existence of liberty 'as such' entailed not a disavowal of the content of liberty, but a disavowal of liberty as a neutral or impartial concept that could be universally employed. Progressive liberals were led to the inevitably ideological stance of regarding liberty as part of a particular cluster of values, a package that could not be taken apart under any circumstances. As this had been their critique of traditional liberals, the difference could only lie in the intellectual and emotional attractiveness of the package.

Unlike some modern approaches to the notion of liberty, progressive liberals did not want to detach the concept from the values which embellished it. Neither did they seek an objective, technical definition that could be universally accepted without reference to other human ends.[257] Their emphasis on the subjectivity of 'feeling free' did not fall foul of the present-day critique that feeling free is a state of mind or desire that has to be satisfied, and hence a feeling of unfreedom can easily be avoided by eradicating that desire.[258] Progressive liberals, of both left and centre variety, believed conversely that liberty was the function of the satisfaction of specific desires, whose eradication would by definition destroy the capacity to be free. At the same time, progressive liberals disagreed among themselves over the sets of desires and activities they sought to promote, because they differed in holding to a more social or less social interpretation of human nature, that in turn determined their view of the development of personality. The empirical data progressive liberals used to determine those desires and activities were the subjective judgements of the individual participants in the political system. But because human rationality allowed for a considerable overlap of perceptions among individuals, such judge-

[257] For a typical approach, see Oppenheim, *Political Concepts*, pp. 53–95.

[258] See Berlin, 'Introduction', *Four Essays on Liberty*, p. xxxviii; Oppenheim, *Political Concepts*, p. 91.

ments were not spread over too wide and contradictory a range.[259] Nevertheless, progressive liberals also insisted on moral and value criteria—development, autonomy, life—in order to ascertain which types of interference or restrictions on actions were acceptable.[260] Conceptions of human nature were fundamental to this assessment and part and parcel of any analysis of the concept of liberty.

6. POWER: THE BLIND SPOT OF LIBERALISM

The essential question must remain: why did both the centrist and left variants of liberalism fail to make sufficient political impact to revive liberalism as a political force and, especially, to make inroads into the post-1918 enfranchised generation? Previous chapters have suggested that part of the answer can be found in miscomprehensions and misperceptions related to the rise of the Labour movement and its apparent divergence from liberal aims and ideology. But another serious weakness of liberal theory can be found in its attitude to the concept and phenomenon of power. Fundamental to the liberal persuasion was the belief that the expression and the representation of individual wills through the political process was the correct and only way of resolving conflict. The methods through which liberty and political justice had been attained throughout the nineteenth century still seemed adequate and, indeed, exclusive of any other. Social reform was first and foremost a question of putting items on the statute-book. This crucial legacy of liberalism resulted in an inability to face up to the realities of political power. Power was misunderstood rather than ignored, because liberals connected it primarily with two issues: equal access to the political process, by means of the vote, redistribution of seats and, later, proportional representation; and the application of reason to provide a harmonious transcending, not merely resolution, of conflict. The dual error lay in the assumption

259 Max Weber's comment is pertinent here: 'We associate the highest measure of an empirical "feeling of freedom" with those actions which we are conscious of performing rationally–i.e. in the absence of physical and psychic "coercion," emotional "affects" and "accidental" disturbances of the clarity of judgment, in which we pursue a clearly perceived end by "means" which are the most adequate in accordance with the extent of our knowledge. . .' (*The Methodology of the Social Sciences* [New York, 1949], pp. 124–5).

260 This would include what Benn and Weinstein call 'being a free person' (S. Benn and W. L. Weinstein, 'Being Free to Act, and Being a Free Man', *Mind*, 80 (1971)).

that equal political power would be attained through the extension of democratic processes alone, and in the further assumption that, in a world within human reach, the political techniques of representation could adequately solve increasingly salient economic and social disputes. In the main, these beliefs continued to assert themselves in the inter-war period.

One of the strongest exponents of this view was Hobhouse. Writing about the rights of nations to self-determination, he commented: 'To push this principle through would be to destroy the notion that government is power, and to substitute for it the principle that government is the collective will of the people governed.'[261] Buttressed no doubt by the intense wartime reaction to the state, this nevertheless was a perspective that broke with theories of power and sovereignty, both past and present, and offered instead a bowdlerized version that hinged on human intelligence and reason as the source of social organization and activity. Historically the state had been used for internal and external protection, maintained Hobhouse,

> and this gave colour to the mistaken view that the State essentially is force or rests on force. In reality force is nothing but an instrument, and it is an instrument that breaks in the hand if there is not intelligent will to guide it . . . State organisation, in fact, does not rest upon force, but effective force rests upon effective organisation, and effective organisation is at bottom a matter, not of external constraints, but of inner psychology.[262]

Although there was a hint here of the *idea* of the state, Hobhouse clearly believed it to be the outcome of the evolutionary realization of his principle of harmony. Freedom did not depend on coercing those who endangered the rest but antithetically—a view that classical liberals would hardly have held—on abandoning coercion altogether, for 'a community is free in the degree in which will replaces force as the basis of social relations'.[263] Indeed, Hobhouse's attitude to property was conditioned by his assertion that 'if property is in one aspect freedom, it is under another aspect power'.[264] Hence the old solution liberals had always preferred to the problem of power—to neutralize it by distributing it widely

261 [L. T. Hobhouse], 'The Day of Intercession', *MG*, 2.1.1915.
262 [L. T. Hobhouse], 'The Ideal of the State', *MG*, 6.11.1926.
263 Hobhouse, *The Elements of Social Justice*, p. 88.
264 Ibid., p. 156.

and evenly—would *ipso facto* also work with respect to the more menacing facets of property.

Hobhouse saw the permanent function of liberalism 'not in trying to undo organisation, but in turning it to the service of freedom and equality of conditions, and, more specifically, in preventing the increased power of the State from being used for repression at home and abroad'. This represented a particular liberal position that could conceive of organization as virtually detached from power, of power as invariably available for evil, and of freedom and equality as perfect antidotes to the wielding of power. All these presuppositions begged the question. Nor was Hobhouse unique in these assumptions for, if as one liberal plainly stated, force 'was the one weapon which [liberals] abhor',[265] the problem was that most liberals did not distinguish between force and power. Indeed, the legacy of the liberal fear of all monopolies *qua* concentrations of power was a hopelessly ambiguous attitude to the state. Thus while Hobhouse reflected the Weberian insight that the state was unique in wielding the physical power of society (though he failed to use the qualifying 'legitimate'),[266] he and like-minded liberals were intensely unhappy with that state of affairs. Hobhouse would have agreed with the *Nation* that 'power must be divided and dispersed', because the state, by means of the government, proclaimed 'an all-inclusive sovereignty' and 'gather[ed] to itself all power and responsibility'.[267] The sharing of power was both the set method of containing monopolies and had the added attraction of offering an ethically and politically astute enlargement of the circle of citizenship.[268] But for Hobhouse an acute difficulty had arisen. For one who laid claim to the title of sociologist, his analysis of the social fact of power was made to give way to value judgements and to wishful thinking that could conceive of 'suitable organs impartially constituted' that would command general acceptance.[269] It was to no small extent an indication of the confusion that sociology as social philosophy was undergoing at the time.

There was, however, another way of dealing with the dangers of concentrated power. In the hands of individuals or private organizations such concentration was potentially harmful, but in the

265 Herbert, 'The Liberal Summer School', 324.
266 [L. T. Hobhouse], 'The Omnipotent State', *MG*, 30.9.1916.
267 'A Treaty with Labor', *Nation*, 26.7.1919.
268 See Chapter 3.
269 Cf. Hobhouse, 'The Problem', p. 276.

hands of the state this was not inevitably the case. While beset by the fear of the state in some of its existing forms, liberals retained their faith, nourished by their turn-of-the-century ideologues, in the possibility of a benevolent state. Here too liberal optimism papered over the cracks in the realities of state and governmental behaviour, an optimism generated by a misunderstanding of the phenomenon of power, and one that consolidated liberal alienation from the frontline of British politics. This stance was reflected in Muir's writings when, in contradistinction to his concern about the perniciousness of economic power in the hands of industrial combinations, he hailed the development in the political sphere of

> a democratically controlled State, which (whatever its defects) stands outside the economic conflict, and is able to perform, and has in many respects, though imperfectly, succeeded in performing, the function of safeguarding and protecting all men against the abuses of power.

This function, Muir believed, could be discharged 'with impartiality'.[270]

Such an attitude was more than a glossing over of the complexities of the democratic process. It contained within it the heritages of many strands of British political thinking: the scientism of Benthamite utilitarianism, with its search for objective criteria of governmental action; the ethical conception of the state as a repository of the social will for good, as developed by the British Idealists;[271] and the new liberalism of the previous generation, with its faith in an interventionist state that would rise above any sectional calls upon its powers. Added to all this was a paradoxical appreciation that the First World War, while augmenting the power of the state to control individual lives, had also emphasized the workman's power and importance and made him aware of the necessity of using his power. This power would consequently have to be recognised by the state.[272] As the agent of communal power, it was there to be utilized in the service of social reform and to construct a more prosperous and equitable society.[273] The extension of political power to all was a paradigmatic liberal position that

[270] Muir, *Liberalism and Industry*, pp. 67, 75.

[271] The most recent expression of this position had been stated by Hetherington and Muirhead in *Social Purpose*, pp. 251–2.

[272] 'A Constitution for Industry', *Nation*, 30.6.1917.

[273] 'The Future of Liberalism and Labour. IV. The Riddle of Socialism', *Nation*, 9.1.1926.

perceived the individual and the community as the only units of political action. As Samuel summarized it, the past transfer of political power to the whole body of the nation was intended 'as the means of remedying the monstrous abuses under which the masses of the people were then suffering'.[274] The introduction of industrial democracy did not fundamentally alter this position, nor suggest to liberals that the industrial unit was a new and visible type of *political* entity.

Part of the problem was due to the tendency of the democratic tradition, as Burns formulated it, to be 'concerned chiefly with the *source* of power, not with the nature of power'. Writing against the backdrop of the rise of European dictatorships, Burns recognized that the moral authority of the state had to be supported by physical force.[275] But power was initially for Burns a choice between force and authority—the two related to each other inversely—and like many of his generation he did not investigate its other forms, nor pause to ask whether power relationships and conflict were endemic to societies. His comments on Marxism are illuminating in this connection:

> Marx (and Laski) are simply Hegel reversed . . . what [Marx] thought was the same as Hegel, i.e. that there is no distinction between *value* and *fact*. Hegel thought the Messiah had come (the Prussian State); & Marx (being a Jew) thought *one more* 'Last Judgment' was to come. But both believed that *Force* was what mattered; for Good and Evil were equivalent to Strong and Weak—i.e. there is *no* 'moral order'. Laski has swallowed that whole, in his theory that 'the State' is simply the 'power' of a particular class. I thought at Oxford they taught T. H. Green![276]

Ignoring the specific interpretation of Marx, this passage is rich with pointers to the liberal mentality. To hold to a strong distinction between fact and value often resulted in certain phenomena—such as, in the above analysis, the state—being endowed with neutrality, or in Barker's self-contradictory statement that 'it is the ideology of democracy to have no ideology'.[277] To insist on a 'moral order' was also a new liberal characteristic, with the concomitant that politics could ultimately be divorced from immoralities such as the wielding of power by a class. Indeed, Burns's

[274] Samuel, 'The Political Outlook', 409.

[275] C. D. Burns, *The Challenge to Democracy* (London, 1934), p. 243.

[276] Hammond Papers, vol. 25, Burns to Hammond, 13.8.1936.

[277] Barker, *The Citizen's Choice*, p. 13.

insistence on a search for goodness or rightness behind all political compulsion led him to dismiss the study of power and wealth 'as if they were merely natural forces such as electricity'. Though force existed separately from moral authority, in the end the facts had to be guided by the values: physical compulsion should only be a means of moral authority.[278]

Once again it was Hobson who, among liberals, contributed the most astute observations to the discussion, though his analysis was not immune from some of the defects of liberal theory. Unlike his friend Hobhouse, Hobson drew the crucial distinction between dominating and creative power. And with less equivocation than Burns, he stated: 'Power is not evil in itself, nor is the desire to exercise power. The desire to realize one's personality by exercising power over one's environment is a normal, wholesome impulse.' Power was an aspect of human nature, necessary for the attainment of human ends. Furthermore, force could be a means of justice, for 'Force applied selfishly by individuals or sections is bad. Force applied socially by organized society is good.'[279] The beneficial and proper role of power in society accorded with Hobson's perception of the individual as creative and expressive as well as rational, and of society as the source of worthy intentions and valuable activities. In contradistinction to Burns, he decried the 'ultimately false antithesis between physical and moral force'. Morality used methods of coercion, despite an appeal to 'reason and good feeling', that were 'at least as degrading to humanity'.[280] Though this was in effect the Millite public opinion, Hobson seemed to argue that morality itself was not averse to brutal persuasion, if rational appeal failed.[281] During and immediately following the war and as part of his distaste for its progenitors, Hobson associated the use of force with social and economic malaise. Though power and property could be

[278] C. D. Burns, *Civilisation: The Next Step* (London, 1938), pp. 33–5.

[279] Hobson, *Democracy After the War*, p. 23. Or, in another version, 'to hold power and not to use it is a waste: to hold power and not to use it well is a moral evil' (Hobson, 'Will America Stop Another War?', *New Republic*, 30.6.1937).

[280] J. A. Hobson, 'Notes on Law and Order. IV. Arms and Man', *Nation*, 5.12.1925.

[281] This referred to existing morality rather than the rational exercise of power and force by the community. The interpretation that Hobson's limited endorsement of force may have propelled him beyond the liberal tradition (Allett, *New Liberalism*, pp. 213–14, 258) is questionable. Welfare-liberalism permitted *limited* compulsion in order to guarantee liberty as self-development; nor can liberalism be reduced to the pursuit of liberty alone.

instruments of a wholesome personality, the misuse of one was often translated into the misuse of the other. In terms of his under-consumptionist analysis, the surplus left after the payment of basic production costs went 'to the stronger party as the spoils of actual or potential class war. Strikes and lock-outs are not the wholly irrational and wasteful actions they appear at first sight. In default of any more reasonable or equitable way of distributing the surplus among the claimants, they rank as a natural and necessary process.'[282]

Thus while Hobson went along with Hobhouse's identification of property as an urge for power, he was reluctant to oversimplify 'this will-to-power, treating it as if it were a mere lust of tyranny'[283] and in that respect differed from Hobhouse. First, the use of force was required to remedy current social defects. In part this was necessary because 'the crust of custom and the appeal of shorter-sighted selfishness require to be broken by an enlightened authority wielding the needed coercive power'.[284] More importantly, the question depended on the consequences of class conflict. The retrieval of status and human dignity by the working class could, at present, justify the use of force, other channels being unavailable. But unlike many socialists Hobson did not hold to the inevitability of class conflict, as various measures of social reform and power-sharing could, and were already, mitigating its intensity.[285] Here Hobson displayed his liberal colours, arguing that the threat of physical coercion, either by violence or through strikes, 'paralyses all the latent liberalism in the classes and wields them into a stiff, unyielding body'.[286] Hope lay in the emergence, both in class and in national antagonisms, of a higher level of consciousness that carried some element of rationality.[287]

Secondly, Hobson did not share Hobhouse's vision of a substitution of force by reason. His delving into psychology extracted a concession of the impossibility of extinguishing human conflict totally, even in its physical manifestations.[288] He refused 'to

[282] Hobson, *Problems of a New World*, p. 26. But see Hobson's later views on strikes, as discussed in Chapter 6.

[283] Hobson, *Democracy and a Changing Civilisation*, p. 68.

[284] Hobson, 'Democracy, Liberty and Force', 40.

[285] Ibid., 43.

[286] Hobson, *Problems of a New World*, pp. 207–8.

[287] Hobson, *Democracy and a Changing Civilisation*, p. 160.

[288] Hobson, 'The Ethical Movement and the Natural Man', 676.

countenance an opposition between reason and physical force', because 'the real conflict is between the unified force of the whole organism operating as reasonable authority through the brain, and one or more of the organic forces operating separately on its own account'[289]—yet another version of Hobson's strong antipathy to particularism. Hence he mooted the possibility of a limited reconciliation between reason and morality on the one hand and force on the other, while bearing in mind that many aspects of force were antithetical to reason.[290]

For Hobson organicism, creativity, and human welfare constituted the rationale of the use of power. Power was an instrument for eradicating separatism and anti-social behaviour. Like his co-liberals, Hobson had no sympathy for power anchored in class structure as a long-term phenomenon, denied any power role to groups in society, and believed that power could be minimized. But unlike them it could not be wished away entirely, nor was it socially beneficial for all forms of power to disappear. Unlike them, too, Hobson did not entertain a merely political solution to the problems that power introduced. He rejected 'that easy optimistic faith in a widening franchise as the all-sufficient instrument of good government which prevailed throughout the Victorian era in this country'[291] and which, as we have seen, influenced post-Edwardian thought to seek answers to the problems of a rising working class in terms of 'economic democracy' and representation. These were necessary but insufficient conditions for the creation of an organic citizenry, as long as they ignored the issues of equality, property, and power that all demanded a different ethical outlook.

The intellectual influences that acted on the liberal mentality in the period under consideration were both complex and eclectic. At a time when scientific as well as ethical certainties were under challenge, and while diverse, ill-thought out, and often half-baked nourishment was its only fare, liberalism could not expect a halting of the processes of fragmentation it was undergoing. Among its political rivals, Marxism was frequently presented as a dilettantist adventure, conservatism as the inability to think intelligently on politics, moderate socialism as utopian or dogmatic, and fascism, not surprisingly, as beyond the pale. The age was not conducive to

[289] J. A. Hobson, 'Force Necessary to Government', *HJ*, 33 (1934), 332.
[290] Hobson, *Problems of a New World*, p. 206.
[291] Hobson, 'Democracy, Liberty and Force', 36.

great thoughts, certainly not in the sphere of political theory. Nevertheless, both centrist-liberalism and left-liberalism maintained a semblance of coherence, even if a patchy one, and cautiously moved forwards into new areas, a movement which, though often tentative, furthered the ideological causes they were espousing together and separately. Left-liberalism, especially, still had a cutting edge and contributed to radical inter-war political thinking. An examination, in the next chapter, of the persistence of central liberal tenets among some socialist theorists may help to demonstrate this appeal of radical liberalism, as well as to broaden the base of the argument advanced in Chapter 6—that the span of liberal ideology was uncontainable within the Liberal party as it had now become.

8

SOCIALISM WITH A LIBERAL FACE

THIS chapter will attempt to take up a theme by way of illustration rather than exhaustive treatment. The question of the permeation of liberalism into Labour and socialist positions is largely unexplored in British studies, in part because it is a perspective that has always gone against the grain of the argument presented by the Fabians and other analysts of British socialism. The following pages will assess the prevalence of liberal assumptions in the thought of two British socialists, H. J. Laski and R. H. Tawney. The *New Statesman*, especially the contributions of G. D. H. Cole, also affords insight into the emergence of liberal notions as central components of socialist ideas. These cases will demonstrate the spread of liberalism outside its conventional domain. Often this was without the explicit acknowledgement of thinkers who expressed unmistakable liberal views alongside the other tenets they preferred to stress.[1] Perhaps permeation is not altogether the correct word, as the intellectual tradition of British socialism was nourished in a rich liberal soil from the outset. Clearly, major ingredients of liberal ideology were preserved, even developed, within the scope of British socialist thought.[2] This is not to argue that all self-styled socialists were liberals in disguise. Rather, it is a restatement, from another perspective, of the assertion put forward in Chapter 6 that the structure of liberal ideology does not correspond with the party structure. This time, however, the emphasis is on a heavy ideological overlap between the core, adjacent, and peripheral beliefs of British socialism and liberalism, even if the internal arrangements of the respective ideologies exhibit important differences. The consumption, assimilation, and dissemination of liberal essentials by the above-named thinkers is, it is contended, sufficient to establish the case this chapter wishes to make; it is recognized of course that the range and intensity of its argument can be augmented.

[1] See the remarks in Chapter 1 on the limitations of exploring intentions as a tool for the analysis of ideological predispositions.

[2] See the perceptive remarks in Greenleaf, *The British Political Tradition*, vol. ii. *The Ideological Heritage*, pp. 412–17.

1. H. J. LASKI

The example of Laski is especially interesting. The nature of his arguments underwent many permutations between the wars; in some manifestations there was little to choose between him and left-liberals. At all times in the period under discussion until the 1930s there were significant elements in Laski's thinking, notably his ideas on liberty and individuality, that were shared with liberals, but between 1925 and 1930 these became core components of his theories rather than merely adjacent to socialist or guild socialist fundamentals. Hence there is little justification for not classifying him as a liberal during those years. The young Laski had come under many of the influences that had moulded liberal thought, such as Mill and Green, but he was also an avid reader and well-abreast of new liberal literature. Hobson especially earned repeated compliments in the extensive book reviewing that Laski engaged in. Much evidence for Laski's voracious appetite for books exists in the voluminous correspondence he conducted with the American Justice Oliver Wendell Holmes. Among the entries: 'I've been re-reading Green on *Political Obligation* with profit'; 'Hobhouse, *Elements of Social Justice*, quite suggestive without being at all thrilling' (this could have summed up the man himself); 'I read an admirable book of J. A. Hobson's called *Free Thought in the Social Sciences* . . . It is a study of the obstacles to disinterestedness in thinking . . . its account of the use of scientific method in political economy as the tool of preconceived desire is, I think, beautifully done, especially as it becomes fatal both to Marshall and to Marx.'[3] This latter remark corroborates an affinity between Laski and Hobsonian thought, buttressed by Laski's reading habits and, not least, by his close association with Massingham's *Nation*; he too resigned from the *Nation* in early 1923 in protest against the latter's effective dismissal.

Once Laski had returned from his legal schooling in the USA, he became a lively, if junior, member of the intellectual set of left-liberals, despite his flirtation with alternative ideologies. The most

[3] *Holmes–Laski Letters*, edited by M. DeWolfe Howe (London, 1953), 3.10.1917, 8.12.1921, 6.2.1926. It is, however, worth noting Laski's high opinion of Hobhouse, as when he expressed puzzlement by the failure of others 'to see what a big person he is' (*Guardian* Archives, Scott Papers, A/210/13, Laski to Scott, 14.11.1927).

significant of those was Laski's long attachment to pluralism and guild socialism. But as has been shown in Chapter 2, there were distinct feelings of attraction towards guild socialism among liberals, and it is hardly surprising to find them projected in the opposite direction as well. In fact, Laski justified pluralism through its adherence to core liberal beliefs. It was only because pluralism afforded the best protection for liberal essentials that a case for it could be made. In one of the main expositions of his early pluralist views, *Authority in the Modern State*, this message was dominant. It was based on the affirmation that state and society are separate, an assertion levelled against those operating either within or outside the liberal tradition and who would, Laski was convinced, damage the aspects of liberal theory he valued most. Despite his admiration for Green, Laski warned that

> The realisation of individual virtue in the common good is a conception fine enough, in all conscience, to suffuse with a glamour of which the treachery is too late discovered the processes by which it moves along the way. The conception is yet inadequate because it fails to particularise those upon whom it is intended that benefit shall be conferred.[4]

What irked Laski was the potential subsuming of the individual by the state. It was not only that some social relationships could never be expressed through the state.[5] Beyond that lurked a real liberal anxiety—the fear of concentrated and unlimited power. The 'internal limitation upon the power of the state' was a means to 'the greatest truth to which history bears witness that the only real security for social well-being is the free exercise of men's minds'.[6] Consequently Laski subscribed to the full range of liberal core ideas, especially and repeatedly stressing the distribution of power, the notion of the state as a means to the realization of individual rights, and an individualism that regarded human development as the ultimate end of social life. Pluralism served all those liberal ends:

> It denies the oneness of society and the state . . . It sees man as a being who wishes to realise himself as a member of society. It refers back each action upon which judgment is to be passed to the conscience of the individual. It insists that the supreme arbiter of the event is the totality of such cons-

[4] H. J. Laski, *Authority in the Modern State* (New Haven, 1919), p. 20.
[5] Ibid., p. 26.
[6] Ibid., p. 55.

ciences. It does not deny that the individual is influenced by the thousand associations with which he is in contact; but it is unable to perceive that he is absorbed by them.[7]

For Laski, then, the individual was retained as the unit of social analysis. As he wrote: 'The problem today . . . is the restoration of man to his place at the centre of social life.' Like others of his generation, Laski entertained the idea of mind in reference to personal self-realization, but also postulated the idea of a group mind. The latter, however, was not to be confused with a general will. Unlike Hobson, to whom Laski constantly acknowledged intellectual debts, the idea of a group mind was essentially individualistic and thus closer to mainstream liberal philosophical assumptions. It preserved the notion of an aggregate, 'a number of men who, actuated by some common purpose, are capable of a unified activity'.[8]

The contention that the young Laski used pluralism primarily as a vehicle for liberalism—a vehicle he believed to be more efficient and more true to liberalism than the existing liberal structure—can be strengthened by reference to a wide range of positions which show him in sympathy with the concerns of his left-liberal colleagues. Foremost among them at the end of the war was the retreat from the state, though one that preserved the lingering liberal faith in the state as arbiter among individuals and groups, and as true representative of the communal good. As Laski noted himself, one of the main sources of historical unrest was the perversion of the role of the state when powerful interest groups used its political power to further their economic concerns. 'The only way out of such an impasse is the neutralisation of the state; and it cannot be neutralised save by the division of the power that is today concentrated in its hands.' The end was the new liberal one of an ethical politics; the technique was different. Whereas new liberals, prior to their disillusionment with the state, had believed that a rational democracy would obviate the need to oppose it, Laski assumed the formation of a benevolent state not through a *carte blanche* for responsible action, but by weakening it and bringing to bear on it an institutional and constitutional edifice that reflected the group nature of society. In so doing, the overlap between Laski's ideas and the traditional liberal predilection for decentralization is

[7] Ibid., p. 65.
[8] Ibid., pp. 90, 68.

notable: 'The truth obviously is that the state must organise itself on lines which admit to the full the opportunity for the realisation of personal and corporate initiative . . . The federalism and the decentralisation [this theory] implies are, in fact, the basis upon which the state of the future can be erected.'[9] On this evidence, Laski was somewhat to the 'right' of those left-liberals who placed their faith in the operation of a rational, harmonious community organized on collective lines. Significantly, he cited Muir with approval when condemning the growth of a new bureaucracy out of the original 'immense promise' of the 'socialised' new liberalism of 1906. For Laski, as for many inter-war liberals, the failure of the new liberalism was not in its social vision or in its egalitarian over-sensitivity to the condition of the people question. It failed because of doubts 'whether the regime it involved was compatible with individual freedom'.[10]

This latter critique constitutes a further mark of affinity between Laski and post-war liberalism, linking his theories of the state with the concepts of individuality and liberty. 'The real significance of freedom' was that it alone enabled 'the individuality of men to become manifest'.[11] It was to the pillar of liberalism, Mill, that Laski turned for guidance. As he explained to Holmes, announcing his intention to write *Authority in the Modern State*: 'A good book is to be written (I am going to write it) on the decline of liberty as a result of the increased power of the state. In that aspect I think we have still a damned lot to learn from J. S. Mill.'[12] Some of the things Laski had learned were revealed in an article he wrote on the fiftieth anniversary of Mill's death. Mill's evocation of the riches of individuality had of course caught Laski's imagination. But like the new liberals half a generation earlier, Laski saw Mill as connecting the socially oriented theories of modern progressivism with the radicalism of an older age, thus playing a bridging role in British intellectual history. From the vantage point of the 1920s Laski invoked Mill for the dual purpose of reinforcing current trends as well as cautioning against some of their costs. Mill had exposed the limitations of private enterprise; he had pointed the way towards industrial co-operation and self-government; he had put a seal of

[9] Ibid., pp. 385–6.
[10] Ibid., pp. 109–10.
[11] Ibid., p. 120.
[12] *Holmes–Laski Letters*, 28.11.1917.

permanence on the severance of individualism from *laissez-faire*; he had infused society with a regard for human rights; he had stressed the importance of individual responsibility for active democratic citizenship. These objectives were Laski's as well, and they constituted the heart and soul of the liberal tradition exemplified by Mill. True,

> We should, perhaps, state Mill's problem [the optimization of the individual] differently; and the experience of half a century would make us emphasize more firmly the degree to which the preservation of individuality depends upon the positive character of social control. But the ideal of Mill is still as noble an ideal as a man may desire: the perception that the eminent worth of human personality is too precious to be degraded by institutions.[13]

Even Mill's concept of the state had a lesson for posterity: 'The State was for Mill, as it was also for Bentham, the great reserve force of society which interferes to prevent the capture of the engines of social power by sinister interests.' A modified social utilitarianism had been one of the great inputs of the new liberalism into the British political tradition; but Laski preferred the residual role that Mill assigned to the state, rather than the central and dominant one that other progressives favoured.

Taking his cue from Mill, Laski explained that 'the emphasis upon freedom is made because it is believed that only in such fashion can the ethical significance of personality obtain its due recognition'.[14] His very marked individualism survived his early sympathy for pluralism, and in the mid-1920s he was still writing of the citizen: 'His true self . . . is the self that is isolated from his fellows, and contributes the fruit of isolated meditation to the common good which, collectively, they seek to bring into being.'[15] Further, 'it is a grave error to assume that men in general are, at least actively and continuously, political creatures. The context of their lives which is, for the majority, the most important is a private context.'[16] These passages are remarkable when set in the intellectual milieu of their times, and certainly more individualistic than anything the inheritors of the new liberal mantle would have associated

[13] *Nation*, 28.4.1923.
[14] Laski, *Authority in the Modern State*, p. 121.
[15] Laski, *The Grammar of Politics*, p. 31.
[16] Ibid., pp. 18–19.

themselves with.[17] Indeed, this conception of social structure was far more consonant with centrist-liberal attitudes, though the adjacent centrist-liberal ideas did not follow. But in his denial of the primacy of politics Laski was reverting to a pre-communitarian position, alien not only to the Hegelian–Marxist tradition but also to the Aristotelian legacy which had so powerfully, via the universities, infiltrated British political thought at the turn of the century. The philosophical alignment was, rather, to a mid-nineteenth-century view in which public activity was voluntary and dependent upon concepts of individual, rather than social, good.

Laski's interest in liberty seemed to increase throughout the first post-war decade. His early treatment reflects the problematics that left-liberals were grappling with, and which Laski must have been exposed to during his regular attendance at the weekly lunches of the pre-1923 *Nation*.[18] If liberty was the condition for individuality, social organization had to guarantee it by the conventional liberal means of dispersing power. In floating the proposal for a British Bill of Rights, based on his American experience, Laski pointed to the menacing increase in state activity: 'the human needs the satisfaction of which history has demonstrated to be essential must be put beyond the control of any organ of the state.'[19] Thus Laski was at one with the renewed interest that most progressives were showing in the preservation of liberty, but at the same time capable, as in the final analysis many progressives would have been, of writing that 'there is a sense in which Rousseau's paradox becomes pregnant with new meaning and it may in the end be true that men must be forced to be free'.[20] Concerted action, if not by the community then within the group, was needed to propel individuals out of their indifference into creative and responsible activity and in order to realize personality. Here the early Laski still retained a more public and political conception of human nature. He was prepared to translate the implications of Mill's emphasis on the moral and mental benefits of political activity for the individual into a more social notion of useful human activity. This was precisely the unresolved tension that post-war liberalism had bequeathed to its practitioners.

[17] See Hobson and Hobhouse on organicism in Chapter 7, Section 2. W. H. Greenleaf, 'Laski and British Socialism', *History of Political Thought*, 2 (1981), 573–91, convincingly demonstrates this libertarian streak in Laski's thought.

[18] See K. Martin, *Harold Laski* (London, 1969), pp. 50–1.

[19] Laski, *Authority in the Modern State*, pp. 101–2.

[20] Ibid., p. 108.

As before, this tension was attached to a revised Benthamism in which the 'absence of governmental interference has ceased to seem an ultimate ideal'[21] but also in which 'the good life is one day to be achieved by the majority of men and women'.[22]

Laski later spelled out this neo-utilitarianism in greater detail. The recognition of a unique social good that arose as a consequence of community life was

> a special adaptation of the Benthamite theory to the special needs of our time. It follows Bentham in its insistence that social good is the product of co-ordinated intelligence; that, though the difficulties be admittedly great, we must plan our way to the end in view. It follows Bentham, also, though from a different basis, in urging that social good means the avoidance of misery and the attainment of happiness. It applies reason, that is, to the task of discovering ways in which wants can be satisfied; and it evaluates the quality of the wants according to the degree in which, when satisfied, they minister to the permanent happiness of the whole community.

Like the new liberals before him, Laski rescued the rationality-, reformist-, planning-, and happiness-cum-welfare-maximizing aspects of Benthamism from the master himself, carefully jettisoning his individualist/atomistic presuppositions, his ensnarement in futile mathematical formulae, and his eschewal of history. As Laski remarked on this latter point: '. . . the value of reason is to be found in the degree to which it makes possible the future, not less than the immediate, harmony of impulses.'[23]

It might have appeared that Laski was slipping even further down the path to traditional liberalism in the mid-1920s when he observed that 'Liberty means absence of restraint; it is essentially a negative thing.'[24] The spurious distinction between negative and positive liberty did not however follow. Earlier Laski had acknowledged liberty 'in the sense of the positive and equal opportunity of self-realisation' while remarking that it had not been established in any genuine sense.[25] In *The Grammar of Politics* he pointed out the social fact that 'regulation . . . is the consequence of gregariousness; for we cannot live together without common rules'. Not all

[21] Ibid., p. 98.

[22] Ibid., p. 108.

[23] Laski, *The Grammar of Politics*, pp. 24–5. See also Freeden, *The New Liberalism*, pp. 12–15.

[24] Laski, *The Grammar of Politics*, p. 142.

[25] Laski, *Authority in the Modern State*, p. 37.

rules frustrated creativity and the end of personal development. When Laski concluded that 'to permit such compulsion is to invade liberty; but it is not necessarily to destroy the end liberty seeks to serve'[26] (that end being the opportunity for people to be their best selves) he adopted a position that differed both from classical liberalism and from the Idealism he opposed. Unlike those who inhabited the meeting ground between liberalism and Idealism, Laski denied that compulsion itself was tantamount to real liberty, or an expression of rational self-control. On the other hand, by distinguishing between liberty and other desirable ends or, in fact, demoting liberty to a means to such ends, Laski dissociated himself from libertarians for whom liberty was the ultimate end to be attained at whatever cost to other values. His position was thus well within the range designated by progressive liberals to the concept of liberty. Liberty was part of a cluster of social goods and the pursuit of one had to be conducted by making adjustments in the pursuit of the others.[27] Laski's dismissal of Mill's distinction between self-regarding and other-regarding actions was also consonant with new liberal doctrine and its notions of social interdependence. Once the idea of a sacrosanct area of individual life was ruled out, the notion of negative liberty as the protection of such an area from infringements evaporated. But the notion of positive liberty as the affirmation by society or the state of a rational type of thought and action, as a model that required conformity, was equally unacceptable. Freedom was 'opportunities which history has shown to be essential to the development of personality'—an authentic liberal-progressive perspective that offered 'avenues of choice' to the individual but neither forced him to walk them nor recommended a route. 'It is only to say that I alone can make that best self, and that without those freedoms I have not the means of manufacture at my disposal.'[28]

Laski's most comprehensive treatment of liberty appeared in his *Liberty in the Modern State*. This book is exceptional for being one of the best expositions of liberty since that of Mill and wholly in the spirit of the latter. Again, though even more subtly, Laski rendered the distinction between negative and positive liberty superfluous: 'I mean by liberty the absence of restraint upon the existence of those

[26] Laski, *The Grammar of Politics*, p. 142.
[27] See Chapter 7, Section 5.
[28] Laski, *The Grammar of Politics*, p. 144.

social conditions which, in modern civilization, are the necessary guarantees of individual happiness.'[29] Although couched in 'negative' terms, the absence of restraint did not apply to the activities of other people as it would have in individualist definitions, but to conditions that could affect happiness. The turn of phrase was curious, though, suggesting as it did that such conditions naturally existed and were merely hampered through some subsequent occurrence. Despite the mention of social conditions, liberty was accorded, in the best liberal tradition, a developmental content implying 'power to expand, the choice by the individual of his own way of life without imposed prohibitions from without'. Recanting his earlier position, Laski now conceded that 'Men cannot, as Rousseau claimed, be forced into freedom', nor did they 'as Hegel insisted, find their freedom in obedience to the law'. Reverting to a liberal subjectivist stance, he went on to say: 'They are free when the rules under which they live leave them without a sense of frustration in realms they deem significant.'[30]

This was arguably the best liberal statement on the nature of liberty produced between the wars. It reflected the embarrassment of liberals with force and power, and as a last resort appealed to a liberal empirical criterion in order to distinguish between permissible and impermissible compulsion: compulsion which individuals dislike and resent is unfreedom. Admittedly, this yardstick is a nebulous one. The question to be asked, though, is not the one of philosophical validity, but which tradition of political thinking did Laski's analysis have most in common with? The answer is, unhesitatingly, the liberal one. Once again the predominant liberal themes emerged in Laski's writings: the limitation of political power, the right to education, the access to knowledge. The right to education became fundamental to human freedom, claimed Laski, 'once the mastery of Nature by science transformed the sources of power'.[31] Here was the new liberal association of human development and evolution with the increasing rational assertion by man, through his mind and his artifacts, over his fate. The absence of free information (an issue liberals were preoccupied with during the

[29] H. J. Laski, *Liberty in the Modern State* (Harmondsworth, 1937; 1st edn. 1930), p. 49.

[30] Ibid. Compare this with the subjectivist approach to liberty by left-liberals, as examined in the previous chapter.

[31] Ibid., p. 51.

1920s) was also 'a denial of the power to use liberty for great ends'.[32] Following on from this, Laski attempted to demolish the Idealist position, drawing heavily and explicitly on Hobhouse's *The Metaphysical Theory of the State*.[33] What demands attention is not Laski's anti-Idealism as such, but his employment of a critique that was entirely liberal. The denial of an exclusive positive concept of liberty as well as a minimalist negative one, the dismissal of a real will ('The ultimate and inescapable fact in politics is the final variety of human wills'[34]), the rejection of the unified state as the highest expression of the individual, and an insistence on the problematics and conditionality of political obligation, were all at the heart of Hobhouse's polemic.[35]

The longest chapter of Laski's book was devoted to the freedom of the mind, a fine treatise in the spirit of the second chapter of *On Liberty*, though obviously speaking the language of a later generation. Just occasionally the perspective differed, as when Laski stated that 'it is socially most important to leave the individual as uninhibited as possible in forming his own way of life'.[36] This insistence on a social point of view to justify liberty was, of course, a conclusion that Hobson had drawn before the war with the aid of the organic analogy, though the ostensibly socialist Laski was more reluctant to voice it than the openly 'liberal' Hobson. By the mid-1920s the gap between Laski and left-liberals had narrowed further. He became reconciled to the idea of a more actively engaged state, at about the same time that post-war liberal animosity towards it had begun to abate. By then Laski was prepared to regard the state as 'the final legal depository of the social will' and as setting 'the perspective of all other organisations'.[37] In resurrecting the modified utilitarianism of the new liberals and Fabians, Laski saw the state as an organization 'for enabling the mass of men to realise social good on the largest possible scale'. Though the state was not identical with society, it possessed power because it had duties and hence was a responsible agency, 'subject to a moral test of adequacy'.[38] Laski's theory of the state thus attempted to fuse a legal-

[32] Ibid.
[33] See Laski's acknowledgement, ibid., p. 61.
[34] Ibid., p. 59.
[35] See above, pp. 33–9.
[36] Laski, *Liberty in the Modern State*, p. 151.
[37] Laski, *The Grammar of Politics*, p. 21.
[38] Ibid., pp. 25, 28.

istic reference to sovereignty, an ethical approach to ends and duties, and a utilitarian concentration on the attainment of happiness and the satisfaction of individual wants. In all those he drew sustenance from different phases of the liberal tradition. He also echoed the new liberal aspiration, or fallacy, concerning the neutrality of the state: '. . . the will of the state is in its nature morally neutral',[39] thus assuming, perhaps unwisely, that a moral input by individuals into the state would be reflected in its decision-making. But simultaneously, he harked back to the older liberal realization that 'the will of the State, in fact, is the will of government as that will is accepted by the citizens over whom it rules'.[40] This was a more 'realist' viewpoint of the state as a possibly dangerous agency, in which responsibility would have to be induced by insisting that it periodically make a convincing rational case for the renewal of its powers. Parallel to the stress on state responsibility was the Millite affirmation that 'no man can be a good citizen unless he personally interest himself in the affairs of the State'.[41]

Of especial interest is Laski's treatment of the consumer/producer relationship, which had so disturbed liberals in the immediate post-war period. In 1918 he tended to argue for the division of functions between the state—'as primarily a body of consumers'[42]—and bodies of producers, mainly trade unions. It was difficult, he believed, to see any permanent basis of reconciliation between the interests of capital and labour in production, but it was possible to conceive of an adjustment between the various producer groups and the state as respresenting the consumer. Laski's tentative solution resembled the later plan drawn up by the Webbs, consisting of 'two bodies similar in character to a national legislature',[43] without settling ultimate sovereignty on either. Liberals, as we have seen, were loath to accept such proposals. Remarkably, Laski himself came over to the views of progressive liberals some years later. He conceded that 'no man's activities are confined to a single function. It is necessary to safeguard his interest as a user of services he has no part in producing. It is essential, in other words, to protect him as a consumer. The co-ordination of functions is the

[39] Ibid., p. 36.
[40] Ibid., p. 56.
[41] Ibid., p. 63.
[42] Laski, *Authority in the Modern State*, p. 85.
[43] Ibid., p. 88.

sphere in which, to that end, the State must operate.'[44] The retention of the state as the supreme social organization was entirely at one with the progressive liberal spirit, as was its designation as a regulatory and directive institution, rather than one that undertook functions and services itself. Crucial, too, was the identification of consumption with the status of citizenship, a connection that had always been central to Hobson's concept of man in a political setting.

Laski also employed the notion of equality in similar fashion to progressive liberals. He had, after all, commended Hobhouse's *The Elements of Social Justice* with the words: 'Nothing in the book is better than the treatment of equality.'[45] Like left-liberals, Laski came by equality through pursuing the implications of liberty in the economic sphere and, concurrently, through the development of a more refined idea of citizenship. In classic liberal terms, Laski first identified equality as 'the absence of special privilege'[46] and secondly as 'adequate opportunities'. Significantly, he added: 'By adequate opportunities we cannot imply equal opportunities in a sense that implies identity of original chance. The native endowments of men are by no means equal.'[47] Equality was an extension of self-government because its absence meant the rule of limited numbers and the wielding of undue influence; it was, *pro tanto*, essential to freedom. All this was liberalism of the most general kind, based on accepted nineteenth-century notions that 'a democratic state regards its members as equally entitled to happiness'.[48] How far Laski's analysis was removed from many socialist doctrines is evident from his examination of the guidelines for the distribution of social goods. Unlike some egalitarians, he was satisfied with a theory that began by catering to a 'minimum basis of civilisation' but then allowed for markedly differential rewards. 'One man is not entitled to a house of twenty rooms until all people are adequately housed . . . We may . . . have Belgravias, if their existence is a necessary condition of social welfare; but we are not entitled to have Belgravias until we have secured the impossibility of Poplar's existence.'[49] This philosophy would have appealed to the

[44] Laski, *The Grammar of Politics*, pp. 69, 75.
[45] *Nation*, 13.5.1922.
[46] Laski, *The Grammar of Politics*, p. 153.
[47] Ibid., p. 154.
[48] Ibid., pp. 156–7.
[49] Ibid., pp. 157–8.

most cautious of liberal progressives; indeed, to many of the more socially conscious conservatives. Laski, however, had more to say on the subject. There is in fact an extraordinary resemblance between his arguments and those now familiarized by John Rawls, as the following passage indicates:

> The idea of equality is obviously an idea of levelling. It is an attempt to give each man as similar a chance as possible to utilize what powers he may possess. It means that he is to count in the framing of decisions where these affect him, that whatever legal rights inhere in any other man as a citizen, shall inhere in him also; that where differences of treatment are meted out by society to different persons, those differences shall be capable of explanation in terms of the common good.[50]

Rawls's two principles[51] are distinctly discernible in embryonic form: the equal liberty to formulate the rules of the game, and the condoning of inequalities only when socially beneficial. Equal access to the political process remained for Laski as for all liberals a defining trait of their ideology. In addition Laski enunciated the further left-liberal position that the 'idea of equality . . . is such an organization of opportunity that no man's personality suffers frustration to the private benefit of others'.[52] That is to say, the end of social organization was individual self-expression, universally applied, and valued by criteria of social utility.

The above discussion does not attempt to offer a comprehensive survey of Laski's thought, nor does it take into account his increasingly Marxist views in the 1930s. What is suggested is that at all times until the early 1930s, and arguably beyond that, elements of liberal thought played a key role in forming Laski's ideas, and that between his pluralist and Marxist phases he was to all intents and purposes a left-liberal. This point must be made because in the past Laski's thought has been examined in isolation and within the context of the socialist/Labourite tradition. A 'horizontal' consideration of his idea-environment rather than a misconceived 'vertical' location of Laski in a 'socialist' tradition reinforces the claim that

[50] Laski, *Liberty in the Modern State*, pp. 53–4.

[51] 'First: each person is to have an equal right to the most extensive basic liberty compatible with a similar liberty for others. Second: social and economic inequalities are to be arranged so that they are both (*a*) reasonably expected to be to everyone's advantage, and (*b*) attached to positions and offices open to all.' (J. Rawls, *A Theory of Justice* [Oxford, 1973], p. 60.)

[52] Laski, *Liberty in the Modern State*, p. 54.

the boundaries of liberal ideology were not institutional, and that previous delimitations of liberalism within party political confines have ignored the impact of left-liberalism between the wars. On issues of social policy, workers' participation, and state regulation of the interests of workers, consumers and investors, there was complete accord between Laski and progressive liberals. He extended, as did left-liberals, the arguments against concentrated political power to economic power as well.[53] On the other hand, he was more sympathetic to trade unions than liberals were, and more sanguine about the capacity of human nature to overcome the need for pecuniary egoistical motivation in order to achieve its best. But these differences do not alter the fundamental liberal structure of Laski's thought in the period referred to above.

What was Laski's own approach to liberalism? The answer is not immediately available, partly because most of his explicit work on liberalism was written during his Marxist period, partly because Labour party members who were (ideologically speaking) left-liberals were often unaware of, or unwilling to publicize, their affinity with liberalism. Instead, they concentrated on attacking centrist-liberal varieties of thought. In his early work Laski consciously related to the liberal origins of his assumptions, as when he wrote in the context of defending freedom: '. . . to destroy spontaneity is to prevent the advent of liberalism.'[54] On the political level, too, Laski supported an alliance with the new Manchester Liberalism, adding that 'in the broadest sense, Liberalism is more necessary in this tangled and chaotic world than it was before the war'.[55] And to Holmes he wrote about his sympathy with Robert Cecil's 'liberal' programme, 'which agrees quite largely with my standpoint and even more with Massingham's'.[56] Of course, Laski criticized liberalism, but mainly because political Liberalism had failed to rise to recent challenges. When he wrote that 'English Liberalism has suffered eclipse because, broadly speaking, it was unable to discover an industrial philosophy suitable to the wants of the new electorate',[57] he was referring to the inadequacies of the Liberal leadership on the one hand and the lack of understanding

[53] Ibid., p. 171.
[54] Laski, *Authority in the Modern State*, p. 121.
[55] *Nation*, 21.5.1921.
[56] *Holmes–Laski Letters*, 15.5.1922.
[57] Laski, *Liberty in the Modern State*, p. 181.

displayed by centrist-liberals towards the problems of labour on the other. Hence liberal industrial policy, as it emerged after the war, 'did not fit into the character of Liberal Leadership' and the centrist Muir came under attack for declaring animosity towards trade unions. The liberalism Muir represented was magnified by Laski into liberalism *in toto*, to the exclusion of left-liberalism, and consequently—though even then exaggeratedly—was labelled as 'an atomistic philosophy applicable to a world in which employer and worker confronted each other, as individuals, on equal terms', and —more accurately—as a 'middle-class outlook'.[58]

In later years Laski wrote two works exclusively on liberalism. The major one, *The Rise of European Liberalism*, acknowledged liberalism as 'the outstanding doctrine of Western Civilization',[59] but reverted to the typecast socialist claim that liberalism had failed as an ideology, being linked to narrow concepts of property, class and contract. Indeed, it was because Laski now abandoned liberal socialism in favour of Marxism that he could jettison the progressive liberalism he had supported. Paradoxically, it was only as a Marxist that he could concede the liberalness of British socialism. It was 'a body of doctrine upon which the emphasis of John Stuart Mill's ideas was far more profound than that of Marx'[60]—an observation that equally applied to Laski's own thinking in the 1920s. In 1940 Laski supplemented this study with a Hobhouse Memorial Trust Lecture on *The Decline of Liberalism*. For the first time he conceded a distinction between 'two aspects of liberalism, the one negative, the other positive, the one atomic, the other organic, the one finding the essence of the individual in his antagonism to the state, the other finding his essence in the context given him by the state'.[61] But to his mind this was a crisis; he did not allow for the possibility that the second stream was a successful example of ideological evolution, successful in its assimilation of moderate theories of social reform and communitarianism. For Laski the weakness of liberalism lay in its failure to adapt. If indeed this was the case, the failure of liberalism was no more pronounced than that of other ideologies competing for hegemony. Again, Laski's new Marxist

[58] Ibid., pp. 182–3.

[59] H. J. Laski, *The Rise of European Liberalism* (London, 1962; 1st edn. 1936), p. 5.

[60] Ibid., p. 157.

[61] H. J. Laski, *The Decline of Liberalism* (L. T. Hobhouse Memorial Trust Lecture No. 10, Oxford, 1940), p. 7.

vantage-point opened his eyes to the characteristics of his own early years: '. . . those of us who are still in middle age cannot but remember how, in 1919, men dared widely to hope that the ideals of liberal democracy had entered upon a long period of triumphant recognition.'[62] But Laski's memory served him ill when he tried to summarize Hobhouse's achievements. Hobhouse's doctrine had a deeper and wider social content than Green's but, though rejecting Bentham's anti-historicism, 'fell into the opposite error of divorcing the process of history from the deliberately willed effort of individuals to plan social change in a wholesale way'.[63]

To accuse liberals of holding to inexorable laws of history and to deny the role of individual will in liberal reformist thought, was a curious conclusion coming from a Marxist. The deliberate planning of institutions had become as much liberal as Marxist (though less totalist). If liberals were occasionally guilty of naïve optimism or a belief in the march of progress, so were Marxists. A reformist, institution-moulding inclination was certainly at the heart of the progressive liberalism that had originally taken its cue from Bentham. Yet even when fundamentally critical of liberalism, Laski was prepared to contemplate its survival in a radically altered form; a form, in fact, that left-liberals had tried to give it themselves. This 'reinvigoration of the doctrinal content of liberalism' had to be based on 'a new conception of property in which social ownership and control replace individual ownership and control'—a position on which left-liberals would have met Laski more than half-way.[64] It meant planning, and a reconciliation of liberty with equality, and the end of economic insecurity. Implicitly acknowledging the flexibility of liberal ideology and its capacity to surround its core principles with new adjacent ideas, Laski concluded: 'A liberalism which attempts this task has still great prospects before it, for it could then draw to its support interests and ideas which now seem alien from its purpose.'

Finally, it is instructive to reverse the perspective we have employed and to examine the regard in which Laski was held by contemporary liberals and the ways in which they consumed and assimilated his ideas. The *Nation* was highly complimentary about

[62] Ibid., p. 4.

[63] Ibid., p. 12.

[64] Ibid., pp. 22–3. See Chapter 7, Section 5. Clarke, *Liberals and Social Democrats*, p. 153, also remarks on this affinity.

Laski's *Authority in the Modern State*, despite his guild socialist and almost syndicalist views. It welcomed especially, in deference to an older liberalism, Laski's eschewal of organicism and his reduction of the state to its members. Its reviewer identified Laski's main thesis as a concern for the attainment of liberty through 'intensifying the active participation of men in the business of government' and placed his advocacy of the legitimate limitation of the state within the framework of 'the old doctrine of natural rights, though not open to the same theoretical criticisms'.[65] Laski's *The Grammar of Politics* which, we have contended, was a left-liberal work, was hailed by fellow progressive liberals who bestowed on it their seal of approval. Even the centrist Muir described Laski's approach as constituting

> essentially a liberal philosophy. It asserts the ultimate sanctity of individuality, and recognises that individual inspiration and initiative are the driving forces of all progress . . . It exalts individual liberty as the supreme end of political action . . . preaches the utmost possible extension of the practice of self-government . . . and . . . the moral values of responsibility. . . . All this is pure and undiluted Liberalism.

On practical issues, Muir saw Laski advocating 'the Liberal Industrial policy'. His fault lay mainly in his 'cocksureness', in his proneness to exaggeration, and—the only substantive point of criticism —in his obsession with committees, which Muir evidently feared as bureaucratization creeping in by the back door.[66]

Wallas, too, accepted most of Laski's proposals and welcomed his book for ignoring the boundaries between politics on the one hand and law and economics on the other. But, again like Muir, he worried about the proliferation of committee work that Laski's proposals entailed. Wallas was by then removed from the frontiers of progressivism, and his review is revealing for what it did not say more than for what it did.[67] While Wallas still saddled Laski with his former sins of pluralism, no longer evident in this work, Morris Ginsberg—Hobhouse's close collaborator—praised the book's great importance from the opposite end as synthesizing and indicating 'the further trend of a significant movement in politics in recent times both in this country and abroad. It may be said to mark the

[65] 'Liberty and Law', *Nation*, 16.8.1919.
[66] R. M[uir], 'The Philosophy of Politics', *WW*, 11.7.1925.
[67] G. Wallas, 'A Grammar of Politics', *MG*, 10.8.1925.

end of the so-called "attack on the State," and to be essentially a vindication of the territorial State, while at the same time denying that sovereignty is a necessary attribute of it'. The test of the state, Laski now seemed to be arguing, was not its will, but the moral character of what was willed. Laski was therefore seen to be an advocate of an ethical, interventionist politics whose aim was to secure freedom, and welcomed into the left-liberal community. The enthusiastic conclusion was: 'Both on the side of theory and of practice Mr Laski's book must undoubtedly rank among the ablest contributions made to political science in our time.'[68] Laski's book stimulated Hobson to re-evaluate current attitudes towards the state and to declare it both as 'a very disagreeable necessity' and 'more necessary than ever before'. Now that Laski had opted for the primacy of political over non-political considerations, Hobson saw himself in full accord with Laski's new position: 'One of the conspicuous merits of Mr. Laski's book is the rectification of the intellectual balance.' If Hobson still had a bone of contention to pick with Laski, it was over Hobson's familiar insistence that the idea of the social good might be thought to include a 'directly operative social or "general" will making for this good'.[69] This had been Haldane's complaint when reviewing Laski's *The Foundations of Sovereignty*. For the Idealist Haldane, Laski's refusal to accept the reality of the general will was the outcome of a metaphysical assumption that the community was a mere concourse of social atoms, mutually exclusive in their individualities.[70] The use of 'metaphysical' may have been a case of the pot calling the kettle black, but both Haldane's and Hobson's reservations indicated that Laski was more centrally situated within the historical liberal tradition than they were, in his refusal to derive a communitarian approach from the new social construct that Idealists and new liberals had tried to put at the disposal of liberalism. Hobson was perplexed by Laski's 'streak of individualism based upon his powerful sense of ultimate individual rights in virtue of the uniqueness of each personality'.[71] Nevertheless, the mutual acclaim of Hobson and Laski for each other clearly reinforces the liberal interpretation of Laski's thought. Indeed, Laski was not only fulsome in his

[68] M. Ginsberg, review in *HJ*, 24 (1925), 388–90.
[69] Hobson, 'The Reformulation of Politics', 430–2.
[70] R. B. Haldane, 'On Sovereignty', *Nation*, 25.3.1922.
[71] Hobson, 'The Reformulation of Politics', 432.

praise for Hobson as 'one of the most alert and freshly vigorous minds now writing upon public affairs' but specifically identified the substance of his work as 'likely to be the clue to a wise liberalism in the next generation'.[72]

2. R. H. TAWNEY

The question of delimiting the liberal ideological community becomes intriguing when one turns to R. H. Tawney. He was not a liberal in the sense that Laski surely was for a period of his life. However, liberal notions served Tawney as points of reference; he shared terms of discourse with left-liberals; and many, though not all, of his theses were arrived at in a climate of ideas that reflected the outer progressive reaches of liberalism. In terms of ideological structure, Tawney held some core beliefs in common with liberals, whereas other liberal beliefs, though not as central to him as to them, nevertheless appeared on the periphery of his system of ideas. The notion of a system of ideas is certainly apt in Tawney's case, in view of his repeated exhortation to Englishmen to construct a map of political theory and principles.[73] Tawney's affinities with Hobson are of some significance. By the end of the war he had read a number of Hobson's more important works, which were demonstrably instrumental in fashioning some of his ideas.[74] The two shared a common respect for Ruskin and the role—perhaps more symbolic than effective—Ruskin had played in shifting economic thought away from an obsessional concentration on production and productivity and towards a recognition of a just system of payment for services. Above all, both men subscribed to Ruskin's superimposition of a unified ethical universe on the discrete and individualistic worlds of economics and politics.[75]

In Tawney's first major book, published in 1921, he developed a theory of property explicitly borrowed from Hobson's distinction between property and improperty. Like other left-liberals, Tawney did not reject the institution of private property, but he remained inimical to its excesses. He acknowledged the right of private

[72] H. J. L[aski], 'Surveying the Wreck', *Nation*, 23.4.1921.

[73] E.g. Tawney, *The Acquisitive Society*, pp. 1–3, 223.

[74] Tawney later called Hobson 'the greatest of economic humanists' (review of Hobson's *Wealth and Life*, *Political Quarterly*, 1 [1930], 276).

[75] Tawney, of course, conducted his arguments within a strong Christian ethical framework (cf. Greenleaf, *The British Political Tradition*, vol. ii, pp. 443–9).

property not only for personal services and for possessions necessary to health and comfort, but property in land, tools used by their owners and even—less socialistically—property in copyright and patents.[76] Tawney frequently defended property in the best liberal tradition. It was an aid to creative work, always remembering that the creativity of individuals was not only, or even primarily, for their own benefit, but for society at large. Building on that basis, Tawney reiterated two items on the progressive liberal agenda: first, proprietary rights had to be widely distributed; second, property was one way of organizing the fundamental need for security.[77] Unlike centrist-liberals, Tawney allowed for far greater flexibility in interpreting this latter precept, extending property to cover annuities and insurance, and detaching it from the traditional body of rights that currently accompanied ownership.[78] His praise for the Liberal Budget of 1909 was consistent with this understanding of property, because 'it was felt to involve the doctrine that property is not an absolute right, but that it may properly be accompanied by special obligations, a doctrine which, if carried to its logical conclusion, would destroy its sanctity by making ownership no longer absolute but conditional'.[79] As we have seen, this was the very conclusion that left-liberals had arrived at. Though notably more sanguine than liberals about the possibilities of enlisting non-economic motives in the service of industry,[80] Tawney shrugged off any associations with revolutionary or maximalist socialism. Those of his persuasion, he wrote, will not desire to establish any visionary communism, for they will realize that the free disposal of a sufficiency of personal possessions is the condition of a healthy and self-respecting life, and will seek to distribute more widely the property rights which make them today the privilege of a minority.[81]

The ethical rule of reciprocity which had guided Hobson and J. M. Robertson in the past[82] served as an organizing tenet with

[76] Tawney, *The Acquisitive Society*, pp. 66–7.

[77] Ibid., pp. 63, 65, 95.

[78] Ibid., pp. 82–5.

[79] Ibid., p. 25.

[80] Ibid., pp. 192 ff. See, by contrast, the *Saturday Westminster Gazette* review of Tawney's *The Acquisitive Society* ('The Case Against Capitalism', 21.5.1921).

[81] Tawney, *The Acquisitive Society*, pp. 94–5. See also R. Terrill, *R. H. Tawney and His Times: Socialism as Fellowship* (London, 1974), p. 166. While Terrill's analysis is illuminating and bears out the interpretation offered here, he does not recognize the closeness of Tawney's views to contemporary liberal ones. Cf. pp. 152, 200.

[82] Cf. Freeden, *The New Liberalism*, pp. 109, 222–4.

reference to which Tawney developed his ideas on social function:

> The first principle is that industry should be subordinated to the community in such a way as to render the best service technically possible, that those who render that service faithfully should be honourably paid, and that those who render no service should not be paid at all, because it is of the essence of a function that it should find its meaning in the satisfaction, not of itself, but of the end which it serves. The second is that its direction and government should be in the hands of persons who are responsible to those who are directed and governed, because it is the condition of economic freedom that men should not be ruled by an authority which they cannot control . . . It is a question first of Function, and secondly of Freedom.[83]

This passage expressed the assumption common to non-pluralist progressives that the community was the ultimate arbiter of sectional behaviour. It subscribed to the liberal appreciation of excellence in performance and of reward for services. As liberals had been doing for two generations, it singled out the idle rich for opprobrium. Furthermore, it saw the question of industrial democracy as an extension of liberty and self-determination, and those terms were defined within the liberal-democratic context of accountability. The very notion of function was entirely compatible with the left-liberal stress on communal ends, as well as overlapping with what Idealists were calling social purpose.[84] In fact, when in 1929 Tawney returned to the idea of social function, he discussed it in language resembling the deliberations leading to the Liberal Yellow Book: 'The important question is not whether an undertaking is described as private or public; it is whether, if it is private, adequate guarantees can be established that it performs a public function, and whether, if it is public, it performs it effectively.'[85] Tawney also quoted directly from the Yellow Book when echoing the liberal demand that industry should operate under conditions of complete publicity.[86]

On nationalization, too, Tawney was far from adopting the stance that opponents of socialism attributed to its adherents. He saw it as 'a word which is neither very felicitous nor free from ambiguity . . . It is an unfortunate chance that English-speaking peoples employ one word to express what in France and Germany are expressed by

[83] Tawney, *The Acquisitive Society*, pp. 7–8.
[84] Ibid., p. 9. See Hetherington and Muirhead, *Social Purpose*, p. 10.
[85] R. H. Tawney, *Equality* (London, 1938; 1st edn. 1931), p. 237.
[86] Ibid., p. 240.

two, *étatisation* or *Verstaatlichung* and *socialisation* or *Sozialisierung*.' As a result, public ownership was confused with 'placing industry under the machinery of the political state'. This failed to take account of federal or decentralized solutions to public control; instead, 'the administrative systems obtaining in a society which has nationalized its foundation industries will, in fact, be as various as in one that resigns them to private ownership'.[87] It was this flexibility that showed a close affinity to liberal experimentalism, although that experimentalism, unlike Tawney's, displayed a more sceptical approach to the initial question of whether to nationalize or not. However, no liberal could have put it better when Tawney concluded that 'nationalization, then, is not an end, but a means to an end, and when the question of ownership has been settled the question of administration remains for solution'.[88]

Tawney exhibited the common equivocation with respect to liberalism that characterized most Labour stalwarts, yet his acknowledgement of the liberal heritage is obvious. The generation of democracy by liberals was a necessary but not sufficient condition of conflict-reduction between the privileged and the rest, and of the construction of a system based on human dignity. 'Liberalism left the conflict to take its course; by its refusal to face the brutal realities of the economic system, it destroyed itself as a party, though it remains a moral power.'[89] This was, no doubt, a subliminal reference to the distinction between the institution and the ideology, though, focusing as he did on centrist-liberalism, Tawney was acutely aware of its ideological shortcomings. But Tawney's conception of socialism had an unmistakably liberal content: 'Socialism accepts, therefore, the principles, which are the corner-stones of democracy, that authority, to justify its title, must rest on consent; that power is tolerable only so far as it is accountable to the public.'[90] He went further than centrist-liberals in stressing equality, but in similar fashion to left-liberals, issued a clear warning to those socialists who would seek, 'whether in the name of economic efficiency or of social equality, to reduce the variety of individual character and genius to a drab and monotonous uniformity'.[91] This

[87] Tawney, *The Acquisitive Society*, pp. 139–40, 141–2.

[88] Ibid., p. 149.

[89] Tawney, *Equality*, p. 259.

[90] Ibid., p. 260.

[91] Ibid., p. 84. This bears comparison with Clement Attlee's comment: 'I think myself that socialism must take the vital parts of liberalism with it . . . the realization

liberal acceptance of natural human differences as the foundation of a healthy social life was limited by the following observation, one which, again, left-liberals would have applauded: 'Differences of character and capacity between human beings, however important on their own plane, are of minor significance compared with the capital fact of their common humanity.'[92] Ultimately, Tawney's very socialism was conceived as an extension of liberalism. Its object was to apply principles recognized in the civil and political spheres to economic and social organization.[93] This economic freedom signified 'not merely the absence of repression but also the opportunity of self-organization'.[94] This was an extension of liberty that liberals had long undertaken themselves.

The aim of this analysis is not to contest the importance of Tawney, nor to belittle the considerable impact he had on his generation. Yet to draw attention to the influence on liberals of Tawney's writings does not suggest the absorption by them of an external ideology so much as a give-and-take within a community of ideas that defined left-liberalism, and to which various individuals made different contributions. Tawney's *The Acquisitive Society* and his later *Equality* struck just the right notes among left-liberals, as acknowledgements in books by Hobson, Burns, and Laski indicate.[95] At the same time, one must remember Tawney's long involvement, as contributor, in the left-liberal *Manchester Guardian*, and the formative influence new liberal ideas had on him.[96] Even his well-publicized examination of the concept of equality did not signal a departure from liberalism. His views on equality were in the main entirely compatible with those of his left-liberal colleagues, not because they reproduced his analyses, but because his was a liberal socialism. Tawney did not oppose the acquisition of wealth as such, but made it 'contingent upon the discharge of social obligations, which sought to proportion remuneration to service'.[97] To desire equality meant for him

of the value of the individual and the value of variety, but I consider that that can only be achieved through socialism.' ('Economic Justice Under Democracy', in *Constructive Democracy* [London, 1938], p. 123).

[92] Ibid., p. 260. [93] Ibid.

[94] R. H. Tawney, *The Radical Tradition* (Harmondsworth, 1964), p. 107.

[95] See e.g. Hobson, *Free-Thought in the Social Sciences*, p. 7; Laski, *A Grammar of Politics*, preface; Burns, *Industry and Civilisation*, p. 7.

[96] See Terrill, *R. H. Tawney and His Times*, pp. 24, 122, 203.

[97] Tawney, *The Acquisitive Society*, p. 31.

to hold that, while . . . natural endowments differ profoundly, it is a mark of a civilized society to aim at eliminating such inequalities as have their source, not in individual differences, but in its own organization, and that individual differences, which are a source of social energy, are more likely to ripen and find expression if social inequalities are, as far as practicable, diminished.[98]

In contrast to those who sought to organize society with a view to allowing the development of exceptional talent, Tawney saw that as a necessary but not sufficient condition for social well-being. Because a community required unity as well as diversity, the pursuit of equality had a dual function: to enable the provision for common needs side by side with the chance for true talent to rise.[99] This combination of communitarianism with developmental individualism was identical to the formula left-liberals had evolved. Hence, the progressive liberal definition of equality meant 'not only that exceptional men should be free to exercise their exceptional powers, but that common men should be free to make the most of their common humanity'.[100] The practical measures Tawney subscribed to—equalization through health, education, provision for contingencies in the lives of wage-earners, and inheritance duties—were all part of the progressive equipment. Most telling was Tawney's abstention from making any absolute appeal to equality. As he significantly observed,

The spiritual energy of human beings, in all the wealth of their infinite diversities, is the end to which external arrangements, whether political or economic, are merely means. Hence institutions which guarantee to men the opportunity of becoming the best of which they are capable are the supreme political good, and liberty is rightly preferred to equality, when the two are in conflict.

Indeed, though not all the meanings put on the concept of equality conflicted with liberty, some inequalities were completely compatible with it.[101]

The one important area in which Tawney and, for that matter, other moderate socialists, differed from left-liberals, was on the subject of power. Though he, too, was as aware as they of the moral evils of concentrated power,[102] Tawney exhibited a greater realism,

[98] Tawney, *Equality*, p. 39.
[99] Ibid., pp. 117–18.
[100] Ibid., p. 119.
[101] Ibid., p. 208.
[102] Terrill, *R. H. Tawney and His Times*, pp. 138–54.

supported by an understanding of power that did not, as with liberals, try to neutralize it by vesting it in the community, but accepted that inequality of power was inherent in the nature of organized society and was—as the ability to act—the condition of liberty.[103] Burns's and Hobson's opinions notwithstanding,[104] left-liberals, as has been shown, were unable to dissociate power from the moral dilemmas it provoked, and hence reluctant to accept it as part of the political process. Tawney displayed no such reluctance. He dismissed progressive liberal solutions to the incorporation of workers into industrial life, observing that under present conditions the 'idea that industrial peace can be secured merely by the exercise of tact and forbearance is based on the idea that there is a fundamental identity of interest between the different groups engaged in it . . . The disputes which matter are not caused by a misunderstanding of identity of interests, but by a better understanding of diversity of interests.'[105] Tawney adopted a more simple approach to power, defining it as 'the capacity of an individual, or group of individuals, to modify the conduct of other individuals or groups in the manner which he desires, and to prevent his own conduct being modified in the manner in which he does not'[106]—a formulation modern political scientists would recognize. Among British progressives only Russell handled power similarly when he argued that it was the fundamental concept in social science, though a large part of his detailed study of power related to moral attitudes towards it and offered typical liberal solutions for 'taming' it.[107] In contrast, Barker delivered a lecture on the foundations of politics which evaded the question of power entirely, substituting for it moral obligation.[108]

Looking back on the 1930s, Tawney felt that British socialism had to 'wear a local garb' and adapt to the psychology 'of the workers of

[103] Tawney, *Equality*, pp. 208–14.

[104] See above Chapter 7, Section 6. Indeed, Tawney rightly claimed that even Burns was 'more interested in values than in forces'. ('The Future of Society', *NS*, 26.11.1938.)

[105] Tawney, *The Acquisitive Society*, p. 43. For Tawney, purpose and an understanding of social function, rather than the harmony and individual rights believed in by left-liberals, would bring conflict under control (ibid., p. 45). Tawney also advocated unequivocal obedience to the state in wartime, in contradistinction to most left-liberals (cf. J. M. Winter, *Socialism and the Challenge of War: Ideas and Politics in Britain 1912–1918* [London, 1974], pp. 167–8).

[106] Tawney, *Equality*, p. 200.

[107] B. Russell, *Power* (London, 1975. 1st edn. 1938), pp. 186–207.

[108] Barker, *The Citizen's Choice*, pp. 125–48.

a particular country at a particular period'.[109] That political psychology had

> been steeped for two centuries in a liberal tradition, and the collapse of political Liberalism has not effaced the imprint. The result is the existence of a body of opinion, larger, probably, than in most other countries, which is sensitive on such subjects as personal liberty, freedom of speech and meeting, tolerance, the exclusion of violence from politics, parliamentary government—what, broadly, it regards as fair play and the guarantees for it. The only version of socialism which, as things are to-day, has the smallest chance of winning mass support, is one which accepts that position.[110]

What this section has tried to demonstrate is both this conscious assimilation of political liberalism into the socialism of Tawney and the close, and rarely acknowledged, affinity that his social and economic views had with his left-liberal colleagues. The question of power apart, Tawney's opus—even his development of the notion of fellowship—was but a variation on a theme whose resonance still stirred the passions and thoughts of progressives on the political and moral left.

3. THE *NEW STATESMAN*

A perusal of the pages of the *New Statesman* also supplies highly instructive evidence on the parallels between Labour party circles and left-liberalism. Naturally, the problem of analysis is an acute one, for Labour party supporters were at pains to stress irreconcilable differences with Liberals, to magnify the weaknesses of the Liberal party, and to underplay the relevance of liberal principles whenever possible. Changing tactics, depending on the fortunes of the Labour party in and out of power, further confuse the issues. Yet behind all this one can detect a grudging recognition of the force of left-liberalism, however much that recognition faltered on the characteristic unwillingness to distinguish ideas from institutions. G. D. H. Cole, who made sporadic appearances on the pages of the *New Statesman*, was representative of this attitude. Cole was less of an academic mind than Laski and less single-minded and succinct in his conception of socialism than Tawney, and his thought abounds with fluctuations and inconsistencies. The follow-

[109] Tawney, *Equality*, p. 265.
[110] Ibid., p. 266.

ing argument must not be taken as an assertion that either Cole or the *New Statesman* were liberal, but as a further instance of the extension of the boundaries of progressive liberalism into socialist ideology. In the words of the *New Statesman*'s editor, Clifford Sharp, commenting in 1924 on the policies of the Liberal and Labour parties, 'the programmes of the two parties are practically identical, so identical, indeed, that disputes have arisen as to who has stolen this or that item from the other'.[111] If this was true on the party political level, it was far more so on the ideological one; but instead of postulating the possibility of the theft of policies, it is more fruitful to consider the possibility of spontaneous combustion among socialist and liberal progressives alike, nourished by a common reformist heritage and confronted with the same socio-economic problems urgently demanding attention. Within this broad community of ideas certain exchanges took place, resulting in mutual influence or 'permeation'. To contend, however, that liberal ideas were deeply rooted in British progressive thought is not to suggest that a monolithic progressive ideology was taking shape. It is intended to demonstrate the variety of ideological structures available to progressives and to show, further, that strong and easily identifiable liberal components were widely shared. This does not mean that all progressive ideologies were liberalism masquerading as something else, but that liberal ideas still offered a viable perspective on politics. Those ideas were often unmistakably at the centre of ideological postures, but even when more peripheral, as in the case of the *New Statesman* and Cole, underscored the common ground that kept liberal essentials alive and ensured that the heritage of the new liberalism remained a distinct contribution to the British political tradition.

It is interesting to find Cole implicitly acknowledging the role of the new liberalism in the early stages of his thought: 'we find ourselves in many cases treating the "New Liberalism" as an embryonic state of Socialist ideas leading deviously to our own goal by way of Radical Collectivism', he wrote before the war.[112] Soon, however, he switched allegiance to pluralism and differed from left-liberals in focusing on the role of the productive units of society rather than on that of the consumer. As has repeatedly been argued

[111] [C. Sharp], 'Labour and its Allies', *NS*, 12.1.1924.

[112] Quoted in A. W. Wright, *G. D. H. Cole and Socialist Democracy* (Oxford, 1979), p. 19.

above, the pluralist position to which Cole subscribed retained elements which liberals held dear: voluntarism, democratic self-government, and the ascription of a moral co-ordinating role to the state, expressing a national will and seeking to reify an ethical interpretation of community. Cole's midway position between producers and consumers which emerged after the war maintained the appeal to the general interest and the eschewal of sectionalism that was a hallmark of liberal thinking. During the 1920s Cole continued to move with the times, reflecting as did liberals the more sombre mood of economic depression. For Cole, this meant a reappraisal of socialism. The 'critical hostility' towards the state, he wrote in 1924, caused the pre-war 'well-defined' structure of socialist ideas to collapse in ruins. Moreover, concessions were being made to property 'which differ little in practice from admissions of right'. This 'eclectic and accommodating' socialism was not notably different from what liberals, or even conservatives, could agree on.[113]

By 1926 the developments within socialism had, to Cole's mind, gone even further, the prominent issue being nationalization. But rather than voicing his reservations, he lent these developments qualified approval. After reading Keynes's 'The End of Laissez-Faire' Cole mused on the changes:

> In a real sense, we are, of course, all opportunists nowadays. If *laissez-faire* has been battered to pieces, Social Democracy has suffered some nasty jolts in the long voyage from the eighteen-eighties to the nineteen-twenties. Nobody thinks nowadays that we have merely to nationalise, or socialise, all our industries, and everything else will be added unto us. The forms of social ownership and control have been reconsidered, and we have come, even the hottest Socialists among us, to see that the social principle may have to be applied in as many different ways as there are services to which it can be applied at all.[114]

This was no instantaneous conversion to Keynes's liberal perspective, but the culmination of the gradual filtration of liberal social-policy proposals, as well as the new realities of industrial life, into the language of public debate. If in the past socialism was almost synonymous with the nationalization of industry, the increasing efficiency of the capitalist trust had changed all this. Nationaliz-

[113] [G. D. H. Cole], 'English Socialism in 1924', *NS*, 6.9.1924.
[114] [G. D. H. Cole], 'The Close of a System', *NS*, 24.7.1926.

ation had meant both public control and combination rather than competition. Now that efficiency could be secured by other means, 'the position among Socialists is not that they have ceased to desire public ownership, but that they have ceased to believe in it with the old fervent faith'. Hence, a new *de facto* consensus was being forged on what was, mainly due to liberal efforts, becoming the central industrial question of the 1920s: '. . . the inevitable effect of this [attention to the efficiency potential of nationalization] is to shift the emphasis from the broad question of public *versus* private ownership to the particular and intricate questions of industrial administration and economic policy.'[115] The ground had been prepared for a grudging yet admiring acceptance of the Liberal Yellow Book. And when it appeared, Cole was at his most conciliatory towards a centrist-liberalism even more removed from him than the philosophy of his left-liberal contemporaries. He appeared to be won over by the thesis of the Yellow Book 'that the age-long controversy between Individualism and Socialism—which still divides the main forces in the political field—is really in process of settling itself'. Although socialists would be reluctant to accept that the semi-socialized type of enterprise would render socialism redundant, and although they preferred the concentration of capital in the hands of the state, rather than opting for the liberal path of diffusion, the underlying thesis of this 'most competent and comprehensive study' of the economic problems of the country embodied 'a large element of truth'. Both liberals and socialists now appeared to entertain a whole range of solutions to the problems of ownership and control which had much in common. 'Certainly', Cole concluded, 'if we were content to concentrate on the points of agreement, we could find in [the Yellow Book] quite enough to serve as the basis for—let us say—a five years' positive programme of co-operation between Liberalism and Labour.'[116] By 1931 this convergence was almost complete. Cole accepted the public corporation model, publicly appointed yet owning privately subscribed capital, which liberals had welcomed, as a 'step towards Socialism' and announced: '. . . the coming form of socialisation will be the public utility corporation rather than the direct administration of industries either by the State or by municipal bodies.'[117] Moreover,

[115] [G. D. H. Cole], 'Where is Socialism Going?', *NS*, 27.8.1927.
[116] [G. D. H. Cole],'Liberalism and the Industrial Future', *NS*, 11.2.1928.
[117] [G. D. H. Cole], 'Public Control', *NS*, 25.4.1931.

for Cole as indeed for Tawney, efficiency and productivity—those virtues of centrist-liberalism—were vital immediate goals that had to be accepted in the present age. Especially salient in Cole's writings was the repeated message that, in tandem with redistribution, production would have to be increased 'before most people can hope to live at more than a desperately meagre standard'.[118] This augmented efficiency would, however, only be achieved by industrial reorganization and not at the expense of workers' wages.[119]

Perhaps the most startling affinity between the *New Statesman* socialists and liberals occurred over the property issue. Captioning one of his essays 'The Diffusion of Ownership' in the best centrist-liberal tradition, Cole argued for increased private holdings in public enterprises. This would both be highly favourable to public enterprise itself and would contribute towards a more equitable distribution of the rewards of industry among the workers. The emphatic conclusion was that 'the broadening of the basis of ownership has nothing to do with the conflict between Socialism and private enterprise. A community in which all the vital services were run directly under communal control could have as broad a basis of ownership as might be desired—with the State and the Local Authorities as the safe care-takers and insurers of the private savings of the people.'[120] Written so soon after the publication of the Yellow Book, Cole must have been keenly aware of his choice of language and terms, yet he met that document more than half-way. But this was no socialist flash-in-the-pan. Kingsley Martin—Sharp's successor at the *New Statesman*—repeated this new truth some years later: 'For ninety per cent. of the population Socialism would mean more property; it is a method of diffusing private property, not abolishing it.' Indeed, it was a defect of socialist thinking to suggest that the attack on property was also directed at personal property. Quite the reverse, argued Martin: only socialism, not capitalism, could guarantee the security of individual property that underpinned individual liberty.[121]

If for many liberals and socialists alike, nationalization demarcated the two ideologies, the restatement of the case for nationalization and personal property in the pages of the *New Statesman* adds significant weight to the contention that overlap and continu-

[118] [G. D. H. Cole], 'Where is Socialism Going?', *NS*, 27.8.1927.
[119] [G. D. H. Cole], 'The Limits of Socialism', *NS*, 17.5.1930.
[120] [G. D. H. Cole], 'The Diffusion of Ownership', *NS*, 24.3.1928.
[121] K. Martin, 'Liberty and Property', *NS*, 13.10.1934.

ity with liberalism were characteristic of the broader progressive outlook. This is not to ignore that fact that such overlap took place in the context of differing idea-environments; indeed, as a reviewer had commented on Masterman and the trade-union leader J. H. Thomas, 'at the moment Mr. Thomas and Mr. Masterman may have reached a common position, but they are revolving in different orbits round different centres'.[122] Cole himself was cognizant of this when he claimed that to the Liberal and Labour parties 'the same or similar measures mean quite different things' and that 'the idea behind them is essentially different'.[123] Still, it is evident that the overlap was not the simple consequence of liberal receptiveness to socialist ideas. The experimental attitude of liberals to nationalization directed them to consider it for some basic services and industries; indeed, for left-liberals socialization was more than experimentalism, being the practical recognition of the claim of society to be a producer of values in its own right. Cole, understandably, was ambivalent about these similarities and their origins. He repeatedly pleaded for a ditching of ultimate ideological labels which nominally divided the Liberal and Labour parties —private ownership or nationalization—and for remembering the new received wisdom that 'what does matter is not ownership but control and management'. While the Liberal party was prepared 'to contemplate a considerable growth in the element of State control', the Labour party was retreating from the direct conduct of nationalized services by state officials.[124] Cole also frequently praised Lloyd George for having 'carried Liberalism a long way from its old faith in the sovereign virtue of letting private enterprise alone' and hailed *We Can Conquer Unemployment* and even more so *How to Tackle Unemployment* as sound and sensible.[125] But while conceding convergence, he was clearly embarrassed by it, as when predicting a large measure of agreement between the two parties 'only because, on broad lines, what ought to be done is so obvious that any party that means to do anything at all is bound to come, within certain limits, to the same conclusions'.[126] By implication, Cole was admitting a close ideological affinity between liberals and

122 'The Party With a Past', *NS*, 13.11.1920.

123 [G. D. H. Cole], 'The Policy of Labour', *NS*, 14.7.1928.

124 [G. D. H. Cole], 'Concerning Nationalisation', *NS*, 21.7.1928.

125 [G. D. H. Cole], 'The Two Problems of Unemployment', *NS*, 30.3.1929; 'Can We Conquer Unemployment?' *NS*, 23.3.1929; 'Mr. Lloyd George Returns to the Attack', *NS*, 8.11.1930.

126 [G. D. H. Cole], 'Can We Conquer Unemployment?', *NS*, 23.3.1929.

socialists on the central domestic political issue of the 1920s—an industrial policy.

The *New Statesman* itself displayed an ambiguous attitude towards liberalism. Sharp was 'soft' on liberalism and prone to statements that irritated his colleagues, despite frequent attacks on the Liberal party, including assertions that 'the Liberal and Labour Parties are enemies and not allies, and are likely for a long time to come to remain so'.[127] Remarkably, he took the Trevelyan line[128] when comparing the two parties: 'It is a difference not of principle or even of opinion—for a Masterman, let us say, must be judged to stand to the "Left" of a [J. H.] Thomas—but of motive and of driving force.' The question was one of organizational efficiency, of zest and youth, but not of ideology—an assessment that many liberals had sadly come to accept. For Sharp, there existed a 'natural affinity' between liberalism and Labour.[129] Writing in the *Daily News* for a liberal readership at the time of the first Labour administration, he expressed confidence in the future of the Liberal party, denied the existence of any line of demarcation between it and the Labour party, and called for a *bloc des gauches* led by a minority Liberal government.[130] Even in 1930 his enthusiasm for liberalism was in direct proportion to his capacity for political misjudgement. His opinion that 'the two-party system has disappeared, probably for ever' was as premature as his false evaluation of the Liberal party as 'likely to remain the ultimate controlling factor in the political life of the country for many years to come'. What he claimed for liberalism, though, was not a plea 'in any party sense', but more a system of beliefs: 'Few of us are strict Socialists, few of us are true-blue Tories. Liberalism is the obvious middle way at the present moment.' Astutely, Sharp identified one major reason for the Labour fear of liberalism: 'The Labour Party, we think, is quite wrong in believing that it has anything to lose by being friendly to the Liberals. It seems to have a sort of "inferiority complex"—a

[127] [C. Sharp], 'Labour and Its Allies', *NS*, 12.1.1924. This reflected Labour's new confidence, almost arrogance, in power.

[128] See above, p. 210.

[129] [C. Sharp], 'Labour and its Allies' *NS*, 12.1.1924. Sharp repeated this theme in the run-up to the 1929 elections and beyond. Cf. 'The Coming Liberal–Labour Alliance', *NS*, 10.11.1928; 'A Question of Cordiality', *NS*, 8.6.1929.

[130] C. Sharp, 'The Liberal and Labour Parties: An English Bloc des Gauches?', *DN*, 24.5.1924. The *Daily News* endorsed Sharp's views heartily in its leader of the same day. Cf. also above, p. 217.

feeling, that is to say, that if it ever admits any appreciation of the virtues of Liberalism it will endanger its own soul—not to mention its electoral organisation.'[131] As we have seen, the *New Statesman* had previously rallied to the indirect defence of liberalism when protecting it from the claims of the soi-disant liberal Ernest Benn.[132] Echoing the liberal plaint, the responsibility for the weakness of progressive forces was astonishingly lain at the door of the Labour party. The theoretical socialism to which it paid lip service and its class character were alienating potential voters. 'True Liberalism', to the contrary, was 'primarily a capacity for moving with the times and taking a generous view of all that is novel.'[133] In general the view of the *New Statesman* was that, whatever the shortcomings of party Liberalism, it was important that all men should be liberals, in the sense of desiring to liberate human beings from restrictions on their development.[134] In that sense socialism was but a liberalism for the times.

The purpose of this chapter has been to demonstrate the heavy penetration of liberal ideas into varieties of British socialist thought. It is arguable whether the mainstreams of British socialism were ever other than liberal in many of their central assumptions. Hobhouse's comment on an early article by Attlee is therefore an attractive one. Referring to the realization of 'the revolutionary trinity—Liberty, Equality, and Fraternity' through the medium of social and economic organization, Hobhouse observed: 'It is this discovery, due principally to T. H. Green, which gave rise to the social liberalism of recent times and to its twin, the ethical Socialism described by Major Attlee.'[135] The point is, however, that many socialists believed their ideology to be manifestly distinct from liberalism, and some of them did at times stray far from liberal fields. The liberal components of socialist thought existed on two levels. The first, and ostensibly more obvious one, related to the essentials of political and civil liberty which socialists often adopted unquestioningly, only to proceed from that base to construct what they imagined was a new socio-economic ideology. In that

131 [C. Sharp], 'Liberalism', *NS*, 25.1.1930.

132 See above, p. 267.

133 '"True Liberalism"', *NS*, 4.9.1926.

134 'The Two Liberalisms', *NS*, 31.1.1920. Wright, *G. D. H. Cole and Socialist Democracy*, pp. 68–9, 98, 235, shows how the question of individual freedom had preoccupied Cole, and continued to do so after the Second World War.

135 [L. T. Hobhouse], 'What is Socialism?', *MG*, 10.6.1924.

fundamental sense much of British socialism was liberal-socialism. The main thrust of this chapter, however, has been to argue that on a second level there was much more in common between socialism and liberalism in the critical areas of social theory that involved community, industrial and economic policy, and state responsibility. Their understanding of human nature and the conditions for its development overlapped, and they shared an acceptance of social pluralism. Nor will it do to insist, as socialists have been wont to do, that most of these areas reflected the influence of socialist thought. The bulk of those ideas, in slightly different form, had been available before the war under the aegis of the new liberalism. After the war, as previous chapters have shown, they constituted distinctive features of progressive liberalism, mostly of the left variety, but with more than a hint of centrist policies. As one moves into the 1930s, however, the possibility of a co-operative alliance, in thought or action, between liberalism and socialism or Labour diminished, despite a few faint-hearted attempts at reconciliation. While socialist theory became radicalized, under the impact of internal and external developments, liberalism as ideology and as organization went into a decline. What liberalism failed to achieve in the 1920s, it was further removed from attaining in the 1930s. That latter decade, to which we now turn, was even less conducive to profound political thought. Liberalism was marking time, but time was slipping away.

9

A DECADE OF DORMANCY

For many who lived through the 1930s the decade seemed one of perpetual crisis and conflict. But whereas periods of upheaval, even despair, will often fire people's imaginations and kindle a spirit of prophecy, the dominant currents of political thinking in England at that time retreated even further into weariness and complacency.[1] As the decade unfolded, fascism—for which more than one British socialist had expressed admiration in the 1920s—lost its compelling aura of vitality as its German variant loomed menacingly on the international scene. Inside Britain, a lack-lustre Labour government had left in its wake an economic and political crisis that gravely shook the self-confidence of the nation, calling up a die-hard conservatism which forced a retreat just short of a rout on progressive opinion. The Liberal party, severely diminished by external competition and internal strife experienced yet another split, into Samuelites and [J. A.] Simonites, the latter fast assimilating into Conservatism. Communism alone attracted the enthusiasm of small groups, but served more to channel a romantic backlash to the perplexities of the times than to reshape effectively social thought and action. In moving forward from liberalism,[2] it repopularized a nineteenth-century image of a materialist, capitalist liberalism cut off from social life. Conservatism stood still, while liberalism and moderate socialism submerged beneath the political surface, emerging periodically to survey the bleak horizon and to signal their continued presence, but operating with barely enough intellectual resources to remain bouyant.

In these depleted circumstances the quality of political argument deteriorated further. If conflict is functional, it was as a consequence of its exacerbation in the European arena that British resolve hardened to withstand its stiff test at the end of the decade.

[1] The philosopher C. E. M. Joad dated this decline *c.*1926, pointing to the end of analysis, purpose and reconstruction in politics and the abandonment of the assumption 'that you can refashion the world by legislation' ('The End of an Epoch', *NS*, 1, 8.12.1934).

[2] Thus the title of a book by Stephen Spender (*Forward from Liberalism* [London, 1937]).

To do this, though, it had to sacrifice the finesse and complexity of political discussion in order to concentrate on an ideological battle that was presented in increasingly simplistic terms, of black and red against white. At the same time, and of central interest to our concerns, the struggle of democracy against fascism and bolshevism was imperceptibly but pivotally becoming, in the hands of progressives, a struggle over the nature of democracy in Britain itself.

1. DEMOCRACY ON THE DEFENSIVE

Any discussion of democracy in the 1930s must recognize the existence of two levels. On the one hand, the very essence of democracy suddenly came under a challenge in the domain of ideas that was rapidly transmuted into a physical struggle for survival. Another certitude of modern British ideology was being undermined. Hobson gave vent to this mood:

> Until the post-War era, democracy, in the sense of popular self-government, was making such advances in most countries of the world as to be considered the natural goal of political evolution. Even those who distrusted it believed it to be inevitable. Now democracy is in several countries displaced by dictatorship, and everywhere it is discredited. Is this a merely temporary set-back . . .?[3]

On the other hand, the debate over democracy was associated with the social and ethical ends endorsed by progressives and the extent to which popular self-government was imperative to those ends. The notion of democracy was harnessed to explore their nature as part of the continuous effort of liberal theorists to extend, radicalize or adapt basic concepts beyond their Victorian applications.

The battle of ideas was on the surface stark and simple. 'Every State is defending its particular *raison d'être* before the Bar of Europe, the Bar of the world at large', wrote Barker.[4] 'The world to-day seems to be faced by a choice between two sharply conflicting conceptions of government and of social organisation, which are loosely and very inadequately described by the terms "democracy" and "dictatorship"', propounded Muir on the eve of the war.[5] Muir and many fellow contemporaries identified this inadequacy as the

[3] Hobson, *Democracy and a Changing Civilisation*, p. vii.
[4] Barker, *The Citizen's Choice*, p. 45.
[5] R. Muir, *Future for Democracy* (London, 1939), p. 1.

expression of a cherished and valued culture by means of a single word. For the defence of democracy was conducted, as the defence of any ideological position must be, with a mixture of passion and reason. An observation made a few years earlier on the left wing of conservatism is edifying: 'The Conservative Party hesitated to accept Democracy; but Democracy, having become established, has become the traditional form of government which Conservatives support.'[6] Even Hobson recognized the truth in this perspective: 'the universal acceptance of democracy as the normal and natural form of government'.[7] On the side of reason, however, democracy symbolized, as Barker put it, a free world of discussion and competition of ideas and actions.[8] For him, as for Muir and countless other progressives, liberty rather than democracy was at stake. Nevertheless, many conceded that the liberal-democratic state would have to beat dictatorships at their own game in order to command allegiance and maintain their inner strength. Samuel reflected a new urgency among liberals in a speech in 1934: 'Those who advocate dictatorships are ready to sacrifice liberty for the sake of efficiency. We must secure both. It is essential that democracy should show itself efficient, energetic, constructive. This Government is failing to do that . . . you cannot meet Blackshirts and Brownshirts with nightshirts.'[9] As in other periods of national crisis and emergency, the potency of efficient action was conjured up by liberals to bolster the abstract appeals of right and morality. Progressives could of course argue that the democratic principle of equal opportunities for obtaining influence 'will allow those who are more competent, honest and public-spirited to secure power'.[10] But committed democrats were feeling the squeeze, and it often came from within. G. B. Shaw and Wells, especially, had amidst great publicity proffered visions of social élites, *samurai*, or an 'open conspiracy' of dedicated politico-religious leaders of men,[11] which compelled liberals to react. Hobson was concerned at the readiness of 'advanced' thinkers to accept the failure of democracy. The denial of the common sense and political merit of the ordinary

[6] R. Boothby *et al.* (eds.), *Industry and the State* (London, 1927), p. 142.

[7] Hobson, *Democracy and a Changing Civilisation*, p. 3.

[8] Barker, *The Citizen's Choice*, p. 48.

[9] *MG*, 5.3.1934.

[10] C. D. Burns, *Democracy* (London, 1935), p. 101.

[11] See, *inter alia*, Shaw's *The Apple Cart* (1930) and Wells's *The Open Conspiracy* (1928).

citizen flew in the face of 'a certain natural wisdom of the people', he countered.[12] Elsewhere he asserted that 'this whole conception of government by an élite is vitiated by the assumption that the common man has nothing of value to contribute'.[13] Hobhouse accused Wells of 'impressionism and a defence of whatever reflects the mood of the moment' and suggested that the only acceptable minorities in a democracy were those that won the confidence of the majority by means of persuasion.[14]

Nevertheless, the image of fascism was not without impact. The leadership principle had provoked a feeling of deficiency among democrats, who reacted with a corresponding bow in the direction of élitism. The following statement commanded general assent: 'The democratic system of government is on its trial. It will only survive if it can produce a policy equal to the problems of our time and a leadership capable of evoking the co-operation and enthusiasm necessary to carry it through.'[15] If leadership was one of the attractions of dictatorship, democracy could not be found wanting on that score. Burns devoted an entire chapter to this question. Echoing the truths apparently made evident by dictatorships, he observed:

> The democratic tradition, like dictatorship, requires the establishment of authority. The first act of common folk, therefore, in making the new community is to *find leaders*. Specialists advise; but those chosen to carry out the treatment cannot merely advise. They must command . . . This is the chief problem of leadership—not how to lead, but how to choose a leader.[16]

This was not to diminish their accountability or denigrate the importance of non-leaders. But it was a reminder to progressives that communities and collectivities needed direction and organization. As one of the younger liberals, A. Herbert, remarked in 1932, 'any Liberal will admit that democracy is not in fact proving, as it was intended that it should, the sieve for finding the best leaders of the

[12] J. A. Hobson, 'Must We Scrap Democracy?', *Nation*, 3.12.1927.

[13] Hobson, *Democracy and a Changing Civilisation*, p. 76.

[14] L. T. Hobhouse, 'Democracy Under Revision', letter to the Editor, *MG*, 22.3.1927.

[15] *The Next Five Years: An Essay in Political Agreement* (London, 1935), p. 7. Cf. A. Zimmern, 'Learning and Leadership' and A. Salter, 'The Challenge to Democracy' in *Constructive Democracy* (London, 1938), published by the Association for Education in Citizenship, of which E. D. Simon was chairman.

[16] Burns, *The Challenge to Democracy*, pp. 237–8. Italics in original.

peoples, at this time particularly, when strong leadership is the paramount necessity'. The answer for many liberals was to acknowledge the need for an increased 'delegation of functions to expert bodies',[17] though the specific problem of a democracy was, as Hobson observed, to enable the common sense of the people to secure such services as part of a co-operative, rather than élitist, enterprise.[18] Nevertheless, by the 1930s progressive liberals would have felt uneasy with Masterman's formulation of liberal belief as vested in 'Government by an aristocracy of intelligence; of energy; of character'. For Masterman this was part of the appeal to education and enlightenment, an appeal that was developing distinct conservative undertones.[19] As Rowntree had pointed out, government by educated democracy was the safest government in the world.[20] This view, though, had had its challengers in the immediate post-war period. Hobhouse warned against 'the familiar remedy of more education' as being unsound: 'The educated classes must supply in some respect the worst elements of public opinion, and support many of the worst measures. Give us someone to educate our educators and you may solve the problem. Otherwise bitter experience must be the teacher.'[21] A decade later the faith in a cultured minority had waned further. Even a controlled and responsible technocracy would lack the wisdom and learning which liberals had come to associate with government.

The debate on democracy was, however, the more incisive at the second level. Naturally, it was not restricted to the 1930s. As we have seen, the extension of citizenship from the political to the economic sphere and the issue of workers' participation had been a focus of discussion from the end of the First World War. The heat of the war and its controversies had bunched progressive liberals together in a united effort to preserve individual liberty, which was to remain 'the first ingredient of democracy'.[22] Initially, as Havelock Ellis saw it, 'Freedom again grows glorious, and the ideals of Individualism become, for the first time among us, truly

[17] Herbert, 'The Liberal Summer School', 325.

[18] Hobson, *Democracy and a Changing Civilisation*, p. 80.

[19] Masterman, *The New Liberalism*, p. 213.

[20] Rowntree, 'Prospects and Tasks of Social Reconstruction', 9.

[21] L. T. Hobhouse, 'Democracy and Civilization', *Sociological Review*, 13 (1921), 134.

[22] Hobson, *Democracy and a Changing Civilisation*, p. 130.

Democratic.'[23] Democracy was therefore, in the first instance, an extension of the liberal stress on participation and social membership to walks of life which were now recognized as important to human autonomy, but which were currently—as in industry—failing to provide for such autonomy.[24] A divide was soon to emerge. Centrist-liberals and left-liberals could move together only part of the way. For Muir, the ultimate justification for establishing a democratic system was the attainment of liberty. Democracy was above all self-government and it entailed self-determination.[25] This was at first acceptable and sufficient to left-liberals, and when Hobhouse differentiated between a narrow and a wide sense of democracy, he was well within the mainstream liberal terminology. In the first sense democracy denoted popular sovereignty; in the second 'a far-reaching conception of life and society—for all that can be summed up in the phrase a free, co-operative commonwealth . . . the releasing of the springs of spontaneous energy and common goodwill'.[26] Even Hobson, as we have seen, reproached Americans for appealing 'from the libertarian to the equalitarian factor in democracy'.[27] Concurrently and with growing frequency, left-liberals began to unravel the complexities of the term. Hobson uncovered two further dimensions, always at the centre of his analyses. First, democracy was the only system that enabled the control and neutralization of an otherwise hostile state. It was thus a solution to the problem of concentrated power as well as to that of individual development. Secondly, democracy 'makes the appeal to the power of a self-directing people . . . as the goal of co-operative endeavour and the instrument for the attainment or support of all the special forms through which the common life finds expression'.[28] Here an element re-emerged that centrist-liberals preferred not to acknowledge: the existence of communal needs and forms of behaviour that, especially for Hobson, converged on the notion of social self-determination.

Despite Hobson's earlier organicism, he was now reluctant to harness the conscious direction of the co-operative will of individuals

23 H. Ellis, 'The Future of Socialism', *Nation*, 13.10.1917. Cf. Chapter 2.

24 See Chapter 3.

25 R. Muir, 'The Liberal Ideal', *Nation*, 11.8.1923; *Future for Democracy*, pp. 1–2.

26 Hobhouse, 'Democracy and Civilization', 128.

27 J. A. Hobson, '1. The Good American. The American Attitude Towards Liberty', *Nation*, 7.2.1920. See above, p. 247.

28 Hobson, *Democracy After the War*, pp. 156, 158.

to the idea of an impartial and correct public policy. This road was, albeit, open for his close colleague, Burns, to travel and in so doing he exceeded the reasonable bounds of liberalism. The aspect of democracy that Burns chose to highlight was 'the hypothesis that all men are equal'. This he took to mean as the denial of inherited privileges and, even more importantly, as 'the assertion that a man who is a good carpenter is an integral part of the community, no less than the man who is a good poet'. The most fundamental characteristic of democracy was fraternity, 'acting as if one's actions were part of a whole with the actions of other men, co-operating in a common enterprise'.[29] This organicism, suggesting mutuality rather than the supersession of individuality by the will of a group, was consonant with Hobson's approach. So was the identification of the 'common man', his will and welfare, as the rationale of the political system. Burns, however, deviated from the paths of his progressive colleagues in suggesting what even Rousseau had stopped short of doing. He announced that 'a common good can be conceived by common men without reference to their share in it', and that this 'common good is not mine or yours but the good of a larger whole', entirely the product of human interaction.[30] The illiberal assumption was the dispensing with the individual as the ultimate location of the good and the reasonable. The proposition that the common good was the outcome of a relationship detached from the individuals entering into it, had moved some way from the left-liberal attempt to balance private and communal personality as equally valid facets of human nature. The logical consequence of Burns's position was to entertain the probability of discovering right answers to political questions. His insistence that 'the moral authority of a democratic Government is based not upon the "will" of the people but upon the fact that such a "will" is right or is itself in contact with what is good'[31] was not only at odds with the centrist-liberal preference for experimentation as reflecting the tentativeness of human knowledge, but conflicted with the left-liberal goal of harmony. Harmony was a working ideal, a reduction of conflict to the point where common purposes could be attained. But those purposes were forged by individuals

[29] C. D. Burns, *Democracy: Its Defects and Advantages* (London, 1929), pp. 22–3.

[30] Ibid., p. 91.

[31] Burns, *Democracy* (1935), p. 80.

and could not do away entirely with errors and contradictions, even on issues of public morality.[32]

In the final analysis, the distinction between centrist-liberalism and left-liberalism on the topic of democracy relates to the idea-environment in which each group enveloped the concept. Centrist-liberals surrounded democracy with liberty, personal autonomy and self-realization, regarding it as a system that served individual ends. Left-liberals, while recognizing the importance of liberty as the original purpose of democracy, wanted to detach from its environment an anti-social individualism.[33] As Burns argued:

> Democracy is not merely equal chances in a game of grab, although this seems to be believed in some circles in America and Great Britain. Individual liberty to take what a man's better brains make him able to take, is violently opposed to democracy . . . The democratic ideal is therefore misrepresented because only one element in it is understood: autonomy is taken to mean independence without obligations. But it cannot be too strongly stated that a democratic man or a democratic community is not only one which is independent but also one which is imaginatively sympathetic.[34]

Although later events elicited from Burns a consideration of leadership, he was still strongly anti-élitist in his refusal to echo liberal Millite tenets concerning the social value of the enlightened or talented few. He also adapted the new psychology to transcend an intellectualist, élitist rationalism: 'now we know that community between men is at least as deep down in the nature of man as any individuality or separateness between them: and we know that reasoning is not merely calculation nor separable from emotions.'[35] Hobson too was arriving at similar conclusions about the idea-environment of democracy. Commenting on the democratic triad of liberty, equality, fraternity, he wrote: 'The second term of the democratic triad, viz. equality, has been too exclusively linked up with the conditions needed to attain liberty, too little with the

[32] See Hobhouse, *The Elements of Social Justice*, pp. 22–7, 46, 71; Hobson, *Democracy and a Changing Civilisation*, pp. 119–21.

[33] Burns, *The Challenge to Democracy*, pp. 85–6; Hobson, *Democracy and a Changing Civilisation*, p. 130; Burns, *Democracy* (1935), p. 42.

[34] Burns, *Democracy* (1929), pp. 181, 205.

[35] Burns, *Democracy* (1935), p. 43. This is in interesting contrast to Burns's 'pre-psychology' position, when he bemoaned a corroding deficiency in the English democratic ideal: the lack of appreciation for intellectual qualities and the critical intellect ('Ideals of Democracy in England', 443).

neglected element fraternity, comradeship, co-operation, community.'[36]

2. THE LIBERAL SUMMER SCHOOL: DOWNHILL YEARS

The decline of liberalism as an organized political and intellectual force during the 1930s is epitomized by the virtual elimination of its central cabal and powerhouse, the Summer Schools. Though these continued to meet until the war, no new gospels emanated from their midst, almost as if all energy had been expended on the creation of the Yellow Book. Even the demise of the Liberal party could not account for the rapid collapse of the Summer School movement, for the only major Liberal publication of the 1930s, *The Liberal Way*, was produced by the National Liberal Federation. True, the guiding hand behind this document was that of Muir, but this was in his capacity as president of the NLF rather than as Summer School pundit. Perhaps most indicative, the press, with the exception of local newspapers, Liberal party publications and those renowned liberal institutions—the *Manchester Guardian* and the *News Chronicle*—ceased to show interest in the LSS. It had become an uninspired meeting of speech-makers, almost devoid of controversy and debate, a place where party stalwarts could go for a week's rest and listen politely to addresses from the podium.

The last display of fireworks from the LSS was, significantly, occasioned by the ideas of an outsider to liberalism, H. G. Wells. Wells had tailored his views on an élitist, revolutionary party of leadership and initiative to the shape of his audience and had called, in highly charged terms, for Liberal Fascisti and enlightened Nazis to provide a 'competent receiver for the present disorders of a bankrupt world'.[37] He now proposed to abandon Parliamentarianism in favour of a vague liberal progressive world state which nevertheless emulated the style of the dictatorships in organization, discipline and propaganda, and prompted the *News Chronicle* to describe it as 'calling in Satan to cast out Beelzebub'.[38] Sadly, but with justification, the 1932 LSS was overshadowed by Wells's address. Lothian, Layton, and Arthur Salter also spoke, or should one say

[36] Hobson, *Democracy and a Changing Civilisation*, pp. 83–4.

[37] *MG*, 1.8.1932. Cf. above, p. 162.

[38] 'Labour's Critics', *NC*, 1.8.1932. See also H. G. Wells, 'Project of a World Society', *NS*, 20.8.1932.

ran, but collected no prizes. Lothian suggested that capitalism was failing due to political intervention: nationalism was hindering it through tariffs and armaments, democracy by taxing profits. As the way to private initiative was barred, and the quickest way back to prosperity—the Manchester School—was now ruled out, Lothian feared the only alternative to be a Russian-type five year plan, 'the Communist substitute for individual initiative'.[39] These words were prophetic for, as shall be discussed below, a British attempt to match the Russian conception was produced three years later. Layton, with the economic crisis still firmly in mind, spoke of a limited free trade group as a beginning to the re-establishment of commerce on an international basis. Salter, mirroring the new concern with competent leadership, proposed constitutional changes to increase the role of the executive and diminish that of Parliament.[40]

The written word continued to intrude upon LSS activities. The 1932 session was also the focus of a debate that revolved round a slim volume—entitled *Whither Britain*?—published by Hubert Phillips and six colleagues.[41] It purported to be a necessary update to the Yellow Book, since the latter was on some issues either silent or already behind the times, but in effect had little new to offer. Its main thrust was to insist somewhat more stridently than the Yellow Book on state intervention in both monetary and industrial policy, with less consideration for centrist-liberal reservations. It urged the state by means of the public corporation to 'decide when competition becomes wasteful, to protect the community from exploitation and to secure efficiency in the absence of competitive urge'. It was Keynesian in demanding an increase in consumption and the utilization of the state to bring savings and capital investments together. It pressed for greater contact between capital and labour under the aegis of a national industrial commission. And it was significantly at variance with centrist-liberal dogma when asking: '. . . have we not been prone to exaggerate the scope of activities whereof the mainsprings are individual competition, and the incentive is private profit?' There were 'hundreds of thousands to whom profit-making does not exist as a psychological factor'.[42]

[39] *MG*, 1.8.1932.

[40] Herbert, 'The Liberal Summer School', 323–5.

[41] Hubert Phillips (chairman), A. Holgate, R. Moelwyn Hughes, T. Elder Jones, I. Lloyd, J. Menken, A. Sainsbury, *Whither Britain? A Radical Answer* (London, 1932).

[42] Ibid., pp. 46–7, 64–6, 67–8, 70. See also above, pp. 116–18, on Phillips.

The debate on *Whither Britain*? well illustrated the conundrum that the corpus of liberalism presented even to its adherents. The editor of the *News Chronicle*, referring to the authors collectively as Mr. 36 on account of their average age, was hard-pressed to pick out its salient points. But he hailed the volume as a 'keen, unprejudiced and reasoned valuation of the present condition of our country', and sympathized with its aim of a closer union of progressive and radical forces.[43] The LSS, however, acting as host to some of the seven authors who expounded on their views, reacted with some confusion. H. L. Nathan, soon to join the Labour party, found it a first-class piece of work, but Dingle Foot, now frequently allying himself with the less progressive sections of liberalism, defended the Liberals in Parliament from any implicit attack by the authors. It was indeed in their outspoken anti-government views, rather than in their proposals, that the real 'radicalism' of the *Whither Britain*? group revealed itself, for Foot provoked Phillips into a reply that 'mixed humour and devastating criticism of the Government in a fashion that no one at the school has equalled'.[44]

The book and the debate it occasioned served as catalysts for a number of viewpoints on liberalism. On the one side Robert Bernays, the Liberal MP, bemoaned the fact that 'the Liberal intelligentsia, in spite of the general drift of all the three parties in these last two years of crisis to the Right, remains aggressively Radical'. This would be fatal to a party that needed the support of its right wing in order to forestall degenerating into a radical rump.[45] Nathan was quick to reply that the radicals had always been the driving force of the Liberal party, reaffirming his allegiance to the Yellow Book's cohesive philosophy.[46] But this only raised a new problem: what then was radicalism? Herbert thought that *Whither Britain*? presented a straightforward, sincere case for planning 'without any staggeringly new idea or revolutionary proposal' and that it created expectations which could scarcely be fulfilled. The survey of monetary problems was 'devastatingly orthodox' (a somewhat unkind remark for 1932); the book ultimately lacked 'a deep emotional appeal' (a shrewd assessment of liberal weaknesses) and gave

[43] T. Clarke, 'Mr. 36 and the Young Men', *NC*, 3.8.1932.
[44] *NC*, 4.8.1932.
[45] R. Bernays, 'Notes of the Day', *NC*, 4.8.1932.
[46] Major Nathan, 'The Liberals of the Right', *NC*, 6.8.1932.

no hint 'that Liberalism comprehends the human side of politics'.[47] Herbert had correctly located *Whither Britain*? within the liberal spectrum; one cannot but agree with Cole that 'these Radicals, apart from their not being revolutionary, turn out to be not so very radical after all', rather these young men wrote as if they were 'middle-aged in a middle-aged world'. Cole's assessment was: 'If this is Radicalism—and it doubtless is, in relation to the "National" Liberalism of these days—it is none the less Radicalism without a sting; and one feels again and again that it lacks the driving force of democratic revolt which gave the old Radicalism its human appeal.'[48] If *Whither Britain*? had any claims to radicalism, it was because it had been written in the tradition of the Yellow Book; and in an increasingly conservative world it did not take much to be radical. The slight left-of-liberal-centre of the Yellow Book had become the new yardstick of a progressive liberalism, forgetful of its truly radical left wing.[49]

1933 saw the *Manchester Guardian* rallying to the defence of the LSS. The session that year, it claimed, was 'highly successful', and it continued:

> It is, we admit, vastly irritating of Liberalism to be such an unconscionable time in dying, and why, year after year, the Summer School of a political faith alleged to be moribund should continue to be better attended, more popular, and more successful than that of any other party must naturally remain . . . an . . . exasperating mystery.[50]

But there is no smoke without fire, and this comparison gave no indication of the problems facing the LSS. By mid-decade attendance had declined dramatically in relation to the 1920s; 1934 seeing only 250 members and 1935 only 450.[51] The LSS secretary reported an alarming difficulty in finding lecturers.[52] At the same time, the international crisis loomed large over the LSS, and a liberalism under continual attack reacted with confusion and lack of clear direction. Barker gave a talk defending liberal democracy on the lines of centrist-liberalism, committed to 'the intrinsic value of

[47] Herbert, 'The Liberal Summer School', 326–7.
[48] G. D. H. Cole, 'Revolution or Reform', *NS*, 3.9.1932.
[49] See also 'Appeal from the Old to the New Whigs', *NS*, 15.10.1932, which called upon liberals to abandon Whiggery and take to Radicalism.
[50] 'Liberalism in the World', *MG*, 10.8.1933.
[51] *MG*, 2.8.1935.
[52] Layton Papers, Sydney Brown to Layton, 19.5.1936.

human personality' and to a 'new economic liberty . . . which will make every worker a free man co-operating freely in a free system of industry'.[53] The repetitive message was an incantation of past glories, and invoked the response from one liberal that 'Professor Barker did his best to turn it [the inquest on democracy] into an orgy of reaction . . . He is a Victorian survival, mesmerised by the vote like a child with a new toy'.[54] Other speakers were Salter, D. Robertson, and Rowntree, as well as J. B. S. Haldane with a critical survey of eugenics.

By 1934 the main theme of the LSS had become the defence of liberty, in view of the situation in Europe.[55] In this context, and with the French example in mind, considerable interest was directed towards a proposal by A. L. Rowse to establish a common front of the Labour and Liberal parties against fascism. Rowse, speaking as a member of the Labour party, caused a 'constant stir' during his address and, in the eyes of the *Manchester Guardian*'s correspondent, 'resembled a little the wolf in the fable of Little Red Riding Hood'. Tempers rose, as one member asked Rowse 'point-blank whether he meant that the Liberal party should go over in a body to the Labour party'. Nevertheless, Megan Lloyd George sympathized with the idea and was ticked off by Samuel for suggesting that both parties were too sectarian. Later on, Lothian delivered an attack on socialism that seemed to set the seal on the refusal of official Liberalism to countenance any co-operation with the Labour party, especially on the basis of the latter's new programme, 'For Socialism and Peace'.[56] The *News Chronicle* located the blame for the failure of the left to consolidate 'in the sterile sands of party dogma', though it was sympathetic towards Rowse's 'realist' Labour point of view.[57] Despite the heat generated by this particular issue, however, one observer felt that it lacked 'the bright-red corpuscles of really effective life', that it was further proof that passion had died out of politics and that 'the old thunder of Radicalism rumbles only occasionally—and then in the distance'.[58]

[53] Barker, *The Citizen's Choice*, pp. 40–1.

[54] L. H. Jackson, 'The Liberal Summer School at Cambridge', *FV*, (Sep. 1933), 89.

[55] *MG*, 27.7.1934.

[56] *MG*, 4.8.1934. Lothian's position had previously been endorsed by Samuel in his inaugural address ('Liberty, Liberalism and Labour').

[57] 'Parties and Progress', *NC*, 4.8.1934.

[58] D. Keir, 'Passion in Politics', *NC*, 10.8.1934.

The 1935 LSS had little to offer, though it gave somewhat qualified support to *The Next Five Years* and the Council of Action for Peace and Reconstruction,[59] of which more below. It is the 1936 session that bears comparison with the 1934 LSS for the radical change of heart now revealed by the proposal for a popular front. Liberals and other progressives, backed by American and European adherents of the idea, spoke of 'the value of the name "Popular" as a counter-cry to the Government's "National"' and recommended co-operation on the basis of a definite short-term programme.[60] Though Foot opposed the proposal, the discussion was generally in favour of a popular front.[61] Rowse commented, with a mixture of satisfaction and frustration: 'I gather that this year the whole balance of opinion at the Liberal Summer School was in favour of a Popular Front. How like politics that is: a year after the horse has bolted, to think of shutting the stable door.'[62] Layton[63] and the *News Chronicle* came out in support of a front. The newspaper wrote emphatically: 'This year's Liberal Summer School has reflected and made articulate the thoughts and the feelings of Progressives throughout the country.'[64] Outside Summer School circles, uncommitted progressives such as Julian Huxley were pressing for a front, without which 'liberal and progressive thought, activity and past achievements are likely to be overwhelmed'.[65] Harold Macmillan, too, spoke favourably of a united front, or a progressive alliance, in the interests of liberty and reconstruction.[66] Muir, by now an undisguised representative of official Liberalism, attempted to dampen this new enthusiasm. With unusual frankness for a party spokesman, he argued that under the present electoral system, with its minimal control over the behaviour of local organizations, a popular front would reduce the Liberal party to an appendage of the Labour party. He was prepared to tolerate Parliamentary co-operation, but no extra-Parliamentary moves in that direction. Muir saw the unconvincing

59 *NC*, 2.8.1935. Samuel pointed out that those movements omitted support for industrial partnership of the workers and greater diffusion of property.

60 *MG*, 31.7.1936.

61 *NC*, 1.8.1936. See also D. Foot, 'The Popular Front: A Liberal View', *New Outlook*, Oct. 1936.

62 A. L. Rowse, 'A British Popular Front?', FR, 146 (1936), 329.

63 See also W. Layton, letter, 'A People's Front', *New Outlook*, Aug. 1936.

64 'Democracy at the Crossroads', *NC*, 6.8.1936.

65 J. S. Huxley, letter, 'The Popular Front', *New Outlook*, Sept. 1936.

66 H. Macmillan, 'In Defence of Liberty', *New Outlook*, Oct. 1936.

choice as between a revived Liberal party and a new (liberal) party based on *The Next Five Years* group or Lloyd George's Council of Action.[67] For Rowse, on the other hand, the problem was one of a generation gap, made somewhat easier by the Liberal shedding of the Simonites. But the Liberal leader Sinclair was also insistent on having a non-socialist alternative to the government and hoped that *The Next Five Years* would play an important role, as 'it occupies a strategic position at the juncture of the main bodies of Left opinion'.[68] In the last analysis, the need was to 'bring new forces, and new men, to the top in their respective parties—the co-operators, instead of the non-co-operators who have ruled in each so long, to the mutual sterilizing of both'.[69] The Liberal party, however, was too obsessed with maintaining its separate identity to contemplate any blurring of distinctions, no matter how detrimental they were to the future of the party. The small surge of opinion within the LSS came to nothing, accentuating its total loss of influence.

The remaining years were increasingly taken up with discussions of peace, dictatorship, democracy and communism,[70] and the domestic debates that punctuated them were timid and of decreasing relevance. Simon believed that the LSS had 'finished its career as a research body' and turned to other forums, such as the Association for Education in Citizenship, as 'a much more effective means of getting over the kind of things we want than the Liberal Summer Schools'.[71] Layton hoped otherwise, but his suggestion to initiate a new LSS investigation to update the Yellow Book on the subjects of monetary policy and free trade came to nothing.[72] Amidst the perceived perils to peace and, understandably, a resurrection of the First World War liberal concern with a possible assault on British liberties by means of the Official Secrets Act,[73] Muir aired his ideas on the wider diffusion of limited property rights.[74] The only other domestic theme seriously to occupy the

[67] R. Muir, 'Popular Front in Britain', *MG*, 18. 19.9.1936.

[68] *MG*, 31.7.1936.

[69] Rowse, 'A British Popular Front?', 334–5.

[70] 'Liberals in Conference', *MG*, 29.7.1937.

[71] Layton Papers, Simon to Sydney Brown, 9.9.1937; Simon to Layton, 17.3.1936.

[72] Layton Papers, Layton to Lloyd George, 19.12.1937.

[73] *MG*, 1.8.1938. Dingle Foot had attempted to amend the Act during 1938 (*Liberal Magazine*, 46 (1938), p. 332). See Lloyd George Papers, G/11/8/8. See also R. Douglas, *The History of the Liberal Party 1895–1970* (London, 1971), p. 241.

[74] *MG*, 1.8.1938. See Chapter 7, Section 4.

attentions of the LSS was family endowment, mirroring the growing national unease with under-population.[75] The economist R. F. Harrod, addressing the Summer School, warned against a 'rapid decline in the population, reducing Britain to the position of a second-rate Power'. Though many liberals had, during the 1930s, accepted some of the milder proposals of eugenists, such as voluntary sterilization,[76] the notoriety of Nazi eugenics had ruled out any further action on those lines. Confronted once again with a pre-war physical efficiency scare, liberals therefore looked in the direction of providing material assistance to encourage larger families, possibly financed on an insurance basis.[77] By 1939 liberals regarded the subject as good 'copy' for an election issue. Both Richard Titmuss and L. J. Cadbury, of Bournville fame, treated the question of 'the community's future citizens'. The former surveyed the incidence of infant mortality; the latter returned to methods of compensating families for the disadvantages of parenthood. For the businessman Cadbury, a declining population would mean a stationary state. This would be a psychological blow to an industry reared on the expectation of expansion. 'What is wanted,' announced Cadbury, 'is a redistribution of the nation's income more in proportion to family responsibilities.'[78] Although, as the *Manchester Guardian* pointed out, this was no novel liberal departure, allowances having been advocated both in the Yellow Book and in *The Liberal Way* of 1934, the campaign was seen as a quick—and by now scientifically validated—way of 'making a substantial impression on the problem of poverty'. It was also a useful rallying cry for Liberals to present progressive public opinion with, as the Labour party and the TUC were divided on the question.[79] The issue of family allowances was, in fact, a theme that progressives had been debating for a generation. Its re-emergence within the confines of the LSS had as much to do with the insecurity and fears generated by the international crisis as with a genuine desire for social reform. As Samuel conceded during another debate:

> . . . Liberalism had not shown in recent years the elements of passion with regard to social conditions that the times required. Lately it had been pushed

[75] Cf. e.g. E. Charles, *The Menace of Under-Population* (London, 1936).

[76] See Freeden, 'Eugenics and Progressive Thought: A Study in Ideological Affinity'.

[77] *MG*, 3.8.1938.

[78] *MG*, 10.8.1939; *NC*, 10.8.1939.

[79] 'Family Allowances', *MG*, 10.8.1939.

into the background by the international situation, and also many Liberals coming from the middle classes were more in touch with employers than with trade unions.[80]

This was a tacit admission that the social profile of the latter-day liberal had changed. What had happened to liberalism was, however, rather a different matter, and necessitates a perspective that by no means could be contained within the Summer School movement.

3. LEFT AND CENTRE: THE GULF ACKNOWLEDGED

By the mid-1930s official Liberalism had recovered sufficiently to produce a small number of books and documents in the reformist tradition. First came Samuel's 'Liberal Address to the Nation' which, as the *News Chronicle* saw it, was a 'timely review of problems' that insisted on economic reconstruction and national development in order to satisfy social justice. Nevertheless, the leader complained about Samuel's too cautious approach to improving the financial and banking mechanism.[81] This was closely followed by Muir's *The Liberal Way*, which aroused little excitement, though the *Manchester Guardian* loyally praised its 'generous temper and broad comprehensiveness'.[82] But with Muir hardening in his centrist mould, the divide between left-liberals and centrist-liberals appeared unbridgeable. In the past, his own preachings and those of the LSS had suggested that the choice between individualism and socialism or, put less emotively, between private and public enterprise, was becoming spurious under new methods of industrial organization. Now Muir retreated to an older philosophy with respect to one of the main questions he put to his readers: 'Free Enterprise versus State Control. Do we believe that individual enterprise and initiative are still, as always, the mainspring of human progress? Or do we intend to bring all enterprise under the deadening control of the State?'[83] Even centrist-liberalism, certainly of the Keynesian variety, had striven strenuously to avoid such dichotomies. Muir's tone had also degenerated, as when he wrote:

[80] *MG*, 7.8.1939.

[81] See the *Liberal Magazine*, 42 (1934), pp. 156–60, and 'The Liberal Address', *NC*, 16.3.1934.

[82] 'The Forward View', *MG*, 27.3.1934.

[83] [R. Muir], *The Liberal Way* (London, 1934), p. 16.

'It is significant, but not surprising, that all these [European] dictatorships have sprung from the Socialist movement.'[84] And a slight but telling adjustment in phrasing seemed even to deny the wisdom of the hard-fought and won redistributionary ethic of the new liberalism: 'The serious thing about this process of redistribution is that the money is transferred in the main from producers—whether employers or workers—to non-producers who make no addition to the nation's wealth in return for what they receive—*rentiers*, old people, widows, orphans, children, sick folk, and unemployed workers.'[85] Muir's ignorance of Keynesian and Hobsonian theories and his eschewal of the Yellow Book's treatment of credit was only matched by the willingness of the 1934 National Liberal Federation conference to endorse his analysis, and thus further alienate itself from newer and more pungent progressive thought. Muir did, of course, recognize the social justice of redistribution, but was more concerned that 'the goose that lays the golden eggs may be killed'. Most of the book, however, was devoted to a restatement of liberal social policy, as an alternative to a planned economy. Yet it asserted also that, within limited spheres, 'it is absurd to speak as if State-planning was a wholly new and unheard-of idea'.[86] It was becoming sadly evident that a party denied all effective hope of power could lose the urge to work out an attractive and distinctive policy. Liberals were now burdened with the frustration of not needing to formulate programmes that had to stand the test of practical politics, and the consequent lack of incisiveness was plain to see. State regulation was designed to attain peace, justice, liberty, and individual self-development, but all this was harnessed to the notions of efficiency and productivity, as discussed above.[87] It was difficult to determine which social ends social reform served, for a 'Bismarckian', capitalist-oriented justification was omnipresent: '. . . progress has to be gradual if it is to be secure . . . By improving the health, fitness, and mental capacity of the people, Social Reform also improves their ability to produce wealth.'[88] This was hardly calculated to bring the masses flocking to the liberal fold, but it may have been intended to reassure the business interests the party depended on.

[84] Ibid., p. 23.
[85] Ibid., pp. 107–8.
[86] Ibid., p. 134.
[87] See Chapter 5.
[88] *The Liberal Way*, p. 183.

The centrist-liberal and party activist, Lothian, voiced the general sense of despair in a note he wrote on Liberal policy in late 1933. From the party point of view Liberalism was in an almost hopeless position. It was impossible to return to free trade—battle-cry of the Liberal past—because of the competitive nature of economic nationalism throughout the world. Lothian urged either the formulation of a new constructive policy, or the support of one of the other two parties with a view to strengthening their liberal elements. The constructive policy he was contemplating—a 'modernised form of Liberal Social Reform'—reiterated the reliance on private enterprise as the driving force of economic life, regulated in the interests of the whole community by a democratically elected government.[89] As we shall see, however, he was more friendly towards the idea of planning than Muir professed to be. As the former Philip Kerr, member of the Liberal Industrial Inquiry, Lothian stood by the ideas of the Yellow Book. With the passing of time, even the novelty of the document was beginning to wear off. Having been harnessed to the Liberal cause in one election, it could hardly have been brought out and dusted for another.

Lothian was as anti-Labour as Muir, but more genuinely perturbed at the economic and social ills still rampant in British society. In 1939 he wrote to Muir suggesting that a more scientific analysis of the distribution of property should be undertaken by Liberals, and he also recommended the organization of taxation or a capital levy so that a considerable proportion of income would pass to the state for redistribution to social services. Muir, referring Lothian to his *Future for Democracy* replied predictably: 'I find no satisfaction in the system whereby crushing taxation of the rich is used to provide social amenities for the poor . . . The present system undermines self-reliance and cultivates the mischievous habit of looking to the State.'[90] No wonder that a reviewer wrote of Muir's book: 'What is undeniably Liberal . . . is his description of general principles and controlling and limiting rules; and for this awed astonishment alone is suitable. Time has stood still. When I first read political literature at all—thirty years ago—exactly these phrases were being used, and the same arguments victoriously shouted from six hundred and fifteen

[89] Lothian Papers, GD40/17/146 (8.9.1933).

[90] Lothian Papers, GD40/17/392, Lothian to Muir (24.5.1939); Muir to Lothian (4.6.1939).

Liberal platforms.'[91] For Lothian too the choice was ineluctably between liberal social reform and communism or Marxist socialism. But he repeatedly showed concern about ways of raising the standard of living, about excessive inequalities of wealth, and about the control of monopolies.[92] A revised capitalism on the above lines and one which, as centrist-liberals were arguing in the 1930s, diffused ownership and introduced a strong democratic element, summed up this ideological position.[93] J. A. Spender congratulated Lothian on the published exposition of his views, adding: 'The present drift which is converting Liberalism into something called vaguely "going to the left" disturbs me. It blurs all the boundaries and leaves the public without any coherent idea of what Liberalism is or what a Liberal candidate stands for or, indeed, why he should be standing at all, when a Labour man is in the field.'[94] This succinctly epitomizes both the tensions within liberal ideology and the institutional constraints that prevented official Liberalism from moving any further to the left, even if it had been so inclined.

Liberals in the 1930s were fatally caught between a desire to remain progressive and a fear, now reinforced by political impotence, of the Labour party. For those who had not joined that party, the problems seemed insurmountable. E. T. Scott, at the helm of the *Manchester Guardian*, wrote despondently to Hammond: 'The general drift of politics seems to me terribly bad. I doubt if we shall ever get away again from the war of the classes.'[95] And a few months later he aptly reflected the opposing pulls of heart and wallet on Liberalism:

> . . . it seems to me broadly that politics are getting into an ugly shape and that we shall be driven more and more to take an anti-property line. And that is fatal to a 2d. paper. I myself feel that I am getting much more of a socialistic way of thinking (or rather feeling), but the more I look at the socialist party the less I like it.[96]

This appeared to vindicate Muir's earlier observation: '. . . the feeling against the Labour party is much more intense than I had realized, although my own feeling on that head has always been stronger than

[91] R. Postgate, 'The Liberal Book Club', *NS*, 6.5.1939 (referring to the Edwardian heyday of Liberal electioneering).
[92] Lothian Papers, GD40/17/440 (Dec. 1934).
[93] Lothian, *Liberalism in the Modern World*, pp. 9–11, 25, 29–30.
[94] Lothian Papers, Spender to Lothian, GD40/17/278, 29.1.1934.
[95] Hammond Papers, vol. 35, Scott to Hammond, 30.8.1931.
[96] Hammond Papers, vol. 35, Scott to Hammond, 16.11.1931.

that of many others in the inner councils of the Party and in the House.'[97] By the end of the decade official Liberals were still adamant that their main enemy was not conservatism but socialism. Shortly before the outbreak of war, Samuel attempted to raise the issues of home affairs in preparation for a possible election. Reflecting on the 'distressed areas', unemployment, and the decline of the export trade, he wrote: 'The fundamental fact is that these things have happened during a period when the country has been under almost continuous Conservative rule. And if we ask what in turn is the cause of that, the answer clearly is—the rise of the Labour Party, and its adoption of Socialism as its policy.' Yet Samuel also knew what was wrong with the Liberal party. Referring to its 'trinity of great purposes—Peace, Liberty and Social Justice', he noted that

> the party has been inclined to stress the first two and to leave the third somewhat in the background. This is mainly due, no doubt, to the conditions of our times—the pressing urgency of questions of Peace and of Liberty. But it may also be due to traditions inherited from the nineteenth century, which need to be adapted to the circumstances of the twentieth.[98]

Too late the Liberal leadership was realizing that the divide between progressive liberalism and the party had become permanent. The breach between left and centre was irreparable, compounded by the further metamorphosis of some centrist intellectuals, as later described by Gilbert Murray: 'I find myself growing "conservative", in the sense that I am terribly anxious to preserve civilization and Liberality.'[99]

The starkest indication of the parting of the ways came in an exchange of letters between those two former colleagues, inspirers of the Summer School movement, Simon and Muir. While Muir was moving steadily to the right of the liberal centre and emphatically endorsing capitalism,[100] Simon was abandoning his always uneasy centrism for a more left-inclined, social-liberalism.[101] The first and most significant exchange came in 1934. Simon took exception to an attack by Muir on the Labour party and wrote:

97 Samuel Papers, Muir memorandum, A/73/10, 8.5.1930.

98 *A Westminster Newsletter*, July 1939 (Samuel Papers, A/69, Pt. II).

99 Hammond Papers, vol. 30, Murray to Barbara Hammond, 10.1.1946.

100 R. Muir, 'Has Capitalism Broken Down?', *CR*, 151 (1937), 650–7.

101 Already in 1929 Muir had voiced his distrust of Simon on industrial matters: 'his sympathies are too labourish, and he is too apt to be influenced by the emotions of the moment' (Layton Papers, Muir to Layton, undated [1929]).

I think the difference between us is that you tend to identify liberty with the Liberal Party . . . I don't believe the Liberal Party is the road to liberty now, but my aim is similar: what I want is a social order in which every child shall have an equal opportunity to grow up as a free and responsible citizen, and to develop his or her faculties and personality to the highest degree of which he or she is capable.

Simon, as we have seen, now emphasized the dependence of liberty on equality, and declared his intention to pursue a career through the Labour party: '. . . I do feel, when I go to a Labour group to discuss, that they are the people who really want what I do, far more than I feel it with most Liberals.' Nostalgically, he recalled:

We had an interesting time with the Summer School; it was a tragedy for us (and perhaps for the country) when our success in getting the Party to adopt our policy was followed by the collapse of the Party. I don't see any real possibility of its getting power again; and I am sure it does not stand for the abolition of privilege with one-tenth the zeal of the Labour Party.[102]

Muir's reply reflected a mixture of political realism and ideological dogmatism. He appreciated Simon's feeling that, careerwise, 'continued loyalty to the Liberal party is a handicap'. And he conceded that 'it seems highly probable that, as an effective political force, the Liberal party is all-but extinct'. But he regarded a change of party as intellectually dishonest and refused to dismiss the seriousness of the Labour intention to nationalize. Furthermore, the control of the Labour party by the trade-union bosses 'simply outrages my ideas of what is politically decent'. This resulted in a class dictatorship, aided by 'a rigging of the electoral machinery' which created 'no alternative, except this rule of the stupid, other than determinism and Toryism. If I have to make a choice, I prefer Toryism.' Muir ended on a strongly personal note, as was his wont, which symbolized the general feeling of decline, helplessness and failure among Liberal loyalists:

. . . if the choice is between apparently beating the air on behalf of the things in which I believe, and forswearing or at any rate qualifying my beliefs in the hope of getting into a position in which I can achieve something real, my choice is immediately and instinctively in favour of going on beating the air, for at least, then, I shall be clean; and perhaps something may sometime result even from my feeble activities. Long since—indeed, ever since you drew me into politics, and before that—I

[102] Simon Papers, M11/16/32, Simon to Muir, 2.2.1934.

have felt this inherent difficulty in the political life . . . while I can never cease to be a politician—never cease, that is, to desire that what capacity I possess should be used for the reshaping of society—I am more and more tempted to put my strength into writing and non-party preaching.[103]

A second exchange, in a slightly more ideological vein, took place when Muir sent the manuscript of his *Civilization and Liberty* to Simon for comment, in the early months of the Second World War. Simon complained that Muir was 'definitely unfair to Socialism; there are several bits which would, I think, unnecessarily infuriate every socialist. Your references to Marx are none too kind; if I remember aright the only thinker you mention with approval in connection with the whole social revolution is the Liberal philosopher T. H. Green'.[104] Simon's criticism was justified, and left unheeded in the final version. Muir saw Marxism as an 'extreme form of the Socialist doctrine, which foreshadowed a bleak prospect of violence and slaughter', associated with force rather than reason.[105] He retorted huffily:

I am not going to justify my genuine beliefs merely to placate possible readers, and I haven't written anything which I don't believe to be true . . . E.g. the statement that all the totalitarians have begun by being Socialists, and that this may be due to the fact that Socialism glorifies the State. That is surely *true*, and, if true, important. You say I only mention a Liberal philosopher T. H. Green with approval. Can you name to me *any* Socialist philosopher who can be named in the same breath with him? Karl Marx? I just *cannot* take him seriously; his premisses are unsound, and they don't bear his conclusions; they are the outpourings of a dyspeptic.[106]

British thinkers may have found it generally difficult to agree on Marx or understand him; what was more alarming was their growing inability to agree on liberalism. Between Muir and Simon that ideology was being stretched to the limits of its tolerance.

4. PLANNING: THE LOGIC OF LIBERAL ACTION

Although, as the above sections indicate, liberalism had lost its sparkle, the decade was not one of complete desolation for liberal

103 Simon Papers, M11/16/32, Muir to Simon, 15.2.1934.

104 Simon Papers, M11/16/32, Simon to Muir, 11.12.1939.

105 R. Muir, *Civilization and Liberty* (London, 1940), p. 247.

106 Muir to Simon, Simon Papers, M11/16/32, 12.12.1939. This curious juxtaposition of Green and Marx is worth comparing to the similar views of the left-liberal Burns. See above, p. 289.

ideals. Nor was it entirely true that liberalism had experienced a total polarization, for counterbalancing forces were working towards creating a link, however tenuous, between left and centre. To appreciate these developments, one must cast one's eye back over the previous few years. The different currents of state regulation, of economic and industrial restructuring, and of rationalization which have been examined in past chapters, began to converge from the early 1930s round a concept of considerable looseness—planning. The importance of this concept was precisely in the structural connection it afforded between different ideological positions, all sharing the term, though surrounding it with dissimilar idea-environments. Mistakenly, this has led to the assumption that a consensus of progressive opinion was being moulded, whereas in fact it merely allowed for a limited agreement on the necessity for central communal foresight. The device of combining to protect a concept of symbolic, even if at the time minimally practical, merit, was of great significance in enabling the survival of diverse progressive views in a hostile climate and in facilitating their re-emergence when conditions were more propitious. Planning was, of course, implicit in some of the recommendations of the Yellow Book. Keynes, never one to be worried by the ideological implications of a word, had repeatedly sought 'to substitute for the operation of natural forces a scheme of collective planning'.[107] Observers of the 1931 LSS recognized that '"planning" has for years been the keynote of the Summer School . . . and we are reminded again that what is wanted now is both more planning and less, more of the good and a great deal less of the bad'.[108] Planning was also salient in Hobson's writings at the time, calling in 1931 for an urgent extension of 'conscious social planning' from the small through the large business unit and finally to the economic system as a whole. This meant 'a public economic policy, systematic and organic' to replace both non-interventionist attitudes and 'general Socialism'. It would be 'skilled and knowledgeable adaptation of State policy to an economic system varying in its structure and in

[107] J. M. Keynes, 'Sir Oswald Mosley's Manifesto', *Nation*, 13.12.1930. Winch, *Economics and Policy*, p. 226, notes the difference between Keynes's macroeconomic approach to planning and the microeconomics of industrial reorganization.

[108] Herbert, 'The Liberal Summer School', 325–6. Cf. also Foot, 'The Liberal Summer School', 327.

the stimuli which it applies to the minds of active agents of production'.[109] Hobson's planning predictably took on a personal hue, as when he wrote: '. . . in that planning the most critical issue will be that of the proper moral relation between the individual and society, or, as I would prefer to put it, between personality and community. This is the problem of relating adequate economic incentives to economic needs.'[110] But this also entailed a recognition of the limits of planning. There were needs which catered to individual qualities and which therefore demanded 'the personal freedom of production outside the compass of collective planning'.[111]

But other interesting voices were being heard, and not only from within the liberal camp. One of the most remarkable came from a group of conservatives and was first expressed in a book entitled *Industry and the State*, which appeared a year before the Yellow Book and, although less ambitious, anticipated in print some of the latter's arguments. The four MPs under whose name the book appeared—Robert Boothby, John de V. Loder, Harold Macmillan and Oliver Stanley—seemed in many ways close to centrist-liberalism.[112] They questioned the divide between individualism and collectivism, suggesting instead that these were 'but two ways of looking at the same thing—both necessary, and each the complement of the other . . . The rights of the individual and of the community exist side by side, and it is one of the principal functions of Government to arrange their harmonious correlation.'[113] They even asserted, in new liberal language, that 'men are not merely units in the industrial machine, but living contributors to a living organism'.[114] They recommended state-inspired extension of credit facilities, an economic general staff, the extension of property-ownership, labour co-partnership, and the detachment of ownership from management, using among others the public corporation model. Underlying these views was the conviction that it was the

109 Hobson, 'The State as an Organ of Rationalisation', 44. See also J. A. Hobson, *The Modern State* (London, 1931), p. 25.

110 J. A. Hobson, *Poverty in Plenty* (London, 1931), p. 87.

111 J. A. Hobson, 'A British Socialism. II', *NS*, 1.2.1936.

112 Macmillan had commended the Yellow Book as the official abandonment of *laissez-faire* by the Liberal party while pointing out its resemblance to *Industry and the State*. 'I do not complain of plagiarism; I rejoice in it' was his unfounded comment (*Hansard*, 5th Ser. CCXIII 755 [14.2.1928]).

113 Boothby *et al.*, *Industry and the State*, p. 138.

114 Ibid., p. 143.

duty of governments to aid progress and that 'Conservative policy should therefore concentrate upon devising an intervention which shall be complete, not intermittent'. Like the liberal ethos, it rejected a priori socialist or individualist theory, preferring instead 'the angle of inductive and experimental thought'.[115] Ideologically, though, this intervention remained true to individualist assumptions and, unlike progressive liberalism, did not regard wide-ranging and permanent state regulation as inevitable:

> It should be the object of Conservative policy, resting on sound Conservative tradition . . . to create a system under which industry should be as far as possible self-governing, and where Government interference would be scarcely ever required in future. It should attempt by one great creative act of interference now to limit future spasmodic interference. It should, in fine, by an act of Government institute a system of self-government.[116]

Macmillan, however, was to take the latent case for planning an important step further. In a book published in 1933 he announced: 'A few years ago we might safely have proceeded on the principle of trial and error. To-day it is vitally important to be right.' He now made it quite clear that 'a return to the old days' of absence of organization was 'technically, politically and economically impossible'.[117] Planning, for Macmillan, was not an idealistic stance but a necessary means to control markets and to bring individual producers within the control of a central direction. Though he still believed in limited industrial self-direction, the stress was on co-ordination and regulation through a central economic council. Yet, in contradistinction to left-liberalism, the idea-environment of planning remained distinctly conservative, for 'the alternative to bold reconstruction under quasi-monopoly powers may be a deterioration in political conditions which will plunge us into violent social conflict with the risk of social disintegration'.[118] Planning had nothing to do with man's social nature; quite the reverse, it was dictated by his fundamental unsociability. In a later article, Macmillan repeated that 'the urge towards planning is con-

[115] Ibid., pp. 30, 166, 176–7.
[116] Ibid., p. 180.
[117] H. Macmillan, *Reconstruction: A Plea for a National Policy* (London, 1933), pp. 3, 16. See also H. Macmillan, *Winds of Change 1914–1939* (London, 1966), pp. 355–70.
[118] Macmillan, *Reconstruction*, p. 22.

tinuous and insistent' and saw it as an extension of authority that was 'necessary in order to preserve that basis of economic stability on which civil liberty must rest'. This was part of an 'intelligent creative effort to keep social organisation adequate to, and in harmony with, the changing needs of a developing society'.[119] No wonder that Hobson welcomed Macmillan's 'bold and thoughtful scheme'. Even though Hobson felt that Macmillan had underplayed the role of government, due to excessive fear of bureaucracy, there was an undeniable common ground: 'If "control" will suffice then let it be "control". Nobody wants national ownership and operation on their own account.'[120]

Nevertheless, 'planning' was still an umbrella that sheltered various views seeking refuge from numerous ills. As Burns emphasized, 'that word has become a sacred symbol without exact meaning'. For him it referred to directive central control of industry and agriculture—a notion that was less ambitious than that of Hobson. But he cautioned against the tendency to reduce planning to a 'producers' plan', which would be little more than the previous adoption by business interests of the term 'rationalization'.[121] On the other hand, Samuel commended an article in the *Economist* for pointing out to Labour leaders that planning, in the sense they were using it, was 'out of the main current of twentieth-century developments'.[122] Simply, the Labour party had associated planning with nationalization and, as so often before, liberals were loath to use a word that had been co-opted for a confusingly different political usage. Lothian, though, saw planning as the essence of modern social reform and very much on the lines of the Yellow Book.[123] It was not governmental interference with the responsibility of business executives, but the enforcement of business and agricultural conformity to higher public and humanitarian standards.[124] Later, he too felt compelled to spell out why planning in the Labour sense—or, rather, in his interpretation of Labour policy—was untenable: '. . . if we want to "plan" in the Socialist sense we

119 H. Macmillan, 'Is Planning a Threat to Liberty?', *Listener*, 15.8.1934.

120 J. A. H[obson], 'Controlled Capitalism', *NS*, 16.12.1933.

121 Burns, *The Challenge to Democracy*, pp. 153–5.

122 Samuel, 'Liberty, Liberalism and Labour', 266, quoting from the *Economist*, 28.7.1934.

123 Lothian Papers, GD40/17/146, 8.9.1933.

124 Lothian, *Liberalism in the Modern World*, p. 32.

must begin by controlling consumption, by forbidding private initiative, and abolishing the piece [*sic*] system.'[125]

5. THE MIDDLE GROUND: AN EXERCISE IN PROGRESSIVE MINIMALISM

There is a case, on the evidence of the previous section, for arguing that progressive liberalism, however timid in its institutional incarnations, was still conducting an independent life. Indeed, the changes within the conservative sector that have been noted above must be seen as a triumph for the liberal ideas of the 1920s, and it is no coincidence that Keynes and Hobson were among the few authorities that Macmillan cited in his books.[126] The concept of planning, then, served a useful social purpose of labelling those who wished to be counted among progressive reformers. The 1930s also saw the founding of a non-party group, Political and Economic Planning (PEP), but for the purposes of this study the most notable activity concerned the *The Next Five Years* group, previously known as the Liberty and Democratic Leadership group. In 1935, the group published the most important political and ideological statement to appear in Britain of the 1930s—important, not because of an innovative content but because it signalled the survival of the new trends of political thought even in a period when they were most isolated from governmental circles, and because it was living proof that the political beliefs of progressives overlapped sufficiently for a common denominator to be discerned. That common denominator was broad enough to constitute a future mainstream in British politics, however improbable it seemed at the time. *The Next Five Years: An Essay in Political Agreement* was the product of a small number of people—Arthur Salter, Geoffrey Crowther, Macmillan, and Clifford Allen among them—but the range of individuals who appended their signature is astonishing. Some liberals and progressives can be singled out: Norman Angell, Barker, L. J. Cadbury, H. A. L. Fisher, A. G. Gardiner, G. P. Gooch, Hammond, Hobson, J. S. Huxley, Layton, A. D. Lindsay,

[125] Lothian, 'Liberalism and Labour', *NS*, 27.4.1935 (for 'piece' read 'price'). See rebuttal by C. R. Attlee, 'Liberalism and Labour', letter to the Editor, *NS*, 4.5.1935. Beveridge believed planning, though essential, was unnatural to democracy 'as breathing under water' ('Planning Under Democracy' in *Constructive Democracy*, p. 135).

[126] Macmillan, *Reconstruction*, p. 59.

Muirhead, Gilbert Murray, Rathbone, Rowntree, and even Wells.[127] Notably absent were Muir and, more surprisingly, Simon. Many political figures who had signed the 1934 manifesto—'Liberty and Democratic Leadership'—such as Samuel, Dalton, Lansbury, and Bevin, also went their separate ways.

To go through *The Next Five Years* would be an exercise in repetition, as there was little, if anything, in the book that had not already been said before. It is, however, useful to identify some of the themes which, although essentially liberal, had now lost that exclusive epithet, and attested to the permeation power of liberalism. That this was not a *consensus* document but one of ideological and policy *overlap* was clarified at the outset: 'Those who, in the Foreword, endorse the book have different political associations, and divergent views as to ultimate doctrine and policy; but they are agreed, without sacrificing principles or ultimate objectives, upon a programme which should be pursued in the years immediately ahead.'[128] Notwithstanding, this was more than the limited co-operation envisaged, for example, by some members of the Liberal and Labour parties, for it comprised a succinct summing-up of an ideological position that closely resembled centrist-liberalism. Mastering war and poverty were its main challenges, buttressed, as has been shown,[129] by a determination to support political liberty and democracy. The heritage to be guarded was a liberal one, containing liberty and political equality as well as an extension of economic equality and an eschewal of sectionalism. Yet again, the authors stated that 'the historic controversy between individualism and socialism—between the idea of a wholly competitive capitalistic system and one of State ownership, regulation, and control—appears largely beside the mark'.[130] The notion of a mixed system was the only realistic one. Similarly, the position that liberals, in Simon's and Hobson's wake, had adopted after 1930 with regard to free trade was formalized. A limited tariff policy was acceptable together with the expansion of export markets. Finally came a rejection of 'muddling through' and—with a faint echo of organicism—an insistence that 'the Government should plan its policy *as a whole*'. As the book put it, this was not planning that would replace the price system,

127 *The Next Five Years*, pp. v–x.
128 Ibid., p.1.
129 See above, p. 332.
130 *The Next Five Years*, p. 5.

but part and parcel of the necessary responsibilities of the state. 'The real alternative to planning in this sense is not freedom but improvization.'[131] A government planning committee was proposed, in tandem with the resurrection of the idea of an economic general staff. Mirroring the debates over syndicalism a decade earlier, the authors gave assurance that such a functional body would not be an 'economic parliament' rivalling the territorial, elected Parliament.[132] Indeed *The Next Five Years* lent credence to Layton's plaint about the Yellow Book that 'the proposals which we expounded regarding industrial democracy have clearly slipped to the background'.[133] By the 1930s, the reorganization of industry was directed at employers, not workers. Ironically, the increasing stress on political democracy was paralleled by a jettisoning of industrial democracy.

The centrality of planning was reflected in the titles of the first two chapters of the book: 'Economic Planning', and 'Towards a Plan for Britain'. Indeed, planning itself was not a plan but a reality, for 'by choice or by compulsion we are constantly intervening through our collective organizations in the conduct of the economic life of the community'.[134] The language of the book was distinctly to the left of its proposals. In the seven years that had passed since the appearance of the Yellow Book, the terms of progressive discourse had become more imbued with egalitarian and communitarian allusions. When the authors wrote about the extreme inequality of wealth currently in existence, they described it as 'an inequality which appears to have little to do with the social value of the contributions made', thus harking back to Hobson's new liberal analysis which had always maintained that human relationships could not be contained within any economic equation. With a new urgency, the group declared that 'political democracy cannot for long live alongside an economic system which confers vastly different economic benefits upon different individuals'. Moreover, in contradistinction to centrist-liberal views, which at various times during the inter-war years had seemed more concerned with efficiency than with social justice, the authors stressed the need to maintain the belief that the democratic state was moving towards

[131] Ibid., pp. 6, 13. Italics in original.
[132] Ibid., pp. 18–19.
[133] Layton Papers, Layton to Lloyd George, 19.12.1937.
[134] *The Next Five Years*, p. 23.

economic justice 'as one of the most precious safeguards of our liberties, and we must not, in the eager pursuit of productive efficiency, lose sight of it even for a decade'.[135] *The Next Five Years* accorded greater prominence to the goal of national development than its predecessors, although in practical terms pride of place was allotted to public works, planned electrification and housing—proposals that had already been well aired. Nor did it deny the importance of private industry and commerce, of course; but this too was ultimately the responsibility of the state to encourage. A National Development Board was also mooted. In language that no socialist could dissent from, the authors summed up their vision: 'a programme of National Development could be the embodiment of the social conscience.'[136] Not since Lloyd George's 1909 Budget had liberals put such an ethical and communitarian interpretation on the role of the state in promoting the public interest by means of a development policy. The post-war nervousness about the state was dissipated as the new liberal faith once again shone through. There was

> an admitted need for interference by the State with the free play of industrial competition. The function of statesmanship is not fulfilled by a passive policy of succouring the victims of competition's defects . . . The State must take an active hand and pursue a positive policy.[137]

More significantly, when discussing the constitution of the boards to be appointed to administer schemes for assisting depressed industries, the notion of the state as impartial broker, which had so appealed to new liberals, resurfaced. The recommendation was for the government to arrange for 'a substantial "neutral" element on each Board, which does not represent any section of the industry but is appointed to represent the public interest'.[138] There were other measures from the liberal repertoire. The Keynesian function of regulating credit policy was bestowed on the central bank, and unemployment insurance was differentiated from unemployment assistance in an attempt to restore its actuarial basis and to

[135] Ibid., pp. 25, 39. [136] Ibid., p. 69.

[137] Ibid., pp. 76–7. As Salter explained, the real issue was 'not whether the State should intervene in economic activity, but *as whose servant* it should do so—the public's or privileged economic activity' ('Oxford University By-Election: Sir Arthur Salter on his Candidature', *New Outlook*, Nov. 1936).

[138] *The Next Five Years*, p. 87.

encourage self-reliance. This was complemented by the proposal that the state take over the responsibility for supporting the dependent families of all the unemployed, whether on insurance or relief, in line with the burgeoning interest in the reconstruction and sustenance of the family. A national milk and food policy was also part of this conception, for 'the task of the community is to ensure not merely that no section of the population falls below the minimum standard but that every family has the optimum standard of nutrition'.[139]

The Next Five Years undoubtedly was a progressive liberal document, even if not in the forefront of liberalism, and appealed primarily to those searching for a 'minimum programme' of advanced opinion. It constituted a framework which prevented the fissiparous forces within liberalism from totally fragmenting that ideology and indicated that a broad common ground still existed. Geoffrey Crowther and Salter were responsible for the first section of the book dealing with domestic affairs.[140] Crowther was an active Liberal, later editor of the *Economist* and member of the Liberal reconstruction committee during the Second World War.[141] Salter was an 'ardent' liberal before the First World War who swore by the *Westminster Gazette* and its editor, J. A. Spender. Though he first entered politics in the 1930s and became an Independent MP in 1937, he 1937, he occupied a slot only too typical of many of the individuals this book has examined, in that he detached liberalism from Liberalism:

> . . . in the first war, during my international work [as a civil servant], and when the Liberal party split up and the Labour party took its place as the main rival to Conservatism, I found myself falling away from any kind of party allegiance and developing in my own mind a kind of selective compromise, in which elements of the Liberal, the right of Labour and the left of Conservatism, all had a place.

[139] Ibid., pp. 197–8. Later the group published a 'Programme of Priorities' which spelt out policies on housing, nutrition and suggested the creation of a public medical service to include non-insured as well as dependants of insured workers. It also proposed a series of interrelated measures on unemployment, linking family assistance, education, and the systematic location of industries into a concerted plan (*New Outlook*, Mar. 1937). See also Megan Lloyd George, 'The Short-Term Programme', loc. cit.

[140] B. Pimlott, *Labour and the Left in the 1930s* (Cambridge, 1977), p. 145.

[141] See P. Addison, *The Road to 1945* (London, 1977), p. 181.

Especially in the 1930s, he felt, 'the party divisions had ceased to correspond with any clear-cut divisions of public opinion'.[142] In attempting to adumbrate this fundamentally liberal ideology, Salter hoped to develop a 'truly national policy'. *The Next Five Years* was the product of this viewpoint: 'We did not aim at the creation of any new party. We hoped to formulate an outline of policy corresponding with the views of many in every party, and of the increasing number of those who had no party allegiance, and so to "permeate" each party, and narrow the differences between the rivals.'[143] Theirs was the advocacy of a 'left centre, moderate, progressive, constructive policy'.[144] Nevertheless, in Salter's opinion, *The Next Five Years* had only a limited success, not enough to inspire hopes for a practical effect. Given the complexion of the government in power, that was hardly surprising.

The *News Chronicle* commented on the signatories to the document that it was 'the most remarkable collection of experience and talent which has ever proclaimed its agreement on so comprehensive and detailed a statement of policy'. It found *The Next Five Years* 'refreshingly free from vague generalities or appeals to the shibboleths of Party doctrine'.[145] Lothian, too, endorsed the document whole-heartedly, and called it the best political programme since the Yellow Book. He thought that the Liberals and the right wing of the Labour party would support it, but recognized there was no party to present it to the electorate.[146] Lothian became a member of the executive committee of the group, which he saw primarily as an instrument for proving the falsehood of Labour's nationalization policies.[147] The group had local branches, too, Gilbert Murray becoming president of the Oxford section.[148] Hobson welcomed the efforts of the group as 'a progressive Liberalism', himself sounding like the Liberal sympathizer he used to be:

It seems possible that, if our electoral system were worked along the lines of Proportional Representation, a powerful Liberal Party could be created on

[142] A. Salter, *Memoirs of a Public Servant* (London, 1961), pp. 243, 44.
[143] Ibid., p. 244.
[144] 'Oxford University By-Election: Sir Arthur Salter on his Candidature', *New Outlook*, Nov. 1936.
[145] 'Five Fateful Years', *NC*, 26.7.1934.
[146] Lothian Papers, GD40/17/312, Memo, 20.12.1935.
[147] Ibid., Lothian to Allen Young, 12.3.1936.
[148] Lothian Papers, GD40/17/331.

this platform. For the rank and file of Labour is not enamoured of bureaucratic rule, and, if there were a reasonable likelihood of coalition with a powerful Liberal Party along the lines of the 'Five Years' Plan,' many electors who now vote Labour, without a close Labour attachment, would vote Liberal.

Here also lay Hobson's predilections, 'for this progressive Liberal policy is nearer to the average electoral mind than any full-blown Socialism'. This was the middle course which Hobson regarded as essential to progressive government in Britain.[149]

Lloyd George, though apparently consulted about *The Next Five Years*,[150] preferred to launch his own parallel group: the Council of Action for Peace and Reconstruction, founded in 1935.[151] It was perhaps a final attempt on his part to revitalize his ebbing fortunes, but came to nothing. Ostensibly non-party, the members of the Council included many of the old faces, notably Layton, Lothian and Eleanor Rathbone, though Snowden also lent his name to the list.[152] Muir thought it might conceivably lead to the formation of a middle party, basically liberal in character, but decided it was too nonconformist and too narrow in its range.[153] By the mid-1930s, in Lord Elton's words, there were 'many varieties of Planner'. He himself had signed *The Next Five Years* and may be excused for thinking at the time that 'the very ubiquity of "Planning" to-day is evidence of the all-pervasiveness of Collectivism'.[154] In fact, it was far from that. It was a British model of planning that respected self-direction in industry and combined individualism, capitalism and communal control.

The reaction of socialists to *The Next Five Years* was voiced by Cole, who saw in it an attempt at a Liberal come-back by people

149 Hobson, *Confessions of an Economic Heretic*, pp. 124–6.

150 Pimlott, *Labour and the Left*, p. 145.

151 *NC*, 3.7.1935. See A. Marwick, 'Middle Opinion in the Thirties: Planning, Progress and Political "Agreement"', *English Historical Review*, 79 (1964), 295–6.

152 'After the Convention', *NC*, 3.7.1935; *Peace and Reconstruction* (1935). The policy objectives of the Council of Action reiterated the Liberal programmes of the previous decade. They included a plan of national development to consist, among others, of housing, regional development, road construction, and the supply of electricity; industrial reorganization; national investment; agricultural revival; a return to free trade principles (rejecting the notion of limited self-sufficiency that Keynes and others had supported); social services, and a minimalist safeguarding of workers' rights.

153 Samuel Papers, A/155/IX/42, Muir to Samuel, 19.11.1935.

154 Lord Elton, 'England's Age of Collectivism', *FR*, 143 (1935), 582.

'who are prepared to re-draft Liberalism in terms of post-war problems, and not afraid of a dash of Socialism as long as it is kept quite clear of dreadful things, such as the class-war'. Cole believed it well reflected progressive opinion:

> I am suggesting that the collective mind of the British electorate, as far as it has one, has got just about as far as the measure of 'political agreement' embodied in *The Next Five Years*. It is not Socialist, but it is mildly socialistic. It wants peace, and progressive social reform, and some curbing of the excesses of predatory Big Business.

If Cole refused to accept or to sign it, this was due to his fundamental assumption that it was impossible to satisfy capitalists and workers at once. He nevertheless conceded—significantly, one may say with the aid of hindsight—that if 'a new situation develops, *The Next Five Years* may come to seem prophetic; but, if we escape war, is a new situation of the sort required at all likely to arrive in the near future?'[155]

6. INTERNATIONALISM AND PROGRESSIVE LIBERALISM

One of the two parts of *The Next Five Years* was devoted to international relations, and although they have deliberately been excluded from the remit of this study, a brief link-up with some of the themes of progressive liberalism is in order. It is, after all, important to remember that much energy of liberals, as of others, was directed during the 1930s to the international scene. The weakness of domestic liberal thought has something to do with the channelling of interest abroad, though that is no excuse for its unimaginativeness. In fact, liberal thinking on international issues produced no new formulas or perspectives that were not being applied to internal liberalism. Quite the reverse obtained. Progressive liberals, of left and centrist complexions, simply extended their domestically focused concepts and analyses to the relations among peoples as well as people. The notion of peace among nations re-emphasized the renunciation of force as a method of human interaction and invoked human reason as the alternative and true path to human cooperation and development.[156] The preferred means to attain

[155] G. D. H. Cole, 'Chants of Progress', *Political Quarterly*, 6 (1935), 534–5, 538.

[156] *The Liberal Way*, p. 33.

this—the League of Nations—embodied the liberal faith in machinery and institutional devices for conciliation and conflict-resolution, very much on the lines liberals had proposed for industry, though they occasionally came up with ideas to diminish the League's lack of compulsory powers.[157] But on the whole, here as elsewhere, their unease and *naïveté* when confronted with the realities of political power were unmistakable. Could it have been that, because their proposals were so remote from the possibility of political realization, liberals and other progressives stressed the appeal to ethics to a far greater extent than when debating domestic issues? They drew an often facile analogy between personal and state morality, were optimistic about the possibility of discussion replacing violence, and hopeful that the common factor in humanity would outweigh the differences among peoples.[158] For Muir, for example, the League provided 'an all but perfect exemplification of the Liberal ideal in international relations, since it combines organization for co-operative action with full recognition of the freedom of every member-State'.[159] When associated with the search for security, international activity was hardly distinguishable from Muir's concern for liberty, mutual respect and security within a community. Other liberals fastened upon the idea of self-determination as a connecting thread. When Hobson defined it as 'the power of a person to guide his conduct in each particular case by consideration of the permanent good of the whole self instead of by the satisfaction of some single passing desire', he too transferred this principle to the realm of 'national or group conduct': 'A self-determining community is one that acts and lives by the conscious exercise of a collective will, directed to the general permanent good and secure from external interference in the performance of this self-regarding duty.'[160] And Samuel picked up this last notion of non-intervention and described it as 'the equivalent in international politics to toleration in private life'.[161] In the 1930s the ethical superiority of democracy was bestowed upon the workings of the

[157] Ibid; Samuel, *Belief and Action*, pp. 288 ff.; *The Next Five Years*, pp. 226 ff.

[158] Samuel, *Belief and Action*, pp. 205–6; Burns, *Democracy* (1935), p. 170; Hobson, *Democracy and a Changing Civilisation*, p. 149; G. Murray, *Liberality and Civilization* (London, 1938), pp. 63, 73.

[159] Muir, *Politics and Progress*, p. 89.

[160] Hobson, *Problems of a New World*, p. 251.

[161] Samuel, *Belief and Action*, p. 218.

League, it being 'simply the latest result, in the international sphere, of the development of the democratic tradition'.[162]

All these examples strongly support the suggestion that liberal thinking on international relations was domestic liberalism 'writ large'. This mirroring of principles extended to the divergence between left-liberalism and centrist-liberalism. For while all the above opinions were shared by progressive liberals, left-liberals took their arguments a step further. Hobson—whose organicism could not have allowed for a separatist treatment of the internal and external affairs of a community—set his 'pacific internationalism' within the context of his all out attack on the alliance between capitalism, militarism and imperialism. Nationalism and imperialism were at odds with the spirit of free trade which Hobson never quite abandoned throughout his tirades against the closed state.[163] Behind his approval of the League lay his tenacious pursuit of the notion of interdependence, which 'posits a community of interests between nations to be promoted by active conscious co-operation for the common good'.[164] This led him later on to extend the idea of co-operation beyond the merely political, for 'the pacific and efficient exploitation of natural and human resources of production on a reliable basis of agreement must become the prime economic objective of a League of Nations or any other form of international government'.[165] The internationalization of resources denied the concept of absolute ownership with respect to states as much as Hobson had denied it with respect to individuals. The notion of national sovereignty—as indeed that of individual separateness—had to be relaxed. The culmination of Hobson's international vision was a society of nations 'on a democratic socialistic basis'. Self-determination was coupled to a federalism that underscored the harmony between the parts and the whole. The possibility of a federal world government was an essential component of this scheme.[166] However practical the domestic proposals of left-liberals were, in the international arena their well-meaning idealism appeared to lose touch with the world of political possibilities.

162 Burns, *Democracy* (1935), p. 166.
163 Hobson, *Democracy After the War*, p. 197. See also Chapter 4, Section 5.
164 Hobson, *Problems of a New World*, p. 227.
165 Hobson, *Democracy and a Changing Civilisation*, pp. 133–4.
166 Ibid., pp. 141–9.

7. THE BEVERIDGE REPORT: LIBERALISM APOTHEOSIZED OR ECLIPSED?

It is difficult to end a study of inter-war liberalism without some thoughts on the Beveridge Report, though the reasons for doing so may appear contradictory. On the one hand it was portrayed virtually as a one-man show, the dawn of a new era in social security. On the other it was the apex of a process that had been in progress for over a generation. Its author clearly did not see it as connected to the movements within progressive liberal thought. Indeed, Beveridge officially became a Liberal only after the Report was published and it is no coincidence that he has not figured prominently in the pages of this book. More than most individuals considered here, he vacillated notoriously between political views, and for most of the inter-war period was estranged from liberalism even ideologically. And yet—though he did not acknowledge it at the time—the Report is a highly liberal document in terms of its ideological orientation, as if Beveridge had emerged from outside the march of time to become suddenly and totally immersed in some radical implications of progressive liberalism, which liberals themselves could not voice. Perhaps it was precisely this insulation from the moods and disappointments of left-liberals and centrist-liberals, combined with Beveridge's highly individual character, that enabled a plan of such vigour and incisiveness to be drawn up. It is ironic that the anticipation of war had impoverished discussions on social reform, but its outbreak had released the bogged down build-up of progressive thought and sentiment. The Report was not a direct logical conclusion to inter-war developments, nor was its author central to any of the groups we have examined. Yet in a circuitous way it was the very spirit of progressive liberalism, and Beveridge succeeded in capturing that spirit where others had failed, or were on the point of giving up. Wars, in general, unlock hidden doors of aspiration as well as despair. A popular tide was swelling that demanded a new charter for the people of Britain. Beveridge happened to ride the tide at the right moment, and he had the single-mindedness and self-confidence to compose a document that could shed the tentativeness of pre-war years. But there is no mistaking that Beveridge was high priest rather than prophet of this revitalized progressive spirit.

It is beyond the scope of this study to offer an extended analysis of *Social Insurance and Allied Services*. Instead, some key themes may be referred to the liberal tradition. Detailed and important as the Report was, it had restricted itself to a narrow area of social planning: social insurance and social security. Although allusion was made to the five giants—want, disease, ignorance, squalor, and idleness[167]—the Report concentrated on want and a partial attack on disease and unemployment. It did not retread the path of the inter-war documents with their concern for reorganizing the industrial system and their emphasis on national finance and development. The Report was thus no mainstream liberal programme; indeed, it devoted itself to a number of issues that, though perfectly consonant with liberal principle, had been put into abeyance while liberals moved on to consider other areas of practical import. Its intellectual origins harked back to the new liberalism before 1914[168] and to questions that inter-war liberals had either thought obsolete—as had Keynes in the 1920s—or of lesser urgency. It was also in this sense that the Report was not a product of direct continuity.

Naturally, the Liberal party had not stood still during the war, and within a short time it had, along with the other parties, established a reconstruction committee. But as Addison has commented, 'the parties were following events rather than setting the pace'.[169] Curiously, the public relations officer to the Liberal party had claimed that paternity for much of the Report lay with the Liberal Conference of September 1942:

> The principles and objectives of the Beveridge plan are almost word for word identical with resolutions passed by the Liberal Assembly . . . A Liberal resolution passed at the Assembly says: 'The four social evils that beset the people are ignorance, squalor, idleness and want. The Liberal party is determined to use the power of the State to do whatever is necessary to overcome those evils.'[170]

Unfortunately, the writer was himself afflicted with ignorance, since Beveridge had coined the 'giants' in June and had publicly

167 W. Beveridge, *Social Insurance and Allied Services*, Cmd. 6404 (London, 1942), paras. 8, 456.

168 Cf. P. Alden, 'The Beveridge Report', *CR*, 163 (1943), 7.

169 Addison, *The Road to 1945*, p. 182.

170 *MG*, 9.12.1942.

mentioned them in July 1942.[171] Nevertheless, liberals felt, and rightly, that the Report was 'in the highest Liberal tradition'.[172]

What, then, is the validity of the claim that the Report reflected liberal thinking? It began by enunciating three notions with a liberal pedigree: the rejection of sectional interests as a guideline to policy-making; the realization that social policy should be organized and comprehensive—a recognition of the interconnected, even organic, nature of social problems, and the importance of planning for their solution; and the assertion that social security had to be achieved by co-operation between the state and the individual.[173] Crucially, Beveridge described his plan as 'first and foremost a method of redistributing income' and in so doing retained that prime liberal reformist element which the Cambridge economists had tried to constrict.[174] Buttressed by the findings of Rowntree and others, Beveridge argued that 'want was a needless scandal due to not taking the trouble to prevent it', as it 'could have been abolished before the present war by a redistribution of income within the wage-earning classes, without touching any of the wealthier classes'.[175] This was not a recommendation to desist from including other groups within the income redistribution process, but it was a departure from the position frequently adopted by liberal economists in the 1920s, namely, that redistribution would not solve outstanding problems and that greater productivity was the only cure to social evils.[176] Beveridge spoke of a double distribution through social insurance and children's allowances.[177] This latter theme, although a minor one in the Report, was the main immediate continuity with a liberal policy that he himself had helped to formulate. Both it and the major recommendations partook of a central liberal premiss, that of the sharing of responsibility between the private and public spheres. Though the question of children's allowances was linked to the recent fears concerning the declining birth-rate 'as an expression of the community's direct interest in children', it was considered preferable to split the financial burden of rearing a family between the state and the parents. The

[171] W. H. Beveridge, *Power and Influence* (London, 1953), p. 312.
[172] *MG*, 9.12.1942.
[173] Beveridge, *Social Insurance and Allied Services*, paras. 7–10.
[174] Ibid., para. 457.
[175] Ibid., para. 445.
[176] See above, pp. 102, 146.
[177] Beveridge, *Social Insurance and Allied Services*, para. 14.

children's allowances themselves were 'regarded both as a help to parents in meeting their responsibilities, and as an acceptance of new responsibilities by the community'.[178] As for social insurance, 'the finance of the Plan for Social Security is based . . . on a continuance of the tripartite scheme of contributions established in 1911'.[179] This had always been entirely consistent with the liberal identification of the three units in the socio-industrial field: the individual, the employer, and the community.[180]

In general, the creation of a compulsory, contributory, state-backed system, was a recognition of the role of the community in attending human need. Old misgivings had not been allayed, however. The danger of providing substantial and long-term benefits resurrected the fear that they could reward idleness. Consequently, the Report insisted that 'the correlative of the State's undertaking to ensure adequate benefit for unavoidable interruption of earnings, however long, is enforcement of the citizen's obligation to seek and accept all reasonable opportunities of work, to co-operate in measures designed to save him from habituation to idleness, and to take all proper measures to be well'.[181] The relations between individual and state were put firmly within a moral framework of fair exchange and quid pro quo, that also outlined desirable social behaviour. The traditional liberal notions of contract and obligation were paramount in defining the interaction between the community and its members. For this reason, among others, the idea of free allowances from the state was ruled out. As for national assistance, this was exclusively the domain of the state, but at the further cost of a means test and 'conditions as to behaviour which may seem likely to hasten restoration of earning capacity'.[182]

The Report recommended a comprehensive approach to insurance, 'in respect both of the persons covered and of their needs'.[183] It thus took an important step towards the communal inclusiveness of progressive ideologies—represented by means of the flat rate contributions and benefits. This was for Beveridge an issue of principle which 'has been found to accord best with the sentiments of the British people', namely, 'that in insurance organised by the

178 Ibid., paras. 413, 415.
179 Ibid., para. 277.
180 See Freeden, *The New Liberalism*, pp. 235–6.
181 Beveridge, *Social Insurance and Allied Services*, para. 130.
182 Ibid., para. 369.
183 Ibid., para. 308.

community by use of compulsory powers each individual should stand in on the same terms'. The egalitarian ethos 'that men stand together with their fellows' was also a strong endorsement of the moral and practical ties that knit a community together; in effect, the mechanism of pooling risks was an embodiment of these ideas.[184] At the same time, the spirit of the Report was removed from socialist conceptions of human nature. In a revealing passage, Beveridge defended the pursuit of security as a justifiable, though not exclusive, aim. It was to be understood within the context of an idea-environment that included initiative, adventure, personal responsibility, freedom and enterprise.[185] This had always been the view proffered by centrist-liberals; if Beveridge saw it as constituting the 'British tradition', he may have unknowingly attested to the widespread acceptance of that variety of liberalism. Certainly, the Report echoed no 'essential sociability' doctrine of human nature; rather, it introduced the community as a *partner* to the liberty and happiness of the individual, a partner whose concerted efforts were indispensable for realizing individual interests and expressing individual variety. Allowance was also made for voluntary effort 'by each individual to provide more than [the] minimum for himself and his family'.[186] In his sequel, *Full Employment in a Free Society*, Beveridge reiterated his belief in the protection of essential citizen liberties, which would exclude 'the totalitarian solution of full employment in a society completely planned and regimented'. Yet, more decisively than a number of centrist-liberals, he maintained that the private ownership of the means of production was merely a device: 'it is not an essential citizen liberty in Britain, because it is not and never has been enjoyed by more than a very small proportion of the British people.'[187]

Within hours of its publication, the Beveridge Report had become a national symbol, a message of hope and reassurance that, despite its detractors, cut across political labels. It was a work that, though unmistakably liberal in nature, was too much the product of one man to reflect the richness, complexity and vicissitudes of the liberal generation that had preceded it. In its author's own words, it

[184] Ibid., para. 26.
[185] Ibid., paras. 455–6.
[186] Ibid., para. 9.
[187] W. H. Beveridge, *Full Employment in a Free Society* (London, 1944), pp. 21, 23.

was 'in some ways a revolution, but in more important ways it is a natural development from the past. It is a British revolution.'[188] This implicit extolling of gradualism was, of course, an element shared with all major British ideologies. Nevertheless, the Beveridge Report is a curiously apposite ending to this study in that it is a blend of left-liberalism and centrist-liberalism, while not constituting the immediate logical conclusion to either. The liberal heritage could not be contained in a single demonstrative act; the success of that heritage was a generalized one. By the end of the period under consideration, most progressive intellectuals, political activists, and reformers no longer recognized their principles as explicitly liberal.[189] Liberalism had transcended its distinct institutional and ideological shape and thus, paradoxically, ensured its survival.

[188] Beveridge, *Social Insurance and Allied Services*, para. 31.

[189] The *Manchester Guardian* repeatedly hailed the Report in its leaders but made no mention of a possible connection between it and liberal beliefs.

SELECT BIBLIOGRAPHY

1. UNPUBLISHED SOURCES

Private Papers

Eagar Papers, Reform Club, London
Guardian Archives, John Rylands University of Manchester Library
Hammond Papers, Bodleian Library, Oxford
Henderson Papers, Nuffield College, Oxford
Keynes Papers, Marshall Library, Cambridge
Layton Papers, in private hands (now at Trinity College, Cambridge)
Lloyd George Papers, House of Lords Record Office
Lothian Papers, Scottish Record Office
Murray Papers, Bodleian Library, Oxford
Rainbow Circle Minutes, British Library of Political and Economic Science, London
Samuel Papers, House of Lords Record Office
C. P. Scott Papers, John Rylands University of Manchester Library
E. D. Simon Papers, Central Library, Manchester
Wallas Papers, British Library of Political and Economic Science, London

2. PUBLISHED SOURCES

A. Primary Works

a. Hansard's Parliamentary Debates

b. Newspapers, Periodicals, Yearbooks

Contemporary Review
Daily Chronicle
Daily News
English Review
Fortnightly Review
Forward View
Hibbert Journal
Humanist
International Journal of Ethics
Journal of Philosophical Studies
Liberal Magazine
Liberal Yearbook
Listener
Lloyd George Liberal Magazine
Manchester Guardian
Nation
Nation (New York)
New Outlook
New Republic
New Statesman
News Chronicle
Nineteenth Century and After
Political Quarterly (1914–1916)
Political Quarterly (1930–)

Saturday Westminster Gazette
Sociological Review
The Times
Weekly Westminster
Westminster Gazette

c. Books and Pamphlets

Barker, E., *The Citizen's Choice* (Cambridge, 1937)
—— *Political Thought in England 1848–1914* (London, 1963; 1st edn. 1915)
Beveridge, W. H., *Full Employment in a Free Society* (London, 1944)
—— *Insurance for All and Everything* (London, n.d. [1924])
—— *Social Insurance and Allied Services*, Cmd. 6404 (London, 1942)
—— *et al.*, *Tariffs: The Case Examined* (London, 1931)
Boothby, R., Macmillan, H., Loder, J. de V., Stanley, O., *Industry and the State: A Conservative View* (London, 1927)
Britain's Industrial Future, being the Report of the Liberal Industrial Inquiry (London, 1928)
Burns, C. D., *The Challenge to Democracy* (London, 1934)
—— *Civilisation: The Next Step* (London, 1938)
—— *The Contact Between Minds* (London, 1923)
—— *Democracy* (London, 1935)
—— *Democracy. Its Defects and Advantages* (London, 1929)
—— *Government and Industry* (London, 1921)
—— *Industry and Civilisation* (London, 1925)
—— *Modern Civilization on Trial* (London, 1931)
—— *The Philosophy of Labour* (London, 1925)
—— *Political Ideals* (3rd edn., Oxford, 1919)
—— *Whitehall* (Oxford, 1921)
Charles, E., *The Menace of Under-Population* (London, 1936)
Coal and Power (London, 1924)
Cole, G. D. H., *Guild Socialism Re-Stated* (London, 1920)
Constructive Democracy (London, 1938)
Dodds, E., *Is Liberalism Dead?* (London, 1920)
—— *Liberalism in Action* (London, 1922)
Essays in Liberalism (London, 1922)
Gardner, L. (ed.), *The Hope for Society* (London, 1917)
George, D. Lloyd, the Marquess of Lothian, and Rowntree, B. Seebohm, *How to Tackle Unemployment* (London, 1930)
Ginsberg, M., *The Psychology of Society* (London, 1921)
Green, T. H., *Lectures on the Principles of Political Obligation* (London, 1941)
Hetherington, H. J. W., and Muirhead, J. H., *Social Purpose: A Contribution to a Philosophy of Civic Society* (London, 1918)
Hirst, F. W., *Liberty and Tyranny* (London, 1935)

Hobhouse, L. T., *The Elements of Social Justice* (London, 1922)
—— *Liberalism* (New York, 1964; 1st edn. 1911)
—— *The Metaphysical Theory of the State* (London, 1918)
—— *Questions of War and Peace* (London, 1916)
—— *The Rational Good* (London, 1921)
—— *Social Development* (London, 1966; 1st edn. 1924)
—— *The World in Conflict* (London, 1915)
Hobson, J. A., *The Conditions of Industrial Peace* (London, 1927)
—— *Confessions of an Economic Heretic* (London, 1938)
—— *Democracy and a Changing Civilisation* (London, 1934)
—— *Democracy After the War* (London, 1917)
—— *Free-Thought in the Social Sciences* (London, 1926)
—— *From Capitalism to Socialism* (London, 1932)
—— *God and Mammon* (London, 1931)
—— *Incentives in the New Industrial Order* (London, 1922)
—— *The Modern State* (London, 1931)
—— *The New Protectionism* (New York, 1916)
—— *Poverty in Plenty* (London, 1931)
—— *Problems of a New World* (London, 1921)
—— *Property and Improperty* (London, 1937)
—— *Rationalisation and Unemployment* (London, 1930)
—— *Rationalism and Humanism* (Conway Memorial Lecture, London, 1933)
—— *The Recording Angel* (London, 1932)
—— *Taxation in the New State* (London, 1919)
—— *Towards International Government* (London, 1915)
—— *Towards Social Equality* (L. T. Hobhouse Memorial Trust Lecture No. 1, Oxford, 1931)
—— *Wealth and Life* (London, 1929)
—— and Ginsberg, M., *L. T. Hobhouse: His Life and Work* (London, 1931)
Holmes–Laski Letters, edited by M. DeWoolfe Howe, 2 vols. (London, 1953)
Joad, C. E. M., *Liberty To-Day* (London, 1934)
Jones, H., *The Principles of Citizenship* (London, 1919)
Jones, S., *The Call to Liberalism* (London, 1922)
Keynes, J. M., *The Collected Writings of John Maynard Keynes*, 29 vols. (London, 1971–83)
—— *The Economic Consequences of the Peace* (London, 1919)
—— *Essays in Persuasion* (London, 1931)
—— *The General Theory of Employment, Interest and Money* (London, 1973; 1st edn. 1936)
—— and Henderson, H. D., *Can Lloyd George Do It?* (London, 1929)

The Land and the Nation. Rural Report of the Liberal Land Committee 1923–25 (London, 1925)

Langshaw, H., *Socialism: and the Historical Function of Liberalism* (London, 1925)

Laski, H. J., *Authority in the Modern State* (New Haven, 1919)

—— *The Decline of Liberalism* (L. T. Hobhouse Memorial Trust Lecture No. 10, Oxford, 1940)

—— *The Grammar of Politics* (London, 1925)

—— *Liberty in the Modern State* (Harmondsworth, 1937; 1st edn. 1930)

—— *The Rise of European Liberalism* (London, 1962; 1st edn. 1936)

—— *Studies in Law and Politics* (London, 1932)

The Liberal Way. With a Foreword by R. Muir (London, 1934)

Lothian, Lord, *Liberalism in the Modern World* (London, 1933)

Macmillan, H., *The Middle Way* (London, 1938)

—— *Reconstruction: A Plea for a National Policy* (London, 1933)

Macmurray, J., *Freedom in the Modern World* (London, 1932)

Masterman, C. F. G., *England After War* (London, n.d. [1923])

—— *The New Liberalism* (London, 1920)

McDougall, W., *The Group Mind* (Cambridge, 1920)

McNair, A., *The Problem of the Coal Mines* (London, 1924)

Morrison, H., *Socialisation and Transport* (London, 1933)

Muir, R., *Civilization and Liberty* (London, 1940)

—— *The Faith of a Liberal* (London, 1933)

—— *Future for Democracy* (London, 1939)

—— *Liberalism and Industry* (London, 1920)

—— *The New Liberalism* (London, n.d. [1923])

—— *Politics and Progress* (London, 1923)

—— *Trade Unionism and the Trade Union Bill* (London, 1927)

—— *How Britain is Governed* (London, 1930)

Muirhead, J. H., *German Philosophy and the War* (Oxford, 1915)

—— *German Philosophy in Relation to the War* (London, 1915)

Murray, G., *Liberality and Civilization* (London, 1938)

—— *The Ordeal of this Generation* (London, 1929)

Nathan, H. L. and Williams, H. Heathcote (eds.), *Liberal Points of View* (London, 1927)

—— *Liberalism and Some Problems of To-Day* (London, 1929)

The Next Five Years: An Essay in Political Agreement (London, 1935)

Peace and Reconstruction (London, 1935)

Phillips, H., *The Liberal Outlook* (London, 1929)

—— Holgate, A., Hughes, R. Moelwyn, Jones, T. Elder, Lloyd, I., Menken, J., Sainsbury, A., *Whither Britain? A Radical Answer* (London, 1932)

Rathbone, E., The Disinherited Family (London, 1924)

Robertson, J. M., *Liberalism and Labour* (London, 1921)
—— *The Meaning of Liberalism* (2nd edn., London, 1925)
Russell, B., *Political Ideals* (London, 1977; 1st edn. 1917)
—— *Principles of Social Reconstruction* (London, 1916)
—— *Roads to Freedom: Socialism, Anarchism, and Syndicalism* (3rd edn., London, 1920)
—— *Power* (London, 1975; 1st edn. 1938)
Samuel, H., *Belief and Action* (London, 1937)
—— *The War and Liberty* (London, 1917)
Simon, E. D., *The Anti-Slum Campaign* (London, 1933)
—— *Houses for All* (London, n.d. [1923])
—— *How to Abolish the Slums* (London, 1929)
—— *The Inheritance of Riches* (London, 1925)
—— *Liberalism in Local Government* (London, 1924)
Stamp, J., *Criticism and Other Addresses* (London, 1931)
Tawney, R. H., *The Acquisitive Society* (London, 1945; 1st edn. 1921)
—— *Equality* (London, 1938; 1st edn. 1931)
—— *The Radical Tradition* (Harmondsworth, 1964)
Towns and the Land: Urban Report of the Liberal Land Committee 1923–25 (London, 1925)
Urwick, L., *The Meaning of Rationalisation* (London, 1929)
Villiers, B., *Britain After the Peace: Revolution or Reconstruction* (London, 1918)
—— *England and the New Era* (London, 1920)
Wallas, G., *The Art of Thought* (London, 1926)
—— *The Great Society* (London, 1914)
—— *Men and Ideas* (London, 1940)
—— *Our Social Heritage* (London, 1921)
—— *Social Judgment* (London, 1934)
Webb, S. and B., *A Constitution for the Socialist Commonwealth of Great Britain* (London, 1920)
We Can Conquer Unemployment (London, 1929)
Wells, H. G., *After Democracy* (London, 1932)
—— *The Open Conspiracy* (London, 1928)
Wilson, T. (ed.), *The Political Diaries of C. P. Scott 1911–1928* (London, 1970)

d. Articles

Alden, P., 'A New Liberal Programme: Liberalism and Labour', *CR*, 115 (1919), 396–403
—— 'The Beveridge Report', *CR*, 163 (1943), 7–11
Barker, E., 'Democracy and Social Justice', *CR*, 137 (1930), 300–7.
—— 'The Discredited State', *Political Quarterly*, 5 (1915), 101–121

Beauchamp, Lord, 'The Liberal Party', *CR*, 130 (1926), 1–6.
Birrell, A., 'The Meaning of Liberalism', *CR*, 132 (1927), 273–81
Burns, C. D., 'The Conception of Liberty', *Journal of Philosophical Studies*, 3 (1928), 186–97
—— 'Ideals of Democracy in England', *International Journal of Ethics*, 27 (1916–17), 432–45
—— 'Practical Issues and Social Philosophy', *Journal of Philosophical Studies*, 1 (1926), 354–65
—— 'Productivity and Reconstruction', *International Journal of Ethics*, 28 (1917–18), 393–405
—— 'When Peace Breaks Out', *International Journal of Ethics*, 26 (1915–16), 82–91
Catlin, G. E. C., 'The End of the Liberal Epoch?', *CR*, 149 (1936), 305–13
Chapple, W. A., 'The Function of Liberalism', *CR*, 126 (1924), 308–15
Clay, H., 'Liberalism, Laissez-Faire and Present Industrial Conditions', *HJ*, 24 (1926), 731–41
Cole, G. D. H., 'Chants of Progress', *Political Quarterly*, 6 (1935), 530–40
Coote, C. R., 'What is a Liberal?', *NT*, 89 (1921), 369–84
Corbett, J., 'Sir Herbert Samuel and the Liberal Party', *FR*, 128 (1927), 71–83
Davies, W. W., 'The New Liberalism', *Lloyd George Liberal Magazine* (1921), 7–10
Elton, Lord, 'England's Age of Collectivism', *FR*, 143 (1935), 574–83
Foot, D., 'The Liberal Crisis', *CR*, 139 (1931), 582–8
—— 'The Liberal Summer School', *CR*, 140 (1931), 324–30
Haynes, E. S. P., 'Liberty and the State', *English Review*, 28 (1919), 59–66
Herbert, A., 'The Liberal Summer School', *CR*, 142 (1932), 322–7
Hirst, F. W., 'The Future of Liberalism', *CR*, 127 (1925), 9–14
—— 'Is British Liberalism Alive or Dead?', *CR*, 149 (1936), 420–8
—— 'Liberalism and Liberty', *CR*, 145 (1934), 276–86
Hobhouse, L. T., 'Democracy and Civilization', *Sociological Review*, 13 (1921), 126–135
Hobson, J. A., 'Co-Operative Welfare', *HJ*, 27 (1929), 703–19
—— 'Democracy, Liberty and Force', *HJ*, 34 (1935), 35–44
—— 'Economic Art and Human Welfare', *Journal of Philosophical Studies*, 1 (1926), 467–80
—— 'The Economics of High Productivity', *English Review*, 25 (1917), 225–37
—— 'The Ethical Movement and the Natural Man', *HJ*, 20 (1922), 667–79
—— 'Force Necessary to Government', *HJ*, 33 (1934), 331–42
—— 'Is Democracy an Empty Word?', *HJ*, 34 (1936), 529–38
—— 'The New Industrial Revolution', *CR*, 118 (1920), 638–45
—— 'The Reformulation of Politics', *CR*, 129 (1925), 430–6

—— 'Social Thinkers in Nineteenth-Century England', *CR*, 137 (1930), 453–61
—— 'The State as an Organ of Rationalisation', *Political Quarterly*, 2 (1931), 30–45
Hodgson, S., 'Liberalism', *NT*, 96 (1924), 639–48
—— 'The Opportunity of Liberalism', *NT*, 92 (1922), 183–92
—— 'The Tenth Liberal Summer School', *CR*, 138 (1930), 296–302
Hogge, J. M., 'Free Liberalism', *CR*, 116 (1919), 629–34
Hopkinson, A., 'Liberalism's Epitaph', *English Review*, 46 (1928), 515–22.
James, C. F., 'Liberalism and the Industrial Problem', *NT*, 90 (1921), 798–806
Lilly, W. S., 'The Reward of Labour', *NT*, 81 (1917), 93–108
Lindsay, A. D., 'The State in Recent Political Theory', *Political Quarterly*, 1 (1914), 128–45
Macdonell, J., 'The Modern Conceptions of Liberty', *CR*, 106 (1914), 190–202
Macnamara, T. J., 'Socialism versus Individualism', *Lloyd George Liberal Magazine*, 7 (1923), 510–20
Massingham, H. W., 'The Case for a Labour Government', *FR*, 121 (1924), 118–25
Morris, R. Hopkins, 'Liberalism and the New Parliament', *CR*, 136 (1929), 280–6
Muir, R., 'The Diffusion of Ownership', *CR*, 155 (1939), 152–9
—— 'Has Capitalism Broken Down?', *CR*, 151 (1937), 650–7
—— 'The Liberal Land Policy', *CR*, 129 (1926), 424–32; 554–63
—— 'The Liberal Party', *CR*, 130 (1926), 1–13
—— 'The Liberal Summer School and the Problems of Industry', *CR*, 132 (1927), 282–9
—— 'The Liberal Unemployment Policy', *CR*, 135 (1929), 556–63
—— 'Liberalism and Industry', *CR*, 133 (1928), 555–63
—— 'The Meaning of Liberalism', *CR*, 130 (1926), 545–54
—— 'Mr. Simon's Questions About Free Trade', *Political Quarterly*, 2 (1931), 23–9
—— 'Property and Liberty', *CR*, 154 (1938), 552–9
—— 'Trade Union Reform', *CR*, 131 (1927), 409–14.
Murray, G., 'What Liberalism Stands For', *CR*, 129 (1925), 681–97
Murray, J., 'Can Liberalism Revive?', *CR*, 127 (1925), 714–21
Phillips, H., 'Liberalism and Industrial Relations', *FR*, 130 (1928), 603–11; 730–9
—— 'Liberalism and Industrial Relations', *FR*, 131 (1929), 65–75
Pink, M. Alderton, 'Towards a New Liberalism', *HJ*, 36 (1938), 492–500
Rew, H., 'Liberalism and Agriculture', *CR*, 122 (1922), 442–50

Robertson, J. M., 'The Idea of a Labour Party', *CR*, 113 (1918), 614–20
—— 'The Industrial Future', *CR*, 115 (1919), 257–63
Rowntree, B. Seebohm, 'Labour Unrest and the Need For a National Ideal', *CR*, 116 (1919), 496–503
—— 'Prospects and Tasks of Social Reconstruction', *CR*, 115 (1919), 1–9
Rowse, A. L., 'A British Popular Front?', *FR*, 146 (1936), 328–35
—— 'Mr. Keynes and the Labour Movement', *NT*, 120 (1936), 320–32
—— 'Socialism and Mr. Keynes', *NT*, 112 (1932), 327–42
Runciman, W., 'The Radical Outlook', *CR*, 113 (1918), 1–7.
Russell, B., 'Socialism and Liberal Ideals', *English Review*, 30 (1920), 449–55; 499–508
Samuel, H., 'The Liberal Industrial Report', *CR*, 133 (1928), 277–84
—— 'Liberals and the Labour Movement', *CR*, 132 (1927), 409–21
—— 'Liberty', *CR*, 131 (1927), 566–75
—— 'Liberty, Liberalism and Labour', *CR*, 146 (1934), 257–67
—— 'The Political Outlook', *CR*, 138 (1930), 409–20
Simon, E. D., 'The Liberal Summer School', *CR*, 130 (1926), 298–303
—— 'The Liberal Summer School', *CR*, 136 (1929), 273–9
—— 'Some Questions About Free Trade', *Political Quarterly*, 1 (1930), 479–95
Usher, H. B., 'Liberalism and its Future', *CR*, 123 (1923), 164–9
Wedgwood, J. C., 'Liberalism and Labour. II. From a Labour Standpoint', *NT*, 91 (1922), 216–21

B. Secondary Works

a. Books and Monographs

Addison, P., *The Road to 1945* (London, 1977)
Allett, J., *New Liberalism: The Political Economy of J. A. Hobson* (Toronto, 1981)
Ashworth, W., *An Economic History of England 1870–1939* (London, 1960)
Ayerst, D., *Guardian: Biography of a Newspaper* (London, 1971)
Bentley, M., *The Liberal Mind 1914–1929* (Cambridge, 1977)
—— and Stevenson, J. (eds.), *High and Low Politics in Modern Britain* (Oxford, 1983)
Berlin, I., *Four Essays on Liberty* (Oxford, 1969)
Birke, A., *Pluralismus und Gewerkschaftsautonomie in England: Entstehungsgeschichte einer politischen Theorie* (Stuttgart, 1978)
Briggs, A., *Social Thought and Social Action: A Study of the Work of Seebohm Rowntree 1871–1954* (London, 1961)
Brown, K. D. (ed.), *Essays in Anti-Labour History* (London, 1974)

Campbell, J., *Lloyd George: The Goat in the Wilderness 1922–1931* (London, 1977)
Ceadel, M., *Pacifism in Britain 1914–1945: The Defining of a Faith* (Oxford, 1980)
Clarke, P., *Liberals and Social Democrats* (Cambridge, 1978)
Cline, C. A., *Recruits to Labour: The British Labour Party 1914–1931* (Syracuse, 1963)
Collini, S., *Liberalism and Sociology: L. T. Hobhouse and Political Argument in England 1880–1914* (Cambridge, 1979)
Connolly, W. E., *The Terms of Political Discourse* (Lexington, Mass., 1974)
Currie, R., *Industrial Politics* (Oxford, 1979)
Deane, H. A., *The Political Ideas of Harold J. Laski* (Columbia, 1955)
Douglas, R., *The History of the Liberal Party 1895–1970* (London, 1971)
80th Birthday Book for Ernest Darwin Simon (Stockport, private printing, 1959)
Freeden, M., *The New Liberalism: An Ideology of Social Reform* (Oxford, 1978)
Gaus, G. F., *The Modern Liberal Theory of Man* (London, 1983)
Gilbert, B. B., *British Social Policy 1914–1939* (London, 1970)
Greenleaf, W. H., *The British Political Tradition*, 2 vols. (London, 1983)
Halévy, É., *The Era of Tyrannies* (London, 1967)
Havighurst, A. F., *Radical Journalist: H. W. Massingham* (Cambridge, 1974)
Hearnshaw, L. S., *A Short History of British Psychology 1840–1940* (London, 1964)
Hughes, H. S., *Consciousness and Society 1890–1930* (London, 1974)
Hyams, E., *The New Statesman: The History of the First Fifty Years 1913–1963* (London, 1963)
Johnson, E. S. and Johnson, H. G., *The Shadow of Keynes* (Oxford, 1978)
Johnson, P. B., *Land Fit for Heroes* (Chicago, 1968)
Macnicol, J., *The Movement for Family Allowances 1918–45* (London, 1980)
Manning, D. J., *Liberalism* (London, 1976)
Marwick, A., *The Explosion of British Society 1914–1970* (London, 1971)
Minogue, K., *The Liberal Mind* (London, 1963)
Morgan, K. O., *Consensus and Disunity: The Lloyd George Coalition Government 1918–1922* (Oxford, 1979)
Morgan, K. and J., *Portrait of a Progressive: The Political Career of Christopher, Viscount Addison* (Oxford, 1980)
Mowat, C. L., *Britain Between the Wars 1918–1940* (London, 1968)
Oppenheim, F., *Political Concepts: A Reconstruction* (Oxford, 1981)

Peele, G., and Cook, C. (eds.), *The Politics of Reappraisal 1918–1939* (London, 1975)
Pimlott, B., *Labour and the Left in the 1930s* (Cambridge, 1977)
—— and Cook, C. (eds.), *Trade Unions in British Politics* (London, 1982)
Qualter, T. H., *Graham Wallas and the Great Society* (London, 1980)
Rae, J., *Conscience and Politics* (Oxford, 1970)
C. P. Scott 1846–1932: The Making of the 'Manchester Guardian' (London, 1946)
Skidelsky, R., *Politicians and the Slump: The Labour Government of 1929–1931* (Harmondsworth, 1970)
Slesser, H., *A History of the Liberal Party* (London, n.d., [1944])
Soloway, R. A., *Birth Control and the Population Question 1877–1930* (Chapel Hill, 1982)
Stevenson, J., *British Society 1914–45* (Harmondsworth, 1984)
Stocks, M., *My Commonplace Book* (London, 1970)
Swartz, M., *The Union of Democratic Control in British Politics During the First World War* (Oxford, 1971)
Taylor, A. J. P., *English History 1914–1945* (Harmondsworth, 1970)
Terrill, R., *R. H. Tawney and His Times: Socialism as Fellowship* (London, 1974)
Thirlwall, A. P. (ed.), *Keynes and Laissez-Faire* (London, 1978)
Thomson, R., *The Pelican History of Psychology* (Harmondsworth, 1968)
Weber, M., *The Methodology of the Social Sciences* (New York, 1949)
Wiener, M. J., *Between Two Worlds: The Political Thought of Graham Wallas* (Oxford, 1971)
Wilson, T., *The Downfall of the Liberal Party 1914–1935* (London, 1968)
Winch, D., *Economics and Policy: A Historical Survey* (London, 1972)
Winter, J. M., *Socialism and the Challenge of War: Ideas and Politics in Britain 1912–1918* (London, 1974)
Woolf, Virginia, *The Diary of Virginia Woolf*, vol. ii. 1920–1940, ed. A. O. Bell (Harmondsworth, 1981)
Wright, A.W., *G. D. H. Cole and Socialist Democracy* (Oxford, 1979)

b. Autobiography and Biography

Beveridge, Lord, *Power and Influence* (London, 1953)
Bowle, J., *Viscount Samuel* (London, 1957)
Butler, J. R. M., *Lord Lothian (Philip Kerr) 1882–1940* (London, 1960)
Hammond, J. L., *C. P. Scott of the Manchester Guardian* (London, 1934)
Harris, J., *William Beveridge: A Biography* (Oxford, 1977)
Harrod, R. F., *Keynes* (Harmondsworth, 1972)
Hobhouse, S., *Forty Years and an Epilogue* (London, 1951)
Hodgson, S. (ed.), *Ramsay Muir. An Autobiography and Some Essays* (London, 1943)

Hubback, D., *No Ordinary Press Baron: A Life of Walter Layton* (London, 1985)

Koss, S. E., *Fleet Street Radical: A. G. Gardiner and the* Daily News (London, 1973)

Macmillan, H., *Winds of Change 1914–1939* (London, 1966)

Martin, K., *Father Figures* (London, 1966)

—— *Harold Laski* (London, 1969)

Masterman, L., *C. F. G. Masterman: A Biography* (London, 1939)

Moggridge, D. E., *Keynes* (London, 1980)

Morris, A. J. A., *C. P. Trevelyan 1870–1958: Portrait of a Radical* (Belfast, 1977)

Muirhead, J. H., *Reflections by a Journeyman in Philosophy* (London, 1942)

Salter, A., *Memoirs of a Public Servant* (London, 1961)

Samuel, Viscount, *Memoirs* (London, 1945)

Skidelsky, R., *John Maynard Keynes: Hopes Betrayed 1883–1920* (London, 1983)

Stocks, M., *Eleanor Rathbone: A Biography* (London, 1949)

—— *Ernest Simon of Manchester* (Manchester, 1963)

West, F., *Gilbert Murray: A Life* (London, 1984)

Woolf, L., *An Autobiography*, 2 vols. (Oxford, 1980)

c. *Articles*

Abrams, P., 'The Failure of Social Reform: 1918–1920', *Past and Present*, 24 (1963), 43–64

Benn, S. and Weinstein, W. L., 'Being Free to Act, and Being a Free Man', *Mind*, 80 (1971), 194–211

Freeden, M., 'Eugenics and Progressive Thought: A Study in Ideological Affinity', *Historical Journal*, 22 (1979), 421–43

Gallie, W. B., 'Essentially Contested Concepts', *Proceedings of the Aristotelian Society*, 59 (1955–6), 167–98

Greenleaf, W. H., 'Laski and British Socialism', *History of Political Thought*, 2 (1981), 573–91

Lowe, R., 'The Failure of Consensus in Britain: The National Industrial Conference, 1919–1921', *Historical Journal*, 21 (1978), 649–75

MacCallum, G. C., 'Negative and Positive Freedom' in P. Laslett, W. G. Runciman and Q. Skinner (eds.), *Philosophy, Politics and Society*, 4th Ser. (Oxford, 1972), pp. 174–93

Marwick, A., 'Middle Opinion in the Thirties: Planning, Progress and Political "Agreement"', *English Historical Review*, 79 (1964), 285–98

Matthew, H. C. G., McKibbin, R. I., and Kay, J. A., 'The Franchise Factor in the Rise of the Labour Party', *English Historical Review*, 91 (1976), 723–52

McKibbin, R., 'The Economic Policy of the Second Labour Government 1929–1931', *Past and Present*, 68 (1975), 95–123

Parsons, W., 'Keynes and the Politics of Ideas', *History of Political Thought*, 4 (1983), 367–92

Skinner, Q., 'Meaning and Understanding in the History of Ideas', *History and Theory*, 8 (1969), 3–53

—— 'Some Problems in the Analysis of Political Thought and Action', *Political Theory*, 2 (1974), 277–303

Weinstein, W. L., 'The Concept of Liberty in Nineteenth Century English Political Thought', *Political Studies*, 13 (1965), 145–62

d. *Unpublished Thesis*

Hart, M. W., 'The Decline of the Liberal Party in Parliament and in the Constituencies 1914–1931' (Oxford University D.Phil. Thesis, 1982)

INDEX

D0203623

From Middle Income to Poor

From Middle Income to Poor

Downward Mobility among Displaced Steelworkers

Allison Zippay

PRAEGER

New York
Westport, Connecticut
London

Library of Congress Cataloging-in-Publication Data

Zippay, Allison.
From middle income to poor : downward mobility among displaced steelworkers / Allison Zippay.
p. cm.
Includes bibliographical references and index.
ISBN 0-275-93791-7 (alk. paper)
1. Plant shutdowns—Shenango River Valley (Ohio and Pa.) 2. Unemployed—Shenango River Valley (Ohio and Pa.) 3. Blue-collar workers—Shenango River Valley (Ohio and Pa.) 4. Shenango River Valley (Ohio and Pa.)—Social conditions. I. Title.
HD5708.55.U62S499 1991
331.13'7974893—dc20 91-11077

British Library Cataloguing in Publication Data is available.

Library of Congress Catalog Card Number: 91-11077
ISBN: 0-275-93791-7

First published in 1991

Praeger Publishers, One Madison Avenue, New York, NY 10010
An imprint of Greenwood Publishing Group, Inc.

Printed in the United States of America

The paper used in this book complies with the Permanent Paper Standard issued by the National Information Standards Organization (Z39.48-1984).

10 9 8 7 6 5 4 3 2 1

To Michael, Andrew, and Elizabeth

Contents

Acknowledgments

I would like to express my appreciation to the National Association of Social Workers' (NASW) Center for Social Policy and Practice for their partial funding of this research, and to thank Harry Specht, Lonnie Snowden, and John Quigley for their review of early drafts of this manuscript.

From Middle Income to Poor

1

Introduction

> It was April 21, 1:00 p.m. They called the guys from my department up to the office. "That's it," they said, "we're closing the shop." I was stunned. It was like they had told me my kid had been killed. I had been a metal worker there for 19 years.
>
> former Shenango Valley steelworker

The steady shift in the occupational structure of the United States from a manufacturing to a service economy is by now a familiar and well-chronicled phenomenon. As a percentage of total employment, manufacturing has been in decline since the 1960s, with the number of plant closings accelerating rapidly in the late 1970s and early 1980s. Hundreds of manufacturing plants have terminated operations, displacing millions of factory workers. During the 1980s many of the industries in decline involved steel and heavy manufacturing, and many of the displaced workers were prime-aged males with a history of blue-collar employment.

What has happened to these manufacturing workers? Following the 1983 recession and continuing through the 1980s, national unemployment rates decreased steadily, while the number of newly generated service-sector jobs rose. It is largely assumed that the displaced manufacturing workers have been absorbed into a postindustrial economy.

Yet scattered and troubling reports raise questions regarding the nature of the occupational readjustment of some these workers. Since 1979 one of the fastest-growing demographic groups among the poor has been prime-aged men. There is speculation that some of these new poor may be displaced industrial workers who have failed to secure satisfactory reemployment. Many areas of the country that were hard hit by plant closings continue to be plagued by depressed regional economies and unemployment rates higher than the national average. Many of the service-sector jobs that have replaced manufacturing employment provide wages

and benefits much lower than those in heavy industry. Anecdotal reports from some regions suffering manufacturing decline describe former steelworkers—their skills no longer in demand—now working in low-paid service-sector jobs as janitors, store clerks, and restaurant workers. While the decade of the 1980s was largely regarded as a prosperous one, the economic data from those years indicate that the gains were not evenly distributed. The rich became richer, the poor became poorer, and many members of the working class found their income level slipping. Due in part to the occupational restructuring of the economy, the sharpest losses in earnings and living standards during the 1980s were felt by male blue-collar workers.

What has the decline in manufacturing meant for persons who for decades made their living as mill workers? Do displaced industrial workers represent a new group of underemployed and economically disadvantaged? What has been the nature of their transition from well-paid manufacturing work? This book offers an in-depth examination of one community in which a series of plant closings in the early 1980s left thousands of former manufacturing workers jobless. It traces the aftermath of large-scale economic dislocation in a community that had long built its identity and economy around manufacturing, and offers a glimpse of one segment of the American population that did not share in the prosperity of the 1980s.

The study site is the Shenango Valley in western Pennsylvania, a blue-collar community nine miles east of Youngstown, Ohio, and sixty miles north of Pittsburgh, Pennsylvania, in what was once a center for steel manufacturing and fabrication. In the early 1980s, a series of plant closings in the Shenango Valley area idled an estimated 6,700 mill workers. As in many areas affected by plant closings, reports from the region described a sharp shift in standards of living: extensive downward mobility, chronic unemployment and underemployment, and increased dependence on public assistance.

Using information gathered from interviews with displaced workers and community leaders, this book examines the income and employment status of a sample of former industrial workers from the Shenango Valley several years after the plant closings, and chronicles the workers' attempts to develop new sources of social and economic support. In addition, the study records and interprets the meaning of mill work to people who labored for decades in industrial plants, and the meaning of its demise.

In beginning to look at individual and community responses to the plant closings in the Shenango Valley, it is important to place local reaction within the larger context of a national response to manufacturing decline. Plant closings take on quite different meanings within and

outside a mill community. Societal attitudes regarding the status of manufacturing industries affect the way problems of economic dislocation are addressed and the kinds of resources directed to distressed communities.

While the shock of economic displacement has been hard felt in regions like the Shenango Valley, its reverberations in the larger society have been relatively slight. Despite what has been quite massive economic displacement—5.76 million manufacturing jobs lost in the early 1980s alone—there has been little public, government, or media outcry regarding factory shutdowns. In contrast, the economic troubles of family farmers in the Midwest during the 1980s attracted a barrage of national attention and concern, including celebrity benefits for "farm aid." No such rallying around the mill towns and mill workers occurred.

Part of the reason for the lack of attention may be that, as the country moves toward a technological and information-oriented economy, heavy manufacturing represents a process and occupation people would prefer to let pass. People act on the basis of the images and conceptions they ascribe to social organization. In a country that glorifies upward mobility, materialism, and the sophistication of high technology, a rusting manufacturing plant may be a negative physical metaphor—a blight on the postindustrial landscape. Heavy manufacturing was lost, in part, to foreign competition, a failure of capital. Its image carries elements that are both passé and somewhat shameful.

High technology has replaced the machine age, and many economists argue that the new age of information and services represents a progressive stage of economic development. Ronald Reagan, while President, repeatedly proclaimed that the move to a postindustrial, service economy was a great economic advance. While some analysts and economists warn of the competitive disadvantage of a decline in manufacturing and the social and economic costs of deindustrialization, they are a minority voice. The decline of manufacturing can be seen to present a paradox: is this a passing to be mourned or celebrated? To date the demise of the mills has been largely tolerated as a requisite component of economic transition. The lack of national attention may bespeak, in part, a national ambivalence toward heavy industry. The decline of manufacturing has not been mourned. The mills have claim to neither status nor nostalgia.

The mill worker suffers a similar problem of status and image. Unlike farming, mill work has rarely been perceived as noble. A factory job is not a station that is often aspired to. While the family farm evokes themes of pride in hard work, clean living, independence, and self-sufficiency, a manufacturing plant is at odds with important cultural symbols. The mills were largely manned by waves of immigrants, many illiterate and unskilled. Within heavy industry, the mill environment is often grim: noisy, dirty,

smoky, and dim. Over several generations, mill workers gained power and monetary reward through the collective efforts of unions. A rise in dignity was linked to increased earnings achieved through collective bargaining, not by individual initiative. Solidarity is not an idea or experience ensconced in American legend, however. It is not an image preserved in the national cultural and political myths.

While our societal impressions of mills and mill workers may not carry much deference, the meanings attached to manufacturing work within the industrial community of the Shenango Valley hold a different significance. Manufacturing plants have been at the core of the Shenango Valley economy for well over 100 years. As described in the chapters that follow, the life-styles of local residents have been shaped by long-standing blue-collar traditions. With thousands of community residents making a living from factories, mill work carries a special community validation.

Local residents know what it takes to earn a living in a steel mill. Most are familiar with the customs, the hazards, and the rewards of factory work. They understand the hierarchy of manual and skilled labor in their local mills, from floor sweeper to welder. They know the rules of behavior that lead to advancement within the factory system, and they recognize the limits of that advancement. Most remember and appreciate the experiences of previous generations of local mill workers, who endured poor environmental conditions and low pay and eventually organized for a better wage. Such knowledge breeds a singular intra-group perception and respect with regard to factory work.

Nevertheless, as in the larger culture, the mills and mill work evoke ambivalence among the people of the Shenango Valley. Immersion in factory work and mill town life has produced both strong attachment and dislike. Most employees recall that the mills were dirty and noisy, and the work often strenuous or tedious. Factories polluted the local environment and were viewed by many as hazards to their health. But at the same time, the mills provided good wages, security, steady employment, and a strong sense of meaning and identity among blue-collar workers. Over the years, rising wages produced a gain in dignity and status. The good wages allowed blue-collar workers to provide a decent existence for their families and enabled many to enjoy the accoutrements of middle-class life, including home ownership, new cars, and vacations. Because of this, factory workers straddled two social classes: while their occupation was categorized as working class, it afforded a middle income. Again, the community of the Shenango Valley offered validation of the unique circumstances of both occupation and life-style.

Despite such intra-community validation, however, it is clear from the comments of displaced workers that there has long been concern that such social acceptance is particular to a mill community. People are well aware of the distinctions of occupational class, that they participate in a work

environment quite different from that of many other Americans. As one former steelworker from the Shenango Valley noted:

> Working in a mill is kind of like another world. Unless you were born and raised in a steel town and accepted that life—I don't think people would work there.

Perhaps awareness of that distinction is one factor that serves to strengthen local community ties and intensify bonds among community members. Social networks in the Shenango Valley tend to be close knit. Most people in the area interact with people much like themselves, that is, people with a current or former economic connection to the mills. Since manufacturing was long the dominant employer, the structure of the local economy has limited the diversity of social circles. Most of the people have lived in the area their whole lives. They share a common work, history, and blue-collar tradition. Friendships often extend over decades.

Linked and fortified by common life circumstances, such tightly knit communities serve as something of a buffer against what might be a condescending larger culture. Within the community one's work and identity are valued and secure; social ties that reinforce one's worth are sustained. Over the years, as reinforcing community associations become tighter and more interlocked, the forces that separate mill communities and manufacturing workers from other social or work groups become sharper; the social stratification becomes more severe.

Interestingly enough, this type of community association, arising in part from the circumstance of an occupational structure that is not highly esteemed outside the community, is often celebrated and mythologized within the larger culture. Tight-knit, supportive networks of friends, neighbors, and relatives represent elements of a gemeinschaft community, that is, a community sustained by strong family and neighborhood bonds, common values, and mutual dependence. In reality, modern communities are comprised of a myriad of formal and informal interactions. Yet longings for home and intimacy lend the image of a gemeinschaft community a nostalgic appeal. As such, the provincialism born of a closed-market mill town and blue-collar enclave may find societal approval as an example of a rare, idealized form of association.

Thus, while the occupational position of displaced workers in the Shenango Valley has not been celebrated, the idealization of their community form, however naive, has been. Ironically, it is to this community structure that displaced workers have been directed during their crisis of job loss. The spate of plant closings in the early 1980s coincided with a presidential administration committed to a vision of economic liberalism that emphasized minimal government intervention in social and economic problem solving. Areas like the Shenango Valley have not been recipients of

novel, federally directed programs of social planning, retraining, and community redevelopment. Rather, the economic growth of the service economy was expected to provide replacement jobs and employment; it was anticipated that the benefits of an expanded economy would trickle down to distressed communities. Beyond the safety net of extant social insurance and public assistance programs, personal networks of friends and family were to provide needed emotional and social support. It was presumed that individual motivation and self-help would lead to successful readjustment, and that the most enterprising would survive. This philosophy of laissez-faire can be seen to have fed a larger lack of societal attention or concern regarding the situation of depressed manufacturing communities. Once more, it was assumed that displaced workers would be absorbed into an expanding service economy.

Again, this case study examines how displaced workers from one community have managed a transition from well-paid manufacturing work. It provides a look at processes of rebuilding as well as processes of decline, including the slide, among some, from middle income to poor. It examines the results of what in some respects has been a test of the efficacy of trickle-down economics.

The following chapters present an analysis of the problem of economic dislocation in light of information gathered from interviews with displaced manufacturing workers from the Shenango Valley.

Chapter 2 sets the plant closings of the Shenango Valley in the context of a national decline in manufacturing. It outlines the extent of recent manufacturing job loss and reviews the literature on the social effects of long-term unemployment and income loss. The study site of the Shenango Valley is described in Chapter 3, with a review of the historical and contemporary blue-collar traditions around which its community life has been organized. Information gathered from interviews with the displaced workers is presented in Chapters 4 through 7 and is organized into four areas: the characteristics of the respondents and their work in the mills (Chapter 4); their income and employment status following the plant closings (Chapter 5); the mobilization of new social and economic resources by displaced workers (Chapter 6); and their psychological responses to the plant closings (Chapter 7). Included are findings regarding job seeking, lifestyle shifts, downward mobility, relocation decisions, use of social services and public assistance, the incidence of depression and other emotional distress, and changes in perceptions of self and community. Finally, Chapter 8 presents a discussion of the findings on changed income and employment status among displaced industrial workers, and recommends actions that could improve the workers' social and economic well-being.

2

Blue-Collar Workers in the 1980s: The Economic and Social Dimensions of a Decline in Manufacturing

During the 1980s the gap between the rich and poor in the United States widened substantially, as the concentration of wealth among the most affluent soared and the wages and income of the poor and working classes declined. While in progress, the 1980s were largely characterized as a time of national pride and material prosperity. Yet scarcely into the 1990s, public opinion appeared to be shifting toward disenchantment with many of the values and economic events of the decade. A Harris Poll released in June 1990, for example, reported that the American population was looking back on the 1980s with a rising degree of criticism, with a majority of adults expressing disapproval of a dominant 1980s value of "everybody making it fast while you can, regardless of what happens to others" and reacting negatively to the statement that "while 30 percent of the top income people got richer, the remaining 70 percent did less well."[1] This shift in perceptions was also marked in Kevin Phillips's widely read book *The Politics of Rich and Poor,* in which a rise is described in public concern over the redistribution of income that occurred during the Reagan era, with its increase in the percentage of persons living below poverty, upsurge in the wealth held by the richest 1 percent of the population, and erosion of the wages of the working class.[2]

To the thousands of displaced industrial workers who did not prosper in the 1980s, this growing awareness of the economic realignment of the decade has most likely come as something of a validation and relief. The conversations that were held with the blue-collar workers who lost jobs to plant closings in the Shenango Valley revealed their extreme agitation with the fact that while the Reagan Administration and the national media were heralding the prosperity of the 1980s, few people seemed to notice or attach much importance to the economic downslide of people like themselves. The experience of the Shenango Valley steelworkers was certainly not unique;

nationwide, millions of workers were struggling to reassemble their lives in the wake of factory shutdowns and a changing economy.

THE DECLINE IN MANUFACTURING

During the early 1980s an estimated 5.6 million manufacturing jobs were lost to plant closures and contractions in the United States.[3] Basic manufacturing industries, including steel, automobiles, and industrial equipment, suffered substantial job and plant losses. Many economists are forecasting continued job losses in the manufacturing sector throughout the 1990s as the United States makes a progressive shift from an industrial to a service economy.[4]

While plant closings in basic industry rose sharply in the late 1970s and 1980s, manufacturing in the United States has, in fact, been in decline since the 1960s. In 1950, manufacturing constituted 50 percent of total employment; by 1990 it represented less than 20 percent, and some economists predict that the percentage of manufacturing jobs in total employment will drop to about 5 to 14 percent by the year 2000.[5] As has been well chronicled, manufacturing firms have limited or ceased U.S. production because plants have moved overseas to take advantage of cheaper labor and materials, foreign manufacturers have gained a competitive edge, U.S. capital has been invested in the non-goods-producing sector, and changes in technology and consumption have altered demands for manufactured goods.[6]

The decline in manufacturing has not affected the country evenly. Hardest hit has been the industrial belt that stretches from St. Louis, Missouri, through the Great Lakes region, including the states of Michigan, Wisconsin, Ohio, Indiana, Illinois, and Pennsylvania. Almost 42 percent of the job losses in manufacturing industries between 1979 and 1984 were concentrated in the Great Lakes and Mid-Atlantic regions. A majority of the workers who were displaced, 59 percent, lived in large urban areas (population over .5 million), with 41 percent in small metropolitan (.1 to .5 million) or rural areas (less than .1 million).[7] In many of these small metropolitan and rural areas, manufacturing industries had been the community's primary source of employment. Typically, the displaced manufacturing workers were males of prime working age with a history of blue-collar employment. Significant job declines have occurred in industries where organized labor was strong and wages relatively high.

While manufacturing has been in decline in the United States, service industries have been expanding, generating millions of new jobs over the past decade. Service industries are generally defined as economic activities whose primary outputs are 'intangible': products such as retail trades, food services, health services, services to business, and information-handling services. Over the past 20 years, 86 percent of the job growth in the U.S. economy has occurred in the service sector, and employment in service

industries currently accounts for about 70 percent of all jobs.[8] Compared with manufacturing, the services have higher concentrations of jobs in both low-paying positions and in management. Many of these low-paying jobs are part time and carry few fringe benefits. A tier of well-paid professional and technical jobs, requiring advanced training and education, contrast with a plethora of $4- to $6-an-hour positions, such as store clerk, clerical or health aide, or hotel or restaurant worker. Paradoxically, while millions of newly generated service-sector jobs contributed to the steady decline in unemployment rates during the 1980s, the nature of much of this employment has left many persons scrambling to make ends meet.[9]

THE NEW POOR AND UNDEREMPLOYED

To what extent has this change in occupational structure resulted in declines in income and employment status among displaced industrial workers? There is increasing evidence that the characteristics of the poor, underemployed, and long-term unemployed in this country are changing as displaced blue-collar workers join their ranks.

Economic data from the 1980s indicate an erosion of income among middle- and lower-class groups. During the 1980s, the number of both affluent and poor households increased, while the share of middle-income households declined.[10] When amounts are adjusted for inflation, workers in private nonagricultural industries earned a weekly average of $186.94 in 1970 and $166.52 in 1989. Blue-collar males have suffered the sharpest drop in earnings. Calculated in constant 1985 dollars, the median earnings of men aged 25 to 35 fell from $10.17 an hour in 1973 to $8.85 in 1987.[11] Since 1979, one of the fastest-growing demographic groups among the poor has been prime-aged men, and the number of working persons whose incomes have fallen below the poverty line has risen by 28 percent.[12] There is speculation that some of these new poor are displaced manufacturing workers who have failed to find satisfactory reemployment.

A few aggregate studies from the mid-1980s lend some support to this supposition. In 1984 the U.S. Bureau of Labor Statistics gathered employment information on 2.5 million persons who had been employed at a manufacturing plant for at least three years and had lost a job due to a plant shutdown or contraction between January 1979 and January 1984.[13] Of these displaced workers, less than 60 percent had found jobs as of January 1984. Approximately 25 percent were unemployed, and the rest had left the labor force. Among the displaced workers who fared worst were those from geographic locales dominated by the declining manufacturing industries of steel and other primary metals. A survey of 220,000 steelworkers who had lost jobs to plant closures and contractions between 1979 and 1983 found that 40 percent were still looking for work in 1984. Among those who were

working, earnings had declined by an average of 40 percent.[14] While the largest financial losses are suffered by displaced workers living in a depressed local economy, analyses of data from the January 1984 Current Population Survey found that a majority of older, poorly educated blue-collar workers experienced large income losses even when they were displaced in a growing local economy.[15]

The trends reported by these aggregate studies are also tentatively supported by a few recent case studies. Researchers at Hull House Associates mailed questionnaires to 6,400 Chicago steelworkers who were laid off from the U.S. Steel Corporation's South Works plants in 1979.[16] With a low response rate of 14 percent, their results describe the circumstances of a nonrepresentative sample of displaced workers. Of those who responded to the survey, 46 percent remained unemployed in 1983. Discouraged by years of job search failure, many reported that they had given up looking for work. Of those who had found jobs, average incomes had dropped from a reported $22,000 in 1979 to $12,000 in 1983. Terry F. Buss and F. Stevens Redburn followed steelworkers laid off in 1977 from the Youngstown Sheet and Tube Company.[17] Initial interviews were conducted with 300 displaced workers during the summers of 1978 and 1979, with a follow-up study of 155 workers completed in 1985. The authors found that in 1985, eight years after the initial layoffs, two-thirds of their sample were either reemployed (32.3 percent) or retired (33.3 percent). Approximately 14.5 percent were unemployed, and 13.4 percent had left the area. Most of the reemployed workers had suffered losses in income and frequent spells of unemployment. A 1986 survey of 401 households in Duquesne, Pennsylvania, a depressed industrial community in the Monongahela Valley near Pittsburgh, found a high 21 percent of the labor force unemployed. Among those who were working, 54 percent were making less than $7 an hour.[18]

These studies of displaced industrial workers are among the first to emerge from the rash of plant closures and contractions in the late 1970s and early 1980s. Their findings on unemployment and underemployment are consistent with the results of other plant closure studies conducted primarily in the 1960s; if and when displaced industrial workers secure reemployment, it is often at reduced income and job status.[19]

Thus, for many contemporary displaced manufacturing workers, job loss may mean prolonged unemployment, or reemployment at irregular or low-paying work. These economic shifts, in turn, affect interpersonal and community relations.

THE SOCIAL AND PSYCHOLOGICAL EFFECTS OF JOB AND INCOME LOSS

In addition to chronic unemployment and income loss, economic dislocation also exacts a toll on social and emotional well-being.

Psychologists list job loss, along with marriage, divorce, and the death of a spouse, as among life's most stress-producing events.[20] In addition to worries over the loss of income and future security, unemployment often triggers doubts regarding self-worth, identity, and personal efficacy. Such feelings can be compounded in situations involving plant closings, because in such circumstances unemployment and income loss are often long term, and there are diminished options for reemployment at previous wage levels.

Research on the social and psychological effects of structural unemployment and income loss has clustered in three time periods: during the Great Depression; in the early 1960s, when automation threatened to displace industrial workers; and recently as a result of the increase in plant closings during the last decade. The most extensive studies of the effects of unemployment and income loss on well-being were conducted in the 1930s during the Great Depression.[21] Though these reports were completed over 50 years ago, the descriptions contained in them are often strikingly similar to more recent accounts of the experiences of persons living in depressed industrial communities in the 1980s.

As with many studies of contemporary displaced workers, the Depression studies focused primarily on persons who had previously held steady employment. Observing families who were experiencing downward mobility as a result of the prolonged unemployment of a primary wage earner, the researchers described patterns of response to joblessness that included anxiety and depression, impaired self-concept, disturbed interpersonal relations, and increased family conflict. Analyzing life-style changes that often accompanied unemployment during the 1930s, Ruth S. Cavan and Katherine H. Ranck found that job loss was often first greeted by workers and their families as a temporary situation—a needed vacation—with the workers holding out high hopes for reemployment at similar wages. As the duration of unemployment increased, the workers became willing to take jobs of lesser skill and pay. To make ends meet, families used credit and savings, sold possessions, cashed insurance policies, moved in with relatives, and limited their social activities. Applications for public relief were viewed as a last resort and a humiliating experience.[22] Such changes in life-style were also accompanied by attitudinal shifts. Reviewing Depression-era literature on the psychology of unemployment, Philip Eisenberg and Paul F. Lazarsfeld described a *process* of response to long-term unemployment and income loss.

> We find that all writers who have described the course of unemployment seem to agree on the following points: first there is shock, which is followed by an active hunt for a job, during which the individual is still optimistic and unresigned; he still maintains an unbroken attitude. Second, when all efforts fail, the

> individual becomes pessimistic, anxious and suffers active distress: this is the most crucial state of all. And third, the individual becomes fatalistic and adapts himself to his new state but with a narrower scope. He now has a broken attitude.[23]

It was also noted that the long-term loss of income frequently altered family roles, which in turn caused tension and conflict. Edward Wight Bakke observed that as the Depression dragged on, women and children increasingly sought odd jobs to supplement income, necessitating a redistribution of duties within the household.[24] Role reallocation often took place in a tense and emotionally charged atmosphere in which the husband's failure to adequately provide for the family was a central issue. Studies by Mirra Komarovsky[25] and Eli Ginsberg[26] reported that both husbands and wives manifested anxiety, discouragement, and depression. Some drank heavily; others had "nervous breakdowns." Komarovsky concluded that most destructive to the family was an erosion of the primary wage earner's self-concept and sense of self-reliance. The humiliation of downward mobility was seen to cut away at the unemployed man's conception of his masculinity, and he was described as feeling adrift in a society where employment and the wage-earner role were primary sources of self-respect.

Contemporary writings on the social and psychological effects of job loss build on many of the observations of the Depression-era studies. A summary by Craig King[27] of findings from studies of plant closings conducted primarily in the 1960s and 1970s found that reactions to job loss and prolonged unemployment form a pattern of response similar to that described by Eisenberg and Lazarsfeld. Denial and disbelief are often the first responses to rumors of termination, followed by high anxiety as the shutdown is announced and layoffs begin. The initial period of unemployment is often viewed as a time of relaxation, with workers frequently exhibiting optimism and making aggressive efforts to find a new job. Persons still unemployed several months after their job loss may experience insecurity and self-doubt, depression, feelings of inadequacy, mood swings, and marital or interpersonal problems.[28] This may be followed by the onset of malaise and an increase in listlessness and resignation. Variables found to mitigate these deleterious responses included length of unemployment, age, and the presence of another wage earner in the household.[29]

Common reactions to prolonged unemployment and irregular employment also include psychological strains such as diminished self-esteem and lowered satisfaction with life.[30] In a classic work on long-term unemployment conducted in the 1960s, Richard Wilcock and Walter H. Franke suggested that one of the most serious impacts of plant shutdowns was a loss of confidence and increased feelings of uselessness among unemployed workers. They noted that "when he [the displaced

worker] is severed from his job, he discovers that he has lost, in addition to the income and activity, his institutional base in the economic and social system."[31]

Such feelings of detachment, uselessness, and self-doubt can lead to more serious emotional distress. Numerous studies have linked job loss to a rise in mental illness—from mild depression to psychosis.[32] In one of these studies, David Dooley and Ralph Catalano reviewed longitudinal and time-series studies that take into account the temporal position of economic disruption and behavioral disorder, and reported a positive association between job loss and subsequent behavioral or self-reported symptoms. Sidney Cobb and Stanislaw Kasl employed a quasi-experimental research design to collect psychological and physiological information on a group of 100 workers who lost jobs to plant closings, as well as a control group of employees working at a plant that was not threatened with closure.[33] Measurements were taken over two and one-half years, both before and after the plant closings. Their study revealed that job loss and unemployment were linked with an increase in feelings of depression, anger, alienation, and suspicion.

In his much-publicized aggregate studies, Harvey M. Brenner examined the statistical linkages between economic and social health.[34] Analyzing national data from the years 1940–73, Brenner studied associations between indicators of economic stress (including per capita income, the rate of inflation, and the unemployment rate), and indices of social pathology (such as age- and sex-specific mortality rates, mental hospital admission rates, and imprisonment rates). Brenner's work showed that all indices of pathology increased with higher rates of unemployment, and that the patterns had been consistent over several decades. In terms of psychological pathology, Brenner concluded that a 1 percent increase in the aggregate unemployment rate sustained over a six-year period was associated with an additional 920 suicides, 650 homicides, 4,000 state mental hospital admissions, and 3,300 state prison admissions.

This aggregate data is supported by various case study reports. Following the closing of a roller bearing plant in Detroit, 8 of the 2,000 affected workers committed suicide.[35] Unemployed steelworkers from Youngstown, Ohio, displayed greater levels of aggression and anxiety than those who were reemployed.[36] Family arguments, child abuse, and spouse abuse have been found to be exacerbated by job loss, as has alcohol abuse.[37]

Though research indicates a positive association between economic dislocation and emotional distress, the relationship is complex, with numerous mitigating variables. Studies suggest that the basic relationship between job loss and behavioral disorder is moderated by personal and environmental factors. Richard M. Cohn found that the negative psychological effects of unemployment are decreased if employment is not one's primary role, and if job loss can be attributed to the environment rather

than to oneself.[38] Though mental and physical symptoms were seen to get worse with prolonged unemployment, Felicia M. Foltman reported that workers who acquire new jobs at a lower status and lower earnings have even poorer mental health scores than those who remain unemployed.[39] Several researchers have suggested that the presence of a strong social support network—in the form of family and friends—facilitates positive adjustment to job loss.[40] Other factors seen to impact adjustment to job or income loss include age, number of years on the job, education, and the availability of future employment options.[41]

THE EFFECTS OF PLANT CLOSINGS ON LOCAL COMMUNITIES

The economic and interpersonal shifts precipitated by economic dislocation also impact the communities in which displaced workers live and work. Difficulties involving income loss, unemployment, and emotional and physical stress often present displaced workers with novel problem-solving situations requiring special mobilization of community resources. Unfortunately, local towns, particularly those in which the plants were the primary employers, may find it difficult to provide for a new population of vulnerable and needy.

Mill shutdowns often set off a chain of events that have a negative impact on the local economy. The reduced purchasing power of large numbers of unemployed workers often causes local retail purchases to fall. When manufacturing industries go out of business, supplier companies lose sales and may lay off additional workers or go out of business. The departure of a major employer means a major loss of income and commercial property tax revenues for local government. Real estate values may plummet. Money decreases for city and community services—police, fire fighters, roads, schools, social services.[42]

Such effects vary according to community size, the size of the closed plant and its work force, and the importance of the plant to the local economy. In the spate of plant closings in the 1970s and 1980s, many "rust belt" regions in Michigan, Illinois, Ohio, Pennsylvania, and elsewhere suffered extensive job and revenue loss from industries that comprised the core of the local economy. As with the prolonged depression in Appalachia following the collapse of coal mining in the 1950s and 1960s, many of these formerly industrial areas continue to experience depressed economic and social conditions, making them regional "pockets" of high unemployment, poverty, and underemployment.

The economic and financial strains precipitated by plant closings often coincide with rising social service needs. Unemployment and income loss among community residents spur applications for food stamps and public assistance. Emotional stress heightens needs for counseling and crisis services. Structural shifts in the economy call for job retraining and

employment services. At the same time that local revenues decline, community leaders and social service personnel are often faced with the demand for expanded and innovative programs for a new and growing population in need.

Unfortunately for many communities, massive job loss in the manufacturing sector in the 1980s coincided with the Reagan Administration's reductions in federal domestic spending, with tightened eligibility for public assistance, and with the rise of the philosophy of laissez-faire and community self-help. The Omnibus Budget Reconciliation Act (OBRA) of 1981 cut $25 billion in federal domestic spending. The cuts included reductions in programs including Aid to Families with Dependent Children (AFDC), food stamps, housing assistance, legal services, community development, home energy assistance, and numerous others. The Comprehensive Employment and Training Act (CETA) was abolished, eliminating 300,000 public sector jobs. CETA was replaced with the Job Training Partnership Act (JTPA), with funding 40 percent below that of CETA. Despite the loss nationwide of hundreds of thousands of manufacturing jobs, no new federal community or employment development efforts were directed to declining industrial locales. In addition to cuts in employment and social service programs, OBRA also legislated a number of program eligibility changes aimed at limiting access by the working poor to public assistance programs.[43]

These cuts in federal domestic spending and the lack of community development initiatives were in line with the Reagan administration's vision of reduced federal intervention in community social problem solving. Individuals and local communities were encouraged to look to their own initiative rather than to the resources of the federal government in solving social problems. The Administration projected that economic growth and increased work effort would reduce the need for expanded federal social program assistance. Restrictive monetary policy aimed at lowering inflation, with supply-side tax, spending, and regulatory policies, were to spur economic growth, the benefits of which would "trickle down" to the disadvantaged. It was projected that an expanding service economy would absorb workers displaced from industrial jobs; government could best promote their readjustment through initiatives aimed at increasing the demand for labor through economic growth. Cuts in social services and public assistance were expected to make work a more attractive alternative to welfare dependency, and increase work effort and productivity. With an emphasis on increased self-sufficiency and productivity, individuals were encouraged to seek aid from their own private networks of support, as opposed to those of the government. Communities and individuals were asked to look more to family, neighbors, friends, and volunteers for provision of both emotional and material assistance.

SUMMARY

Research to date indicates that a progressive shift in the United States from an industrial to a service economy forecasts continued plant closures and an increase in low-wage service employment. Displaced industrial workers are likely to experience prolonged unemployment and income loss, which may precipitate a host of emotional and interpersonal problems. The communities that have been hardest hit by the industrial decline of the 1980s are often geographically separate from areas of the country experiencing economic expansion, and they frequently represent regional pockets of chronic unemployment and underemployment. The rash of plant closings in the 1970s and 1980s coincided with federal cuts in social spending and regulatory changes that limited social program participation, particularly for persons with some labor market attachment. Federal policy during the last decade encouraged individual and family initiatives in social problem solving, while discouraging government involvement in community development efforts.

How have displaced manufacturing workers from hard-hit industrial communities responded to economic dislocation in the 1980s? To what extent have they succeeded in mobilizing new sources of material, emotional, and community support? How have they fared in the service economy? Little in-depth information is available on changes in living, coping, and resource mobilization among recently displaced workers. Such coping and adaptation include specifics of life-style shifts from middle income to poor, social service utilization, reliance on informal networks of family and friends, and decisions regarding whether or not to remain in an economically depressed area or seek employment elsewhere. Though scattered anecdotal reports have alluded to depressed standards of living in some areas hit by plant closures, little information is available on the long-term effects of their displacement, including the proportion and characteristics of households that fall below the poverty line, as well as those that maintain a middle-income status.

As described in the following chapters, many of the displaced steelworkers from the Shenango Valley represent a new class of poor and underemployed. As with many other locales affected by manufacturing decline, the community has struggled to address novel social and economic problems with minimal public and corporate guidance and support. The experiences of the community's working poor echo those of people in diverse areas across the country: the nation's growing service economy includes a large proportion of irregular, low-paying jobs offering few fringe benefits; these low earners evidence unique social and economic problems and needs. As such, the purview offered by the case study of the Shenango Valley is that of another America: people who suffered the downside of the American dream during the "prosperous" decade of the 1980s.

NOTES

1. Louis Harris, "Public Looks Back on 1980s with Growing Sense of Criticism," *The Harris Poll*, 29 July 1990.

2. Kevin Phillips, *The Politics of Rich and Poor* (New York: Random House, 1990).

3. Office of Technology Assessment, *Technology and Structural Unemployment* (Washington, DC: U.S. Congress).

4. See Daniel Bell, *The Coming of Post-Industrial Society* (New York: Basic, 1973); Ronald K. Shelp, *Beyond Industrialization: Ascendancy of the Global Service Economy* (New York: Praeger, 1981); and John Gershuny and Ian Miles, *The New Service Economy* (New York: Praeger, 1983).

5. Office of Technology Assessment, *Technology and Structural Unemployment*; Malcolm R. Lovell, Jr., "A New Approach to Encourage Reemployment" (paper delivered at the National Issues Forum on Displaced American Workers, Brookings Institution, Washington, DC), December 1983.

6. See Barry Bluestone and Bennett Harrison, *The Deindustrialization of America* (New York: Basic, 1982); Stephen S. Cohen and John Zysman, *Manufacturing Matters* (New York: Basic, 1987).

7. U.S. Department of Labor, Bureau of Labor Statistics, *Displaced Workers Survey* data file, Washington, DC: Bureau of Labor Statistics, January 1986.

8. Cohen and Zysman, *Manufacturing Matters*; U.S. Department of Commerce, Bureau of Economic Analysis, *Survey of Current Business*, June 1981, pp. S-11, S-12.

9. Barry Bluestone and Bennett Harrison, *The Great American Jobs Machine: Low-Wage Work and the Polarization of Wages*, report prepared for the Joint Economic Committee, U.S. Congress (Washington, DC: U.S. Government Printing Office, 1986); William Schmidt, "Hard Work Can't Stop Hard Times," *New York Times*, November 25, 1990, pp. 1, 30.

10. See McKinley Blackburn and David Bloom, "Regional Roulette," *American Demographics* 10, no. 1 (1988): 32–36; Jason DeParle, "Richer Rich, Poorer Poor, and a Fatter Green Book," *New York Times*, May 26, 1991, p. 2E; Phillips, *Politics of Rich and Poor*.

11. Phillips, *Politics of Rich and Poor*, p. 18.

12. Schmidt, "Hard Work," p. 30; William O'Hare, "Poverty in America: Trends and New Patterns," *Population Bulletin* 40, no. 3 (1985): 3–45.

13. U.S. Department of Labor, *Economic Adjustment and Worker Dislocation in a Competitive Society* (Washington, DC: U.S. Government Printing Office, December 1986).

14. Paul O. Flaim and Ellen Sehgal, "Displaced Workers of 1979–83: How Well Have They Fared?" *Monthly Labor Review* 108 (June 1985): 3–16.

15. Marie Howland and George E. Peterson, "Labor Market Conditions and the Reemployment of Displaced Workers," *Industrial and Labor Relations Review* 42, no. 1 (October 1988): 109–122.

16. Julie S. Putterman, *Chicago Steelworkers: The Cost of Unemployment* (Chicago: Hull House Association, January 1985).

17. Terry F. Buss and F. Stevens Redburn, *Shutdown at Youngstown* (Albany, NY: State University of New York Press, 1983); Terry F. Buss and F. Stevens Redburn, "The Closing of Youngstown Sheet and Tube," *Entrepreneurial Economy* 5, no. 5 (1987): 2–5.

18. David E. Biegel, James Cunningham, Hide Yamatani, and Pamela Martz, "Self-Reliance and Blue-Collar Unemployment in a Steel Town," *Social Work* 34, no. 5 (1989): 399–406.

19. See Herbert Hammerman, "Five Case Studies of Displaced Workers," *Monthly Labor Review* 87, no. 6 (1964): 663–70; David B. Lipsky, "Interplant Transfer and Terminated Workers: A Case Study," *Industrial and Labor Relations Review* 23, no. 2 (1970): 191–206; Michael Aiken, Louis A. Ferman, and Harold L. Sheppard, *Economic Failure, Alienation, and Extremism* (Ann Arbor, MI: University of Michigan Press, 1968).

20. T. H. Holmes and R. E. Rahe, "The Social Readjustment Rating Scale," *Journal of Psychosomatic Research* 11 (1967): 213–18.

21. See Robert C. Angell, *The Family Encounters the Depression* (New York: Scribner's, 1936); Edward Wight Bakke, *Citizens without Work* (New Haven, CT: Yale University Press, 1940); Ruth Shonle Cavan and Katherine Howland Ranck, *The Family and the Depression* (Chicago: University of Chicago Press, 1938); Eli Ginsberg, *The Unemployed* (New York: Harper, 1943); Mirra Komarovsky, *The Unemployed Man and His Family* (New York: Octagon, 1940).

22. Cavan and Ranck, *The Family and the Depression.*

23. Philip Eisenberg and Paul F. Lazarsfeld, "The Psychological Effects of Unemployment," *Psychological Bulletin* 35 (1938): 358–90.

24. Bakke, *Citizens without Work.*

25. Komarovsky, *Unemployed Man.*

26. Ginsberg, *The Unemployed.*

27. Craig King, *The Social Impacts of Mass Layoffs* (Ann Arbor, MI: University of Michigan Press, 1982).

28. King, *Social Impacts,* p. 70; Terry Buss and F. Stevens Redburn, *Mass Unemployment: Plant Closings and Community Mental Health* (Beverly Hills, CA: Sage, 1983), 31.

29. Douglas H. Powell and Patricia Joseph Driscoll, "Middle-Class Professionals Face Unemployment," *Society* 10 (1973): 18–26; Alfred Slote, *Termination: The Closing of Baker Plant* (Indianapolis, IN: Bobbs-Merrill, 1969); Thomas D. Taber, Jeffrey T. Walsh, and Robert A. Cooke, "Developing a Community-based Program for Reducing the Impact of a Plant Closing," *Journal of Applied Behavioral Science* 15 (1979): 133–55.

30. Richard M. Cohn, "The Effects of Employment Status Change on Self Attitudes," *Social Psychology* 41 (1978): 81–93; Herbert S. Parnes and Randy King, "Middle-Aged Job Losers," *Industrial Gerontology* 4, no. 2 (1977): 77–95.

31. Richard Wilcock and Walter H. Franke, *Unwanted Workers: Permanent Layoffs and Long-Term Unemployment* (New York: Glencoe, 1963), as cited in Bluestone and Harrison, *Deindustrialization of America,* p. 66.

32. See Buss and Redburn, *Mass Unemployment;* Sidney Cobb and Stanislaw Kasl, *Termination: The Consequences of Job Loss* Report No. 76-1261, Washington, DC: Public Health Service, Center for Disease Control, National Institute for Occupational Safety and Health, U.S. Department of Health, Education, and Welfare, June 1977; P. Komora and M. Clark, "Mental Disease in the Life Crisis," *Mental Hygiene* 19 (1935); David Dooley and Ralph Catalano, "Economic Change as a Cause of Behavioral Disorder," *Psychological Bulletin* 87, no. 3 (1980): 450–68.

33. Cobb and Kasl, *Termination.*

3

Setting: The Shenango Valley Community

The Shenango Valley is located in Western Pennsylvania, 90 miles north of Pittsburgh and 9 miles east of Youngstown, Ohio, in what was once a center for the manufacture and fabrication of steel and steel products. Situated in Mercer County, the area is made up of a cluster of small towns, including Sharon, Farrell, Wheatland, and Hermitage. With a combined population of about 60,000, the towns lie along the Shenango River on the Pennsylvania-Ohio border.

The Shenango Valley is a solidly blue-collar community. Once employing almost 60 percent of the local work force, manufacturing plants have long dominated the physical and economic landscape of the valley and have been a primary factor in shaping the structure and organization of the community. When several mills closed their doors in the early 1980s, many community residents faced both an economic and an identity crisis. In retreat was the source and focus of jobs, income, and collective activity and meaning around which the community had been built.

THE LEGACY OF FRANK BUHL

Every year in the Shenango Valley, Labor Day is celebrated as Buhl Day, in honor of the industrialist Frank Buhl. It was Buhl who opened the valley's first steel mill in 1886, and more than a century later his stature in the community remains great.

Originally from Detroit, the industrialist made the valley his home after marrying a local woman, and proceeded to establish several area steel manufacturing and fabrication mills. Other industrialists followed his lead, and by the turn of the century the Shenango Valley was home to numerous manufacturing plants. In the tradition of the nineteenth-century paternal entrepreneur, Buhl presided over the valley like a provident father. He lived

in a stone mansion on a hill above the flatlands where the valley's manufacturing plants were built. He employed thousands of people; made millions of dollars; bequeathed to the area Buhl Hospital, Buhl Library, and Buhl Park; and endowed numerous other community charities and recreational facilities.

The town has officially declared Frank Buhl its First Citizen. On Labor Day, Buhl Day is celebrated in the lush 300-acre park that bears his name. Thousands of residents congregate each year for a community picnic that includes parades, polka bands, and a spread of ethnic foods. Though many of the mills in the area have closed and many of those in attendance are no longer employed as mill workers, Buhl remains a popular and powerful symbol of the community.

Built with the profits of industry, the hospital, library, park, and other of Buhl's endowments are, in effect, products of the labor of previous generations of workers. To the current generation, these highly valued community assets represent and validate the hard labor of grandparents, relatives, neighbors, and friends on which the factories and the community were built. Buhl was a paternal figure, and to many local citizens his beneficence represents approval of the efforts of his employees. As such, Buhl is a symbol of a company/labor relationship that defined community activities in the Shenango Valley for decades and continues to shape the world view of many local residents. Paternal in orientation, that relationship was grounded in what has been described in other manufacturing towns as a familial "spirit of covenant" or mutual obligation.[1] Manufacturing employers provided for their employees by way of jobs, security, and community-based philanthropy. In return they expected a labor force dependent on and loyal to the factory system.

THE PHYSICAL ENVIRONMENT

Sharon is the central city in the cluster of towns that make up the Shenango Valley. With 18,000 residents, it is among the largest local cities in population and a center for business. Its downtown is small and quiet, with many of its buildings dating to the early 1900s. On the hillsides of State Street—its main thoroughfare—stand a number of stately old houses formerly occupied by industry owners and the city's elite. Most of these large houses are no longer private residences. The Buhl mansion was renovated into the Wilmar School of Beauty and several of the others are funeral homes. Stretching east, State Street turns into a strip of fast-food restaurants and shopping malls—national chain stores that over the past decades have replaced many locally owned shops. Through the center of town, the Shenango River cuts a path perpendicular to State Street. The road that runs along the river is lined with manufacturing plants, and they occupy the same strip of land that was initially developed by industrialists in the early 1900s.

34. Harvey M. Brenner, *Mental Illness and the Economy* (Cambridge, MA: Harvard University Press, 1973); Harvey M. Brenner, *Estimating the Social Costs of National Economic Policy: Implications for Mental and Physical Health and Clinical Aggression*, report prepared for the Joint Economic Committee, U.S. Congress (Washington, DC: U.S. Government Printing Office, 1976).

35. Don Stillman, "The Devastating Impact of Plant Relocations," *Working Papers for a New Society* 5, no. 4 (1978): 42–53, as cited in Bluestone and Harrison, *Deindustrialization of America*, p. 65.

36. Buss and Redburn, Mass Unemployment.

37. See Katherine Briar, "The Effects of Unemployment on Workers and Families," Doctoral diss., School of Social Welfare, University of California, Berkeley, 1976; Blair Justice and David Duncan, "Life Crisis as a Precursor to Child Abuse," *Public Health Reports* 111 (1976); King, *Social Impacts*.

38. Cohn, "Effects of Employment Status Change."

39. Felicia M. Foltman, *White and Blue Collars in a Mill Shutdown* (Ithaca, NY: Cornell University Press, 1968).

40. See Sidney Cobb, "Social Support as a Moderator of Life Stress," *Psychosomatic Medicine* 38 (1976): 300-14; Alfred Dean and Nan Lin. "The Stress-Buffering Role of Social Support: Problems and Prospects for Systematic Investigation," *Journal of Nervous and Mental Disease* 165 (1977): 403-17; Berton H. Kaplan, John Cassel, and Susan Gore, "Social Support and Health," *Medical Care* 15 (1977): 47-58.

41. King, *Social Impacts*.

42. See C & R Associates, *Community Costs of Plant Closings: Bibliography and Survey of t he Literature* Report No. LO362, Washington, DC: Federal Trade Commission, July 1978; Bluestone and Harrison, *Deindustrialization of America*, pp. 67-72.

43. John L. Palmer and Isabel V. Sawhill (eds.), *The Reagan Record* (Cambridge, MA: Ballinger, 1984).

The plants stretch for miles, their frames huge and dark. Several are now boarded up; a few remain in operation. Down the street in front of a working mill, an open door or window shows a glimpse of what looks like an eerie other world: a dim, smoky interior with flashes of sparks or orange molten steel. The factory smokestacks lend a slight sulphur smell to the air. At night, emissions from a steel manufacturing plant light the sky with a soft pink glow. Mill whistles blast at 12 noon and 10 p.m., sounding through the entire community. As such, the mills have long provided something of a sensory cloak to residents of the valley: they tint the sky, cast a sulphur smell, loom large, and send out regular auditory signals.

COMMUNITY LIFE

Manufacturing also overlays community activities. For years, thousands of residents packed a lunch bucket and headed for a factory to make a living. This activity, shared by a majority of the town dwellers, shaped family, social, and community routines.

Much of community life, for example, was organized around the institution of the swing shift. In two-week spells, most factory workers alternately worked a day turn, from 7:00 a.m. to 3:00 p.m.; an afternoon turn, from 3:00 p.m. to 11:00 p.m.; and a midnight turn, from 11:00 p.m. to 7:00 a.m. The downtown rush hour occurred at the 3:00 p.m. shift change, and many family dinners were served at 4:00 p.m. The Steel Cafe and numerous other taverns that line the streets around the mills filled at shift change as some men gathered for the traditional shot of whiskey and a beer after work. Individuals working the midnight turn often tried to sleep during the day, and a good neighbor refrained from mowing the grass when the noise might disturb a neighbor on night shift attempting to nap. Processes as diverse as traffic patterns, meal times, and neighborhood etiquette functioned in accord with the requisites of mill work.

The character and organization of community life has also been affected by the cultivation, among thousands of residents, of the personal attributes required of factory work. A majority of jobs in local mills required various degrees of physical strength. Factory workers would often remark that they had been hired as "a back." Stamina was a marketable asset, and providing for one's family often entailed a traditional male linking of strength and endurance to income. Planning for their futures, men would bid for less physically strenuous jobs as they advanced in age, ensuring their ability to continue to function as providers. For the breadwinner, responsible planning also included staying with one mill over the course of one's work life, because taking a series of jobs at various mills resulted in low seniority and reduced pension benefits upon retirement.

Mill employees were also subject to potential health risks. Though conditions in the mills have been much improved over the decades, many

plants are still full of smoke, soot, and physical hazards. Mill workers speak of the risk of physical injury as an ever-present threat that goes along with the job. Both minor and serious injuries occur: strained backs, broken limbs, burns from welding flash. Fatal industrial accidents in Shenango Valley mills were not uncommon. Workers at a local foundry had a high incidence of siliocis and respiratory ailments, and hearing loss from machine noise is commonplace. There is speculation that an elevated cancer rate in the vicinity is associated with industrial air and water pollutants. Among both mill workers and community residents, risks to health have long been one of the side effects of the manufacturing economy.

HISTORICAL SETTING

The reliance of local residents on manufacturing employers and their immersion in a mill town environment dates back almost to the founding of the area in the late 1700s. The discovery of local deposits of iron ore and blast coal in the early 1800s led to the rapid development of an iron production industry in the Shenango Valley area, and by 1870 the county boasted 458 small manufacturing establishments, many of them iron-producing blast furnaces. The steel plant opened by Frank Buhl in 1886 was among the first of dozens of steel manufacturing and fabrication plants to set up shop in the valley, and by 1900 steel manufacturing had replaced iron production as the area's primary industry. A county historian writing in 1909 asserted that manufacturing "has for years been the largest single resource of the county and the dependence of thousands of people for means of existence."[2]

Immigrant Labor

With the demand for factory labor high, thousands of immigrants, mostly from Italy and Eastern Europe, came to the valley at the turn of the century to work at the Carnegie Steel Company, American Steel Castings, Sharon Steel Works, and numerous other manufacturing plants.

Immigrants coming to the area settled within walking distance of the mills, in neighborhoods populated by ethnic groups that included Hungarian, Polish, Slovak, Croatian, Italian, German, and Rumanian. Most of the immigrants had come from peasant villages, so their initiation into factory work and mill town life was often difficult and bewildering. The congested neighborhoods surrounding the factories were a jangle of foreign languages, foods, and customs. Between the emissions from factory smokestacks and those from home coal stoves, the air in town was often thick with soot and dust and smelled of sulphur.

Before coming to the United States, most immigrants had worked on farms in their native countries. Now they labored inside dimly lit plants that were noisy, filthy, and dangerous. Their lack of education and language

skills was no barrier to employment. Newly arrived immigrants worked common labor jobs in the lowest ranks of the manufacturing and steel industries. Making a living as a mill worker required physical strength and the stamina to withstand heavy labor and 10- or 12-hour work days in a grimy, hot, hazardous mill. Death or serious injury on the job were frequent. The Pittsburgh Survey, conducted in the early 1900s, conservatively estimated that 25 percent of recent immigrants who worked in steel mills were injured or killed on the job each year.[3] In addition to being dangerous, the employment was also intermittent. Long layoffs accompanied downturns in the business cycle, with annual stretches of joblessness and lost income the norm for most immigrant mill workers.

Despite what were often difficult working and living conditions, immigrants lined up by the thousands for factory jobs in areas like the Shenango Valley. There was not much choice—the factories were the providers of the means of existence. In search of an alternative to the rural poverty of their home villages, the immigrants put up with filth, danger, and hard labor in exchange for a job and the hope of upward mobility. Most believed this was a necessary sacrifice toward a better life. They gained a reputation as hard workers intent on saving money. As one immigrant described his work in a Western Pennsylvania steel mill, "A good job, save money, work all time, go home, sleep, no spend."[4]

Social Networks Among Immigrant Workers

The harshness of factory work was buffered somewhat by tightly knit networks of ethnic cohorts. Arriving in a strange country and work environment, the immigrants most often sought relatives and compatriots as neighbors and friends. In what has been described as "chain migration," the immigrants often moved to areas like the Shenango Valley in the wake of family and acquaintances who had come before them.[5] These contacts helped arrange for housing and employment and provided a support system for the newcomers. Many new arrivals initially moved in with close and extended family, who then helped them find a factory job. Many mill workers labored alongside relatives and acquaintances from their home villages.

Ethnic groups also organized their own religious and social activities. They formed churches with native-language priests and ministers that carried on the customs and celebrations of the old country and provided social assistance, such as aid to the sick and elderly.

The ethnic groups also had their own social clubs—often called "homes"—where members gathered for drinks, conversation, and music. Walking the streets of the ethnic neighborhoods, one would come across the Slovenian Home, Italian Club, Serbian Home, and many others.

Ethnic groups also provided mutual help in the form of "lodges" or

benefit societies. Given the vagaries and dangers of factory work and the absence of government social insurance programs, these lodges were established to provide a cash benefit to dues-paying members who lost wages due to injury, illness, or death.

Thus, with the rise of manufacturing in the Shenango Valley, the local community was built in large part by ethnic and immigrant groups who organized their lives around familiar, densely knit networks of friends and kin. These associates provided both emotional and material support in an alien living and working environment. Across the various ethnic groups living in the valley, a shared identity and loyalty to the community developed, as residents found their lives conditioned by common past and present experiences. The social world of the Shenango Valley consisted of tightly knit ethnic clusters representing a dozen languages and "old country" cultures, united by their community of residence and occupational identity as mill workers.

Industrial Collapse and Revitalization

The influx of immigrants and rapid industrial development in the Shenango Valley continued until the Great Depression, when the manufacturing boom collapsed. Plants closed or drastically curtailed operations, and all but a fraction of the area's mill workers were laid off. For over a decade, the blue-collar population suffered prolonged unemployment and income loss. The situation did not turn around until the second world war, when orders for military hardware once again brought a boom to local industry.

With the mills running at full capacity, the area actually experienced a labor shortage. Local women stepped in to assume factory labor jobs, and companies recruited black workers from Southern states to fill vacant industrial slots. Representing a new wave of immigrant labor, the black workers settled in neighborhoods contiguous to the mills where European immigrants had previously been concentrated. Many of the black workers and virtually all of the female laborers subsequently suffered layoffs in the late 1940s, as returning GIs made claim to industrial slots. Blacks were not rehired in the mills in large numbers until the mid-1960s. Women were not recruited for laborer positions again until the early 1970s, and their numbers never exceeded 1 or 2 percent of total employees.

After the war, industrial production remained steady, as goods were manufactured for consumer items, and through the 1950s and 1960s manufacturing employed a majority of the local work force. Steel manufacturing and fabrication, electrical transformer production, and pipe and tube manufactures fueled the local economy. Unions, which had gained recognition in local mills in the mid-1930s, grew in strength, and the United Steelworkers of America (USWA) and the International Union of Electrical and Radio and Machine Workers became the dominant labor unions in the

area. During the 1960s, the civil rights movement and a prosperous economy served as catalysts for the increased hiring of black mill workers. Conditions in the mills improved somewhat; the plants were cleaner and safer. Wages and benefits rose steadily. For the most part, the blue-collar workers employed in the mills gained a middle-income status. Through the 1960s there was a sense among valley residents that the mill workers were getting their due—that the sacrifices of grandparents, the organizing efforts of union members, and the workers' long-term loyalty to local companies had paid off in terms of a reasonably comfortable living standard.

In line with national trends, manufacturing began to show signs of decline in the early 1970s. Plants slowly but steadily stabilized or decreased the size of their work forces, primarily by failing to replace retirees. Nevertheless, a rising standard of living and a sense of security in the jobs provided by local industry persisted in the valley through the mid-1970s. Although local manufacturing companies were increasingly being sold to nonlocal owners or business conglomerates—the Buhls, for instance, had long since divested their plants—there continued to be a perception that industry had a familial commitment to the valley. Local residents, media, and town officials expressed the opinion that industry appreciated a labor force that was loyal, skilled, and conditioned to factory work. Local mill workers felt that they had kept their part of the labor covenant; upon retirement most had worked upwards of 25 years in the local plants. Likewise, town officials continued to do everything they could to accommodate industry owners, including backing away from demands for stricter pollution standards. It was assumed that industry would continue to find the valley a favorable manufacturing site. Through the 1970s, steel manufacturing and fabrication, pipe and tube manufactures, and electrical transformer manufacturing remained the valley's core industries. Local plants, including those of Westinghouse, Sharon Steel, National Castings, Shenango Furnace, General American Transportation Corporation (GATX), and Wheatland Tube, employed approximately 14,000 workers.

THE COMMUNITY BEFORE THE PLANT CLOSINGS

Prior to the wave of plant closings that hit the Shenango Valley in the early 1980s, manufacturing remained—as it had been for decades—the primary employer and central organizing force in the community. At the turn of the century, manufacturing had shaped immigration, work, living conditions, and social interaction. Similarly, in the 1980s, manufacturing continued to condition numerous aspects of community life, including the physical environment, population flow, income and employment, health, recreation, and social relations.

The area retains a strong ethnic character, and as in previous generations, social networks are often intimate and closely knit. The Italian Home, Serbian Club, Slovak Home, and others still have sizable memberships, and

there are numerous local ethnic dance and entertainment groups. Many local churches can still be identified with distinct Eastern European, Italian, or other immigrant groups, with their social activities, weddings, and food sales retaining ethnic and "old country" traditions. The valley contains 97 churches, and they are important social as well as religious centers.

Over the years, the Shenango Valley population has grown steadily older. Though some young people remain in the valley to work in the mills, many depart after high school in search of better job opportunities or to go to college. A majority of those who go do not return, leaving the valley to an older, more homogeneous, home-bound, working-class population. Among those who work the mills, many are second- and third-generation factory workers who have lived in the valley most of their lives.

As in previous decades, social groups tend to overlap. Neighbors are also coworkers; kin are church fellows; and coworkers include family. The social circles of the majority of residents are quite similar. Their acquaintances tend to be blue collar, of moderate income, and long-time valley residents. Primary-group ties are generally strong, and relations among neighbors, families, and friends often go back decades. Working in a mill often takes on a primary-group form, as men labor 20 to 40 years with coworkers who include relatives and neighbors as well as friends.

Hunting, fishing, and hiking are among the favored leisure pursuits of local residents. The first day of deer-hunting season is a local school holiday, and cabins in the nearby Allegheny mountains are a popular retreat. Many people spend much of their spare time constructing and fixing things: in making woodcrafts, house remodeling, working on cars. Bowling, bingo, and church activities are popular. There are also a community symphony and an arts council.

In its 1985 nationwide ranking of community quality of life, Rand McNally listed Sharon, Pennsylvania, as the "least cultured" town in the United States. In a tongue-in-cheek response printed in the local newspaper, one valley resident commented, "Cultureless! Why, the *National Enquirer* can be found in every library in the Valley. And no house is more than a 20-minute drive from a Pennsylvania Lotto machine." Nevertheless, most valley residents have a profound attachment to their community, and its people, history, and working-class roots. Nonresidents, including the writers at Rand McNally, may not value the blue-collar life-style, but most valley residents would consider that the writers' loss.

As described, manufacturing and community have been tightly interwoven in the Shenango Valley for decades. Manufacturing has permeated both physical and social settings. It has influenced what people breathe, with whom they interact, and the attributes they must have to make a living. Many residents of the valley share a common understanding of blue-collar work and a loyalty to the community they have built, and their dense social networks have intensified their personal commitment and attachment to the area.

THE PLANT SHUTDOWNS

In 1977, on what is referred to as Black Monday, 4,000 steelworkers lost jobs in nearby Youngstown, Ohio, when the Youngstown Sheet and Tube Corporation closed its doors. The shutdown stunned the residents of the area. Over the next five years, Youngstown lost an additional 6,000 manufacturing jobs to plant closings.

In the Shenango Valley, tension was mounting between labor and plant management. During the late 1970s, management at several plants had undergone frequent change. Virtually all of the plants in the Shenango Valley were now owned by out-of-town operators. Workers began to complain of a lack of reinvestment in the plants and the community. Management asserted that wages and benefits were too high, profits too low. Unions were asked to grant concessions; some accepted them, others did not. Shutdown notices began. Between 1981 and 1984, seven local plants terminated operations. Within a four-year period an estimated 6,700 manufacturing workers lost jobs. The shutdowns had a ripple effect on the local economy; in addition to the mills, several supplier companies and retail businesses left the area. The Shenango Valley suffered its worst unemployment since the Great Depression, with the jobless rate peaking at 24 percent in January 1983.

Thus, the plant closings that hit the Shenango Valley in the early 1980s disrupted social and economic relations that had evolved over generations. A conception of manufacturing as integral to community no longer held. Local industry, now owned by out-of-town operators and subject to national and international economic pressures, was not obligated to or dependent on Shenango Valley workers for its labor or profits. A dense, interdependent community network was losing its primary economic connection. In retreat was a force that had linked community residents, activities, and institutions for decades.

NOTES

1. Paula Nesbitt, *Beyond Plant Closure: A New Strategy for Corporate Social Responsibility,* paper presented at the annual meeting of the Society for the Study of Social Problems (SSSP), August 1988.

2. J. G. White, *History of Mercer County, Pennsylvania* (Chicago: Lewis, 1909).

3. C. Eastman, *Work Accidents and the Law* (New York: Charities Publication Committee, 1910).

4. Charles Walker, *Steel: The Diary of a Furnace Worker* (Boston: Atlantic Monthly Press, 1922), cited in David Brody, *Steelworkers in America* (Cambridge, MA: Harvard University Press, 1960), p. 100.

5. John S. MacDonald and Leatrice MacDonald, "Chain Migration, Ethnic Neighborhood Formation, and Social Networks," *Milbank Memorial Fund Quarterly* 42 (1964): 92–97.

4

Mill Work and Mill Workers

> The hardest thing when the plant closes is this—you could have been the best steel pourer that mill ever had and it no longer means a thing.
>
> former steelworker, National Castings

Four years after the first plant closings, interviews were held with over 100 former steelworkers from the Shenango Valley. They were asked to describe their work in the mills and to discuss the changes that had taken place in their lives since the shutdowns. These men and women were eager to talk. They had much to say about their unemployment, their job hunts, and their diminished wages and work opportunities. They were also anxious to talk about the mills and the jobs they had held there for 10, 20, or 30 years. These displaced workers offered vivid stories of their labor as steelworkers. Years of immersion in mill work had shaped their emotional and economic responses to job loss, and they provided rich descriptions of the nature of their attachment to the factory system, as well as of the dynamics of their separation from the mills.

In beginning to trace the changes that had occurred among these blue-collar workers, we start with a description of their demographic characteristics, their incomes as mill workers, and their mill work environment.

CHARACTERISTICS OF THE DISPLACED WORKERS

In-person interviews were conducted in the fall of 1987 with 102 randomly selected displaced workers who were residing in the Shenango Valley. All of those interviewed had been employed as hourly manufacturing workers at two local steel fabrication plants, GATX and National Castings, which had closed in 1983 and 1984. The names of these

displaced workers were drawn at random from the United Steelworkers of America (USWA) lists of union employees at these plants. The respondents were representative of the population of hourly manufacturing workers employed by these mills. Interviews were also conducted with 10 displaced workers who had relocated from the Shenango Valley and with 22 directors of local social service agencies. The characteristics of these two latter groups of respondents are given in later chapters. The methodology for the study is detailed in Appendix A.

The 102 survey respondents who were residing in the Shenango Valley were primarily males with a history of blue-collar employment. The majority were long-time valley residents and had been employed in the mills most of their working lives. The characteristics of these persons are summarized in Tables 4.1 and 4.2.

At the time of the interview, the respondents had been laid off from their manufacturing jobs for between 4 and 7 years. Approximately two-thirds had lost their jobs at the time of the mill shutdowns in 1983 and 1984, while the remainder had been laid off between 1980 and 1982, prior to the plant closings.

Of these displaced workers, 50 had been employed at GATX, and 52 at National Castings. GATX had manufactured and assembled railroad tank cars, and National Castings had made steel parts for railroad cars and included a foundry where steel was produced and poured. National Castings had terminated operations in May 1983, a few weeks after its union employees had voted not to accept wage and benefit concessions requested by the company management. GATX had closed in February 1984, about six months after its local union had accepted benefit concessions—a move that management had intimated would prevent a plant closing. The managements of both plants cited lackluster sales and profits among the reasons for termination.

Of the 102 persons interviewed, 99 were male and 3 female; 86 percent were white and 14 percent black. The respondents averaged 16 years' seniority at the mills, though many had worked from 30 to 40 years there. Their mean age was 44.

The educational levels of the displaced workers were quite varied: 77 percent were high school but not college graduates, of whom 17 percent had completed some college-level work and many had postsecondary vocational training; 4 percent of the workers were college graduates, with degrees in teaching, anthropology, or business. At the other extreme, 19 percent had not graduated from high school, and six of these indicated that they were illiterate.

While employed at the mills, the respondents held a variety of skilled, semiskilled, and manual-labor jobs, such as welder, inspector, millwright, general laborer, crane operator, wood pattern maker, machine operator, shipper, core maker, chipper and grinder, electrician, and coiler. Most had followed in the steps of their fathers and grandfathers as blue-collar

Table 4.1
Demographics of Displaced Workers

N = 102	
Sex	
Male	97%
Female	3%
Race	
White	86%
Black	14%
Age	
Mean	44
Range	26–69
Education	
High school not completed	19%
High school graduate, no college	60%
Some college	17%
College graduate	4%
Religious preference	
Catholic	40%
Protestant	57%
Jewish	0%
Other	3%
Marital status	
Married	82%
Widowed	2%
Divorced	5%
Separated	2%
Never married	9%
Household size	
Mean	3.2

Table 4.2
Manufacturing Work Experience of Displaced Workers

N = 102	
Previous employment	
National Castings	51%
GATX	49%
Union membership	
United Steelworkers of America	100%
Year of job loss	
1980	3%
1981	13%
1982	22%
1983	36%
1984	26%
Number of years of seniority	
Mean	16
Range	2–41
Earnings	
Average hourly wage	$12
Median annual individual income	$25,000
Range, annual individual income	$14,000–$35,000

manufacturing workers, with 73 percent reporting that their fathers had been employed in manufacturing, often at the same plants as their offspring. Most of the respondents were also long-time residents of the Shenango Valley; over three-quarters of them had been born and raised there. Those in the remaining quarter averaged 28 years of residence in the area.

Most of the displaced workers reported a strong attachment to the community in which they had lived for so long. Many commented that they enjoyed the company of close-knit family, friends, and neighbors; the slow pace of small-town life; and the accessibility to nearby woods and mountains. Their involvement with home and family was strong. Most had extended family in the area, with 80 percent indicating that

they had seven or more relatives residing in the valley. The majority, 82 percent, were homeowners. Eighty-two percent were married, and many still had children at home or in college. Their average household size was 3.2 persons.

Beyond home and family, hunting and fishing were their most frequently reported leisure pursuits. Most respondents belonged to at least one club or organization, such as a fraternal lodge, ethnic club, or sports team. Most were also church members, with 64 percent attending church regularly.

While employed at the mills, a majority of the displaced workers enjoyed a middle income. At the time of the plant closings, all of those interviewed were members of the United Steelworkers of America. While employed at the plants, they averaged hourly wages of $12* and an annual median individual income of $25,000.

In summary, the respondents in the survey sample tended to be persons with deep roots in the home community. Their connection to mill work extended back over decades, with most being second- and third-generation mill workers. A majority had been born and raised in the Shenango Valley and had been employed most of their working years in the plants. Though blue-collar workers, they had enjoyed a middle-income status.

THE MILL ENVIRONMENT

The mills in which the displaced workers spent most of their working lives were frequently described by them as like "another world": dark, noisy, dirty, cold in the winter, hot in the summer, dangerous, and often frightening. Though their work had given them middle-income wages, there was an acknowledgment among them that the nature and conditions of their employment had been in a realm very different from that known by nonmanufacturing middle-class employees. Mill work carried a distinct physical and social reality. That reality inspired both strong attachment and dislike, and it deeply affected their reaction and adaptation to the subsequent closing of the mills.

In the accounts that follow, the displaced workers describe the conditions and experiences of working in the mills of GATX and National Castings. Their comments are cited verbatim. Some of the citations contain repetitions; the persons interviewed frequently drew on similar images and phrases in describing their experiences in the mills.

> It was almost a surreal image. Dark, with smoke and dust in the air. Little fires everywhere. I had expected it to be more spacious and clean, with central heating.

---

*Hourly rate includes average piecework rates. It does not include the dollar value of fringe benefits.

> It was kind of an eerie-lookin' place, like a fun house. Dark—it was always brighter outside. Machinery and steel everywhere. And busy—everyone always running somewhere.
>
> Your first impression was: dirt. The first day I came to work I walked down the steps into the foundry. There was steam and smoke belching. Like hell itself. I said, "Oh God, what have I done?" I would come home dirty—the dust settles on your clothes. And I would have a mill smell. You stink like the mill.
>
> It's about the most scariest place you can walk into—dirty, dark, dingy, noisy. The temperature inside was always worse than that outside—hotter or colder. I was just out of high school—just had my eighteenth birthday when I started there. I got a lunch bucket as a birthday present.
>
> You would enter the foundry from upstairs. Walk down steps and into a dungeon. A dark hole. Then you'd be hit with the noise and the dirt. The plant was so old the windows were stained brown; a brown light would filter in. You could hear the noise from the street, the banging on steel. There were lots of sparks and sand in the air. It was very dangerous—you had to watch the molten steel.

While inducing such apprehension, the plants were also described by some as holding an air of excitement. Several former mill workers expressed awe or intrigue with the production process.

> It was a marvel what they could manufacture! It was a maze of heavy machinery, and mind-boggling to see the equipment and then the finished product.
>
> It looked exciting to me when I first walked in. It was fascinating to watch the steel production process. It was dangerous and looked dangerous. A new person coming in would be amazed at some of the things people were doing on the job. . . . My first impression was, I'd like to try the work for the thrill of it.

As mentioned earlier, the displaced workers were employed in a variety of mill jobs ranging from highly skilled to manual. Much of the work, though not all of it, involved varying degrees of physical labor. As it had in previous generations, their ability to make a living as a mill worker often required stamina or strength.

> I was a chipper and burner—chipped frames with a hammer and chisel. It was hard physical work—that's why my hands are all beat up.
>
> I did a lot of sledgehammer work. And lifted steel plates—about 200 pounds. Got a bad back out of it. The pain is still terrible.
>
> I lifted 110 pounds about 200 times a day. Picked up blocks of hard sand, put them down on the next board and scraped off the burrs. I'm in heavy construction now, but in terms of physical labor the work I do now doesn't compare at all—doesn't even come close—to the physical labor I did in the mill.

Because of the difficult conditions of mill work, it was not unusual for newly hired men to quit after their first day on the job. Those interviewed frequently alluded to the fact that they, as long-time plant employees, had accepted or put up with a work life that many others would not have tolerated. These acknowledgments often appeared to carry both a self-congratulatory and self-abasing tone: a sense of pride at having endured difficult work situations, mixed with chagrin at having swallowed poor labor conditions.

> It was hot and dirty and hard work. A lot of new guys came in and walked right back out.
>
> A lot of people hired would come in and go right back out, they were so terrified. You sense the danger as soon as you walk in. The smell would hit you—smell of burning steel and asbestos. A sulphur smell. Sparks would be flying everywhere, noisy. I didn't think I would last there too long, myself. But then you get used to it.
>
> I came from the Carolinas in 1942. My brother was here and he sent for me. I was just a young dude. I wasn't afraid to work and I could put up with the smoke and dirt. Even then a lot of guys would work one day and quit—they couldn't take the dirt.
>
> Working in a mill is kind of like another world. Unless you were born and raised in a steel town and accepted that life—I don't think people would work there.

The tolerance of difficult working conditions also extended to acceptance of the risk of physical injury, a given element of mill work. Writing about industrial accidents and working-class life, Levison has noted,

"All the clichés and pleasant notions of how the old class divisions . . . have disappeared are exposed as hollow phrases by the simple fact that American workers must accept serious injury and even death as part of their daily reality while the middle class does not."[1]

Such a condition of employment had been routine to these displaced workers. Of those surveyed, 85 percent reported that they had been injured while working in the mills, some seriously. Many had witnessed severe or fatal injuries. And most had accepted the threat as part of the job. They spoke matter-of-factly about the ever-present danger of physical harm. Their descriptions of mill accidents were sometimes startling for the casual manner in which they were told, suggesting a numbing effect of daily exposure to danger. In other instances, the vividness of their recountings underscored the trauma of many of the experiences.

Asked why injuries had occurred, some of those interviewed asserted that the mill operators had been at fault for unsafe conditions. A majority, however, expressed the opinion that injury was most often a matter of an individual's bad luck or inattentiveness. Caution, they said, reduced the chances of injury, but getting hurt was often a matter of being in the wrong place at the wrong time.

In describing their own injuries, the matter of luck was repeatedly mentioned. But rather than focusing on their bad luck, they most often spoke of their good fortune in not having been hurt worse.

> I realized the first time I walked in there that it was every man for himself. You assume the risk of injury when you take the job. Once I had a stack of steel fall on my legs. I thought they were severed. So I was relieved to find out I had just broken both and crushed one.

> I got hurt plenty. See all these burn marks on my arms? I was a welder since 1946. I never got disfigured, though.

> I got blown out of a gas furnace once. It was a malfunction. I was in front of it and a big flame came shooting out—whoomp. The pressure was so extreme I was thrown into the air—did a flip and landed on all fours. It was midnight turn, about 2:00 a.m. It was a very cold night; there was snow outside and a full moon. It felt like slow motion when I was flipped through the air, and I remember seeing the moon and the snow, so serene. I was lucky—only sprained my neck. That's the kind of danger that you have to accept as part of the job.

> A buddy of mine was killed when a piece of steel fell off a crane. We had just had a cup of coffee together. Ten minutes later he

> was dead. Another time a man fell in a tank and suffocated. I was the one who pulled him out.
>
> I seen three men killed. One fell off a ladder. Another got knocked in the head with a ladle. And once they were pouring steel and a man got hit—opened him right up and you could see his entrails. There were many accidents. But you just can't quit over that.

Acceptance of the hazards of mill employment also extended to the potential for illness due to environmental pollution. The mill workers continually made reference to the dirt, dust, and fumes in the air at the plants. They described respiratory and other ailments affecting themselves and their coworkers and speculated that they were attributable to the work environment. Despite expressed anxiety about the pollution, however, they repeatedly described it as something one had to accept as part of the job. A worker put up with a less than ideal situation because the work was steady and the wages were good.

> If a ray of sunlight would hit, you would see dust particles glittering in the air, going into your lungs, sitting on your sandwich. You realize it is not the best environment, but you also realize the money is good, and you "eat" it. As a family man it is your best hope for a decent existence in society.
>
> I worried at first about the dirt and my lungs. But then you get used to it. If you want to make a living, that's what you put up with.

Such tolerance for difficult working conditions did not mean that they were viewed with indifference, however. When asked to recall their job dislikes, these persons most frequently listed these same environmental hazards and conditions: the noise, dirt, extreme heat and cold, and risk of physical injury. In what can appear as a strange contradiction, however, the dirt, noise, and danger were often not considered negative enough to affect overall job satisfaction. Though expressing dislike for poor working conditions, many persons also indicated a strong attachment to the mills.

A surprisingly large percentage of the displaced workers reported high satisfaction with their former plant jobs. Though the plant shutdowns and subsequent unemployment and income loss most likely enhanced memories of work in the mills, a sizable 50 percent asserted that they had been very satisfied with their jobs at the plant, and 41 percent said they had been somewhat satisfied. Interestingly enough, when asked about job likes and dislikes, 20 percent of the respondents said there was "nothing really" that they had disliked about these jobs. When probed, they most often responded

by talking about what they liked about mill work. On the opposite extreme, a much lower 9 percent reported strong dislike or hatred of work in the mills.

Again, job dislikes were primarily focused on environmental conditions: the lack of central heating, the dirt and noise, and the threat of physical injury. Other dislikes included the shift changes, particularly the midnight turn, and jobs that required heavy physical labor or were tedious. Extreme dislike of mill work was most frequent among the younger respondents.

Among job satisfactions, good money topped the list. For many it was the wages and benefits that compensated for difficult working conditions and enhanced work satisfaction, while for some, money was the sole enjoyment: 10 percent commented that good wages and benefits were the only things they liked about the mill. The remaining 90 percent, however, listed numerous other job likes: steady work; security; job tasks that were interesting or nonroutine; working with one's hands; a good foreman; camaraderie among coworkers; and a sense of accomplishment in a job done well. Often, job satisfaction was linked to their advancement over the years to a coveted work station. As men gained seniority, they "bid" on positions that were more skilled, less physically demanding, and less dirty. Long years spent in one mill often paid off in terms of more comfortable work.

As with the list of job dislikes, likes often included specific physical conditions: a department that was heated or cleaner than other shops; a window to look out. Since the shift changes, particularly the midnight turn, were generally disliked, a job that allowed a steady day turn was highly valued. Other elements of a favored job included work that was varied in its tasks, required skill or craft, and allowed some autonomy.

> I worked in the pattern shop. Everyone had a bench. You had all your tools behind you. There was a window you could look out of. We had metalworkers and woodworkers. It was very precise work and the guys were good. The old-timers would show you how to do it. I loved my work. I had worked my way up from laborer to pattern maker.

> It felt good to produce a useful product—there was a sense of accomplishment.

> I liked repairing things—working with my hands. And there was some prestige in that you fixed things other people couldn't; that felt good.

Relationships with Coworkers

Very striking in their descriptions of the enjoyable aspects of work in the mill were the number of references to camaraderie with fellow workers.

Much of the satisfaction with plant work was derived from relationships with coworkers, built over many years. Since the days when the immigrants first came to the area, the mills had often taken on a primary group form as workers labored alongside friends, neighbors, and relatives. As described by the former mill workers, that primary group contained its share of diverse personalities—from "crooks to preachers"—and not all of the respondents were impressed with the character of all of their coworkers. But even among unlike individuals there was evident a common bond or identification as members of a shared work environment. Strong connections had developed among those who had worked together 10, 20, or 30 years. Clearly, these displaced workers indicated a strong social as well as economic attachment to the mills.

> People were friendly, like one big family. I had lots of friends already working there when I started—it's not like I walked into a place full of strangers.

> You worked with a strange array of people, from highly intelligent to illiterate. The guys were OK—there was a certain amount of what you call bonding. You get to know people's idiosyncrasies after ten years.

> We were like a family. It was like working with brothers—everyone kidding and knowing all about each other.

> There was a mix of people. You worked with people from crooks to preachers. There were oddballs there—not everyone was somebody you'd want to be best friends with. But they were still part of the crew.

> It was a family thing—like a big family. Everyone knew each other and was connected. There were 15 in our department. I liked the guys and liked my work. I got along with everyone from top down. You'd come in the morning and everyone would be saying "Hi, George. How ya doin'?" It felt good.

Many of those interviewed indicated that their sense of connection with fellow mill workers also extended back to previous generations of plant employees. Again, a majority of the displaced workers had fathers, grandfathers, uncles, and other relatives who had worked in the mills. The experiences of the older generations were routinely relayed to those who were younger.

Most displaced workers had knowledge of the history of the mills and the labor struggles that had resulted in higher wages and better working

conditions. It appeared that one reason for their tolerance of grim environmental conditions was their understanding of how much worse conditions had been in past decades. Many described the "old days" as told to them by older workers or as they themselves had experienced them: the soot that used to hang in the air surrounding the mills; sand in the foundry so thick "you couldn't see your hand in front of you"; the lack of showers, lockers, and cafeterias in the plants; and the low wages and minimal benefits. They indicated an appreciation for the struggles of earlier workers, in both suffering through such conditions and effecting changes in them, primarily through union activities.

There was also an expression of respect for the skill and craftsmanship of previous generations of workers and among the "old-timers," mill veterans of 25 or 30 years. Many of the displaced workers said that the mill operators did not have to spend much money on job training because they relied on the old-timers to do it. The passing of skills from one generation to the next was a frequent component of their descriptions of mill experiences.

> The old-timers would teach the young ones. You learned your craft on the job.

> I was an interior linings operator; the work was very precise and had to be just right. When I first got the job it was hell. I couldn't get it right and the other guys cussed me. Then an old-timer took me aside. He was great. He was patient and took the time to teach me. In a few months I had the job down.

> There was lots to learn on the job, and the older guys broke me in. Then I would know how to break in a younger guy and they would thank me.

> My dad got me a job at the mill. He was a welder and I was a laborer. After my shift he would take me down to the welding booth and show me what he knew and let me practice. I eventually got a job as a welder.

These connections with veteran mill workers intensified personal identifications with the plants, as well as with the occupation of mill worker. For many, the attachment to the mills was deep-rooted, spanning generations. As one man noted, the mills were, "in your blood." This attachment, and its implications for adjustment to the aftermath of the plant closings, was described in numerous conversations.

> I had a hard time leaving the mills. I'm kind of a textbook mill hunk: my grandfather worked in the mills; I was a third-generation

> mill worker. My roots were there, and it is hard to get it out of your system. It's hard to explain, but there is a lot of psychological stuff that goes along with these mill closings. That's all part of this transition. It's part of what makes you depressed afterwards.

As such, the mills formed an environment that had provided its workers with both economic and social support, a sense of connection and identity, and a source of both strong attachment and dislike. With the plant closings, the physical and social reality to which the behavior of local manufacturing workers had long been attuned was gone. The displaced workers lost good wages and benefits, seniority and security, and an attachment to a community of mill workers. Many forfeited jobs they had coveted and worked for years to obtain. They were forced out of a relationship with an industry and employer that had provided an occupational identity and a means of existence for generations. At the same time, however, they were freed of daily exposure to pollution and noise, the threat of physical injury, and other difficult aspects of factory work. But while the displaced workers did gain a release from such elements, they also lost the justification for having put up with grim environmental conditions most of their working lives. Their loyalty to the factory system was no longer of any economic or social significance. When the plants shut down, these men and women were severed from a complex set of mill-centered expectations and associations that had long been integral to personal and community functioning. The effects of this dislocation are the focus of the next three chapters.

NOTE

1. Cited in Paul Fussell, *Class* (New York: Ballantine, 1983), p. 70.

5

The Downward Slide: Changes in Income and Employment

> Reagan kept saying the economy was getting better. Which economy? For who? They acted like we didn't exist.
>
> former core maker, National Castings

As discussed in Chapter 4, a majority of the displaced workers enjoyed a middle-class income while employed in the mills. At the time of the plant closings, they averaged hourly wages of $12 and an annual median individual income of $25,000. These numbers stand in stark contrast with their subsequent economic status. Four years after the first closings, unemployment remained high and wages had plummeted.

At the time of the survey interview, 35 percent of the 102 respondents were not working. Of that 35 percent, 2 percent were on disability, 8 percent had retired, 14 percent were unemployed and actively seeking work, and 11 percent were discouraged workers—they had actively looked for work for several years but had given up because of the perceived futility of the search. A majority of the displaced workers had experienced a long spell of unemployment following the plant closings, with their joblessness averaging 1.6 years and ranging from two weeks to five years. Income and employment figures for the displaced workers are summarized in Table 5.1.

Among the 65 percent who were working, average hourly wages were $6.50. Approximately one-half of these jobs paid no benefits. Among all of the respondents, median household income was $14,500, well below the national family median ($30,853 in 1987) and considerably lower than the respondents' median individual income while employed at the plant.

Certainly among the most startling findings was that 29 percent of the displaced workers reported household incomes that fell below the federal poverty line. Among those whose income fell below poverty, 47 percent

Table 5.1
Employment and Income Status Among Displaced Workers

N=102	
Employment status	
Employed	65%
Unemployed	14%
Retired	8%
Discouraged	11%
Disabled	2%
Employment sector*	
Services	60%
Manufacturing	22%
Other blue-collar	8%
Professional/managerial	10%
Full-time/part-time*	
Employed full-time	70%
Employed part-time (less than 30 hrs/wk)	30%
Length of unemployment following job loss	
Mean	1.6 years
Range	2 weeks–5 years
Household income	
Median	$14,500
Range	$2,124–$43,000
Hourly wages*	
Mean	$6.50
Mode	3.35
Changes in household income since plant closings	
Increased	7%
Stayed same	6%
Decreased	87%

* N = 65

were working. Another 15 percent had household incomes up to 125 percent above the poverty line. Downward mobility had been experienced by an overwhelming majority of the displaced workers, with 87 percent reporting a decrease in household income since the plant closings. This downward slide was sometimes accompanied by drastic changes in material circumstances: eight had had a home foreclosed; several had had vehicles repossessed; and many had eventually found themselves on welfare.

CHARACTERISTICS OF JOBS OBTAINED

As expected, a majority of the displaced workers who did obtain jobs following the plant closings were reemployed in the service sector. Janitor was the occupation they most frequently held, followed by delivery truck driver and security guard. Others included school bus driver, salesclerk, teacher's aide, hospital orderly, school crossing guard, gas station attendant, salesman, meat cutter, and paramedic. Of the 65 who were working, 60 percent held service-sector jobs; another 22 percent had secured employment in manufacturing, and 8 percent held other blue-collar jobs, such as carpenter and construction worker. A tier of these former manufacturing workers—10 percent—had moved into professional or managerial jobs.

In contrast with their previous history of steady, well paid employment, work for the majority of the displaced steelworkers was now often irregular and low-paying. Many had minimum-wage and part-time jobs in the service sector. Among those who found work, 36 percent were paid the minimum wage of $3.35 an hour in the first job they secured after the plant closings, and 72 percent worked for $5.00 an hour or less. These displaced workers typically hopped from one low-paying job to another, gaining incremental wage increases—$3.35, to $3.75, to $4.50. Their average time on each job was only eight months. They would quit to find better wages or, in many cases, were laid off due to slack business. As mentioned above, many of these jobs carried no fringe benefits—a sharp change from the generous benefit packages offered by the mills—and almost one-third of those who were employed were working 30 hours per week or less. Among these, 90 percent were working part time involuntarily. Such involuntary part-time work at low wages kept many households at or near the poverty line.

This pattern of lower-paying, irregular work also held for the minority of displaced workers who were able to secure manufacturing or other blue-collar employment. Wages for blue-collar and manufacturing jobs tended to be higher than for service jobs—an average of $8.60 versus $4.56 an hour—but they were still well below the mill wages of $12 an hour that these individuals had previously earned. In addition, the work was often intermittent and insecure and carried lower fringe benefits. Their low seniority left many of these workers vulnerable to frequent layoffs, and

many of the manufacturing jobs were in nonunion shops. Though 100 percent of these displaced workers had been union members prior to the shutdowns, only 12 percent were represented by a union at the time of the interview.

The exception to this pattern of irregular and low-paid work was found among the tier of displaced workers who had made status climbs into managerial and professional jobs. Their new occupations included attorney, business manager, and small-business owner, and their annual individual incomes averaged $23,000. The specifics of their climb out of working-class occupations are discussed in Chapter 6.

THOSE WHO FARED WORST

Among those interviewed, those most likely to experience prolonged unemployment and income loss were middle-aged men, persons with low education, women, and blacks.

As might be expected, poverty was highest among those with low educational credentials. Of persons with less than a high school education, 38 percent reported household incomes below the poverty line, versus 25 percent of those with at least a high school diploma. Poverty was higher among blacks than whites, with 36 percent of blacks reporting household incomes below poverty versus, 26 percent of whites. Of the three women in the survey sample, all had household incomes below poverty. Poverty rates also varied among age groups. Poverty was *lowest* among those over 51 years of age, with a rate of 24 percent. Pension benefits helped keep some older respondents out of the lowest-income category. Poverty was *highest* among those who were 41 to 50 years old, with a rate of 30 percent.

Age, education, and race were also associated with differences in hourly wage rates. Again, as would be expected, low education was linked with low hourly wages. Blacks had lower hourly wage rates than whites, and age was strongly associated with hourly earnings, with younger persons more likely to be making more. The average age of persons earning $5 an hour or under was 43, while those making over $5 an hour had a mean age of 36. Younger workers also had higher educational levels and were more likely to have secured new jobs in manufacturing.

The unemployment, like the poverty, was highest among those in the 41 to 50 age group, with 30 percent of persons in that age group unemployed. These figures lend support to the claims of numerous middle-aged respondents who maintained that employers prefer younger, stronger workers and are apt to discriminate against job applicants who are over 45. Unemployment did not vary by race, and lower education was not associated with higher rates of unemployment. The demographics of discouraged workers—those who had actively looked for work but had given up the search—were strikingly different from those of both the

employed and the unemployed. Discouraged workers were older, with a mean age of 56, and 50 percent had less than a high school education.

SOCIAL NETWORKS AND ECONOMIC STATUS

Persons with low income and employment status also differed from the sample as a whole with regard to the characteristics of their social networks. In the 1980s many policymakers asserted that economically disadvantaged persons should be encouraged to increase their reliance on family and friends—as opposed to the government—as sources of support. To investigate the characteristics of the social networks of the displaced workers and the ways in which these networks were utilized after job loss, the displaced workers in the survey were asked questions about the nature and functions of their circle of family and acquaintances.[1] These questions measured the size of the respondents' social networks (the total number of acquaintances), their composition (the number of family, friends, neighbors, and work cohorts), their degree of intimacy (the number of network contacts who were very close friends, as opposed to more distant acquaintances), and their supportive functions (in providing emotional and material assistance).

Persons with income below the poverty line and those without a labor market attachment were found to have networks significantly smaller in size and higher in intimacy than those of the overall sample. The findings suggest that tightly knit social networks—those small in size and high in intimacy—are negatively associated with employment and household income among displaced workers.

Among persons who reported household incomes below poverty, total network size averaged 22.5 persons. The average proportion of intimate ties was 52 percent. In contrast, persons with incomes above the poverty line had a total network size of 42.8 and an intimacy ratio of 43 percent. Similarly, persons who were not working (including those who were unemployed or retired and discouraged workers) had a mean network size of 25.4 and an intimacy ratio of 50 percent. Those who were employed had networks averaging 43.9 persons and an intimacy ratio of 42 percent.[2]

Persons who had low income and employment status also had a higher percentage of kin in their social networks. They had fewer organizational affiliations—they were less likely to belong to any clubs or groups. While most had strong supportive ties—persons who served as confidants—only a minority could name a person in their social network who could assist them with a job lead.

As such, poor persons and those who were not working had a smaller number of personal network resources on which to draw. In addition, their extant network contacts were more intimate and family oriented, containing fewer "weak" ties with more distant associates. Without information on the social networks of these persons prior to changes in income and

employment, it is unclear whether smaller networks are an antecedent or a consequence of lowered status. As discussed further in Chapter 8, the critical point is that those who currently have less in the way of money and employment opportunity also have fewer and less diverse personal resources on which to draw.

Summary

Several years after the plant closings, the population of displaced workers was found to have suffered quite severe income loss and downward mobility, with a substantial number dropping below the poverty line. Almost one-half of those with incomes below poverty were working. Most of those who were reemployed held jobs in the service sector, at wages considerably below what they had previously earned in the mills. A high percentage remained unemployed or were too discouraged to continue looking for work. A minority of displaced workers had secured manufacturing jobs, and a few have made climbs into managerial or professional positions. Those persons with less than a high school education and those in the 41- to 50-year-old age group had fared the worst in terms of low wages and prolonged unemployment, and the poor and unemployed were found to have the fewest personal acquaintances from whom to seek assistance in times of need.

THE PROCESS OF ADJUSTMENT: RESPONSES TO JOB AND INCOME LOSS

How have these displaced workers adjusted to their downward mobility? What have been their emotional and behavioral reactions to job and income loss?

As described in Chapter 2, some previous studies of structural unemployment describe a *process* of response to long-term joblessness and income loss in a sequence that includes shock, denial, anxiety, anger, optimism, depression, and resignation. Such responses are similar to those of trauma, grieving, and loss. The reactions to job termination described by the displaced workers from the Shenango Valley in many ways paralleled responses detailed in the literature. Denial, shock, and anger were often the initial responses to news of the plant closings, followed by rising anxiety as the job layoffs began. The weeks immediately following termination were often described as a period of diminished apprehension, with the displaced workers frequently exhibiting optimism and making active efforts to find a new job. Persons still unemployed several months after their job loss often reported rising feelings of insecurity and self-doubt, with some exhibiting deep depression, extreme anger, and interpersonal problems. In some cases

this phase was followed by one marked by apathy and resignation. These patterns surfaced in the displaced workers' descriptions of the aftermath of the plant closings and are illustrated in the comments that follow.

Shock and Anger: Reaction to the News of the Shutdowns

Though rumors of shutdowns had circulated at both GATX and National Castings for some time, and plant closings in nearby Youngstown, Ohio, had already left thousands of persons unemployed, most of the displaced workers reported feeling shock when they heard the news of the closings.

> It was a feeling of someone slapping you in the face. . . .
>
> I was stunned. I saw so many other plants shutting down that I knew it was coming. But when they said, "That's it, Boys," it was still a gut feeling of shock.

As with many traumatic situations, those interviewed could often recall quite vividly where they had been and what they were doing when they heard the news.

> I was sittin' over there in that orange chair and my wife was in the kitchen fryin' hamburg. The mailman came to the door with a registered letter—that's how I found out, by registered letter.
>
> The wife and I were driving to the clothing outlet in Erie when we heard it on the radio.

Shock at the news was commonly accompanied by disbelief. Numerous workers reported that they simply had not accepted the company announcement. Many at first thought that the company management was bluffing to extract further concessions from the union. Others assumed the closing was not permanent and anticipated being rehired in a subsequent reopening of the plant. Such responses were conditioned in part by past experiences. For years the mills had regularly laid off portions of their work force during slack periods and rehired when business picked up. Also, both GATX and National Castings had been in operation since the early 1900s and were viewed by many as inviolable community institutions, a perception that intensified the incredulity at their closing. Among some displaced workers, such denial persisted for years; there were a few persons who, at the time of the interview, continued to insist that the companies would eventually "come to their senses" and reopen the plants and rehire their former employees.

Among the mill workers, the shock and disbelief at the news of the shutdowns were also intermingled with feelings of sadness and disappointment, a reaction not often referred to in the literature on unemployment. More than one-half of those interviewed indicated that the shock was accompanied by a strong feeling of sadness and a realization that a secure source of income and support was ending.

> I was more sad than anything else. You reach your niche in a mill and you think you'll retire there. It's awful to think that you have to start over from scratch after 26 years in one job.

> When I heard the news I felt sad. Sad and very disappointed. You have a smile on your face but in your brain you know you are in trouble.

> I felt let down and sad. I had served them well.

Such sadness was frequently followed or combined with frustration and anger. Many of the displaced workers felt betrayed by the companies—they were surprised and upset that their loyalty to the mills had not been met by company loyalty to the Shenango Valley. Defending their productivity and pointing to the profitability of both plants, many asserted that the shutdowns were unjust. Workers at GATX felt exploited by the company after concessions had been greeted with a closing announcement. Workers at National Castings felt that the company had used the veto of concessions as an excuse to close the plants. Frustration escalated into anger. Some men lashed out verbally or physically; others reported "holding it in" and smoldering.

> I was completely shocked and surprised by the closing, and I was a recording official for the union. We had just settled a contract and given concessions in August; in October they announced that they were closing the plant. The company called all the union reps into the office and told us they were closing. I had so much anger, they had to hold me down. I could have choked 'em.

> I felt so bitter and angry. I punched holes in walls.

> I was so mad. Mad at the company. I wanted to scream at someone but I didn't. And it just eats at you.

Underlying this anger was apprehension. As the date of their job termination drew closer, many said that their anxiety surged. The mills were familar territory. Few of the steelworkers had much job experience outside

the plants, and few had a sense of what other kinds of work they could do or what would be available. As unemployment approached, many recalled having trouble sleeping. Others remarked on the intrusive and nagging thoughts they had had about their future ability to pay their bills and obtain work.

> I was very nervous. I was used to a ritual and I thought it would be hard to start over. I kept thinking, Could I handle it? What would I do with the rest of my life? Where would I go?

> You worry. I sat down with a pencil and paper and figured out my bills over and over.

> You wonder how you'll make a go of it. My daughter was getting married one month after the shutdown. The other was about to go to college. I was worried.

These feelings of anxiety, anger, and sadness surfaced in descriptions of violent and emotional outbursts on the last day of work, as they faced the loss of a long-term source of both social and economic support.

> It was the last day of work and I was having lunch in the cafeteria with a buddy I'd worked with for about five years. I was eatin' my sandwich and I looked up across the table at him and I seen he had tears in his eyes. Then he picked up his lunch bucket and smashed it against the cafeteria wall.

> I seen guys cryin' at the gate on the last day of work. Guys meeting their wives and the two of them cryin' together.

> After my shift was done I walked out into the parking lot with the six guys I'd worked with for 15 years. We was all real close—used to change clothes together, argue, joke. We knew everything about each other. We walked out into the parking lot, and all shook hands, one after the other. Then we left. . . .
>
> I have a 25-year-old son at home. He's a beautiful kid and full of ideas—save the whales, save the environment, that kind of thing. When I got home that day my son says, "Dad, how do you feel?"
>
> I says, "Very sad, Son."
>
> He says, "Dad, this is the best thing that ever happened to you. You ain't going to come home dirty no more. No more noise pollution. No more eating dirt every day. No more strain on your legs."

But I said, "Son, I have six children and I have bills to pay. And I'm 55 years old."

He don't really understand what a sad thing it is.

Initial Phases of Unemployment

As described above, numerous displaced workers commented that the first weeks of unemployment were unexpectedly experienced as a time of diminished apprehension. Several persons noted that there was a physical relief—to be away from the dirt, din, and heavy labor. Anxiety over future job prospects was present but quelled for a short period, while people took stock and devised a follow-up plan of action.

Though almost all of the displaced workers suffered income loss immediately following the plant closings, the financial blow of job loss was buffered and delayed at first by the availability of unemployment insurance and the receipt, by some, of severance benefits. Unemployment insurance was available to most of the displaced workers for up to 52 weeks, because high local and national unemployment rates during the 1983 recession had resulted in federal and state extensions well beyond the usual 26-week collection period. In addition, most plant employees who did not qualify for a pension received severance pay, which averaged about $1,600. These displaced workers were not eligible for Trade Adjustment Assistance (TAA).

During this initial period of unemployment, many reported that they had had naive and overly optimistic expectations of finding another job at wages similar to what they had made in the mills. This wave of optimism most often led to an active job search, beginning two or three months following job loss.

Job searches typically began with registration at the Pennsylvania Job Service, Office of Employment and Security and a series of informal inquiries among close acquaintances—particularly those who were employed in blue-collar trades or who held jobs in the handful of local plants still in operation. Next, the displaced workers typically applied in person to almost every mill still in operation within a 60-mile radius of the valley, with many holding out for jobs and wages similar to what they had had before. Job inquiries were then extended to local stores, hospitals, restaurants, and other small businesses. As detailed in Chapter 6, some sought schooling, retraining, and out-of-state job opportunities. As time wore on and their unemployment insurance neared expiration, wage and occupational expectations shifted and anxiety rose. These displaced workers were searching for work with thousands of other former mill workers. Several reported filing up to 100 applications, with perhaps one or two calls for interviews. They were pressured to take any wages and whatever work they could get. Again, 36 percent of those who found reemployment worked for $3.35 an hour in their first job following the plant closing, while 72 percent

worked for $5 an hour or under.

Not surprisingly, the optimism that spurred most initial job search efforts was often fleeting. Lack of success in securing employment or decent wages left many dispirited. As the optimism waned, it was frequently replaced by heightened insecurity and diminished self-esteem, anger, marital and interpersonal conflict, and depression. Months at home while unemployed greatly increased personal and household tensions. When their unemployment insurance benefits were exhausted, those who were still without jobs often experienced a sharp rise in anxiety and emotional distress. Particularly among those who remained unemployed or took very low-paying jobs, resignation or apathy ensued. This slide from optimism to discouragement was described over and over by the persons interviewed.

> When the unemployment [insurance] ran out I panicked. I had thought there would be another job for me. When there wasn't I got scared. I thought, Wow, what am I going to do? There seemed to be nowhere to go.

> The first few months weren't so bad. I did things around the house and worked on the car. Then it hit. You go looking for a job and get desperate. The temper kicks in and everything gets on your nerves.

> I felt panic when the unemployment ran out. I had tried hard to find another job. Then you start not to care.

> You see, there are three phases to this thing. (1) You ride on unemployment. You kind of enjoy the vacation. And you say to yourself, "I can find another job." (2) You start to get worried. You pound the pavement. (3) You see 500 guys in line for 5 openings. You put in applications and no one calls. You are disgusted and depressed. You throw up your hands. It seems hopeless.

As described by the displaced workers and corroborated by local social service personnel, discouragement over job and income loss has led to a myriad of personal and social problems, including divorce, spouse abuse, alcoholism, and severe depression. The scope of these problems is described in Chapter 7.

The pattern of response to unemployment described above—shock, denial, sadness, anger, anxiety, optimism and distress—was evidenced in a majority of the descriptions of job loss offered by the displaced workers. A minority, however, did not conform to such a pattern. Some persons were

not shocked at the closings or angered by their job loss. Others reported some of these phases but not all. A handful of men who had disliked their mill jobs reported that they had felt more relieved than sad at the news of the closings. Older workers who opted for early retirement frequently suffered less anxiety about their future, but were often deeply saddened by the shutdowns. Those most likely to report the entire sequence of responses, from shock to distress and resignation, were those who had suffered prolonged unemployment or sharp income loss after the closings.

Thus, as described by the displaced workers, responses to job termination and unemployment were marked by distinct changes in emotion and outlook. Clearly, the duration and intensity of some of these phases were shaped, in part, by the respondent's success in securing satisfactory reemployment. A good job eased distress, while affect deteriorated most severely among those whose economic or employment status did not improve over time. What troubled many of the displaced workers was that an early *positive* response to unemployment—a response marked by an optimistic attitude and an aggressive job hunt—often had little impact on their subsequent income and employment status. As described in the next chapter, active and enthusiastic efforts to mobilize new skills and resources had widely varying results.

NOTES

1. Information on respondents' social networks was collected using a network map that solicited data on network size, categories of association, and degree of intimacy. Respondents were asked to mark on a pie chart the initials of persons whom they knew and with whom they interacted within different categories. These persons could reside in any part of the country. Categories of association were charted as friends, family and relatives, neighbors, current work associates, and former coworkers from the manufacturing plant. Concentric circles emanating from a center point (representing the respondent) signified zones of social intimacy, with primary relations marked by the area closest to the respondent. Network members, indicated by initials, were placed within categories and intimacy zones.

Other questions obtained information on the supportive functions of these network ties. Respondents were asked to list members of their social network with whom they could talk about a personal problem, borrow $500, obtain a job-hunting lead, or ask to watch their house when they were away. Information was also collected on respondents' participation in community organizations, including churches, sports teams, and social clubs.

2. A test for the differences between the mean network sizes of persons who were employed and those who were unemployed was statistically significant ($t = 2.89$; $df = 90.20$, $p \langle .005$), as were the differences in mean network sizes for persons with incomes above and below the poverty level ($t = -3.77$; $df = 94.82$, $p \langle .000$). For more detail see Allison Zippay, "The Limits of Intimates: Social Networks and Economic Status Among Displaced Industrial Workers," *Journal of Applied Social Sciences* 15, no. 1 (1990): 75–95.

6

The Process of Rebuilding: Mobilizing New Sources of Support

> You eat hamburg and hotdogs instead of steaks and chops. Don't buy clothes. My wife cut out bowling and I cut out my sports club. Our bills are always late.
>
> former crane operator, GATX

How have families with a history of well-paid blue-collar employment responded to quite dramatic changes in their income and employment status? Income loss often necessitated substantial changes in life-style, and many displaced workers sold possessions, scrambled for odd jobs, delayed medical care, and eventually approached social service agencies for assistance. As with their reactions to unemployment, such life-style shifts often followed a sequence of phases, as the former mill workers sought to assemble new sources of economic and social assistance.

In so doing, the displaced workers drew on a mix of personal and organizational resources. Desiring self-sufficiency, most looked to personal means and assistance from family and friends for material or emotional support. As these resources were exhausted or proved inadequate, many turned to community organizations. In the commentary that follows, the displaced workers describe how they attempted to conserve existing resources and develop new ones. Changes in their living conditions, sources of income, and social service utilization are surveyed, as are their attempts to mobilize new employment resources through job training, job search, and relocation.

THE COMMUNITY CONTEXT

As the displaced workers moved to restructure their lives, they discovered a community that, like its residents, was reeling from the effects of economic dislocation. The departure of major employers had sent city tax

revenues plummeting, necessitating cuts in municipal services. Retail businesses languished. Real estate values plunged, and, as Illustration 6.1 shows, houses could be purchased for as little as $7,000. As lines at the food stamp office, job training center, and other social service agencies lengthened, these organizations were faced with cuts in funding enacted by the Reagan Administration's Omnibus Budget Reconciliation Act (OBRA) of 1981, and also with a decline in private contributions precipitated by the departure of local corporate donors.

Unemployment was high nationally as well as locally. The plant closings coincided with the recession of 1982–83, and job prospects in other locales were dim. While unemployment in the valley was nearing 25 percent, no coordinated local, state, or federal response to mass joblessness was undertaken. To the contrary, under President Reagan the federal government was retreating from involvement in social problem solving.

Beyond the staple of unemployment insurance, displaced workers frequently looked initially to personal networks—friends, neighbors, relatives—as a sustaining resource. As noted earlier, the Shenango Valley is a very close-knit community, with most people sharing an identification with working-class culture and the experience of mill work. Social bonds are strong and interlocking; relatives are neighbors, neighbors are also coworkers and friends. As the displaced workers began the task of reordering their lives, they did so within a tightly bound community of associates. Yet many of these associates were also facing unemployment and income loss and were thus limited in the assistance they could provide.

LIFE-STYLE SHIFTS: CUTTING CONSUMPTION

As soon as the plant closing notices went out, most mill workers began curbing their spending. The first expenditures to go were "frills"—vacations, meals at restaurants, and unnecessary purchases such as extra clothing or household goods. As unemployment dragged on, cuts were made in necessities—weekly grocery bills were limited, and electricity and other utilities conserved. When their unemployment insurance ran out, those who remained jobless or who took work at greatly reduced pay tapped personal assets and reserves; savings accounts were drained and some insurance policies cashed. Many sold their cars, and at least five of the respondents had their vehicles repossessed. Others sold possessions, such as guns or motorcycles, to gather extra cash.

Cost cutting also affected children. Those interviewed frequently commented, with chagrin, that they had had to stop buying extras for their kids. Higher education, a mainstay of upward mobility among the offspring of blue-collar workers, was also affected; several persons noted that their older children had delayed college, dropped out, or switched to less expensive schools during their unemployment.

Illustration 6.1
A Real Estate Agency's Listings of Houses For Sale in the Shenango Valley, September 1987

REINHARDT'S AGENCY, Inc.

Need An Excellent Starter Home? Investors — Note The Rental Potential!

607 WOOD WAY **$7,900**	691 FISHER HILL, SHARON **$29,900**
535 DAVIS ST., SHARON 3 bedrooms, 2 car garage **$11,100**	137-139 THIRD AVE., SHARON Side-by-Side Duplex **$6,500**
368 SHARPSVILLE AVE., SHARON Tri-Plex **$6,500**	810 SPRUCE AVE., SHARON 2 bedrooms, new kitchen **$13,500**
129 FIFTH AVE., SHARON 3 bedroom home **$15,000**	SIDE-BY-SIDE DUPLEX Located in West Middlesex on a dead end street. Each unit has 2 bedrooms, family room, modern kitchen & baths.
376 ORCHARD AVE., SHARON 4 bedrooms **$10,000**	414 GRANT ST., SHARON 4 bedroom home **$16,500**

REINHARDT'S AGENCY, Inc.
105 SOUTH WATER AVE. • SHARON, PA 16146 • (412) 347-4527
218 NORTH ERIE ST. • MERCER, PA 16137 • (412) 662-2900

As personal resources were depleted, some displaced workers turned to their families for assistance. Parents loaned money to children, and adult children gave cash to needy parents. Several displaced workers moved in with their parents or in-laws to save money. Parents also helped their children by buying groceries, making a mortgage payment, or assisting with child care. Often, however, the parents as well as their adult children were grappling with job loss and lowered incomes.

> Our families help when they can—but both our dads lost their mill jobs.
>
> I sold a motorcycle, snowmobile, and new car. Did away with all the frills, the enjoyment things.
>
> We took out lower insurance on our cars. Our son was about to go to Carnegie Mellon University, and he had to switch to Penn State off campus. We had to stop buying things for the kids.
>
> We couldn't pay our mortage, so we just paid the interest to the bank. We needed a new car but drove our junker. Bought nothing. This is embarrassing, but for a while we even watched TV by candlelight to save on the lights.
>
> We used all our savings and cut back on everything. Had to take it one day at a time. Our truck was repossessed. My wife had garage sales and sold things that were lying around the house, like a bike.

Such cost-cutting measures would have been adequate to sustain some of the displaced workers through a temporary period of unemployment before they regained work and decent wages. For most, however, such curtailment had continued into the time of the interview. Again, at the time of the survey, 87 percent had experienced a decrease in household income; 29 percent were living below the poverty line; and 15 percent had incomes up to 125 percent above poverty. People who until five years before had enjoyed a middle-class life-style now reported difficulty paying bills, buying cars, and providing for their children. Numerous displaced workers reported delaying visits to the doctor because of the cost. Bartering goods and services became a more common means of exchange—people swapped a roofing job for auto repair, or firewood for used furniture. Social life was an often reported casuality of reduced income. Almost all of the displaced workers who suffered income loss reported restricting their social activities to save money, a move that often limited their contacts with their network supports. Many restricted or

stopped activities such as bowling, going out with friends, club memberships, visits to bars, and entertaining.

In reading the descriptions of life-style shifts among these displaced workers, it can be somewhat startling to recall that these are the voices of people who until recently had had a steady job and a middle income.

> We've cut out all the extras. We buy things on sale and use coupons. My wife is a thrifty shopper. We do crafts for pocket money. Our payments are slow but we make them. We were about to give up a campsite we had but the camp director has let us run camp activities in exchange for the site.

> You do without. A bill is always waiting. I need new glasses. We don't go to the doctor. My wife wants more kids but we can't afford them. I pay $20 a month on my mortgage.

> We tried all our resources—my mother and father helped, we sold a car and used our savings. When the kids ask for ice cream you have to say no. That hurts.

> I cut wood for my stove so I don't use so much heat. I grows a lot in the garden and can food. And I does all my own mechanic work on the car. Those are big savings. My house is paid off—I paid cash for it. But I'm behind in my utility bills.

The reference in the last comment to the displaced worker having paid cash for a house underscores an interesting paradox among the group. As mentioned earlier, 87 percent of those interviewed were homeowners. Housing prices in the area had long been modest, even before real estate values dropped in the wake of the plant closings. As noted earlier, at the time of the survey houses could be purchased for between $7,000 and $30,000; saving to pay cash for a house was not preposterous. Local residents have a reputation for disliking debt, and it was not uncommon for families to increase their mortgage payments to rid themselves of liability more quickly. In fact, at the time of the interview, 27 percent reported that they had already paid off the mortgage on their house. Because of this, many of the displaced workers who now fell into the poor or low-income category had property assets. Some people who had slipped in status from middle income to poor may not have had enough money to pay utility bills, but owned their homes outright.

It is important to note, however, that not all those who had purchased homes were free of housing worries. Younger people and those who had bought homes within the previous 15 years were the most likely to be having trouble meeting house payments, and some had lost their homes. Of the 102

respondents, eight had had a bank foreclose on their property since the plant closings.

SOURCES OF INCOME

In addition to restricting consumption and altering spending patterns, life-style shifts following the plant closings also involved securing new sources of income, including unemployment insurance and company pensions, income from odd jobs, earnings from children and spouses, and assistance from social service programs. As described below, these new financial means were often accompanied by changes in family roles and relationships and altered patterns of dependency.

Social Insurance and Early Retirement

As described in Chapter 5, most displaced workers intially secured income through unemployment insurance, which provided a measure of financial security for several months after the plant shutdowns.

For 34 percent of the respondents, income was also supplemented by a company pension. Pensioners ranged in age from 43 to 65, with a mean age of 54. To be eligible for a pension, mill workers had to have at least 20 years of seniority and be 40 years old. Pensions averaged $350 a month and increased with age and seniority. Though pension benefits offered a supplement to income, they were not considered by most to be adequate income. And while the displaced workers appreciated the income generated by the pensions, few welcomed the forced early retirement that frequently ensued.

Of the 34 persons who received a pension, only 6 had retired voluntarily after the plant closings. The rest had pursued an active job search. Many of these, however, had had difficulty finding employment. With upwards of 20 years' seniority, they had no recent job search experience and little work experience outside the mills. As older workers, they had fewer educational credentials. In describing their job searches, most said they faced age discrimination, with employers favoring younger men for blue-collar and manual labor. At the time of the interview, 15 of the 34 pensioners were employed, with wages averaging $4.50 an hour; 2 were still unemployed and actively seeking work; another 2 had decided to retire after an unsuccessful job search; and 8 were classified as discouraged workers—they were no longer actively looking for work because of past job search failure, but did not consider themselves retired because of their desire to secure work in the future.

In describing their status as pensioners, the refrain heard over and over among these men, whether retired, unemployed, or employed, was, "I didn't want to retire."

> I was not happy to take early retirement. I have two kids to raise. Two in college. Looking for a job for $3.35 an hour at age 45 was humiliating.

> I wasn't ready to retire—financially or otherwise. I was forced to. Nobody wants you at 57.

> It was winter when I lost my job and I went crazy. I'm a workaholic and can't sit still. I didn't want early retirement! And I was worried financially.

Changes in the Family Economy

Odd Jobs

During their initial unemployment, many displaced workers supplemented their social insurance income with earnings from odd jobs. While unemployed, most picked up various types of piecework—they mowed grass, fixed roofs, and painted houses. Such work, however, rarely provided much supplemental income. With so many unemployed mill workers in town, the surplus of labor brought down wages and spread the available work thin. Some displaced workers tried a variety of novel efforts to get extra cash. One rented a garage and washed cars by hand, $1.00 a car. Several sold handmade woodcrafts, and one cut firewood to sell. Among persons who are still unemployed or employed at low wages, odd jobs remain a common source of extra money.

Working Family Members

Additional income also came from family members. Children frequently picked up paper routes or odd jobs, and teenagers took on whatever work they could find. Most important to family economic stability, however, was the employment of a spouse.

At the time of the plant closings, the mill worker was most often the primary breadwinner in these households. With the loss of the mill job, however, the dynamics of the family economy often changed dramatically. In many households the female spouse became the primary earner, while the displaced worker remained unemployed or underemployed.

At the time of the interview, 70 percent of the respondents' spouses were working. Of that number, 35 percent had gone to work following the plant closings because the household needed extra money. Because the types of work available locally—low-wage, part-time, service-sector jobs—were those traditionally held by women, it was often considered easier for the women to assume these jobs than for the men, who were used to a factory setting and heavy labor. It was most often the woman of the household who

first took a job making hamburgers at McDonald's or as a sales clerk at J. C. Penney. Among spouses, 90 percent held service-sector jobs. Men who eventually took low-paying service-sector jobs often did so later than their wives; they first held out for higher pay or manufacturing work. It is interesting to note that several female spouses assumed the role of primary breadwinner because of wage advancements in traditionally female professions. Spouses who were teachers and nurses, for example, earned wages that were often much higher than those that many of the displaced workers could command.

Househusbands

Underscoring such role reversals was the fact that 9 percent of the respondents identified themselves as househusbands. They cooked, cleaned, or took care of the children while their wives worked. Some of the former steelworkers, though not all, expressed discomfort with this new role.

> I took a minimum-wage job as a cook. My wife is a medical secretary. Sure I felt degraded in the job, and the wife made more money than me. We have two small kids, and it wasn't worth paying a babysitter for me to work for $3.35. So I quit to take care of them. At least I'm getting a chance to raise the kids.

> It's hard on a man financially and psychologically. It is hard to see the wife take over as breadwinner.

> My problem is this, I'm a househusband. My wife went to work because I went everywhere and couldn't find a job—nobody wants a guy at age 60. She wants to quit but we need the money. I sit around the house a lot during the day. I've been very depressed. I clean and then cook supper for the wife—I make great stuffed peppers and stuffed cabbage. I play accordian in a polka band, and on Friday night we go out to practice. The wife complains about that, but she works! She talks to people, goes out for lunch. I sit home all day. It drives you crazy being cooped up like this.

The importance of spouse earnings to a family's economic viability is illustrated in Table 6.1, in which household income is paired with the number of spouse earners. In the lowest-income category, 0 to $10,999, only 17 percent of the households have two working spouses, while in the top category, $31,000+, 100 percent of the households have two. Prior to the plant closings most of the households could maintain an income in excess of $20,000 through the salary of one mill worker. At the time of the survey, however, that income most often required two earners.

Table 6.1
Household Income and Number of Spouse Earners

N = 102

Household Income	% of Married Respondents	% of Households with Two Spouse Earners
0-$10,999 N = 36	67	17
$11,000-$15,999 N = 21	75	30
$16,000-$19,999 N = 17	82	52
$20,000-$25,999 N = 15	100	53
$26,000-$30,999 N = 8	100	62
$31,000+ N = 5	100	100

Social Service Utilization

In beginning to arrange alternate sources of material and social support, all of those interviewed were initially linked to the social service system via insurance programs such as social security, unemployment insurance, and company pensions. Beyond that, most relied on personal and family assets during initial phases of unemployment. As personal or family resources were depleted or proved inadequate, however, most of the displaced workers were moved to seek social service assistance. This represented a novel experience for long-time workers, who typically had little previous interaction with social service providers. Likewise, the situation was a new one for the service providers, who faced a new and growing clientele in need.

The use of social service programs by the displaced workers is summarized in Table 6.2. Their extensive use of a variety of social services marks a dramatic change in sources of economic and social support for this population. At the time of the survey interview, 18 percent reported using some form of public assistance: food stamps, general assistance, Aid to Families with Dependent Children–Unemployed (AFDC-U), or Supplemental Security Income (SSI); 36 percent were benefiting from a social

Table 6.2
Social Service Utilization Among Displaced Workers in the Years Following the Plant Closings

N = 102

Service	% of Respondents Using Service (fall 1987)	% of Respondents Who Used Service in the Three Yrs Immediately Following the Plant Closings (1983–86)
Unemployment insurance	3	96
Social security	10	10
Pension	34	32
Food stamps	18	35
AFDC-U	7	14
General assistance	1	11
SSI	3	5
Mortgage assistance	6	6
Utility bill assistance	25	36
Church programs	10	16
Counseling	6	13
Food pantries/ government food distribution	31	64
Other	6	13

insurance program, such as social security, a company pension, or unemployment compensation; and 39 percent were using other social service programs, such as utility bill assistance, counseling services, or government surplus food distribution. In total, 69 percent were utilizing some type of social service program, with most participating in more than one program.

Though high, these figures represent a drop in usage compared to the first

three years after the plant closings, during which 38 percent had used some form of public assistance. As all of the displaced workers collected unemployment insurance, social security, or a pension, 100 percent had benefited from at least one social insurance program. In addition, 70 percent had used some other type of social service.

In examining changes in social service utilization following the plant closings, the reports from the displaced workers were supplemented by information gathered from interviews with executives at 22 local social service agencies (Appendix B). In line with respondent reports of increased use of social services, agency statistics showed a dramatic increase in caseloads following the mill shutdowns. The Mercer County Assistance Office (public welfare), for example, saw cases go from 7,200 in 1981 to 13,000 in 1983, leveling to 12,000 in 1987. The Women Infants and Children Supplemental Food Program (WIC) served 11,908 women and children in Mercer County in 1981; 37,517 in 1983; and 45,123 in 1986. Alternatives for Women, the local battered women's shelter, reported a 100 percent increase in clients served in the year after the first plant closings. The Emergency Management Office in Mercer distributed government surplus food to 4,000 families in 1981; 12,000 in 1983; and 8,000 in 1986.

As reported by agency executives, these dramatic increases in demand for services often coincided with budget cuts. Some agencies lost money through federal government cuts in domestic spending enacted in the first several years of the Reagan administration. Many lost private funding because corporate donors left the area as businesses closed, and because the local United Way was forced to cut allocations when its contributions dropped from about $2 million in 1981 to $.9 million in 1983. Many organizations reported that their fund raising could not keep up with the expense of rising caseloads, and some were forced to cut staff at a time when demands for services were soaring.

Though the Shenango Valley boasts a large number of social service organizations, few agencies were able to offer services specific to the needs of the new population of displaced workers. The extant programs had not been established with displaced workers in mind. Many of the programs were targeted to the poorest, most needy clients, and newly unemployed persons with property assets were often ineligible for services. The special needs of displaced workers, such as health insurance or relocation assistance, had not previously been addressed by local social service programs. Of the 22 agency executives interviewed, only 4 reported that they had altered programs to accommodate the special problems of displaced workers. Most said they simply lacked the resources and staff to handle this new population of needy. Others were bound by federal or state eligibility mandates and could not change their program structure to admit displaced workers.

In response to this situation, a coalition of clergy, union representatives, and community members organized a group called the Concerned Citizens

for the Unemployed to provide some special services to the jobless. Formed in 1983, the group solicited private donations and federal emergency management funds to establish a community food bank and a county-wide string of 23 food pantries. A few other grassroots efforts were also organized. Local churches offered food, clothing, and emergency cash assistance to unemployed parishioners. The Salvation Army collected money to be used to help the jobless pay utility bills. As regional unemployment skyrocketed, the state of Pennsylvania implemented a mortgage assistance program for displaced workers under which the state would pay interest on a mortgage for three years on homes on which the bank had begun to foreclose.

As such, a patchwork of services for displaced workers developed. In making their way through this system of services, it is interesting to note that the displaced workers once again drew on their personal networks, with most of them finding out about services through word of mouth. In considering approaching a social service agency, many said that they or their spouses had first checked with relatives, neighbors, or friends to get any information they could on what it was like to apply and the types of services offered. A well-informed network often spurred service use.

Other means of connection with social services included union publications and contacts with intake workers at the employment office. Only four agencies reported doing any outreach to displaced workers, citing limited resources and already high caseloads.

The Stigma of Dependency

Many displaced workers reported that their decision to seek social assistance was among the most degrading in a series of downward life-style shifts. The majority of the displaced workers—74 percent—reported having been hesitant to apply for assistance. The most frequently reported reason for this hesitancy was pride. They did not want to accept charity or give in to dependency.

> It's pride that makes you hesitant to go. When we got food stamps we went to a grocery store where no one knew us. Lots of people do that, you know. You just hate to be seen doing it.

> You feel funny. We wanted to make it on our own. I felt others were worse off.

> We take care of things on our own. We were determined to be self-sufficient. You don't want to admit you need help.

> My pride is way up here [gestures to ceiling] even though my wallet is down here [gestures to floor].

While many displaced workers did participate in social service programs, others intentionally stayed away. The numbers of persons eligible for service were much higher than the recipient rates. Though 29 percent reported household income below the poverty line, only 18 percent said they were participating in public assistance programs. Pride had kept many from applying. Others, as homeowners, feared the lien on their property that was required for receipt of some forms of public assistance.

> I'm too proud. I know I could have qualified for food stamps and fuel assistance, but I didn't want to do it. You don't want to feel like you are scraping bottom.
>
> We live on the wife's minimum wage. We don't like to take charity from nobody. For welfare, we don't want no lien on the house.
>
> I'd like to go for food stamps but I'm afraid they'll put a lien on my trailer.
>
> I'm sure we qualify for food stamps but I don't want to apply. Just feel funny, ashamed. I'd go before I'd starve, but not 'til then.

Lack of experience and information also interfered with usage. Most workers had not previously made extensive use of social service programs and were not familiar with what was available.

> To tell you the truth, I haven't gone for anything 'cause I don't even know what's out there.
>
> Seems like more of a bother than a good. Not worth the time, wait, and aggravation. It always seemed a hassle to find out what was around.

Limited participation in social service programs—particularly in public assistance—was also a result of program eligibility requirements. The federal "100 hours rule" denies cash public assistance to able-bodied individuals who have worked 100 hours in one month. Many displaced workers whose income fell below poverty were working, most in excess of 100 hours. The displaced workers also expressed frustration with asset requirements. Again, most were homeowners; to receive cash public assistance one had to sell the home or accept a lien on the property that required that all cash assistance be repaid upon sale of the home. Both food stamps and AFDC also have very low asset ceilings ($2,000 and $1,000, respectively), so that participants must have exhausted almost all savings

and sold newer vehicles to qualify. In addition, receipt of AFDC-U in Pennsylvania carries a workfare requirement; nonexempt able-bodied individuals must work off the cost of their benefits at a community-service job. Because most of these highly stigmatized jobs are in visible locales—for example, as janitors at local elementary schools—the requirement has deterred participation among displaced workers.

Many also expressed discouragement and frustration over their lack of access to medicaid or health insurance. Following their job loss, many of the displaced workers attempted to secure assistance with health costs, and were stunned to learn that Medicaid was only available to recipients of AFDC. At the time of the interview, 17 percent of the displaced workers were without health insurance, while another 15 percent were paying their own premiums—a hefty financial burden for low-income persons.

Diminished Resistance to Public Assistance

Though initially hesitant to use social programs, many of the displaced workers eventually came to rationalize that, as taxpayers, they had paid for public programs and were entitled to them. Also, with so many of their friends and former coworkers using the services, the stigma associated with participation began to decrease.

> At first I felt funny. But you'd be surprised how many people use the programs. So I decided I might as well.

> I'm not hesitant, because I paid for the services when I was working and I'm entitled to them now.

> It was a new experience. I had heard about the programs through the union. I didn't want to use them, but we had no choice.

The lessening of this initial reluctance was also observed by social service personnel. Echoing the displaced workers, agency executives said that pride and inexperience were factors that had made the former mill workers hesitant to seek assistance. However, they noted that attitudinal changes occurred over time, as displaced workers began to accept a status marked by increased dependence.

> Initially they are very hesitant to come here [welfare office]. They feel a stigma about coming in, but that is changing. Look at our waiting room—it is blue collar, former middle class.

> A lot of these guys are very angry at being in a position of having to ask for help after having worked for everything their whole

> lives. Many of these are the same people who criticized welfare recipients as "lazy bums." Now they are welfare recipients, but they know they themselves aren't bums. Attitudes change—maybe they see that it is a matter of circumstances. They resist coming for help for a long time, until they are very needy. Then resignation sets in and they begin to accept their dependence.

Numerous agency executives reported that because of the pride of male displaced workers, it was most often the wife who first approached an agency for services. In seeking assistance, the women reportedly often initiated interaction with comments like, "My husband doesn't know I'm calling," or "I can't get him to come in, but we're at the end of our rope." There was a sense among agency personnel that as the men became depressed over job search failure or low-wage employment, the women in many families actually experienced a rise in self-esteem, as they assumed pivotal roles in managing household budgets, taking on jobs to increase household earnings, and mobilizing social service resources.

> Men equated the mill with success and masculinity. They had a vision of the future which evaporated, and they get depressed. Women are not happy about the situation, but they are taking hold and attempting to keep the family intact. This crisis has become an opportunity for them, and many have a key role in building. They look for work, call social services, manage the family.

> A mother has children to feed and clothe. She is driven. She can't let pride stand in her way. She's the one who seeks out social services.

Agency personnel frequently expressed exasperation, however, that families often waited until all other resources were exhausted before seeking social assistance, asserting that it was much more difficult to pull families out of poverty when they had so few resources left. Among the families of displaced workers, however, this was regarded as appropriate behavior. They tried to preserve self-sufficiency as long as possible, delaying application to social service agencies. Also, eligibility requirements for public assistance demand that persons have limited or no resources in order to participate, virtually mandating prior exhaustion of assets.

Lack of Advocacy for Expanded Services

Following the plant closings, no efforts were undertaken by the displaced workers themselves to organize support services or to advocate for

expanded services. Their concern was to preserve self-sufficiency, not increase their dependency. Many also assumed that their situation would be temporary; few believed that their income loss and need for services would be long term.

Other than the efforts of the Concerned Citizens for the Unemployed, no joint plan of action or assessment occurred among local social service providers. One agency executive commented that while local social service providers were connected—they met and talked regularly—they were not coordinated in their efforts to address the problems of the displaced worker. This lack of coordination was attributed, in part, to staggering increases in caseloads, coinciding with cuts in funding. The problem of mass unemployment and the rise of a new class of poor and low-income people was novel and overwhelming to them. Struggling to maintain day-to-day operations, many agency personnel reported that they felt they were left with no time or energy to devote to broader, coordinating activities. For most agencies, neither guidance nor additional resources for dealing with this new social problem were forthcoming from the federal, state, or local governments.

As identified by both the displaced workers and agency personnel, the primary gaps and problems in services to displaced workers included a lack of health insurance; eligibility requirements for public assistance that blocked or discouraged access to the working poor and persons with property assets; lack of relocation assistance; and a lack of counseling and support groups directed specifically to the problems of the jobless.

Thus, though most displaced workers clung to the prospect of self-sufficiency, their joblessness immediately placed them in a position of dependency, as they were linked to social insurance programs including unemployment insurance and pensions. To supplement these formal supports, the displaced workers drew on personal resources, as well as the material and social assets of relatives, neighbors, and friends. As these were exhausted or proved inadequate, assistance from formal social services was sought. Meanwhile, hope for greater self-sufficiency was sustained through an ongoing employment search.

PURSUING NEW EMPLOYMENT OPPORTUNITIES

Policy debates concerning the decline in the number of manufacturing jobs and the situation of displaced workers often emphasize the responsibility of former manufacturing workers to adapt themselves to a postindustrial economy via retraining or relocation. Displaced workers are encouraged to seek out more prosperous economic sectors and geographic locales. In the Shenango Valley, numerous displaced workers attempted to mobilize new employment and economic resources through job training, job search, and relocation, with mixed results.

Job Training and Education

In hopes of increasing their employment options, displaced workers enrolled in programs offered by the JTPA, local colleges, vocational-technical schools, and correspondence courses. Some increased their job and income status as a result of education and training, but most did not.[1]

Of the 102 persons interviewed, 23 percent participated in some type of job retraining or further education. Another 26 percent attempted to enroll in training or education programs but were denied admittance because they did not meet eligibility or admission standards or because underfunded public programs could not accept additional enrollees.

Most displaced workers who sought retraining went first to the local office of the Job Training Partnership Act (JTPA). As the successor to the federal CETA jobs program, JTPA primarily funds on-the-job training and classroom instruction for income-eligible individuals. Because of limited funding, most JTPA programs offer short-term training for entry-level work. Title III of JTPA provided funds for training and related reemployment services targeted specifically to displaced workers; these services were defined broadly to include job counseling and job search assistance as well as retraining. Enacted in 1982, the initial legislation provided $223 million over a 21 month start-up period—a funding level that could support less than 5 percent of those eligible for services. Because of very limited funding and a huge eligible population, many applicants for Title III programs at the Shenango Valley JTPA were turned down for assistance.

In all, 8 of the respondents had completed JTPA-funded retraining or education programs. Another 15 participated in training or education programs that they pursued and paid for themselves; of those 15, 12 had applied to JTPA but had been turned down.

The results of retraining and education varied widely. The displaced workers enrolled in programs ranging from law school to correspondence courses, and job and income advancements were most often dependent on the type and extent of training completed. The average hourly wages of those who participated in training and education were $6.50, the same as the wages of those who did not pursue training. Unemployment among this group was 17 percent, compared to 14 percent in the overall sample. However, higher earnings were observed among four respondents who obtained salaried as opposed to hourly wage jobs in professional, sales, and managerial positions. These salaried personnel averaged annual incomes of $23,000.

Table 6.3 lists the types of training or education pursued by the displaced workers and the types of jobs subsequently obtained. In all, only four persons secured work related to their education or training; one of the four had been funded by JTPA. Among those who had been successful in obtaining training-related jobs were those who had pursued the most

Table 6.3
Types of Training or Education and Subsequent Employment

N = 23

Training/Education	*Subsequent Employment*
JTPA funded	
Auto mechanics, 9 months of vocational technical school	teaching assistant, school for the disabled
Computer repair, 9 months of vocational technical school	janitor
Locksmithing, correspondence school	welder
Business administration, Bachelor's degree	business manager
Refrigeration repair, 6 months of vocational technical school	construction worker
computer programming, 15 months of vocational technical school	appliance salesman
Business administration, Associate degree	unemployed (laid off from job as business manager)
GED	unemployed
Funded by respondents	
Accounting, currently working on BA	security guard
Liberal arts, 1 year at Penn State	teacher's aide, school for the disabled
Bartending, 2 months	factory worker
Bible school, 2 years	department store clerk

Table 6.3 (cont.)

Business school, 1 semester	unemployed
Liberal arts, 1 semester at Penn State	factory supervisor
Typing course	factory supervisor
Medical technology, Associate degree	medical technician
Engine repair, correspondence course	welder
Law, Juris Doctor	attorney
Computer repair, 1 year of vocational technical school	cable TV installer
Currently working on BA	dishwasher
Mechanics, correspondence course	unemployed
Paramedic training, 6 months at vocational technical school	paramedic
Education, 1 year at Penn State	salesman

advanced training: law school, a bachelor's degree in business, and an associate's degree in medical technology. All of those who pursued advanced training had previously had some college-level work. Personal contacts were also key in their educational decisions: the father of the displaced worker who studied law was an attorney; the man who was studying accounting had been encouraged to do so by a brother-in-law who was a CPA; the displaced worker who pursued a business degree had several friends who were college-educated businessmen.

Those who were not successful in obtaining training-related employment most often blamed the type of training they received. Some were sheepish at having been lured into worthless programs, often at a substantial cost.

These included, for example, a correspondence course in engine repair and "mixology" (bartending) school. Several said their training had been much too elementary, barely offering preparation at an entry level. One man described his experiences as follows:

> There was an auto mechanics program in Detroit that I wanted to go to—a very intensive GM program. That's what I needed, and that's what I qualified for. But they [JTPA] refused to pay for it. Instead they sent me to a local trade school for nine months. It was lousy. I was in with a bunch of 18-year-olds; they called me Grandpa. I already knew everything they went over. It was much too basic. A person couldn't get a job with what they offered.

A few of the others acknowledged that they might be able to find training-related work if they chose to relocate.

Those who pursued training were younger than the sample as a whole, with a mean age of 39 as compared to 44. All but one were married, and all of those who were married had a working spouse. These displaced workers made it quite clear that the earnings of their spouse were a crucial factor in enabling them to engage in retraining or education. None were stipended for their schooling, and the earnings of the spouse helped support the family during this time. These men were also better educated than the sample as a whole; except for the person who was enrolled in a GED program, all had a high school diploma and several had some college.

Futile Attempts to Obtain Training

As mentioned above, almost a quarter of those interviewed had attempted to enroll in training or education programs through JTPA but had been turned down. This was due primarily to insufficient program funding.

JTPA was constructed as a program of the private sector in partnership with local government. State governors are authorized to designate local job training Service Delivery Areas (SDAs). Elected government officials within SDAs appoint business and civic representatives to a Private Industry Council (PIC), which in conjunction with the local government, plans and implements training and education programs in accord with the needs of the local job market.

Unfortunately, the Shenango Valley JTPA experienced difficulties that proved disadvantageous to local displaced workers. When National Castings and GATX closed their doors in 1983 and 1984, the local JTPA was in the midst of a fiscal and management crisis. Funds had been misused and depleted, and the office was being reorganized. Those who phoned or applied for service were sometimes given confusing or inaccurate information about program availability. Following the announcement of

their plant shutdown, the owners of GATX pledged a contribution of $300,000 to the local office of the JTPA. Funding problems persisted, however, and available resources fell far short of need. In addition, local JTPA officials struggled with the problem of arranging training programs that would prove useful or productive, given the depressed local and regional economy.

Given its limited resources, the local JTPA used testing to weed out applicants. Of the 102 respondents, 26 percent reported that they had applied for JTPA training but had been turned down because their test scores were too low or because funds had been depleted. Rejection by JTPA often compounded already strong feelings of insecurity and worthlessness.

> I applied to JTPA and told them I was interested in computers or entrepreneurship. They tested me and I guess my scores were low. They said I couldn't participate. Guess they didn't want to waste their money on me.

> I applied to JTPA. They said there was no more money available. I don't know why. I figured that's my life, that's my luck. I live under a dark shadow.

> They gave me a test and told me I couldn't work at a factory 'cause my dexterity was bad. I was so upset. Then I got a job on my own at Wheatland Tube. I'd like to show 'em what job I got!

While many displaced workers applied for training and were turned down, another segment of respondents, 32 percent, inquired about JTPA but decided not to participate. A primary reason for their nonparticipation in further training was fear or dislike of schooling. Many displaced workers believed that the only type of retraining that would lead to a good job was that which required mental rather than manual skills, such as computer science, business, and accounting. Many people who had gone into the mills after high school had done so because they disliked school or had not done well at academics. They avoided further education because of a fear of failure in the classroom.

> I'm embarrassed to say that I can't write or spell. So I never applied.

> I'm afraid of school. I'm no good at it.

> I am a skilled welder—I didn't think I needed training. And I can't stand to sit at a desk and go to school. I'm a builder, a maker. That's me.

> I quit school in the ninth grade. I have no school smarts. I can't be trained to run a computer.

Others turned away from JTPA because they thought the training would get them nowhere. Some were frustrated by short-term programs that offered only entry-level training. Many did not think jobs would be available in the areas in which training was offered. Several found it impossible to go through training or education programs without a stipend that could help support their family while they were in school. Other displaced workers who already held jobs found they were disqualified from participating because of a federal regulation that deemed ineligible those whose current hourly wages were more than one-half their mill wage, even if the job was part time or a dead end.

> I considered JTPA but it was a waste. I have so many qualifications I could teach the classes—bodywork, millwright, pipe fitter, spray painter. If I couldn't get a job no one could. I took their test and they said I should be a metallurgist. But there was no money available to support my wife and kids while I was in school.

> I looked at JTPA but it was unrealistic. They would give one year training in electrical or machine work—I have buddies with 10-20 years' experience in that and no job! I could teach training classes in sheet metal and air conditioning, for God's sake!

> I considered it, but I had construction skills and I had gone to electrician's school. I didn't need training, I needed work.

Thus, attempts at mobilizing new employment opportunities through education and training were successful for some, but stymied by a variety of personal and programmatic difficulties for many others.

Job Searches

Following the plant closings, new employment opportunities were also pursued through extensive job hunts. As described in Chapter 5, most of the displaced workers in the survey had begun an active job search two or three months following their job loss. These searches utilized both informal and formal channels: inquiries among friends were the most common initial job search methods, followed by contact with the Pennsylvania Job Service, Office of Employment and Security (a requirement for receipt of unemployment insurance). Most of the searchers next began in-person inquiries at every mill still in operation in

the vicinity. Job hunts were then extended to retail stores, restaurants, hospitals, and other small businesses and community organizations.

The most effective job-hunt method involved personal contacts; 74 percent of the respondents who were employed had obtained their jobs through a relative, friend, or acquaintance. Another 8 percent had found jobs through the employment office, 5 percent through newspaper ads, 10 percent through in-person applications, and 3 percent by other methods. The most desirable jobs—those with high pay, benefits, and security—were most often obtained through personal contacts.

As long-time mill employees, many displaced workers had little work experience outside the plants, and lacked job hunt information and experience. Help with the job search came from a variety of sources. College-educated children frequently aided their unemployed parents with resume writing, and spouses often did the layout and typing. Many displaced workers attended job-search or resume-writing workshops sponsored by JTPA and the Pennsylvania Job Service.

As described by the displaced workers, job searches often involved dogged attempts, encompassing scores of inquiries. Competing for work with over 6,000 other displaced workers, many described exhausting and discouraging job hunts and asserted that the best hope for landing a job was to "know someone."

> I was unemployed one year. I went through the phone books and newspapers and went to all the plants and talked to everyone. I looked and looked and came up with nothing. Then my brother got me a job selling potato chips.

> I sent out over 100 resumes. I sent one to every mill, went to the employment office religiously, answered newspaper ads, filled out a civil service application, and took an exam to be a mailman. Nothing happened. I was unemployed two years and got a janitor job at an apartment building. Now I'm a janitor at a mill.

> I put in resumes everywhere from Grove City to Youngstown. I knocked on doors and pounded the pavement. My son was a college grad and he wrote a resume for me. I used everyone in my network—called up my old boss at GATX. Especially at my age [51] you have to use everyone you know. And that's the only way you get a job—connections.

> I was in the car every day. One day I'd go to Youngstown, then Warren, Niles, Salem. I went everywhere. It never occurred to me that I wouldn't find a job. I'm experienced and a good worker. I tried so hard, and I couldn't believe what was happening. I kept

saying, In two weeks I'll have a job. I was unemployed one and a half years—I finally got a job as a janitor.

These often very aggressive job hunts yielded good jobs for some and part-time, low-paying, or no employment for many others. It is critical to note that the widespread apathy and resignation prevalent at the time of the study among many of those interviewed was clearly a consequence of, rather than an antecedent to, situations of unemployment and low-income. In tracing job search histories, it is evident that the overwhelming majority of the displaced workers who are poor, low-income, unemployed, or discouraged had previously looked actively for work. Their discouragement had most often been preceded by optimism and vigorous job searches.

In contrast with their work in the mills, jobs obtained after the plant closings have often been of short duration and have involved frequent lay offs. So rapid, in fact, is job turnover that for some job seeking has often become ongoing, a way of life. Cycles of unemployment and employment have changed dramatically, and are marked by a high rate of employee termination due primarily to a slack demand for work.

First I was a part-time janitor. Then I got a job at Austin Tool and Dye for one year, off and on, and got laid off. Then I got a welder job at T. Bruce Campbell's and got laid off. I got a carpenter's apprentice, and now I'm laid off that and waiting to be called back.

I've had a series of jobs. I worked one month at Masury Steel and was laid off. Then I had a temporary job with the city of Sharon cleaning streets. I worked six months at Yorga Trucking washing trucks for $3.35 an hour, then got laid off. I worked seven months at a supermarket stocking shelves for $3.35 an hour, but couldn't stand it. Now I do yard work for a nursery. I was an electrician at the mill.

I was unemployed for two years. Got a job as a gofer at a lumber place for $4.45 an hour, no benefits. Then my brother got me a job in Ashtabula at a fiberglass plant. Drove 65 miles each way for one year, $7 an hour, no benefits. I've been laid off from there now for a year.

Again, because so many of the displaced workers were still seeking improvement over their low-paying employment or lack of employment, they were still persevering in their job hunts.

> Right now I have a job that pays $4.00 an hour, so I'm always lookin'. I always hit the employment office; it seems senseless, but you never know. I listen for jobs word of mouth, and I put in applications everywhere . . . but really the only way to get a job around here is to know someone.

> I went to college to get an associate's degree in business management. I got a temporary job in production planning at Sharon Steel—it lasted 16 months. My job hunt now consists of newspaper ads and word of mouth. I keep this scrapbook [pulls out notebook full of want-ad clippings]. I paste each ad I answer in here, with the date I applied. You see there are about 50 here now. I've also sent blind resumes to every bank and financial institution around here.

The displaced workers frequently expressed frustration with official unemployment statistics, which they say have masked their employment experiences. While the unemployment rate in the Shenango Valley dropped from a high of 24 percent in 1983 to about 8 percent in 1987, the nature of employment had changed radically. Again, many of the jobs are part time, short term, low wage, nonunion and pay no benefits. The displaced workers complained that simply quoting a lowered unemployment rate without discussing working conditions served to veil their poor income and employment situations. Moreover, the statistics were misleading, they said, because they failed to count those discouraged workers who had stopped looking for work and those who had been forced to retire early.

Upward Mobility: From Blue Collar to White Collar

As noted in Chapter 5, six displaced workers had been successful in making occupational shifts from blue-collar to managerial or professional positions. This group was comprised of an attorney, a business school teacher, a district sales manager, a corporate contract administrator, and two small business owners (a taxidermist and a florist).

These respondents were slightly younger than the sample as a whole, with an average age of 40. Three had had some college education before entering the mills. All were white males, and all but one were married. The average household income for this group was $29,000.

What factors precipitated their climb from working-class occupations? The attorney and the contract administrator had been among the displaced workers who pursued higher education after the plant closures. As noted in an earlier discussion, both had personal contacts who influenced their educational decisions; the father of the attorney was a lawyer, and the contract administrator had several friends who held managerial positions in business. Both commented that they had taken a job at the plant when they were young because of the good wages and the need to support a wife and young children, and that they had become "trapped" by the security and high earnings at the mill. They had completed some college work before entering the plants, and both asserted that they had always felt that they could "do better" than labor in a manufacturing plant. The shutdowns were a spur to a career shift, with the closures viewed as an opportunity for change. Both men had spouses with professional jobs who had worked while their husbands went to school full time, and both commented that they could not have completed the schooling necessary for a career shift without the financial and emotional support of their spouses.

Following the plant closures, two displaced workers opened their own businesses, as a taxidermist and a florist. In discussing their career changes, both of these men said that they had always felt confined by the mills and disliked working for others, and both had always harbored a dream of opening a business. As mill workers they had pursued hobbies of taxidermy and flower arranging. One was a high school graduate; the other had an eighth grade education. After the plant closings, each pursued a similar business development strategy. They borrowed books from the town library on small business management and read everything they could on the subject. They talked to other small business owners, consulted the chamber of commerce, and sought a business loan from a local bank. Both had working spouses who supported them and their families while they established their businesses.

The business school teacher and the district sales manager had obtained their jobs through personal acquaintances who held managerial or professional positions. Both had worked a series of lower-paid service-sector jobs before their personal connections helped them secure their current positions. As with other college-educated persons who had worked as laborers in the mills, the business school teacher, 36 years old, described being "caught" by the security and good wages of the mill. Failing to find a teaching job following graduation from college, he had accepted a mill job because it was the highest-paying work he could find and he needed to support his family. He had never intended to remain a factory worker, but rising wages and generous benefits made it difficult to quit, and he did not leave until the plant closed.

What distinguishes these occupationally mobile respondents from the sample as a whole? All had personal contacts who held higher-status positions and who encouraged and facilitated their career moves. Most of the six said they could not have made the transition without the financial support of a working spouse. Most of these men were also slightly younger and better educated than the average respondent. Beyond these characteristics, all seemed confident in their mental or managerial abilities. Though this self-assurance was most likely a result, in part, of their

job-search success, perhaps it also preceded and contributed to their pursuit of a higher-status occupation.

WHY STAY? DECISIONS TO LEAVE OR REMAIN IN THE VALLEY

Despite some success stories, the job search experiences of most of the displaced workers had not been positive. In the wake of the plant closings, the situation in the Shenango Valley included downward mobility, limited job opportunities, high social-service needs, and a community hard pressed to meet those needs. The question often arises, why did people not leave the area?

In fact, it is estimated that 10 to 15 percent of the displaced workers from the Shenango Valley had relocated. An additional 20 percent had traveled to other states to look for work but decided not to move. Another 5 percent had relocated and later returned.

Relocation

Of the 15 persons from the sample who were known to have moved from the Shenango Valley, 10 were located and interviewed by telephone. All but one, a retiree, were employed, and their average hourly wages and total household income were higher than those of persons who had not relocated.

Among the 10 relocators who were contacted, hourly wages averaged $9.00 and total household income averaged $29,000, compared to hourly wages of $6.50 and an average household income of $14,500 among persons who remained in the valley. All but one were married, and their high household incomes were due in part to the employment of their spouse. As with the larger sample, their mean age was 44. Six had at least a high school diploma, and four did not. Three were black and seven white. Three had moved to the Chicago area, one to central Pennsylvania, one to Ohio, and the remaining five to Southern states. Three of the respondents had obtained manufacturing jobs; two had blue-collar positions as a construction worker and a shipper; and the other four had service-sector positions including a car salesman, a sales representative, a medical technician, and a corrections officer.

All of those who had relocated had done so with the assistance of a friend or relative. Most went to a location where a friend or relative lived, and that person provided them with a place to stay and assistance with a job search. Often the out-of-town contact played a role in instigating the move. For example, the three who had moved to Chicago went there to work in a plant owned by the company that had managed National Castings because a former supervisor called one respondent to offer him a job. The other two followed the first, who as a valley friend and neighbor, provided their job connection.

While the hourly wages of those who had relocated were higher than the wages of those who remained in the Shenango Valley, most were still lower than the wages earned at GATX and National Castings. The ones who found manufacturing jobs were all employed in nonunion shops, with salaries and benefits much lower than had been made in the Shenango Valley plants. The jobs also offered less security, and six relocators had already experienced layoffs. The three who moved to Chicago to work at a manufacturing plant were laid off within nine months; however, all three subsequently found manufacturing jobs at another Chicago-area plant. Three other relocators had also been laid off from their first job but found other employment.

Most of the men who had relocated remarked that their relocation had involved great emotional strain and practical difficulties. For many it had meant a lower standard of housing. While all had been homeowners in the Shenango Valley, all but two were renting their housing in their new location. Several had been unable to sell their Shenango Valley homes and had eventually rented them. Relocation also produced family stress. Most reported that their families were reluctant to leave the Shenango Valley and that the move had triggered marital strain and distress among their children and spouses. All but one of the relocators made the initial move alone, waiting to send for their families until they felt that their new employment was secure and satisfactory. At the time of the interview, all but three men had been joined by their families. Those who had not been joined by their families said they felt their job situation was still too insecure to warrant uprooting their wife and children.

It is interesting to note that, following the plant closings, those who had eventually relocated had been out of work slightly longer than the rest of sample—1.9 years compared to 1.6 years. Most said that their relocation was a move of last resort, after all other employment possibilities in the valley had been exhausted, and had been encouraged by a friend or relative in an out-of-town community who offered assistance. Several noted that they would like to return to the valley if they could find suitable employment there.

Relocation and Return

Some recent studies on plant closings refer to the substantial numbers of displaced workers who leave their hometowns to accept other employment but later return.[2] In the Shenango Valley, stories and rumors abound regarding the numbers of displaced workers who have left the area, only to return because of the hardships experienced out of town. One often-told story, for example, is about a family who sold its house, moved to Florida, and had to hitch a ride back to the valley in a pickup truck after job failures left the family penniless. In fact, 5 of the 102 survey respondents reported that they had indeed moved from the valley to accept other employment and

later returned. In each case the displaced workers—all male—had made the initial move alone. Those who had families had left them in the Shenango Valley with the intention of sending for them when they were settled. Their stays had ranged from six weeks to two years, and averaged six months.

The five who moved and returned were younger than the overall sample, with a mean age of 35. All but one were married. Two had found out-of-state jobs by answering newspaper ads. The other three had moved to towns in which a close relative lived, and that relative had provided initial housing and helped with job arrangements. Their employment included spray painter at a factory in Texas, computer programmer in Texas, and factory worker in Southern California. Their out-of-state wages had averaged $9.00 an hour.

All five described the great effort, expense, and anxiety that went into relocation and their discouragement at watching their arrangements collapse. Three had returned because of job difficulties: one was laid off, and two found their wages too low or the work too insecure to support a family. The other two had returned because their families were unhappy in their new locale. Their stories had fueled the rumors and anxiety about out-of-town work that prevailed among the local displaced workers.

> I answered an ad in the paper for an "expert spray painter" for a place in Texas. They told me I would teach spray painting and promised big wages and a promotion. So I went down. After I'd been there six weeks and taught their guys how to paint they went back on their promises. Said I would just be a laborer and cut my pay. The whole thing was fishy. I think they just wanted to pick my brain and then dump me. It was nonunion; what could I do? I came back here. Luckily my family hadn't moved down yet.

> I went to Kentucky to try and start a business in steel fabrication with my brother-in-law. I brought my savings, and we were going to use his intelligence and my back. I was very optimistic and assertive. I wanted something better for my family. The prospects for the business looked good. We put the house up for sale and the family was going to join me when it sold.
>
> Things didn't work out . . . we decided to forgo the business. So I looked for a job—could only find work at $6.00 an hour with no security. I felt I'd get stuck in a low-paying job. Meanwhile we had no offers on the house.
>
> I came back to the valley and worked as a janitor, $4.00 an hour, no benefits. I was so depressed I cried. I was there for a year.
>
> Then I went to visit some friends in Lancaster and looked for a job there. Got a job as a welder for $7.00 an hour, no benefits.

> We put the house up for sale again and I moved down. But the whole thing was shaky from the start. The boss couldn't give me steady work or any commitment of job security. It was a circus. I decided it was too risky, too insecure. We hadn't sold the house yet, so I came back.

Out-of-State Job Searches

Another large group, numbering 20 persons, had traveled out of state to look for work but had decided not to relocate. Those who had ventured to other states differed little from the larger sample with regard to age, education, or marital status. A smaller percentage were homeowners (74 percent vs. 87 percent), a factor that might have made it easier to consider relocating. Those who traveled long distances to look for work did hold a feature in common: a network contact, usually a close relative or friend, who offered a place to stay and assistance with their job search.

While some had chosen not to move because they did not like the geography or life-style of the places they visited, the primary reason for not relocating was a lack of job search success. The jobs they found paid wages too low to compensate for a higher cost of living and did not provide security.

> I went out West to look for work and came back. All I could find was $6.00-an-hour jobs. The cost of living is high, and both husband and wife have to work just to survive.

> I went to Florida to look for work. The wages were higher, but so was the cost of living. Nothin' seemed secure and I had no place to live.

> I went to West Virginia and applied to mills down there. But they were laying off and closing too.

> My son lives in Washington, D.C., and I went down to see if I could find some construction work there. I decided not to move because it was just too fast for me. High gear and wide open—that's not for me.

Decisions to Remain in the Area

While some displaced workers had traveled out of state to seek work opportunities, others merely entertained the idea of relocation. Of those who have remained in the area, 62 percent said they considered leaving, but few thought they would actually go. Asked about the likelihood of their leaving

in the next five years, only 8 percent reported that it was very likely they would leave; 23 percent said it was somewhat likely; 24 percent said it was not too likely; and 46 percent reported it was not at all likely.

There were many reasons behind the hesitancy to move. As described in Chapter 3, most residents of the Shenango Valley have lived there their whole lives and feel a strong attachment to the area. Most have close-knit family and friends and a strong identification with the working-class culture. Many reported a reluctance to leave elderly parents who live in the area. Others felt that they themselves were too old to uproot.

Such attachments are more difficult to break because of the practical complications of relocation. Many of the displaced workers had no family, friends, or job contacts elsewhere. They had never lived outside the valley and did not know a lot about other places. Aware of the national decline in manufacturing, they feared there would be no jobs for which they were qualified in other locales. They had heard the tales of low wages and irregular work from those who moved from the valley and later returned.

It is also difficult to sell a house in the area. Again, 87 percent of the respondents were homeowners. Already modest, real estate values had declined since the plant closings. As indicated by the real estate ads in Illustration 6.1, houses could be bought for $7,000 to $30,000. There were dozens for sale and few buyers. Even if one were successful in selling, the price would barely have covered a down payment in many parts of the country, particularly in areas such as the Northeast or West Coast where jobs were more abundant. Numerous displaced workers expressed the opinion that they were better off making $5.00 per hour in the Shenango Valley, secure in a home and with a community of friends, than working for $8.00 or $9.00 an hour in an area where they could not afford a home and would be apart from community supports.

Many also feared that, as new employees, they would be vulnerable to lay offs. They felt that being laid off from work in a strange town—minus an affordable home and a ready support network—would be much more devastating than being down and out in the Shenango Valley.

Finally, relocation was made difficult by the fact that no social programs of relocation assistance existed. Many did not have the cash to travel to job interviews, move furniture, and establish a new household. Welfare recipients could receive a few hundred dollars toward the costs of moving; otherwise, no help was available to local displaced workers who wished to relocate. This paucity of assistance applied to information as well as cash. Knowledge of jobs and opportunities in other locales was difficult to obtain outside of personal contacts. The information provided by the local Pennsylvania Job Service and JTPA was limited and fragmented.

In talking about relocation, displaced workers disclosed strong feelings of attachment to their community, as well as anxiety about the unknown.

> If you leave the area it is like stepping into the Twilight Zone. You don't know where you'll be or what you'll get.

> I heard so many stories of people who left and could only make $6.00 an hour. At least here I own my own home and have family who won't let me starve.

> We looked in different newspapers and talked to people. Where could we go? To do what?

> I was afraid to go. My brother went to Oklahoma and had a terrible time—the oil boom collapsed and he is just scraping by. At least here we have family and a house, and we like the valley.

> I have no idea where to go and I couldn't afford to leave. If you go and get laid off, then what happens? I think I'll be here forever.

Individual versus Community Mobilization: A Lack of Collective Action

It is interesting to note that most of the methods used by the displaced workers to mobilize new sources of social and economic support involved individual efforts. Aside from the actions of the Concerned Citizens for the Unemployed in organizing a county-wide food bank, no collective efforts were undertaken by the displaced workers to protest the plant closings, rally media attention, or organize or lobby for expanded employment, job training, and social services. Some displaced workers discussed among themselves the idea of a worker buyout of the plants, but no action was taken. This was due in part to their observation of the difficulties that displaced workers in neighboring Youngstown faced when they attempted to obtain worker control of a steel plant there in the late 1970s. In addition to stubbornly clinging to a belief in self-sufficiency and individualism, many displaced workers also appeared to lack the confidence, know-how, and political connections needed to organize collective efforts. As noted in Chapter 7, however, many were plagued by feelings of guilt that they had not done more as a group to protest and respond to the closings.

SUMMARY

Several years after the plant closings, some displaced workers had managed a transition into secure, well-paying jobs. Such factors as age, education, and personal contacts had facilitated their reemployment in a changed economy. Despite what had often been very active efforts, however, most of those interviewed had not been able to establish satisfying or

improved employment opportunities. As will be described in Chapter 7, years of unrewarded attempts at finding satisfactory reemployment have disturbed the psychological well-being and shaken the world views of many of these displaced workers.

NOTES

1. See Allison Zippay, "Job Training and Relocation Experiences among Displaced Industrial Workers," *Evaluation Review* 15, no. 5 (1991): 555–70.

2. Terry F. Buss and F. Stevens Redburn, *Shutdown at Youngstown* (Albany: NY: State University of New York Press, 1983); Richard Swigart, *Managing Plant Closings and Occupational Readjustment* (Washington, DC: National Center of Occupational Readjustment, 1984).

7

The Emotional Toll: Depression, Anger, and Mistrust

The downward mobility of many displaced workers has taken an emotional toll. Four years after the first plant closings, many reported lingering depression and anger and a growing sense of futility. The experience of dislocation had affected their expectations for the future; most felt vulnerable and distrusted the prospects for themselves and the larger community. Among many, bitterness over the plant closings had spilled over into an animosity toward institutions such as big business, labor unions, and the government.

LINGERING DEPRESSION AND ANGER

At the time of the interviews, a startlingly high number of displaced workers said that they continued to be plagued by anger and depression. Over half reported a prolonged struggle with feelings of frustration and loss and uncertainty over how they could settle these emotions. Many continued to be haunted by the events surrounding the shutdowns. Asked which community services they were presently in need of, most first mentioned job services. The second most frequently listed item was psychological counseling.

Issues that continued to distress the former mill workers included a loss of self-sufficiency, an inability to find satisfactory reemployment, a loss of pride, a sense of betrayal by the company owners who had closed the plants, and a loss of the sense of belonging and camaraderie that had characterized interaction in the mills. As the respondents discussed these issues, their comments were often strikingly intense, with sharp and emotional expressions of anger and despondency.

As illustrated in Table 7.1, depression and interpersonal difficulties were experienced by a majority of the displaced workers in the months

Table 7.1
Affective Responses to Job Loss in the Months Following the Plant Closings

N = 102	
Depression	
Increased	76%
Same	21%
Decreased	3%
Temper/irritability	
Increased	50%
Same	44%
Decreased	6%
Relations with spouse	
Better	11%
Same	35%
Worse	53%
Alcohol consumption	
Increased	28%
Same	57%
None	8%
Decreased	7%

immediately following the plant closings. An increase in feelings of depression following their job loss was reported by 76 percent; worsened marital relations by 53 percent; problems with temper and irritability by 50 percent; and increased alcohol consumption by 28 percent. Many indicated that these reactions had developed in the first several months after their job loss, ebbed to varying degrees while they searched for jobs, and intensified as the months and years dragged on and their income and employment status failed to improve.

As the displaced workers described their current problems and feelings, references to low self-esteem and a sense of personal failure often surfaced. These comments were most frequent among the unemployed and persons who had been reemployed but at lower wages.

> It's hard emotionally and socially. You can't find a good job and feel terrible about yourself. You bang your head against the wall. You can't help feeling that way.

> It's like you are a piece of paper that someone crumpled up and threw into the wastebasket.

Shaken self-confidence was often accompanied by a jarred sense of purpose and identity. Several years after the plant closings, many still seemed to be at loose ends, having been unable to secure a new or respected occupational identity. Mill work had provided a sense of security and order that many had not been able to recapture.

> It's like the earth opened up and just sucked us in.

> I've felt lost about no job and no place to get one.

> I'm still angry and upset. You begin to wonder what life is all about—what it all means. What are you going to be doing in the future?

The former mill workers also made frequent references to feelings of abandonment. Many still felt stung by what they perceived as a betrayal on the part of company owners. Again, many respondents had worked most of their adult lives at the plants, in what were often difficult conditions. Many felt that the company owners had disregarded their employees' loyalty to and tolerance of the factory system. Belief in the paternal responsibility of mill operators to the local community persisted, and numerous displaced workers continued to look at the plant closings as a personal affront.

> I gave them the best years of my life. Then I was gone with the wind.

> You are rejected—that's what hurts. They don't want you.

> I still feel angry. It was a big part of my life. I didn't like being abandoned.

> Why did they do this to me? I didn't deserve this. To this day it still bothers me.

Many also continued to believe that the work of several generations of steelworkers had been slighted, and that the labor of their fathers and grandfathers had been spurned.

> I keep thinking, "Is this all they cared about us?" My uncle had scars all over his arms. Especially all those guys who worked so long. They paid their dues there.

> By closing down they lost the meaning of those old-timers who worked so hard for 30 cents an hour to build the mills and build the country.

Others were nagged by feelings of guilt that they, as steelworkers, had not done more to protest the plant closings collectively.

> We went to the slaughter like a bunch of sheep.

> If we had all stuck together this might not have happened—the plants might not have closed.

Their feelings of frustration and loss had frequently translated into increased irritability. Many described their difficulties with flaring anger or smoldering resentment. Frustration over the plant closings and declines in income and employment status had strained interpersonal relations, as some displaced workers took out their discontent on spouses, family, and friends. Again, over 50 percent of those interviewed stated that their marital relations had suffered following the job loss, and five displaced workers blamed their recent marital breakups on strains caused by job loss. Many described tense or violent home scenes. As noted in the previous chapter, the local shelter for battered women reported a 100 percent increase in clients served in the first year after the plant closings. In some homes such tensions had continued.

> My wife says my temper is terrible. She's right. I'm very frustrated. Tensions build—I'm home all day with the kids. We've got no enjoyment money to get out of the house. It's a vicious cycle. I've been edgy and irritable, and relations with the family are bad.

> I see friends for whom everything has fallen apart. People have marital problems. Maybe these marriages weren't so strong to begin with, but the job loss was the last straw. It kicks people over the edge.

Increases in personal tensions and anger were also felt outside the home.

> I still feel depressed. I don't cope very well. I scream at the neighbors. I'm not happy. It gets worse as it goes. I'm meaner

> now than I ever was—like an animal. I know I could probably use some counseling.

Some displaced workers with young children expressed concern about the effect that their unhappiness and changed home life might have on their offspring. They worried about the children's exposure to increased household tension and anxiety. Some said they saw a decline in the quality of their children's schoolwork; others said they felt their children were more anxious.

Linked to some problems of household tension and anxiety was an increase in alcohol consumption. About 28 percent of those interviewed said that their drinking had increased after the plant closings, but how much of that increase represented substance abuse is difficult to gauge. A handful of respondents commented that they were currently drinking too much. Four said they drank heavily after their job loss and eventually quit with the aid of Alcoholics Anonymous or another treatment program. Local social service personnel reported a steady stream of alcohol-related problems among former mill workers and their families. Those who had battled their own alcoholism described the links between alcohol and distress.

> I couldn't find work and I felt inadequate. I drank with my buddies and we all felt inadequate together. It was very negative and destructive.

> At first I went to the bars a lot. You go down there and talk to the guys about your problems. It's like a release valve. And then there comes a point where you realize it's not doing you any good. It's making you worse. I quit.

> A lot of us drank heavy. All go to a bar and feel sorry for each other 'til we had no feelings. I almost lost my family and myself.

By far the most pervasive and lingering response to the plant closings has been depression. Again and again, displaced workers spoke of an inability to overcome feelings of sadness and despondency. Their comments were often startling for the sharp pain they expressed. As mentioned earlier, their unhappiness and depression stemmed from factors including a lack of job search success, loss of pride, and loss of their identity as blue-collar workers. Such despondency was most common in persons who had suffered a drop in income or employment status.

> I thought I would have no trouble getting another job. But I've tried so hard—there is nothing here for me and I feel very

> depressed. I haven't even told my wife this, but sometimes I go down to the cellar and just cry my eyes out.
>
> My doctor says I'm suffering from depression. My wife says I'll get over it. But how do you get over it? . . . I've had some bad dreams. I've had them several times. I dream I hear the presses running and the guys kidding each other. A couple of times I jumped out of bed in the morning—thought I was going to work. And then you remember you aren't.
>
> You look and look for work and no one wants you. It seems like there is no future.

Many related stories of continuing struggles with separation and loss. Several of these accounts contained haunting images of the idle, empty mills—images that evoked the bereavement that many experienced.

> I knew a guy who was one of the last to leave [the mill]—he helped ship the equipment out. He said the place is big and empty and still. That long plant with a hush over everything. You hear the wind outside. I think of things—what does my shop look like now? When I drive past I think of that and I feel sad.
>
> It's all very confusing. After I retired I bought a motorcycle. I'd always wanted one and a friend sold me a $2,000 Honda for $500. I'm 69 and I still ride it almost every day. Anyway, I jump on my motorcycle and I ride down to the plant—down to the parking lot over to the gate where I went in for 41 years. And I just look. And I say, It seems impossible that you can put all of your life into a place and then it is gone. It's like a dream. Sometimes I have to pinch myself—was it real? The grass is growing high there now.
>
> I keep thinking about these things. After GA [GATX] closed I got a temporary job as a security guard for a plant that had made parts for GA. I'd walk through the plant at midnight with a flashlight, and my flashlight would shine on a part that I myself had applied at GA. But GA was shut down. That made me real sad—see those parts and nowhere for them to go.

Three respondents expressed extreme despair and spoke of suicide. All three of these had incomes below the poverty line. Two of them were working, but for minimum wage.

> I'm still very depressed. How do I deal with it? I avoid people just like I tried to avoid you. I don't talk to no one about it or anything. The state mortgage program has run out and now I owe the bank $1,900. They are foreclosing now. I don't know what we are going to do or what will happen with the house or family. It is hard to swallow. You don't feel like a man. If I had an insurance policy to leave I would take a gun and blow my head off. Sometimes I just feel like doing that anyway.

Continuum of Responses

Such deep distress represents the extreme of a continuum of responses among the displaced workers to their changed income and employment status, with their anxieties ranging from mild to severe. A majority of those interviewed continued to be disturbed by some degree of emotional or interpersonal difficulty. These emotional disturbances had spurred domestic violence, fed alcoholism, discouraged their job searches, and spawned suicidal thoughts.

At the other end of the spectrum, a minority of the displaced workers appeared to be relatively free of distress. As illustrated in Table 7.1, some displaced workers said they had not suffered depression or anger or had marital problems. Whereas job loss had precipitated marital strife in some homes, in others the respondents reported that the trauma had strengthened their relationships as they and their spouses weathered the crisis together. While some increased their alcohol consumption after job loss, others reduced their drinking, explaining that they had no money to spend on alcohol or that they no longer drank the traditional shot and a beer after the mill shift. Eight said they were happy to be out of the mills and pleased with their new jobs or careers.

What influences such variations in response? Of the variables measured in this study, low economic status was the factor most often associated with distress. In comparing respondents who reported such problems as excessive anger and depression with those who did not, variations were found in income and employment status. Among those who did not report emotional troubles, household income averaged $17,000, compared to $13,000 for the distressed respondents. Among the group that did not report depression, all were currently employed, while 20 percent of those who did report depression were jobless.

Methods of Coping

In discussing the disturbances that have accompanied changes in income and employment status, the displaced workers also described a variety of ways of coping with distress. Some said that they talked about their

problems with friends, family, or former coworkers. Several mentioned that they coped by "keeping busy" with household projects or other activities that provided distraction. Others found solace in religion. The fact that many of their neighbors or acquaintances were in a similar situation provided some comfort and support.

A surprising number of respondents, however, said that they had not sought friends or family for counsel. Clinging to an ideal of self-sufficiency and independence, many said that they had tried thinking through problems themselves, or tried to cope by seeking solitude through fishing, hunting, or another sports activity.

> I tried to work through my problems on my own—I didn't talk to anyone.

> I blocked out a lot of thoughts—and I'd go on long jogs.

> I grab my fishin' pole and just go sit in the woods. Takes the pressure off. When you are sittin' fishin' you have a lot of time to yourself to sit and think.

> I don't do anything to cope—I just sit and smolder.

Others would pick one person—their spouse, a friend, or a minister or priest—to confide in.

> I have been very depressed and sad and bitter. I finally went and talked to my priest. He said I needed to get the bitterness out of my heart and soul . . . . I had gotten snappy with my wife, and the priest said I have to watch it.

> I can see how people turn to drink. Sometimes I wouldn't want to go home—wife kept asking me what I was going to do. I finally talked to a friend to let off steam.

It might be assumed that, given the close-knit nature of associations in the Shenango Valley, the displaced workers would have had ready and adequate support systems to help them in dealing with distress resulting from job loss. It is true that the large numbers of displaced workers in the Shenango Valley provided a supportive environment, to the extent that the respondents did not feel they were alone in experiencing difficulty. Yet numerous people maintained that neither they nor their network of acquaintances were equipped to handle the novel and complex problems and emotions that continued to trouble them years after the plant closings.

It is interesting to note that the personal networks of persons experiencing prolonged depression did not lack close ties. In fact, those suffering from depression reported a higher percentage of close personal ties than the sample as a whole (50 percent vs. 41 percent). The depressed individuals had intimate friends; however, their personal contacts were simply unable or unequipped to provide the emotional assistance they needed. When most of one's acquaintances are also experiencing job and income loss, fresh insights and new resources many not be forthcoming from them. Mutual support alone is not necessarily effective in solving emotional and social difficulties.

Again, when the displaced workers were asked what community services they were most in need of, "counseling services" was the second most frequent response. Approximately 13 percent of those interviewed had sought counseling with a member of the clergy or a therapist at some point following their job loss. Many others indicated that they wished there were counseling or support groups directed specifically to problems of displaced workers and their families.

> I'm not a weak person, but it has been very difficult to readjust [this respondent had completed a B.A. in business and secured a managerial job]. I think we needed help, some kind of counseling or therapy.

> I'd say we desperately need some kind of counseling; . . . we need advice on how to cope. There should be some kind of support groups for families.

> I would suggest that the government hire a person that is just there to listen—they could just put them in the employment office or something. Just someone who could listen to a bitch. We need something like that.

It is interesting to note that many of the respondents were eager to discuss the subject of counseling because of a recent experience that involved the response of the American Red Cross to a local natural disaster. About two years after the first plant closings, a tornado hit the Shenango Valley, killing several people and causing extensive damage to one community. In the aftermath of the disaster, the Red Cross sent counselors to visit and talk with families who had been affected by the tornado. Several displaced workers had been recipients of these visits, or had had friends or family who were. The counseling was perceived by most as extremely helpful. Several commented that, in similar fashion, there should have been a "disaster team" that visited families affected by the plant closings, to offer advice on coping skills. People who had

previously been very suspicious of counseling services were now receptive to them.

Thus, while some displaced workers had managed a social and emotional adjustment to economic displacement, many were left with unresolved personal and interpersonal distress. For many, this sense of personal uneasiness had also produced discomfort with the broader community environment.

Changing Attitudes toward Community

The experience of dislocation had changed the way many viewed their surroundings. Frustration and anger regarding declines in personal income and employment status had fed a growing apprehension toward the political and economic systems which the respondents regarded as having circumscribed their opportunities. Failed attempts to secure decent employment and wages had left people frustrated in their personal lives, and angry and distrustful of institutions including business, unions, and government.

Such doubt and alienation were expressed across several arenas. While 90 percent of the respondents said they were registered Democrats, 50 percent said neither political party represented their interests. Almost 50 percent said the unions did not represent their interests. And 87 percent said the federal government, then under the Reagan Administration, was not at all concerned about displaced workers. They talked a great deal about big business and big money ruling the country. Many said average workers had been brought to their knees through a nationwide plan to break the unions and lower wages. While most viewed the future as holding little hope for improvement, a few talked of the need for radical action to bring about change.

Plant Closings and Big Business

The former mill workers were quick to voice their opinions on the reasons for the plant closings, and related the experience of the shutdowns to their growing distrust of big business.

Most respondents cited several interrelated reasons for the plant closings: corporate desire for cheaper, nonunion labor; poor management; a slowdown in factory orders; and lack of modernization and capital investment in the plants. Many spoke bitterly about corporate greed and a management focus on profit maximization. Some complained that while both GATX and National Castings were turning a profit when they closed, the percentage of profit had not satisfied corporate headquarters. After shutting down their Shenango Valley plants, both mills had transferred operations to extant nonunion shops in other parts of the country. Orders at the Shenango Valley plants had gone down, said respondents, because of

decreased market demand and heightened competition. Many believed that steel mills had been unable to compete with foreign manufacturers because new corporate managers had more interest in the bottom line than in the manufacturing process. They said greed and lack of modernization had cost U.S. mills their competitive edge.

> They drained the plants—kept taking out and not putting back in. It's just like a house—it will fall apart if it is not modernized.

> There is too much greed. The companies just wanted to maximize profit.

> The plants and the machinery were old. They were overrun by competition. The new management came in and didn't know how to fix things. The old engineers would come right down to the floor and set it right. If it wasn't in the book the new engineers didn't know about it. They lost business that way.

The role of high wages and employee greed in the shutdowns was hotly debated. Some displaced workers felt that wages for some factory jobs had gotten too high, and that union demands had been out of bounds. Others thought benefits—particularly vacation time—had become too generous. However, the majority felt that, given the conditions and hazards of factory work, their wages had been fair. They maintained that their average $12 hourly pay at the Shenango Valley mills had been below that for the steel industry as a whole. While they acknowledged that all plants employed some men who "slept" on the job, most felt strongly that the overall quality of the work force and their manufactured products had been high, and that wages had not been a primary cause of the closings.

> I don't think wages were a prominent factor. Companies didn't modernize for years. There was no money spent on capital investments. Early on there was no competition and rising wages and slack management didn't hurt their profits. Then others caught up. The competition hit and it was too late.

In discussing the flight of the mills from the Shenango Valley, many people bemoaned the loss of community-based company owners, such as the Buhls, to out-of-state conglomerates, whose executives had had little knowledge of or concern for the town and its inhabitants.

> It used to be a company owner closed his plant and he hurt his neighbors. No more. The old industrialists are gone—plants

> today are run by accountants. The original Buhl types are gone—the guy that would actually come down to the plant, have coffee with the guys, get his shoes dirty, go home and have his chauffeur wipe them clean. The largest corporations are here to exploit any economy or country they want—the government allows that. All loyalty to country and community is gone.

Many of the displaced workers expressed great anger and bitterness toward the owners of GATX and National Castings. These sentiments spilled over into a general dislike and distrust of industry and big business. Many expressed the conviction that they were victims of a nationwide plan, engineered by big business, to reduce wages among the working class.

> Industry thought wages were getting out of hand and they needed to curb inflation somehow . . . it is a national trend.

> What happened was the working man got too high. He bought vehicles, boats, made decent money. They seen it and decided it was time to pound him back down. Pound down the peons, that's what I call it. They have beat you down to where you'll take any kind of work.

> You work your whole life and then they want to pay you $3.35. They have us on our knees.

> Business just wants more profits. They feel the American people make too much for common labor jobs. They are trying to force wages down.

> The people with the money shut the mills down. They keep money from the working man to control him.

Ambivalence toward the Unions

Business was not the only target of ire; the doubts and discontent among these blue-collar workers extended to unions as well as corporations. While most of the displaced workers said they were strong believers in unions, many said they felt that union leadership had become corrupt and had sided more often with the corporations than with the workers. Forty-seven percent of the respondents said they felt the unions had not represented their interests during negotiations regarding the plant closings.

Those who felt supported by the union's efforts said that, given the difficult circumstances of the shutdowns, the union representatives had

done what they could. Those who were critical of the unions most often pointed to a weak and greedy leadership.

> The union was run by a handful of guys who forgot where they came from.

> I am dedicated to the union. The world has to have unions. But something happened. It blew up in our face.

> Unions were with the company. . . . the union was big business itself.

Some felt that their local union representatives were unprepared to deal with the complicated issues involved in a plant closing.

> I think the union officials were not qualified to negotiate for us—they were out of their league. They were competing with college-trained negotiators. The situation was too complex for them.

> The union leadership had limited knowledge and skills. They didn't know alternatives or national issues. For example, they could have negotiated a clause that the concessions we gave in August didn't hold if the plant closed within a certain period of time.

Others pointed a finger at themselves.

> The union people selled us out. But we have to take responsibility. We put them in there.

Mistrust of Government

In addition to business and unions, institutional mistrust was also extended to government. As mentioned above, while 90 percent of the respondents identified themselves as registered Democrats, 50 percent said that neither political party represented their interests. This disaffection appeared to be colored by the perception that the Democrats, as well as the Republicans, were increasingly allied with the interests of big business and had moved too far from the people. The Democrats were also in disfavor because of events associated with the Carter Administration. Local steel mills had begun to close while Carter was in office, and his administration had issued no response to the shutdowns. The Carter Administration had also turned down a request from a coalition of neighboring Youngstown steelworkers for a government loan that would have helped the workers purchase the recently closed Youngstown Sheet and Tube Company.

Consequently, executive-level Democrats were also viewed as having largely ignored the plight of displaced industrial workers.

While the respondents reported growing disaffection with the Democratic party, however, their harshest comments were directed at the Republicans, whose interests, they contended, were clearly aligned with those of the rich. Of those interviewed, 87 percent asserted that the federal government under the Reagan administration, had not been at all concerned about the situation of displaced workers. The Reagan administration was widely perceived as being out of touch with the social and economic issues affecting low-income and working-class groups. Many respondents lambasted official employment statistics, a "boom" economy characterized by jobs that paid minimum wages, and trickle-down economics.

> Worst mistake this country ever made was putting a movie star in office. He lives in a fantasy world. He says just pick up the paper to get a job. Yeah, at $3.35 an hour!

> This is an economically depressed area; there are part-time and minimum-wage jobs. That's what the Republican Administration wanted—to bring down wages. I don't believe the employment statistics. Look at the welfare roles. That's where people are.

> Their philosophy is trickle down—it is structural displacement, and the government should keep its hands off and the people will eventually come out of it. But it isn't working that way.

A common complaint among the displaced workers was that the federal government had "abandoned" the Shenango Valley and other depressed areas. Many complained about policies that allowed generous funding for foreign aid, but not regional redevelopment.

> They don't do nothin'. They are lending billions to other countries and not helping here.

> They abandoned us. They give money to El Salvador—why not Pennsylvania?

> The situation is impossible for local towns to bring new businesses here. We needed government help.

Reagan was widely viewed as a union buster, with his firing of the air traffic controllers in 1981 described by many as the most disturbing in a series of nationwide moves to weaken unions and keep wages down.

> What I got to say about Reagan you don't want to hear. He was out to bust the unions. The whole country should have gone out when the air traffic controllers went on strike.

> They are out to bust the unions. . . . I don't understand any of it, but I blame Reagan. Ever since he broke the traffic controllers it snowballed, like a sickness.

> Reagan says he supports Lech Walesa, but he doesn't support solidarity in this country.

Comments regarding Republican politics and politicians also touched frequently on issues of class.

> Reagan and the Republicans are fat-cat rich boys. They have no concept of what it's like to live on $50,000 a year, let alone $10,000. He's surrounded by his own kind.

> A lot of times you don't see the whole picture. I thought the end product benefited everyone. But since the shutdowns I can't help but feel the last Administration has gone the wrong way. They are for big business, and the little guy doesn't count for much.

> Reagan and Nixon—they let the rich population take over the government. The rich help each other get richer.

Many expressed the view that laws protect corporate interests at the expense of workers. Having observed mill owners operating within the legal system as they took over profitable plants, drained them of cash, and shut them down, many had a shaken faith in law and justice.

> Government is for big business. They aren't interested in us. The laws we have protect the rich man, not the poor man.

> The courts always rule in favor of the corporations.

> Companies bleed a plant, then close it. That's legal! No laws to prevent it.

So strong was their feeling that government had been remiss that several displaced workers used the Soviet Union and principles of socialism to illustrate their vision of a preferred approach to economic and social welfare.

> The poor will get poorer and the rich richer. I feel very angry and

> it is wrong. We are a consuming nation, but we can't consume if we don't make money. The Communist governments at least take care of people.
>
> Having no medical benefits has been the worst. Even in Russia they give medical benefits.
>
> I wonder if the Communists don't have the right idea—to spread the riches, make it more equal for everyone.
>
> People say the economy is booming. With what? Fast food jobs and no health insurance. Even in Russia they give people health care.
>
> There is so much greed. We have too many millionaires. We need to equalize it. They've busted up the middle class.
>
> The government should put limitations on certain salaries. Why should football players make $60,000 a week? They should equalize wages. Of course they will never do that. The middle class will shrink. I think more and more you'll see a high class and a low class, with the middle shrinking.

A few had harsh words for capitalists and the current capitalist system.

> The country has a supposedly democratic government, but capitalism is not democratic. Capitalism is being conducted improperly—it's rape. We are all being raped. The U.S. government spends its time overthrowing other governments or controlling them. Business has its thumb over us all. I am a capitalist—I'm not against capitalism. But it should be democratic capitalism, conducted the proper way.
>
> This is a new Appalachia. Low wages, lost households. If I were a capitalist I would love this turn of events. They have lots of serfs to exploit. There is lots of money to be made on cheap labor here.

Frustrated by a perception that government had largely abandoned the average working man, many displaced workers described themselves as having been "beaten" by the system. Their views of the powers of ordinary citizens tended to be cynical, and few expressed confidence that they could influence government and make it more responsive to the needs of displaced workers. During the survey interview, the respondents were asked which of two statements they believed more strongly to be true: "The average citizen can have an influence on government decisions," or "This world is run

by the few people in power and there is not much the average guy can do about it." Sixty-eight percent believed the second statement to be more true.

Elaborating this position, several described a sense of being manipulated by larger powers. Many felt that their economic destiny was in the hands of omnipotent corporate interests.

> A few people are up in glass towers playing chess with us. "Let's see what we can do with them next." They're making pawns of us.

> There is a transition happening throughout the world—everything is changing to services. It's an experiment—they just want to see what happens. We aren't producing anything now, just importing. I think that if they want to they can push a button and turn the whole thing around again. They are either very stupid or very intelligent. But they are doing it on purpose.

While the majority of the displaced workers indicated a sense of powerlessness, a minority clung to the belief that average citizens can effect change: 30 percent saw more truth in the statement that "the average citizen can have an influence on government decisions." Indicating some degree of confidence in citizen input, a majority said they usually voted in national elections, and 28 percent said they had written or phoned a legislator about a social or community issue; many had been in touch with the local state representative who is well known in the community.

Some of those who felt that they could have an influence on government decisions thought it was time for people to take matters into their own hands and unite around common issues. While expressing the need for collective action, few of those interviewed saw themselves as organizers. Rather, they appeared to be waiting for "people" or "someone" to lead such a cause.

> People need to organize. We should have a coalition of working people, not just unemployed. Right now people aren't being heard. They have lost interest.

> You vote and what happens? Nothing. Someone needs to organize.

> The government does what it wants. But people need to be more involved. We need a revolution. I lost a truck and my house.

PERSPECTIVES ON THE FUTURE

As with their views on citizen input, the respondents' visions of the future were more often pessimistic than hopeful. A majority described the future

as holding little promise of improvement, for either the community or themselves. When asked how they viewed the prospects for the Shenango Valley, 58 percent said conditions would stay the same or get worse, while 29 percent felt the situation would get better, and 10 percent did not know what to expect.

> I see zero for the valley and zero for the American economy.

> In ten years this place will be dead—industry will be gone. Nothing to take its place. Town slowly dries up. People retire and die. Young ones leave.

> I can hardly get it out, but I don't see the mills coming back. It is very hard to admit that. To get the words out.

Many displaced workers said they had resigned themselves to low wages and service-sector jobs.

> We will survive. We just won't have as many material things. We'll have to do without.

> You set your sights lower. Material goods aren't everything.

Others described the inevitability of economic transition and change. Some discussed the injustice of falling victim to such a transition, yet accepted it as part of the change process.

> The plant closings were due. It was a turn, like a century. This is the computer era.

> Our economy just changed. It came to the end of the industrial era.

> It's a changeover now, and it takes time for it. Some are going to gain, some are going to lose. It's not fair that a person loses, but that's the way it is.

As is often the case with persons who have suffered trauma or displacement, many of the respondents conveyed a sense of vulnerability and uncertainty with regard to the future. The plant closings had disrupted the long-standing order of mill employment. Previous sources of security had collapsed, and the present and future seemed unsteady.

> You just don't trust the future anymore. Nothing is secure now.

> There is no security anymore. Who knows what I'll be doing in ten years?

> The experience makes me skeptical of the future. It was tough to go through. I don't think it strengthened me spiritually or morally.

In reflecting on the experience of dislocation, many described an intensified belief in the importance of individualism and self-reliance. Again, references to their distrust of social, political, and economic environments figured heavily in discussions of "lessons learned" from the experience.

> I believe this taught people a good lesson: don't put your confidence in no mill or no person.

> I tell my son, "You don't ever want to grow up to be dependent on anyone else."

> It makes you feel like—live for today. You don't learn a lesson from it. You start not to care.

> My advice is this: if you have a job, put your money away. Leave go those fancy things early in life. They close those mills overnight.

While institutional distrust prevailed, some displaced workers described the experience of the plant closings as having heightened their sense of linkage or identification with other Americans who had suffered hard times or misfortune.

> I was always against able-bodied men sitting around. I never believed in people with their hands out. But I don't think it's true anymore. There are so few jobs now.

> My attitude toward those who are bad off changed. I was more able to associate with them.

> You have to live it to understand it. People will laugh at people on food stamps. But it can happen to them. It can happen to anyone.

Again, though most displaced workers expressed a pessimistic vision of the future, a minority clung to the view that conditions in the Shenango Valley would improve. Some held out a hope that industry would return

and once again take a more personal interest in the valley and its people.

> Things are very bleak now, but my dream is that some industry will recognize that we have very hard working and understanding people here.
>
> We have a quality work force. If they [industry] get stung overseas they may come back here. They want cheap labor, but the quality isn't as high. If they are smart they will be back.

Others saw a future in small business or in the capacity of local residents to rebuild the local economy.

> I think positive things will come of all this. A lot of small businesses are opening up. We are still at the bottom of the mountain—but we are capable of climbing it.
>
> I believe we will prosper without steel. We are near Pittsburgh and lakes and colleges. I think we can attract interesting people and small businesses.

Many of the displaced workers who expressed optimism for the future were persons who had been successful in securing satisfactory employment for themselves. However, there was also a core of people who, despite a grim personal situation, believed that the future held promise. Their comments often made reference to a refusal to give up the fight for decent employment opportunities or to let go of a belief in the potential for organization and solidarity among the working class.

> I tell my son, if you get slapped in the face, pick yourself up and keep fighting. I tell him, you and I are like chickens scratching in the back yard. We aren't rich, we aren't poor. We just scratch, scratch, scratch to get by. It may be tiring, but you don't lie down. You have to keep fighting.
>
> I see a time when the kids today will have to do what my grandfather did 60 years ago—organize for a decent wage. The old-timers did it, and we had it handed to us on a silver platter. We held on to it for a while. Now it's gone and the youngsters will have to pick up and organize, just like in the 1920s and 1930s. It's the only way things will change.

Thus, these blue-collar workers presented a mixed set of responses. In talking with them, the most overwhelming impressions were of cynicism,

sadness, anger, withdrawal, and loss. Yet a minority remained optimistic. Some were volatile in their expressions of anger regarding the plant closings, while others were more passive and resigned. Some viewed their lives and the future as futile, while others carried a hope or determination that conditions would eventually turn in a positive direction. Their vision of change ranged from small business development to labor organization to revolution. Clearly, the extent of their alienation with regard to current economic and political institutions was significant. These people, for the most part, had believed and participated in a vision of society that equated hard work and motivation with economic reward, an ideology many no longer trusted. Minus a reaffirmation of that vision and an improved income and employment status, such alienation was unlikely to dissipate.

8

Out of Sight, Out of Mind

> It's like the earth opened up and we were swallowed into a big hole. Out of sight, out of mind.
>
> former welder, GATX

For the employees of GATX and National Castings, mill work carried a host of complex and sometimes contradictory meanings. For many, factory employment meant camaraderie, good earnings, and security. To some, it simultaneously represented pollution, danger, and hard physical work. It often involved self-effacing acceptance of uncomfortable working conditions, combined with pride in having the stamina to endure such an environment. Today, many displaced workers are embittered because their loyalty to the factory system and their tolerance of its undesirable working conditions were betrayed. Many are angry at what they perceive as abandonment. Those who have experienced reduced income or employment status are often resentful of their low wages and frustrated because their persistence and motivation in seeking reemployment have not yielded economic rewards.

It is stunning how sharp and obsessive their expressions of anger, depression, anxiety, and betrayal remained. Four years after the first closings, many of the displaced workers who participated in the survey were still deeply distressed over the loss of the mills. Factors contributing to this situation included the method and tone of the societal response to the decline in manufacturing, and the fact that these men and women had tried hard, but failed, to improve their economic position. Within the broader society, there has been scant acknowledgment of the downward mobility experienced by many displaced industrial workers, and there has been no plan for the social and economic revitalization of depressed communities. While popular images of the 1980s heralded the decade's affluent and

upwardly mobile, the increase in the numbers of working poor and low-income persons was scarcely noted. The resolution of problems of economic dislocation in communities like the Shenango Valley requires political recognition of the social stresses and employment difficulties that have confronted many displaced workers, and it also calls for more aggressive efforts to renew the economic viability of distressed regions.

ACKNOWLEDGING CHANGES IN EMPLOYMENT CONDITIONS

Clearly, there is a new group of poor and low-income persons in the Shenango Valley. These "new poor" are also likely to be present in communities throughout other areas of the country that have lost large numbers of industrial jobs to plant closings in recent years. The nationwide increase in the number of prime-aged males living below the poverty line most likely reflects, in part, the increase in the number of former industrial workers who have not secured steady or well-paying reemployment.

Official unemployment statistics do not provide an accurate picture of recent downward shifts in the structure and rewards of employment. Sharp feelings of frustration among many of the displaced workers surveyed reflected, in part, their sense that their labor market difficulties have not been recognized. While unemployment rates in the Shenango Valley and nationwide fell steadily after 1983, for many, employment conditions deteriorated rather than improved. The newly generated jobs are primarily in the service sector, and many are entry level, pay low wages, and carry minimal benefits and job security. Declines in wages and job security are also evident in the manufacturing sector. The available manufacturing jobs are increasingly found in nonunion shops, again with low benefits and little job security. Many displaced workers are involuntarily employed part time. Many are working poor. Work is often irregular and short term, and many of the new employees are vulnerable to frequent layoffs. Those displaced workers who have dropped out of the labor force because of discouragement over lack of job search success are not counted in unemployment figures.

One way to better gauge recent changes in the nature of employment is to return to the use of a subemployment index. The subemployment index was used by the U.S. Labor Department for a period in the 1960s to measure labor maladjustment not recorded by unemployment statistics. A subemployment index includes a tabulation of the number of persons who have dropped out of the labor force because of discouragement, those who are working part time involuntarily, and heads of households under age 65 who work full time but earn poverty-level wages. Using these criteria, the subemployment index among the sample of Shenango Valley respondents would be approximately 36 percent. Coupled with the unemployment rate of 14 percent, the measure of labor maladjustment would be 50 percent.

Such a measurement provides a more realistic depiction of the labor

market difficulties experienced by this and other low-income populations. It is one method of furthering awareness of the problem of underemployment among low-income groups, and it provides a more precise informational base for problem-solving efforts.

MOBILIZING NEW SOCIAL AND ECONOMIC RESOURCES

In responding to reduced income and employment status, most displaced workers acted in accord with cultural norms that emphasize personal motivation and self-sufficiency. They cut back on living expenses, looked for work, drew on personal assets, and solicited material and emotional support from family, friends, and neighbors. What has angered and frustrated many of the displaced workers is that, despite these initiatives, they have been unable to improve their income and employment status substantially, or to find relief from depression and anxiety.

Clearly, policies that stress reliance on trickle-down economics and local networks of social support to rally distressed people and communities have been inadequate. With regard to the mobilization of new sources of social and economic support, the findings suggest a need for public and private interventions in areas including relocation, job training, social service provision, and community development.

Relocation

As described earlier, policy debates concerning the situation of displaced workers often emphasize the responsibility of former manufacturing workers to adjust to a depressed local labor market by seeking employment in other geographic locales. In this study we found that many displaced workers were motivated to explore relocation as a means to improve their economic situation: an estimated 35 percent had either relocated or actively searched for jobs in other locales; and 62 percent had considered relocating. Most respondents, however, were unable to negotiate or accept the practical and social difficulties involved in a move.

In an area like the Shenango Valley, relocation involves enormous practical and psychological obstacles. Many local residents know little about other areas of the country, and information on out-of-state job opportunities is not readily available. Many people do not have the money to make long-distance phone calls to potential employers, travel to job interviews, and cover moving expenses. Houses in a depressed community are difficult to sell and property values low. For many, it is difficult to sever ties with a tightly knit home community. The available service-sector jobs often offer low wages and little job security. Most of those who traveled to other areas to look for work chose not to relocate because they could not find employment at an adequate wage.

The displaced workers who relocated did improve their employment status; with the exception of one retiree, all were working, and at wages higher than those who remained in the valley. As reported by the relocators, however, there were social costs to moving: marital stress, separation from their family and home community, and a lower standard of housing. Those who relocated were also vulnerable to frequent lay-offs, and their average hourly wages were lower than those they had previously earned in the Shenango Valley plants.

As noted above, social programs of relocation assistance were not available to the displaced workers in the Shenango Valley. As a response to economic displacement, their relocation efforts were most often individual endeavors accomplished with the aid of friends and relatives. In the manner of the "chain migration" of early immigrants who came from Europe to work in the mills, displaced workers most frequently relocated in the trail of family and friends, who offered housing and job assistance. In addition, these acquaintances provided social support and facilitated a psychological transition. By trailing a friend or relative who had some knowledge of and connection to the Shenango Valley, the displaced workers could sustain some link to their past identity and milieu. Their stories and experiences suggest that relocation is difficult for those who do not have such personal connections to job and social supports. Individual initiative alone was seldom enough to muster the resources necessary for relocation.

If relocation is to be considered an important element of labor readjustment, then government, corporate, and union assistance must be forthcoming. Such assistance could include collectively bargained transfer provisions; subsidies for moving expenses; computerized out-of-state job listings through the federal Employment Service; phone banks available for long-distance calls for job searches; arrangement for local recruitment by out-of-state firms; and provision of information on various geographical locales. Given that people prefer to move to locations where they have some personal contacts, a data bank could keep updated lists of relocators, putting displaced workers in touch with others from their area who have moved. It is important to note that most of the displaced workers who relocated did not leave the locale until they felt they had tried all job possibilities in the valley—a time period averaging over two years. Assistance programs should be designed to extend relocation benefits to blue-collar workers for several years after a plant shutdown. Various forms of such relocation assistance are routinely provided to professional and managerial staff at plants and corporations that experience a closure or contraction.

Job Training

As with relocation, many displaced workers were motivated to seek job training as a means to improve their employment status. Approximately 49

percent either participated in or attempted to enroll in job training or education. These efforts, however, were often thwarted. While 34 persons applied to the JTPA program, only eight participated in some form of federally funded training. Many were denied admittance to the program because they did not meet admission standards, or because the program could not accept additional enrollees. Of those who did participate in retraining, only a few obtained training-related jobs. Short-term, entry-level training did not enhance their employability or wages; those who had income gains had completed the most advanced training.

Given the limited availability of social program assistance, most persons who desired further education had to arrange and finance it themselves—a difficult task for those with low incomes and skills. Clearly, the resources and objectives of the JTPA program were inadequate. Large numbers of displaced workers were denied entrance to job training because of a lack of funding. The use of testing to screen eligibles diminished the self-esteem of persons already suffering from feelings of depression and low self-worth. The opportunity costs associated with a lack of stipends for schooling or retraining made it impossible for many persons, particularly those with young families, to consider participation in JTPA. Individuals with no high school education tended to avoid retraining programs because they lacked confidence in their ability to complete classroom work, and the local job program did not provide outreach to this group. In addition, the short-term training offered to many participants was not sufficient to increase their employability.

Programs to provide education and upgrade training should be a key element of efforts to reduce the labor market difficulties of displaced workers whose skills have become redundant. A program better targeted to the needs of displaced workers could include stipends for classroom training and education; encouragement of advanced or longer-term training; outreach to those who did not complete high school; more aggressive placement efforts; relocation assistance; and increased funding. As discussed below, such programs would also have to be linked to ongoing economic development efforts. In addition, public service employment could be made available to persons whose poor skills and training are a hindrance to labor market participation. In distressed communities that suffer because of scarce tax resources, a deteriorating infrastructure, and a surplus of labor, a public works program would appear to have many benefits for both individuals and the municipality. Some of these suggested changes have been enacted in the 1989 Economic Dislocation and Worker Assistance Act (EDWAA), which has replaced JTPA Title III.[1]

It could be argued that job training should be available to displaced workers as an entitlement, that their long-term loyalty to factory employers could be exchanged for the opportunity for higher education and job skills. Entitlement to skill upgrading or retraining could sharpen the competitive

edge of the nation's work force, encouraging workers to retool to meet the demands of a changing economy. Experiments in entitlement to retraining have recently been instituted at some corporations.[2] Typically, union employees contribute a percentage of gross pay to a fund matched by the corporation. That contribution entitles the employees to training and education services while employed, as well as following termination from the company. Variations on this concept could include the involvement of government, educational institutions, and private foundations in funding and organizing such efforts. Increasingly, business leaders have publicly expressed concern that our work force is not educationally equipped to meet the future needs of an information-oriented economy. Experiments in expanded investments in human capital would encourage a more dynamic and competitive work force.

Social Services

Immediately following their job loss, the displaced workers were linked to a well-organized system of social insurance and supplemental assistance programs that offered a measure of temporary income support to the newly jobless. True to their design, such provisions as unemployment insurance and severance pay were successful in providing a financial buffer in the first several months following job loss. With the lapse of these temporary supports, however, new problems associated with long-term unemployment, income loss, and emotional distress surfaced. The extant social service system lacked the resources and the mandate to address a new population in need. Gaps in services included the lack of health insurance, and the restricted eligibility for public assistance.

Many of these service needs are similar to those faced by low-income and working-poor persons throughout the country. Public assistance programs have been targeted to the poorest of the poor and those with a limited attachment to the labor market. Persons who live on the margin of poverty, who have some earnings, or who have property assets have difficulty obtaining some forms of assistance. Several policy analysts have suggested such reform efforts as the expansion of medicaid and establishment of regulations requiring businesses to provide health benefits to employees; elimination of the AFDC-U "100 hours rule," which cuts aid to able-bodied heads of household when their work effort exceeds 100 hours in one month; and higher asset limits for the receipt of public assistance.[3] A common complaint among caseworkers in the Shenango Valley was that displaced workers who qualified for public assistance had become so destitute that it was difficult to reverse their dependency. Requiring individuals to exhaust most assets in order to qualify for public assistance deepens their poverty and immobility.

Other needed reforms are specific to the situation of displaced workers. A major plant closing, particularly one in a small community, must be acknowledged as a traumatic occurrence that requires extracommunity assistance. Just as the American Red Cross is ready to mobilize assistance following a natural disaster, so too should a team of community service personnel be available to offer financial and technical assistance to local communities following a plant closing. In the Shenango Valley, local social services and community agencies were left virtually alone to solve problems that had their roots in national and international economic shifts. The situation was overwhelming. The social service agencies did not have enough funds or personnel to handle great increases in demand for services. They did not have the resources or the mandate to respond to a new population of distressed persons. These agencies needed supplemental staff, money, and sanction to assemble services specific to the needs of displaced workers, services such as counseling programs and cash assistance funds. In addition, as described below, their efforts needed to be supported by ongoing community and economic development efforts. Obviously, minus good jobs and wages, no amount of service provision can effect long-term change.

As community agencies prepare a response to plant closings, it is also important that they attend to the dynamic phases of response that are common among displaced workers: shock, denial, anger, optimism, depression, and distress. The initial phases of shock and denial often have a numbing effect, with displaced workers reporting a state of inactivity or lack of ability to formulate future plans. Social service personnel from towns experiencing plant closings have reported that displaced workers seldom utilize counseling services made available immediately following a plant closing.[4] Few people are moved to seek counseling when in the stage of shock and denial. More helpful at this point could be meetings with fellow workers at which the details of the closing could be discussed and debated, emotional responses to the closing shared, and information disseminated on programs such as unemployment insurance, pensions, and severance benefits. Federal legislation passed in 1988 that requires plants to give a 60-day termination notice should aid the readjustment of displaced workers; by the time termination occurs, the employees should have begun to emerge from the stage of denial and shock and be ready to begin resource mobilization.[5]

As they move into a phase of optimism, active job search, and planning for the future, displaced workers could be offered participation in job clubs, where former coworkers get together to exchange information on job hunt strategies and receive information on resume writing, training programs, and relocation. Following this, counseling and support groups should be set up in anticipation of the anxiety and distress that are likely to follow in persons who do not secure adequate reemployment and who are having

difficulty with the transition. Again, numerous survey respondents commented that they wished that group or family counseling were available to help them cope with their anger and depression stemming from long-term job and income loss.

The experiences of displaced workers from the Shenango Valley also suggest improved methods of outreach. Because it is generally female spouses of displaced workers who first approach social service agencies for assistance, information on available services should be disseminated to them as well as to their husbands. Currently, limited outreach is most often targeted to displaced workers through union and employment offices. Research also suggests that people are less hesitant to use services when they feel they have contributed to them and are entitled to them. Outreach workers could emphasize that displaced workers, as taxpayers, have paid into public social services.

FRUSTRATED EFFORT: THE PROCESS OF DOWNWARD MOBILITY

Despite active attempts to mobilize new sources of social and economic support, many displaced workers have not succeeded in improving their income or employment status. The fact that large numbers of persons in the Shenango Valley have suffered long-term income loss offers a unique glimpse at the process of downward mobility and the slide, among some, into poverty and dependency. Analysis of the antecedents of this downward slide challenges some common assumptions regarding the character of dependent populations. The experiences of these former steelworkers also raise questions regarding the process of attitudinal change that sometimes accompanies downward mobility.

Contrary to common notions of poverty and dependency, it was clear from this study that apathy and lack of motivation among the respondents were a consequence of rather than an antecedent to situations of unemployment and low income. Following job loss, the job searches of those who were poor and unemployed at the time of the survey had not differed in effort from the job searches of those who had obtained work at good wages. Rather, those who had been successful at obtaining good jobs had higher skills, more marketable personal assets (including age and education), and better job contacts in their personal networks. Those who had become resigned or apathetic typically had had the least marketable personal assets and the least diverse social networks. For example, high rates of both poverty and unemployment among the 41- to 50-year-old age group certainly pointed to age discrimination, supporting the assertions of numerous displaced workers that employers did not want men over 40 for manual work. It is also significant that 50 percent of the discouraged workers did not have a high school diploma. In addition, their average age was 56, and their network size was the smallest of any subgroup in the sample.

Among this group of respondents, it would appear that loss of motivation and downward mobility had been spurred by job search failures linked to nonmarketable personal and demographic characteristics. Such findings question the assumptions of some social policy analysts that low motivation normally precedes and predicts low-income status.

In studying upward mobility and changes in class position, sociologists speak of "status incongruity," in which people are caught between two worlds and do not yet know the rules of their new position. Among displaced workers in the Shenango Valley, a status incongruity can be observed among those who have shifted *downward*, from middle income to poor or low income. Following a shift in economic position, displaced workers initially cling to the rules and behaviors of their former income or employment status. They are hesitant to seek social service assistance. They use food stamps at grocery stores where they will not be recognized. They keep up dogged job hunts and accept minimum-wage jobs rather than remain idle. However, as described by both social service personnel and the displaced workers, there comes a point at which attitudes and behavior among some people begin to change. After a period of economic struggle, some families accept public assistance and begin to perceive it as an entitlement. Job hunts stop and resignation sets in.

Continually thwarted motivation and lack of reward for job search and employment efforts may also spur alienation from social and political institutions. Among some persons, attitude changes are evident in a growing distrust of unions, politicians, and big business and a loss of faith in the power of the average citizen. The study raises the question, at what point and under what circumstances do attitudes change? Among some, frustration of effort is associated with dulled motivation. At what point do resignation, alienation, and disinterest replace motivation and belief in the political and economic system? Of late, much attention has been focused on the growth of an American underclass, that is, persons who experience chronic poverty and aberrant or dependent behavior. The experiences of displaced workers who are now suffering long-term poverty, dependency, and discouragement may provide clues as to how such a state of being and thinking evolves.

SOCIAL NETWORK MOBILIZATION

The displacement of workers from manufacturing jobs in the Shenango Valley disrupted long-established social and economic relations. In mobilizing new sources of material, emotional, and community support, these men and women tapped personal and organizational resource networks in their efforts to find new employment, relocate, and utilize social services. Their extant network relations both facilitated and restricted such resource mobilization.

The social networks of most of the displaced workers in the survey were tightly knit and family oriented, with deep roots in their home community. These networks have certainly provided them with strong and invaluable material and social supports as they have weathered the crisis of displacement. Among these displaced workers, dense networks of friends and family were the most frequently utilized supportive resource.

It can be argued that such tightly knit networks can also limit opportunity mobility and adaptation to situations requiring new skills and information. As suggested by numerous network analysts, dense networks can be encapsulating, making economic and social transitions difficult.[6] Networks that are intimate and stable can provide strong, supportive, and integrative bonds, but they can also function as a tether. Associates who share very similar social worlds may lack access to information and experiences that differ from those known locally. Most people in the Shenango Valley regularly interact with persons much like themselves: people who were long-time valley residents and who are current or former mill workers. When a situation such as a plant closing demands new forms of social and economic support, persons in a tight-knit network may have difficulty responding because they lack the needed "weak ties"—less intimate and more diverse associates—that are of primary importance in providing access to new information.[7] Close friends are likely to share a similar social milieu, while more distant acquaintances are likely to live in somewhat different social environments. When seeking resources that are not readily available, individuals are more likely to obtain them by connecting with less intimate acquaintances, who are apt to possess bridging ties to different social worlds. The more varied one's social contacts, the greater one's access to a wide range of resources.

In an economically depressed community in which most persons are in a similar situation, information on how to deal with novel experiences is not readily available. As was clear from the respondents' comments, friends and family often do not have the resources or ability to deal with new situations such as severe depression, job procurement, or relocation.

The importance of diverse ties in facilitating reemployment is evident in the experiences of the respondents. The overwhelming majority of persons who obtained employment did so through personal contacts. Again and again, people described extensive job hunts involving numerous personal inquiries and applications, with no employment offers. Rather, job offers most often came via acquaintances who had a connection with a person or business that needed an employee. The larger and more diverse their social network, the greater the chance of obtaining a job offer. Among persons who obtained professional or managerial jobs, the personal contact that facilitated employment was most often an acquaintance of higher occupational status. All of the respondents who enrolled in advanced training or education had a personal friend in a professional or white-collar

position who guided and influenced that action: for example, the attorney's father was a lawyer, and the man studying to be an accountant had a brother-in-law who was a CPA.

Likewise, it is significant that the social networks of persons in poverty and those lacking a labor market attachment were smaller and more intimate than those of persons who were not poor and who were employed. Again, the temporal aspect of this situation is unclear. Certainly, low incomes and unemployment are associated with social isolation. As reported by the displaced workers, activities such as club memberships, entertaining friends, and participation in groups like bowling leagues are often limited or eliminated when incomes decline. Likewise, withdrawal from the work force ends daily contact with fellow employees. On the other hand, it might also be true that persons who were now poor or unemployed had had fewer personal contacts before their manufacturing job loss, a circumstance that could have contributed to their current situation. Again, whether smaller networks are an antecedent to or consequence of diminished status is unknown. The critical fact at present is that those who have the least in terms of income and employment also have the fewest personal supports on which to draw. They are the most in need of external supports and connections.

In addition to limiting access to new information, small, tightly knit networks might also be linked to a lack of social cohesion and ability to effect collective action. It has been argued that densely knit social clusters are socially fragmenting, as opposed to cohesive.[8] This is because dense cliques are often void of connecting ties among one another and lack links to extracommunity power sources. In the Shenango Valley, displaced workers did not succeed in organizing to protest the plant closings or to bring additional jobs or social services to the locale. Though some discussed the possibility of a worker-owned plant, after regional union officials refused to back the effort, the matter was not pursued. Though a group of clergy, citizens, and union representatives did organize a food bank after the shutdowns, the displaced workers themselves did not band together to call for supplemental job or social services. In part, this was due to a desire to retain an image of self-sufficiency and to a reluctance to admit downward mobility. But it can also be postulated as due in part to a lack of bridging ties to persons who were familiar with the operation of broader social or economic systems, and who had access to alternate resources. While tightly bound neighborhood clusters can provide strong interpersonal support, they offer few means of establishing the wider alliances critical to resource mobilization.

Within the Shenango Valley community, tight-knit and intimate networks can be seen as a product, in part, of a long-standing economic structure that has circumscribed social and economic interaction. Such a network form was in the interests of capital and the manufacturing employers. A lack of other employment opportunities in the area bred a

dependence on and loyalty to the factory system. With the departure of the factories, the weave and function of local networks was disrupted, and associations that had served the interests of a manufacturing economy were not particularly adaptable to the mobilization of new and alternate social and economic resources. People have suffered from the limitations of their social circles and from the fact that they reside in a one-industry region. Dense networks have provided most displaced workers with a significant measure of social and economic support. However, many persons experiencing job and income loss have found that close friends and family are not equipped to deal with the scope of their problems, or that the supportive resources of such contacts have been exhausted. Extra-community supports need to function as "weak ties," assisting local residents with resource mobilization.

LINKS TO ECONOMIC DEVELOPMENT EFFORTS

Clearly, efforts to expand local job training, relocation assistance, and a variety of social service programs must be linked to broader economic development efforts and macroeconomic policies that promote balanced economic growth. External efforts are needed to stimulate regional redevelopment. At bottom, the difficulties of displaced workers are structural in nature, rooted in an economy in which there is a mismatch between labor supply and demand. An economic development corporation established in the Shenango Valley following the plant closings was successful in attracting a few small businesses to the area. But though they try, local business and economic leaders have neither the connections nor the clout to lure significant new business to the community. Those new jobs that have come to the valley are primarily connected with restaurants and retail stores, and pay low wages. Depressed regions of the country need state and national assistance with economic development. Several economic analysts have proposed policies focused on industrial reorganization, as opposed to abandonment. Others have called for efforts to improve the wage-and-benefit structure of jobs in the growing service economy. If our culture is to celebrate and preserve the local community, it must be prepared to develop and support its economic viability through ongoing development efforts.

WORKING HARD, WORKING POOR

Several years after the plant closings, many displaced workers from the Shenango Valley remained troubled by changes in their income and employment status. Many were underemployed, and over one-quarter had slid in status from middle income to poor. Persistent yet unsuccessful efforts to regain satisfactory employment had left many people bitter and

mistrusting of business and government. Many were working hard but remained poor or low income. Clearly, the benefits of an expanding service economy had not trickled down to many of these displaced workers. Their experiences document the paradox of the 1980s: great increases in wealth and job creation have been accompanied by a growing underemployed, low-income population.

NOTES

1. EDWAA includes several important modifications over JTPA Title III: the establishment of state-level "rapid response" teams to mobilize and coordinate local job training and social services following a plant closing; a stronger emphasis on remedial training for persons with low education; stipended training for displaced workers who have exhausted their unemployment benefits; and certificates that can be used to defer the start of retraining or to permit workers to seek their own training. Unfortunately, no plans for public-sector employment and strengthened relocation assistance have been enacted, and advanced training has not been promoted. Many of the EDWAA components are optional services, including stipended training, relocation assistance, advanced training, and training certificates. Because the EDWAA appropriation is not high ($287 million in 1989), it is expected that some grantees will not be able to implement the more costly, though perhaps more effective, program options.

2. For example, the Alliance for Employee Growth and Development, a partnership between AT&T and the Communications Workers of America.

3. See David Ellwood, *Poor Support* (NY: Basic, 1988); Phoebe Cottingham and David Ellwood (eds.), *Welfare Policy for the 1990s* (Cambridge, MA: Harvard University Press, 1989).

4. Terry Buss and F. Stevens Redburn, *Mass Unemployment: Plant Closings and Community Mental Health* (Beverly Hills: Sage, 1983); David Biegel, James Cunningham, Hide Yamatani, and Pamela Martz, "Self-reliance and Blue-collar Unemployment in a Steel Town," *Social Work* 34, no. 5 (1989): 399–406.

5. The Worker Adjustment and Retraining Notification Act (WARN) (Public Law 100-379) became effective February 4, 1989. It requires employers who have 100 or more employees to provide notice 60 days in advance of covered plant closings and covered mass layoffs.

6.. Mark Granovetter, *Getting a Job: A Study of Contacts and Careers* (Cambridge, MA: Harvard University Press, 1974); J. C. Mitchell (ed.), *Social Networks in Urban Situations* (Manchester, England: Manchester University Press, 1969); B. A. Paux, *The Second Generation* (Capetown, South Africa: Oxford University Press, 1963).

7. Mark Granovetter, "The Strength of Weak Ties," *American Journal of Sociology* 78 (1973): 1360–80; Peter d'Abbs, *Social Support Networks* (Melbourne, Australia: Institute of Family Studies, 1982).

8. Mark Granovetter, "The Strength of Weak Ties: A Network Theory Revisited," in Peter Marsden and Nan Lin (eds.), *Social Structure and Network Analysis* (Beverly Hills, CA: Sage, 1982): 105–130.

Appendix A: Survey Methodology

RESEARCH DESIGN

The study utilized a cross-sectional survey research design. In-person interviews were conducted with three groups of respondents: 102 displaced workers residing in the Shenango Valley in Western Pennsylvania; 10 displaced workers from the Shenango Valley who, following their job loss, relocated beyond a 60 mile radius of the area; and 22 directors of community service organizations located in the Shenango Valley and Mercer County.

Survey Populations and Sampling

Displaced Manufacturing Workers

For this study, displaced manufacturing workers were defined as members of the United Steelworkers of America (USWA) who had previously been employed as hourly workers at the Shenango Valley steel fabrication plants of National Castings and the General American Transportation Corporation (GATX) and had lost jobs due to a labor force contraction or shutdown at these plants between 1979 and 1984.

Both National Castings and GATX were steel fabrication mills that made parts for railroad cars. National Castings, with 1,400 employees, terminated operations in May 1983. GATX, which employed 1,600, closed in February 1984. These plants were selected as study sites because characteristics of their employees and details of the plant shutdowns were compatible with the study's research objectives: both plants were located in the Shenango Valley and employed primarily Shenango Valley residents; both plants were represented by USWA; and both employed hourly workers at a variety of skill levels, from manual laborer to skilled tradesman.

A systematic random sampling method was used to select the respondents. The sampling frame consisted of persons on the United Steelworkers of America (USWA) employee lists for National Castings and GATX who were residents of the Shenango Valley and who were employed or laid off awaiting callback at the time of the plant shutdowns. The USWA roster of hourly employees at National Castings numbered 1,050, with the names listed in alphabetical order. The USWA list of hourly workers from GATX numbered 950, with the names in order of seniority. Every tenth name on each list was selected for this study. Persons from this list with addresses outside the Shenango Valley were eliminated from the sample. From the names remaining, every second person was contacted for an interview. Replacement names were drawn at random from the names remaining on this list. Fifty-five employees from each plant were targeted for interviews.

Directors of Community Service Organizations

The population of directors of community service organizations was defined as executive-level, administrative staff members of private and public nonprofit organizations that were located in the Mercer County–Shenango Valley area and that offered community services to Shenango Valley residents, including cash assistance, counseling, information and referral, employment services, economic development, legal services, and housing, food, and clothing assistance. (These organizations are listed in Appendix B.) The United Way of Mercer County publishes a directory of public and private nonprofit organizations located in Mercer County, which served as the sampling frame.

DATA COLLECTION

Administering the Survey

Three different questionnaires were administered to the three groups of respondents. Each was pretested using in-person interviews with respondents drawn from the sampling frames. Each respondent was sent a letter describing the study and requesting his or her participation in an interview, and a follow-up phone call was made to answer questions regarding the study and to schedule an interview appointment. All of the interviews were conducted by the author.

Locating the Respondents

Current addresses and phone numbers for the persons selected for the sample were located through the local phone and city directories. Those who

were not listed in these directories were tracked via post office forwarding, inquiries among former coworkers, and inquiries among persons listed in the local phone and city directories who had the same last names as the respondents. Those who had a listed address but an unlisted telephone number or no telephone were requested by letter to call the researcher and set up an interview time.

Interviews

Displaced Workers Residing in the Shenango Valley

The interviews with persons residing in the Shenango Valley were conducted in the respondents' homes and at community locations, including the public library and the local union hall. The respondents were offered the choice of having the interview conducted in their home or at another community location, because it was found during pretesting that some respondents were uneasy about having a stranger come to their home, while others had activities in their households that did not permit an uninterrupted hour-long interview. In eight cases, respondents who refused to participate in a face-to-face interview were surveyed by telephone. Telephone interviews were conducted only when respondents had repeatedly refused an in-person interview.

The interviews were conducted from September through November 1987. On average, they took one hour to administer. The survey questions were both closed- and open-ended and elicited quantitative as well as qualitative information on current employment status; level of income before manufacturing job loss; current income levels and sources; changes in life-style since loss of job; methods and contacts in job hunting; factors impacting decisions to remain in or leave the area; political orientation; social service utilization; current human service problems and needs; and social network ties and characteristics.

Displaced Workers Who Relocated

Persons who relocated were interviewed by telephone in December 1987 and January and February 1988. The interview schedule was an abbreviated version of the one administered to displaced workers residing in the Shenango Valley, and took approximately one half hour to administer. Information was collected on the respondents' current and past employment and income status, changes in life-style since job loss and relocation, methods and contacts in job hunting, factors impacting their decisions to leave the area, and their relocation experiences.

Directors of Community Service Organizations

Directors of community service organizations were interviewed from

August through November 1987. Closed- and open-ended questions were designed to determine the types of services offered, client characteristics, changes in demand for services over the past five years, changes in funding and service provision over these years, and agency participation in or development of programs specifically designed to aid displaced workers. Information was also collected on agency characteristics, including program goals, age, funding sources, and staff size.

Response Rate

In total, 102 displaced workers who resided in the Shenango Valley were interviewed, with a response rate of 84 percent. Of the persons contacted for interviews, ten refused to participate in the study and ten of those initially selected through random sampling were not listed in the phone or city directories and could not be located through either post office forwarding or inquiries among former coworkers or relatives.

Of the fifteen displaced workers who were known to have relocated from the Shenango Valley, ten were interviewed by telephone, for a response rate of 67 percent. Attempts to find current addresses or phone numbers for the remaining five persons were unsuccessful.

DATA ANALYSIS

Quantitative data were analyzed using the Statistical Package for the Social Sciences (SPSSx). Frequency distributions and descriptive statistics were examined for all variables, and contingency tables using the chi-square were used to analyze relationships among categorical variables such as demographic characteristics and poverty and employment status. Difference of means (t) tests were conducted among groups including persons who were over and under age 40, the unemployed and employed, and the poor and nonpoor, for variables including social network characteristics and wage rates. A Pearson correlation matrix was generated for continuous variables including age, household income, network size, and social service utilization. Qualitative information collected from open-ended questions was examined using comparative analysis. The responses were read for their descriptive detail of life-style changes and for evidence of attitudinal and behavioral patterns of adjustment to economic dislocation. In addition to overall trends, patterns of response were compared among groups including the poor and nonpoor, employed and unemployed, those over age 40, and those who relocated.

Appendix B: Community Service Organizations Surveyed

Alternatives for Women (AW/ARE) (shelter for battered women)
Sharon, PA

Catholic Social Services
Sharon, PA

Community Action Agency
Farrell, PA

Community Food Warehouse
Farrell, PA

Community Mental Health and Counseling Center
Hermitage, PA

Drug and Alcohol Rehabilitation Services
Sharon, PA

Emergency Management Office (government surplus food distribution)
Mercer, PA

Farrell Redevelopment Authority
Farrell, PA

Mercer County Assistance Office (public welfare department)
Hermitage, PA

Mercer County Children and Youth Services
Mercer, PA

Mercer County Information, Referral, and Service Center
Sharon, PA

Northwestern Legal Services
Sharon, PA

Pennsylvania Job Service,
Office of Employment and Security
Sharon, PA

Private Industry Council/Job Training Partnership Act
Sharon, PA

Salvation Army
Sharon, PA

Sharon Community Development Department
Sharon, PA

Sharon General Hospital, Department of Social Work
Sharon, PA

Shenango Valley Primary Health Care Center
Sharon, PA

Shenango Valley Urban League
Sharon, PA

Southwest Gardens Economic Development Center
Farrell, PA

St. Paul's Catholic Center (food and clothing distribution)
Farrell, PA

United Way of Mercer County
Sharon, PA

Bibliography

Addison, John T., & Portugal, Pedro. (1989, July). Job displacement, related wage changes, and duration of unemployment. *Journal of Labor Economics*, 7: 281–302.

Aiken, Michael, Ferman, Louis A., & Sheppard, Harold L. (1968). *Economic failure, alienation, and extremism*. Ann Arbor, MI: University of Michigan Press.

Alperovitz, Gar, & Faux, Jeff. (1984). *Rebuilding America*. New York: Pantheon.

American Iron and Steel Institute. (1980). *Steel at the crossroads: The American steel industry in the 1980s*. Washington, DC: American Iron and Steel Institute.

Angell, Robert C. (1936). *The family encounters the depression*. New York: Scribner's.

Appelbaum, Eileen. (1984). High tech and the structural employment problems of the 1980s. In Collins, Eileen, & Tanner, Lucretia Dewey (Eds.), *American jobs and the changing industrial base*. Cambridge, MA: Ballinger.

Aronson, Robert, & McKersie, Robert B. (1980). *Economic consequences of plant shutdowns in New York State*. Ithaca, NY: New York State School of Industrial and Labor Relations.

Bailey, Thomas R. (1988). Market forces and private sector processes in government policy: The Job Training Partnership Act. *Journal of Policy Analysis and Management*, 7(2): 300–315.

Bakke, Edward Wight. (1940). *Citizens without work*. New Haven, CT: Yale University Press.

———. (1940). *The unemployed worker*. New Haven, CT: Yale University Press.

Beckett, Joyce O. (1988). Plant closings: How older workers are affected. *Social Work*, 33(1): 29–33.

Bell, Daniel. (1973). *The coming of post-industrial society: A venture in social forecasting*. New York: Basic Books.

Bell, Thomas. (1976). *Out of this furnace*. Pittsburgh, PA: University of Pittsburgh Press. (Original work published in 1941.)

Bensman, David, & Lynch, Roberta. (1987). *Rusted dreams: Hard times in a steel community*. New York: McGraw-Hill.

Biegel, David E., Cunningham, James, Yamatani, Hide, & Martz, Pamela. (1989). Self-reliance and blue-collar unemployment in a steel town. *Social Work*, 34(5): 399–406.

Birch, David C. (1979). *The job generation process.* Cambridge, MA: MIT Press.

Bluestone, Barry. (1984, September). Is deindustrialization a myth? Capital mobility versus absorptive capacity in the U.S. economy. *Annals of the American Academy of Political and Social Science,* 475: 39–51.

———. (1988, Fall). Deindustrialization and unemployment in America. *Review of Black Political Economy,* 17: 29–44.

Bluestone, Barry, & Harrison, Bennett. (1982). *The deindustrialization of America.* New York: Basic.

———. (1986). *The great American jobs machine: Low-wage work and the polarization of wages.* (Report prepared for the Joint Economic Committee, U.S. Congress.) Washington, DC: U.S. Government Printing Office.

Bodnar, John. (1977). *Immigration and industrialization: Ethnicity in an American mill town, 1870–1940.* Pittsburgh, PA: University of Pittsburgh Press.

Brenner, Harvey M. (1973). *Mental illness and the economy.* Cambridge, MA: Harvard University Press.

———. (1976). *Estimating the social costs of national economic policy: Implications for mental and physical health and clinical aggression.* (Report prepared for the Joint Economic Committee, U.S. Congress). Washington, DC: U.S. Government Printing Office.

Briar, Katherine. (1976). "The effects of unemployment on workers and families." (Doctoral Diss., School of Social Welfare, University of California, Berkeley).

Brody, David. (1960). *Steelworkers in America.* Cambridge, MA: Harvard University Press.

Burke, Ronald J. (1986, April). Reemployment on a poorer job after a plant closing. *Psychological Reports,* 58: 559–70.

Buss, Terry F., & Redburn, F. Stevens. (1983). *Mass unemployment: Plant closings and community mental health.* Beverly Hills,CA: Sage.

———. (1983). *Shutdown at Youngstown.* Albany, NY: State University of New York Press.

Buss, Terry F., Redburn, F. Stevens, & Costa, Frank (Eds.). (1983). Reemploying, retraining, and relocating displaced workers. *Journal of Health and Human Resources Administration,* 6, Special Symposium Issue.

C & R Associates. (1978, July). *Community costs of plant closings: Bibliography and survey of the literature.* (Report No. L0362). Washington, DC: Federal Trade Commission.

Cairns, Cathy, & Cunningham, Jim (Eds.). (1986). *Aliquippa update: A Pittsburgh milltown struggles to come back, 1984–86.* Pittsburgh, PA: River Communities Project, School of Social Work, University of Pittsburgh.

Catalano, Ralph, & Dooley, David. (1977, September). Economic predictors of depressed mood and stressful life events. *Journal of Health and Social Behavior,* 18: 292–307.

Cavan, Ruth Shonle, & Ranck, Katherine Howland. (1938). *The family and the depression.* Chicago: University of Chicago Press.

Clague, Ewan, Couper, Walter J., & Bakke, E. Wight. (1934). *After the shutdown.* New Haven, CT: Yale University, Institute of Human Relations.

Cobb, Sidney. (1976). Social support as a moderator of life stress. *Psychosomatic Medicine,* 38: 300–314.

Cobb, Sidney, et al. (1966). The health of people changing jobs: A description of a longitudinal study. *American Journal of Public Health,* 56: 1476–81.

Cobb, Sidney, & Kasl, Stanislaw. (1977, June). *Termination: The consequences of job loss.* (Report No. 76-1261). Washington, DC: Public Health Service, Center for Disease Control, National Institute for Occupational Safety and Health, U.S. Department of Health, Education and Welfare.

Cohen, Stephen S., & Zysman, John. (1987). *Manufacturing matters.* New York: Basic.

Cohn, Richard M. (1978). The effects of employment status change on self attitudes. *Social Psychology,* 41: 81–93.

Collins, Eileen, & Tanner, Lucretia Dewey (Eds.). (1984). *American jobs and the changing industrial base.* Cambridge, MA: Ballinger.

Cook, Robert F. (1987). *Worker dislocation: Case studies of causes and cures.* Kalamazoo, MI: W.E. Upjohn Institute for Employment Research.

Coontz, Phyllis D., Martin, Judith A., & Sites, Edward W. (1989, December) *Steeltown fathers: Rearing children in an era of industrial decline.* Pittsburgh, PA: River Communities Project, School of Social Work, University of Pittsburgh.

Cunningham, James, & Martz, Pamela (Eds.). (1986). *Steel people: Survival and resilience in Pittsburgh's Mon Valley.* Pittsburgh, PA: River Communities Project, School of Social Work, University of Pittsburgh.

Dickerson, Dennis C. (1986). *Out of the crucible: Black steelworkers in Western Pennsylvania, 1875–1980.* Albany, NY: State University of New York Press.

Dooley, David, & Catalano, Ralph. (1980). Economic change as a cause of behavioral disorder. *Psychological Bulletin,* 87(3): 450–68.

Dorsey, John W. (1967). The Mack Truck case: A study in unemployment. In Otto Eckstein (Ed.), *Studies in the economics of income maintenance.* Washington, DC: Brookings Institution.

Dow, Leslie M., Jr. (1977, Summer). High weeds in Detroit: The irregular economy among a network of Appalachian migrants. *Urban Anthropology,* 6: 111–28.

Drennan, Jan. (1988). Responding to industrial plant closings and the unemployed. *Social Work,* 33(1): 50–52.

Eisenberg, Philip, & Lazarsfeld, Paul F. (1938, June). The psychological effects of unemployment. *Psychological Bulletin,* 35: 358–90.

Ferman, Louis A. (1971). Regional unemployment, poverty, and relocation: A social service view. *Poverty and Human Resources Abstracts,* 6: 499–517.

Ferman, Louis A., & Gordus, Jeanne P. (Eds.). (1980). *Mental health and the economy.* Kalamazoo, MI: Upjohn Institute for Employment Research.

Flaim, Paul O., & Sehgal, Ellen. (1985, June). Displaced workers of 1979–83: How well have they fared? *Monthly Labor Review,* 108: 13–17.

Foltman, Felicia M. (1968). *White and blue collars in a mill shutdown.* Ithaca, NY: Cornell University Press.

Fuechtmann, Thomas G. (1989). *Steeple and stacks: Religion and steel crisis in Youngstown.* New York: Cambridge University Press.

Gershuny, John, & Miles, Ian. (1983). *The new service economy.* New York: Praeger.

Ginsberg, Eli. (1943). *The unemployed.* New York: Harper.

Gordus, Jeanne Prial. (1984). The human resource implications of plant shutdowns. *Annals of the American Academy of Political and Social Science,* 475 (September): 66–79.

Gordus, Jeanne Prial, Jorley, Paul, & Ferman, Louis. (1981). *Plant closings and economic dislocation.* Kalamazoo, MI: W. E. Upjohn Institute for Employment Research.

Hallman, Howard W. (1980). *Community-based employment programs.* Baltimore: John Hopkins University Press.

Hammerman, Herbert. (1964). Five case studies of displaced workers. *Monthly Labor Review*, 87(6): 663–70.

Hammermesh, Daniel S. (1987). The costs of worker displacement. *Quarterly Journal of Economics*, 102(1): 51–75.

Hanson, Gary B., et al. (1980). *Hardrock miners in a shutdown: A case study of the post-layoff experience of displaced lead-zinc-silver miners*. Logan, UT: Economic Research Center, Utah State University.

Hanson, Gary B., Bentley, Marion T., & Skidmore, Mark H. (1981, February). *Plant shutdowns, people and communities: A selected bibliography*. Logan, UT: Utah Center for Productivity and Quality of Working Life, Utah State University.

Harris, Candee. (1984, September). The magnitude of job loss from plant closings and the generation of replacement jobs: Some recent evidence. *Annals of the American Academy of Political and Social Science*, 475: 15–27.

Hoerr, John P. (1988). *And the wolf finally came: The decline of the American steel industry*. Pittsburgh, PA: University of Pittsburgh Press.

Holen, Arlene. (1976, November). *Losses to workers displaced by plant closure or layoff: A survey of the literature*. (CRC 313). Arlington, VA: Center for Naval Analyses.

Horvath, Francis W. (1987, June). The pulse of economic change: Displaced workers of 1981–85. *Monthly Labor Review*, 110: 3–12.

Howland, Marie. (1988). *Plant closings and worker displacement: The regional issues*. Kalamazoo, MI: W. E. Upjohn Institute for Employment Research.

Howland, Marie, & Peterson, G. E. (1988, October). Labor market conditions and the reemployment of displaced workers. *Industrial Labor Relations Review*, 42: 109–22.

Jacobson, Louis S. (1984, March). A tale of employment decline in two cities: How bad was the worst of times? *Industrial and Labor Relations Review*, 105(3): 40–44.

Jacobson, Louis S. (1978). Earnings losses of workers displaced from manufacturing industries. In William G. Dewald (Ed.), *The impact of international trade and investment on employment*. Washington, DC: U.S. Government Printing Office.

Jahoda, Marie J., Lazarsfeld, Paul F., & Zeisel, Hans. (1933). *Marienthal: The sociography of an unemployed community*. New York: Aldine-Atherton (1971 ed.).

Justice, Blair, & Duncan, David. (1976). Life crisis as a precursor to child abuse. *Public Health Reports*, 114.

Kaplan, Berton H., Cassel, John, & Gore, Susan. (1977, May). Social support and health. *Medical Care*, 15(5): 47–58 (supplement).

Kasarda, John. (1980, December). The implication of contemporary redistribution trends for national urban policy. *Social Science Quarterly*, 61(3,4): 373–400.

Kasl, Stanislaw, Gore, Susan, & Cobb, Sidney. (1975, March–April). The experience of losing a job: Reported changes in health, symptoms, and illness behavior. *Psychosomatic Medicine*, 37(2): 106–22.

Kasl, Stanislaw, & Cobb, Sidney. (1979, December). Some mental health consequences of plant closings and job loss. In Louis A. Ferman & Jeanne P. Gordus (Eds.), *Mental health and the economy*. Kalamazoo, MI: W. E. Upjohn Institute for Employment Research.

King, Craig. (1982). *The social impacts of mass layoffs*. Ann Arbor, MI: University of Michigan Press.

Kinicki, Angelo J. (1985, March). Personal consequences of plant closings: A model and preliminary test. *Human Relations*, 38: 197–212.

Kochan, Thomas A., Katz, Harry C., & McKersie, Robert B. (1986). *The transformation of American industrial relations.* New York: Basic.

Komarovsky, Mirra. (1940). *The unemployed man and his family.* New York: Octagon.

Komora, P., & Clark, M. (1935). Mental disease in the life crisis. *Mental Hygiene,* 19.

Kornblum, William. (1974). *Blue-collar community.* Chicago: University of Chicago Press.

Kornhauser, Arthur W. (1965). *Mental health of the industrial worker.* New York: Wiley.

Kruse, Douglas L. (1988). International trade and the labor market experience of displaced workers. *Industrial and Labor Relations Review,* 41(3): 402–17.

Kulik, Jane, et al. (1982). *Reemploying displaced workers: The implementation of the Downriver Community Conference Economic Readjustment Program.* Cambridge, MA: Abt Associates.

Lapham, Lewis. (1988). *Money and class in America.* New York: Weidenfeld & Nicolson.

Lazornick, William. (1981, March). Competition, specialization, and industrial decline. *Journal of Economic History,* 41(1): 31–38.

Lebergott, Stanley (Ed.). (1964). *Men without work: The economics of unemployment.* Englewood Cliffs, NJ: Prentice-Hall.

Levy, Frank. (1987). *Dollars and dreams: The changing American income distribution.* NY: Russell Sage.

Liem, R., & Raymon, Paula. (1982). Health and social costs of unemployment. *American Psychologist,* 37: 1116–23.

Lipsky, David B. (1970). Interplant transfer and terminated workers: A case study. *Industrial and Labor Relations Review,* 23(2): 191–206.

Lustig, R. Jeffrey. (1985, March). The politics of shutdown: Community, property, corporatism. *Journal of Economic Issues,* 19: 123–52.

Lynd, Staughton. (1982). *The fight against shutdowns: Youngstown's steel mill closings.* San Pedro, CA: Singlejack Books.

MacDonald, John S., & MacDonald, Leatrice. (1964). Chain migration, ethnic neighborhood formation, and social networks. *Milbank Memorial Fund Quarterly,* 42: 82–97.

Mann, Michael. (1973). *Workers on the move: The sociology of relocation.* New York: Cambridge University Press.

Mauer, Harry. (1979). *Not working: An oral history of the unemployed.* New York: Holt, Rinehart & Winston.

Maxwell, Nan C. (1989, April). Labor market effects from involuntary job losses in layoffs, plant closings: The role of human capital in facilitating reemployment and reduced wage losses. *American Journal of Economics and Sociology,* 48: 129–41.

McKenzie, Richard B. (1984). *Fugitive industry: The economics and politics of deindustrialization.* Cambridge, MA: Ballinger.

Metzgar, Jack. (1980, September-October). Plant shutdowns and worker response: The case of Johnstown, Pa. *Socialist Review,* 10(5): 18–19.

Mick, Stephen S. (1975). Social and personal costs of plant shutdowns. *Industrial Relations,* 14: 203–8.

Myers, Charles A., & MacLaurin, W. Rupert. (1943). *The movement of factory workers.* New York: Wiley.

Newman, Katherine S. (1985). Turning your back on tradition: Symbolic analysis and moral critique in a plant shutdown. *Urban Anthropology,* 14(1–3): 109–50.

Northeast-Midwest Institute. (1982). *Shutdown: A guide for communities facing plant closings.* Washington, DC: Northeast-Midwest Institute.

Office of Planning and Policy Development. (1982, June). *Planning guidebook for communities facing a plant closure or mass layoff.* Sacramento: State of California.

Office of Technology Assessment. (1986). *Technology and structural unemployment: Reemploying displaced adults.* Washington DC: U.S. Congress.

Owen, J. P., & Belzung, L. D. (1967, January). An epilogue to job displacement: A case study of structural unemployment. *Southern Economic Journal,* 33(3): 395–408.

Pappas, George. (1989). *The magic city: Unemployment in a working-class community.* Ithaca, NY: Cornell University.

Parnes, Herbert S., & King, Randy. (1977, Spring). Middle-aged job losers. *Industrial Gerontology,* 4(2): 77–95.

Perrucci, Carolyn C., et al. (1988). *Plant closings: International context and social costs.* New York: de Gruyter.

Phillips, Kevin. (1990). *The politics of rich and poor: Wealth and the American electorate in the Reagan aftermath.* New York: Random House.

Podgursky, Michael. (1988). Job displacement and labor market adjustment. In Richard Cyert & David Mowery (Eds.), *Studies in technology, employment, and policy.* Cambridge, MA: Ballinger.

———. (1987, Fall). Duration of joblessness following displacement. *Industrial Relations,* 26: 213–26.

———. (1987, October). Job displacement and earnings loss: Evidence from the displaced worker survey. *Industrial and Labor Relations Review,* 41: 17–29.

Policy and Management Associates, Inc. (1978, April). *Socio-economic costs and benefits of the Community Worker Ownership Plan to the Youngstown-Warren SMSA,* Washington, DC: National Center of Economic Alternatives.

Putterman, Julie S. (1985, January). *Chicago steelworkers: The cost of unemployment.* Chicago: Hull House Association.

Raymon, Paula. (1982). The world of not working: An evaluation of urban social service response to unemployment. *Journal of Health and Human Resources Administration,* 4: 319–33.

Redburn, F. Stevens, & Buss, Terry F. (Eds.). (1981). *Public policy for distressed communities.* Lexington, MA: Heath.

Reynolds, Stanley S. (1988, November). Plant closings and exit behavior in declining industries. *Economica,* 55: 493–503.

Rones, Philip. (1984, February). Recent recessions swell ranks of long-term unemployed. *Monthly Labor Review,* 107(2): 25–29.

Root, Kenneth A. (1979). *Perspectives for community organizations on job closings and job dislocation.* Ames, IA: Iowa University.

———. (1984, September). The human response to plant closures. *Annals of the American Academy of Political and Social Science,* 478: 52–65.

Ruhm, Christopher. (1987). The economic consequences of labor mobility. *Industrial and Labor Relations Review,* 41(1): 30–42.

Schultz, George P., & Weber, Arnold R. (1966). *Strategies for displaced workers.* New York: Harper & Row.

Sheehan, Michael F. (1985, October). Plant closings and the community: The instrumental value of public enterprise in countering corporate flight. *American Journal of Economics and Sociology,* 44: 423–33.

Shelp, Ronald K. (1981). *Beyond industrialization: Ascendancy of the global service economy.* New York: Praeger.

Sheppard, Harold, Ferman, Louis A., & Faber, Seymour. (1960). *Too old to work—too young to retire: A case study of a permanent plant shutdown.* (Report to Special Committee of Unemployment Problems, U. S. Senate). Washington, DC: U.S. Government Printing Office.

Shostak, Arthur B., & Gomberg, William (Eds.). (1964). *Blue-collar world: Studies of the American worker.* Englewood Cliffs, NJ: Prentice-Hall.

Siegel, Lewis B. (1987, October). BLS surveys mass layoffs and plant closings in 1986. *Monthly Labor Review,* 110: 39–40.

Slote, Alfred. (1969). *Termination: The closing at Baker Plant.* Indianapolis, IN: Bobbs-Merrill.

Smith, Luke A., & Fowler, I. A. (1964). Plant relocation and worker migration. In Arthur B. Shostak & W. Gomberg (eds.), *Blue-collar world: Studies of the American worker.* Englewood Cliffs, NJ: Prentice-Hall.

Staudohar, Paul D., & Brown, Holly E. (Eds.). (1987). *Deindustrialization and plant closure.* Lexington, MA: Heath.

Stern, James L. (1973, January). Consequences of plant closure. *Journal of Human Resources,* 7: 3–25.

Stern, James L., Root, Kenneth A., & Hills, Stephen M. (1974, October). The influence of social-psychological traits and job search patterns on the earnings of workers affected by plant closure. *Industrial and Labor Relations Review,* 28(1): 103–21.

Stillman, Don. (1978, July/August). The devastating impact of plant relocations. *Working Papers for a New Society,* 5(4): 42–53.

Strange, William. (1977). *Job loss: A psychosocial study of worker reactions to a plant closing.* Washington, DC: Employment and Training Administration.

Summers, Gene F. (Ed.). (1984, September). Deindustrialization: Restructuring the economy. *Annals of the American Academy of Political and Social Science,* 475.

Taber, Thomas D., Walsh, Jeffrey T., & Cooke, Robert A. (1979). Developing a community-based program for reducing the impact of a plant closing. *Journal of Applied Behavioral Science,* 15: 133–155.

Tausky, Curt, & Piedmont, E. B. (1967-68, Winter). The meaning of work and unemployment: Implications for mental health. *International Journal of Social Psychiatry,* 14(1): 44–49.

U.S. Department of Labor, Bureau of Labor Statistics. (1985). *Workers without jobs: A chartbook on unemployment.* Washington, DC: Bureau of Labor Statistics.

U.S. Department of Labor, Secretary of Labor's Task Force on Economic Adjustment and Worker Dislocation. (1986, December). *Economic adjustment and worker dislocation in a competitive society.* Washington, DC: U.S. Government Printing Office.

Walker, Charles. (1922). *Steel: The diary of a furnace worker.* Boston: Atlantic Monthly Press.

———. (1950). *Steeltown: An industrial case history of the conflict between progress and security.* New York: Harper.

Way, Harold E., & Weiss, Carla M. (1988). *Plant closings: A selected bibliography of materials published through 1985.* Ithaca, NY: School of Industrial and Labor Relations, Cornell University.

Wilcock, Richard, & Franke, Walter H. (1963). *Unwanted workers: Permanent layoffs and long-term unemployment*. New York: Glencoe.

Wright, Helen Russel. (1934, March). The families of the unemployed in Chicago. *Social Service Review*, 8: 17–30.

Wu, Sen-Yuan, & Korman, Hyman. (1987). Socioeconomic impacts of disinvestment on communities in New York State. *American Journal of Economics and Sociology*, 46(3): 261–71.

Yamatani, Hide, Maguire, Lambert, Rogers, Robin, & O'Kennedy, Mary Lou. (1989, November). *The impact of social/economic change on households among six communities in Western Pennsylvania*. Pittsburgh, PA: River Communities Project, School of Social Work, University of Pittsburgh.

Young, Edwin. (1963). The Armour experience: A case study in plant shutdowns. In G. Somers, E. Cushman, & N. Weinberg (Eds.), *Adjusting to technological change*. New York: Harper & Row.

Zippay, Allison. (1991). Job training and relocation experiences among displaced industrial workers. *Evaluation Review*, 15(5): 555–70.

Zippay, Allison. (1990/91, Fall/Winter). The limits of intimates: Social networks and economic status among displaced industrial workers. *Journal of Applied Social Sciences*, 15(1): 75–95.

Index

ABOUT THE AUTHOR

ALLISON ZIPPAY is an assistant professor of policy and planning at the School of Social Work, Rutgers University. She received a Ph.D. from the University of California, Berkeley, and has served as a teaching fellow at Harvard University and as a planning consultant to numerous community service agencies. Her research and writing focus on poverty, underemployment, and community planning.